Opera Omnia

Space, Time, and Science

Opera Omnia

I. Mysticism and Spirituality
Part 1: Mysticism, Fullness of Life
Part 2: Spirituality, the Way of Life

II. Religion and Religions

III. Christianity
Part 1: The Christian Tradition (1961–1967)
Part 2: A Christophany

IV. Hinduism
Part 1: The Vedic Experience: Mantramanjari
Part 2: The Dharma of India

V. Buddhism

VI. Cultures and Religions in Dialogue
Part 1: Pluralism and Interculturality
Part 2: Intercultural and Interreligious Dialogue

VII. Hinduism and Christianity

VIII. Trinitarian and Cosmotheandric Vision

IX. Mystery and Hermeneutics
Part 1: Myth, Symbol, and Ritual
Part 2: Faith, Hermeneutics, and Word

X. Philosophy and Theology
Part 1: The Rhythm of Being
Part 2: Philosophical and Theological Thought

XI. Sacred Secularity

XII. Space, Time, and Science

Opera Omnia

Volume XII
Space, Time, and Science

Raimon Panikkar

Edited by Milena Carrara Pavan

ORBIS BOOKS
Maryknoll, New York 10545

Library of Congress Cataloging-in-Publication Data

Names: Panikkar, Raimon, 1918–2010, author. | Carrara Pavan, Milena, editor.
Title: Space, time, and science / Raimon Panikkar ; edited by Milena Carrara Pavan.
Description: Maryknoll, NY : Orbis Books, [2022] | Series: Opera omnia ; volume xii | Includes bibliographical references and index.
Identifiers: LCCN 2022003402 (print) | LCCN 2022003403 (ebook) | ISBN 9781626984967 (print) | ISBN 9781608339587 (ebook)
Subjects: LCSH: Religion and science. | Time—Religious aspects. | Space—Religious aspects. | Space and time—Religious aspects. | Science—Philosophy. | Space and time. | Space. | Time.
Classification: LCC BL240.3 .P355 2022 (print) | LCC BL240.3 (ebook) | DDC 201/.65—dc23/eng20220524
LC record available at https://lccn.loc.gov/2022003402
LC ebook record available at https://lccn.loc.gov/2022003403

Series Foreword

All the writings it is my privilege and responsibility to present in this series are not the fruit of mere speculation but, rather, autobiographical—that is, they were first inspired by a life and praxis that have been only subsequently molded into writing.

This *Opera Omnia* ranges over a span of some seventy years, during which I dedicated myself to exploring further the meaning of a more justified and fulfilled human lifetime. I did not live for the sake of writing, but I wrote to live in a more conscious way so as to help my fellows with thoughts not only from my own mind but also springing from a superior Source, which may perhaps be called Spirit—although I do not claim that my writings are in any way inspired. However, I do not believe that we are isolated monads, but that each of us is a microcosm that mirrors and impacts the macrocosm of reality as a whole—as most cultures believed when they spoke of the Body of Śiva, the communion of the saints, the Mystical Body, *karman*, and so forth.

The decision to publish this collection of my writings has been somewhat trying, and more than once I have had to overcome the temptation to abandon the attempt, the reason being that, though I fully subscribe to the Latin saying *scripta manent*, I also firmly believe that what actually matters in the final analysis is to live out Life, as witnessed by the great masters who, as Thomas Aquinas remarks in the *Summa* about Pythagoras and Socrates (but not about Buddha, of whom he could not have known), did not write a single word.

In the twilight of life I found myself in a dark forest, for the straight path had been lost and I had shed all my certainties. It is undoubtedly to the merit of Sante Bagnoli, and of his publishing house Jaca Book, that I owe the initiative of bringing out this *Opera Omnia*, and all my gratitude goes to him. This work includes practically all that has appeared in book form, although some chapters have been inserted into different volumes as befitted their topics. Numerous articles have been added to present a more complete picture of my way of thinking, but occasional pieces and almost all my interviews have been left out.

I would like to make some practical comments which apply to all the volumes:

1. In quoting references, I have preferred to cite my previously published works following the general scheme of my publications.

2. Subject matter rather than chronology has been considered in the selection, and thus the style may sometimes appear uneven.

3. Even if each of these works aspires to be a self-sufficient whole, some ideas recur because they are functional to understanding the text, although the avoidance of unnecessary duplication has led to a number of omissions.

4. The publisher's preference for the *Opera Omnia* to be put into an organic whole by the author while still alive has many obvious positive features. Should the author outlive the printer's run, however, he will be hard put to help himself from introducing alterations, revisions, or merely adding to his original written works.

I thank my various translators, who have rendered the various languages I have happened to write in into the spirit of multiculturalism—which I believe is ever relevant in a world where cultures encounter each other in mutual enrichment, provided they do not mislay their specificity. I am particularly grateful to Milena Carrara Pavan, to whom I have entrusted the publication of all my written works, which she knows deeply, having been at my side in dedication and sensitivity during the last twenty years of my life.

R.P.

Contents

SECTION II

SCIENCE AND TECHNOLOGY

ABBREVIATIONS

Hindū Scriptures

AV	*Atharva-veda*
BG	*Bhagavad-gītā*
BGB	*Bhagavad-gītā-bhāṣya*
BhagP	*Bhāgavata-purāṇa*
BP	*Brahma-purāṇa*
BS	*Brahma-sūtra*
BSB	*Brahma-sūtra-bhāṣya*
BU	*Bṛhadāraṇyaka-upaniṣad*
BUB	*Bṛhadāraṇyaka--Upaniṣad-bhāṣya*
CU	*Chāndogya-Upaniṣad*
GopB	*Gopatha-brāhmaṇa*
IsU	*Īśa-Upaniṣad*
JabU	*Jabala-Upaniṣad*
KathU	*Kaṭha-upaniṣad*
KausU	*Kauṣītaki-Upaniṣad*
KenU	*Kena-Upaniṣad*
KenUB	*Kena-Upaniṣad-bhāṣya*
MaitU	*Maitrī-upaniṣad*
MandU	*Māṇḍūkja-upaniṣad*
MāṇḍKār	*Māṇḍūkya-Kārikā*
MB	*Mahābhārata*
MundU	*Muṇḍūkya-Upaniṣad*
NarS	*Nārada-sūtra*
P	*Purāṇa*
PrasnU	*Praśna-Upaniṣad*
RV	*Ṛg-Veda*
S	*Sūtra*
SantPar	*Mahābhārata-Śānti-parvan*
SB	*Śatapatha-brāhmaṇa*
SU	*Śvetāśvatara-Upaniṣad*
TB	*Taittirīya-brāhmaṇa*
TMB	*Tāṇḍya-māha-brāhmaṇa*
TS	*Taittirīya-saṃhitā*

TU	*Taittirīya-Upaniṣad*
U	*Upaniṣad*
Vākyap	*Vākyapadīya (Bhartṛhari)*
VisnuP	*Viṣṇu-purāṇa*
YS	*Yoga-sūtra*

Christian Scriptures

1 Cor	*First Corinthians*
2 Cor	*Second Corinthians*
1 Jn	*First John*
2 Jn	*Second John*
1 Pet	*First Peter*
Acts	*Acts of the Apostles*
Col	*Colossians*
Dan	*Daniel*
Eph	*Ephesians*
Ex	*Exodus*
Ezek	*Ezekiel*
Gen	*Genesis*
Heb	*Hebrews*
Is	*Isaiah*
Jn	*John*
Lk	*Luke*
Mic	*Micah*
Mk	*Mark*
Mt	*Matthew*
Prov	*Proverbs*
Ps	*Psalms*
Qo	*Qohèlet*
Rev	*Revelation*
Rom	*Romans*
Sir	*Sirach (Ecclesiasticus)*
Song	*Song of Songs*
Tit	*Titus*
Wis	*Wisdom*

Others

Denz.-Schön.	*H. J. D. Denzinger, Enchiridion symbolorum, definitionum et declarationum de rebus fidei et morum, A. Schönmetzer (ed.), Barcelona: Herder, 1973*
ST	*Thomas Aquinas, Summa Theologiae*

Introduction

Volume XII, the last one in the structure of this *Opera Omnia*, includes articles and books dealing with science that were published in the early years of my production. Even though their contents and style may now sound quite outdated, I nonetheless decided to insert them here as a reminder of that period and the issues in which I was then interested. In particular the prologue, "A Synthetic Vision of the Universe," is remarkably outdated, but it presents some insights that I still consider meaningful.

The theme of this book starts with the conception of time linked to a scientific vision of reality.

> *Omnia tempus habent*[1]
> *[All things have a time of their own]*

This time is not something that envelops the being externally, but an integral and specific dimension of each being that *is*, in the sense that it *has a duration*, and its duration consists precisely in the fact that it *is* this particular being and not another.

The time of the technological civilization has caused a profound conflict within Man by altering his life rhythm. Should Man refuse technology or, on the contrary, reinforce it and be integrated in progress? This is an inescapable conflict.

At this point it should be noted that technology has an ontonomic nature, and therefore an intrinsic relationship both with the world and with Man. In fact, the relationship between Man and technology is as deep and intimate as that between technology and nature. Man generates technology by starting from nature. Technology is originally produced by Man's interest in the earth and matter.

> *Et tempus non erit amplius*[2]
> *[And time will be no longer]*

The Running-Out of Time

Every cosmovision based on the idea of creation implies a belief in the finiteness of time and space. This finiteness leads us to imagine a beginning of time, and also an end. Now, time is not infinite—not because it all gets used up, like a sort of path along which Man is traveling, but because Man too is not infinite. The end of time does not mean, therefore, that the path suddenly vanishes, leaving things unfinished. The finiteness of time means that time runs out because things reach a fullness of existence. Time finishes because beings reach their end. The end of time means the end of Being inasmuch as Being is temporal.

We have spoken of the running-out of time because the temporal dimension is the one closest to our way of conceiving the human situation; but we could equally well have

---

[1] Qo 3:1 as it was translated in the Vulgate Bible.
[2] Rev 10:6.

considered the coming to an end, or the contraction, of space. We speak of the conquest of space, but we should not forget that this mastery of space means a diminution of space as distance, and therefore a diminution of space as such.

In this perspective, we try to see how, by a paradoxical somersault, technology can serve, on the one hand, to reconcile Man with nature, and on the other to humanize the cosmos.

The Reintegration of Man into Nature

Technology allows a new relationship between Man and Nature—that is, a relationship of *ontonomy*.

Almost all civilizations lead Man to self-awareness. If "primitive" Man considered himself as an object among objects, and felt lost within the cosmos that he was part of, civilized Man is becoming increasingly self-aware and no longer considers himself as part of "nature," or as an "object," but as a "spectator" of the world. It is the age of knowledge, and above all reflexive knowledge.

Technology cuts the ground away from under Man's feet and removes his support; it breaks both its natural and rational rhythm and turns Man into a thing once more, but in a very particular way. Through technology, Man loses his rhythm and imposes vertiginous rhythms on nature; through technology, Man ceases to be a passive spectator of the universe and becomes an actor. Activism is one of the illnesses of our century because it has found favorable conditions as a reaction to an essentialist immobility.

So, technology reduces the distance between Man and nature, and perhaps also matter, to its true proportions. (This distance had led Man to believe that he was the king of nature, the center of the universe, and belonged to a different "class" from the rest of creation.) Technology helps us rediscover our kinship with matter, and our common destiny with the universe.

Technology can kill Man, but it can also help him to achieve his being. One should not forget that Man, a temporal being and a pilgrim, is not isolated, but forms a whole with the world and with others, and is part of a universe that is also transitory and in a state of gestation.

Nature's Entry into Man

A preliminary consideration is necessary: this "nature" that Man is reentering by means of technology is no longer the pure and simple nature of a subjugated world, as it might seem in the age of heteronomy, but a different nature, transformed by Man's very entry into it.

This is a field to be approached with great prudence. Technology also wounds the cosmic rhythms and transforms nature in a way complementary to that in which it transforms Man. Today we talk of an "anthropization" of nature. In any case, it is a fact that nature is elevated insofar as it is, so to speak, taken on by technology. Thanks to technology, matter imitates Man more closely; and a machine is nothing more than an imitation of Man. All machines are anthropomorphic. We are told that machines are to replace human beings in their activities, their work and tasks, and this is true, but they do so precisely by imitating Man. Nature thus acquires a human aspect and arouses within itself latent possibilities; one could say that it undergoes a process of spiritualization. The phenomenology of technology reveals a certain convergence: Man and nature are traveling toward a common goal in one and the same movement. All the works of Teilhard de Chardin, in particular *L'Avenir de l'Homme*, develop this theme in full.

This dynamic process is still happening, and will continue, and we think we can detect a participation of the machine in this dynamism. In fact, the machine transmits something human to matter; human orders are obeyed and carried out by nature; human structures are copied and followed by machines. A machine may be a poor imitation of Man from our point of view, but from nature's point of view, the machine represents an important achievement of matter.

Of course a machine is not a living organism, but it should be added that the organism of which the machine aspires to be a part is not its pure mechanical structure, but a more complex structure, of which Man is also a part. The complete organism of the machine is supramaterial. In the same way that a finger, or a stomach, when it is cut off from its vital function and from its connection with the totality of the organism is dead and no longer has any vital function, so a machine, when removed from its "vital" link with Man and society, is dead and no longer organically related to the technological supra-organism. It has no life or meaning in or for itself, but this is also true of any part of a living organism. Since Man, as such, has believed over these last centuries that he is the outcome and perfect achievement of creation, one can understand his resistance toward allowing his primacy to be taken from him by an organism in which he would be no more than an organ. It is evident that in this symbiosis between Man and machine the individual loses his autarchy.

And so, it is no longer a question of rediscovering Man's place in the cosmos, nor of reviving the old discussion on anthropomorphism and cosmocentrism. Since its first beginnings, science has believed it could destroy the anthropocentric idea of the world, but the universe without Man is lost, just as Man is lost without the universe.

Man and Science

We must bear in mind the antinomy between modern cosmology and traditional cosmologies.

What we are trying to say is very simple. We have relativized all the past conceptions of the world; we speak about the Aztec universe, Hindū cosmology, and so on, and anthropologists explain how every culture constructs its own vision of the world in which it lives. It seems however that modern Man does not wish to apply that vision to himself and, when it comes to present-day science, he makes it into an absolute, converting it into the model through which he judges all the other cosmovisions, considering it to be a definitive acquisition of the human spirit. For some, the Moon is a Goddess, for others it is a living being, for others the home of their ancestors, and for others still it is the symbol of certain rhythms; but "we know perfectly well" that it is an inert mass orbiting at a certain distance from the Earth, with craters we can see. Furthermore, we believe that we have a deep knowledge of it because we have gathered specimens from its soil and our feet have stepped on it. In short, we believe we have demythologized and demystified the moon.

We started by saying that what we want to say is very simple, but it is also serious, difficult, and dangerous. It is *serious* insofar as it delineates the destiny of the world, the meaning of human experience over the last six thousand years. It is *difficult* because it implies a synthetic vision, on the one hand, and a selective one, on the other, in order to catch the global meaning of the situation that has been arrived at not only by Man but also by the life of our universe. It is *dangerous* in that it conditions our actions. We may be wrong in our judgment or run the risk of falling prey to facile simplifications, but this is no excuse for not taking sides, because even to abstain is in itself a decision. And practice is always dangerous.

Over the last centuries of Western tradition there has been such fear of looking obscurantist toward the success of modern science that no one has dared to actually state out loud the radical incompatibility between a scientific vision of the universe and the Christian tradition. Where are the "heavens" in Newtonian space? What does the Ascension of Mary in body and soul imply? *What* is present in the Eucharist? What is the meaning of Angels and Archangels, of Thrones and Cherubs, who sing to the glory of God? The very resurrection of Christ is mere nonsense if one accepts the scientific conception of the human body. It is true that Christianity scorned reason and identified faith with a series of more or less superstitious beliefs, and abused its power: hence its sense of guilt (of which it is arguably aware) that it then attempts to redeem by going in completely the opposite direction and embracing the scientific cosmovision uncritically. Here, however, we restrict ourselves to only one point: *neither science nor modern technology represent a cultural invariant; they are neither neutral nor universal and thus "universalizable" without destroying other cultures.*

It is not by chance that modern science and technology were born in the bosom of Western culture of a Mediterranean, Christian, and Atlantic origin. In fact they are not only bound de facto to Western culture but they are also bound de jure: they have a common destiny. So-called modernization, a problem reflected in two-thirds of the world, is the equivalent of Westernization. De facto, despite the efforts to reap the "benefits" of science and technology, experience demonstrates that it is not possible to avoid introducing the lifestyle and thought of the West. De facto, moreover, technology cannot establish itself without planting its roots in the soil and subsoil. To simplify, one could say that the roots correspond to the Christian desire to save the world, the soil to the Hellenic desire for knowledge, and the subsoil to the pragmatic vision of reality.

Introducing modern scientific ideology into two-thirds of the world, when it is not something that has been generated in the bosom of their own culture, is like the strategy of the Trojan horse. Within the bowels of technology there lies hidden a whole host of basic notions that, when transplanted from their natural environment, unbalance and destroy the basic intuitions of other cultures—with the obvious risk of reactions, rebellions, and catastrophes.

My thesis is not that some, or all, or almost all the cultures, if the march of humanity so demanded, need to die. Nor does it say that Western culture is evil or that other cultures are sublime. Instead, it suggests that science and technology (not Western culture tout court) only represent one aspect of the human spirit. Of course, this does not mean that all scientists and technocrats are perverse. Not all of those who enforced slavery in the past were human monsters, nor were all the crusaders criminals or all the colonialists oppressors. However it has taken us several centuries to realize this. What we lack nowadays is not only a judgment of the past or a *Generalreformation der ganzen Welt*, as the *Rosicrucians* (Johannes Valentinus Andreae) have been preaching since the seventeenth century; we do not merely need a reform but rather a fundamental transformation, a radical *metanoia*, but this does not mean that we must go back to a romantic or unreal kind of primitivism.

The thesis does not affirm but does suggest that technology can become dehumanizing and consequently very negative, even though individually one can make good use of it: from the point of view of an individualistic mentality, this is quite evident despite the danger of despotism of every sort (there is something artificial about wanting to restrict the possession of atomic weapons just to some countries, considered to be morally superior to others). This reasoning does not, however, bear in mind the intrinsic dynamism of the proliferation, that is, cancer, of the technological system, which surfaces not only in phenomena like the arms race, but in general all throughout the industrial world linked to the market economy. This is why we are moved to advocate not the destruction of technology but rather our emancipation from it.

Let us now consider universality: *neither science nor technology is universal.* On the contrary, they derive from premises that are bound to a certain type of culture.

What has caused confusion, even among the greatest scientists, is the almost magical power of words. Today we still call "science" the continuation and perfecting of Galileo's "new science," which is so "new" that it is no longer science in the traditional sense. Traditionally, science meant knowledge, and knowledge was understood to be that faculty of the human spirit by which Man could come into contact with reality so as to participate and commune with it for a spiritual rebirth, thanks to a natural communion with reality: *similia similibus cognoscuntur.*[3]

The field of philosophy has also been invaded by the scientific mentality. The influence of the new science on illustrious minds such as those of Descartes, Kant, Hume, Berkeley, and others is well known. In a subtle way, this influence is still there today. For example, it has actually been possible to write that knowing is interpreting. In that case, philosophy would be pure *hermeneutics.* Certainly there is an interpretative dimension to every cognitive process, but knowing is far more than simply interpreting; knowing is more than "decoding" a written work, reducing the distance between a subject and an object. Knowing is more than deciphering a message. To know is to identify with the known thing, to be part of it, albeit at the necessary critical distance. One cannot really know if one is not convinced of the truth of that which one knows. To know is a process of conversion. It implies communion, a loving embrace that places us in communion with reality; the interpretative aspect is merely one element. *Hermeneutics requires nothing more than reflection; not so does knowledge.* Reflective knowledge, as such, is aware and interprets but, as a form of knowledge, possesses something that hermeneutics cannot grasp.

Modern culture has created a "fourth world" to replace the world of Gods, Men, and Things because, as it feels insecure in itself, it has attempted to escape to the realm of a fourth world that it is able to control. It is important to underline the need of modern Man to create a world that he can control, a world where life can be lived in peace and without fear. But he is beginning to regret the loss of cosmic trust (in *ṛta, dharma, ordo, kosmos*); in other words, the trust that Reality is something we have been given and with which we can identify; that Reality is to be experienced, first of all, and then known, and thirdly transformed by living it.

Modern Man has lost this basic trust, this attitude of respect for Reality. Nowadays it is has become necessary to examine everything, to discover all the secrets, to split the atom, to have everything one has not yet, and ensure that everything one needs is available by relying only on one's own power, one's own intelligence, and what one can directly control.

Perhaps this is what the *novum* of modernity consists in. Life in the three worlds implied a certain trust in reality, in what we had been given. Things worked well enough, so to speak, but thanks to an intrinsic dynamism and not because of an extrinsic *chiquenaude* (Descartes), a mechanical impulse. Nature is wise. It must be watched over, listened to, and also improved on—because these are natural impulses too. The classical purpose of alchemy consisted in completing the work of creation that the Creator himself urged us to finish. Here the dignity of Man was quite clear: he was called on to participate in a *synergheia* with the Divine.

All this changed with the technological complex that Man has created for his own benefit. Today he no longer needs to fear the Gods (by virtue of Science), live in dread of nature (Technology), or be terrorized by other people (Democracy). But he does need to be constantly vigilant in order to prevent energy running out, or the System collapsing. It is not by chance that so-called terrorism is becoming the obsession of the technocrats.

---

[3] Shared likeness is the ground of knowledge.

This fourth world is not able to recycle itself, but it *can* fall apart, resources could run out, and it could self-destruct together with the whole of humanity, including life itself on the planet. The temptation of mass suicide ("cosmicide") is a *novum* in the history of human consciousness.

Simple trust in Reality has been lost. The world, the planet, and even Being, in a sense, could cease to be. Nothing guarantees its permanence. If time had a beginning, it can also have an end. Non-Being could prevail over Being. The human adventure is expanding and turning into a cosmic destiny. An external God does not seem inclined to intervene—considering His silence in the face of the worst human disasters.

The fact that both science and technology were born in Western Europe is not just a historical accident: science and technology cannot even be understood except in their cultural context. One could say that at least mathematics is universal, but we cannot be sure about this either: without going back as far as Pythagoras, we could cite Cassiodorus who in the sixth century defined *music* as "the science of numbers." But there is more. The very concept of universality implies a notion of objectivity, that is, a possibility of abstraction from any form of subjectivity, which is certainly not a cultural invariant that could be defined as universal.

Finally, *neither science nor technology is "universalizable"* without steamrollering all the other cultures and reducing them to just relatively exotic folklore or tourist industries for the benefit of the "first world," as we are already witnessing.

There is a basic assumption behind our thesis: the legitimacy of cultural pluralism and the overcoming of a monodirectional evolutionism. Let us suppose that the evolution of humanity has no reason to go in a single, linear direction. Evidently one could think that up to now humanity has proceeded virtually in darkness, but at last *Homo technologicus* can bring together the whole heritage of humanity within himself, so that everything converges in a single type of Man, the representative of the technocratic civilization of today and forged upon the scientific model. If such analyses were valid, the consequence would be that this is the only path for humanity to follow. The other cultures would be destined to being absorbed by scientific civilization.

This ideology is far more widespread today than we might think. One frequently hears the statement that 90 percent of the great "inventors" of humanity have lived in the last fifty years, and that, before technological progress, Man's life on earth was not much more than a desperate, savage fight for survival. Other cultures are tolerated like accidental, perhaps exotic, extras, and other religions as a *praeparatio technologica* for the new superman. There is a great difference between Nietzsche, Aurobindo, Teilhard, and the modern technocrats, but they all share a certain centripetal vision of reality. Our thesis states, instead, that Reality is multicolored, and denies the universal validity of the "monochrome" vision of modern science.

* * *

The volume is made up of two sections, although the contents are constantly interwoven.

The first section concerns time and space, which is a subject that forms the basis of a vision of reality, not only from a philosophical point of view but also from a scientific one. Because the subject of time is perceived differently from Western and Eastern viewpoints, the section has been divided into two visions: the Eastern vision underlines the aspect that is more closely linked to Being, while the Western one is more linear, with a beginning and an end, an alpha and an omega.

The second section deals with a more Western conception of science. It begins with an article dedicated to Max Planck, the founder of quantum physics with philosophical repercussions, which is followed by an outline of my doctoral thesis in science, *The Ontonomy of Science* (1961). The section concludes with a leap of almost half a century with an essay on modern science leading on to technology, "The Narrow Door of Knowledge." Two articles underline the importance of becoming emancipated from science and technology, not so much as a rejection of their value but more as an overcoming of their conditioning.

PROLOGUE:
A SYNTHETIC VISION OF THE UNIVERSE

Et sine ipso factum est nihil.

—Jn 1:3

Preliminary Note

I would not want this pause in my journey, which has come about halfway through my life, to be interpreted as a complacent look at the past. It is, in fact, quite the opposite. My interests—many of which have resulted in a dozen or so still unpublished studies—are focused on a Christocentric experience of reality, and any digression from this I feel would be regrettable.

If I have agreed to republish these studies and notes, it is because I am convinced that they have some value with regard to what I would still like to say. Their purpose is to provide a remote introduction to the one Christian theme. If the being of the contingent entity is found at the end, as the first cause, the problematic value of these pages is also rooted in its future, as is the life of every human being. It is for this reason that we are forbidden from judging our brother.

These pages do not express the central concern of the author; they were written simply as a means of clearing the way toward that hidden path where, as on the horizon, heaven and earth meet, time and eternity join hands, and no noise or words are heard. In rereading them, I was greatly tempted to redo everything, reformulate the problems, add a new bibliography after further consultations—in a word, to retrace the entire journey. I decided against this, however, because one does not set up scaffolding again after it has allowed us to reach heights from which we can, in all honesty, no longer go back.

My only hope is that these pages will allow someone to venture further, where concepts matter little and ideas themselves are secondary.

* * *

Reviewing these essays after many years, I cannot help but feel the full weight of the admission that Thomas Aquinas made to Brother Reginald. The only thing that persuades me not to imitate him, and let all these writings sink into oblivion, is the humble recognition that their author is not the Dominican friar of Roccasecca, and also the suspicion that my potential readers may not wish to remain as silent as Brother Reginaldo.

Rome, Feast of St. Michael the Archangel
September 29, 1960

The Problem

Sicut nullus potest videre pulchritudinem carminis,
nisi aspectus eius feratur super totum versum;
sic nullus videt pulchritudinem ordinis
et regiminis universi, nisi eam totam speculetur.[1]

—Bonaventure, *Breviloqium, prol.,* 2

We are not aware of how the internal organs of a living being function when they are healthy. When something goes from being natural to becoming a problem, it does not always indicate a step from naturalness to criticism; many times it is a sign that that something has suffered some damage, and our attention, awakened by the pain, turns to curing the problem.

Never before have we considered the world in its totality, human life in its complexity, and God in His infinity and transcendence a problem. Western Man, in a process that is conspicuously illustrated in the history of thought, lost God at the end of the Middle Ages, lost himself in the century of the Enlightenment and in Idealism, and has again gone astray in contemporary times, in our technological era. He has stopped believing in God *efficaciously*, he has lost the sense of his own being, and he does not know what to do in order to fill the void that faces "every Man who comes to this world."[2]

But just as pain, to a certain degree, is one of the organism's defense mechanisms and an indicator of malady, so our current restlessness—which is not the constitutive restlessness of the "wayfarer" but the uneasiness of the unhealthy—is also an indicator of its own infirmity, as well as the place where curing can begin. The cure must be radical, as evil has reached an extreme point. Having lost God, Man can no longer resort to finding refuge in himself and in Nature, or to hurling himself upon the world in an attempt to escape from his own self— seeing that loss and escape are correlative, as is confirmed by Adam, who *lost* his innocence and *escaped* to hide. Contemporary Man *feels* thrown out, hurled into this world: a world that eludes him, that causes him anguish and that, despite the fact that he has discovered many of its particular laws—as the marvelous productions of technology prove—dominates him in its general rhythm, in its cosmic order, and mocks him by making sure that those same products of civilization have the capacity to destroy him (even materially) and further intensify his unhappiness.

Man must be saved, redeemed. Who will be the redeemer? Politics, Art, Philosophy, and Religion all claim to have the power to do so.

In order to be able to judiciously decide upon the remedy, we must first examine the evil. But since this is not the place to present an in-depth analysis of modern Man, a single affirmation about the current illness of humanity will suffice: *evil is universal.* The restlessness, or uneasiness—as we defined it earlier—extends to all spheres of life, and anyone who does not notice it is a fool. This is not an exaggeration. In the last few centuries, where can we find a vision of the world that is not an idealist lucubration?—that is, one that, once its premises are accepted, even if it represents a prodigious exercise in dialectics and explains certain theoretical problems satisfactorily, has a real effect on Man's concrete activities and on his innermost yearnings: not his rational ones, but rather those related to love? The great

---

[1] "No one can see the beauty of a poem unless he reads it through, and no one can see the beauty of the universal order and providence if he does not contemplate the whole of it."

[2] Jn 1:9 (in the Vulgate version).

scandal of the current era is that the cultivation of Science, of sciences, the cultivation of intelligence, in brief, of the most noble faculty Man possesses and the one through which he most resembles his Creator, very often does not lead him any closer to God; it may not even clear the path toward Him.

Thus, we can only allow for a remedy that presents a universality as extended as evil itself—as Man himself. Even philosophy is going to seem limited. When philosophy separated from theology, it described itself as a *rational explanation of reality*; today it attributes the mission of saving Man to itself and claims to possess the power of salvation. Perhaps modern philosophy—or at least part of it—is an attempt at salvation; but it is nothing more than that: an *attempt*. This leads us to think that it is trying to save something that is falling apart for a different reason. Philosophy wants to save Man, not because Man breaks down without philosophy (philosophy did not claim this mission before) but simply because he is breaking down. Man perishes because he has lost faith. And since Man drowns without faith, philosophy would like to substitute it, to be a surrogate of religion. Therein lies the apparent greatness and the real tragedy of philosophy today.

Present-day evil lies on the lack of unity, on the displacement of problems, and on the absence of harmony. An untold number of tendencies, attractions, and values are claiming man's attention, and he himself cultivates and produces valuable works; but he has lost both his sense of totality and his way in the path to unity. Yet he cannot abandon this path. The unity toward which, ultimately, every man tends is Divinity itself, and the force that impels us toward this unity is the same one that draws us to God. Contemporary Man lives "torn apart" (in the etymological and also in the figurative sense of the word); his actions do not flow from the internal unity that unites every being and his actions. Instead, these become a juxtaposed series of activities. The *scientist* lives *with* his specialized problem, and he tries to live *off* of it as well—which is even more severe—without, often, relating it to the whole, either of his life or of science.

The *religious Man* tries to find the harmony of the cosmos, but, as a general rule, the bonds that tie him to the diverse spheres of the world are, in many cases, external and predominantly individual, which is not enough to tackle the human problem. Religion has become disconnected from life in the consciousness and the practice of the majority; it has become a watertight compartment, or, at most, a special and specialized "virtue."

The *philosopher* examines the meaning of being, but, generally, he does not find it, perhaps because the ultimate and integral meaning of existence escapes the very possibility of philosophy. Moreover, he does not know how to descend from general connections to less abstract realizations. His systems are plagued with gaps and rifts—not simply de facto, but de jure.

We believe that the evil of our current times is characterized by a lack of *synthesis*, and perhaps also by the fact that, consciously, we do not miss this synthesis enough; a synthesis that unifies (without making uniform) all of human life, that embraces Man in his totality, that makes him saintly and wise, strong and humble; that gives meaning to all the sciences and an ultimate end to all actions; that achieves peace for Man, peace for his scientific restlessness (which means neither repose nor solution to all his problems), peace for his longing to better himself, peace for his desires of happiness, and peace even to people among themselves. A synthesis that does not scorn even the most minute human atom, but rather puts it in its place, following a vision of the whole and a particular mission.

What is this synthesis? Is it possible? May it be the same as philosophy? These, and analogous questions, are what I briefly attend to in what follows.

Theory: Analysis of the Concept

Unitatis curam habe, qua nihil melius.[3]
St. Ignatius of Polycarp, *Letter to the Polycarp*

Etymology

What does "synthesis" mean? Philology is the first, or the last, thing we turn to in order to elucidate a concept. It is already apparent in Greek that σύνθεσις comes from the root (τι) θη(μι), which means "to place." Θέσις is the act of placing. Thus συν-θεσις is the act of placing together. The ending -σις means something active. "Synthesis" therefore possesses a dynamic, active character; it is an ideal, it is fulfillment.

Which things we must place together, and how we must place them together, are two problems that are posed by the mere word. For a universal synthesis, as the one we are searching for, we will simply have to place all things together. We must include everything that is thinkable. The relationship between what is thinkable, what exists, what is possible, and so on does not alter the problem in any way. We are referring to the most absolute totality.

However, the real problem lies in the small particle συν. To place jointly, to place *conjointly*, means to place some things next to each other following a certain sense of order; it means not leaving anything unconnected, without an *internal* relationship to everything else that exists—because Man must not place things at his own will, but according to the place that each one of them *requires*. Synthesis means *placing together in an ordered fashion*. Therefore, the entire question lies in searching for the *cosmic order* according to which everything must be placed—an order that is not an external bond that restricts the freedom of beings, but rather the maximum exponent of their perfection and, hence, of their freedom. We have elsewhere called this order *ontonomy*.

We must first address a previous issue whose solution can help us determine whether we can go forward or we have to recognize that we are facing a utopian and fruitless enterprise. Is this synthesis possible? And, analogously, does this order really exist?

In order to address these issues we must further elucidate the characteristics of this synthesis whose feasibility we are trying to determine. In other words, we must carry out a phenomenological analysis of what the *synthesis-in-itself* is.

Essence

Ex multis ratio colligit unam et simplicem veritatem.[4]
Thomas Aquinas. In *Boethius's De Trinitate,* q.6, a.1, ad 3

Chemistry has laid claim to the word "synthesis"; the field applies this term to the process of organic composition, which becomes more and more important every day. Leaving aside its definition as a substitute or as something artificial—as in the expression "synthetic product"—we are left with what is technically referred to as chemical synthesis.

In order to achieve chemical synthesis, the first thing we need is to gather all the elements that must be synthesized—be it in their elemental stage or as part of a more complex compound. These elements, or the products that contain them, must come into contact. Before that, chemists (as Nature requires) need a set of determined, favorable physical conditions, because any synthesis can only occur at a given pressure, temperature, and so on. The different elements are

---

[3] "Take care of unity, as there is nothing better than this."
[4] "Reason collects one simple truth out of many things."

put together in order for the reaction to occur, yet it may happen—as it often happens—that the synthesis does not take place: there must be a catalyst that acts as an accelerator of the latent energies that lie within the elements. The result, the synthesis (the fruit of the *tree*!) is something different from its components; it is a new product, a superior unity. In order to complete this description, even if briefly, we cannot forget the actual chemist who heats up, cools, separates, or unites—who, in one word, directs the necessary operations, always keeping in sight the ultimate end.

Chemical synthesis is, thus, the formation of a superior unity as of the elements that compose it—and it must always take into account the prerequisites that the nature of each of the substances that intervenes in the synthetic reaction demands. The essence of the universal synthesis we are searching for will also be the reduction of a superior unity of everything that exists, and the method to achieve it will also be conditioned by the nature of the objects that are being synthesized.

It might, at first glance, seem that this synthesis could be found in the classical *concept* of *being*, since this encompasses all of reality. The superior unity, that which coincides in all objects, appears to consist fully and solely in this: in that they *are*. However, mere "coincidence" does not equal synthesis; a common base is not enough for a real communion. Something else is also needed, something that does not let us settle for a purely static unity.

Recent developments in the field of chemistry have discovered the dynamic character of all reactions and, therefore, also of synthesis. In every reaction there is, to a greater or lesser degree, a balance between the components of the reaction and the result; that is, the product is constantly forming and decomposing in equal measure. This is what is missing in the simple unification of all things in the *concept* of "being." Once we reach the concept of being, ridding it of the specific characters (of that which distinguishes *beings*), we can no longer return to beings; that is to say, the reaction is irreversible. One of the elements of the reaction—the specific differences—was volatile, thus the balance becomes completely displaced. Philosophers say that even if the concept of being is the highest in its broadness, it is the lowest for the understanding: it is in fact the poorest in its contents, and one cannot "draw" anything out of it.

The being that logic leads us to is not useful because, once we reach it, we can no longer descend and again unify everything that exists in terms of our acquired synthetic vision. We need a Being that, even if it were different from the elements that lead us to it (that is, different from the creatures), it contained these within itself in a way that allowed us to return to them as of the formed product. We need a synthesis that, while unifying everything, did not make anything disappear and whose unity was not the poorest concept, but the richest: a synthesis that truly contained all of reality, and that was not attained through the path of impoverishment and subtraction (of specific features, so that we are left with the only thing common to all) but rather by way of enrichment (of eminence and transcendence).

The essence of synthesis is to be a unity: not a unity that contains nothing, but rather a unity that contains everything—even if in an imminent manner; a unity that is the harmonic culmination of the immense variety of material beings, as well as of the blossoming flora of feelings, tendencies, volitions, and thoughts that simmer in the depths—and on the surface—of all that exists. We need a synthesis that really saves (because Man needs to be saved), a synthesis that imposes an order, a synthesis that gives meaning to the world and to human life, not only in general terms, but even in the smallest details of our daily life.

This synthesis must be the supreme reality: pure Act; the most noble feeling: Love (may the philosophers forgive me—love in itself is not a feeling); the most absolute freedom: Life; the fullest reality: Truth; the most perfect end: Goodness; the most potent personality: Trinity

xxviii SPACE, TIME, AND SCIENCE

(I hope the theologians forgive me—we cannot affirm that the Trinity as such partakes in the composition of any creature). This synthesis must be God!

Logic offered us the formal and empty unity of *being*. The being of logic is not, as we have said, the synthesis we are looking for, among other things because it is not a product of synthesis but of analysis. We reach the concept of being not by synthesizing but by subtracting. And yet the concept of being is really the unification—although formal—of everything. Thus, formally, the synthesis we are looking for must possess the character of being in general, it must be *being*. Vitally, though, we require the exact opposite. The difficulty is resolved, the circle is closed; analysis gives us unity in *being*, synthesis leads to unity in *God*. God is, precisely, Being. God is "He Who Is."[5] God is *essentially* Being: the very Being that is: *ens a se, ipsum esse*—but not the *concept* of being, empty of content and dispossessed of reality. In other words, the synthesis we are looking for (as the particle συν reminds us) must be reconstruction, or at the very least, construction. In metaphysical terms we could call it return, reunification, and in theological terms, recapitulation, redemption; it is something dynamic to carry out, a duty, a goal.

Up until now we have seen that the synthesis of the cosmos, as an object of phenomenological reflection—whether or not it exists in objective reality—must possess the characteristics that have been pointed out, it must be God. God, if He exists, must be the origin of the totality of the universe and He who gives it meaning, that is, order. The *cosmic order* that we have alluded to is none other than the meaning that God has given the world. We are now able to answer the question that we posed.

Possibility

Quia non est impossibile apud Deum omne verbum.[6]

—*Lk 1:37*

Is synthesis possible? This question presents two sides. In the first place, one may ask if this cosmic order—whose existence supposes synthesis—really exists; and, second, if Man can ever know it.

After what we have said, we can sustain that the cosmic order really exists if we can demonstrate the existence of God. If God exists, since He must in essence be the orderer and the universal cause, this order exists, and the characteristics that for us define this synthesis, which indicate a close relationship and harmony between the diverse spheres of being, must be compatible with it.

Let us recall that we are not trying to create a new proposal for philosophy, but rather to develop the concept of a synthetic vision of the universe. And let it not be said that the demonstration of God's existence is assumed at the very beginning of the system (we are not trying to construct a system), because the full acceptance of the concept of Divinity is the fruit of a whole philosophy, and it follows a great part of metaphysics as its culmination. Synthesis is the path of descent that implies having first ascended (ανα-λυσις)[7] and having reached the goal. Consequently, it would make sense to insert a metaphysical system here that arrived at a demonstration of the existence of God and at the determination of His attributes. But

---

[5] Ex 3:14, especially in the Vulgate version.

[9] "For with God nothing shall be impossible."

[7] "Analysis" in its etymological meaning.

this is not the problem at hand, and in order to keep moving forward, we will presuppose such a metaphysical system.

Once the existence of God has been demonstrated, the following question arises: can Man have knowledge of the cosmic order? The possibility of synthesis for Man depends on the answer to this question. Naturally, it is not necessary to have exhaustive knowledge of this order to suspect that it exists.

We have come to a gnoseological problem, to the problem that has tormented us from modernity until well into our own century. Because of God's very nature, what we have been calling "cosmic order" here (that is, the order of things that our minds demand to exist for the harmony and unification of everything in a global synthesis) corresponds to the objective and real order of beings. The first order emerges from God the orderer, and the second from God the creator. Afterward, speaking for a realistic standpoint, that is, recognizing Man's objective and real knowledge, we can simultaneously establish the possibility of knowledge of the cosmic order, and with it, the synthetic vision of all things, even if we do not specify up to what degree. Synthesis is possible—however, does it really exist?

Existence

In lumine tuo videbimus lumen.[8]

Ps 36:9

The answer to the question of existence is very simple: *Ecce!* Behold! It consists in pointing to something existing and verifying if it coincides with the mental paradigm we have of it.

From the descriptions mentioned above we could sift out the criteria necessary to judge whether or not what is presented with the pretension of total synthesis is truly such, but the criteria of universality should be enough, as it is the most appropriate and the simplest. In fact, if we could apply it rigorously, exhaustively, we would have no need for any other one. A completely universal solution—fully "catholic"—cannot be false.

Only Philosophy and Religion present themselves with this required claim to universality.

Philosophy is clearly insufficient. Theoretically, it encompasses the whole sphere of knowledge, as a science of ultimate causes and of being in its entirety, but it is a fact that philosophy, as it is understood in the West, does not make Man happier or better. It is a fact that many philosophers who have delved into the foundation of human problems with great subtlety have not achieved personal synthesis in their own lives, the concordance of knowledge with action—which proves that *their own* being was not unified, that all their knowledge did not have a decisive influence on their being. Furthermore, philosophy does not appease the authentic human angst. I cannot leave the resolution of the personal mysteries of my destiny purely in the hands of reason, all the more when twenty-five centuries of philosophy show me the sad spectacle of a disturbing discrepancy between different philosophical systems, as well as the discrepancies between these and human life.

Philosophy undeniably comes close to a certain synthesis. But it is a partial synthesis, truncated in its base and in its vertex. *In its base* because, along with the intellect, Man possesses other faculties that should also be integrated in a universal synthesis. *In its vertex* because even within the sphere of the intellect, it leaves synthesis incomplete, without forcing

---

[8] "In thy light shall we see light."

it to end or to penetrate into Ultimate Reality—or even hoping that it might. A complete synthesis can make use of philosophy, but the two cannot coincide.

Religion is capable of a greater synthesis, but merely on a personal level. The meaning of life has been resolved for the saint, the person for whom religious values possess their full force; he or she has found the path to happiness in the union between Goodness and Truth. Religion takes Man in his entirety and impresses a unitary direction upon his entire being and doing, simultaneously giving him strength (grace) to get closer to his ideal, to God—even if in a discontinuous and asymptotic way.

But the synthesis we need cannot be verified on a total level. Philosophy may make Man wise, religion may make him saintly; but we must still verify the union, achieve synthesis between these two values. The saint may have achieved Goodness. Perhaps the wise man has reached Truth; but there may still be divorce between Goodness and Truth. Human wisdom is folly in the eyes of God.[9]

It is true that within the field of religion there are two types of wisdom superior to metaphysical knowledge, though these take us outside of the merely religious field and place us within a full Christianity—and Christianity contains much of what the pure essence of religion demands. Even so, neither *theological wisdom*, which assumes a faith of inspiration, nor *wisdom as a gift of the Holy Spirit* constitute the last step of synthesis. Wisdom as a divinely "infused gift" is the seed of divine life. He who possesses it achieves the *highest* synthesis that Man is capable of achieving on earth; however, he does not yet know the cosmic order that reigns in the world in full detail; there are many things he cannot see clearly because of their height and his poor eyesight. There may even be a subject of inspired wisdom who possesses neither theology nor metaphysics. This is the highest synthesis but not the most *complete*—the most elevated, but not the deepest.

The ultimate human synthesis is the result of the development of a previous divine seed; the strengthening of human vision so that it may be elevated and deep, sublime and complete; it is *beatific vision*; it is seeing God face-to-face and seeing God in everything. The blessed are not only saintly and happy, they are also wise. They see the first and last connections of things in God. Their entire lives are simply participations in the Pure Act. They have already *con-verted* into God.

Thus, synthesis exists: it is the possession of God, it is the entire world in its fulfillment, it is the return and the recapitulation of the cosmos, it is its definitive state or, in Christian terms, the new heaven and the new earth where God will be in all.[10] The only thing left to do is see how this synthesis may be achieved.

Fulfillment

Beati mundo corde quoniam ipsi Deum videbunt.[11]

—*Mt 5:8*

Returning to the earth once again, Man can now ask how he can get closer to his goal—not only to be able to one day possess a full synthesis, preparing himself for a good death, but also to be able to achieve, in whatever measure possible, even down here, a synthetic vision of

---

[9] See 1 Cor 1:20.
[10] 1 Cor 15:28.
[11] "Blessed are the pure in heart: for they shall see God."

the universe. Only the thirsty will be quenched,[12] and those who, in this world, do not feel the need to reach perfection, to reach the maximum synthesis that their forces will allow, to move toward God, is not worthy of the kingdom of heaven. A *full* life is the only preparation for death. Preparation for death consists in preparation for *life* in all of its meanings.

To whom will Man entrust himself in order to be able to achieve this synthesis, which coincides with his own end?

If God is the synthesis, the only way to reach this synthesis will be through *union with God*. However, since this union cannot be fully achieved in this world, it makes sense to wonder how close one may get.

The "re-ligation" with God is given to us by means of "religion." The restoration of human nature makes the union with God possible again. After Man's fall, this union can once again be reached—thanks to Redemption—with the correct disposition of the will and with the love of charity, and without any need for the whole of one's being to be already disposed toward God. That is to say, order is reestablished by its own eminence as soon as what is superior returns to its proper seat, and without requiring (not yet, here on earth) a complete "rebuilding" of the individual. This is what we have been calling *personal synthesis*. If Man joins God through love, his entire being participates in that union, because Man is a unity; synthesis is truly personal. Besides goodwill, right intention, the saint may have an innocent ignorance of the inferior orders or an internal disorder of these. Temptation, the inclination to evil, and so on, never completely disappear here on earth. One might even be ignorant of what happens within one's own self.

But, furthermore, a *reconstruction of the original cosmic order*[13] is often mentioned, whose culmination—although not necessarily so—is the elevation of Man to a new sphere. This is *objective synthesis*. Strictly speaking, it is not the reestablishment of an old ordination, but rather the *implantation of a new order*.

Man will, therefore, come closer to achieving synthesis by having *sanctity* in the personal order and aspiring to *truth* with all his soul in the objective order. By saying "with all his soul" we mean aspiring toward complete truth without limitations of any sort, without any hidden desire that truth be anything other than what it is. What matters is not philosophy, or theology, or science as such. What matters is the harmonic solution to all of the problems that Man's life on earth, in all its complexity, presents, from the material—and economical—problem of physical existence to the problem of our destiny, and including all purely intellectual problems. In short, we are interested in uniting the personal and the objective syntheses. And for this, Man must turn to all the solutions that are available to him.

How is objective synthesis achieved? Certainly, it is not independent of personal synthesis; what's more, the ideal of all personal syntheses is to reach the highest possible degree of objectivity, to ground every union with God, not only in the correct disposition of the will—elevated by grace—but also in the correct disposition of all of one's being, aiming at God.

From everything we have said, we can deduce that achieving objective synthesis consists in cooperating in the reestablishment—or, better yet, in the reformation—of the universal order that Redemption initiated by laying the foundation, the cornerstone, pointing in the right direction and giving Man the strength to continue the work. Every human being on earth must be, in this sense, "co-redeemer."

There are two necessary prerequisites to get close to objective synthesis: knowing this order in some way and having the strength to achieve it.

---

[12] See Mt 5:6.

[13] The ἀποκατάστασις; see Acts 3:21.

We have seen that philosophy and religion are both insufficient to reach an objective synthesis. The former makes our vision of things deeper, but it lacks the required height and strength to make us achieve it. The latter elevates our being, but it does not necessarily illuminate our intellect. It is then necessary to verify its sublimation, in order to be able to reach a superior unity. We must elevate philosophy and turn it into *theology*. We must put religion into effect, making it deeper, bringing it to life, turning it into *Christianity*. The intimate rapport of theology and Christianity (which potentially contain philosophy and religion) constitutes what can justly be called *Christian synthesis*, the objective synthesis we have been looking for. Theology reveals the order of things, and Christianity confers the necessary strength (grace) to achieve the synthesis.

Perhaps it would be more accurate to speak of "theological philosophy" instead of theology. What we consider essential is that the rational knowledge of philosophy is "in-formed" by a superior form of knowledge: faith.

This is not the place to go into further disquisitions. We merely wish to point out the existence of a latent set of problems.

Man is a unity, and it is he who confers unity to his search for truth when, with a sincere attitude, he turns to all the means within his reach to press forward in the *path to synthesis*, for which his heart and his intellect necessarily long. The only factor that must condition whether he appeals to one or the other means of capturing reality is the actual structure of reality itself, since, needless to say, he is not *creating* synthesis but *discovering* it, realizing it—reenacting it, to put it more precisely.

The senses, certain affective intuition, reason, moral instruction, purely intellectual intuition, faith, and, within this, a certain experience of the Divine are the instruments Man possesses to capture the truth.

Since Man is essentially rational (this is his defining characteristic), reason always has the last word. As a result, even if, ultimately, faith must prevail (since it is the superior mode of knowledge), everything is coated in the form of the rational. And even though the malady caused by our present-day lack of synthesis is primarily due to a shortage of faith, the battle must be waged *in* intelligence, and victory must be obtained *by* intelligence—under the guidance of faith. Consequently, even if faith presents itself as a superior form of knowledge, it must always be used in accordance with reason, which is able to perceive the reasonability (not the rationality) of faith itself. If I wish to investigate the structure of matter, I will fix my eyes on it and describe it; but if I possess a microscope, I will use this instead of only relying on my eyesight. Why should I abstain from using a microscope when it exists? If faith gives me a deeper vision of the world, I will turn to it. Needless to say, I do not abdicate my reason because of this, as I do not disregard my sight when using the microscope. The microscope makes no sense for a blind man; faith means nothing to a being that is not rational. But faith is also a gift from God. Only he who possess a microscope will be able to "see" what the microscope discovers for him; only the *grace* of faith will make us discover this new dimension of things.

On the other hand, even if the knowledges that faith gives us are the guiding principles of our investigation into truth, we must apply our entire being in this investigation. In its own way, faith resolves the problem of personal synthesis, it gives our vision the necessary *height*; but only with the help of all the other human faculties can it also give the fecundity and penetration that our vision needs in order to shed some light on the cosmic order. Faith shows us the goal, though veiled and imperfectly, and it indicates the path; but this path must still be traveled. And this is Man's task in his pilgrimage on this planet! We not only have to walk along this path step by step, but we must also plant plenty of milestones along the way. We have not yet made the most of the guiding force of faith, even in the purely human terrain.

In the simile with chemical synthesis that we introduced earlier, we spoke of the need for contact, for gathering all the elements in order to synthesize them. This is philosophy's mission: to investigate all the elemental bodies that constitute reality and describe their properties. But synthesis is not achieved without a catalyst: human reason does not have enough strength to synthesize all things. Only a few reactions (the merely dialectical ones, and these in a state of disintegration governed only by common sense) are possible without a catalyst. Faith is the catalyst of reason. Taking this parallelism even further, we could say that the chemist in his laboratory symbolizes the Providence that, in the laboratory of the world, directs Man and the entire universe toward the end for which they have been created, building the definitive synthesis of all beings that constitutes the end and the meaning of creation.

Once we know the cosmic order, every Man must do his part. There is an intimate concatenation between knowing and achieving the cosmic order: they are interdependent. Knowledge—because it requires faith—emerges from the longing to achieve the cosmic order in its personal aspect, being aided by grace; and, simultaneously, its objective achievement presupposes knowledge. The Christian, as such, possesses the seed, the beginning of the solution to all problems, both theoretical and practical. The ultimate and internal meaning of the world is given by Redemption, and it consists in moving toward the kingdom of God.

It is specifically about looking for the intimate connection of this idea with practical life and with all the sciences, even empirical ones. In this way, Christian synthesis gives the entire world meaning. Those who possess it more come closest to the perfect synthesis.

The Dialectics of Synthesis

Omnia in mensura, et numero, et pondere disposuisti.[14]

—*Wis 11:20*

All contributions to truth, wherever they may come from, are in themselves a contribution to synthesis. What is missing is their coordination, their *internal* relation. If the point of departure, the coordinating criteria is a human point of view, it will never be totally objective. The objective point of view would be God's perspective. But "no one has ever seen God: it is the only Son, who is close to the Father's heart, who has made him known."[15] We have God in Jesus Christ, and we can only know Jesus Christ through faith. This is why, earlier, we spoke of faith as that which makes the intellect bear fruit.

We now wish to examine the rational structure that the synthesis should possess from the point of view of the intellect, wherever it may get its content: that is, to scrutinize the dialectics of synthesis.

Until now we have used the term "synthesis" to designate very diverse—though analogous—concepts whose meanings did not lend themselves to misunderstanding because of the context. Now it is necessary to group these concepts.

Absolute synthesis, that which really *is*, which is full Reality, which gives meaning to and unifies everything, is God. We can therefore consider it the synthesis of all that is created. (Up to a certain point, we could call the first one *ontic synthesis* and the second one *onto-logic synthesis*, the work of the *Logos*). The latter may be understood on an eminent plane: then

---

[14] "You have ordered all things by measure and number and weight."
[15] Jn 1:18.

the *cosmic synthesis*, the alpha and omega of creation, would be Jesus Christ; or as the internal ordainment of every being toward God, constituting the *cosmic order* of which we already spoke. Within this order there is a complex being endowed with a special characteristic that we are interested in studying further: Man, a being created with its own powers of ordination, endowed with freedom: *human synthesis*.

We have also already seen that the *perfect* human *synthesis* is constituted by beatific vision; but because it cannot be achieved in this world, we inquired after its terrestrial substitutes. It is then that we distinguished between a *personal synthesis* consisting of the union with God on earth, and an *objective synthesis*. The former is only an incomplete part of the latter; it is like its first stage, as all personal syntheses possess an objective base (there can be no saintliness with a completely false vision of reality) even though it may later follow a subjective path. Any objective synthesis needs a personal starting point, just as it needs faith as an indispensable element. Within the same personal synthesis we can consider a purely natural approach to God and a supernatural union. For the latter we have reserved the term *sanctity*. Personal synthesis could also be called *moral synthesis*, since it is Man's attempt to reach his maximum perfection; this is the preferred realm of freedom.

Objective synthesis has also been called *Christian synthesis* because it coincides with the full and total development of Christianity. Christianity is not only *a* religion, it is Man's perfection and his maximum development; it endows him with his highest dignity as the authentic son of God. *Terrestrial synthesis* is not independent of cosmic synthesis. Man is an integral part of it, and cosmic order is, in turn, seen through Man. Moreover, Man is a microcosm, and in this sense, the order of creation is reflected in his very being.

If objective synthesis represents an ordination of all the strata of the human being, we have to distinguish the diverse existing ontological spheres. Within each sphere is a synthesis that represents its systematic ordination. These are the *external syntheses*, all of them partial. We will later have to organize them according to the Whole: we will constitute a *heterogeneous synthesis*, which must be a *total synthesis* that coincides with objective synthesis.

The following diagram outlines everything we have just said:

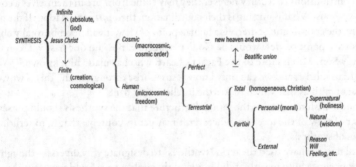

Each external synthesis will be directed by the special structure of each particular ontic sphere. Reality itself is what conditions the method we use to approach it.

Heterogeneous synthesis offers even greater complexity. We have already seen the preeminence of faith and the role of reason in any terrestrial synthesis. All the same, some points still need to be further developed.

A total synthesis cannot be merely *rational*. Man is much more than pure reason. The supralogical connections that synthesis strives for cannot be only the fruit of reasoning. When we say that they cannot be merely rational, what we wish to express is that an ultimate synthetic vision of the world cannot be the logical consequence of simple rational speculation. Reason is not the most elevated organ Man possesses for the discovery of reality. Its primary function is not to discover, not even to investigate, but rather to explain, to demonstrate. One demonstrates a known thesis; one explains a given solution. Within its field, reason is certainly autonomous—nobody doubts this—but nowhere it is written that its field is universal, nor that it has absolute independence. Reason does not consider the pressing issues of human life. We only search for what we already know; and this guiding principle or previous knowledge cannot belong to reason, since then we would already rationally know that which we must rationally explain, instead.

Synthesis, on the other hand, must be *reasonable*—which does not mean rationalizable. Even if Man participates in other forms of knowledge, reason is his characteristic form of knowledge, and with it he can and must judge the value of the rest of the instruments he can turn to in order to grasp the truth. Even if our faith is not—and cannot be—rational, it is reasonable that we have faith; the reasons for its credibility are rational. There is such a thing as "judging by sympathy" (*per modum inclinationis*), but its correlate of judging by science, by knowledge of causes, also exists. This is true even in the philosophical field. True philosophy possesses logical rigor, but its building blocks are made up of intuitions; it resists the assaults of logic, but it does not allow logic to supervise the construction.

In brief, it is reasonable to say that human reason is not the guiding principle of everything. *Reasonable* is the synthesis that, independently of its content, finds the connecting threads between data logical and finds a *formally rational* structure. In contrast, something is rationalizable, or simply *rational*, when reason penetrates the data and completely dissolves them, that is, when it reaches the primary logical principles that show themselves to be rational—even if they are not necessarily so—inasmuch as they are the very basis of rational thinking. The facts are here, thus, *materially* rational.

The path to synthesis essentially consists in looking for—and to a certain point, finding—the bonds that connect things, which are not precisely joined by logical ties just because they belong to heterogeneous spheres. These connections, these essential constants of the world, these invariants of the universe, will give *meaning* to things and processes. *Being* is given to the intellect, and its *meaning* is also given when the intellect learns the order of the being in question within the scale of beings. Meaning is thus the intellection of a being according to the Whole. This is why synthesis ultimately gives us the meaning of things, and to aspire to a human synthesis is nothing more than the desire to find *meaning to all of life*.

Through faith we know not only the authentic meaning of things—which coincides with the goals God has revealed that He carries on with the world, both globally and particularly—but also that this meaning is not a prolongation of the meanings given to us by the intellect, but rather different and sometimes apparently contrary to these, because faith lies on a superior level. Grace does not destroy nature, but rather supposes and perfects it. The perfection of a fallen nature is above all a reestablishment that is often accompanied by painful amputations—not of limbs, to be sure, but of the shapeless growths that have developed attached to them. The Beatitudes, for example, are not a continuation of the human ideal, rather they propose a new, divine ideal to a fallen nature that is different from the pure ideal that our rational mind can forge.

This is why doing without faith in the construction of a total synthesis will not get us as far as we would go with it; indeed, it will also make us end up in error. In other words, a non-Christian *philosophy* is not necessarily false, but a non-Christian *synthesis* is necessarily false in that it is missing fundamental data for the construction of said synthesis. Philosophy can be freely used when we deem convenient to do so—a full synthesis cannot stop walking the path until the end—but if it ignores the Christian ontological and axiological trans-formation, it will draw consequences that do not exist because meanwhile a new order of things has intervened.

The synthesis of the universe must include a certain number of principles—of all the orders—from which the foundation of a synthesis that embraces all of reality may be built. These principles must be compatible and independent, really "principles," that is, not derived from others, and they must also be sufficient in number so that nothing, *on principle*, is left out.

One may dialectically state that a synthesis is not true, in the first place, if it is not complete, that is, if we can find an authentic problem that it does not contemplate—which is obviously different from not being able to find an immediate solution for it. In the second place, if it is contradictory, or if through it, by applying reason alone, we reach an obvious contradiction. Now then, can we say that a synthesis is true simply when neither of these cases occur? That is, are completeness and noncontradiction the only criteria of truth for a synthesis? We already pointed out that the mere criteria of universality ("catholicity") is enough to guarantee truth. This assumes that there can only be one explanatory system of the world; that there is only *one* synthesis; that any other attempt will, sooner or later, arrive at a contradiction. The problem of the world only allows for one singular solution, once all the data have been gathered. Even if these data are not exhaustively known by Man, his knowledge of them does not introduce such arbitrary parameters so as to affect the solution with radical insecurity.

Now then, what criteria can there be to know that we possess all the data? If synthesis were the work of reason, we could never a priori know that we possess the totality of elements we have to synthesize. But since it is not a fruit of our dialectical reason, since it does not require an exhaustive analysis of what exists in order to reach the peak of the system from where we would have to descend while showing the synthesis, this criteria is given by the—material as well as formal—eminence of the principles from which we start. This makes it impossible to complete the synthesis here on earth, though it does not make synthesis itself impossible. This compels the synthesis to be open, to leave room—although a limited amount of room—for the Unknown, for Mystery, for evolution, development, perfection, growth; so that there is room for the visions that are infra-, supra-, or a-rational, as are, for example, the (respectively) mythical, mystical, and symbolic, giving each one its corresponding value. This compels the synthesis to be humble, to recognize that the building of human wisdom is still under construction, and that Man does not supervise it.

Synthesis is neither a closed system nor a monolithic and finished conclusion. Synthesis is essentially dynamic, and it is also *in the process of becoming*, like Man. The principles we have alluded to can be known, but the foundations are not completely laid out and the building is far from complete. Moreover, here on earth, synthesis can never wave the flag of a finished construction; its roof is always open, it is the sky and the stars.

For this very same reason, the synthesis we search for is compatible with a plurality of philosophical and even theological systems. Strictly speaking, synthesis is discovered as it is being built according to a "master plan" that only the Father knows. . . .[16]

---

[16] See Mk 13:32.

SECTION I

SPACE AND TIME

Part 1

ORIENT

1

TIME AND HISTORY IN THE TRADITION OF INDIA

Kāla and Karman

"Above time has been placed a vessel full to overflowing."[1]

The existence of the universe—and hence the history of Man and of the cosmos—is under the sway of two superior forces: *kāla* (time) and *karman* (the act).[2]

The first part of this study is accordingly devoted to time, and the second, which is shorter, to history. We approach the problem of time by following the various paths of the tradition that is summed up in a passage of Bhartṛhari: "The vision of time varies according to whether time is regarded as power, the Self, or a divinity. In a state of ignorance [time] is the first thing to manifest itself, but in the state of wisdom it disappears."[3]

Time

Time as the Fruit of Ritual Action

In the earliest experience of *Vedic* India, time was perceived as the actual existence of the beings we describe as temporal. There is no such thing as empty time. "Time" is an abstraction that does not exist. What does exist is the (chronological) flux of beings, and this process makes sacrifice possible.

Time is born with sacrifice, and it is by sacrifice that time is once again destroyed. This concept is at the root of the intimate relationship between worship and time, and provides us with a key to the understanding of the central place of sacrifice and Man's participation in the unfolding of time. In this sense, time is something that Man makes, in close collaboration with the Gods: time, that is, the continuing existence of beings, is a theandric product.[4]

In the *Vedas*, in the Saṃhitā period, we find several words to designate time, for example, *āyus*, life-time, life span,[5] or *ṛtu*, the right time for sacrifice, the season.[6] Abstract time is of

---

[1] *AV* XIX.53.3: *Pūrṇaḥ kumbho dhi kālā āhitaḥ* . . .

[2] Despite India's close connection with Buddhism, the fact that Buddhism developed outside India, and that Indian Buddhism alone would require a separate study, will provide us an excuse for this limitation of the field to India—although we are the first to deplore such a limitation.

[3] Bhartṛhari, *Vākyap* II.233.

[4] See my *Le mystère du culte dans l'Hindouisme et le Christianisme*, in particular, the chapter "Le culte et le Temps," pp. 43–52 (Paris: Cerf, 1970). In Volume VII of this *Opera Omnia*.

[5] See *RV* X.17.4.

[6] See *RV* I.49.3 and 84.18.

no interest to the *ṛṣis*, the poet-sages of the *Vedas*, for whom there is no continuity of time apart from ritual activity or the act of a God (for instance, Indra).

> This time ... has no reality, that is to effectiveness, except in the moments in which divine or sacred acts are concerted. .... In this succession of acts linking moments it would be vain to look for a given continuity: continuity is no more than the fruit of the constructive activity which recommences day after day.[7]

In the *Vedas* the unit of time is the day, which is the center of all experience of time.[8] Dawn and twilight are "junctions," the most "critical" moments in the whole day. It is "from day to day" (*dive dive*)[9] and by dint of the daily sacrifice, the *agnihotra*, that time endures and existence continues. Hence the well-known saying "If the priest did not offer up the sacrifice of fire every morning, the sun would not rise."[10]

Later, as the sacrifice became increasingly elaborate, and the building of the fire altar in the *Brāhmaṇas* stretched out over a year, the year became the larger unit of time. The sacrifice remained the foundation of the temporal structure, each brick of the altar corresponding to one day in the year.

It was the *Puruṣa*, the cosmic Man of the *Ṛg-Veda*[11] and Prajāpati in the *Brāhmaṇas*, who was originally immolated in order that the world might exist: the world exists only by virtue of this primordial sacrificial act.[12] In a second act—which is, however, performed in the reverse order—the sacrifice reconstitutes the Lord of living beings. Since Prajāpati is identified with time, symbolized by the year,[13] this reconstitution corresponds to the consolidation of time, the structuring of the year. In the *Vedas* this activity is frequently compared to that of weaving.[14] It is the weft being made up of the day and the night[15] and ritual moments.[16]

Another very ancient image that represents the rhythm of time is that of the wheel (*cakra*), the symbol of the solar cycle. This image plays a vital part, even today, both in speculations on time and as a folk symbol of the "cycle" of existence.

To sum up, in this intuitive *Vedic* view of time there is, first, the idea of a relationship between time and the act of worship (*karman* in the intrinsic sense of the word) that is so close that the one does not exist without the other; and second, the *Vedic* Man—unlike Man in subsequent periods—aspires either to long life or to a certain kind of continuity that does not seem to be guaranteed by the cosmological events.[17]

---

[7] L. Silburn, *Instant and Cause* (Paris: Vrin, 1955), 43.

[8] See *RV* X.37.9 etc., and *SB* IX.4.4.15 for the continuation of tradition, for example.

[9] See, e.g., *RV* I.1.3; X.37.7.

[10] *SB* II.3.1.5.

[11] See *RV* X.90.

[12] See my "La Faute Originante ou l'Immolation Créatrice. Le Mythe de Prajapati," in E. Castelli, ed., *Le Mythe de la Peine* (Paris: Aubier, 1967), 65–100, esp. 70–79. In this *Opera Omnia*, Volume IX, Part 1.

[13] See *SB* V.2.1.2; VII.1.2.11; X.4.3.3, and also *BU* I.5.14; *Praśna-upaniṣad*, I.9, etc.

[14] See *RV* IV.13.4; V.5.6; *AV* X.8.37ff., etc.

[15] See *AV* X.7.42–43, etc.

[16] See *RV* III.3.6; X.130.1–2, etc.

[17] See *RV* II.33, etc.

Time as a Cosmic Power

A second fundamental intuitive notion of time, which is moreover akin to the first, goes so far as to consider time as a cosmic power that is the *fons et origo* of reality. Not only is this a very ancient concept, for which there are analogies in other civilizations, but above all it is a widely held popular view, belonging probably to the less brahmanic stratum of Indic tradition. This would explain why nearly all orthodox schools reacted vigorously against what they called *kālavāda*, that is, the doctrine that places time at the center of reality and ascribes to it a universal causality. Any vehement negation presupposes precisely the existence, even the predominance, of that which is denied: thus the markedly a-temporal and transtemporal tendency of a certain kind of Hinduism might be accounted for precisely by the important role played by absolute time in the outlook of the period.

Time as an Absolute Principle: Fate

We leave aside here the question whether the concept of absolute time was imported into India from Babylon or Greece,[18] and to what extent this concept is traceable to Iranian influences.[19] Our primary concern is with the importance of this doctrine from the period of the *Atharva-veda* onward. The exaltation of Great Time in two hymns of this *Veda* is the earliest expression of this vision of Time as "the creator of the creator," Prajāpati, who is *brahman* (the ultimate principle of the universe) itself:

1. *Time draws [the chariot like] a horse with seven reins,*
   a thousand-eyed, fruitful-loined, immune to age.
   Astride it are poets who understand inspired songs.
   Its wheels are everything that exists.

2. *Thus time draws seven wheels,*
   it has seven hubs, its axle is [called] non-death.
   On the hither side of all these existences
   it advances, first among the gods.

3. *A full vessel has been placed above Time.*
   We see [Time] even though it is
   in many places [at once].
   Opposite all these existences
   Time [is also seated], they say, in the highest firmament.

4. *In oneness Time bore these existences,*
   in oneness it encompassed them around.
   Time the father became time their son.
   No glory higher than his.

5. *Time engendered Heaven above,*
   Time also [engendered] the Earths we see.
   Set in motion by Time, things which were
   and shall be are assigned their place.

---

[18] See O. von Wesendonck, "*Kālavāda* and the Zervanite System," *Journal of the Royal Asiatic Society* (January 1931): 108–9.

[19] See J. Schleftelowitz, *Die Zeit als Schicksalsgöttin in der Indischen und Iranischen Religion* (Stuttgart: Kohlhammer, 1929).

6. Time created the Earth; in Time burns the Sun;
    in Time [yes], Time, the eye sees far off all existences.
7. In Time is consciousness; in Time,
    breath; in Time is concentrated the name.
    As Time unfolds
    all creatures rejoice in it.
8. In Time is [sacred] Fervour, in Time [yes], in Time
    is concentrated the all-powerful brahman.
    Time is the lord of all things,
    Time was the father of Prajāpati.[20]

All reality depends on Time, and even sacrifice, which elsewhere in the *Vedas* is considered as the supreme force, is likewise subordinated to Time. It is important to note the relationship, spoken of in practically all texts on time, between absolute time and empirical time, the creator and the creature, father and son,[21] cause and effect. Here space is supported by, and extended in, time.[22] Even inner realities—consciousness and breath—are under the sway of time.[23] A universal dynamism sets everything in motion. To put it succinctly, *kāla* is here the supreme divinity that is subject neither to the personified creator (Prajāpati) nor to the impersonal universal powers of the sacrifice or of *brahman*: "After conquering all worlds by the Word, time advances, the supreme god."[24]

The *Maitrī-Upaniṣad*, which reflects several concepts of time, quotes a sentence from the doctrine of absolute time (*kālavāda*): "From time flow beings, through time they grow old, in time they are destroyed: Time that is amorphous assumes a shape."[25]

There are, accordingly, two aspects of time: transcendental time and time embodied in the sun, the planets, and the empirical divisions of time.

It is difficult for us to establish all the connections between this ancient *kālavāda* doctrine and the much later texts on time in the *Mahābhārata*, for whatever we know about this doctrine comes mainly from quotations occurring in texts THAT seek to refute it.[26]

Besides, what is reflected in the *Mahābhārata* is more of a popular concept, which probably had a profound influence on the attitude of less "Vedic" circles, namely the concept of time as fate.[27] A certain Hindū passivity, which is almost fatalistic, too readily ascribed to a Muslim influence in India, has its roots in this vision of time.

The most frequent quotation attributed to the *kālavāda* is the following: "Time ripens beings, time enfolds creatures: Time keeps watch when all are asleep. Time is hard to overcome."[28]

While it is obvious from the *Mahābhārata* that many different views have been held about time, the predominating one certainly seems to be that of an insurmountable fate.

---

[20] *AV* XXI.53.1–8, from the French translation by L. Renou in *Hymnes Spéculatifs du Veda* (vv. 9 and 10 have been deleted) (Paris, 1956).

[21] Ibid., 54.3 (from Renou, *Hymnes Spéculatifs du Veda*).

[22] Ibid., 54.2 (from Renou, *Hymnes Spéculatifs du Veda*).

[23] Ibid., 53.7 (from Renou, *Hymnes Spéculatifs du Veda*).

[24] Ibid., 54.6 (from Renou, *Hymnes Spéculatifs du Veda*).

[25] *MaitU* VI.14.

[26] See Gaudapāda's reference, in *MāṇḍKār* 8, to the *kālacintakāḥs*, "those who reflect on time" and regard it as the origin of everything.

[27] *Kāla* is very close to *niyati* and *daiva*.

[28] *Mahābhārata* (from now on: *MB*) XII.231.25; XII.227.79; etc. See, however, "But no one here on earth knows Him in whom Time is ripened" (XII.244.2).

[Time is] the Lord who works change in beings—that which cannot be understood and that from which there is no return. Time is the destiny [flux: *gati*] of everything; if one does not follow it, where can one go? Whether you try to flee from it or remain motionless, you cannot escape from time. The five senses cannot grasp it. Some say that [*kāla*] is Fire, and others that it is the Lord of the creatures [Prajāpati]. Some conceive of time as a season, others as a month, a day, or even an instant. . . . There are those who say that it is the hour [*muhūrta*]: but that which is uniquely One has many forms. Time must be acknowledged as that which controls everything that exists.[29]

Here, as in many other texts, time is perceived as indivisible and omnipotent, beyond divisible and measurable time.

Time is the cause of all; it is time that creates and destroys,[30] that binds people by its links[31] and causes their joys and sufferings, regardless of their actions.[32] According to this conception, Man is purely and simply delivered up to fate, and his actions and efforts are powerless to alter his lot. In the end, the destructive aspect dominates: it is Time that hastens the progress of all beings toward dissolution.[33] Time is compared to an ocean where one can see neither the other shore nor any island of refuge.[34] Time becomes the great destructive power, sometimes synonymous with death.[35]

The frequently expressed idea that time "matures" or ripens beings simply means that it leads to old age and ultimately to death. The Buddhist view of the impermanence of existence, in the context of an ever-fluctuating and fleeting dynamic motion, seems to have influenced this vision of time.[36]

The *Purāṇas* still retain echoes of the conception of Time as a divinity, but they often attempt to integrate it in their respective theologies. The statement that *kāla* is without beginning and without end, ageless, omnipresent, and supremely free, that it is the great Lord,[37] is a continuation of the ancient *kālavāda*: "Time, being infinite, caused the end; being without a beginning, creates the beginning, the immutable."[38] However, the *Purāṇas* tend to regard time rather as a divine power.

Time as a Power of God

The *Atharva-veda* already spoke of "a full vessel placed above time,"[39] and time can be visualized as forever replenished from that source. This fullness beyond time can be understood in the light of the *Maitri-Upaniṣad*, according to which "*brahman* has two forms: time and timelessness."[40] Thus there is no longer absolute time or relative

---

[29] *MB* XII.224.5–54.

[30] *MB* XII.227.73.

[31] *MB* XII.227.81–82.

[32] *MB* XII.227.85.

[33] *MB* XII.227.103.

[34] *MB* XII.231.23 and 27.

[35] See *MB* XII.27.44, which speaks of "the ocean of time infested by great crocodiles of decrepitude and death."

[36] Even Gods are subject to impermanence. See the dialogue between Bali and Indra in *MB* XII.224.

[37] See *VisnuP*, I.2.26, etc.

[38] *BhagP*, IV.11.19.

[39] *AV* XIX.53.3.

[40] *Akāla, MaitU* VI.15.

time, but time on the one hand and, on the other, pure timeless transcendence. This is evidence of a radical transformation that springs from the *Vedic* concept of sacrifice but which did not produce its full impact until the Upaniṣadic and Vedāntic period: the eternal is no longer thought of as limitless time or absolute time, but as something that transcends any kind of temporality. The vessel full of time, from which time flows out, is not itself temporal: it contains time while being itself timeless: "Time ripens [matures] all beings in the great Self—in which time itself is matured: he who knows this knows the *Veda*."[41]

But this transition does not take place smoothly or without controversy: theism, of which one of the earliest documentary testimonies is the *Śvetāśvatara-Upaniṣad*, attacks the *kālavāda* as materialistic and atheistic: "Some sages say that [the cause of the world] is nature, others say time. They are mistaken, it is the power of God which cause *brahman*'s wheel to turn in this world."[42]

Time is not an independent reality; it is the Lord who is the "knower and creator of time,"[43] and time is His instrument.[44] The *Upaniṣad* emphasizes the transcendence of the Lord vis-à-vis time: "He is the origin. . . . He is beyond threefold time. . . . He is higher, He is other than the tree [of the world], other than time and forms."[45] "He, Rudra, repossesses the worlds at the end of time."[46]

In both the Śivite and Viṣṇavite theologies, any reality that is not identical with the God—though very frequently identified with Him—becomes His power or *śakti*. Because of its cosmological importance, time is one of the God's earliest powers: *kālaśakti*, his instrument in the creation, preservation, and destruction of the universe. However, in the *Purāṇ as* there are many doctrines regarding time. For instance, the *Śiva-purāṇa* recognizes three levels of time, from which we can trace the process by which absolute time was absorbed by Śivaism. In its first stage, time is not different from Śiva, it is eternal. In its second stage, it becomes the power of Śiva, Śiva being the innermost essence (*ātman*) of time. Śiva rules the universe by means of time. In the third stage, time is considered as a limiting principle, being the product of *māyā*, cosmic illusion. Only in this last stage is time divided up, and causes succession, duration, and limitation. What has happened is that the transcendent absolute aspect of time has been transferred into the sphere of the God, and its empirical aspect into the sphere of the *māyā*, that which veils reality. However, the concept of *kālaśakti* creates a certain balance between these two extremes.

Viṣṇavism accepts the same theory. In the *Mahābhārata* the preeminent place of time is expressed as follows: "Beyond the spirit is intelligence, beyond intelligence Great Time, [but] beyond time is Lord Viṣṇu, from whom proceeds all the universe."[47]

In the *Bhagavad-gītā* it is Kṛṣṇa who is identified with time, in its indestructible[48] but destroying aspect.[49]

---

41 Ibid.
42 *SU* VI.1.
43 *SU* VI.2.
44 *SU* VI.3.
45 *SU* VI.5–6.
46 See *SU* III.2.
47 *Śāntiparva* 199.11.
48 *BG* X.33.
49 *BG* XI.32.

About the divine immanence the *Bhagāvata-purāṇa* says, "The Lord penetrates all existences by his own power (*ātmamāyā*): within he takes the form or the spirit [*puruṣa*]; on the outside [he takes] the form of time [*kālā-rupa*]."[50]

The cosmological role of *kāla* is frequently described in the *Purāṇas*, according to which time exists in a latent state during the dissolution of the world, and is awakened by the God at the moment of the re-creation.[51]

Yet *kāla* is, and remains, more closely linked to Śiva than to Viṣṇu, and it is its destructive aspect that dominates all other cosmological aspects. Śiva himself is called *mahākāla*, Great Time, meaning death.[52] The destructive Goddess Kālī is perhaps the female counterpart of the God Rudra-Śiva, who is identified with time.[53]

The conception of *kālaśakti* profoundly influenced Hindū thought. Even a philosopher like Bhartṛhari describes it as the first power of the One: "Because they depend on its time-power, which is held to be responsible for differentiation, the six transformations [*pariṇāmas*] like birth, etc., become the cause of the variety of existence."[54]

And the first commentary explains that this power is independent (*svātantrya śakti*) and the cause of everything.[55]

The two concepts dealt with so far encompass a great variety of views, but they have in common the fact that they belong to a religious universe: whether they deal with ritual time or with time as an absolute or divine power, these concepts represent two aspects of time as a sacred value, though many others have been traditionally held.

Time Devoid of Real Power

For some civilizations, the "overflowing vessel" of time has shattered into countless pieces, and all that remains are the different temporal parameters of the different spheres of reality. For others, the vessel is, as noted above, the symbol of the Author of time.[56] But there is still another view, which has found illustrious adherents in India: the view of time as the supreme form of cosmic illusion.[57]

It is relatively easy to trace back the development of this thought. When the anthropomorphic features of the "vessel above time" recede, the vessel ceases to be the lord of temporal reality, becomes its impersonal cause, and takes over the full import of its reality, so that everything that overflows from it is no longer fully real.[58]

Time thus becomes devoid of reality, or at least of any power over reality.

It even becomes the symbol of illusion. The vessel above time always remains full to overflowing, since it never really empties; there is no time that runs out, nothing falls from

---

[50] *BhagP* III.26.18. See also *VisnuP* I.2.14.

[51] See *BhagP* III.8.11, etc.

[52] This intuition is of fairly ancient date; it occurs already in the *Brāhmaṇas*, where Prajāpati is identified with time and death. See Silburn, op. cit., 53ff.

[53] Despite her other etymology: "the Black (Goddess)."

[54] *Vākyap* I.3.

[55] *Vṛtti* on *Vākyap* I.3.

[56] See *kālākura* in *SU* VI.2 (and VI.16), quoted above, or the "lord of the past and the future" in *KU* IV.13 (II.1.13).

[57] See the notion of *nitya-anitya-vastu-viveka*, "discerning between the temporal and the eternal," in Śaṅkara, *BSB* I.1.1. See also *Vivekachudamani* 20.

[58] See *MU* I.1.1 with the reduction of past, present, and future to the *Om*.

the timeless vessel.[59] The eternal here devours time.[60] Time here belongs to *māyā,* interpreted as illusion; it is based on *avidyā,* or cosmic ignorance. It is merely something superimposed on the Absolute, *brahman.*[61]

Philosophical speculation subsequently sought to modify this vision, and we can now see that much of Indic philosophy might be characterized by the degree of reality that different systems ascribe to time.

Linguistic Hermeneutics

Indic philosophy took an interest in time starting primarily from a consideration of grammar and language, but also (this is striking in Yoga) on the basis of a spiritual desire to transcend time. The other philosophical systems gave little thought to time; at most, they included it in their systematization of the factors of existence, without however basing their conception of the universe on the phenomenon of time.[62]

We limit ourselves here to referring—by way of example—to the analyses of time carried out by the philosopher of language, Bhartṛhari, in his *Vākyapadīya.* In his chapter on time[63] Bhartṛhari studies the concepts of time that existed in his day[64] and expounds his own views.

It is obvious that time is closely linked to action, for, as stated in a Tantric text, space is a limitation of form and time of action.[65] Bhartṛhari maintains that time, as an absolute, is only differentiated and divided up because of actions (*kriyābhedas*),[66] for there is no perceptible time without some action, which suggests a *before* and an *after,* speed or slowness.[67] An action consists of a succession of instants (*sakramas*). In the analysis of its two functions, the role of time is described in detail: the permissive force (*abhyamljña*) and the preventing or retaining force (*pratibandha*). These are the two functions of time that keep the order of the universe: without them, everything would be produced or destroyed simultaneously.[68]

The first function enables the virtual to become real, to blossom in time; the second prevents things from materializing before their time and ensures that they do not continue beyond their allotted time. Thus time is called the secondary[69] or efficient[70] cause, which alone can regulate and activate the other causes.

Some schools of philosophy have denied the existence of time independent from action.[71] Bhartṛhari, on the contrary, only recognizes the existence of time as such, utterly independent of any division between time past, future, and present.[72] In his opinion, it is the sequence of

---

[59] See *The Doctrine of Sattvaśūnya* in the *Tattvatraya* of the Rāmānuja school (Chowkhamba Sanskrit Series, no. 22), p. 62: "Time is empty of being. It is (merely) the cause of the modification of nature and of its evolution."

[60] See *BG* XI.32.

[61] See, for example, T. M. P. Mahadevan, *Time and the Timeless* (Madras, 1954).

[62] See E. Frauwallner, *Geschichte der Indischen Philosophie,* vol. 2 (Salzburg, 1956), 111.

[63] *Klasamuddeśa,* in *Vākyap* III.9.

[64] Fifth century and early sixth century, according to Frauwallner.

[65] See *Tripura Rahasya* XI.46.

[66] See *Vākyap* III.9.32. See also *Nyayamanjari,* Kashi Sanskrit Series (1936), 123–27.

[67] See Satyavrat Śastri, *Essays on Indology* (Delhi, 1963), 174ff.

[68] See *Vākyap* I.3 with *vṛtti,* and III.9.3–8.

[69] *Sahakarikāraṇa:* see *vṛtti* on *Vākyap* I.3, etc.

[70] *Nimittakāraṇa.*

[71] See for example Yuktidīpika, quoted by Satyavrat Śastri, op. cit., 192.

[72] There is a certain correspondence between *trikāla,* triple time, and *triloka,* the three worlds.

actions that makes us speak of past, future, and present, time itself being always the same. In other words, we speak of the past because an action is completed, and we think of the future when we imagine coming events. The proof of the existence of time in the present is more difficult to establish, and implies a detailed analysis of grammatical usage, which we do not study in this essay.

Time is called the pure mirror that reflects the real form of beings.[73] It is time that, so to speak, strips the reality of things.

Lastly, the grammarian/philosopher Bhartṛhari recognizes that any action would be impossible without time, whether we try to make it relative or not. A purely mental concept cannot get away from a fact.[74]

Already in the *Mahābhāṣya* and in Kaiyaṭa's commentary thereon we find the affirmation that it is change (*pariṇāma*) in beings that forces us to accept the reality of time.[75]

These examples are sufficient to show that both empirical and phenomenological analyses can be found in the Indic tradition. Yet the fact remains, and significantly so, that language is the starting point of these reflections. Other analyses—to be found in Yoga and Buddhism, which are just as detailed—show a purely spiritual concern, and do not lead to an empirical affirmation but rather to the negation of any objective reality of time.

The Interiorization and Transcending of Time

The *Vedas* sought the continuity of time through the sacrificial act, but the *Upaniṣads* began to question the permanence of this act and this continuity.[76] Immortality, the sole concern of the Upaniṣadic sages,[77] was no longer ensured by the performance of rite. Continuity was no longer to be found externally, in the ritual or the cosmos, but internally, within Man, or more exactly within the Self, the *ātman*. And yet cosmic connotations are not lacking in this new vision.

One of the first factors to be descried in the search for this continuity is the breath of life, *prāṇa*.[78] *Prāṇa* is, in the first place, the life principle and the individual aspect (*adhyātma*) of the unabating, omnipresent cosmic wind (*vāyu*).[79] Second, *prāṇa* is not merely physiological breath, but the rhythm of respiration that also becomes a spiritual exercise (*vrata*) to overcome death.[80] This is the beginning of yoga exercises to control breathing (*prāṇayama*). If even the sun is said to rise and fall in the *prāṇa*, one begins to realize the cosmological importance of breath. Later on, *prāṇa* is identified with immortality (*amṛta*)[81] and *brahman* itself. The important point is that respiration corresponds to an internal time, and it is the mastering of this internal rhythm, especially in yoga, that leads to the transcending of time—both externally and internally.

---

[73] See *Vākyap* III.9.

[74] Ibid.

[75] *Mahābhāṣya* II.2.5 and Kayaṭṭa's *Pradīpa*.

[76] See *KU* II.10–11, etc.

[77] See, for example, *BU* IV.5.3.

[78] See the competition among the vital organs, which is won by *prāṇa* since the other organs depend on it: *BU* I.5.21–23.

[79] See *BU* I.5.22: "As *prāṇa* is the central breath, so Vayu [the air] is the central divinity. Other divinities interrupt their activity, but not Vayu. Vayu is the divinity which knows no rest."

[80] See *BU* I.5.23: "This is why one must ... observe one single practice. One must breathe out and in, in order to avoid succumbing to Mṛtyu the evil [one]."

[81] See *BU* I.6.3.

The transition from the ritual time of the *Vedas* to the interiorized time of the *Upaniṣads* occurs evidently at the point where respiration, interpreted as a sacrifice, takes the place of the sacrifice of fire (*agnihotra*).[82]

In addition, the *Upaniṣads* look for what is beyond the past and the future;[83] they seek infinitude (*bhūman*)[84] and plenitude (*pūrṇam*), which they find symbolized more in space than in time: the atmosphere, infinite space (*ākāśa*), is also present in the innermost chambers of the heart (*hṛdākāśa*).

The *Kālacakratantra* contains a distant echo of this interiorization of time as a spiritual exercise designed to transcend time: the yogi "relates inhalation and exhalation with day and night, and then with fortnights, months and years, gradually working up to the major cosmic cycles."[85] The purpose of this and other similar practices is clearly to succeed in discovering the unreality of time,[86] and eventually to transcend it.

From the Upaniṣadic period onward, both time—succession and duration—and the universe of the act (*karman*) are divested of their value, and at the end of this process the doctrine of the cycle of existences (*saṃsāra*) will give rise to a negative conception of time. The metaphysical schools that have liberation (*mokṣa*) as their goal tend, in theory, to deny time any real value, and seek to achieve a state of existence that is beyond time—to use a yoga term, "the cessation of mental states,"[87] one of which is time.

In order to affirm the relativity of time, these schools envisage time as an intellectual conceit having no counterpart in any "real thing." This almost psychological reduction of time is expressed, for instance, in the *Yoga Vāsiṣṭha*, which tries to show the unreality of instants and cosmic ages.[88] It says that, depending on the mental state of the subject, an instant may appear as a *kalpa* (eon) or, contrariwise, an eon may be experienced as a single instant.[89] In short, time per se does not exist. He who is absorbed in meditation knows neither day nor night,[90] and in the end, self-knowledge, illumination, encompasses all the future within one instant.[91]

The philosophical schools following the *Upaniṣads* and Buddhism take the instant, *kṣaṇa*, as their fulcrum for the "leap into timelessness." Here it should be noted that the doctrine of instantaneousness and the "propitious instant of liberation"[92] profoundly influenced Hindū spiritual teachings.

So, the interiorization of time, the first step toward transcending it, leads toward the discovery of "subtle time," the infinitely small unit of time, in which time and eternity, movement and stability meet, since "it is on the stasis [*sthiti*] of time that all quietude depends."[93]

In his *Yoga-sutra*, Patañjali recommends "meditation on the instant and the succession of instants in order to attain knowledge born of discernment."[94]

---

[82] The entire *Prāṇagnihotra-upaniṣad* is based on this substitution.
[83] See *KU* II.14 (1.2.14).
[84] See *CU* VII.24.1, etc.
[85] Quoted by M. Eliade in *Images et Symboles* (Paris: Gallimard, 1952), 113.
[86] Ibid., 112: "By working in this way on his breathing, the yogi works directly on experienced time."
[87] *Cittavṛtti*.
[88] See *Yoga Vāsiṣṭha* III.20.29.
[89] See ibid., III.60.21; III.103.14, etc.
[90] See ibid., III.60.25–26.
[91] See ibid., III.60.171.
[92] See Silburn, op. cit., 403ff.
[93] See ibid.
[94] *YS* III.52.

The commentary defines the instant—the sole "real" facet of time—in terms of atoms (*aṇus*) and their movement.[95] The succession of instants and units of time—here the influence of Buddhism is clear—are not real (*na asti vastu-samāhāraḥ*), but exist solely in the mind (*buddhi*) as an intellectual or verbal concept. Time is empty of reality (*vastuśunya*: without substance), and the yogis admit only the present instant, without past or future. Hence the purpose of meditation (*saṃyama*) is to attain the perception of the instant, which is pure and—paradoxically—unflawed by temporality, for it is this subtle time (*sūkṣma*) that is the springboard for the timeless and the eternal. Transformations (*pariṇāmas*) are not denied, but they are reduced to the sole instantaneous dimension of time.

Not only in Buddhism, but also in other philosophical schools, the instant acquires a kairological connotation—in other words, salvation, the awakening, the release from the yoke of time, may be achieved at any instant, or else at the propitious instant (and here, a certain notion of grace is implied).

The Śivism of Kashmir (the Trika school) goes still further: "Since no time unites instants in one substance, the yogi will be able to separate and penetrate the liberating interstitial vacuum [*madhya*] in between two successive instants."[96]

According to this system, the instant is described as the vibration of consciousness; it is the eternal present that alone confers plenitude and felicity,[97] a state governed by neither space nor time.[98] It is through the instant that one penetrates into timeless reality.

*   *   *

Can we now try to define more closely the concept of time in traditional India?

We have quoted the richly evocative symbol of the overflowing vessel. We may perhaps hazard a guess as to some aspects of this vessel overflowing with time.

The first aspect is the co-extensiveness of time and beings. There is time so long as beings exist, and beings exist so long as they have time (to exist).

The second aspect is that the same degree of reality exists between beings and time. If beings are regarded as real, unreal, or halfway between (*sadasadanirvacaniya*),[99] time partakes of the same degree of reality.

Although language is inadequate to express the third aspect, most systems of India hold that time, and beings with it, does not exhaust the whole of reality. The vessel that contains time makes time possible, but is not itself temporal.

History

The very notion of history raises some preliminary problems of terminology. Are we talking about the concept of history, or about the way in which history is experienced, or about the historical dimension of Man? Should we start from a Western conception of history and look for corresponding elements in other cultures? Obviously, we do not seek to express Indic categories in Western terms, nor vice versa. Our object is rather to discover

---

[95] Vyasa Bhaṣya on *YS* III.52.

[96] L. Silburn, *Le Vijnana Bhairava* (Paris: De Boccard, 1961), 69.

[97] See Abhinavagupta, *Parātrivṇśika*, quoted by Silburn, *Le Vijnana Bhairava*, 62.

[98] *Digdeśakālaśunya*, in Silburn, *Le Vijnana Bhairava*, op. cit., vol. 22, p. 76, where the experience of plenitude beyond time is once again linked to the practice of respiration; see also vol. 24.

[99] See *BG* IX.19 and later Vedantic speculations; see, for example, *BS Bhaṣya* I.3.19; I.4.3; II.1.27; etc.

the intuitive views of India and to situate them in the Indic world of thought, where they may possibly occupy a place homologous to that occupied by history in Western thought.[100]

A further comment is appropriate here: it seems that the "idea" of history and of historicity (as distinct from the "experience" of history) makes its appearance precisely at the time of a break with, or a deep crisis in, tradition. It is when tradition is challenged that one most fully realizes the historical character of existence: reflection needs a certain perspective. The West is going through a crisis concerning its own tradition, and is keenly aware of its historicity. India, on the contrary, and despite its manifold crises, is still living in tradition, without a perspective of historical self-reflection, that is, without being fully convinced of "living through" history. There are, admittedly, some very diverse historical levels within the modern culture of India, but "history" in India is mainly the living of tradition, rather than any subsequent reflection on this culture.[101]

As to tradition itself, the concept that has played, and still plays, a role comparable to that of the "historicity of Man" in Western philosophy might be said to be *karman*.[102]

Karman and the Historical Dimension of Man

In dealing with time, we saw that action is intimately linked with time. Both in the world of the *Vedas* and in the analysis of factual experience, it is often the deed, the human or divine action, that determines time. Apart from certain doctrines of absolute time, the law that governs time and history—taken together as a whole—is the law of *karman*.

Karman is in the first place action, then the residuum of the action that produces good or bad results[103] and that lives on after the person,[104] and lastly, the law that governs the retribution of actions and the network of interconnections between the *karmans* of beings. This "universal causality," as the law of *karman* is commonly known, explains virtually all the relations in the universe, and goes far beyond any individual conception of transmigration. *Karman* combines personal elements (the repercussion of each action unto the outermost limits of the cosmos) with impersonal ones (the element of "creatureliness" that all beings have in common) in such a way that *karman* may be said to be inexhaustible, that is, without end, as the aggregate of the residues of human acts. The beings who attain *mokṣa* may be released from their *karmans*, but the *karman* as such has not ended.

Who then is the subject of *karman*? While today's Western world tends to regard the individual, or particular individuals, as the subject or subjects of history, India tends to deny that the illusory ego can provide the subject of *karman*. Śaṅkara's saying has become classic: "There is no transmigrant [subject] other than the Lord."[105]

Karman as a universal law does not reflect the externals of history, an explanation of events (though such an explanation may be inferred from it), but rather the inner historicity, subtle and hence invisible. A reflection on *karman* is more than a reflection on the causes of events.

---

[100] See my "La loi du *karma* et la dimension historique de l'homme," in E. Castelli, ed., *Herméneutique et Eschatologie* (Paris: Aubier, 1971), 205–30. In Volume IX, Part 1 of this *Opera Omnia*.

[101] Therefore, the sources we cite as to modern Indian culture are not so much modern books on history (which are, in any case, quite rare) as rather a certain contemporary school of phenomenology.

[102] See my article quoted above.

[103] See *BU* IV.4.6.

[104] See *BU* III.2.13, etc.

[105] *BSB* I.1.5: *satyam neśvarād anyaḥ saṃsāri.* Literally: "In truth, no other than the Lord (trans) migrates."

Furthermore, the very term "event" should be understood not as connoting something that happens externally, or even as an external change in a constellation of space and time, that is, a change in the position of beings, but as a *karmic* modification, that is, a modification in a being's *karman*. This is a question of anthropological incidences, rather than sociological accidents—of achievements rather than occurrences.

The question of Man's freedom with respect to his own or the universal *karman* has also concerned the Indic mind. Philosophical and religious schools have proposed different paths for escaping from what appears to be determined and have defended the free human act (*puruṣakāra*), that is, Man's power to break the actual chain of the causality of actions and reactions. Some of the more deterministic views come very close to the interpretation of *kāla* as fate.[106] And it was to get away from these views that, on the one hand, the idea of *puruṣakara* (which is, for example, basic to Yoga: Man's own effort to transcend his *karman*) and, on the other, the doctrines of divine grace were developed.

This having been said, no school or religion in India, perhaps even in all Asia, would deny the law of *karman*, however diversely interpreted.

The relationship between *karman* and time, the counterpart of the relationship existing between historicity and time in Western thought, is twofold.

In the first place, time's raison d'être is precisely the existence of *karman*. So long as *karman* exists in the world, time will be necessary. *Karman* is, as it were, the intrinsic quality of time, that which gives substance and density to time itself.

Second, without time, *karman* would be unrealizable but would remain in a latent state—and without the collaboration of time, so to speak, beings would not be able to attain either their goal, through the performance of their duty in this world, or the liberation, for which the consummation of all *karmans* is a prerequisite.[107] The example of the "liberated during their lifetime" (*jīvanmuktas*) shows this relationship: for the individual who has "raced through" all his or her *karmans*, time has ceased, so to speak. They live outside time, and their bodies are said to continue to exist only until the consumption of all the subtle vestiges of *karman*, of which their bodies are but the condensation.

Karman is thus linked less to history, in the sense of historiography, than to the intrinsic historical character of beings, whereby their past determines the present and the future, and not *one* of their actions is wasted or without repercussions. The structure of reality is based on this historicity, which makes reciprocal interactions possible throughout the world, in a pattern of universal solidarity.

Myth and History: Itihāsa and Purāṇa

A people's vision of history indicates how it understands its own past and absorbs it into the present. But it is not so much the written interpretation as the way in which the past is experienced, and continues to be experienced, that bears witness to a people's attitude toward history. India has experienced its past much more through its myths than by interpreting its history as a recollection of past events. This does not mean that there is no such recollection—in certain regions there is even an acute consciousness of history in this sense[108]—but

---

[106] The difference being that *kāla*, in this case, is an external though encompassing power, whereas *karman* is the result of the specific history of each being.

[107] See the two functions of time described by Bhartṛhari, *Vākyap* I.3.

[108] It is enough to quote Śivaji's role in the *Maharashtra*: the king who repelled the Muslim invasion (1627–1680).

there are no criteria for differentiating between myth and history: a disconcerting fact for the Western mind, which does not realize that history is its own myth. Commenting on that great epic, the *Mahābhārata*, G. Dumézil said that it "is not what we think of as history, but what takes the place of history, and renders the same services both to dynasties in search of great ancestors and to a host of listeners longing to hear of a glorious past."[109] In other words, it is myth as the counterpart of history.

The expressions for "mythical history" or "historical myth"—the two are inseparable—are respectively *itihāsa*, "it happened thus," used to designate epic literature, and *purāṇa*, "ancient narrative," used to designate, more specifically, mythical literature in which historical elements are obviously intermingled.[110]

Myth and history should not be correlated to legend and truth, but should be regarded as two different horizons of reality. Only within a historical view does myth appear as legend, that is, as less real than historical facts. Within a mythical view, on the other hand, history is interpreted as inferior to myth. What a Westerner considers as history in the West he would see as myth in India. In other words, what he calls "history" in his own world is experienced as "myth" by Indians. But, conversely, what in India has the degree of reality of history is what, in the West, an Indian would term a "myth." To put it differently, what an Indian in India would call "history" is experienced by Occidentals as myth. From a Western point of view, it is not history that matters to the Indian mind. Whatever is of great importance in a people's historical consciousness is precisely mythical.

The personalities and events that profoundly mark and inspire Indian life (in Western terms, which carry historical weight) inevitably give rise to myths, since any event having what we may call existential "consistency" goes into the realm of myth. "Myth" has a greater degree of reality than "history." This statement might be illustrated by the popular reaction at the time of the birth of Bangladesh.

The process of the creation of myths has not come to an end, and it has been amply proved by Mircea Eliade that "archaic Man" is more interested in archetypes than in the uniqueness of a historical situation.[111]

If it is conceded that this "mythical consciousness" corresponds to the Western "historical consciousness," at least with respect to its function of preserving and integrating the past, it should be said that, while India has not thought profoundly about "history," it has organically assimilated historical facts into "myths." This assimilation might be compared to sacred trees like the *pipal*, the secondary roots of which reach down from the air to the soil, take root again, and sometimes survive even when the trunk has gone.

Reintegration of History

Nearly all Indic traditions have regarded the ultimate meaning of life as a-temporal, and in a certain sense nonhistorical. They have placed greater emphasis on detachment and the surrender of historical values than on temporal commitment, since true history always transcends the temporal. Yet such commitment has not been lacking, and its justification is to be found precisely in a religious conception of secular duty. The teaching of the *Bhagavad-gītā* was, and still is, an outstanding example of this attitude.

---

[109] G. Dumezil, *Mythe et Épopée* (Paris: Gallimard, 1968), 239.

[110] All the *Puraṇas* give, for instance, the genealogies and dynasties of the kings (*yaṃśas*).

[111] See M. Eliade, *Le Mythe de l'Éternel Retour: Archétypes et Répétition* (Paris: Gallimard, 1949), *passim*.

It has been said that it is no accident that the *Bhagavad-gītā* was rediscovered in our time, and that it has provided a spiritual basis for many political movements. The reason is that it teaches that the path of action (*karma-mārga*) is as valid as the traditional paths of knowledge (*jñāna-mārga*) and of loving devotion to a God (*bhakti-mārga*). The advice given by Kṛṣṇa to Arjuna on the battlefield (the plain of Kurukṣetra) was precisely not to relinquish his duty (*svadharma*),[112] but to fulfill his role in a given historical (that is, mythical) situation. Action must be purified (*karmaphalatyāga*),[113] and this "unattached" action alone will preserve the universe and the order of the world (*lokasaṃgraha*).[114]

The great leaders of modern India, like Mahātma Gandhi, Vinoba Bhave, and others, found their source of inspiration in this spirituality of action in the *Bhagavad-gītā*. They purged political action of personal aspirations and gave a divine significance to history. They approached history not as an end in itself—as if a more perfect future society might be the aim of humankind's expectations—but as a duty assigned by God, which must be carried out with total commitment, yet at the same time with the greatest possible detachment.

Gandhi's interpretation of history may be summed up as follows:[115] (1) The meaning of earthly life and the meaning of history are identical; (2) the ultimate meaning of life is a-historical or transhistorical, but at the same time it is conceived as dependent on the social order; (3) since this ultimate meaning of life is transcendent in relation to both history and social structure, Man's hope does not lie in a future utopia; and (4) since the ultimate meaning of life is a-historical, there is no absolute concept of history.

* * *

We might conclude this study with a reference to the familiar metaphor of the circularity of time and history as an expression of the quintessence of Indic experience, while giving it its proper interpretation.

The circularity of time, hence the repetition of history, does not imply that time is infinite or history unlimited—quite the contrary. Circularity is the symbol of contingency, ontological limitation, and closure of time, as well as the enclosure of history and the contingency of events. The circumference is limitless, and the circle indefinite, only in a two-dimensional world. This metaphor from geometry implies, precisely, that reality has other dimensions, and that one must break through encircling time if one is to save oneself and achieve Being. One must escape from the domination of time, not by running toward a future that is always ahead, but by leaping out of the circle.

It there were nothing else but time, the "successive" points of passage through the same point would be absolutely identical; in other words, there would be only one single point. This is the cycle of *saṃsāra* or, perhaps, hell. This is what history would be if we were not able to escape from it.

---

[112] See *BG* II.31 and 33, etc.
[113] See *BG* V.12, etc.
[114] See *BG* III.20 and 25.
[115] From a personal communication from Minoru Kasai, the author of a study on Gandhi's idea of history.

2

Toward A Typology of Time and Temporality in the Ancient Indic Tradition

A first intuition on the nature of time could be formulated by saying that time is lived or experienced as the ontological temperature of being, that is, as that which manifests the activity of every being, and consequently also its existence as intelligible and its degree of reality, be it provisional or ultimate. In other words, time "is the revealer of all beings,"[1] it is the space (to use a conjugated metaphor) that makes the unfolding of beings possible. In this sense, "Time engendered the things that were and that will be";[2] it is (to borrow terms from different schools of thought) the exterior, visible, material, phenomenal dimension of every being. *Brahman* is "the author of time"[3] to the same extent that it is its destroyer.[4]

The degree of reality given to time in the different schools of thought is the same as that given to beings. That is to say, where beings are considered as real, so is time, and where things are considered as less real or unreal, time has the same coefficient of reality. Time is almost never considered in itself, but almost always as the dimension of expansion, that is, of the "temporality" of beings.[5] Time is that expansion that permits the phenomenal consciousness of beings and their extension in the material world (geography and history). Today, in India, the most widely used word to designate time is *kāla*, but it appears just once in the *Ṛg-Veda*, which speaks, instead, of *āyu* or *āyus* (cf. αιων, *aeon*, *saeculum*), which means the vital force, the time of life, the long life, the existential span or duration of every being.[6]

A second intuition, which immediately follows from the previous one—although "historically" it is found "before" (but must we accept the "Western" schema as *the* paradigm?)—shows time as the "product" of divine or ritual action, by the very fact that this very action calls the beings into existence. The reasoning is simple: time is the foundation of all action since there is no action without change and no change without time. "From time all beings emerge."[7] Now, any real change is a modification of the very constitution of beings. But only sacred or ritual action can, by definition, produce such a modification. To recall a

---

[1] *Gauḍapāda Kārika* I.6.8.
[2] *AV* XIX.54.3.
[3] *SU.*
[4] See *BG* XI.32, etc.
[5] An exception would be the two late hymns in *AV* XIX.53 and 54.
[6] *RV* X.42.9.
[7] *MU* VI.14.

quote from the previous chapter, "If the priest did not offer the fire sacrifice every morning, the sun would not rise."[8]

In other words, sacrifice both makes and destroys time; it is sacrifice that reenacts, but in the opposite direction, the sacrificial act of Prajāpati (the Father of the Gods), that is, that act by which, in sacrificing and dismembering himself, He "created" the world.[9] Man, the immolated *puruṣa*, is "remade" by an act of "de-creation" that extends in time, or rather, time is the occasion for the progress of the world toward Him, "in whom the beginning and the end of the universe are united."[10] "He alone is inexhaustible time."[11]

This means that time is not a "given" but a product. It does not arise from the order of quantity, but from that of quality, the same quality of existence itself. Each being has its own time, as it were. Time is the great factor of solitude and isolation. In order to achieve communion, one must transcend time, one must pierce the temporal crust of beings. In time we are separated and fragmented.[12]

Later traditions reunited these two intuitions in the concept of *karman*, which is homologous to the concept of historicity. Every action both produces *karman* and is the fruit of *karman*. *Karman* is a sort of condensation of time, a cosmic link of universal solidarity on that level of reality that we call precisely temporality.[13]

This leads us to a third intuition, often poorly understood and awkwardly expressed when, paying tribute to "modernity," one tries to explain things in the perspective of the other and forgets that the understanding of irreducible elements does not allow such "reductionism." We may *translate* an ultimate insight, but we cannot *reduce* it to other insights without depriving it of its character of ultimacy.

We refer to the so-called circular conception of time and to the popular Indic conception of vast cyclical periods. The circularity of time does not imply that it is infinite, but exactly the opposite, that it is contingent and limited, that it is closed. Hence, in order to achieve or reach reality, one must shatter it, transcend it, escape from its grasp, break the circle. The cycle is not the symbol of infinitude but of finitude, not of opening but of enclosure. The circumference is indefinite only in a two-dimensional world; the geometrical metaphor means precisely that reality has other dimensions, and that one must break the temporal encirclements (and not fall into another super-time) in order to save oneself, in order to reach Being.[14]

The metaphor of circularity also expresses the fact that, from the point of view of temporality, the "second" passage or circuit through the same point on the circle cannot be distinguished from the "first" passage. In a word, points A and A_1 are temporally identical: there is no "second" passage or circuit through the same point. Here we should situate the problem of history and eschatology, even though in a sense that represents an original contribution to modern culture.

---

8 *ŚB* II.3.1.5.

9 See *RV* X.90, etc.

10 *SU* VI.2; *MU* IV.6; *BG* X.32.

11 *BG* X.33.

12 See my *Le mystère du culte dans l'hindouisme et le christianisme* (Paris: Cerf, 1970), 43–52, on "Le culte et le temps" (op. cit.).

13 See my "The Law of Karman and the Historical Dimension of Man," *Philosophy East and West* 23, no. 1 (January 1972): 25–43.

14 One is tempted to quote Augustine's sentence: *Ut ergo tu sis, trascende tempus* (*In Iohannem* 38.10): "Transcend time, so that you can *be*."

Taking Sanskrit as an example, we may perhaps grasp a fourth intuition: the primacy of the static over the dynamic, of being over becoming. It is striking to find that in Sanskrit a positive value is ascribed to most terms of a static nature vis-à-vis those that express movement and change. Its grammar is based on the primacy of the substantive over the verb. The entire structure of Sanskrit rests on juxtaposition, on apposition, on repetition; it revolves around the noun. A majority of verb forms are substantivized. Adjectives are used to express functions that, in Western languages, require auxiliary verbs. Time expressions such as "yesterday" and "tomorrow," "the day *before* yesterday" and "the day *after* tomorrow," "three days *before*" and "three days *later*," are in each case the same word in Hindi, the essential point being the distance from the center, without giving priority to an orientation toward the past or the future.

But here we must understand the situation in its own terms. This primacy of the temporal is not a temporal stasis. The stoppage of time would be death, if it did not carry with it an access into (or rather the discovery of) what is currently designated in negative terms, such as the a-temporal, the immutable, the immortal.[15] In keeping this in mind, we should also cite the divine attribute of the destruction of time as the path toward liberation. Kālī is also the Goddess of Mercy.

Buddhism is a world in itself and presents practically the whole range of conceptions of time. Limiting ourselves to the intuition of the Buddha and within the horizon of India, we could perhaps add another fundamental experience: the radical relativity (*pratītyasamutpāda*) of the entire possible human experience, and hence of "reality" in every sense accessible to Man. "If you meet the Buddha, kill him," says a later tradition. Here time is not gone beyond or transcended: it must be killed, eliminated. There *is* no transcendence, because there is no springboard sufficiently solid from which to jump out of the human condition. *Nirvāṇa* represents the total extinction of all that can be burned, destroyed, extinguished. Hypothetically, if "there is" any reality whatsoever out there, we could know only one thing about it, that it is *not* as we might imagine or think it to *be*, that it has nothing to do with whatever meaning we might give to the word "being," not even if we consider it as transcendent. There *is* nothing, and certainly there is *not* nothing. To say that the other shore *is* not, is as wrong as saying that it *is*. An ontic silence is called for.

Time then is the symbol of Being, of all that is; Being and Time are strictly linked. Time as such is the best proof of the contingency and impermanence of everything. Time is neither rectangular nor circular, but punctual, even though it would—again—be more exact to say "nonpunctual." Being is Time and Time is Being.

All is nonpermanent, *sarvam anityam* (or, in Pāli: *sabbe saṅkhārā aniccā*), all things are transitory. Here indeed is the central Buddhist concept of time.

---

[15] See the *nityānityavastuviveka* of the Vedāntic tradition, e.g., in Śaṅkara, *BSB* I.1.1; etc.

3

TIME AND SACRIFICE

The Sacrifice of Time and the Ritual of Modernity

Abstract[1]

In most traditions, liturgical time does not tally with ordinary, everyday time. The latter is governed by the horizontal succession of daily occurrences. The former would like us to enter into contact with a privileged moment, which appears to be discontinuous when seen from the perspective of linear-chronological time. Liturgical time follows a vertical and/ or a circular time pattern; it is qualitative, ambivalent, and multidirectional (e.g., it moves "backward" as well as "forward").

Theologies of every kind have tried to explain liturgical time by means of various hypotheses, most of which rely on the objectivity of the event, fact, revelation, experience, or any other chrono-genetic moment. The modern sciences of religions, on the contrary, have generally tried to explain liturgical time by referring to the subjectivity of the believer.

Using the paradigms of sacrificial time in the Hindū and Christian traditions, I try here to show that these hypotheses—the objective and the subjective—derive from the philosophical assumptions that underlie, respectively, traditional theologies and the classical history of religions. This paper suggests a possible synthesis by presenting the traditional category of sacrifice as still valid for modernity (although adequately transformed).

Further, this study maintains that we should overcome the subject/object dichotomy at the epistemic level, and the natural/supernatural dualism on the ontological plane, when dealing with ultimate human problems. The nature of time is not an a priori in our minds or, if we extrapolate, in the phenomena themselves, nor is it an a posteriori, that is, detectable only as a "given" external fact. Time is at the crossing point between consciousness and matter.

Finally, I hope to provide a pertinent example for our contemporary situation of a cross-cultural study that tries to relate two different traditional religions and the present-day degree of awareness. My expectation here is to be able to carry out a cultural fecundation, trying to find a field sufficiently wide and deep to allow a cross-fertilization between tradition and modernity.

Introduction

A fundamental reflection on time, if it does not deprive the question of its meaning from the very beginning by assuming that we already know what time is, has to take into account

---

[1] I understand "abstract" literally, that is, that which remains once all that the article says has been abstracted.

what Man has understood time to be.[2] Because neither Man nor time are objectifiable entities, Man's self-understanding belongs to what Man is, and similarly Man's opinions on time
cannot be excluded from fundamental research on the nature of time. In other words, we have
to draw on the global human experience if we want to say something about that universal
deity—speaking with the *Vedas*—that we call by the name of time.[3]

The immediate purpose of this paper is twofold: first, to show the intimate connection
between the human experience of time and the equally human practice of sacrifice. Here
my remarks are based mainly on the Hindū and Christian traditions, although they point
to contemporary Man.

Second, to alleviate the temporal discomfort of modern Man—who longs to overcome
time but does not know how to do it—by a hermeneutics of sacrifice as a mediation between
tradition and modernity. Sacrifice is here understood as the basic human ritual, and my
thesis is that sacrifice is a set of actions by which Man tries to overcome time, that is, either
escape, deny, or integrate it. My second thesis is that this also applies to contemporary Man.
By *time*, I understand the human consciousness of the sequences of events through which
Man deduces the durational structures of himself and the world.

My working hypothesis goes tentatively like this: Man is a temporal being, a being
immersed in time, made of time, and yet constantly dissatisfied with his temporal existence.
He tries by every means to overcome the temporal character of his being. Cultures have
traditionally done this by setting "above time, a brimful vessel"[4] and by exhorting Man to
reach the supratemporal,[5] in other words, by postulating a separate reality in which "there
shall be time no longer."[6]

By contrast, modern Man has broken the jar of eternity and found it empty.[7] Nevertheless,
he has not been cured of his nostalgia for it, nor been able to subdue his temporal unease.[8]
Belief in the transtemporal may be a disease, but Man has found no remedy for it so far. A
hermeneutics of sacrifice may help us to understand the continuity between tradition and
modernity, and thus help us to discover the proper ritual for coping with the ever-recurrent
problem of Man's discomfort with his own temporality.

One could ask at the very outset: But why does one want to overcome time? What
exactly does that mean?

It seems to be a universal human fact that Man is the animal that wants to jump over his
milieu. Like a fish striving to come out of the water, or a bird flying outside the air, or a beast
going beyond the earth, Man seems to want to leap above space and, specifically, beyond time.

---

[2] I will write "Man" throughout this article to express not the male, but the androgynous human
being, and use the morphologically masculine pronoun with an ambivalent meaning.

[3] Having dedicated much of my academic activity to elucidating how we can understand other
people's benefits, I skip here altogether a thematic reflection on the formidable problem of the proper
method for cross-cultural studies.

[4] *AV* XIX.53.3. See chapter 2.

[5] See, e.g., Lk 12:20ff.

[6] Rv 10:6.

[7] Even if modern exegesis is right, the shift of emphasis and even of meaning in the quote just given
is typical. The *AV* also says, "There should be time no longer," and this reflects the classical mentality of
the *quia tempus non erit amplius* of the Vulgate, translating literally the ambivalence of the original οτι
χρονος ουκετι εσται as cosmological time or anthropological (waiting) time. Modern versions translate
χρονος by delay, instead: "There shall be no more delay" (RSV); "Plus de delai!" (BJ).

[8] See Thomas Aquinas saying, "Aeternitas non est aliud quam ipse Deus" [Eternity is nothing but
God himself], *Sum. Theol.*, I, q.10, a.2, ad 3.

And even if this is deemed to be an impossible and alienating dream, it has to be explained to the human animal that he should be fully satisfied to live in his own element. I have cited the three main elements: water, air, earth. Perhaps that fourth element, fire, is the constituent of Man—and *agni*, an "envoy among the Gods,"[9] "navel of the earth,"[10] "king of the waters,"[11] although "the waters are his mothers,"[12] and he "sustains the sky,"[13] "maintains the earth,"[14] and "has linked the two worlds with the light of heaven."[15]

It is not a trifle to be Man: a time-ridden being, "thirsty and hungry" to shed his temporal skin.

Time Sacrificed

A Human Invariant: The Tension
between the Eternal and the Temporal

Among the many theories on the nature of religion and the origin of sacrifice we find a human invariant—although, of course, any given expression of it has to be couched in a concrete language, thus reflecting only one particular philosophical view. But this inherent limitation of language should not prevent us from tackling a universal problem.

This human invariant can be identified as the constitutive tension in human consciousness between being and becoming, the one and the many, identity and difference, the divine and the human, change and continuity or, also, between time and eternity, understanding the latter as either time-less or time-filled.

Incidentally, I note here my conviction that handling this constitutive tension in dialectical terms expresses both the strength and the weakness of Western culture, and that other traditions approach the problem differently.[16] Only a complementary approach can help us to overcome the increasingly dangerous cultural neocolonialism of our times. *Sed de hoc satis* for my purpose here.

This human invariant has its source in the fact that the awakening of human consciousness carries with it an awareness of Man's limitations that entails, at the same time, an almost irresistible desire to peer over at the "other shore."

We could reduce these limitations to three: of knowledge (power), of space (communication), and of time (fullness).

Man does not know everything, he cannot go everywhere, and he cannot encompass the complete temporal span of his own existence. The awareness of Man's limited knowledge of things and his limitation in space are ultimately not as discomforting as the awareness of his temporal limitation. We can easily understand and accept that we cannot know everything and reach everywhere: we realize that we are neither all-powerful nor the entire universe. But the awareness of time limitation implies not only the impossibility of gathering past and future into the lived present, but also the shocking discovery of a normally nonexperienceable

---

[9] See *RV* III.2.8.

[10] See *RV* I.59.2.

[11] See *RV* X.45.5.

[12] See *RV* III.2.9.

[13] See *RV* III.5.10.

[14] See *RV* I.67.5.

[15] See *RV* I.69.1.

[16] It may be noted, in passing, that I have not worded these polarities so as to show them as mutually exclusive, as Being / Non-Being, one / non-one, identical / non-identical, etc.

limit *a quo*, birth; and another, still more intriguing and equally nonexperienceable limit *ad quem*, death. This temporal limitation touches the very core of Man; it is not so much about a consciousness of (a tolerable) finiteness as one of (an irritating) imperfection. That is to say, we experience the limitation as something painful, humiliating, as something that should not be, as an obstacle to be overcome, as a punishment to be suffered, or as an inherent human condition we must learn to accept. Birth and death are two limiting situations that become challenge situations as soon as we think about them.

In short, we experience this limitation as a problem that demands either its solution or its dismissal as a problem. The fact that we cannot even possess ourselves, as it were—that we cannot fully encompass our own existence, that our ego has to trust our feeble memory to gather some fragments of its own past, and is reduced to mere speculation in order to ascertain even a few hints about its own future—remains a standing insult and a constant threat to Man's self-identity. How can I be sure of my own present ego if last year's ego now seems so different, and the future one so unpredictable? My real ego cannot be only today's ego, and yet this seems to be practically all that is left to me. The most astonishing thing, however, remains the fact that we are conscious of this split so that, in a sense, in our present there is a certain presence of our past and our future. Human consciousness seems to be peculiarly transtemporal.[17] In a way, if I want to be my-self, I must somehow gather up all three times and, most probably, transcend time altogether.[18] In sum, conquering time, that is, mastering my temporal dispersion, seems to be the fundamental condition for being my-self. But how to achieve it?

Ways of Handling the Tension

I am assuming here that we feel a tension between the temporal present and—at least—the totality of our temporal existence, and that there is a human urge to cope with this tension. I say "at least" because a traditional statement concerning this tension speaks not only of gathering past, present, and future, but of transcending time altogether. It speaks of time and eternity.[19] Here we may also recall the tremendous rise of historical consciousness in the modern West. History tries to ease the tension between past and present, and also between present and future, by performing the same function in both cases, namely that of linking

---

[17] See Spinoza's "Sentimus experimusque nos aeternos esse" [We feel and experience that we are eternal], in *Ethics* 23.5, or the famous Augustinian sentence "Inquietum est cor nostrum donec requiescat in te" [Our heart is restless until it rests in you] (*Confessions* I.1.1).

[18] See Augustine's sentence "Ut ergo tu sis, trascende tempus" (*In Iohannem* 38.10) [Transcend time, so that you can *be*], or *YS* I.26, saying that for Uśvara, the model of perfect Man, "there is no limitation by time."

[19] Interestingly enough, in Sanskrit we have practically no positive word for eternity, that is, only negation of temporality (except perhaps *nitya* of disputed etymology: *ni-tya* = in-ness, or *ni-ja* = innate). See the common expressions *nitya-anitya* (constant, eternal, and inconstant, temporal); *kāla-akāla* (temporal and a-temporal); and the adverb *nityakālam* (always, at all times, or rather, constantly temporal). In Hebrew we have *holam* and *netsach* for "eternity." The first comes from the root *h-l-m*, to hide (hidden time?). The root of the second means to shine, brightness. There is also a third word, *chad* (related to *chet*, time). Greek, on the other hand, seems to have only the temporal and secular word αιων for "eternity," the meaning of which is *saeculum*, world. See J. R. Wilch, *Time and Event* (Leiden: Brill, 1969), which sums up the state of the question in the Semitic tradition, including J. Barr, *Biblical Words for Time* (London: SCM, 1962).

time with eternity, or at least bringing the different fragments of time together.[20] There seem to be several ways of solving this fundamental human unease (*duḥkha*). We can classify these ways as attempts to overcome the tension or efforts to put up with it.

The first alternative offers two ways out: either denying the very basis of the tension so that it does not have to be surmounted, or trying to transform the conditions of this tension so that it can be conquered.

The first way out is represented by the typical Buddhist solution of denying the existence of the patient altogether. If everything is impermanent and each instant is new, emerging—as it were—from utter nothingness, the cause of the trouble is eliminated. This is the *anātmavāda* preached by the Buddha, the teaching of the nonexistence of the ego, soul, *ātman*, and, in general, of any kind of (permanent) substance. To be sure, the Buddhist denial of the tension is not a mere intellectual discovery: it is rather a personal conquest, an experiential truth that one realizes and thus, in a way, produces. To discover that *saṃsāra* is *nirvāṇa* implies that one has actually converted *saṃsāra* into *nirvāṇa*—and this Buddhist conversion is not just an academic amusement. The tension is not transformed but positively denied.

The second way out, transforming the condition of the tension, offers a double possibility: either Being is ultimately identified with consciousness, and then we have a fundamentally gnoseological transformation, or it is not, and then we have a predominantly ontological transformation.

The first possibility is exemplified by the typical Vedāntic system, which affirms that this is a question of enlarging, expanding, piercing through the ego until the consciousness of the *ātman* emerges, which then realizes its identity with *brahman*, the divine principle without beginning or end, the immortal, the timeless. The gnostic discovery of our true or real nature also belongs here.

With the second possibility, we have the majority of the religious traditions of the world, which believe in the possibility of a real transformation of Man so as to overcome the tension between the temporal and the eternal, this latter standing for any authentic victory over merely temporal existence. As to the ways of this transformation, they are as numerous as the religious traditions themselves.

The second way of dealing with the problem of Man's temporality—putting up with it— dismisses as an alienating and cheap consolation any attempt to escape from the constitutive limitation of the human being. Instead, this alternative accepts our unavoidably temporal human condition. This acceptance can be seen either as noble and beautiful, so that the "humanist" is the real hero,[21] or as a realistic acknowledgment of the human condition, so that the only coherent and true human attitude is despair and absurdity.[22] We could call the former attitude *heroic humanism* and the latter *radical nihilism*.

Sacrifice as a Universal Means of Handling Tension

The above-mentioned scheme is neat and clear, but it is too exclusively theoretical. Historically, in point of fact, the major human traditions are hardly logically consistent. Life

---

[20] From Cicero's history as *magistra vitae* to A. Toynbee's prophetical function of history, there is a continuous line in Western tradition. See, for the latter, his posthumous book *Mankind and Mother Earth* (New York: Oxford University Press, 1976).

[21] Albert Camus could be given here as a modern example.

[22] See E. M. Cioran, *The Trouble with Being Born* (New York: Viking, 1976), and E. Jabès, *The Book of Questions* (Middletown, CT: Wesleyan University Press, 1976), to cite just two French authors who have been translated into English—and J. P. Sartre, of course.

is more powerful than logic, and logical constructs are strictly valid only for logical entities, however helpful they may be at the level of description.

No extreme position is stable. As a Chinese saying has it, nobody can stand for a very long time on his toes. A rigidly consistent position seems to ignore both human weakness, which prevents a posture of constant heroism, and human wisdom, which has surmised that truth is not so esoteric and inaccessible that simple people cannot attain it. In fact, most extreme positions have, in one way or another, reverted to a kind of "middle path."[23]

Radical Buddhism has been forced to deal with the ineffable; orthodox *vedānta* could not help distinguishing two planes of existence; various techniques of salvation have had to relax their rules and commandments; extreme humanisms have had to accept many models (and even nonmodels) of being human; and formerly radical nihilism has recognized that Man is capable of growth and is thus open to transcendence, which may then become the object of hope.

This implies that all those disparate attitudes have something in common, namely a set of rules, devices, and means—even if they are only convictions or intuitions—by which the meaning or end of life is reached. In other words, there seems to be a consensus that the limitation of the ego exists only for the *time being*, that is, for *being in time*—even if this is all that there is. Such a recognition opens the way toward the healing of this scar of temporality.

Coming specifically to our problem, even the most radical views seem to accept the fact that something must be *done* in order to possess authentic humanity and reach the full meaning of human life.

This meaning may be emptiness or a better future, or eternity, justice, revolution—but in any case the human condition demands an act or a series of actions by which it grows, develops, or changes into another stage. In other words, *ritual* is needed to give Man the possibility of disentangling himself from the trappings of the provisional.

Let me explain why I am using the word "ritual" here. The inconvenience of a language that tries to make sense for a plurality of worldviews is that sometimes one is forced to remain vague and almost structuralistically abstract. The advantage, however, is that sometimes one may get at the very core of things. The case in point here is the recovery of the profound meaning of ritual, so often overshadowed by ceremonies and paraphernalia, not only in ritualistic practices but also in the philosophical and theological universes.

Ritual is that act by which Man tries to reach, obtain, express, or do what is otherwise inaccessible by any other means. To worship the moon can be a ritual as long as there is no other way of communicating with "her" on a particular level. To say—obviously with faith—a prayer while taking a medicine is a ritual as long as one does not believe in the total efficiency of biochemicals. To honor the king is a ritual as long as the people believe that the ruler has a power that they cannot control. An embrace of peace can be a ritual when it expresses more than what I can say and do, and a meal becomes a sacramental rite when it not only feeds the body or the mind, but also instills grace into the table-companions. A particular kind of clothes becomes liturgical when it symbolizes what otherwise is not visible or directly graspable . . . just to give some examples instead of elaborating a theory. It is on this common ground, with all of its ambivalence, that the nature and function of sacrifice are placed. This is what we have to explore.

---

[23] The function of philosophies and theologies of all kinds has been not only that of unfolding the consequences of an initial and creative intuition, but also that of adapting the theoretical system to the factual development of tradition. Not only Scriptures or the foundational charisms are *loci theologici*, but also the life of people.

A Small Phenomenology of Sacrifice

A small phenomenology of sacrifice would show the following features.

1. Man is unstable in his human situation. He wants something more, and even something else.

2. In his first attempt to get this *more* and *else*, he stretches his hand out in space in order to obtain the desired fruit and waits in time in order to reach the expected maturity.

3. Soon he realizes that coveted things are beyond the reach of his hand, and that temporal flow alone does not bring the expected results. Something else has to be done: the machine reaches further than the hand, and an internal effort is required to obtain the glory and strength he desires. No wonder an aura of sacredness surrounded the first material tools and the first spiritual exercises.

4. These two efforts cannot be made without help. Man requires the help and collaboration of others who are invested with a higher power: the hero, the elder, the ancestors, and the God. They have a power that ordinary Man has not. Entreaty and supplication, imitation and emulation appear on the scene. The ritual appears.

5. Man comes of age when he makes the first unexpected and somewhat nonlogical discovery that the human fullness he longs for cannot be obtained by a mere prolongation of the means at his disposal. Machines and techniques do not help. A rupture of planes has to take place; Man has to jump outside his given situation, he has to be initiated. He has to perform an act or a series of acts that will make this jump possible, and reach the higher value, state, condition, and so on. This is the place of sacrifice: the act by which Man *transcends* his factual human situation and reaches what he wants: health, riches, a prosperous family, heaven, wisdom, joy, divinity. . . . In other words, the action by means of which Men believe they will fulfill those desires they cannot achieve on their own is the very core of sacrifice. It is that ritual that breaks the planes in order to reach transcendence.

6. This act always takes the form of a rupture: something is destroyed, cut, burned, offered—sacrificed, precisely—in order to reach the transcendent. I have already indicated the pure phenomenological way of understanding transcendence: that which is beyond the actual reach of a given situation, whether it exists by itself or not. It may very well be that the transcendent has an existence of itself, or that there is an initiative coming from it. In fact, an analysis of many religions shows that often it is not Man who takes the initiative or even wants the sacrifice. Often Man escapes, hiding and avoiding contact with the transcendent, and it seems as if it were the latter who compels Man to such religious acts. Even in these cases, what phenomenology detects is the human feeling of a divine initiative and the human response, positive or negative, to the call of transcendence.

7. A philosophical phenomenology, further, can discover the trait we are trying to formulate as the basis for the thesis of this paper, namely that the sacrificer seeks to deal with the temporal situation of Man, in one way or another, in order to save, redeem, enhance, make happy, enrich . . . the human being.

If this means realizing that there is no soul whatever to be saved, the sacrifice will take the form of an enlightenment, which will reveal the emptiness of what we had previously held as substantial. The Buddhist forms of meditation, of which the Zen practices are a clear example, tend to transcend the mental and even reflexive consciousness in order to reach the goal, which is the extinction of all (that we think) there is, including "being" and of course, the "goal."

If it is a question of transforming our situation, whether in the gnoseological or the ontological order, the sacrifice will take the form of a mental sacrifice, or of an ontic sacred action. The "mental sacrifice" of *Bhagavad-gītā*[24] and *Brahma-sūtra*[25] as well as the living sacrifice of an "intellectual worship" of St. Paul[26] and the "spiritual sacrifice" of St. Peter[27] with their corresponding traditional interpretations,[28] belong here. To support the idea that the sacrifice really transforms the structures of reality, we can cite the traditional understanding of it in most major religions.[29]

If, on the contrary, we have simply to accept our humanness as either our dignity or merely our destiny, once again the sacrifice will open our eyes to our factual situation and remove the veil of ignorance and superstition: "from education to revelation" could be the name of this type of sacrifice. We refer here to an immense amount of psychological, anthropological, and sociological literature, plus philosophical and theological studies trying to help the human being work out or recover his fullness, liberation, or happiness.

I do not call these acts "sacrifices" just in an attempt to reduce the rich variety of human efforts to cope with Man's condition to a common denominator, but *because* all these acts are intended to perform the *same* type of function. We should remember that no one has a monopoly on names. Not long ago, for example, Christians considered the word "grace" as being exclusively theirs, inasmuch as grace was understood as saving grace, participation in the divine nature, and, as such, a unique prerogative of those who have been redeemed by Christ, the only Mediator. Now, when dialogue with other religions becomes unavoidable, Christians must reconsider this position, since there is no other word to express the similar state of affairs that exists in other religions. Hence, although interpretations may differ— and such differences have their rightful place—no one can refuse to accept the grace that is claimed to exist also outside Christianity. Similarly, we shall have to speak of sacrifice outside its traditional religious context, if we want to understand the phenomenon of sacrifice in all its human depth.[30]

Now I will describe what is meant by sacrifice in the two traditions I have chosen to discuss, in order to have a basis for the subsequent considerations.

The Vedic Conception of Sacrifice

We may describe the quintessence of the *Vedic* tradition by mentioning a few traits.[31] It is by means of sacrifice that not only Men but also Gods acquire immortality.[32] By means of

---

[24] See *BG* IV.33; IX.22, etc.

[25] See *BS* III.4; III.6, etc.

[26] See Rom 12:1.

[27] See 1 Pet 2:5.

[28] See Śaṅkara, *BSB* I.1.11; I.4.14; *BU/S* III.3.1; III.9.20; and the *Philokalia*, to quote only two important sources.

[29] See, e.g., V. Warnach, "Vom Wesen des kultischen Opfers," in B. Neunheuser, ed., *Opfer Christi und Opfer der Kirche* (Düsseldorf: Patmos, 1960), 29–74.

[30] "-Emic" and "-etic" considerations could be placed here. The terms are taken from *phonemics*, which deals with the sounds of one particular language, and *phonetics*, which attempts to find rules for all languages.

[31] See my *The Vedic Experience* (Berkeley: University of California Press, 1977), for further texts and the contexts of this succinct paragraph. In Volume IV, part 1 of this *Opera Omnia*.

[32] See *SB* II.2.2.8–14, and also IV.6.9.12 as well as JB I.2. The participation in the *aśvamedha* sacrifice results in a victory over death in all the worlds (*SB* XIII.3.5.1; *TB* III.9.15.1).

sacrifice, Man reaches heaven,[33] freedom,[34] happiness,[35] purification of sins,[36] superiority.[37] Sacrifice helps Man overcome his earthly condition.[38] By performing the sacrifice, Man reaches the "navel of the world."[39] Authentic existence is reached only in and through sacrifice.[40] By the sacrificial act, Man reaches the shores of the other world[41] and is saved from the grip of time.[42] In point of fact, *brahmanic* literature would stress that by virtue of sacrifice Man is capable of attaining the full span of his life,[43] for "Man's immortality is a full life-span."[44] The subsequent *jñānic* spirituality would go a step further and proclaim that through the spiritual sacrifice Man is saved (that is, released) from time altogether.[45] To sacrifice is the highest action, because in it Man collaborates with the World and the Gods to sustain the entire universe.[46] In a word, all these and many other utterances make sense only if we discover in sacrifice the ultimate texture of reality—that act thanks to which the universe has come into being[47] and by which it is kept.[48]

One trait emerges from all this: sacrifice is every act by which Man partakes in the power of a supratemporal agency. He reaches beyond the immediate present into the recesses of the past, sometimes even to the beginning of time, and also into the reservoir of the future, in some cases even to the end of time. The sacrificial act may also serve to fulfill this or that earthly desire, but ultimately it differs from every other action because it stretches beyond the ordinary time span and, by rescuing Man from his servitude to time, truly liberates him.

The Christian Conception of Sacrifice

Let us now summarize the Christian-biblical tradition.[49] Central to the Christian tradition is the importance of the sacrifice of Christ as the unique act that, once and for all, gave new life to the world.[50] It is the sacrifice that was already prefigured in the sacrifice of Abel,[51]

---

[33] See *SB* VIII.6.1.10, etc.

[34] See *SB* XI.1,8.5; *CU* II.24.12 (*svārājyāya*, . . .), etc.

[35] See JB II.140 (*śrī*); *TMB* XXIII.4.2 (*ṛddhi*); *TB* III.1.4.10 (sacrificer who has become lucky, *bhagī*).

[36] See *SB* II.3.1.6, with reference to the *agnihotra* sacrifice. See also *SB* XII.8.1.16; XII.3.1.1.

[37] See *SB* XIII.6.1.1, with reference to the *puruṣamedha*. See also *SB* IV.5.3.2.

[38] "Each day the sacrifice is offered, each day the sacrifice is accomplished, each day it links afresh the offerer to heavenly existence, each day the sacrificer penetrates the heavens" (*SB* IX.4.4.15).

[39] See *RV* I.166.35.

[40] See *SB* III.6.2.26.

[41] See *TB* III.9.2.1: *agnihotra* is a ship leading to heaven; *SB* II.3.3.15, etc. Or *TB* III.1.5.11 for the sacrifice as offering the right foundation, the firm ground, *pratiṣṭhā*.

[42] See "When one worships time as if it were *brahman*, it escapes" (*MaitU* VI.14), although we cannot enter into its proper context here.

[43] See *SB* II.2.2.14 (*sarvam āyuvus*).

[44] *TMB* XXII.12.2.

[45] This is one of the main messages of the *Upaniṣads*.

[46] See *BG* III.10–16.20, etc.

[47] See *RV* X.90; *AB* VII.8.2; *SB* I.8.1.1–10, etc.

[48] This is also the function of *dharma*, and *dharma* is intimately connected with sacrifice.

[49] See my *La misa como* consecratio temporis: *la tempiternidad*, in *Sanctum Sacrificium*, proceedings of the Fifth Eucharistic Congress, Zaragoza, 1960, 75–93, for a more detailed discussion on the Christian background.

[50] See Heb 7:26ff.; 9:25ff., etc.

[51] Heb 9:4 and also 1 Jn 3:12; Jude 2. For the Old Testament, see Gen 4:1–25.

Melchizedek,[52] and Abraham.[53] It appears as well in the sacrifices of other religions.[54] Christ is the High Priest for all humanity.[55] In reenacting the sacrifice of Christ in the liturgy, Christians are not duplicating his act, nor simply commemorating it, but entering into a relationship with that act that was at the beginning of the world, has redeemed the cosmos, and continues until the total divinization of the universe.[56] For this reason, the Christian sacrifice forgives sins,[57] has the power of impetration and expiation,[58] and its fruits can reach not only the living but also the dead.[59] That God will ultimately be all in all[60] is not something that will come about automatically, but is the result of the action of Christ, priest, that is, mediator (not just intermediary) of all creation.[61]

A specific trait also characterizes the Christian understanding of the sacrifice of Christ and of Christians, namely that sacrifice is an act that transcends time and space, an act by which past sins are forgiven and future grace is treasured, an act that connects us with the beginning of the world and has eschatological repercussions.[62] Every Christian who shares in the mystery of Christ by means of the sacrifice lifts up his or her life into the life of Christ himself, and by doing so, that person shares in the mystery of the entire cosmotheandric[63] dynamism of the universe.[64]

The Sacrifice of Time

The pattern underlying these two traditions, as well as many others, appears clear enough: Man, the prisoner of time, overcomes his temporal limitation by participating in an act that in itself has transtemporal significance. The ritual of sacrifice *saves* Man from being drowned in his everyday "temporality." By performing the sacrifice, Man becomes a contemporary of the Gods, and of the Gods' creative act at the beginning and end of this universe. By sharing in the sacrifice, the quotidian becomes the tempiternal, that is, that form of existence that does not so much encompass as pierce the three dimensions

---

[52] See Heb 5:6–10; 7:1ff. For the Old Testament, see Gen 14:18; Ps 110:4.

[53] See Heb 6:13ff., etc. For the Old Testament, see Gen 22:1–18.

[54] See B. Neunheuser, ed., op. cit., and especially V. Warnach, art. cit.

[55] See Heb 4:14ff.

[56] See the traditional Roman Catholic doctrine of the sacrifice of the Man, for instance, as proclaimed in the Council of Trent in 1662. See Denzinger-Schönmetzer, ed., *Enchiridion symbolorum, definitionum et declarationum de rebus fidei et moribus,* 34th ed. (Barcelona: Herder, 1967), no. 1738–59.

[57] Giving the *Denzinger* references will spare us further elaboration. See *Denz.-Schon.*, 1740.

[58] See *Denz.-Schon.*, 1753.

[59] See *Denz.-Schon.*, 1743.

[60] See 1 Cor 15:28.

[61] See O. Casel, *Das Christliche Opfermisterium* (Graz, 1968), as a single example of a Christian theology of sacrifice. Who Christ is remains here an open question.

[62] See another text of the already quoted Council of Trent, *Denz.-Schon.*, 1740.

[63] By "cosmotheandric" or "theanthropocosmic" intuition, I mean that vision of reality that sees the Divine, the Human, and the Cosmic as the three ultimate factors present in anything existing. See my contribution to the Second International Symposium on Belief, "La visione cosmoteandrica: il senso religioso emergente del terzo millennio," in R. Caporale, ed., *Vecchi e nuovi dèi* (Turin: Valentino, 1976), 521–44.

[64] This summary, of course, does not do justice to the entire theory of sacrifice, which, according to the same Christian tradition, is essential to any religion: "Remotisque sacrificiis nulla nec esse nec cogitari religio potest" [Without sacrifices, no religion can exist or even be imagined], *Denz.-Schon.*, S3339.

of time, and yet it does not abandon them entirely, in order to uncover the transtemporal core of time itself.[65]

Sacrifice, then, is an act by which time is overcome; it is fundamentally the sacrifice of time. Time is sacrificed, destroyed, pierced through, and a trans-temporal core uncovered. But, again, time exists because of the primordial sacrifice that has called the temporal reality into being. Thus, one could sum up at least these two highly representative traditions by saying, "Time both springs from and dies through ritual."[66] It is sacrifice that makes time, and ultimately creates this temporal world, and it is also sacrifice that destroys time and enables the world to reach its tempiternal core. Let me be emphatic on this. I think that, if we lose sight of this primordial experience, we not only do injustice to most religious traditions of humankind, but we automatically convert our almost immediate ancestors into primitive superstitious and irrational people, not only cutting ourselves off from understanding them but undermining the very ground where we stand. Temporal provincialism ("Only modern Man matters and has the right opinions") is worse than a spatial ghetto mentality ("Only Christians, only Americans, only black people, etc.").

When a Christian or Hindū believer performs the sacrifice, he may have any number of immediate intentions, which may sometimes blur its ultimate meaning. Nevertheless, it is the latter, the underlying and deeper intuition, that vouches for the perseverance and intensity of sacrificial action. Through the sacrifice, believers not only acquire merits, favors, and forgiveness, but also and chiefly they reach salvation, that is, an ontological realm that would otherwise be closed to them. They get in touch with the beginning and the end of time, with their ancestors, and with the eschatological situation of the universe. They collaborate in the functioning of the world and, in a sense, they not only feel that they are not wasting their time, but, on the contrary, they believe they are performing the most fruitful action for themselves, for their fellow beings, and for the entire world.[67] In fact, traditional sacrifice does not save or rescue Man *from* the world, but saves the World—and thus *also* Man. To "kill time" does not mean to waste it, but to pierce it in order to extricate the everlasting from the bondage of the perishable.

To put it in the terms of the broad horizon of traditional religions: in the sacrifice, time itself is sacrificed in order to make room for a transtemporal mode of existence. Man puts his own time, and time as a whole, on the altar of sacrifice and there immolates it, so that once time is sacrificed, Man is liberated from its grasp, that is, he overcomes death, and the World can reveal its transtemporal status. It constitutes the dignity of Man to be able to perform this act.[68] And although he cannot do it by himself, Man steers the cosmos, so to speak, to its proper transtemporal destination.

Now, the popular understanding (mystics being clear exceptions) of the a-temporal status of reality is one of a supratemporal, or even a posttemporal reality, into which the believer

---

[65]   See the notion of *illo tempore*, especially as discussed by M. Eliade in his *The Sacred and the Profane* (New York: Harcourt, Brace & World, 1957 and 1959); *Cosmos and History* (New York: Harper, 1959); *From Primitive to Zen* (New York: Harper, 1967), etc. As for the term and notion of "tempiternity," see my *La misa* . . . , op. cit., and "El presente tempiterno," in A. Vargas-Machuca, ed., *Teología y mundo contemporáneo* (Madrid: Cristianidad, 1975), 133–75. See the next chapter.

[66]   See my *Le mystère du culte*, op cit., 47.

[67]   See the conception of *BG* III.9; IV.23: if all actions are performed as sacrifices, time will be fulfilled and thus redeemed; it is no longer alienation, but fullness.

[68]   "Reverend" is one who can perform the sacrifice in the Christian tradition, as *pūjya* (with the same meaning as a title) is the privilege of the sacrificing castes in Hinduism.

enters—too easily forgetting that the kingdom and *brahman* are within us.[69] The secular mentality, on the contrary, comes closer to the genuine religious insight by interpreting the a-temporal not as supra- but as transtemporal. And this leads us straight to the next step in our fundamental reflection on time.

The Sacrifices of Time

The A-Temporal Nature of the Temporal Act of Consciousness

Before proceeding further, let us insert an ancillary philosophical reflection.

The act of consciousness is certainly a human act. It is a process that *happens* in time and is also *dependent* on the time in which it happens; but, as such, it is *a-temporal*.

The act of consciousness happens *in time* in the sense that all our concomitant actions are subject to time: when I am conscious, the clock does not stop, my breathing continues, my stomach functions, the sun follows its course, and so on. The conscious act happens during that time.

The act of consciousness is also intrinsically dependent *on time*, that is, on the time in which it happens. It is not irrelevant that a conscious act happens at one time or another, because the act itself is a function of the times in which it happens. The actual consciousness of a contemporary of Yājñavalkya is different from the consciousness of a contemporary of Heidegger, because the temporal factor belongs to the act itself, so that its temporal coordinates condition the very nature of that consciousness. In fact, consciousness does not consist in a mere formal structure of thought, but is the integral fact of being conscious of something.

Now, both the "something" of which we are conscious and the "someone" being aware are subjected to time. The subject of this "being conscious" is the temporal and historical person, plunged in his temporal situation. Consciousness (as far as we are conscious of it) is always a person's consciousness, and this person, the conscious subject, is a temporal and even a historical being. Even when we attribute consciousness to the God and/or the Gods, we make them enter into the sphere of time. Furthermore, consciousness is representation, that is, a power that reflects something by being aware of it—and there is no way of defining consciousness outside of consciousness itself. This "something" is what we call "reality," for reality is that which consciousness directly or indirectly represents. Now, the conscious reality of Yājñavalkya's time—and thus of Yājñavalkya—is different from that of Heidegger's time—and thus of Heidegger. This applied also in the most extreme idealistic interpretation of consciousness. Every act of consciousness, by definition, reflects reality, even if this reality were only a projection of the conscious act itself.

On the other hand, the act of consciousness itself is an a-temporal act. Notwithstanding the two facts just mentioned—namely that, as an act, it shares in the temporality of every human process (Man is a temporal being) and that, as consciousness of reality, it depends on the temporal reality itself (Reality is temporal)—it remains nevertheless that the *quo* act of consciousness is not affected by time. When I become aware of something, I do not become conscious of temporality. The act of consciousness (when consciousness "clicks") is an a-temporal moment. An act of consciousness, as such, has no precursor and no sequel. At a second moment, I may become conscious that I was conscious of something, and then situate the first act of consciousness in space and time, but this happens *after* the fact (of consciousness) and is another act altogether.

---

[69] See Lk 17:21; Acts 17:27–28; and *BU* III.7; *KU* V.9; VI.17; *MandU* II.1.9; *MaitU* VI.1, etc.

This can be seen very clearly in the constitutive impossibility of measuring any primary act of consciousness by any physical or even mental apparatus: first, we can only measure the effects (of the conscious act), and second, the act of measuring is already another act, not only different from the original act, but even modifying it. The difference, here, with any other act or phenomenon is that the measuring action cannot but be of the same nature as the measured one. We can measure protons by their mass and velocity, for instance, but we have to measure the act of consciousness by another act of consciousness, in spite of all the intermediaries we may put in between.

But I am saying more than that the act of consciousness is temporally unmeasurable. I am saying that the representation or presentation, the appearing or manifestation of reality that constitutes a conscious act, is, as such, untouched by time. A conscious act dawning upon me is like a new creation. I know on subsequent reflection that a moment before I was not conscious of what was not yet there: I know that my existence is temporal, and that what I am conscious of (that reality that presents itself in the conscious act) may not be an eternal reality. But the act of consciousness itself (that act that, by uniting and separating, creates a subject and an object) is of an a-temporal nature. There is a timeless *ecstasis* behind any true act of understanding. There may be other acts preceding my particular act of consciousness, and many others may also follow it, but there is nothing in the act proper that allows for a προτον or a υστερον, a *prius* and *posterius* of temporal nature.[70]

Moreover, precisely because we have not a perfectly conscious act, because we are not pure consciousness, we go on living in time. If we could become pure consciousness, or see God face-to-face (to rephrase Hindū and biblical terminologies), we would jump outside temporal reality altogether—and we *do* it, "momentarily," each "time" consciousness dawns upon us.

In saying this, I am not parroting Heidegger's analyses, or the Buddhist theory of momentariness, the *yoga* practice of stopping the flow of the mind, the magical or shamanistic device of bringing the world to a standstill, the Christian belief in eternity, or the phenomenological idea of pure awareness. I am describing a fundamental human experience, which may be at the basis of these as well as many other worldviews. I am stressing the fundamental human experience that temporality is a fact of consciousness, but the act of consciousness qua act of consciousness has little to do with temporality.[71]

The act of awareness differs from the reflective act of becoming aware of one's awareness, and also differs—but is not separable—from the object of awareness. It is an act that has no space or time. We may call it instantaneous, but this instant cannot be considered a unit of time, for no amount of these "instants" would ever constitute a temporal succession. Were it not for extrinsic and indirect devices, we would not be able to discover that the act of consciousness happens in time. In fact, the so-called pure sciences often claim to be a-temporal. "Three and two are five" may formulate an a-temporal statement when devoid of its extra-mental truth (three angels and two Gods are five "nothing") and concerning a formal, ideal content in Man's consciousness. Newton's or Einstein's physical laws may be a-temporal only as long as they do not touch the real, that is, do not refer to actual physical events.[72] Even pure formalism depends on the structure of our mind, and our mind is not necessarily eternal.

---

[70] See Aristotle, *Physics* IV.11 (219b1).

[71] "Los fenòmenos espirituales o mentales no duran; los anímicos ocupan tiempo. El entender que $2 + 2 = 4$ se realiza en un instante," as José Ortega y Gasset wrote in 1924 (*Obras Completas*, vol. 2 [Madrid: Revista del Occidente, 1966], 461).

[72] See my chapter "La unidad fisicomatemàtica de tiempo" in *Ontonomia de la Ciencia* (Madrid: Gredos, 1961), 309–551, for the distinction between physical and physico-mathematical time.

The Three Ways of Overcoming Time

We have described Man as a being having a "thirst" to overcome time, and also as possessing the belief in the possibility of doing so. Now, there are three human acts by which Man has traditionally tried to overpower the dominion of time, or at least to master the temporal yoke. There are three temporal ecstasies, as it were—three human victories over time. One tries to encompass the flow of time by knowing everything that is (past, present, and future); another wishes to jump outside time, losing all consciousness of it by falling in love (reaching the a-temporal); and a third one claims to transform time itself, or at least to find its "soul" by working within time (piercing it through).

In order to be brief and stick to the point, I am going to skip philosophical and historical analyses and use what I would like to call a phenomenological irony: *cum etiam vita universa ironiam habere videatur*,[73] the Romans knew well, as expressed by the Spaniard Quintilianus in his *Institutio oratoria*.[74]

Jñānamārga

The first, and most sophisticated, is the way of gnosticism, saving knowledge, *gnôsis, jñāna, visio*. ... If we succeed in knowing authentically, this very act will make us independent of time, or put us outside it. The heap of facts we know and the amount of knowledge we possess are certainly not removed from the grip of time, but pure knowledge and intellectual intuition are just as certainly time-transcending. The sage is one who has already crossed to the other shore of the river of time.

This ideal has haunted Man since he discovered himself to be *Homo sapiens*. Not only gnostics, alchemists, mystics, and occultists had a longing for knowledge, but sober scientists and pure philosophers as well have cherished the dream of deciphering, one day, the mysteries of the Real, not just for the fun of it, but because they believed that liberation, salvation, justice, happiness, and truth were behind that knowledge. "Enlightenment" is a word of many meanings, but most of them apply here.

To the Man who really knows, past, present, and future will yield their hidden and menacing powers; superstition and exploitation will be done with; the kingdom of Truth will emerge. Ignorance is the archenemy, and Education the sociological idol. Whence, otherwise, the sacred aura of futuristic studies?

Once knowledge has discovered all secrets hidden by time, Man is no longer fragmented in temporal bits and pieces. And what was the privilege of an immutable God now becomes the utopian model of the enlightened citizen, the perfect scientist, the true philosopher, the all-knowing sage, the *jīvanmukta*.

Bhaktimārga

Love, *agapê, bhakti, amor* is another a-temporal human experience. The genuine act of love seems to be untouched by the temporal factor. That love wants eternity is something every poet knows and sings about: it would make no sense to want to love for five minutes; this would not be real love. It is quite another matter, of course, that love may fade away after five minutes.

---

[73] The whole life seems to have its own irony.

[74] Is it also an irony that he was probably the first rhetorician being paid by the State?

If the sage is the model of the first way, the saint is the ideal of this second attempt. The saint is the genuinely happy and perfect human being; he is a lord over time. The saint is above the miseries of time—the temporal is here synonymous with the transitory, fallacious, and ultimately contemptible. Salvation and happiness can only be found above the fleeting and deceptive appearances of temporal things.[75]

It is not surprising that many religions have stressed either knowledge or love as the way by which Man reaches salvation, liberation, happiness, fulfillment. However this may be, the saving effects of both paths are linked to overcoming the flow of time and being freed from the bite of temporality, *saṃsāra*.

Karmamārga

There is yet another way, which traditionally seems to have been the most important and prominent way to reach the end of human life toward which religions of every type, ancient and modern, claim to lead. This is the way of action: *karmamārga*, the ritual performance of certain acts by means of which the desired fulfillment is attained. Religion here is, first of all, "orthopraxis."

Although the other two ways also reinterpreted the sacrifice according to their own perspective, here, in this third way, we have—strictly speaking—the place of sacrifice, or at least of the primordial meaning of it. And here, significantly enough, the most ancient religious traditions of humankind meet the most modern trends of secular Man. Here work redeems Man. Admittedly, the work is sacred, not merely a profane activity, but nothing prevents it from being utterly secular. Let me stress that the *sacred* is opposed to the *profane*, not to the *secular*.[76] We are now ready to pick up the thread of our discourse.

The Modern Secular Sacrifice

When comparing our contemporary situation with problems of the past, we have to take the different horizons of intelligibility into consideration; in other words, we have to consider the different myths underlying the cultures we are addressing. Now, the myth of an epoch or a culture is the spontaneous or unproblematic horizon against which facts and events are situated, so that Man may understand them. The myth offers the ultimate ground of intelligibility for a given culture or subculture; it is that horizon in which we believe without believing that we believe in it, so much so that we take it for granted. For instance, history is a criterion for truth: a fact is taken to be real if it can be proved to be a historical fact. This is a rather modern Western myth, probably of Semitic origins, but not universal at all within human experience. This is why we can easily detect the myth of others without being aware of our own myths, just as we instinctively detect the accent foreign people have in speaking our language, but we are not aware of our own accent—unless, of course, others draw our attention to it.

To speak of sacrifice as the proper ritual for overcoming time may be easily accepted by historians of religions when dealing with other people and cultures. But the question becomes much more delicate when applied to our present-day situation. I submit that the function and scope of the Science of Religion is not just to study some exotic culture but to investigate the

---

[75] See the many Buddhist parables, as well as the *terrena despicere* (despising earthly things) and "Ibi fixa sunt corda ubi vera gaudia" [Our hearts tend toward the only true joys] of the Latin Christian liturgy.

[76] See my *Worship and Secular Man* (Maryknoll, NY: Orbis Books, 1973), 9–13; and chapter 2, "Secularization," 28–55. In Volume IX, Part 1 of this *Opera Omnia*.

religious dimension of Man—ourselves and our culture included. This understanding of religious studies, as the study of the ultimate self-understanding of Man, shows that the underlying insights of the traditional doctrines of sacrifice are still alive and valid in contemporary secular society. Further, this perspective may help us not only to understand our modern situation, but also to reform and transform it by setting it in a wider and deeper context. This is all the more relevant as the two traditional ways, knowledge and love, seem today to be on the wane after centuries of predominance in the religious world: *Homo sapiens* and *Homo amans* are increasingly giving way to *Homo faber* and *Homo agens*. It seems to be a modern axiom that not by knowing or loving are we going to save and justify our lives, but by making and acting.

The Sacredness of Secular Work

What has been said so far should not be understood as either saying that the ways of contemplation or wisdom (*jñanamārga*) and those of love and devotion (*bhaktimārga*) are obsolete, or that the traditional *karmamārga* is what modern secularized Man is performing. Rather, I am detecting a connecting link with, and a growing point from, tradition.

If "the clock, not the steam-engine, is the key-machine of the modern industrial age,"[77] a new experience of time should accordingly dawn in the postindustrial age.[78] The power of the methods of thought is not just that they provide us with a way (ὁδός) toward the Real, but that they shape and assist in the creation of the very reality they claim to help us discover.[79]

To be sure, modern secularized Man is not performing the *Vedic* or Christian sacrifice; the understanding of action has also evolved. But, in a sense, he *is* performing sacrificial actions: the efforts of the good citizen to increase the welfare of society; the concern of the genuine intellectual for the well-being of his fellow beings; the sincere ideal of the scientist in working for the progress of the world; and the pains the honest national or international official takes for the elimination of poverty, disease, hunger, injustice, and the like could be given as examples. We should not minimize the religious *pathos* behind such attitudes, even if entirely secular.

The work-ethic mentality is not the privilege of Anglo-Saxon Protestantism only. Other Christians, as well as Muslims, communists, socialists, and humanists, share this belief: Man justifies his existence by his work. The principle enunciated by St. Paul—"He who does not work should not eat"[80]—has never been better followed than nowadays. Perhaps this is a latent feature in all cultures of Abrahamitic origin. Work is the way in which Man believes he repays his debt to society and to the past, and by which he justifies his existence, for he believes he is collaborating in building a more just and human society.[81] Work is sacred and rightly demands a kind of sacred consecration to it. The full-fledged human being is the worker.[82]

---

[77] L. Mumford, *Technics and Civilization* (New York: Harcourt, Brace & World, 1934), 14.

[78] "The bells of the clock tower almost defined urban existence. Time-keeping passed into time-serving and time-accounting and time-rationing. As this took place, Eternity ceased gradually to serve as the measure and focus of human action" (ibid.).

[79] "The application of quantitative method of thought to the study of nature had its first manifestation in the regular measurement of time" (ibid., 12).

[80] 2 Thess 3:10.

[81] See the many "theologies of work," so popular some decades ago, trying to counteract the Marxist *pathos*: "To work is to collaborate in the creative act of God." See the pioneer article by M. D. Chenu, "Pour une théologie du travail," *Espri* (January 1952). *Theology of Work*, the English translation of his French book, is of 1965.

[82] See the liturgy, and the theological justification of it, of the first day of May as the feast of St. Joseph

Nor is this all.[83] Work seems to be the heir of traditional sacrifice, and in fact, most laws and regulations of modern civilization spell out the rituals for duly performing this grandiose sacrifice of the working community. Work, we hear in different tones, is no longer the task of slaves but of free citizens; work ennobles; "work is worship."[84] The work of everyone allows a nation to be prosperous and rich, and citizens to reach a well-deserved "paradise of abundance," freedom, and happiness. *Karmamārga* is the way to salvation; educators, doctors, lawyers, engineers, and politicians are the dignified and well-honored priests of this modern religiousness. Modern banks are better kept and adorned with tapestry, pictures, flowers than churches. The sacred hours are not the time of leisure or prayer, but the working hours.[85]

Here, with as much accuracy as in the most orthodox traditional religions, time is regulated and considered sacred. Working hours are reckoned as the most precious hours of daily activity, to the point of being meticulously calculated to the exact minute. Other hours are less important. An employee working overtime is paid more, precisely because he or she "sacrifices" more time. To "take up your time" or to ask for "some of your time" without compensation amounts to exploitation or plain robbery. . . . By means of work the ordinary citizen becomes contemporary with the founder's dream, myth, or idea that inspires him to work.[86] He also reaches the ideal of the end of times, when the hardships endemic to work will be taken away and life will be filled with justice and joy.[87] If we produce enough "time-saving" gadgets for everyone, they will redeem us from the effort of pain connected with work. . . . The sacrifice, the sacrificer, and the sacrificed, like in the *Vedas* and the New Testament, ultimately coalesce.

In sum, modern work claims to liberate Man from the tight spots of time and to allow him both to rescue his life from the chains of a time-bound existence and to justify his life by allowing him to collaborate in the "salvation" of the world.

All traditional motives of sacrifice have been preserved in the process of being transplanted into another horizon. We have here a typical example of transmythicization.

The Secular Sacrifice

It is quite clear now, in this last quarter of the twentieth century, especially in the most technologically developed countries, that the foregoing description sounds like a caricature. Modern work tends to turn people into slaves, exploitation has not decreased, even free time has been downgraded to mere recovery for a better future production; the success of the fittest, of the winners in "free" competition, means misery for the others; technology devours its own fathers, and so on.

---

the Laborer in the Roman Catholic Church, instituted by Pius XII in 1955. See also the idea and the ideal of *consecratio mundi* carried out by Catholic Action and secular spiritualities within the same church.

[83] See the first article of the *Constitution of the Spanish Republic* of 1931: "España es una Repùblica democràtica de *trabajadores* de toda clase" (my underlining). Not citizen but worker is the title of the "people."

[84] A common slogan in modern India, as well as, "Cleanness is (next to) godliness."

[85] Shops and officers used to open at ten o'clock in the morning in a tropical country like India, because the best hours of the morning were supposed to be consecrated to prayer, study, and leisure. Modern India is slowly "catching up," and modern business makes a more "rational" effort by beginning "work" at "better" times.

[86] The Communist ideology is a typical instance, and many of the bicentennial speeches of 1976 in the United States are another example.

[87] See K. Marx and F. Engels, *Communist Manifesto*.

I am not arguing for or against anything at the moment, but trying to understand this central aspect of modernity by describing the fundamental thrust of the secular attitude, and detecting its deep roots in tradition. Attempting another sketchy overview of human civilization in the perspective of this paper, I would suggest the following.

The ancient ages were characterized by the *theological belief* that Man's life was part of a divine adventure. The rituals expressed the struggle of Men and Gods, all together. The first Hellenistic and the *Vedic* periods could be given as examples.

The middle ages are represented by the *cosmological belief* that Man's dignity consists in collaborating in the sustenance of the World. The ancient rituals and sacred mysteries are thus converted into expressions of, and means for, the human participation in the destiny of the universe. The *Bhagavad-gītā*, the Hellenic and Christian mysteries here come to mind.

Modernity is shaped by the *humanistic belief* that Man's life justifies itself by being of service to humanity and working together for the progress of society. The ancient rituals have been transformed into the ethical behavior of the community, be it a nation, a State, a party, a Church, an academia, or any other group.

The present-day situation discloses itself in the crisis of modernity and in Man's impotence to go back to the other two attitudes. The ancient rituals have not died, and in fact many new forms of old religions—though ephemerally—appear.

This paper tries to show that both the merely traditional concepts of sacrifice and their modern secular versions are incapable of satisfying the deep urges and authentic needs of contemporary Man. And yet, we cannot do without them, nor can we artificially concoct new eclectic ways. Here is the place for a mutual fecundation between the old and the new, and the hope that such an encounter, if authentic, may produce a new being when "time ripens."[88] This is what we are exploring.

The secular attitude is not only, or not primarily, an attack against established religions, but the fruit of an experience of the real, and hence ultimately positive, character of time. Temporality is an intrinsic and essential feature of all beings and of Being itself. To be sure, not only can Being be "said in many ways,"[89] but Time also has many meanings.[90]

Now, in the modern world, precisely because the uncritical enthusiasms of the first hour have subsided, there is both room and need for sacrifice, meant as the redemption of time. In a secular world, the liberating sacrifice cannot liberate us from time (coextensive with being): that would amount to annihilation or, at least, alienation; neither can it free us from a merely cosmological temporality, and so relieve us from our earthly and human condition. Here redemption of time does not mean setting us free from time, in order to fly into an a-temporal realm. It rather means our redemption from inauthentic time, surreptitious time, boring time, the dictatorship of time, and especially the mirage of an all-dominating time, which exhausts every dimension of our being.

The question then becomes: How to live an authentic life, cleansed of all the excrescences of wasted and inauthentic time? How can we justify our existence? In other terms, how can we save our lives? Rather than a sharp and negative criticism of the evils of modern society (easy to make, and true as it may be), it will be more constructive to point to the profound,

---

[88] It is significant that the two Indo-European roots related to time, *di* (to part, cut, distribute) and *ten* (to extend, stretch, dilate, expand) are both related to words signifying sacrifice. See J. Pokorny, *Indogermanisches etymologisches Wörterbuch* (Bern-Munich: Francke, 1959).

[89] See Aristotle, *Metaphysics* IV.2 (297; 1003a33).

[90] See as a pertinent example J. T. Fraser, ed., *The Voices of Time* (New York: Braziller, 1966); *Of Time, Passion, and Knowledge* (New York: Braziller, 1975).

underlying, and mostly unconscious dynamisms crossing the very attempts of modern Man to master his human condition. The dimension of time is deep and central enough to provide us with a clue to some fundamental issues.

The place and function of sacrifice are precisely here. The essence of sacrifice is not the lamb, the flower, the bread, or a particular rubric, but the ritual through which Man finds salvation, that is, more specifically, overcomes the dominion of time and is rescued from its slavery.

Secular sacrifice, in accordance with the belief of secular Man, does not take us away from time, transporting us to some a-temporal realm. Such an independent kingdom does not exist for him. Secular sacrifice does not save us from time; rather, it saves time itself, because time needs to be redeemed, purified, sublimated—so as, eventually, to make it reveal its tempiternal core. But to accomplish this, it has to be a genuine sacrifice and not a mere pantomime of it.

Humankind cannot go back to a pretechnological age. We cannot take refuge in the deserts, the monasteries, or even within ourselves: the modern world is more pervasive than the glitter of the big city, the lords of the ancient *Bourgs*, the *paṇḍits* and priests of old institutions. *Jñanamārga* and *bhaktimārga*, important and necessary as they may be, are neither self-sufficient nor de facto possible without the balancing complement of *karmamārga*, the way of action.

I am not simply justifying modernity or being callously uncritical of the sorry condition of modern society, but neither do I want merely to condemn modernity or restore tradition. Rather, I am undertaking the task of discovering the radical continuity of our society with tradition, without falling into a *laudatoris temporis acti*[91] attitude that would not help—besides not being true. If we discover the common roots, we may find a possibility of regeneration without alienation.

The many attempts of secular Man to master time, for instance, show the same deep concern as the more traditional forms of religiousness. One typical example in technological society is the sacred character that speed has acquired. This is especially true of acceleration. By increasing speed, one increases power, efficiency, pleasure, and so on, and so the ideal becomes to increase velocity itself: acceleration.[92] But it has not taken many centuries to discover the precarious nature of such an outlet. Speed does not touch the core of Man, however it may increase the range of his possibilities. We may read faster, have more information available, accomplish more operations that would otherwise be lengthy and complicated, choose among many more options, and so on. But we do not necessarily enhance the quality of life or Man's real power, for either time seems unlimited (and always demands more, so that we cannot stop and enjoy what we have attained) or we ourselves seem limited (and so we are unable to enjoy the possibilities open to us), even if we accept the technological world as efficient and equitable.

The redemption of time, which secular Man does not understand as escaping from time but as its purification, cannot be brought about by making time go faster, nor by trying to slow it down, and eventually stop it altogether. Neither accelerating time, on the one hand, as the pure secularist would recommend, nor stopping it, on the other hand, as the old shaman would commend, would help us to "win our lives." Both extremes—creating a better technology, or humanizing it, as well as destroying it, or dispensing with it—are, in my opinion, not only *practically* ineffective, they are also *theoretically* wrong. Mere patchworks and efforts aiming at a reform of a mortally wounded system will not do. But to stop the entire machinery of

---

[91] Praiser of past times.

[92] See my *Technique et temps: la technocronie*, in *Tecnica e casistica*, ed. E. Castelli (Padua: CEDAM, 1964), 195–229.

the world would prove utopian, even for a selected elite. Neither attitude would bring a balanced and proper solution, even if it were possible.

The Sacrifice of the Secular

If the most salient feature of our modern culture is its secular mentality, and the core of secularity is recognizing the central and inescapable character of time, modernity's basic issue would be to discover how Man can become the master of time. Now, while agreeing with the secular mentality that time is constitutive of Being and thus coextensive with it (so that there is no being—and no Being—untouched by time), one should immediately add that there is not just *one* property of Being. This is the crux of the issue. Time may be a transcendental in the sense of the Aristotelian Scholastic philosophy, that is, a property inherent in any being qua being, but it is not the only one. Of course, the only property incompatible with time as a transcendental would be no-time, but not the super- or transtemporal. Time may be coextensive with Being, but Being is not exhausted by it.

In other words, is there any way for modern Man to discover something built in the very heart of time, inseparable from time, and yet not to be confused with it? This is what I have called *tempiternity*, which is neither an everlasting time nor a "posttemporal" eternity, but the very "soul of time," as it were. Without it, time is a corpse; but a soul without its body is a mere abstraction.

Now, sacrifice is that set of actions that reach the tempiternal core of Reality, and thus gives us, first, an awareness of the transcendental value of our authentic acts, and, second, the possibility of acting with the full power inherent to those acts.

"What are you doing?" asks the master builder of the Cologne cathedral to the stonecutters.

"Cutting stones," answers one of them.

"Earning the bread for my family," says a second one.

"Building a cathedral," proudly voices a third.

My contention is that this awareness is more than a merely subjective disposition. In point of fact, it is the third attitude that literally *builds* the cathedral. Let me make this a little more explicit.

First of all, a sacrifice, an act, an action, needs to be performed. Human life is a project. Man cannot cease to strive for something greater than himself, at any given moment. He is unfinished, and this unfulfillment impels him to act. But not every act is a sacrifice. A sacrificial act is always an act that attains some type of fulfillment, even if only partially so, or for the time being. This is why the sacrificial act produces a certain rupture of planes, a certain discontinuity, and a leap into another order. Sacrifice does not bring about any homogeneous evolution, but revolution, mutation. The classical word is *salvation*.[93] Here lies its sacred character, a quality that is by no means absent from the secular mentality. Sacrifice, then, has to be an act by virtue of which Man overcomes his "ordinary," banal existence. Modern Man has to work, certainly, but not just for the sake of it, or to have a job for earning his livelihood. He has to regain the consciousness that his activity is a *praxis* and not a mere *poiêsis*,[94] in the Aristotelian sense of the terms.

---

[93] Shall I offer this explanation for the startling sentence that "the kingdom of God suffers violence" (Mt 11:12)? It is not the automatic happy ending of a rosy discipleship, but the new life after an act of total renunciation.

[94] A deeply human act, not simply any action. [*Editorial note*]

Further, this sacrifice cannot be the mere repetition of old, although respectable, rituals. It must correspond to our present degree of consciousness. Generally speaking, traditional rituals are heteronomous: there is a supreme authority, whether it be God, Book, or Tradition, that prescribes what is to be done.

For those who believe that this supreme authority embodies all truth, there is no conflict. But for those who see that Man changes while the religious source remains immutable, a problem arises.

The secular mentality reacts to this with its own autonomous rituals: each individual, group, or nation is absolute, sovereign. Thus, anything that fosters one's growth or fulfills one's needs is permissible. Perhaps the only exception is the pragmatic "rule of thumb" whereby I limit my freedom where it impinges on the freedom of others—since, if I irritate my neighbor unnecessarily, and he is powerful enough to eliminate me, he will do it. This untenable position has led to modern forms of authoritarianism, be they of the State, money, intelligence, and so on. Mere reactions become reactionary, and will not do.

This consideration leads us to the third feature of sacrifice. We have said that it has to be an act, that is, action including involvement, commitment, praxis, work. We have said that it has to be adequate for our present times. We now add that it has to be the reenactment of something primordial, fundamentally human, basic, traditional—to use different words with different connotations. It must have a link with the past and its roots in the human ground. It can neither be absolute newness, nor an uncritical and automatic prolongation of the past. It must be a renewal.

Today, there is an increasing awareness that neither unlimited and unhampered growth (autonomy) nor artificial or dictatorial compulsion (heteronomy) will—lastingly—solve any human problem. Only through an intrinsic mastery that discovers the *optimum* not with the *maximum* (population, wealth, prestige, etc.) but with the harmonious relation of the Whole, within an *ontonomic* order, can we hope for just solutions.[95]

The ontonomic order recognizes the constitutive interdependence of every sphere of being. Hence, compulsion and enforcement are as deleterious as unbridled anarchy, even if they are exercised in the name of freedom. This realization would then elicit the discovery of the tempiternal core of reality not as something separable from time, or still to come in a contradictory after-time, but in the very midst of time. It would also enable us to discover all those values that, being independent of space and time, allow a person to achieve one's realization even under externally difficult or socially painful conditions. The many forms of these sacrificial acts, by means of which the human being acquires sovereignty over himself, that is freedom from the conditioning of life, are the rituals of the *sacred sacrifice of secular Man*.

Combining the three points just mentioned, it suffices to say that secular sacrifice is not a new kind of ritualistic act, but a spirit or a degree of consciousness present in Man's liturgical actions. First of all, it will manifest itself in viewing the traditional religions in a new light, enabling us to discover their underlying intention. Second, it will find new means of expression, which obviously cannot be preplanned, much less postulated. Third, it will set us before the Unexpected and put our lives at stake—perhaps for death, hopefully for resurrection.

Santa Barbara, California
April 1977

---

[95] For an elaborated discussion on the metaphysical foundation for an ontonomic order, see my "Le concept d'ontonomie," in *Actes du XIe Congrès International de Philosophie*, Brussels, August 20–26, 1953 (Louvain: Nauwelaerts, 1953), 3:182–88.

Part 2

WEST

1

CIRCULAR TIME

Temporization and Temporality *

Behold, now is the acceptable time; behold, now is the day of salvation.

—*2 Cor 6:2*

Introduction

I would like to offer an example of transcultural theological thought while keeping three great contemporary, although traditional, theological concepts in mind: the *Heilsgeschichte*, the *Teología de la Liberación*, and theological observations about the *absolute Zukunft*. Even though I am walking alone and this is all new terrain, I believe that this issue is well known. After a somewhat autobiographical, existential, sociotheological deliberation, I will try to expose, without further additives, what seems to me to be at the least an enlightening corrective, if not a fundamental complement to the three above-mentioned problems. I would like to offer these thoughts as an example of theological cross-fertilization that could be the result of the integration of two cultural traditions: India's subjective experience of time and the Western problem to which we have alluded elsewhere.[1]

If I were to enter into direct dialogue with the aforesaid trends, I would say, for example, that the *Heilsgeschichte* is not simply a history of salvation that brings about the salvation *of* history—that is to say, historical salvation and the salvation of history itself—but it describes salvation *in* history, which is equivalent to affirming that salvation is a transhistorical event, and that salvation brings us to deliverance while freeing us *from* the grasp of history itself. Salvation, both personal salvation and the prototypical act of Christ, arises *in* and *through* history, but it is not in itself a historical act. Historically, Man is not saved, but dies. Man is

---

* Original text: "Le temps circulaire: Temporisation et temporalité," in *Temporalité et Alienation*, ed. E. Castelli (Paris: Aubier, 1975). It includes a short part from a previous essay in Spanish, "El presente tempiterno. Una postilla a la historia de la salvación y a la teologia de la liberación," in Vargas Machuka, *Teologia y mundo contemporaneo. Homage a Karl Rahner* (Madrid: Cristianidad, 1975).

[1] See my essays on "La Misa como *consecratio temporis*: la tempiternidad," in *Sanctum Sacrificium*, Zaragoza (V Congreso Eucarístico Nacional) 1961, 75–93; "La loi du *karma* et la dimension historique de l'homme," in E. Castelli, ed., *La théologie de l'histoire. Herméneutique et eschatologie* (Paris: Aubier, 1971), 205–30; "Toward a Typology of Time and Temporality in the Ancient Indian Tradition," *Philosophy East and West* 24, no. 2 (April 1974): 161–64; *Le mystère du culte dans l'hindouisme et le Christianisme* (Paris: Cerf, 1970), chapter 3: "Le culte et le temps," 43–52; "Temps et histoire dans la tradition de l'Inde," in *Les cultures et le temps* (Paris: Payot/UNESCO, 1975), 73–101 (see previous chapters).

saved precisely when he does not allow history to swallow him whole. Man is saved when he "saves himself from" history.[2] I would add that the liberation found in liberation theology is not only Man's liberation from oppressive social structures, but particularly his liberation from time and, by consequence, from the dream of a purely temporal deliverance. Second, this release from time is not so that Man is turned into an angel or a timeless being, but it lets him achieve ownership of the temporal.[3] Third, the alienation from which Man must be freed is the menacing alienation of time, which devours his entire existence and monopolizes his whole being. Man alienates himself and loses human dignity when he dives into the temporal world as if it were his only environment, and where he consequently drowns in the ocean of time. In addition, I would like to point out that any concept implying a tyrannical eternity and a monopolizing a-temporality would be even more alienating.[4] We should not lose sight of this issue throughout this study. I would like, however, to proceed with a certain independence from the issue in order to be able to philosophize, theologically, from another perspective that also belongs to the human experience.

Sociotheological Interlude

All that could be said about the current situation of humankind would not even give a faint idea of the truth, because it would be the language of the privileged minority, which both asks the question and is more or less interested in finding the answer. The two-thirds of humankind—who are the victims in this situation—do not have the occasion, the capability, or the will to read or to listen to that which could be said.[5] They are just as powerless as a fetus or an unborn child. Talking about what could happen to those who may or may not be born in nine months is sarcastically sad and could be an example of a preoccupation for the future at the expense of the present, when millions of human beings probably will not live a full life because of hunger, cold, heat, avoidable infections—in short, infra-animal conditions—and are completely forlorn. Here we are talking about endemic situations that go from bad to worse, in spite of all good words, good intentions, and numerous efforts. A genocide by omission can be greater and crueler than any clearly sinful "purges."

We must face the human situation in all its plainness. For the current generation, for the millions of human beings in Asia and Africa in 1975, there is neither hope nor solution in temporality. We cannot continue to let ourselves be led astray by utopian solutions for the future, and abandon the current generations without even a burial. Or, yes, we may act consistently and maintain that it was necessary to sacrifice fifteen million Ukrainians, ten or more million Chinese, six million Jews, and that we must abandon unto death an even

---

[2] From this perspective we could, perhaps, bridge Cullmann's and Bultmann's positions. The existential participation of each person is fundamental, but it is possible only because of an event that happened within history that reveals a certain fullness of history (of history of salvation).

[3] Here, we could also complete Gutiérrez's thesis, and especially J. B. Metz's thesis about political theology. Political activity is essentially religious and theological, but it does not exhaust the religious dimension, and it cannot be interpreted one-dimensionally.

[4] We obviously make reference to an overcoming of the Marxist doctrine—without going back to a previous viewpoint—and to the current Marxist analyses. The exploitation of Man by an economy of privilege and the alliance of traditional religious feelings with factors of alienation cannot be forgotten. Nonetheless, this does not justify another—and worse—alienation in which Man's center of gravity is moved from an "eternal" future to a temporal future.

[5] The FAO meeting on world hunger in November 1974 (after this essay had already been written) tragically confirms all that I would like to show.

greater quantity of anonymous victims in our future plans—without even letting them wear a martyr's aureole for posterity or providing a humane ritual for their premature death.

If these thoughts are not welcome in the theological debate, it is theology that excommunicates itself from Man. If, at the same time, it is not a philosophical problem, it will then be philosophy that mutilates itself.

The pertinent consideration to make here, philosophical and theological in nature, seems to me to be the one that springs from the direct experience, even if at different degrees, of sharing life with that suffering part of humanity. I only speak here about the experience in India today, and will not make moral or social considerations, but rather a fundamental philosophical-theological reflection. An authentic speculation does not *look* at reality: it *reflects* the same reality from a critical point of view, all the while aware that the image of reality participates in reality itself, thus having the power to change it. The philosophical-theological sciences have often sought refuge in the fortresses of their concepts, escaping reality instead of reflecting upon it and being able, by so doing, to correct its image, thereby modifying reality itself.

In India there are at least 250 million people living in such precarious conditions that they are beneath a humane and even animal standard of living.[6] And even though we are about to praise these populations, this will not improve the situation, but rather worsen it. It is a sin, an insult to humanity, a sort of original sin committed by each individual in our day and age,[7] to let almost two-thirds of humanity die because of the special organization of the other third.[8]

These peoples do not aspire to a better future; they do not believe in it, and they do not even have the necessary strength to imagine it as a real possibility beyond escapist dreams with a purely hallucinatory compensation.[9] They do not even conceive of any form of liberation—in the Western understanding of the word—as possible, nor as comprehensible. They

---

[6] This would not simply require a better world distribution of goods, nor does it mean that the responsibility only belongs to the "rich" countries. The disparity between the favored people and the needy ones grows in parallel with the poverty of a country. If, in the wealthiest countries, 25 percent of the population live below the "normal" standard as to assistance and subsistence, they are the 60 percent worldwide; in India, on the other hand, up to 85 percent live below this standard, and only a privileged 15 percent have access to assistance and subsistence. Over the past twenty-five years, the increase in the material standard of life in India has only touched 10 or 15 percent of the population, whereas the remaining percentage has remained at the same level as before, if not worsened. Another example: 80 percent of the Indian population lives in rural areas, and the number of hospital beds and doctors in these areas only reaches 30 percent and 20 percent, respectively. (Figures gathered at a medical meeting in New Delhi, published by the *Hindustan Times* [New Delhi], September 9, 1974).

[7] In 1950, the University of Freiburg invited me to lecture on *Die Kultursünde des Abendlandes* (the cultural sins of the West), which has had some repercussions in this sense.

[8] The modern world is beginning to discover that today's technological organization (both in the "first" and in the "second" world) is not even theoretically close to being a solution to the problem that it is partially guilty of creating. According to UN documents, in 1939, 40 percent of the world's peoples were suffering from below-standard food intake; in 1956, this number grew to 60 percent, and the catastrophic forecasts for the year 2000 seem tragically inevitable.

[9] In India, where 3 percent of agricultural families have more than 50 acres of cultivable land, 57.6 percent of those families own less than 2.5 acres (5 acres being the minimum necessary to sustain a family). If, in 1960–61, the percentage of residents in these towns living below the subsistence level was 38 percent, in 1967–68 their number reached 57 percent. See B. Böttger, "Indische Perspektiven," *Neues Hochland* 66, no. 3 (May–June 1974): 235–45.

do not have a sense of history or of any sort of historical ideal. If these people are liberated, it is not by history. History has turned its back on them and has even become their greatest enemy. It is by history that they have been ceaselessly exploited.[10]

To inculcate in these populations the three previously mentioned theological concepts would (maybe!) "open their eyes," "educate," "civilize," and "convert" them. It would also, however, devastate them, make them lose the meaning of life, and put them in a position to commit universal suicide. This recalls many cases of suicide in our Western world, when some "privileged" members of society enter into contact with a clear view of a life that is different from their own, and are then confronted with the impossibility of living that life.

Both the internal experience and life in common with this underdeveloped world present a new aspect of the problem. This problem is very difficult to expose because the least exaggeration in any direction could completely deform the truth and have heavy practical consequences. It is not about glorifying the poor or the forlorn, nor is it about portraying the ideal of the "good savage," of the "happy poor man," or about superficially remembering that the poor are "blessed." It is also not about representing them as degraded human beings or lacking human dignity. Undoubtedly, they suffer and lead such a precarious existence that, if one does not live it, it is just as intolerable as it is unimaginable. However, they reflect the profundity of a life that is as bare as their bodies are naked and their stomachs are empty. They evoke a freedom that makes them capable of everything, either good or bad, of one thing or another, because they have neither obstacles nor bonds of any kind. It is precisely how to understand these people, our brothers, that I would like to deal with in depth. How and why do these beings survive? Why do they not destroy themselves or rebel against the others?[11] I repeat that, in the end, their experience is a nontransferable one, like all forms of experience, but maybe it can become communicable to others through theological meditation.

Phenomenological Approximation

Even though comparative and contrasting knowledge is not the only way to come to a form of intelligibility, we use this method here because it is dominant in modern science. Subsequently, we notice three significant absences in the way of living temporality in India, which contrast with the common experience of time in the technologized Western world. It could be that the latter has won in discrimination or lost in depth, but our current approach is purely phenomenological. In essence, this absence constitutes one characteristic derived from the subjective experience of cyclical time, but for more clarity, we proceed with a tripartite division.

---

[10] There are few differences between those who have exploited the masses or have taken advantage of their exploitation—be they Mongols, Britons, *zamindars* [a caste of great hereditary landowners in the Indian Subcontinent; abolished in the 1950s (n.d.t.)], loan sharks, *brahmans*, politicians, government officers, or representatives of God; but what is certain is that liberation did not come to those peoples through history.

[11] The *practice* of revolution presupposes a certain preconditional *theory* to revolution. The idea of revolution is linked to different, very particular forms of thought that are contrary to the mentality of these peoples for whom I would like to speak in this study. See my article "Philosophy and Revolution," *Philosophy East and West* 22, no. 4 (July 1973): 315–22, where I have tried to show that, in order to have an effective revolution, and for it to make sense, a determined form of philosophy is necessary because it makes it thinkable.

The Time of Waiting

In daily life, we must often wait for a visitor who does not pop up, a bus that does not come, or an idea that never stops crystallizing. "He who waits despairs," says a Castilian proverb, but, for the average Hindū Man, it is neither about waiting nor despairing. He does not grow impatient because he does not anxiously tie himself to an uncertain future time in which he hopes that an event will take place. He does not wait because, consciously or not, he does not eliminate the present time.

It is not only about the fact that the porter, the most informed person on the platform, invariably responds to the question "When will the train arrive?" with "In the morning" or "Soon." It is also not about an employee of an airline company who says—naturally and without any personal obligation to offer excuses—to the almost desperate tourist that he can take advantage of the fact that the plane is not going to leave that day, and take a break. It is not about simple anecdotes, but something more profound. It is about life events that are not lived in function of time, as if time were only in function of what I expect of it and from it. In some ways, it is about an experience of the seigniory of time, because time is not at the service of other things.

Ultimately, there is not a *time* of waiting. Not because there is a lack of desire for an event to happen, but because that determined moment, however important it may be in my life (I am going to get some work, to organize the marriage of my daughter, to make a deal . . .), is not *temporally* independent and, by consequence, separable from the concrete moment in which it happens. Time is not a train rail on which events can arrive late. The temporal coefficient is intrinsic to the event itself. This is why, incidentally, there is no great need to date it, that is, to refer it to an ideal time with Cartesian coordinates. History is not a succession of dates, but a connection between events. Each thing brings its own time with itself. We may want the train to arrive early or on time, but we cannot wait for (hope for) the very meeting, the kiss, the transaction that we will have with the person who is on the train, because this act brings its own time with itself, and wanting to anticipate it would mean to idealize it, to convert it into an unreal daydream. During a night of insomnia, I can want the sun to rise before its time, but I cannot hope that the day will break *and* remain in the shadows of the night. We cannot expect that the sun will rise in the middle of the night. The meeting with the sun itself will bring the time of its light.

There are no interstitial moments to fill the voids. Each event comes in its own time. Thus, from each thing's time, we can understand the true nature of events. Is it not here where we can find the justification of astrology in India? Anthropological-cosmical harmony consists in that the subjective order of having a time for each thing corresponds to the objective principle that each thing exists in its own time.

There is no "pastime" because, strictly speaking, time does not pass. Events succeed one another, more or less important in nature, and their individual times fade away along with each of them. A game in India is not a pastime, but a very special time. During the game, we are living the present without the weight of the past or the anxiety of the future. The game is not a pastime, even if by playing we "kill" the empty and teleological time.

This attitude may persist insofar as "free" time and "possibility" time do not count, since time is not (yet?) monetized or quantified—in such a way that "waiting" a few minutes or a few hours has no importance as long as we are comfortable. But it is also possible that this could be due to another vision of things, which considers them as inseparable from time, from which they come. It is also possible that a religious tradition that does not hope for any Messiah, and is not anxious to "leave Babylon" and return to the motherland "where milk and honey flow," has not developed a sense of temporality as a formal domain of possibilities that Man's creating activity can convert into (historical) facts. However, it is still possible that this depends on a vital experience of both present time and reality, in a depth beyond time, allowing Man to discover that possibility-time is infinitely inferior to the coefficient of the inherent reality of what actually happens.

It is not, however, the time for us to explore why there is an absence of despair—which is to me incontestable—for the late arrival of things and the absence of the meaning itself of waiting.[12]

Wasted Time

A big part of the "educative" efforts in a school system more or less copied from Western patterns (again, phenomenology does not provide value judgments) consists in instilling a sense of responsibility linked to an awareness of not losing or "wasting" time. Nonetheless, someone living in one of the country's university campuses will find, to his surprise and/or amazement—depending on the case—the most generous dilapidation of time. And let us not speak of daily life when it is not under the constraints of work. In fact, the very phrase "to lose time" makes no sense. We can lose a ring, we can break a machine, we can upset a project, but we cannot lose time, much in the same way that we cannot lose the moon or lose suffering.

In order for us to lose time, time would need to be something in itself, or capable of disengaging from the events to which it is connected. However, we have seen that this is not the case. Wanting to use "foreign" terms to formulate the experience of time in India in order to reach a form of intelligibility, we could speak of a type of "conservation law" for time, much like there are energy conservation laws. During such a time, and thanks to it, we can do different things, both good and bad, productive and destructive, without haste or worry, because time always seems to be there, at our disposal, as if there were time for everything. "It is not because you wake early that the day breaks earlier." Once I scandalized a "disciple" in India who could not understand my resistance to devoting all twenty-four hours of the day to him. What did I have to "lose" since he would let me do all that I wanted, as long as we shared our time together? Could I tell him that I would be losing my time by being with him? Would convincing him that he would better benefit from his time by being alone, or away from me, make sense? Another example: "Master, I have been following you for three years, and I have not yet found a thing"—"Did you lose anything?" was the disarming answer of the Master.

Being able to do something better than what we have done, and therefore having the conviction of our own responsibility, has nothing to do with the Western idea of losing time because you could have taken better advantage of it by doing something better. There is no Newtonian, "spatial" time (or divine *sensorium*[13]) where events take place. There *are* events, and with each event comes its own desire and its own time.

Effectively, time does not get lost because it cannot lose itself; it only transforms itself, like energy. Time is lived, in one shape or another. Therefore, there is nothing to fear, nothing to doubt. No one can steal it, not even death, as we will see. There is a time for everything, even for dying.

---

[12] See the interesting points of contact offered by Pedro Laín-Entralgo in his study "La espera y la esperanza," *Revista de Occidente* (1957), and the works of E. Castelli, *Les présupposés d'une théologie de l'histoire* (Paris: Vrin, 1954); *L'enquête quotidienne* (Paris: PUF, 1959); and *Le temps invertébré* (Paris: Aubier, 1970).

[13] An expression taken from Francis Bacon. [*Editorial note*]

Accelerated Time

We cannot accelerate the growth of a plant by pulling on its stem or on its leaves. And if, at any given moment, we have been able to make time go by more quickly than at its natural rhythm, there is a form of elasticity in time that then puts it back in its place—as if it were bouncing—at a lower speed, in order to regain its rhythm and reestablish balance. I was not able to convince my travel companions that airfare is more expensive than traveling by train because a plane is faster. They finally agreed that it is more expensive because it is more comfortable, like with a seat in first class and a seat in second class, even though you arrive at the same time in both cases.

There are certainly different speeds, and each being has its own, but what cannot be accepted is the acceleration of those speeds. We could say that the Hindū countryman has the intuition, proper to relativism, that the faster you go the more the moving mass diminishes. That time can be accelerated means that things can get smaller, and that the artificial sphere can penetrate the entrails of the natural, the normal dimension. We can accelerate elementary particles, but what would happen if we accelerated fundamental elements, like the sun, the moon, and other planets? Could we make the Earth rotate around the sun at different speeds depending on our every whim? Can we accelerate Man as such? What does an accelerated "life" mean?

Elsewhere, I have tried to show that the acceleration of time is a characteristic of the second-degree instrument, and that elementary matter has a degree of acceleration much higher than that of organic matter, which in turn is much higher than that of vital matter, in turn higher than that of human matter.

The second-degree machine accelerates time and, by accelerating it, changes the structure of things. Here again, a quantitative change produces a qualitative transformation. It is not surprising that a survival instinct for our own identity provides resistance to such exogenous variations. In other words, there is a level of acceleration proper to each type of being, which, once passed, produces the death or the mutation of the accelerated body. The acceleration of time in technological civilization has already created a mechanical-human hybrid that can easily be made out in the people living in large capital cities: they show a mutation in comparison with the human being represented by a villager who has not undergone this transformation. We cannot recklessly accelerate rhythms. It is impossible to skip the question whether this acceleration is, or is not, a universal cultural necessity or a cancerous growth, or maybe an intermediary phase. In any case, an adequate diagnosis is of great importance.[14]

The characteristics we are stressing here are common to every predominantly agrarian civilization, and, before the machine introduced acceleration, they constituted a large part of the Western pretechnological mentality. We should as well remark that the time of seasons and of agriculture is also cyclical. And all of this would only be in our favor: cyclical time is far from being an aberration. It would be worthwhile, however, to notice a difference: a given cord vibrates with a defined resonance, but, if the originating vibration is too strong, the resounding cord stays flat. Analogously, the growing transformation of the West, for more or less two centuries, has allowed the Western soul to vibrate at an increasingly rapid rhythm without breaking. If, however, everything is done abruptly, barely over the course of two generations, there is nothing astonishing about the cord breaking or becoming paralyzed. The current situation in India does not seem to leave room for an

---

[14] See my contribution to the colloquium on "Tecnica e casistica," *Technique et temps: la technochronie* (Padua: CEDAM, 1964), 195–229, then published in Spanish as *Técnica y tiempo* (Buenos Aires, 1967).

alternative: either it will lose its identity by breaking, or it will become paralyzed in tow of a foreign technology.

What, then, is this time that, in some cases, appears as the carrier of human hope, the instrument of salvation; and, in other cases, a symbol of the smallness and the deciduous nature of things, the obstacle to liberation?

Keeping faithful to our method, we do not give an abstract answer to this question, but rather try to describe the depth of life in traditional India, in order to confront the first, unavoidable, question that we asked: What will happen to these famished and ragged masses of people of our same species and planet? Are we going to tell them to revolt and to sacrifice themselves for a future that they will never be able to attain? Are we going to preach resignation, due to the incapability of finding another solution? What does the *Tao-te Ching* mean when it says, "Happiness is rooted in misery, misery lurks in happiness"?[15]

The Circular Nature of Time

The strength of metaphors is that, once they are thrown into circulation, they escape the hands of their authors; but they are not, as such, independent of the context in which they were created.[16]

The metaphor of the circular nature of time gives us a typical example of the distinctive character of Oriental religions that have afterward been reinterpreted in the context of Cartesian coordinates. The interpretation of texts belongs to compared morphology when the texts are synchronic with the interpreter, and to diachronic hermeneutics when the texts are not. The understanding of the contexts, however, belongs to what I have called *diatopic hermeneutics*. Not having taken this into account has produced *lèse-humanité* misunderstandings.

Here I express my thoughts about one of these misunderstandings: it is a fact that traditional India—which is represented by the millions of people to whom I have alluded in the beginning—among many other cultures, believes in the circular nature of time.[17]

Maybe it would be fitting to explain briefly the following interpretation, which, because of its diatopic standpoint, strays from a certain type of erudite Indological (diachronic) exegesis and from a popular (morphological) interpretation. If the former is represented by a critical and documented vision (but from the outside, and from the perspective of temporal distance), the second represents an authentic and sincere, although excessively superficial, fact of life from the perspective of a distinct morphological situation. Both interpretations—the one sustained by a large part of modern Indologists and the one emerging in popular expressions—are not wrong but incomplete. In fact, by applying a hermeneutic based on the literary genres followed by these two groups of interpretations, we discover that they differ from the one I am defending less because of the fact that they are contradicting opinions than that we must place ourselves on two distinct levels.

We could say to a number of Indologists that they sometimes—not always—apply categories of "foreign intelligibility" to the phenomenon in question. These may help to clarify it

---

[15] *Tao-te Ching*, 58. Literally, "good luck lies on disaster, disaster squats under good luck." [n.d.t.]

[16] I am not going to discuss here the Christian concept of time, or whether it is linear or not. See anyway Cullman's repeated protest that his famous thesis on linear time does not consist in a study about the concept of time, or even about the Christian concept of time, but in an exegesis of the way in which first-generation Christians lived and interpreted the temporal fact of the apparition of Christ.

[17] "To hope for fulfillment in the future, then, is like expecting the purpose of a symphony to be the finale," as acutely Sehdev Gupta said in "The Concept of Time: East and West," *Teilhard Review* 9, no. 2 (June 1974): 40.

under a new angle, but they deform it if they are not completed. To those who represent the popular vision, we could add that their personal thinking is correct, but when they want to explain the phenomenon, they transform it so much that they deform it—a little bit like when a traditional Christian without theological training tries to "imagine" heaven like a garden of delights where God will let us live forever if we have been good on earth. What the listener understands is not what the speaker wants to say. Here, as it often happens, both the truth and the error lie in the interpretation.

In other words, the interpretation I suggest does not want to be polemic but, on the contrary, would like to present a vision of the phenomenon from within thanks to experience and conviction, and to be *also* critical by going beyond a certain legendary language in which this fact of life has generally been expressed. Moreover, I believe that the present interpretation can be plausible for the modern Man, and that it is in line with the tradition from which it comes. Without elaborating upon the principles of diatopic hermeneutics at this moment, we try to apply it to our case.

But let us first try to explain the image of the circular nature of time.

The Circumference Is Undefined

In the first place, this image suggests a circumference, that is, that time is undefined, and that it does not have a temporal start or end; and this is why worrying about beginnings "before" time, as well as torturing ourselves about eschatological-temporal problems, is useless.[18] By definition, every *before* and every *after* belong to time. The circumference of the circle has neither beginning nor end. By straddling time, we will never be able to find its originating point or its end. Every temporal voyage, as such, cannot escape from time and can therefore find no limit to time. There is no way to escape from time if our vehicle is temporal. And we cannot doubt that our "reasoning reason," which also needs time for reflection, is temporal. Every rational thought, and therefore predicative thought, that would like to be extratemporal or think the a-temporal commits undue extrapolation.

An important corollary to this first point clarifies one of the major difficulties of a purely linear thought. For this last notion, it is incomprehensible that both the beginning and the end of any process always be "beyond." The search for the beginning and the eschatological investigation are set to fail.[19] The constant call toward continuously distant limits stops only when we abandon reflexive thought in order to admit, mythically, that one given point is a beginning or an end. But every thought has an unlimited number of antecedents and consequences.[20] The Greek *anankê stênai* (we need to stop [somewhere]) is a natural and pragmatic necessity, but if we artificially impose it, we paralyze the very form of thought. Myth is necessary, but it cannot be imposed. Experiencing the circular nature of time allows us to avoid this aporia: it is useless to try to exit time with instruments that are also—and only—temporal. The question about the beginning and the end is a false question, as Buddha showed by refusing to answer the ultimate questions.[21] He was in harmony with the largest

---

[18] Let us remember the classic argument of St. Thomas Aquinas, according to which we cannot prove that the world had a (temporal) start, and those who would like to show this do not help apologetics. See *Sum. Theol.*, I, q.46.

[19] See Castelli in his Introduction to *Temporalité et Alienation*: "In order to speak about the origin of the world (or of the spoken) one must resolve the problem about the word *origin*" (13).

[20] See A. N. Whitehead, *Essays in Science and Philosophy* (New York: Philosophical Library, 1948), 73, showing that this also includes very simple affirmations like "1 + 1 = 2."

[21] See my reflections on this argument in *El silencio del Dios* (Madrid, 1970), and in my chapter

part of human traditions: "What is above you, do not look for it, and what goes beyond your strengths, do not try."[22] "Leave aside erudition and you will not suffer."[23] "It is unknown for those who understand [it], it is known to those who do not understand [it]."[24]

Not having been *able* to eliminate the question, because it supposes a linear schema of thought, is at the basis of the modern Western Man's twofold anxiety: anxiety for not being able to ever finish anything (the fear of the end) and anxiety for not being able to go back to the origins (the fear of the beginning).[25]

In other words: living time like a circumference frees us from the obsession of "what is new" as the ultimate criterion of authenticity and creativity. Simply because the past is past, it does not mean that it will be surpassed or invalidated.

The Center Is Indistinct

Second, this circular image implies a center, which means that time is indistinct. Each point is equidistant from the center and has the same curvature. From this point of view, there are no privileged moments, be they considered either objectively or subjectively. Objectively, any point of the circumference can be the temporal start or end. Only individual eschatology has a heuristic value. Subjectively, my life can be interrupted at any given moment and does not break insofar as it possesses true life. Death is as close to the child who has just been born as it is to the octogenarian. The anxiety of death has no place in the metaphysical plane. The law of *karman* takes care of my *karmatic* remains so that they effectively live in another subject or subjects, but my person, my uniqueness, is reintegrated into the center, naked and simple like when it left it. The merit belongs to my successors in the *karmatic* order: it is what I provide to history. My *atman* does not need this.

The first noticeable consequence, rich in lessons for discussions about Christian eschatology and its multiple contemporary interpretations, consists in discovering the essentially personal nature of each eschatology. If we move the eschatological problem from the historical domain to the personal domain, then the exegetical discussions find their proper place.[26] From a personal viewpoint—which does not mean individual—if not personalistic, my death coincides with the end of the world. My death, since death is more than the simple physical phenomenon of matter and energy transforming, consists in breaking the spatial-temporal schema of reality. But, outside of space and time, we all coincide.[27] My death is the door that

---

"Le silence et la parole: Le sourire du Bouddha," in E. Castelli, ed., *L'analyse du langage théologique* (Paris, 1969), 121–34. In Volume V of this *Opera Omnia*.

[22] See *Ben Sira* (*Ecclesiasticus*) 3:22, according to the Vulgate. See also Wis 9:13–14; Is 29:14; Ps 30:10; 1 Cor 3:19.

[23] *Tao-te Ching*, XIX, LXIII.

[24] *KenU* II.3.

[25] See Castelli (op. cit., 16) when he writes about the "implicating inexhaustibility . . . the deductibility which brings with itself the anxiety of not being able to finish."

[26] The following, innumerable, and subtle modern theories, handsomely named with imaginative linguistic effort, are well known: "consequent" eschatology (Schweitzer), "realized" eschatology (Dodd), "inaugurated" eschatology (Florovsky), eschatology "in a process of realization" (Jeremias), "proleptic" eschatology (J. A. T. Robinson), "existential" eschatology (Bultmann), "historical-salvific" eschatology (Cullman), etc.

[27] In traditional Christian parlance, this is the same as saying that the particular judgment and the universal judgment coincide. There is no intermediary waiting time—unless we keep on defending a temporal idea of eternity.

opens to salvation,[28] and this is why St. Paul said that he died every day.[29] It is a question of *personal eschatology.*

The practical manifestation of this second characteristic of circular time shows itself not only in the theological interpretation of the eschatological problem but also in personal experience. A clear example is the contemporary sociological studies concerned with Man's attitude toward death and the astonishment of Western scholars in discovering that in India, for example, death does not "hide"—that it is not a private, negative, or even shameful event. Aside from these general thoughts, we can also mention the way in which death is experienced by those who live in cyclical time. Death is the most natural phenomenon of existence. Not only is its presence no longer a trauma, but its reality ceases to appear as an anxiety or a threat. Of course, we fear the suffering and the infirmities of old age, but we are not dismayed by death. Death thwarts my being and interrupts my real life only when I have identified myself with my projects, and it then prevents their fulfillment.[30]

In a way, death is not to be found at the end of my life; my existence is not a race toward death. How could I believe that the more I live, the closer I am to death? The more I live (and *the more*, here, is certainly not quantitative), the more I have life and the more I am, by this fact alone, distanced from the nonlife of death. Death is not *in front* of me but *by* me, and its company allows me to act (as we will describe) with first-time enthusiasm and last-time maturity. In some sense, death is *behind* me, at the beginning of my existence—if we try to translate this intuition into a linear schema.

In other words, experiencing time as equidistant from the center frees us from being obsessed with the future and from the desire to place the meaning of our life in a problematic future time, so that, if our life were to break before this future, it would lose its meaning. True liberation begins when we discover that the ultimate meaning of life, in the last analysis, does not depend on time, and therefore we can live without the obsession of a constant "danger of death."

Personal progress does not consist in a straight and ascending time line but rather in a more marked rapprochement to the center of the circle. But here the metaphor should be corrected, because the center of the circumference is not the circumference, nor is it, in some sense, situated within the circumference.

The Circle Is Limited

Third, the circular image of time suggests a circle, that is, something that is not only limited and finite, but also not infinite or absolute. A circle has a determined surface and thus becomes the symbol of limitation, of contingency. Time is certainly the most fitting symbol of Being; it is its appearance, its clothing. The whole temporal circle is something similar to the projection of an a-temporal point that could be represented by the center of that same circle. From this angle, we understand that the principle characteristic of the a-temporal is not transcendence but immanence.

---

[28] Here Bultmann is right in stressing the importance of the existential decision; but his interpretation is not historically existential, and it presupposes a linear concept of time in which a person's death becomes reality. In this sense, I would say that Cullman is right in defending that the *Heilsgeschichte* corresponds to historical Christian intuition.

[29] 1 Cor 15:31. See the clear eschatological context of the whole passage about the resurrection.

[30] See the well-known expression *Vita mutatur non tollitur* [Life is transformed, not taken away] in the Christian liturgy for the deceased, and the not less known *akāla mṛtyu*, inopportune death, death as setback, in the Indic tradition.

It is instructive to study the value of metaphors.[31] In India, the circular course of time suggests precisely the image of its own limitation and also, as we will see, the impossibility of its repetition. The infinite, in order to exist, that is, in order to emerge in the world, must logically wear a temporal clothing. Time is not a "place" that we cross in order to reach an end; it is rather the envelope that limits us, the costume that renders us visible and, in some ways, individualizes us.

Time is unique precisely because it is finite. This is where the comparison has often been misunderstood because it has been interpreted out of context. "Circular nature" does not mean repetition. It is as impossible to repeat circular time as it is to repeat linear time. Let us use the same metaphor to clarify this argument. Let there be a point A in the temporal circumference, and let us imagine that, after a determined period of time, even a temporal cycle, we return for the second time to the same point, which we now call "A$_1$." Now, the circular nature of time tells us that A is identical to A$_1$. Indeed, if time is the situation on the circumference, nothing temporal can differentiate A from A$_1$. There is no second time or possible distinction. The two moments are one and the same moment.

Therefore, it is not about my returning and returning again, so that I turn and repeat the same cosmic cycle an unlimited number of "times," because this "time" and all "times" would be completely identical and the same "time." There is no repetition, there is only continuity. This is what the popular vision underscores: nothing is lost in the *karmatic* order, all things return and, in some ways, are conserved, but they are in a different subject, in a new and different carrier and, therefore, with no repetition. Having confused the *saṃsāric* circular course of temporal elements with the repetition of the subject was at the origin of the common misunderstanding about the so-called transmigration of souls. Everything in fact transmigrates, *except* the transmigrating subject. This subject is the psychological "I" for elementary psychology; for a philosophical anthropology, it is the characteristic of uniqueness of the personality; and for a theological-*Vedāntic* interpretation, it is Īśvara, the Lord of the universe, God himself, the subject of all change.[32]

Here is the true place of rite. The external appearance of a ritual act takes the shape of a repetition, or—at the very best—of a commemoration, but what the rite claims is much greater. In passing, I would say that the rite excludes the "curious" people, the non-initiated, because by seeing they do not see, and by observing they are mistaken. What the rite wants to achieve is precisely this victory over time, recapturing the a-temporal knot of reality. It does not matter, in this case, that this may be hypostasized in a mythical initiation, in a special time, in a particular eschatology. What does matter is that it represents itself, that is to say that the primordial act becomes truly present again—that there is "true presence" in the ritual act of "re-presenting." Without "contemporaneity" and therefore presence of the totality of time in the present act of worship, there is no true rite.

We have said that time is the symbol of an a-temporal reality. But the symbol is not "another" reality, or "the" reality: it is the symbol "of" reality, the reality "as" symbol, its appearance, its apparition, its manifestation. In order to reach reality we must therefore abandon the symbol and grasp something else—unless we recognize the symbol as such, that is, as an appearance of reality. We must break its meaning as "reality"; and then this broken

---

[31] See Parmenides's "sphere" and Greek cyclical time.

[32] See the famous text of the *Śaṅkara-bhāṣya*, I.1.5: *satiam neśvarad anyah samsāri*: "In truth, there is no other transmigrant than the Lord." See my commentary, "The Law of Karman and the Historical Dimension of Man," *Philosophy East and West* 22, no. 1 (January 1972): 25–43. In this Opera Omnia, Volume IX, Part 1.

symbol will open us up to reality. It is the sacrifice in time that redeems time.[33] It is not by following time to the end that we will reach the Eternal, as if it were "after" the temporal, but rather it is by breaking the circle that we will be able to reach eternity. Time is there precisely to be broken, to be transcended. Man does not aim at the future but at his liberation, even though this becomes reality through and with time. It is not the progress that counts but the perfection, the realization, the rupture of the envelope.

This means that, on top of the purely cosmic or temporal dynamism consisting in following the circle, there is another force in Man that pushes him to transcend time, to break the circle, to abandon the circumference. If we break linear time, the result is still a line, and therefore still a line of time. If we break the circumference, the result is no longer a circumference, and there is no longer time as such.[34] It is by exiting time that we find our liberation. We can see this more concretely by examining how India's "temporal civilization," still alive today in the generations to which we have already alluded, experiences the temporal.

In other words: experiencing time as a closed circle frees us from being obsessed with the present, as if we could have the entire human experience in a purely temporal present. Here, it is important to note that there are two ways of living the present: as a chosen and privileged moment in the temporal event, and as the concentration of all time (past and future) in its perforation into a "tempiternal" present.[35]

Perhaps it would be useful to recall that this study does not seek to present the whole issue of time, or to defend the circular concept of time to the bitter end. I would simply like to give the example of cyclical time and present it in its positive aspects, even if it may be not more satisfactory than linear time. As a matter of fact, every metaphor is imperfect. "Circular" time, like "linear" time, refers to a space that does not fit the specificity of time. At most, time is irreducible to space, and spatial metaphors prevent the understanding of one of the most fundamental characteristics of temporal reality: temporal accumulation, that is, the different degree of "density" that temporal beings present in function of the "quantity" of time that they would have assimilated.[36]

The Theosociological Question

We have provided enough examples to allow us to realize the most distressing and insoluble sides of the question of liberation *in* time or *of* time. It is the theologian's responsibility to ask this question in all of its strength. A third or perhaps half of humanity does not experience time as a linear time; these people are not sensitive to the future or to history; if they have some desire for liberation, it is not in order to perceive themselves as "free" to work and to dedicate themselves to worldly tasks, but rather to liberate themselves from the weight of temporal existence and of the seal that time imprints on Man.

I repeat that the problem is serious, and the balance delicate. I do not deny that social liberation and political justice are urgent, or that a radical transformation of society, even at the risk of overturning the existing status quo, is necessary. But I argue that the simple laying

---

[33] See Eph 5:16; Col 4:5.

[34] See Rev 10:6; we would here translate χρονος ουκετι εσται with: "No more delay!"

[35] The two "presents" clearly appear in the double meaning of Faust's *Augenblick* in his promise to Mephistopheles (*Faust*, II.1699–703) and in his last prayer before death (II.11581–86). In the first phase, the present is purely temporal, it excludes the past, and is contemptuous of the future. In the second phase, the "moment" is transtemporal, tempiternal, and transcends—without negating—the three times by embracing them.

[36] We would like not to be misunderstood: we are not speaking of time, but only of its circular aspect.

of exogenous measures is not the solution, and that a good number of the self-proclaimed spokespeople of these "illiterate" and "poor" masses are not their true representatives, even though we recognize their good intentions and admit that they may be right in a large part of the things they say. Moreover, I maintain that the problem is much deeper than a simple question of technique for a better distribution of goods, because it is about salvation, liberation, fullness, felicity, peace, or (call it as you will) the final destiny of these people, our contemporaries, who cannot hope for better times or purely temporal solutions because such times will not come, nor will these solutions be able to reach them.[37]

The initial dilemma remains: either we eliminate, in one way or another, these human "parasites" who suffer in a cruel and unnecessary way, or we find an authentic solution for them (and not *only* for their descendants). Both the so-called modern technological civilization and contemporary Judeo-Christian-Marxist civilization, no matter the tie that unites them, have a different conception of time from other cultures. In their contacts with these cultures, they introduce—by virtue of their excessive material or spiritual power—a concept of temporal reality that is completely new and that, by penetrating different cultural regions, twists the deepest fibers of the organism that receives them.

In times of cultural "mono-formism" (one king, one Empire, one religion, one Church, one civilization), one would say, in a more or less delicate and nuanced manner, that the "other" concept was simply erroneous and needed to yield to the "true" way of life, thought, or belief. And perhaps it is a remainder of ancient monopolizing ways of thinking that seem to be kept by a certain technological mentality, namely the conviction that this mentality offers *the* valid and universal form of shared human existence. Controlled pluralism, even if only by the "pluralists," and even if only intellectually so, is not true pluralism. Unlike plurality, pluralism belongs to myth. This is why we destroy it when we want to rationally justify it—with the *logos*.

What to do? And—as orthopraxis clearly calls for orthodoxy—what to think? Three negative answers (see below) are unacceptable because they are self-destructive. The three positive answers are, at the very least, problematic.

Negative Answers

Do not think. The first response seems manifestly incongruous: do not think about the problems, do not worry about them, and by consequence, do not do anything, so as to let things improve or worsen on their own. An attitude like this is equivalent to a capital sin against Man and his dignity; here inhibition is a crime of *lèse-humanité*. Not taking a decision is already a compromise with some form of decision. A supposed liberal laissez-faire is not a solution because it contradicts the conditions of free action: it does not let happen.

Act without thinking. This second response seems equally unconvincing: to act, to throw oneself into action without thinking. Not only might this end up with a contrary result but

---

[37] It is interesting to note that, at the World Population Conference held in Bucharest (August 19–30, 1974), immediate causes of political alliances aside, countries known as "developing" agreed that we cannot isolate the problem of population and resolve it separately by following the well-known impatience of "first world" countries, whose propositions were Cartesianly "effective" and "concrete" because they did not "lose the North" but went straight to the "core" of the question. I believe that, here too, we can see the divergence of two mentalities—politics aside. One follows the "scientific" method, already formulated by Descartes, of isolating a problem in order to resolve it; while the other prefers to focus on a general overview, which has a chance for success only if reality is not made of "airtight compartments" but of constitutive relations.

it may also be impossible. Every action implicitly contains, and is fed by, some schema of thought. An action stripped of theory does not exist in Man, and if this theory does not make itself known, it carries with it the overflowing of suffocated ideas and the fury of repressed intentions or, more simply sometimes, the slavery of preceding conditionings and stiffened traditions. It pushes toward ideology, in the worst meaning of the word. Revolution for the sake of revolution, nothing more, can only bring us back to the point of departure—and make us suffer in vain.

Think without acting. Another answer seems to us to be inadequate: thinking without executing, limiting ourselves to diagnostics, to "phenomenology," to "contemplation." This is, at the same time, harmful and unacceptable. In the first place, it would represent an offense and a mockery in the emergency situation in which we find ourselves. It is equivalent to saying that such a way of thinking would be ethically unacceptable. Second, and more importantly, such a thought would not mirror the real situation. The human situation is not a case we can study in vitro or understand from the outside, without taking part or compromising ourselves in the upsetting events of our time. This does not mean that we cannot recognize different degrees of participation or compromise. But he who does not live through the situation of his contemporary Man, or does not feel his own spirit jeopardized by this situation, does not actually understand the situation; he lacks the mental equipment needed to pose the problem.

This does not mean dismissing the importance of a critical distance, or the contemplative, theoretical dimension necessary for such an enterprise. The *templum*, from which we can see the auspicious flight of birds, cannot be set in a private property or an ivory tower isolated from human troubles. Critical distance does not mean isolation any more than contemplative serenity means absence or indifference. "Universities" made of pure "intellectuals" and "monasteries" of pure "spiritual" people are parasitic forms whose diagnoses are simply an insult to the reality in which they live.

Positive Answers

Other, more positive alternatives appear, with more realism. It seems to me that, here too, the major division is tripartite: technologize the world, develop a pluralist coexistence, or find a new solution.

Technoscientific civilization. The first answer seems to be the one that, in fact, has taken the initiative. Since the technological civilization has developed, first in Europe, then in the United States, it has slowly invaded other continents, generally with the most cordial welcome by the minorities that hold public positions among the peoples in question. But now, that is, after the experiences of at least two generations, we begin to hear protests from different sides against a similar approach—protests that are increasing both in number and in vehemence.

On the one hand, even the West has come to criticize its own solutions, and on the other hand, the representatives of other cultures have also begun to realize that a technological civilization is only a new and more subtle form of colonialism. Both the writers' and the consumers' trust in science and technology has begun to weaken. It is a double rift: at the starting point, and at the end point. By studying his own origins, Man discovers that he is something more than a simple *homo mensurans atque faber*, only measuring things and making tools. A purely scientific concept of the universe leaves the human being incomplete. "Science" is incapable of capturing many equally real aspects of the universe. But, moreover, by studying the results given by "science" itself, we discover that it does not reach the expected conclusions because it is unable to include or to assimilate into its calculations imponderable and incommensurable facts about the human condition.

This phenomenon has been sufficiently studied, and therefore there is no need to insist. Technology, in practice, has not given the expected results, and we begin to doubt whether it is able to resolve, even only in theory, the most elementary of human problems.

Cultural coexistence. The second answer seems to acquire more and more strength, thanks to the limited success of the first attempt. In Africa, and especially in Asia, and in a more specific way also in Latin America and socialist countries, the movement is clearly visible, and so it is in the less "privileged" areas of so-called developed countries. All these cultures and subcultures are discovering that their own traditions are something more than pure museum folklore or celebrations, and have begun to think about the possibility of a pluralistic coexistence between the two systems, technology on one side and regional culture on the other. Here we speak of pluralism and tolerance. In the best scenario, science and technology would put themselves at the service of other civilizations, not just at the service of the ones where they were born. But here, too, hesitations about a too-naive optimism are now rising. Coexistence is only possible if the levels of existence are homogeneous. Otherwise, the big fish swallows the little fish: the most powerful, better-off, attractive, the easiest or, if you want, superior civilization dominates and supplants the other civilizations. To dream that scientific and technological values are universal, therefore assimilable everywhere and universally compatible, is beginning to look like a utopia.

A deeper knowledge of human cultures shows that there are no "neutral values," and what we call "the modern technological era" descends directly from a particular civilization presupposing a certain idea about life, which, with or without reason, is far from being universal. To accept technology, and to be a creator of technology, one must have a certain idea about Man, about matter, about time and space, and at the same time about society, all of which notions are far from being shared by other traditions, until now.

Maybe we should reform and perfect the first solution after having checked its short-comings, but the utopia of a possible coexistence of substantially different worldviews as a viable formula must be put aside. Perhaps this could modify technology and prepare us for a new symbiosis. But we would need to study its conditions of viability in order to prevent the birth of a monster.

A new solution. "New solution" is a useless phrase if we do not, at least, perceive its general guidelines or if we do not look for it. It is an adventurous task, but the ecological crisis as well as the two aforementioned sociological crises (the double deception of "developed" and "developing" countries; and the possibility that modern techniques may give humanity a period of peace and justice) seem to prepare the terrain for the search of a new solution that would integrate all of humanity's different experiences. Little by little, positive points emerge from the global consciousness. A certain ethical code, by its own initiative, seems to impose itself more and more; a series of commonly accepted proceedings seems to emerge as well, although slowly. Dialogue, mutual trust, ecumenicalism of all types, encounters between religions, and so on—everything is on the agenda. And although, sometimes, it may only be about somewhat fashionable commonplace, this very fact sufficiently proves that the opposite language—as a monopoly of truth, a unique depository of good and exclusive ownership of material wealth—cannot sustain itself much longer without an instinctive, negative reaction from an immense majority of people.

We are still very far from such a solution. Goodwill and the spontaneous desire for under-standing and harmonious synthesis do exist, and are the foundation for our hope, but besides interests created and disproportionately heavy historical inertias, there are still theoretical problems to explore. We do not yet have a common language (not meaning, of course, *one* language), we have not yet sufficiently studied *diatopic hermeneutics*, which would allow a correct interpretation of cultures and lifestyles that remain generally misunderstood *topoi* or are relegated to a second place. It is not about postulating a global philosophy or one single religion, or even a mono-form culture, but about creating a mythical complex (I cannot find a shorter formula) in which all people on our planet may participate, without it meaning the reduction of the human being to the smallest common denominator of elementary necessities, however important and necessary these are.

To help a new positive solution rise is the reason for this study. And in this perspective, we can now address the specific problem we established in the beginning.

The Theological Problem

We could present the theological problem in its true colors in the following way.

In the world there is suffering, injustice, disorder—or, if you want, sin. A large movement that began in the West, in a more or less disguised or explicit way, claims to bring a solution: the techno-scientific civilization. This worldview is, in fact, supported by two ideals that confer a quite obvious dynamism to it: (a) a more or less spiritualistic ideal belonging to the group of Abrahamitic religions, and (b) a more or less materialistic or humanistic ideal, belonging to the above-mentioned modern secularization. As a matter of fact, the main propagators of technical civilization are Judeo-Christian or Marxist-humanist believers, allowing for a margin of flexibility and interference. Ultimately, these two ideals are not only different manifestations of the same "soul." It is meaningful that both the "first" and the "second" world export the techno-scientific civilization and use it to the same extent. I do not believe that the movement coming from Japan can be considered as an exception at the moment, because the ideology that its propagators have represented until now does not go beyond the rules of the game we have just described. With time, things could change, but a mutation has not (yet?) happened.[38]

If we were to look at it from different points of view, it is clear that Judeo-Christianity and Marxist humanism differ from each other, but, in the perspective that here interests us, both share a similar structure. For example, both have—among other things—a linear concept of time and a similar concept of history. To which point this concept is essential to them is a question that does not concern us now.

Where are liberation, fullness, peace, justice, and salvation? "Clearly, they are in the future," even though the design of this future is very different according to, for example, Marxist and Christian orthodoxies. Here the thesis about an Absolute Future, to be identified with God, regains its whole meaning, but also shows its limits.[39] This thesis, in the Christian-Marxist encounter, is a model of dialogue and an example of the rule that Giordano Bruno already formulated and for which he paid with his life: "The first lesson for those who want to learn the art of discussing is: do not investigate [truth] and do not ask questions according to your

---

[38] A few years ago, I took a study tour in Japan to ask different representatives of Japanese society if they would advise India to follow the Japanese way of technification. To my great surprise, not only did I receive almost no affirmative response, but I was able to note the country's high degree of cultural schizophrenia.

[39] See K. Rahner, *Marxistische Utopie und Christliche Zukunft des Menschen* (Einsiedeln, 1965), 77–88. The fact that we can here hear an echo of the Thomist maxim "Aeternitas non est aliud quam ipse Deus" [Eternity is nothing else than God himself] (*Sum. Theol.*, I, q.10, a.2, ad 3) is secondary as a curiosity, but important for exegesis.

own principles, but according to the principles your adversary admits."[40] From this point of view, speaking about Christianity as a religion of the future,[41] of the absolute future,[42] so absolute that it contains no futuristic intraworldly utopia,[43] is to begin a dialogue with all those who think that "Man is . . . the being that . . . creates himself as he plans his future, and toward that future he plans his reality."[44]

What happens—and it is here that I have based my critique—is that such a "Man" is not the universal Man, because there are other people who understand themselves in different ways, and a Man's self-comprehension belongs to his own constitution.[45] And it is there that our case lies, with regard to the cyclical notion of time shared by a large part of humanity. Should we change it, "convert" it into a linear concept of time? Should we "temporize" these two "times"? Should we begin to see time like a spiral? These three questions correspond to the three answers mentioned in the previous chapter: technologizing, coexistence, and mutation.

I will not hide my sympathy for the third alternative, but the current situation is perhaps not ripe enough for it. The other two concepts—linear time and cyclical time—are so deeply rooted in the two hemispheres of the planet that a positive symbiosis will require us to respect the rhythms of any possible fecundation and preparation through a just temporary synthesis. I must be content with allusions and suggestions, nurturing my hopes by remembering that true fecundation happens first in the entrails of those who, by vocation, find themselves compromised in this task, then in the conscience of the peoples in question.

The interest for the past, reflected in literature and in history as they are cultivated, for example, in the West, is very significant. Equally revealing is the quasi-obsession that sociology and, in general, science in the West show for the future. Only the present seems to be forgotten. It is as if the present were only the intrascendent point of intersection between a past loaded with wealth and a future full of hope, perhaps because the human being, "a man of desire,"[46] is keen on absence. However, the fact that absence is contemplated within the past or the future, and that we do not look for it in the transtemporal (tempiternal) opening of the present time, is what seems to characterize the myth of history in which the current West seems to live.

I can now try to describe the experience of temporality in India that I would call *temporization*, but in order to be brief and concise, I focus on what I believe to be the core of the question. I call it the experience of the *tempiternal present*.[47]

Perhaps the best way to approach this experience is to describe what could be called the unrepeatability of time. But it is sheer banality to speak of the unrepeatability of any authentic action, so I rather call it the *irreducibility of the present*. The past *was*, which means that, in some way, it *is* no longer, if not in the present. The future *will be*, which means that, in some way, it *is* not, if not in the present. Whereas the reality of the past makes a certain reference

---

    [40] See G. Bruno, *Cena de le Ceneri* (Ash supper), Dialogue IV.

    [41] Rahner, *Marxistische Utopie und Christliche Zukunft des Menschen*, 78.

    [42] Ibid., 79.

    [43] Ibid., 82.

    [44] A. Darlap, s.v. "Zukunft" (Future) in *Sacramentum Mundi* (Basel: Herder, 1969), col. 1452.

    [45] A direct discussion of Rahner's thesis would make us ask him why we should not also say that God is the Absolute Past.

    [46] See Dan 9:23 (Vulgate).

    [47] I do not call it "absolute present" because my study is not an anti-thesis to Rahner, and because this *tempiternal present* is not *ab-solute*, that is to say, broken off from the temporal flow condensing in the present.

to the present, and so does the future, the experience of the present can be lived without any necessary reference to the past or the future. This is the experience of the tempiternal present that I would still like to describe.[48]

Not *any* present time is irreducible: only the tempiternal present is, that is, this present in which a true, authentic indeed, and, by consequence, unique action becomes reality.

Any action that can be repeated is no longer unique by this simple fact; therefore its value depends on the largest and optimal quantity of possible repetitions. Its value is accumulative. It is not a definitive action, it is interchangeable, it can come back. Essentially, it is not a real action, and if it is, at most, it is so only in part, not more. Because of this, not fully authentic and, in essence, not totally wanted human actions can be forgiven. We can repent because the action was incomplete and left flaws through which the remorse can penetrate. God forgives every sin to Man—according to the Abrahamitic tradition—except the sin against the Spirit,[49] or the angels' sin. This sin cannot be forgiven because it is not an act that can be repeated in time. Forgiveness would mean annihilation. And if the act must be truly forgiven, this sin would require an impossible repentance because the act is unique and thus cannot be repeated. This would imply an ontological suicide, metaphysically impossible, as being and non-being cannot coexist. It is at this "angelic" level, if you please, that the problem of the subjective experience of "time that cannot be repeated" is placed.[50] It is by virtue of this time that it is worth having lived, it is precisely those acts that we—quite paradoxically—are prepared to repeat incessantly.

The Real is unique, and this is why it cannot be repeated; its value resides in this impossibility of repetition. If what I do today I will be able to equally redo tomorrow, and if I really do repeat it tomorrow, the value of today's action is only a fraction of the total sum of repeatable actions. May not the experience of the uniqueness of our actions be a sign of maturity, rather than of youth? The young people think that they will still have ample opportunities to learn, to redo what they have already done, to repeat such and such experience, to experiment again with what, perhaps, in a given moment, they did not carry out as they had wished. The young people can allow themselves the luxury of making a mistake: it is from this that their spontaneity and optimism spring. If they fail, they will start again better, having learned. The mature man, on the contrary, no longer believes in a time void of content, and therefore no longer counts on the time that he has "in front" of him in order to do and redo things; he has already lost occasions and worn out experiences; he knows that each occasion is unique and that each act is impossible to repeat; he is no longer an apprentice taught by each repetition, but a master for whom each action is creator—or destructor. To what extent this maturity is an asymptotic ideal has nothing to do with the present case. "Time is a child playing," says Heraclitus.[51]

What we could call *sacramental actions*—that is to say, unique acts that have validation during the entire temporal event because they transcend time—constitute another example of what we have just said. Almost all human traditions recognize these acts. Faithfulness to the given word, which has many social repercussions, belongs to this type of act. If there is

---

[48] "On ne se rapproche pas de l'Absolu par un voyage [dans le temps], mais par une extase" (P. Teilhard de Chardin, *La vision du passé* [Paris, 1957], 184): "We do not reach the Absolute by a travel [through time] but by an ecstasy").

[49] See Mt 12:32.

[50] The Aristotelian and medieval distinction between "(truly) human acts" and "(general) acts of Man" could be enriched by a new category, that of tempiternal acts.

[51] Fragm. 52 in H. Diels and W. Kranz, *Die Fragmente der Vorsokratiker* (Berlin, 1934).

not a tempiternal dimension that is manifested at given moments, the promise of faithfulness to God or to humankind no longer has any meaning. How can I compromise myself, now, with regard to something I will do in a future of which I have no knowledge, if there is not something in this *now* that transcends all variants of the future?

If, when I act, I already think about the possible repetition of this act in a near or distant future; if when I live in the present, the past weighs upon me, the future stimulates me, but I already lose the present moment, I only make of this moment a simple crossroads, without its own reality, between a past and a future. I make of it an instrument in function of a something that has already passed, or of another something that has yet to come—and I do this with an aggravating circumstance toward the past, because it did not have better luck, and toward the future, because it too will not have luck: this past and future were also afflicted with many other hypothetical pasts and futures.

All nonauthentic moments in our existence are those in which the tempiternal present remains stifled by the trivial temporal crossroads of psychological haste or epistemological attempts.

One of the conditions for living a-temporal moments is to never want to repeat them, and therefore, to never desire them, or, in some ways, to not even plan them.[52] Another condition for momentary a-temporality is its incompatibility with any previous or concomitant utilitarian thought. A-temporal moments, from the point of view of temporality, are of "time lost," not of time put to use; they lead nowhere and do not prepare any future. Aesthetic enjoyment conserves a lot of this character even in cultures where will and projects dominate. What poets call "first inspiration" cannot be manipulable; a first love cannot be planned. When a husband and a wife, after twenty-five years of marriage, say they would be ready to start *anew*; when he who had been persecuted or suffered for a cause, or he who takes a certain path a quarter of a century before, affirms that they feel ready to start *anew*, this means that this act was unique, that its repetition is impossible, and that is why one cannot feel sorry about it: they are irreversibly transforming acts. When the *shaman* and the mystic want to stop the world, even if for just an instant, they ask for nothing less than this: that our acts be distinct from those of the simple periodic movement of the stars or of the simple biological metabolism of plants and animals—they demand tempiternal acts.

These considerations and others alike can guide us to the central experience of the tempiternity that we seek. India's so-called illiterate generations, as well as many people who have studied "letters," spontaneously live the uniqueness of moments. Starting with customs like the daughter's dowry for marriage, which often plunges a family into debt for a lifetime, to ceremonies like pilgrimages that have a special uniqueness among the ordinary events of life, to acts in daily life made with no consciousness of repetition—all are examples of actions in which time has been broken, and we cannot, because of this, temporally reassemble, that is, repeat them.

We sometimes have the impression that an encounter, a birth, a death, a word, or a smile could reward a lifetime of fatigue and sweat.[53] The present is worth more than all of the lived past and the future that is still to live combined. However, this present, with such density, is

---

[52] In fact, this is a leitmotif in Zen spirituality that could be based on numerous evangelical passages; see, e.g., Mt 6:3 and 25ff; Lk 12:27ff; 21:14, etc.

[53] In response to the extremely "rational" question asked by his boss, the servant who, earning two hundred rupees a month, will never be able to settle, during his lifetime, the debt of five thousand rupees he incurred for the marriage of his daughter, replies—inwardly scandalized by his boss's inhumanity and incomprehension: "It is a unique act!" Time to come does not count.

not a simple amorphous crossroads between a past and a present, nor is it a better time than any other. These are a-temporal moments, maybe because memory is poor, hope is feeble, and spontaneity is far superior to reflection, but also, maybe, because they have pierced the shell of pure temporality. This present is, in some way, a-temporal; it is a tempiternal present, it is a present in which, with innocence and candor, we live the a-temporal dimension of existence without knowing it, and it is a present that has transcended time. Consequently, any passing moment can possess or present this quality of eternal presentiality. It is not that the present stops, according to a poet's desire,[54] but it is as if it were opening itself up, as if it were becoming transparent and letting us see, for a "moment," the open sky,[55] eternity,[56] the true present.[57]

We have spoken about a-temporality in order to introduce the experience of tempiternity, but, more precisely, it is not about a nontemporality dialectically opposed to temporality, or about a-temporality wholly foreign to time. It is about existence itself, discovered in its transtemporal profoundness, or more precisely tempiternal profoundness, as we will see.

To tear one's hair, for example, because in India there are maybe seven million *sādhus*, a-cosmic monks, who do not contribute to the edification of the Earthly City, would show a form of ignorance about the question, and a displacement of the problem. If the economic factor is principal and decisive, if Man's mission on earth is to work this earth, then these men do not have the right to live. If human life finds the roots for its justification in production, usefulness, and efficiency, then all those religious people are pure parasites that suck the blood of the working classes. In a word, if Man's end lies within the line of time, and if the future is the justification for the present acts, then—clearly—the sooner we eliminate all static factors, the sooner society will improve.

We may object that, first, such premises are neither valid nor truthful. Then, that, independently from any criteria of validity, the *fact* is that the society in India does not believe in the truth of such premises; and because of this, even if they may be wrong, we must keep in mind the convictions of those people in order to find any viable solution that may indeed prove to be a solution. My presupposition here is that dictatorially imposed measures, in the long run, may unchain a reaction of opposition and are therefore not real solutions. Anyway, it is not the Indian monks who interest us at the moment, but common people.

Those people cannot believe, or even understand, a message that describes to them a better future, when their multisecular experience shows them that, each time they hear such a sermon, it aims at exploiting them more and making their life harder. The only thing they have is the present, and this cannot be taken from them.

But there is still more to it. It is possible that in India's current situation it will be necessary to take the Christian and Marxist principle seriously: he who does not work, does not eat.[58]

---

[54] See the already cited passage from Goethe's *Faust*, or the equally beautiful fragment from *Cant Espiritual* by J. Maragall: "Aquell que a cap moment li digué *Atura't* / sino al mateix que li dugué la mort, / jo no l'entenc, Senyor, jo que voldria / aturar tants moments de cada dia / per fè'ls eterns a dintre del meu cor" [He who at no moment said "Halt" / save to that which brought him death, / I do not understand him, Lord, I who would like to / halt so many moments of each day / to make them eternal within my heart].

[55] See the triple and very interesting context in Jn 1:51; Mk 1:10; Acts 7:55, on which however we cannot comment now.

[56] See *MaitU* VI.14–16.

[57] See *SU* VI.1ff.

[58] See 2 Thess 3:10 and Gen 3:19.

Of course, religious and spiritualist inflation is one of the worst forms of inflation; but this is only one side of the story. Maybe these "useless" *sadhus* are only the living symbol of a dimension of existence that would have otherwise been more or less lost. We cannot ignore the value of the widespread phenomenon of a West now feeling a spiritual attraction toward the East, and we cannot ignore the "thirst" that India's youth and the youth of other countries feel for Western technology, trying to convince themselves that it has a redemptive value. *Ex oriente lux*: in this case, since we have discovered that the Earth is round, this means that salvation is always exogenous, it always comes from the "other," from the exterior, the East, where the sun rises. And if the East of Europe is Asia, the East of Asia is America.

Yoga, although incredibly misunderstood, is one of the most widespread forms of spirituality in India, and can offer another instructive and meaningful example. Its most fundamental starting point is the primacy of the static element over the dynamic, that is, the achievement of the a-temporal moment passing through the flux of temporal movements; or stopping it all, the dynamism of the spirit and the flux of thoughts included (only temporarily, of course) by passing through the immobility of the body; without which, all other efforts would be in vain—if we can still call "effort" something that does not want, in any form, the "violence" of movement.[59]

These people would well understand (here, Gandhi would be a qualified witness) a Sermon on the Mount not watered down with the vain promises of a nonexistent future. Do we not minimize, not to say erase, all of the Beatitudes' power when we project them into a temporal future? In the first place, because they are not accomplished and, in second place, because they have been exploited in favor of a resignation that is certainly not evangelical.

Ultimately, what is the future envisaged by the Beatitudes? "Blessed are you who are hungry now, for you shall be satisfied; blessed are you who weep now, for you shall laugh."[60] Either everything is simply a bucolic, sentimental, and totally unreal burst of euphoria used to mislead the "blessed poor," or else the benediction of Christ must be accomplished. The traditional interpretation, which gave hope to the Christian peoples and kept them joyful as long as they believed in it, is the temporal interpretation of an eternity that will come later, after; then, in heaven, they would be satisfied and recompensed for all their present suffering in this "vale of tears." We can contest this idea about eternity, but what is not genuine is the substitution of eternity with a temporal paradise to be regained, or stripping the concept of eternity of its temporal scum so much so that people are then left without hope. First because, in a linear future, the poor are not satisfied and those who cry are not comforted.[61] Rather, it seems that those who possess get richer and those who have nothing get even poorer.[62] Next, if there happened to be no eternity "posterior to time," if heaven does not come "after," when will they be satisfied, when will they laugh—those who until now suffer the hunger and the

---

[59] See *YS* I.2: *yogás-citta-vṛitti-nidodhaḥ* [yoga consists in eliminating the fluctuations of the spirit].

[60] Lk 6:21.

[61] According to official declarations made by the president of the World Bank, Robert S. McNamara, in November 1973, according to the distinction made between "relative poverty between nations" and "absolute poverty" as an infrahuman life condition, a third of two billion people in the current world suffer from hunger and malnutrition; 40 percent of the inhabitants of poor countries have a life expectancy twenty years inferior to the norm in other countries; 20 or 25 percent of children die before reaching the age of five; and millions among the survivors are abnormal. It sounds quite like the denial of any literal interpretation of the Beatitudes.

[62] Is it not this the irony of the evangelical parable in Mt 8:12; 25:29, etc.? "To the one who has, more will be given, and from the one who has not, even what he has will be taken away."

thirst of bread and justice? It is here that our "formula of blessing" must be applied. It is at present, in the very *nunc, vvv,* that it has its value.[63] And the good news is about discovering that those who *now* suffer can *now*—in this exact present, which is the *now* of salvation, of realization, of faith—be happy, have peace, and obtain freedom.

The message of salvation, if it must be so, must be within reach for all fortunes and be possible in all situations, and be able to come to realization in all circumstances.

Let us not forget that the truly *universal* story does not deal with a privileged minority that can think about the meaning of life, but with a majority that has lived in circumstances that the minority refers to as abnormal and extraordinary. The slaves, illiterate, "sinners," "nonbelievers," the poor, and the "others," in the last analysis, have almost always been the most numerous in Man's history. What the elites call "ordinary" is, strictly speaking, the extraordinary.

"The kingdom of God is near"[64] not only in a temporal way, but rather it is nearing each of us without "partiality."[65] It is not about a historical prophecy (which did not come to pass) or an affirmation of temporal eschatology (which remains unfulfilled) but rather a proclamation of the good news. That is to say: both the rich and the poor can obtain it; believers, of one kind or another, can reach it, and those who cannot fulfill the plenitude of their human possibilities can enter it as well. The kingdom of God is near because it is not an archaism of the past, or a utopian dream of the future, but an opening of the present. When the present opens up, when it flowers—so to speak—into a tempiternal flower, the kingdom of God appears. Those who will die today, those who will not fulfill any of their ambitions, generations who are visited by inopportune death,[66] the crippled, the poor, and the beggars are also invited to the banquet.[67]

Not *later*, in a future that, in the best case, will come true for our grandchildren, when we have already starved to death; not *later*, in a posttemporal heaven, when everything has already "passed" ("past") and therefore it will be without interest and will no longer be able to bring any solution—but *now*. Now, today, in this moment, the possibility of salvation must exist; now I can realize that naked existence is worth more than anything we can add to it. Now I can realize that the impossibility of repeating my life brings me such pleasure that nothing in the world can pay for it. Now I must be able to experience that I have pierced time and have arrived to a form of existence that I cannot describe, in most cases, but allows me to be happy and even to die at the wanted time—and not with the despair of having only suffered, without having realized any of the dreams that I had flirted with during my lifetime.[68] The quality of life also depends on the quality of death.[69] Learning how to live well is inseparable from learning how to die well.

---

[63] See the famous "invitatory" in the Latin Breviary: "Today, if you hear His voice, do not harden your hearts" (from Ps 94), not only in relation to the *Nunc dimittis* of Simeon (Lk 2:29ff.) in the prayer of compline, but also to *Upaniṣadic* spirituality: *yad ahar eva virajet / tad ahar eva pravrajet* [at the same moment in which someone is disillusioned, / at this same moment they pull back] (*JabU* 4).

[64] Lk 10:9; see Mt 3:2; 10:7.

[65] See Acts 10:34.

[66] It is the concept of *akāla mṛtyu*: inopportune, premature death at a time in which it should not have happened.

[67] See the many parables and teachings about this in the Gospels: Mt 22:8–10; Lk 14, etc.

[68] Isn't this the central message of Solzhenitsyn, that its detractors understood so well?

[69] Christ's sentence to the Good Thief (Lk 23:43) does not mean the annulment of a past life, but rather the culminating point of existence by the redemption of time in its totality.

The quality of life does not improve by simply postponing our encounter with death, by prolonging our temporal existence, as well as it does not if we do not cultivate temporal values. The quality of life depends on quality, not on quantity, even if there is an indispensable quantitative minimum in order for quality to increase. The quality of human life requires a harmonious integration of temporal values and their transtemporal grounds; this is what we have called "tempiternal existence."

But there is more yet. The kingdom of God, when it comes, is not located in space or in time, its arrival is not spectacular, and its time is not foreseeable.[70] "The kingdom of God is *between* you."[71] That is, it is not only *within*, nor exclusively *among* you. It is neither an eternal and purely interior reality "within" the human being, nor is it a sociological and temporal reality "among" human beings. The kingdom of God is in the constitutive relationship between people; it is among the human beings, within them, and their relationship; in the internal solidarity of the whole creation, and in the tempiternal relationship.

It is a well-known fact that the Hindū tradition and, like it, a great number of the other Oriental religious traditions have combined this experience of the tempiternal present with the palliative of the law of *karman*, which lets this realization happen only when the personality is prepared for it. Meantime, the *karmatic* conditionings that each individual carries with himself return to the temporal cycle in order to be overcome when the necessary conditions are accomplished, in such a way that the hope of salvation is strengthened by the multiplicity of occasions. The only person, in this case, is only the one who transcends the entire cosmic envelope that the individual embodied in his or her concrete existence. The rest, because it is not authentic and can therefore be repeated, goes on in the temporal cycle.[72] I perfectly realize the danger of such a discussion if we extrapolate it from its context: the danger of taking advantage of it, whether consciously or not, in order to justify an obviously intolerable status quo. I also realize that such a presentation is unilateral if it reduces itself to a disembodied mysticism, paralyzing all human effort in favor of a better sociotemporal order—but one thing does not prevent the other.

Moreover, the discourse does not only address young people, encouraging them toward a (more and more problematic) tomorrow, but adult people who have already lived and suffered enough to embark upon adventures that, in the best scenario, would be fruitful only in the possible harvests of a hypothetical future. They do not demand opium to cure their pains or promises of a wonderful future to hide their rags. They claim for a faith in the present, a love that does not wait, and a hope that transcends time: it is a thirst for the tempiternal present that is already here, co-extensive to any situation, and which gives us enough peace to leave us with our hands free, and work to improvements, temporal too, in favor of our brethren.

---

[70] See Lk 17:20, when, being asked by the Pharisees on the "when" (ποτε) and "how" of the coming of the Kingdom of God, Jesus answers, "The Kingdom of God is not coming with signs to be observed" (μετα παρατηρησεως). Παρατηρησις, here, is as rich and ambivalent a term as those used in controversies. The Kingdom of God cannot be observed, or localized; we cannot see it, and no legal observance (this is also a meaning of the word) can cause it to arrive, in the same way that no intellectual analysis, or the examination of any picture or omen, could ever unveil it.

[71] The adverb εντος (*intra* in the Vulgate) has been differently interpreted as *within* or *among*; and depending on scholars, a more interior or more sociological interpretation prevails. See the NEB, which is so "poor" in notes that, after having translated *among you*, adds, at the bottom of the page: *within you . . . within your grasp . . . will be among you.* Our interpretation is neither *within* nor *among*, but *between*. The *BG* translates *parmi*, and the "Bible of Montserrat" *enmig*.

[72] We here skip the other problems connected to the issue of the human person, in order not to lose the thread of our discussion. See the passage in the *Śaṅkara-bhāṣya* quoted above.

This liberation from time does not necessarily mean indifference to, or the idolatry of, the temporal business.

They hope for a salvation that is not a temporal salvation. It may happen that this will be achieved through and by history; it may also happen that salvation comes to us by collaborating with history. But the true salvation to which Man aspires is not that of a lost paradise that can be found, but rather of a formidable leap, a leap that loses its nature as soon as it describes itself; a transcendence that contradicts itself in the same moment in which it affirms itself, as it is being pronounced—on the other hand, it is not a dogma that all *can* be said, nor that all may be adequately formulated.

We could be asked: in what way is this solution new? Before answering, let us consider the presuppositions of such a question, which are precisely those that negate our response. The newness of the solution is not a historical or intellectual newness; it is not the thought of a more convincing hypothesis. Its newness rests upon its impossibility of repeating it, on its radical originality, even if its formulation coincides with the oldest of traditions. Its newness rests upon personal application, on nontransferable experiences, on overcoming excessive identification between our being and our thinking about it, on recovering the mythical dimension of our existence, and putting the *logos*, both human and divine, back into its own place.

He/she who cannot wait is a living hope. And if they have faith in something, it is not in the coming of a God disguised as a prophet, Messiah, or liberator, but in a God changed into bread—into love of the present—before their death.

What to do? What to think?—we have asked, and we have answered that only when thought transforms our action, and action transforms our thought, in a nonvicious but vital circle, then we are on the right track. In reality, if the action is not contemplative, it is not action; if the contemplation is not active, it is not really contemplation. Moreover, the dichotomy must be overcome at the anthropological and metaphysical level. To opt for a paralyzing "eternalism" of human activity is as unfruitful and erroneous as limiting oneself to the pure temporality of human action. But there is more still. Trying to juxtapose the two kingdoms, whether in a temporal succession ("first" the earth "here," and "later" heaven "there") or in a personal secession (on the one hand, the field of what is temporal, secular, or purely material or mundane, and on the other hand, the field of the religious, the spiritual, or sacred) is, in the same way, ineffective, producing cultural and human schizophrenia, or even radically erroneous since such airtight compartments do not exist in us or in reality. Neither the autonomy of each sphere nor the heteronomy of either of them can give a solution to the problem. We must find the *ontonomous* relationship between them.

The solution does not consist, besides, in laying the blame on one or the other of the two attitudes, or to think about it with old methods. The past does not return, precisely because it is real insofar as it does *not* repeat itself.

It is therefore unfruitful to accuse technology by saying that it powerlessly tries to resolve a problem that it actually created. It is also useless to attack the masses' passivity and resignation, and then say that, if these masses subsist, it is thanks to them. It is about waking a new consciousness by virtue of which such dichotomies may be solved.

The dimension of "presentiality" that we stress should not be interpreted as a *fuga mundi*, an escape and negation of the world, or in the sense of an exacerbated individuality, as if all was centered on the individual. It is a fundamentally personal dimension, which means that it is concerned with the individual as much as it is with society. It is not about a tendency that wants to counterbalance an excessive activism, but a dimension which comes to imprint the entire life of Man on earth, giving it a temporal and an eternal meaning *at the same time*.

Neither is eternity "later," nor is temporality based "on" eternity. In essence, everything is simplified if we are able to recover the subjective experience of tempiternity.

Here it is not about giving advice or proposing "techniques" for meditation, concentration, or interiority, however useful they may be. It is only about awakening human awareness a little more—an awareness that, in fact, lives tempiternity in itself as a good gift it has received. The most elementary proof of this is that nothing purely temporal satisfies us, nor does anything exclusively eternal gratify us. We cannot disregard the one or the other. The unity of the two begins to crack when one of the dimensions dominates and when eternity is placed "after" time (which is one consequence of the domination of historicity), just like if we hold back temporality in favor of the nontemporal (which is a consequence of the domination of a-temporality).

Maybe the experience of the tempiternal present will be able to inspire us in this new research. Eternity exists neither *outside* time, nor *in* it—without anyway forgetting the metaphorical value of the two prepositions. But time also does not exist *outside* eternity, nor does it exist *in* it. Tempiternity is the very symbol of Reality, just as Being (which is still a temporal Being) is the symbol of a reality that manifests itself only in the Being.

But, truthful to the concrete spirit of this study, oriented toward the action, instead of pursuing this speculative path, I would like to end with a few considerations that respond to the content of the problems posed here at the beginning.

What to do? What to think? In the first place, we must make our thinking arise from our active experience and let our action be inspired by our thinking. But let us see, secondly, what this could mean.

It means, in my opinion, that we have the duty not to look for the fullness of Man in an extratemporal future, waiting for a world that comes "later," and also not in a temporal future, joining some "other" world distinct from the one in which we live, sacrificing it on the altars of utopia, of ideals, or of the kingdom of the Future. This absolutely means that human life must not be paralyzed, or halved by a tendency toward a linear or vertical future, but must be concentrated in the full lived existence of the tempiternal present, that is, *this* present, which includes not only the fruits of the past and the seeds of the future but also a tempiternal knot embracing the entire temporal interval of our existence.

In more positive terms, the experience of the tempiternal present means living the liberation from time—not escaping from it, but embarking upon it with greater freedom: the liberation *from* time *for* the sake of time. This means placing all of one's efforts into the construction of the Earthly City because there is not another city to build, all the while knowing that it is not in the actual city, but in its loyal and passionate construction that we will find joy.

We must certainly free all of Man's atrophied potentials for the construction of a better world, but we need to be pretty clairvoyant in order to see reality in front of our eyes, knowing, at the same time, that the pilgrimage is not finished—not any more than this study . . .

Historical-Religious Reflection

Just as there are four cardinal points on Earth, there are—I believe—four great hypotheses developed by mankind in response to the mystery of suffering, both physical and moral; to the mystery of evil of every sort. I propose a synoptic overview, though it will inevitably be a simplified one.

The schema has a mere indicative value, in the sense that it describes four fundamental directions that could just as well be taken from other examples in human history. It also holds a correlative value, which is to say that it must be understood in its fourfold internal relationship. It does not describe certain human or religious traditions but rather it underscores contrasting characteristics.

We are less interested in speaking of Hinduism, Buddhism, Christianity, or Confucianism here, as we are about penetrating into four attitudes with regard to the nature of time: understood, on the one hand, as unreal, in the negative or the positive, and on the other, as real, also in the negative or the positive.[73]

1. The Hindū vision strongly defends the radical incompatibility between the Absolute, *brahman* (the good God, rational order) on the one hand, and the chaotic world (permanent situations of injustice, inevitable disorder) on the other. No compromise is possible. If this world is real, if suffering is real and, ultimately, if evil is real, then God is a mere figment, a projection of man's weakness, the dream of a prisoner.[74] There is no room for both in the kingdom of Reality. But if God is real, if "being, intelligence, happiness"[75] are authentic attributes of the Real, if the Absolute *is*, then it does not correspond to this world, and this world is appearance, evil is a fiction. In other words, time—as a fundamental characteristic of the universe—is not real; in fact, it is negative. What remains to be done then, is to discover the unreality of the world, the evanescence of time, by means of experiencing the reality of the Absolute.

A Hindū is saved and arrives at bliss when he discovers the eternal and immutable ātman within his own self.[76] A good Hindū will certainly help his brothers, who are still ignorant— because they "do not know," they have not "understood"—but he cannot participate personally in their pain because he knows it is mere illusion. Furthermore, his empathetic suffering could only deteriorate the situation without contributing anything positive other than sentimentality, which is in the long run useless or counterproductive. It would be something like committing an evil in order to help someone escape from it. In order to arrive at this intuition, the Hindū has endured various methods of spirituality in which the ascetical overcoming of pain plays a large part. Faith transcends appearances in order to reach the invisible.

2. The Buddhist vision coincides with the first ethos in claiming that time is not real, but it grants time a positive character, given that time can be escaped through time itself. The cornerstone of Buddhist spirituality consists in finding the path that leads to the elimination of pain, which is real but extinguishable. Once the actuality, the origin, and the cessation of pain are established, the "Four Noble Truths" all point to the fourth one, which, in turn, refers to the "Eightfold Path" that leads to the extinction of pain. The Buddhist saint, *arhat* or *bodhisattva*, has not overcome pain but rather has managed to abandon it, to leave it behind. Therefore, even without real, interpersonal participation, the Buddhist is able to show others the path toward liberation. The Buddha merely smiles and shows the path. Faith is the path.

3. The Semitic or Abrahamic vision—in which one can include Judaism, Christianity, and Islam—considers both time and the world as positive and real. Pain is real, and time is "temporary"; it will not last forever, and pain can become purifying. In Christianity, for

---

[73] See my *Worship and Secular Man* (Maryknoll, NY: Orbis Books, 1973), 9–13, where I deal with this fourfold schema of time.

[74] Allusion to Plato's famous allegory of the cave (*ndt*).

[75] The classical triad *sat–cit–ānanda* (*ndt*).

[76] The *ātman* is a bridge (with immortality, etc.) See *BU* IV.4.22; *CU* VIII.4.1–2: *MundU* 11.2.5; *MaitU* VII.7; SO VI.19.

example, Christ bears humanity's sins and suffering, but does not deny that both can be defeated, the same as death. One does not attain salvation by denying pain or escaping from it, but by going through it and accepting its purifying qualities. In these traditions, the saint is a "suffering servant" who shares in the suffering of the rest of humanity, but without letting himself be overcome by pain. He does suffer, but in peace and even with joy. He lives for others and for the good of others, but his kingdom is not of this world. Christ died, abandoned, on the cross, but he rose from the dead. Faith looks to the goal, to eternal life.

4. The Chinese or humanist vision is like the previous one insofar as it is sensitive to pain and affirms the positivity of time, but it denies that time can be transcended and does not accept the idea that that one can sanctify it in the name of a transtemporal reality. What really matters is time, so that it is madness to try to deny it, useless to try to escape it, and puerile to try to transcend it for a reward. The end of man is yet to come, given that the present is obviously full of injustices and pain. In this tradition, the hero is the prophet, the leader who guides men toward the perfect society, toward an earthly paradise. Faith is not so much a matter of the invisible, or of the path or of eternal life, but of this life itself.

If a historical-religious consideration could provide this quadripartite schema, then a philosophical-sociological reflection could speak to us about the phenomenon of secularization, which is in fact a contemporary phenomenon that serves as the dividing line between tradition and modernity. Marxist humanism is an example of this new atmosphere. Without going into further details now, one can still show how the secularizing movement (which I essentially interpret as that level of Spirit that guarantees the reality, the most positive reality, of the temporal structure of the world) is a notion inherent in every human tradition, especially underlined in the Chinese vision and in our own times taken to the extreme by so-called atheist and Marxist humanisms. It is not a coincidence that Marxism was born on Christian land after having been fertilized by Jewish seed and that today it thrives in China.

This brings us to the present situation of our world in which the great human hypotheses are beginning to influence one another on a universal historical scale, thus providing a unique opportunity to create a synthesis, but likewise a somewhat inevitable confusion between different values and identities.

One of the reasons for our current global crisis is precisely that no single one of the four hypotheses is powerful enough to tackle, on its own, the huge problems of pain and injustice. Our ancient myths are collapsing. A simple phenomenological consideration will argue, against the first vision, that suppressing the evidence of the reality of both this world and of pain in name of a religious a priori is not a good method; and against the second vision it will point to its unreal elitism. Even if a minority is able to attain inner peace and tranquility in the midst of universal pain, the vast majority of human beings are incapable of it, and it is useless to say that they do not want it—then we must ask ourselves why they do not want it, which simply shifts the problem.

The third vision is likewise unsatisfactory in the eyes of experience. Even granting that, in exceptional cases, pain can purify and evil can become an opportunity for good, in practice this is simply not the case for the majority of humanity. Pain brutalizes, suffering embitters, evil reigns, and misery is by no means good. As "temporary" as time may be, this is of little use for those who do not know any other temporal level, in the hope of some supratemporal kingdom where (if it exists) the entire problem of time will somehow be resolved, even dissolved. Neither is the fourth hypothesis satisfactory, not only because of its faith in a future that in itself is not the least bit appealing or because of an absolutely blind faith, contrary to all daily experience, but also because, at root, it makes us evade the problems of the current generation, which is now beginning to realize that the same chorus is being repeated without ever solving the issues.

It goes without saying that this description of the four ethos that are the natural consequence of the four great traditions mentioned above does not consider them to be four models that exclude each other or even the only models that exist within their respective traditions. Moreover, the vitality of a tradition reveals itself precisely in its capacity to grow, that is, to assimilate new experiences, to adapt to new circumstances and to create new solutions without loss of identity. Thus, in fact, these four traditions are presently undergoing a process of reflection and cross-fertilization, which is precisely one of the optimistic "signs of our times."

For example, a good part of the Hindū tradition may insist on an ontological distinction between the two levels, but in time, it will grant some type of reality, even if on an earthly level. The Buddhist tradition may grant primacy to compassion as the fundamental virtue and consider purely individual salvation an aberration. The traditions of Semitic origin, in turn, may develop a less anthropomorphic image of the Divine. And the humanist tradition may envision the future as something more than a prolongation of the present. We find ourselves in the most promising springtime of transcultural fertilization in the history of humankind. Let us try not to miss the train of ideas.

2

KĀLAŚAKTI: THE POWER OF TIME

The Awareness of Time

Time is the revealer of all things.

Gaudapāda-kārikā I.6.8

Time is something that concerns all of us.[1] We are all under the power of time. It is inseparable from human self-consciousness. Man lives "in" time. He is aware "of" time. He reckons "with" time. Time is all-pervading. There is no human being without time-consciousness. Man lives time.

We are all in its grips. We, humans, but also matter, the universe, nonsentient and intelligent beings alike. Everything suffers the bite of time. Time is "the matrix of all differentiation," says Bhartṛhari.

On the other hand, salvation, liberation, enlightenment, divinization, glorification, *nirvāṇa, mukti,* . . . consists in escaping time, being free from it, standing above it, passing beyond it, realizing it, bringing it to its fullness, or transcending or annihilating it.

Time is the Supreme Power in the Universe, the great *deva* (*AV* XIX.54.6): "Upon time all the worlds repose" (*AV* XIX.54.4); "From time all beings emerge" (*MaitU* VI.14). "I am time" (*kālo smi*), says Kṛṣṇa Vāsudeva (*BG* XL.32).

One of the results of modern specialization is that it makes real things difficult to grasp, for who can embrace all details of a single thing?

Modern culture has succeeded in convincing most of our contemporaries that time is so elusive, so difficult, that only exceptional minds like Newton, Einstein, or Prigogine know what time really is. Or, for the more conservatives, that only the *Vedic ṛṣis*, the biblical writers, Śaṅkara, or Aristotle, or, for those more philosophically oriented, Wittgenstein, Nishida, or Heidegger, have an idea of what the essence of time is.

It seems that we are quite resigned to leave it to some special people to tell us what time is—just as we put all our lives in the hands of technological experts, be they medical doctors, economic advisers, politicians, engineers, or computers. It all seems as if we are condemned to be surrounded by and have daily intercourse with life-decisive factors without knowing what they really are.

The dilemma is clear: either we need borrowed knowledge for something so ultimately essential to our life, or its knowledge, after all, is not so important.

If we accept the first horn of the dilemma, most of us will have to live relying on the knowledge of some privileged creatures. This attitude denigrates immediate experience, asks

---

[1] Original text in Kapila Vatsyayan, ed., *Concepts of Time, Ancient and Modern* (New Delhi: Indira Gandhi National Centre for the Arts–Sterling, 1996).

us to believe in the expertise of others and, ultimately, undermines our personal dignity and self-confidence. While religious beliefs conveying this type of alienation are on the wane, this scientific belief is still rampant, although beginning to decline. Contemporary consciousness somehow revolts against this kind of life by proxy. And a sane reflection tells us that authentic faith cannot rely on the belief in the belief of others. If time is so important, it cannot be something whose meaning escapes most of us.

Or, after all, the knowledge of time would be only a luxury for idle people and we would not need to know something with which we are constantly in contact. The knowledge of time would then be not so necessary for life, for human life. Do we only need to handle clocks and watches so as to march at the pace of the megamachine? Should we simply "work" and not worry?

If acceptance of the first horn condemns us to more or less blind belief and inauthentic existence, accepting the second plunges us into a merely instinctive and irrational life. We would not need to know the fundamental "factors" of human life.

Is there any way out? Time is important and inescapable, we cannot renounce the consciousness of time without renouncing our human status. We can live without knowledge of the law of gravitation or the existence of quasars and fractals, but we cannot have a full and even normal human life without reckoning with the time factor in all our human affairs. Knowledge is an inalienable human gift, and reflective knowledge belongs to our human dignity.

The only way out from the dilemma is to discover that there is another type of knowledge, different from the fragmented and specialized information that characterizes a great part of the scientific and philosophical notions of our predominant culture.

What is, then, this knowledge—or, in our case, what is this awareness of time?

The so-often quoted sentence of Augustine—"If no one asks me, I know; if I want to explain it to someone who asks me, I do not know" (*Confessions* XI.14.7)—indicates that question-answer knowledge is not the immediate and most primordial awareness. Any answer to a question, as a certain *Vedānta* would say, is already secondhand knowledge. It is not primal knowledge. It is not saving knowledge. Primal knowledge does not give an answer but solves, that is, dissolves the very question; it makes it transparent. The philosophical and pedagogical consequences are revolutionary. We should be alerted to the intrinsic violence of the questions (including the questionnaires of polls).

We touch here a truly formidable problem, because the awareness of this dilemma upsets our belief in rationality. The rhetoric of Augustine, incidentally, applies to any ultimate issue. All ultimate issues are qualified tautologies. They can only be tautologies, otherwise they are not ultimate, and any further explanation would have to proceed ad infinitum. But we qualify them somewhat by letting the ultimate insight of such tautologies unfold in our awareness without breaking the intuition into further (nonexistent) components.

In our human existence we have to deal not only with time, but also with space, matter, spirit, self, soul, love, and the like, without really having a specialized knowledge of what they are. But what is knowledge?

There are at least two types of knowledge: the one proceeds by "cogitation," in the traditional sense of *co-agitare*, to stir, analyze, interfere. The other proceeds by "intellection," in the traditional sense of *intus-legere*, up to becoming identified with the thing known. We should recover the importance of this latter acception of knowledge, without neglecting specialized cognitions.

In other words, any knowledge that has to proceed by abstractions is not primordial knowledge. Scientific knowledge needs abstractions. Modern science extracts (abstracts) the quantifiable kernel of things and deals with it. It has hardly ever claimed to be saving wisdom, integral knowledge. It is *al-djbr*, algebra. There is no confusion when it utilizes letters, that is, formal signs. But it often uses the same language that people use in their daily lives. Time is a case in point, and sometimes this confuses people and scientists (Stephen Hawking, for instance). The reality of time—whatever this may be—is not identical to a scientific parameter. Philosophical knowledge should know better, but a certain type of philosophy has forgotten its primary character and simply deals with abstracted aspects of the real, abandoning the Whole.

We have too often forgotten that the "thing" out of which abstraction abstracts the quantitative parameters, or even the qualitative features, is the *real thing*. There is a predominant, widespread Platonic presupposition in the West, and an idealistic assumption in the East, that the "magma," that is, the original and complete thing, from which abstraction has abstracted the thoughts, is negligible, unimportant, and ultimately not-real; only essences, and immutable essences at that, are taken to be real. Nature may well be written in mathematical characters, as it has been said, but Reality is not script alone—and, besides, "the letter kills," as it has also been said.[2] Of course, those philosophical systems will inverse the order and defend that things are the mere appearance of the real essence(s).

The second type of knowledge, *gnôsis, jñāna*, wisdom, does not proceed by abstractions, nor by inferences, either inductive or deductive. It proceeds by intellectual intuition and integral experience. This holistic and thoroughly loving knowledge easily degenerates into false mysticism when it specializes and cuts its constitutive links with the intellect and the senses, with the *noêsis* and the *aisthêsis*. Let the knower of the Whole (*kṛtsna-vin*) not interfere with those who do not know the Whole, warns the *Bhagavad-gītā* (III.29; cf. XVIII.20), echoed by St. Paul (1 Cor 13:12) and so many others.

Perhaps the conscious "will to knowledge" has spoiled the original character of pure *sophia*, experiential awareness. It has introduced a "will to power" that has substituted the "love of knowledge" with the desire of dominion. We have to wonder whether it is possible to have a new innocent reflection. Precritical thinking is a reflection that reflects on a thing, but not on itself. We know that we know something, but we leave it at that: we have confidence in our knowledge. The postcritical innocent reflection includes the subject in the very reflection. We know that, when knowing something, this knowledge of the thing belongs also to our knowledge; we involve the knower. This is the crux of contemporary philosophy: the subject-object split.

If reflection were only an epistemological act, this new innocent reflection would not be possible. It would have to go back to the epistemic subject: epistemologically, I only "know *X*" when "I know that I know *X*." This epistemology becomes critical epistemology when it also studies the nature (conditions of possibility, and what not) of my "knowing *X*." But if reflection is more than just epistemologically knowing that I (the subject) have grasped something (an object), if it is an awareness in which object and subject are merged together, then there may be a knowledge that is not solely an epistemological activity, that is, an object-directed cognition, which then needs to go back to retrieve the neglected subject. This is precisely the new innocent reflection which does not harm (*nocere*) the object in the act of knowledge, because it *equally* involves the subject. To know is, then, not just to bring an object to a subject (a chasing, called "apprehending," grasping of the object), but a growth of consciousness that includes the knower as much as the known in the very act of knowledge.

---

[2] See 2 Cor 3:6.

This type of knowledge is not a purely objective cognition, which would then become a trophy of what I call "hunter's epistemology." Nor is it a merely subjective knowledge, the result of keeping the conquest of knowledge for the benefit of the psychological ego ("gatherer's epistemology"). It is rather an awareness of the existing links that constitute Reality and a creation of new ones. We can know only because we can (old *cunnan*) be conscious of *what is*, disclosing it to our triple experience (aesthetic, noetic, mystical), which itself forms part of Reality.

Now, this holistic, and thus saving, knowledge is itself under the power of time. It is not absolute or immutable knowledge; it is integral knowledge within a particular horizon, within a particular *mythos*. The holistic knowledge of a Pythagoras or Vyāsa is neither immutable nor absolute. The holistic knowledge that we should attempt to attain must certainly spring from a so-called *philosophia perennis*, but it cannot be reduced to a retrieval or repetition of an immutable past. We cannot ignore the innovations of specialized science. We should, on the contrary, try to integrate them into a new experience of Reality. But all is under the power of time. *Kālaśakti* is here equally at work.

Coming now back to our case, we ask whether there is an immediate awareness of time that is not an abstraction, that is, a picking up of the element "time" from the rest of the given reality.

But isn't time itself already an abstraction? Here is the heart of the matter.

An abstraction of what? It should be, obviously, of events, of what we call temporal things. We would then abstract the concept of time from temporal events, substantiate time, and make a concept out of it, a sort of intellectual substance.

It may be that we need abstractions in order to reach a certain intellectual understanding of things. But we should then never forget that there are abstractions of something more primordial, and keep constantly in mind the link between the abstracted idea and the thing out of which we drew the idea.

If the concept of time is an abstraction, it should be an abstraction of temporal things, we said. And here we discover two astonishing facts. We discover that we previously have to detect the temporality of things in order to abstract the concept of time from them. And that everything is temporal, for we do not know any a-temporal thing. Time seems to stick to everything. Time and Being, some philosophers would say, belong together. Every being is temporal; although this does not mean that it is *only* temporal.

We should then say that time is an aspect of the Real, rather than an abstraction. It is a perspective under which we envision all things, rather than a sublation of an ingredient of reality that we succeeded in isolating like in a chemical experiment.

Under which aspect do we envisage things when we speak of their temporal dimension?

Here again, we detect a startling fact. In order to detect the temporality of objects, we have to detect the temporality of the subject as well. Time implies a certain persistence of the objects past and a certain duration of the subject while the future comes. We may call it memory, or the mere awareness that we also need to be temporal in order to have the awareness of time.

Time is neither merely objective (time does not belong to objects only) nor purely subjective (time does not exclusively belong to subjects). To speak of time "in itself" is as meaningless as of a time exclusively "for us." The very concept of "real time" is not possible within a dualistic epistemology starting from the split between a knowing subject and a known object. If we put ourselves out of the picture, we cannot obtain the concept of time, which entails a link with the past (or the future) still lingering (or glimmering) in the present. Time implies change, duration, succession, a certain "passing" that still lasts when it has already gone—or when it is still to come.

Space can be *somehow* objectified. The subject is, at least, more easily left out of the picture. This does not occur with time. This may be the reason why modern science has reduced time to another dimension of space: we can then measure time. But time is more than a mere measurement of space by means of speed. It is more than ds/dv.

"*Kāla* [time] is not manifested by *adhvā* [space, distance, course, orbit, way, journey] but by *kriyā* [action, work, doing]," says Vāsyāyana in his *Nyāya Bhāṣa* (II.39). We should not reduce time to space, he warns us.

Summing up, we cannot abstract time from anything because everything, including our consciousness, is already temporal. If we were to abstract time from Being, we would abstract the whole of Being. Nothing would remain. It remains Nothingness, Emptiness, *śūnyatā*, *asat*, Non-Being, the timeless. Many traditions would say that by overcoming time we reach the Divine: utter Nothingness, Silence. . . . As we indicate later, the path to realization, the way to Reality, consists in overcoming, not in suppressing, time. This is what I call *tempiternity*, against temporality on the one hand and timelessness (eternity) on the other.

A simple reflection can show us the intimate connection between time and nothingness. The experience of time requires the consciousness of past, present, and future; it requires a certain flow, change, movement. But our experience as a direct touch with reality can only be *in* and *of* the present.

The past *is-not*. The future *is-not-yet*. The past qua past is annihilated when we bring it to our consciousness. The future ceases to be future when it *is*, when it has come to be. The events of the past have passed, they *are* not, they were. And yet we may remember them, that is, they become again present in our mind. Something similar can be said about future events. In both cases, we cannot skip the non-being. Both, past and future, are at least tinged with non-being. Time has been traditionally linked with the experience of contingency, limitation, nothingness.

This long preface was needed in order to prevent the misunderstanding that the reflection on time has to be a specialized subject matter of some particular discipline.

What, then, is time?

We may quote any number of acute definitions and adduce a useful amount of types of time: psychological, musical, physical, mathematical, rhythmic, cyclical, linear. . . . But the prior question is about the *what* of which we want to give a definition or offer a classification. What is that "thing"? How shall we recognize it?

We have already said that we cannot understand the nature of time if we forget the "understander." Time is so pervasive that it equally permeates the questioner and the question, let alone the answer. We are thus obliged to affirm that everything open to a conscious human experience is temporal, although this does not allow us to say that everything is *only* temporal.

In sum, prior to the divisions in physical and psychological times, before the talk about time in the arts or time in the different human traditions, is there any justification in applying the same word "time" when approaching all those and other similar questions? Contemporary philosophy would ask whether there is any phenomenology of time. Is there anything, appearing in human consciousness, that we may describe as time? We now turn to this question, before trying to overcome the dilemma we posed at the beginning.

"Phenomenology" of Time

Ut ergo tu sis, transcende tempus.[3]

—Augustine, *Tractates on the Gospel of John* 38.10

We cannot escape time, we said. Our conscious life is embedded in time. We have an immediate consciousness of something we may call temporality. But can we *think* time? We can certainly think about things, and discover that they present a temporal nature. This means that we experience things whose entity is not exhausted in a moment because they last. We experience *ek-sistence*. Existence amounts to the temporal character of things.

The word *existentia*, in fact, was introduced—by Marius Victorinus—in order to distinguish the "following" of beings from their *substantia* (ουσια) and *subsistentia* (υποστασις). Playing both with etymology and the history of the word, we could say that the *sistere extra causas* of *ek-sistence* (which translates υπαρξις, from υπαρχω = υπο-αρχω: to begin, to take the initiative from below) already suggests that we are aware of beings by becoming conscious of their existence, that is, their beginning to be, their emerging from the bottom of nothingness into the presentiality of reality. In a word, existence is already a temporal intuition.

We experience ourselves, too, as unfinished beings, that is, as beings going on, continuing in our own existence. Our temporal life is *distentio animi*, says Augustine (*Confessions* XI.29). We experience ourselves as unfinished in the sense of not-yet-finished, that is, in the making, living, growing, becoming.

All this implies memory, which is the "faculty" or power that allows the past to reappear (that is, to make it manifest) in the *now*. Alongside with memory (of the past) we also have expectation (of the future), which allows us to think about the future also, that is, to re-present (now) ourselves or things in a later state.

From the *now* we jump backward toward the past and forward toward the future. We may ponder this double fact of past and future. We may easily, although inadequately, objectify the past by materializing it, converting time into a dumping ground of past actions. We similarly may objectify the future by "spatializing" it, converting time into one dimension of a four-dimensional field. But we cannot objectify the present because, even if we were to consider it as the intersection between past and future, the "place" (moment) of the intersection depends exclusively on the subject (observer, spectator). We experience the temporal character of things because we (the experiencers) are temporal: our consciousness, as it were, stretches (along time) so as to embrace the (temporal) flow of events. In a word, we discover temporality in things because we are temporal.

But this entails a very important consequence: there can be no *pure* phenomenology of time. Time cannot be a pure *noêma*. We need, at least, a lingering of a prior state of consciousness while aware of the second one.

This is, after all, not startling, because we well know that there is no such *thing* as time. Time is not a "thing in itself" (*Ding an sich*). It exists nowhere. We may have a notion, but not a *noêma* of time. For the notion of time we need not one, but two particular phenomena, plus an awareness of their link. Let us analyze this.

We become aware of time when we perceive change. We speak of change when we perceive a situation A, another situation B, and N, our awareness of AB.

Now, what is the kind of relationship between this trinity that constitutes time? For the sake of brevity, I reduce the analysis to its bare elements.

---

[3] "Transcend time, so that you can *be*."

There is a situation A: the birth of a child, the death of a friend, the last solar eclipse, the promise of selling a property, the dropping of the atom bomb, the fall of a stone, the movement of a molecule, the thought of leaving one's spouse. . . .

There is a change from A to B, which can be as varied as the examples above: that child has been born, the friend is no more, the particular eclipse has gone, that promise has been held or broken, the same place has changed, the very thought has persisted. . . .

There is an awareness of A, an awareness of B, and an awareness of their relationship N. It is A that has changed into B. The perception of A and B is not simultaneous, and yet the perception of the relationship between A and B has to be somewhat simultaneous, or else we would have two unrelated states of unconsciousness. And here begins the difficulty, or rather the encounter with the irreducibility of temporal experience to one single act of consciousness. There are two observations, two different acts of consciousness. But their relationship is one. This relationship touches the core of time.

What is this relationship? It is, at least, an awareness of the difference between A and B. Yet we could not be aware of any difference if not against a background of identity. But we would not be aware of any identity if there were not a difference in some point. In a word, identity and difference are correlative. The "two" different observations are not one, they are consciousness of A and consciousness of B. But they are not "two" absolutely disconnected observations. Two means 1 + 1, where the second observation is precisely another homogeneous (second) 1, which we could add to the first 1. But this is not our case.

The second observation or act of consciousness is not independent from the first; it is the very awareness of the mutation of A into B. In other words, the awareness of the difference is an a-dualist consciousness, an observation that is neither one single nor two single observations, as it were, but a non-second observation, which is non-second precisely because it is still connected with the first, without being it. So, it is negating the second, as an independent observation, how we relate them. It is neither one nor two. It is a-dualist, *adva howitic*, says Indic wisdom.

The observer becomes aware of N, that is, of the change of A into B. This awareness is a-dualist. The A-B-N relation is the specific interplay of this tri-une event in the field of consciousness. This interplay is what we call time.

Time is not in the things alone. An observer must be there. "If there were no soul [ψυχη] there would be no time [χρονος]," said Aristotle (*Physics* IV.14; 223a26). Without an observer, we could not speak of time. Without an observer, we could not speak of beauty either. But there is a fundamental difference. The beholder of beauty is needed to discover beauty in things because the relation with the beholder is essential. Beauty is a relation. But the observer of time must, above and beyond, discover a sui generis relationship between two "moments" in the event itself. The relationship is also between those moments of the thing, not with the observer alone.

This means that is not in the observer alone either. Without things changing from situation A to B, there would be no time. If there were just one thing, one absolutely unchanging thing, there would be no time. If there were one single unchanging observer in the universe and one single thing, there would be no time. The observer can only observe time if there is a change in the observation. In simpler words, *one* observation of *one* thing does not yield the notion of time. There must be a change in both the observer and the thing, that is, in the subject and the object. The observer has "two" observations corresponding to the moments A and B of the thing. The link between the "two" observations, which negates their duality without letting them coalesce into one, yields the consciousness of time.

In sum, we need "three" elements to have the notion of time: "two" different situations in mutual relationship, and a consciousness of that state of affairs. Time has a triadic structure.

Kant is right: time lies at the basis of all intuitions, but it is an intuition that reflects a change both inside and outside our intuition. The very experience of time demands both a subjective and an objective factor; it entails a link between things or events and the consciousness of it. Time, being neither subjective nor objective, is prior to the epistemological split between subject and object. If things and consciousness were not already temporal, there would be no reflective consciousness of anything because consciousness is already a temporal process. Time seems to be inherent to Reality itself. A pure consciousness without objects (of that consciousness) would not be conscious of anything and thus would not be consciousness of time. Consciousness of time needs at least one change in the object of consciousness. It needs at least a consciousness of A, which is followed by a consciousness of B, otherwise it would not be conscious of anything, not even of A. It would stick to A and be unable to move toward a reflective consciousness of A. A real consciousness of time requires (1) the consciousness of A, (2) the reflective consciousness of A, and (3) the consciousness of ceasing to be the consciousness of A, that is, of the distinction between (1) and (2).

Phenomenology, in the sense of Husserl, is not applicable to the understanding of the temporal phenomenon, because time, that is, the very temporal structure of our consciousness and of the phenomena appearing there, is already a presupposition of the phenomenological analysis. On the one hand, time, as the temporal-spatial-material "reality" of things, enters into the famous εποχη: it should be put in brackets. Phenomenology does not deal with the nature or behavior of things. On the other hand, time belongs to the nature of both our objects of consciousness and our consciousness itself. We are presupposing time all along the phenomenological analysis. This is something more than the so-well-studied "epistemological circle": in order to know an object, we have to (already) know that it is an object. It is a very special case of the "methodological circle": the method we follow derives from the nature of the phenomenon being studied, which appears as such precisely because we follow the method.

But the impossibility of phenomenology of time is due to a more important reason than the fact that time does not appear in a pure phenomenological analysis. The main impossibility is not due to the fact that there is no permanent *noêma* in a single act of consciousness. This timeless act, assuming it is possible, would not anyway give us the experience of time. The deeper reason manifests itself in the fact that the experience of time is already presupposed in any reflective act. We cannot define time because time is already presupposed in any definition. We have to circumambulate (define) the *definiendum*; and this already requires time.

This circle means that the concept of time lies in the very concept of a concept because any concept presupposes precisely the factor of time: the concept of time is presupposed in any concept. This is what a certain philosophical language calls "transcendental," that is, something that transcends all its manifestations without being separable from them. Time, like Being, is "something" we carry along all our conceptions, including the very conception of time.

This means that thinking is a temporal process not only because it happens "in" time. It is also intrinsically temporal inasmuch as the very principles of identity and noncontradiction, required for thinking, have the time factor inherently built in them. A is A only if the predicate A keeps on being A. A cannot be A and non-A, if they have to be such at the same time, at least.

But the consciousness of this unbreakable circle is not barren. It reveals to us that there is some consciousness outside the circle, which is precisely that awareness that allows us to recognize the circle as a circle. In other words, it is the revelation that we cannot transcend time. This consciousness of our limits, this awareness of the impossibility of transcending our contingency, in a very particular way, has already transcended it. We recall the etymological wisdom of contingency: *con-tingere*, we touch upon the limit, bottom, or ceiling of our being. "Something" else dawns here.

But we are now only concerned with the phenomenology of time. And we assert that, strictly speaking, it is not possible because the temporal structure of both consciousness and things is the very condition of possibility of phenomenology. Time in this sense is a "given," a gift, and before analyzing it, we must become aware of it by receiving it. It is the "feminine" aspect of awareness, different, but not separable from the more "masculine" function of the same intellect. We can only grasp reality if we are also aware that we are "grasped" by it. We understand when we *stand-under*.

Time Is the Life of Being

ζωη χρονος του ειναι
[Life is the time of being]

—*Hesychius, Lexicon*

If our introductory remarks are correct, our conclusion must be very simple: the very experience of time amounts to the experience of reality. We experience time as we experience reality (to be). Our experience of time depends on our own awareness of life, of our life. Time is just the word for something that does not *belong* to us, but *is* us. We are temporal beings. We may be more than just temporal beings, but we are certainly not less than temporal beings, and if we eliminate temporality we destroy ourselves.

In this sense, I have inverted the Greek intuition for purely heuristic reasons. It comes ultimately to the same. Plotinus, in fact, describes time as "the life of the Soul" (*Enneads* III.7.11), and Bartṛhari calls time "the soul of the universe" (*Vākyapadīya*, III.9.12) and "the *svātantryaśakti* of *brahman*." Both life and time are ultimate.

We should remember that here the Greek word is *zôê* (ζωη), not *bios* (βιος). The expression χρονος του βιου, "the time of life," as in the *Second Letter of Clemens* (1.6), means precisely the limited duration of our individual lives. The Greeks, when speaking about the limited period of time in a Life of which we only live a portion, said επι του της ζωης αυτου χρονου (for the period [time] of life of [enjoyed by] someone). Anyway, these academic differences, like the distinction between καιρος and χρονος, were often blurred, not always respected. *Zôê* is life as such, life indestructible, life "eternal," as the Gospels say. "Life does not die" (*na jīvo mriyata*), says one *Upaniṣad* (*CU* VI.2.3). *Bios*, on the other hand, is private life, individualized life, as it were, finite life. "*Prāṇa* is *brahma*," says another *Upaniṣad* (*KausU* II.1), and specifies, "He [Indra] said: I am life [*prāṇosmi*], revere me as life immortal," or literally, as (temporal) life (and as) immortality (*āyur amṛtam*). "Life is *prāṇa, prāṇa* is life [*āyuḥ prāṇaḥ, prāṇo vā āyuḥ*]: it is immortality" (*KausU* III.2). My personal interpretation of it is that the *Upaniṣad* correlates temporal life, *āyus* (αιων, aeon, age), with immortal life (*prāṇa*).

All this amounts to saying that the conception of time is simply dependent on our conception of reality, and the basic experience of life (reality, Being, the world) will condition our notion of time. We project on time, as it were, our basic *Lebensgefühl*.[4] For some, time will be an image of eternity; for others, the power of *brahman*, the Supreme God or the supreme magician, the measure of all things or the soul of universe, and so on. In a word, the problem of

---

4 Feeling / perception of life.

time is not a question of a thing called time: it is the issue of Reality, the issue of Being. "Time is aptly described as a mimic of eternity," says Plotinus, echoing Plato (*Timaeus* 37D), "that seeks to break up in its fragmentary flight the permanence of its exemplar" (*Enneads* I.5.7).[5]

If we believe that this world is non-real, like some *māyāvādins*, time will be non-real. If we believe in two worlds, like some Greeks, time will be the image of the other world. If we believe that this world is evil, time will be the contradiction to the eternal, as some Gnostics affirm. If we believe that this world is here for us to merit another one, time will be the passage to the eternal, as most Christians and Muslims say. If we believe that the world is a measurable entity, time will be the specific ratio between space and speed, and so on.

At any rate, the power of time cannot be denied. The main problem consists in the relationship between time (be it illusory or real) with what could be called Being, *brahman*, Reality, the universe. Time is the link, as it were, with the other side of time. Time relates to temporal beings, but these beings are *in* and *of* the world; and if they *are* the world, they have something to do with Being.

A new dilemma appears here. It is a dilemma that has almost tortured the Indic mind for centuries: either time is real or it is not. If it is real, Reality is temporal, all is in progress, all changes, all is empirical, *vyāvahārika, saṃsārika*. If time is not real, the entire world is an illusion, life on earth is without ultimate relevance, the "real thing" is transcendent, invisible *pāramārthika*.

My contention, which tries to continue and deepen an almost perennial human insight, is that time is real, and Reality itself presents an a-dualist polarity that "includes" the eternal without "excluding" the temporal. (We should overcome the spatial connotations of these two words in order to avoid contradiction.)

In order to maintain the formal parallelism, we examine this problem under the light of the correlate to time, that is, eternity, to use this term in spite of its etymon (*aeternus* from *aevus, aetas,* αιων, Sanskrit *āyus,* age; and also the Gothic *aiw,* always). In other words, the difficulty with time does not lie with it, but with what it "reveals," "points to," "implies," namely, that which has sometimes been called eternity. *Nityānitya-vastu-viveka,* "discernment between the eternal and temporal things," says *Vedāntic* wisdom (*nitya*: continual, perpetual, related to *ni-ja*: innate, in-born) is essential in order to know what we really are, what Reality truly is. "Time is difficult to overcome," says the *Rāmāyaṇa* (*kālo hi dur atikramaḥ,* in III.72.16).

Let us introduce the question trying to show how a reflection on time leads to its other side. In thinking about time, there is something we cannot get rid of: our present point of reference, our temporal stand in the present. We may be able to think eternity, future, past, Being, Nothingness, and what not. It all may be problematic. But one standpoint we cannot eliminate: the present as the point of reference, of departure or arrival, as the point from which and on which we stand for whatever operation of our consciousness. We may remember the past and even foresee the future, but it always happens from the platform of the *now*.

But this *now* seems to reveal something "else" or "more." On the one hand, the *now* seems to convey a temporal revelation, something more than a past that has come to be, and a passage to a future that will be. It looks like intersection with something vertical as well. There is a novelty in the present that does not come from the past and that does not determinate the future exhaustively. We experience it as *freedom*. It is neither fully conditioned by the past, nor does it completely determine the future. (Otherwise, when the future becomes the present, it would be a fully conditioned present).

---

[5] Mackenna translation.

This freedom, which is only in the *now*, is somewhat untouched by time. It is the "gate" to eternity. But, on the other hand, eternity reveals itself temporally in the *now*. The moment is temporal, it is a crossing of the past and the future. But "at the same time" it manifests in itself (for us and "now") something of another nature. It is not an indefinite past or a never-ending future. Nor is it the integration of all those "realms." It is something of another order, which appears in the temporal moment. It is the *tempiternal* moment of the *now*, the present, the *nunc stans* and not the *nunc fluens*. We could here refer to the human experience of the zenith and the solstice since the Neolithic period. The sun must somewhat stop when it changes direction. The stone must somewhat stop when, after having been thrown vertically into the air, it "begins" to fall. "The *now* is the link of time . . . and it is a limit of time," said Aristotle (*Physics* IV.13 [222a]. Cf. also VIII.8 [261b ff.]). A similar argument could be found in the famous introduction to the *tat tvam asi* (*CU* VI.12—for instance: the nothingness is the eternal).

We may continue our philosophical reflection on the intrinsic relationship between time and eternity by considering the apparent paradox that the most immediate awareness of nothingness or non-being is linked with our thought about time. The very thought of nothingness, which is so central in most Eastern philosophies, and not only there, is the immediate result of our temporal awareness.

In fact, what is the past, from the only standpoint in which we can have a direct experience of it, namely, the present? What is the past, if not something that *is-not*, that has disappeared? What is the future, if not something that is equally nonexistent? We may not have an experience of nothingness in the strict sense of an immediate awareness of non-being. But we are conscious of nothingness by our temporal awareness of something that is no-longer or not-yet present. The past is our tomb of, and the future our monument to, nothingness—from our only possible, present standpoint. Time is (also) the revealer of Nothingness, we could say, complementing Gaudapāda.

In sum, in the present we have the doorway both to nothingness and to eternity. If we link the two, we will almost automatically overcome the loose and improper, although popular meaning of eternity as a never-ending (and never begotten) time, an indefinite time. While this is a legitimate notion—although it leads to pitiful debates (eternity and *big bang*, creation and evolution, etc.)—it is not what we understand by eternity, following a long tradition adumbrated by Plato and developed by Plotinus.

Eternity is not an infinite time; nor is it the negation of time, as well as the nothingness of the past or the future, in our present experience, is not the negation of the past or the future.

We cannot eliminate the temporal present where we stand, even if we may experience something of another nature in it. The *nunc stans et permanens* has been suggested as a description of eternity. The *nunc* (now) is not just the lasting of the instant, the temporality of the present, the freezing of the moment. It is rather the radically *novum* (new) in-stant, as the etymology suggests (including the English "now," akin to "new"). The Indo-European root *nu* is related both to *nunc* and *novus*, now and new. In the present *now*, both the past/future and the eternal meet. If we are too obsessed with the past or too worried about the future, we may overlook the eternal of each instant.

In spite of the fact that we may be only indirectly conscious of that timelessness, no self-consciousness of it can discard the temporal moment in which the act happens. Reflective consciousness is always temporal consciousness. We cannot shed off temporality. This does not only depend on the fact that we are always situated in time and space. The fact is that time itself is inherent in the act of consciousness, although we may remember (and therefore rescue from the past) that the foundation of that act of consciousness was somehow "outside" the temporal flow. The *now*, in a word, is inherently inserted in any act of which we can be aware.

We are saying that not only is the moment the temporal revelation of eternity, but that eternity is the eternal revelation of time. What does this mean?

It means that we cannot separate the two. The moment is such not only because it stands at the crossing between past and future, but also because it simply stands, although it does not stop (temporally). It is immediately (temporally) followed by the subsequent moment, but it has a consistency of its own: a "con-sistency" (not a mere "dis-tension" or "ex-tension") that gives each moment its message, its personality, as it were: its eternity.

The present is not a mere crossing of past and future: it is rather the encounter of time and eternity. The present would be nothing, if eternity were not already "in" it. The present is not a short time, not even an infinitesimally short time. We should know this since Zeno of Elea. The passage from past to future, happening in the present, reveals the eternal to us. Otherwise there would be no present.

The *citta-vṛtti-nirodha* of *Yoga-sūtra* I.2 (dealing with the processes of the mind) may be interpreted as "the door to the awareness of eternity."

Now, this eternity is not something temporal. Between the moment A and the immediate subsequent moment B there is nothing. There is not a third moment C. If there were a C, we could always intercalate shorter moments. There are infinite intermediate numbers between 2 and 3, but eternity is not an infinitely small time. It belongs to another order. Between A and B there "is" nothing. And this nothingness is eternity.

Time belongs to Being. Being is precisely *be*-ing. Being is temporal. Being is a verb. Being and time belong together. A timeless Being would be "dead." It would stifle itself. It could not breathe, it could not be. Being has to "be being." And this act implies activity, dynamism, life. This movement may not be an actualization of a dormant potentiality, it may be pure act, pure activity. It may not be a linear temporal unfolding, going somewhere where it has not previously been. But it has to be novelty, a throbbing, a rhythm. Being is more than becoming. "Be-coming" is a transient state, it is a coming-to-be. But when the becoming has come to *be*, this "be" itself is not static, but it is *be*-ing.

Nothingness "is" another name for the eternal. Nothingness *is-not*. We cannot say, therefore, that it is static. It is not a substance, that is, an "under-being." Eternity is not the substantial platform, the "stand" of time, an ontic *pratiṣṭhā*. Time does not repose on eternity, no more than eternity decomposes itself in the flow of time. "In time all things disappear" (*MaitU* VI.14). But this going to rest, stopping to go, disappearing (*niyacchanti*) is more—not less—than time. Time has yielded its fruit, as it were.

Nothingness is not the basis of Being, no more than eternity is the ground of time. Neither nothingness nor eternity are capable of offering a basis, a ground, a substance. The relationship is of another order. Neither nothingness nor eternity have a consistency of their own. Nothingness *is-not*, and eternity does not *ex-sist*. It has neither "ex-tension" nor "dis-tension." All these tensions and "sistences" belong to space and time as attributes of Being.

Now, what does it mean that the "two" belong together? What is their glue? There is no glue, because they are not two. Time and eternity, like Being and Nothingness, are neither two nor one. They belong together. What is togetherness? Who or what brings them together? Nobody, nothing! This is what allows us to say that, in spite of not being one and the same thing, there are not two things.

Here is the proper place of the *Advaitic* intuition. Or rather, of the trinitarian insight, for the "relation" between the "two" is a "third" that maintains the constitutive polarity that eliminates any oneness without falling into any dualness.

When I say *advaita*, I do not mean monism. Monism claims that there is one single degree of reality: what is not the real, *satyasya sat*, is unreal. All the rest is appearance, which only appears so to the non-enlightened ones, therefore not even a real appearance.

When I say *advaita*, I do not mean dualism either. Dualism claims that there are at least two incommunicable types of reality. The universe is a two- or multistory building with no ultimate communion of those levels with each other: a universe with two or more irreducible orders of reality.

When I say *advaita*, I mean that the subject and the object are not two, without being one; that the Divine and/or the Cosmic and/or the Human are not two, without being the same. And this without falling into contradiction, because the very nature of Reality is polar, each pole being constitutive of the Whole. And without falling into irrationalism either, because all the rights of reason are respected and acknowledged, just without absolutizing reason. Each rational statement is relative—in the sense of relativity and not relativism—to a particular context, and emerges out of a particular *mythos* or horizon of intelligibility that is taken for granted.

Long ago, I introduced the notion of *tempiternity* to express this *Advaitic* relationship. I have also attempted to describe the cosmotheandric or theo-anthropo-cosmic or *ādhi-daivika-ātmika-bhautika* insight as the holistic knowledge of the Divine, the Human, and the Cosmic. Time, along with space (with matter and energy), are definitive and constitutive dimensions of Reality. All is temporal. But the Whole is not only temporal.

Time and Being show this *Advaitic* character. They are not one. We should not confuse them. Eternity is another attribute of Being, but they are not two either. There is no a-temporal Being besides a temporal one. There would be a contradiction, if time and eternity were on the same level.

But *advaita* does not only deny. It is not mere negative attitude, it means also affirming a-duality. And this affirmation is worth considering. The positive aspect of *advaita* is not synthesis, that is, bringing together, as if the original state were separateness. We do not identify Being and Time or time with eternity. We do not synthesize them or bring them together. We simply do not separate them. *Advaita* is a primordial intuition. Time and Being, in our example, are not composed. We do not need to put them together by affirming that they are not two, that the separatedness is only a "weakness" or an "imperative" of our awareness. (We do not discuss *advaita* now, but try to apply the *Advaitic* intuition to our case.)

Precisely because *advaita* is a primordial intuition, it affirms a-duality. If it affirmed unity, it would become monism: the identification of Time and Being in our case, or of time and eternity. *Advaita* affirms the radical and constitutive polarity of the Real. At the same time it recognizes both the power of reason (Time and Being *appear* as two) and the overcoming of it (they *are* not two). *Advaita* is rational, but not rationalistic. Our experience of time is a case in point.

My contention is that this holistic vision was often indiscriminate, uncritical, and blurred. Distinctions were needed. But these distinctions led to specializations, and the latter to the present-day fragmentation. It is important and urgent to integrate the fragments into a more holistic union, without abandoning the insight of our specialized disciplines.

* * *

In an attempt to sum up, in a cross-cultural way, the human experience regarding time as the symbol of the Real, we could distinguish three kairological moments.

Calendar Time

Since the prehistoric era, Man has experienced time in connection with the cyclical periods within himself and in the outside world: periods of rest and activity, hunger and fullness, youth and old age, day and night, summer and winter, and so forth.

We may say that the first temporal experience of Man is the rhythm of life. Time is rhythm, but rhythm is not repetition. The consciousness of repetition springs with the institution of the calendar. It has been called the Neolithic metamorphosis. It is the first temporal revolution. The heterogeneity of time, the incomparability of the *now* and the uniqueness of each day was complete (cf. still Mt 6:34). Calendar time introduces the uniformity of the second day, the third winter, and the like. Quantity enters into the human consciousness of time. Time begins to be considered as having parts and, except—mainly—for the present, the past and the future are now projected onto a more or less uniform canvas: the common shape of the past fifth year will begin to blur and be hardly distinguishable from the sixth year, except for the number separating the years. Time is seen as unlimited, "cyclical."

Chronological Time

When many calendars conflict with each other, we need a new degree of abstraction, a new and more thorough quantification. The still rhythmic and qualitative calendar is substituted by a pragmatic and often arbitrary chronology. It offers an allegedly neutral and universal point of reference. The fact that the Christian Era is called by some "Common Era" is an example of both: the pretension to neutrality, claiming to overcome ideological contents (of Christian origin, in this case) and the pretension of being universal (to call this era "common" is the acme of colonialist culture-centrism). To begin a time reckoning with the *big bang* would not be less ideologically loaded.

What interests us here, however, is the move toward quantification and abstraction. Time is then seen as a chronological parameter, a quantitative factor, and most expeditiously linked to space and movement as an anonymous fourth dimension. It is the time of modern science.

The possibility of another realm is not denied by modern science. It would be the field of timelessness. Time would then be one thing and timelessness another. This apparent tolerance is easily misleading. The introduction of dualism (time is one separate thing and timelessness another totally different entity) kills reality like the child of the famous Solomonic judgment. And here begins modern cultural schizophrenia, in which the fragmentation of knowledge leads to the fragmentation of the knower.

Ontological Time

If the first vision of reality could be called monistic (time and eternity coalesce), and the second dualistic (time has nothing to do with eternity), this vision may be named a-dualist or *Advaitic* (time and eternity are distinct but not separable). The notion of eternity will not, therefore, concern timelessness as a second level of reality, or a second story of an a-temporal reality with no connection with the temporal whatsoever, but it will rather concern *tempiternity*.

"Above time is set a brimful vessel," sings the *Atharva-veda* (XIX.53.3). Eternity is not just the absence of time but its fullness. "Aeternitas includit omne tempus" (Eternity includes all time), says Thomas Aquinas (*Sum. theol.*, I, q.13, a.1, ad 1), and he insists, "omnia tempora" (all times) (I, q.10, a.2), "totum tempus" (all the time) (I, q.14, a.13), not to leave any doubt. Eternity is neither separated from, nor juxtaposed to time. It is co-extensive with it, they embrace mutually. The word "tempiternity" expresses this *Advaitic* relationship. It is the *intemporale tempus* of Nicholas of Cusa (*De aequalitate* III.374), the *niṣkala kāla* of Śaṅkara (*Vivekacūḍāmaṇi* 497). "Beginningless time and the present moment are the same," said Huang Po (*Chun Chou* 31).

In point of fact, eternity is neither indefinite time, nor timelessness, nor even timefulness, if we interpret this last word as a sort of integer between $-\infty$ and $+\infty$ time. The fullness is not of "all times" but of the present (for the past and the future *are-not*), as we already said. We may reach the fullness of the present by experiencing the *trikālābādhyatva* of Indic tradition: "The unremovability of the three times," that which can never be removed away once we eliminate the past, the present, and the future. The *trikālābādhyatva* as that which can never be contradicted at any time (past, present, future) is a criterion for truth for some Vedantins. The full passage in the quoted text by Nicholas of Cusa says, "The soul, which is a-temporal time, sees in its essence the past, the present, and the future [and] calls the past memory, the present intellect, [and] the future will."

"Ontological time" is only a philosophical and, for many, secularized expression of probably one of the oldest and most universal experiences of humanity. This primordial human experience was at the basis of calendar time since the Babylonians, Egyptians, and Meso-Americans. Time is one aspect of Reality, as I said. Time is one revelation of the Deity; or rather, the temporal display of things reveals the many Deities that are at work (alive) in Reality, as they said. This old and traditional language, if well understood, may help us to better describe the human experience of "the mystery of time."

Time is the door to eternity: we find this said almost everywhere. But this threshold is not only the "last time," death. It is not the future time (of death, of which hardly anybody has the experience), but the real time, that is, the present time. Time is a deity. In time, our destiny and that of the Gods coalesce—we have here the basis of what later on was called astrology: the facets (measures) of time are manifestations (measures) of Gods, Men, and the cosmos alike; they are the Divinities, not just hidden (as for many modern people) but patent for Man.

It is through time, living it, and not just sliding on it, how we become what we truly "are"—where this "are" is not a fleeting present, but it is not "as we were" or "as we shall be" either. This "are" is not only the crossroad of past and future, but a deity. Every day has its own divinity: each event is a divine, a human, and a cosmic happening: each happening is a "moment" in Life. Earth, sun, moon, stars (as also matter, fire, water, wind) are divine precisely because they move, and they move because they are aspects of Life, "measures" of time. They reveal time to us. Any Aztec or Maya child would understand it, let alone a Babylonian or Egyptian child. Time is the Life of Being, we said, in a more philosophical parlance.

Now the discussion comes full circle. Time, like Being, is the most immediately "given" reality to us, and therefore the most mysterious when we deal with it as an object, and most deceiving if we handle it as an adjective of a subject. We *are* it. We cannot speak of it without somewhat splitting it. We should rather let time speak through us, be in us, "time" us.

Time is the Life of Being. Time is the very life of our own being. We experience time in the same measure as we experience life. Our life is distended: we call time life's distension. Our life is fragmented: we call time its fragmentation. Reality, as much as it is fragmented, is temporal. The experience and measurement of the different fragmentations will give us different notions of different times.

The *kālaśakti*, the power of time, reveals herself as a *śakti* of the Divine, of Śiva, one tradition will say; of Reality, we may translate in a more general way.

3

THE END OF HISTORY*

The Threefold Structure of Human Time-Consciousness

Hoti krónos oûkéti ésti[1]

Rev 10:6

Introductory Remarks

The *historia,* that is, the inquiry into contemporary events, leads me to think that we are not only at the end of *an* historical period—as many analysts today would agree[2]—but that we are ending *the* historical period of humankind, which is to say that we are *at the beginning of the end of the myth of history*.[3] In order to catch a glimpse of what a posthistorical myth may represent, I shall describe it in relation to prehistorical and historical consciousness. The main elements of a posthistorical myth are already present—or else we could not speak of it intelligibly—but its contours have not yet emerged for most people.[4] These three

---

* *Original text:* in *Teilhard de Chardin and the Unity of Knowledge* (New York: Paulist Press, 1983), and then in *The Cosmotheandric Experience,* Part 2 (Maryknoll, NY: Orbis Books, 1993), as part of the Proceedings of Centenary Symposium held at Georgetown University, Washington, DC, May 1–3, 1981.

¹ "For there shall be no more time." The traditional translations say, "That there shall (should) be time no longer" *RV* (*AV*). The NEG translates, "There shall be, no more delay." Other readings: *tardança* (Monserrat), *délai* (Jerusalem), *dilación de tiempo* (Martín Nieto), *tiempo* (Nácar-Colunga). The Vulgate says, *Quia tempus non erit amplius.*

² Compare, for example, Lewis Mumford, *The Conduct of Life* (New York: Harcourt, Brace, Jovanich, 1951, 1970), esp. chapter 8, "The Drama of Renewal." Mumford includes many such critiques.

³ The author is fully aware of the difficulty and danger of hurried syntheses and generalized overviews; but for many decades he has been concentrating on the problem of a "Vision de sintesis de universo" (*Arbor* 1 [1944]), and would like to offer these late reflections as an homage on the centenary of his birth to Pierre Teilhard de Chardin, who was not afraid of breaking all anthropomorphic scales and applying to Man the parameters of the evolution of the cosmos.

⁴ "Il est difficile de saisir l'intelligibilité d'un mythe à partir de l'autre, mais on doit admettre qu'une bonne partie du monde aujourd'hui est atterrée à la pensée de la possibilité d'un cataclysme à l'échelle planétaire, tandis que toute une autre partie de l'humanité n'est pas trap touchée par le déclin historique de la race humaine [It is difficult to grasp from one myth the intelligibility of another, but we must admit that much of the world today is terrified by the thought of a possible cataclysm on a planetary scale, while a whole other part of mankind shows little concern for the historical decline of

forms of consciousness are all human. This is why I speak of three moments of human time-consciousness, or rather of the threefold structure of human time-consciousness. These three moments should not be interpreted chronologically, that is, as though they followed one after the other. They are qualitatively different and yet intertwined, coexisting in one way or another, in the human race and the human person as well. The nonhistorical type is very much alive today, and transhistorical consciousness is equally present in our times. They are three modes of consciousness that are neither mutually exclusive nor dialectically opposed, but *kairologically* related.[5] I mean by this word the qualitative aspect of human time that represents at once the dominance of one mode over the others, according to idiosyncrasies of all sorts, and a certain temporal sequence that accords with the unfolding of individual and, especially, collective life.

The question of vocabulary is almost insurmountable here. Each word has a home. It may have received some hospitality in other neighborhoods, but hardly a word today has international citizenship, let alone global validity. Speaking within the historical myth, history must be the central point of reference; therefore I have called these three periods nonhistorical, historical, and transhistorical. But this is only a device to introduce the three moments mentioned. First of all, they are not periods in the mass media sense of the word, but rather in the more complex sense suggested by the etymology of the word *period*: ways around, or recurring ways of being human.[6] Second, I might have called them *past-directed, future-oriented,* and *present-centered* time-consciousnesses, but because most writers and readers of our so-called literate contemporary cultures live within the prevalent historical moment, I shall not deny history the importance it has. Granting history this centrality, the three moments might be called prehistorical, historical, and posthistorical. But this would not do justice to the ahistorical moments. My preference would be to call them kairological, historical, and secular.[7] But I shall remain with the compromise of nonhistorical, historical, and transhistorical.[8]

---

the human race]," R. Panikkar, *L'eau et la mort*, ed. M. M. Olivetti, *Philosophie et religion face à la mort* (Paris: Aubier, 1981), 500.

[5] After years of using this word, I find that Romano Guardini had the following scheme: "Das Dasein verwirklicht sich in der Zeit" [Existence is realized in time], and, consequently, "heissen die drei Teile der Christlichen Lehre von der Daseinzeit die Archelogie, Eschatologie und Kairologie" [these three divisions of the Christian doctrine concerning existence in time are called archaeology, eschatology and kairology]. He describes the latter as the doctrine of the moment: "wie die laufende Zeit gegenwärtig und damit das Dasein in jeweils unwiederbringlicher Einmaligkeit dem Menschen anvertraut wird; abermals das Dasein des Einzelnen und der auf ihn hin bestehenden Welt" [time becoming the present in its fleeting course, thereby entrusting existence to man in irrevocable, unalterable, unique fashion—that is, his own existence and that of the world related to him]. *Die letzten Dinge* [Le cose ultime] (Würzburg: Werkbind-Verlag, 1940), introduction (n.p.); English translation: R. Guardini, *The Last Things* (New York: Pantheon, 1954), ii.

[6] The word *period* comes from the Greek *perí* (around) and *hódos* (way, manner). See "episode" (*epi-eis-hódos*), "method" (*meta-hódos*), etc.

[7] The *kairos* would emphasize the nonlinear and especially nonhomogeneous aspect of time, over against the *chronos*, notwithstanding the fact that *kairos* and *chronos* were often used indiscriminately in Greek. *Secular* would underscore the experience of the *saeculum* as the temporal life span of both the world and the human being.

[8] I had hesitated between *para-historical* and *meta-historical*, but the current use of the first prefix and the different utilization of the second one in different contexts has led me to use the prefix *trans-*, though I must insist on its secondary meaning—that is, not so much in the sense of trans-cendence, of going *beyond*, as of trans-parency, passing *through*.

There may be no more formidable problem than the problem of time.[9] We are speaking here of a threefold human time-consciousness. The difficulty in communicating what I would like to say lies in the fact that from each of these time-consciousnesses we tend to scan the entire temporal spectrum. Most of my readers, as already noted, will tend to comprehend any human temporality in historical categories. Prehistorical Man generally does not know how to read or write, or at least does not make much of it.[10] And transhistorical consciousness does not much feel the need of that skill. And yet, bear in mind, the three modes are not mutually exclusive. In each one of us there exist more or less latent forms of nonhistorical and transhistorical time-consciousness, although modern Man may "historicize" them when thinking about them in our rational and historically conscious parameters. Those moments for which we would have given our entire life, those artistic experiences that seem to be atemporal, the realms of life that open up in deep meditation, besides the peak and ecstatic experiences in the face of the mysteries of life, suffering, and death, could be adduced as examples of human consciousnesses that are irreducible to historical consciousness.

These three moments not only form a triad in our own individual lives, they are also analogously present in the collective unfolding of human existence, although in any given culture and from a sociological viewpoint one of them may predominate over the others.[11] And because the lives of most book writers and readers unfold in historical time, I somehow have to pay tribute to it by using a presentation and a language still tainted with historical overtones, as the very words pre-, post-, and even non-, para-, and trans- "historical" betray.

The argument of this study is as follows: Man is a temporal being.[12] His experience of time has three focal points: the past, the future, and the present. The predominance of one or another of these foci makes up the three kairological moments to which I have alluded. The development of all three time-experiences accounts for the maturity of the human being phylogenetically and ontogenetically. When the past is the paradigm through which we experience time, we have the nonhistorical moment (memory and faith are central); when it is the future, historical consciousness prevails (the will and hope are predominant); and when past and future are lived in terms of the present, we share in the transhistorical experience of reality (the intellect and love become fundamental).[13]

These three moments in human consciousness correspond to three periods of human existence on Earth—in the indicated sense of the word *period*. We could even date these periods.

Until the invention of writing, Man could not project all his creations into the future; the past had the most powerful grip on him. Tradition was paramount. Time comes from a Beginning. *Mythos.*

With the invention of writing, human specialization becomes possible.

---

[9] For the complexity of the human experience of time, see J. T. Fraser, ed., *The Voices of Time* (New York: Braziller, 1966), his *Of Time, Passion and Knowledge* (New York: Braziller 1975), and J. T. Fraser et al., eds., *The Study of Time III* (New York: Springer, 1978), all works of the International Society for the Study of Time. I have completed a bibliography on "time" of more than fifteen hundred entries.

[10] I say generally because nonhistorical consciousness is prevalent in many of the Asian and African cultures of today—using this last word in a chronocentric historical way.

[11] We shall not discuss here the evolution of this threefold consciousness or, for that matter, how far prehistorical Man can be said also to possess historical and transhistorical consciousness.

[12] I state again that Man with a capital "M" refers to the entire human being—*anthropos*—previous to the differentiation of the sexes.

[13] It would require an elaborated anthropology to properly explicate these parentheses.

Progress is a sacred word. Time marches forward. The future belongs to God and God to the future. *History*.

When Man split the atom, the seemingly indestructible elements on which the entire world rested showed their vulnerability. The human technological miracle has itself been fissioned. The atoms of all sorts (spiritual and intellectual as well) are no longer indestructible. The past is broken, and the future collapses. The present is the only time left. And it is this experience that opens the door to the predominance of the *Mystical*.

Before the description of these three moments, a criteriological description will be helpful.

Methodological Reflection

The Subject Matter: Man

Let us be clear that these three moments of human consciousness do not mean three different objects of consciousness, that is, three different ways of looking at the world, while the human subject remains unchallenged and, so, unchanged. They represent rather three different modes of being human, precisely because consciousness defines Man. Man is that speaking animal, which speaks because it has something to say, that is, because it possesses a self-consciousness that makes it aware of its own consciousness. And because of this, it speaks. The human animal speaks, not because it is aware of things and actions (as other animals also are), but because it is aware of itself doing this. And to communicate its subjective (reflective) intentions, it needs words. I would call it a *speaking consciousness, śabda-brahman*.[14]

In other words, if Man is essentially self-conscious, how can we know what Man is, without taking into account all that human beings have *understood* themselves to be? The "object" Man of the study of Man also embraces the "subject" Man who undertakes the study. But this Man is not only I or we, the investigators. It is everybody, Everyman.[15] The study of Man entails the study of what humans think of themselves. Is such an enterprise possible? Possible perhaps, provided we keep it all the while open and provisional, that is, maintain the awareness that we do not have access to the universal range of human experience.[16]

As if this were not enough, another difficulty arises: Man reveals himself not only in thinking but also in doing. How then can such a study be accomplished without taking into account all that Man has done? In fact, actions are as much crystallizations or revelations of Man's understanding of himself and the universe as are his theoretical reflections.[17] Now in the West, since Aristotle at least, Man's actions have been divided into those that return for the perfection of the agent—activities like feeling and understanding—and those that are

---

[14] See Bhartṛhari's memorable beginning: "The Brahman who is without beginning or end, whose very essence is the Word, who is the cause of the manifested phonemes, who appears as the objects, from whom the creation of the world proceeds" [*Anadinidhanam brahma śabdatattvaṃ yad akṣaram / vivartate 'rthabhavena prakriya jagato yataḥ*].

[15] See the fifteenth-century European play *Everyman*, possibly of Buddhist origin according to the author of a new version. See Frederick Frank, *Every One* (Garden City, NY: Doubleday, 1978).

[16] "Global perspective," "total awareness," "universal outlook," and similar expressions are useful and well-intentioned signs of the will to overcome dangerous provincialism, but they are impossible ideals for any single human being. This universalism could in its turn become a new source of totalitarian or colonialist attitudes: "We have the global vision, we know better and impose our ideas upon you—for your own benefit, of course!"

[17] "Thinking" here stands for the overall human intellectual activity, related to consciousness and including, of course, the (conscious) will and thus love.

directed *ad extra* for the perfection of something else.[18] We do not refer to the former, the *poiesis,* but to the latter, the human *praxis.*[19] Human *praxis* reveals what Man is, just as much as does *theoria.* Humans think, and all their thinking belongs to what Man is, but humans also act, and all their activity belongs to human nature as well, even if the meaning of those acts has not reached reflective consciousness.

The attempt to reach such theoretical awareness is the task of philosophy. The study of such praxis is history.[20] The unfolding of such events is *Geschichte.*[21] Both history and *Geschichte* belong to anthropology. I understand anthropology as the *telling* of what Man is. *Geschichte* tells us what Man is through his deeds. History tells us what Man is by the interpretation of his deeds. *Geschichte* offers the praxis, history the theory of Man's constructs—and both, obviously, in relation to human (historical) facts. But history also means that dimension of human consciousness that makes the study of human praxis meaningful. It is historical consciousness that undertakes the study of history, precisely because it is convinced of the revelatory character of such an enterprise.[22] The study of history will tell us what Man is, as long as we believe Man to be a historical being.[23] This is extremely important and has often been overlooked. History is what it claims to be, namely *magistra vitae,* the revelation of what Man is, the "unfolding of human reason" and the like, insofar as Man believes himself a historical being. In short, history is history inasmuch as we are in or believe in the myth of history. All this discourse would have no meaning were we not somewhat convinced that we are historical beings living in history as our proper world, as the proper environment of the fish is water. What then does it mean, in this context, that the historical period is coming to an end? It does not mean that we cease to take an interest in human praxis. It does not mean that we jump altogether outside time and space. Historicity should not be confounded with temporality. The phrase means that Man ceases to consider himself as *only* a historical being, or *the* historical being, *Dasein,* and by this very fact ceases to be a merely historical being.[24]

---

[18]   See Aristotle, *Metaphysics* IX.8 (1050a23–b2), etc.

[19]   Paradoxically, we could say that if this praxis reveals Reason for Hegel, it should be shaped by Reason for Marx. See also the texts of Kant, Gentz, and Rehberg in *Uber Theorie und Praxis,* with an Introduction by D. Henrich (Frankfurt a.M.: Suhrkamp, 1967), for the discussion surrounding Kant's polemical paper.

[20]   The meaning of the root, *aid,* from which *historía* comes, is to see, to know. See *eídos,* idea; *histír,* the erudite, he who knows and witnesses, the judge. *Historikós, -e, -ón,* means exact, precise (scientific), and *historéi* to inquire, observe, examine.

[21]   Hegel distinguishes History as *historia rerum gestarurn,* the subjective aspect, and as *res gestae,* the objective aspect, in *Vorlesungen uber die Philosophie der Geschichte* (*Lectures on the Philosophy of History*), *Werke,* ed. H. Glockner, XI.97.

[22]   See Hegel's central and masterful *Die Vernunft in der Geschichte* (*Reason in History*), and the well-known quotation at the end of his *Philosophy of History:* "For the history of the world is nothing but the development of the idea of freedom." Trans. J. Sibree, *Great Books of the Western World,* ed. R.M. Hutchins, *Hegel* (Chicago: Encyclopedia Britannica, 1952), 369.

[23]   See W. Dilthey's description of his enterprise of a "Critique of Historical Reason": *"d.h, des Vermögens der Menschen, sich selber und die von ihm geschaffene Gesellschaft und Geschichte zu erkennen"* [i.e. the ability of people to recognize themselves and the history and society they have created], *Gesammelte Schriften* (*Selected Writings*), I.116 (in Scholtz, art. *Geschichte),* J. Ritter, ed., *Historischen Wörterbuch der Philosophie* (Darmstad: Wissenschaftliche Buchsgesellschaft, 1974), 3:382. Dilthey sees clearly, "Dass der, welcher Geschichte erforscht, derselbe ist der die Geschichte macht" (He who studies history is the same as he who makes history), *Schriften,* VII.278 (ibid.).

[24]   See M. Heidegger's first description: "Geschichte ist das in der Zeit sich begebende spezifische

It means that Men begin to question whether the study, or knowledge, of what they do and think exhaustively reveals what they are and gives them the clue to life, happiness, and/or truth.[25] It means that the fulfillment of human life is no longer seen exclusively, or even mainly, in the historical unfolding (individual or collective) but also, or rather, in transtemporal experiences (not atemporal but tempiternal), as I shall try to spell out.

We should insist on this for a moment. The peculiar nature of the human being also consists in the *who* that *thinks* and *does,* besides the *what* that is thought and done. This constitutes the fundamental distinction between the so-called natural, that is, physical sciences, and philosophical anthropology, that is, the humanities. The former intend to know *objects* (however modified by and dependent on the investigator); the latter seek to understand *subjects* (even if incompletely covered by the investigation). When science studies Man, it wants to know the object Man: what Man *is.* When philosophy (or should I say philosophical philosophy, to distinguish it from a certain modern scientific philosophy?) takes aim at the same target, it wants to understand the subject Man: who Man is and even who I, a Man, *am* and you are. The epistemological paradigm of the natural sciences is: "S is P." It strives to find the P fitting to S. The epistemological paradigm of at least some philosophy is "What am I?" so that it may also answer "What you are" and be able to formulate "Who Man is."[26]

Our particular case still needs a second degree of sophistication. Our problem has to do with more than the well-known fact that the humanities cannot be totally objectified—since individual viewpoints also belong to the "subject matter." It has to do as well with the fact that the particular human awareness of an entire group of cultures (the historical ones) is called into question. This is possible only if we recognize the validity of a truly transcultural invariant, which we can only locate extrinsically through a genuine cross-cultural approach to the ultimate problems of human awareness. We cannot deny a priori the possibility of another human a priori. But the burden of proof lies in our capacity to show that this genre of discourse also makes sense.

The transcultural is a kind of homeomorphic equivalent to what European philosophy since Kant has called the transcendental—that is, that which, being an a priori condition of our understanding, is given in any reality we understand, but always in the very form in which we understand it. Similarly, the transcultural does not stand alone. There is nothing just transcultural, since we are always in a certain culture, even if it is a new or nontraditional one. Yet the cross-cultural approach to reality opens us up to the discernment of something— although obviously not a "thing in itself"—present in the differing homeomorphic notions of different cultures. It is rather that which allows the cross-cultural correlations and makes us aware that we are dealing with a homeomorphic notion.[27]

Geschehen des existierenden Daseins" [History is the specific happening of ex-sisting being-there unfolding in time], *Sein und Zeit (Being and Time),* 12th ed. (Tübingen: Niemeyer, 1972), §73, p. 379. And also, "Das Dasein hat faktisch je seine 'Geschichte' und kann dergleichen haben, weil das Sein dieses Seienden durch Geschichtlichkeit konstituiert wird" [Being-there always has its "history," and it can have something of the sort because the being of this being is constituted by historicity], §74, p. 382. Obviously the entire work should be consulted, especially the last two chapters of the book. We cannot now enter into the complete problematic.

[25] See Schelling's saying that the only content of philosophy is history (K. F. A. Schelling, ed., *Werke* 1382ff.). In Ritter, op. cit., III.363. An idea that the Romantics will also reiterate.

[26] See R. Panikkar, "Words and Terms," *Archivio di Filosofia,* ed. M. M. Olivetti (Rome, 1980), 117–33, in Vol. IX, Part 2 of this *Opera Omnia.*

[27] "Homeomorphism is not the same thing as an analogy; it represents a peculiar functional

We know, for instance, that *dharma* cannot be rendered simply by "justice." It may also mean religion, righteousness, duty, right, feature, character, and still have many other meanings. Likewise, we know that religion is not only *dharma*, it is also *bhakti*, *karma-niṣtra*, *niyama*, *sādhana*, *pūjā*, and many other words, each of them covering only a part of the meaning of the original. The relation is not univocal, one to one. Now if we are familiar with these two worlds of *dharma* and *religion*, we shall detect that the numerous English words standing for *dharma* have little or nothing in common in the English linguistic world, and yet they all express *dharma*. Something similar could be put the other way around regarding the word *religion*. When we detect that the former series are all "dharmic" words and the latter "religious" words, we approach the transcultural. For an adequate interpretation we need a cross-cultural approach. We need to understand, for instance, what *dharma* means in the *Gītā* and be able to render that meaning in English, or what *religio* means in the Vulgate and be able to put it into Sanskrit. It is when we discover that the relation is not bi-univocal that we may be able to choose the appropriate word, taking into consideration the transcultural factor. Only when I know that *dharma* means all those words in English, *religion* all those words in Sanskrit and yet univocally none of them; only when I choose the right word because something has dawned upon me that finds its proper expression in the language into which I am translating, almost as a new creation; only then am I in touch with the transcultural: it is not *dharma*, or religion, or duty, or *puja*—and yet it allows me to find the appropriate word. Generally it happens because we know the context and then find the proper word, but this only postpones the problem, because the context also has to be known by means of words.[28] We are touching the problem of the experience before its expression. There is no experience without expression, and yet they are not the same.[29]

The case of time is paradigmatic here. We may have a cross-cultural understanding of time. Different cultures have different experiences and understandings of the human and cosmic rhythms. What I am attempting here is to group these cultures in larger units according to one particular fundamental feature, that of "time." Time has to do with past, present, and future, with the flow of events, with change, movement, and the like. Time has to do with living and with being. But all these realities are lived and experienced differently by different human traditions. A cross-cultural understanding will show the differences and the similarities. But it is only with an awareness of the transcultural character of time that we may be able to detect the three modes of human time-consciousness that we are about to elaborate here.

In order to prepare the way for an intelligible discourse, we shall have to disclose the parameters of our investigation.

The Human Scale: The Astrological Rhythm

Between the cosmic yardstick of a Teilhard de Chardin, comprising hundreds of thousands of years, on the one hand, and the journalistic vision of mere days or weeks, the sociological perspective of decades, or the historical angle of some centuries, on the other, lies

---

equivalence discovered through a topological transformation." It is "a kind of existential functional analogy" (R. Panikkar, *The Intrareligious Dialogue* [New York: Paulist Press, 1978], xxii).

[28] See G. Steiner, *After Babel: Aspects of Language and Translation* (London: Oxford University Press, 1975), and the abundant bibliography.

[29] See R. Panikkar, "The Supreme Experience," *Myth, Faith, and Hermeneutics* (New York: Paulist Press, 1979), chapter 10, in Vol. I, Part 1 of this *Opera Omnia*.

the astrological meter of the Earth's rhythm.[30] This is the natural equinoctial rhythm of the Earth around the Sun, which takes twenty-five thousand years for its axis to precess round to the same alignment. This is the so-called Platonic or cosmic year. Each astrological month would then last twenty-one hundred years. If we entered the period of Aquarius around 1950, ending the month of Pisces which began circa 150 BCE, my own perspective would be to situate the following reflections against the backdrop of the beginnings of what we call human history, which coincides with the two previous periods, that is, Aries, from about 2250 BCE, and Taurus, which began around the year 4350 BCE.[31] Human history thus has a memory of roughly six thousand years.[32] Can we say something meaningful on this scale?

I would like to venture some ideas, based not on astrological considerations, important as these are, but on my own diachronical and diatopical experiences of cultures and peoples we know.[33]

All the different rhythms are legitimate. The individual's need for food cannot be dealt with on a yearly or even weekly basis; it is a daily concern. Politics cannot bypass or ignore the situation of the generation actually living within the *polis*. Historians have a wider span, natural scientists another, and philosophers would tend to further enlarge their perspective and somehow generate theories or opinions *sub specie aeternitatis*, or at least *in mundo sublunari*, that is, valid for the human condition as such—sociology of knowledge notwithstanding.

Yet there is an intermediate span which has all too often been neglected, because it needs different scales and yardsticks.[34] There are problems too small to be measured by physical or biological laws and too big to be treated in merely sociological categories. This is what I call the astrological scale. This scale is precisely defined by the magnitude of those phenomena which relate to Man as homo sapiens and to the solar system within the more comprehensive rhythms of our galactic system. I should not be misunderstood. What has been said should not be interpreted in historical categories, as if we were speaking of the human historical clock measured in astronomical units. I am speaking not so much about a Newtonian or Einsteinian solar system, but about Man. The human scale is not just a larger meter than the historical one, but that meter capable of measuring the changes in human time-consciousness. It is not our time-perception that is at stake here, but our own temporal being, which has in the last centuries of Western civilization all too often (though not always) been identified with historical being.

The true yardstick here is human language. It is somewhat disturbing to see human problems approached with superhuman paradigms like those of the astronomical and biological

---

[30] Cf., for details and justifications, the study by Alfons Rosenberg, *Durchbruch zur Zukunft. Der Mensch im Wassernannzeitalter* [Breakthrough to the future: Man in the age of Aquarius] (Bietigheim/Württ: Turm Verlag, n.d.; 2nd ed., 1971).

[31] For the beginnings of the Aquarian Age, See the controversy surrounding Marilyn Ferguson's book *The Aquarian Conspiracy* (Los Angeles: J. P. Tarcher, 1980) in Forum 11, no. 1 (1980): 27–46, although my perspective here is probably more radical.

[32] Interestingly enough, the literal reckoning of the age of the world according to the Bible would be precisely six thousand years.

[33] See an example of such experience in my study "El presente tempiterno: Una apostilla a la historia de la salvación y a la teología de la liberación," in *Teología y mundo contemporáneo* (Homenaje a K. Rahner), ed. A. Vargas-Machuca (Madrid: Christiandad, 1975), 133–75, where an alternative is suggested to the dilemma of non-Western cultures either perishing or accepting historicity.

[34] The epochal daring of Teilhard de Chardin consists in projecting straightaway the miniscule homo sapiens into the galactic destiny of the universe. The present study may well provide a missing link between the cosmological macro-level and the anthropological micro-level.

cycles. But it is equally unsatisfactory to tackle issues regarding Man and the nature of reality as experienced by the human being with limited calipers valid only for much more restricted phenomena. If the danger of the former is vagueness, from lack of concrete data, the latter approach runs the risk of oversimplification by unwarranted extrapolation.

Historical studies have to limit themselves to written documents, and prehistorical research concentrates on human tools. Language, I submit, is the human *metron* par excellence. It measures the *humanum*, and it is more than just a tool or a document. It is human nature incarnated. Not only has the *Logos* become flesh; the flesh also becomes *Logos*. In language we have the crystallization of human experience and its tradition.[35] Human language is not a mere record of the past. It bears witness to human nature in the present. We should learn not only to decipher past documents but also to read language.

And here the wisdom of prehistorical Man, as well as the teachings of the great masters of the historical period—perceived in a cross-cultural light—come to our aid without our having to escape into superhuman or metacosmic utopias. They have all paid the utmost attention to language. Teilhard de Chardin or Hindū cosmology may well be true in their contexts, but just as we should avoid using centimeters and seconds to evaluate our present human situation, we should equally eschew using light-years for human measurements.[36] The destiny of the human race cannot be judged only from the White House or the Kremlin, but also not exclusively from Mount Wilson, the Sri Aurobindo Ashram, or a biological laboratory. Our scale is neither that of the United States presidential elections nor that of the zoo-biological species.[37] I am taking into account human consciousness of the last twenty thousand years, at least, and human memory of the six thousand elapsed historical years, in order to project our reflections into the coming millennia.[38] Within this middle range the human scale may be preserved. And it is here that transhistorical consciousness may shed some light on the excruciating predicament of our times.[39]

---

[35] We cannot readily pursue the argument further here. Cf., as a single reference because it is not very well known, F. Ebner's *Das Wort und die geistigen Realitäten* (*The Word and the Spiritual Realities*) and *Zum Problem der Sprache und des Wortes* (*On the Problem of Language and Words*), both reprinted in *Schriften I* (Munich: Kösel, 1963).

[36] I am not contesting the legitimacy of Teilhard's approach. I am perhaps offering the vital connection between history and cosmology. But I refrain from discussing the problem of evolution.

[37] "Nur die gesamte Menschheitsgeschichte vermag die Massstäbe für den Sinn des gegenwärtigen Geschehens zu geben" [Only human history as a whole can provide the standards for the meaning of present events], wrote Karl Jaspers in 1949, just after the Second World War, *Vom Ursprung und Ziel der Geschichte* [*The Origin and Goal of History*] (Frankfurt a.M.: Fischer, 1956), 11. One generation later, I dare to add that the application of this scale leads to the conclusion that we are on the brink of the mutation already suggested. This is what Jaspers seems to indicate at the end of his book: "Die Auffassung der Geschichte im Ganzen führt über die Geschichte hinaus" [The apprehension of history as a whole leads beyond history] (262).

[38] One thing seems certain: our solar system has already lived half its life span. The planet Earth is a mortal macro-organism. Our boundaries are not only spatial, but temporal as well. From this perspective, we are all prisoners. But this is not our question here.

[39] To lump Genghis Khan and the Mongol invasion of Europe together with the French Revolution and the Chinese Cultural Revolution, to toss the Punic Wars into the same sack with the last two world wars—because all are but microscopic moments of a cosmic evolution toward a noosphere—may help us to discern a general direction of the universe, but it tends to blur the equally necessary distinction between the exploits of a Hannibal and those of a Hitler.

The Crossing of the Human Ways:
A Threefold Typology

The diachronical character of the contemporary scene, together with a proper cross-cultural methodology, makes possible our enterprise here. We do not need to travel back thousands of years in order to find a nonhistorical experience of reality. It may suffice to travel perhaps some thousands of miles at most, but for many, only some few yards beyond their habitats. We live in a diachronical world. We are the contemporaries of Paleolithic peoples, Confucian sages, Vedantic *paṇḍits*, Renaissance women, and electronic engineers. As to the cross-cultural sensitivities aroused here, many of the people aware of this problematic today are equally conscious that a single culture or a single way of thinking simply cannot do justice to the contemporary human situation. If we succeed in entering into nonhistorical human consciousness and also in detecting glimpses of the transhistorical, we may be able to describe in an intelligible manner the breakdown of the historical myth that we perceive to be occurring in our midst.

I should repeat that this threefold typology does not represent three watertight, isolated compartments. In each human being and in each culture there lie more or less dormant the other two less predominant types. This, among other factors, is what makes for the irreducibility of human life, even on a theoretical level, to purely logical or rational parameters. In an over-condensed way, I may describe this typology as follows:

When we say and believe, "The origins of humankind and/or of the Earth are in a heterogeneous principle—that is, in a transcendent point that has no direct connection with our present situation, although it explains it—this principle has to be the most important factor of reality, but we cannot properly know it or direct it. We can at most entreat it. God is one name for such a principle, but by whatever name, there it is: sovereign, inscrutable, and transcendent. Although ever-present, this principle was at the origin of everything, the very source. The past then must be the most important category. Thus tradition is paramount. We have to find our way across this middle world, the *antarikṣa*..."; when we respond positively to such a set of ideas, then we are in a nonhistorical frame of mind. The criterion of truth is what was and ever shall be. Authority is spontaneously recognized as an essential element in the order of reality. Memory is power.

When we say and believe, "In the Beginning was a specific Act of the God, an actually spoken Word of the Divine, a Birth of the God or the Hero—or the Foundation of the City, the Constitution, the Event, the dateable Big Bang—this Beginning is important, it is indeed the beginning, but we must continue it, we must take life into our own hands and construct the future. Destiny does not depend on the whims of the Gods but on us, our behavior, and our thoughts as well. The future is the relevant category. Thus freedom is paramount; we are marching toward an eschatology which is the fruit of our deeds . . ."; when we respond positively to such a set of ideas, then we are in a historical world. The criterion of truth is evidence of the fact, and fact is something that strikes our mind and compels it because of its unmistakable and undeniable spatiotemporal parameters. Creativity is spontaneously recognized as an essential element in the order of reality. To measure (distances to the Beginning and in-between and to the Goal) is to think. This measuring is knowledge, and brings power.

When we say and believe, "There was neither Principle nor Event at the Beginning; each moment is its own beginning and end; to discharge on the past the burden of the present or to postpone for the future what we cannot deal with now is the greatest temptation on Earth; the present is the most important factor of reality because only the present has full ontological weight, as it were; life is neither a second edition of a heavenly paradigm nor a project pro-jected into a more or less ideal future, neither a reminiscence nor a trial, nor a mission, nor capital that will yield interest; we have to pierce the crust of shallow temporality in order to find the core of it all, and thus happiness . . ."; when we respond positively to such a set of ideas, then we are in a transhistorical mentality. The criterion of truth is the personal experience about which there can be no doubt. Freedom is spontaneously recognized as the most essential element of reality. To have insight into, that is, to realize the nature of things, brings power.

We are dealing here with fundamental attitudes toward reality. From the platform of one attitude we are entitled to say that we do not understand the other one or that we do not agree with it, but this does not cancel out those other basic human experiences. And the fact that they are human makes them part and parcel of how Man has understood himself to be, and thus of what Man is. To put the same thing differently: cross-cultural studies do not deal only or even mainly with how "we" (with our categories and from our perspective) understand "others" but with how others have understood themselves in a way that we may also come to understand, or at least surmise—because the encounter with the other has not only enlarged our field of vision but also changed our own stance. It is certainly legitimate that from a certain point of view, for instance that of modern science, we try to understand the totality of the real and that we declare ourselves ready to change our own parameters, should the "object" of our investigation so require. Every worldview has an inbuilt and legitimate claim to truth and thus to universality. Nobody can from the outside dictate the flexibility of any mode of knowledge or way of life.[40] This is what makes dialogue possible and fruitful. But there are patterns of intelligibility, metaphysical options, basic attitudes, and/or fundamental human perspectives that seem to be mutually incompatible, sometimes incomprehensible or even wrong, and yet are nevertheless represented in the human panorama. This is what makes for the seriousness of pluralism, as we are still going to see.[41] It is not the object of science, in our example, which is not universal, but the scientific perspective. Science is one way of looking at and thus of being in the world, but not the only possible way indeed. We are dealing here with something more fundamental than different ways of thinking.[42] We are dealing with different possible ways of being human—all of them connected, however, in and with the *dia-logos*.[43]

Be this as it may, this set of human perceptions of reality, including the reality of Man, entitles us to cross the historical frontier and speak of a transhistorical human consciousness, already kairologically present in the prevalent historical consciousness of contemporary Western Man.

---

[40] How often a Roman Catholic is confronted with outsiders who tell him or her, "But you cannot speak this way as a Catholic!" for they have learned in the Baltimore Catechism what Catholics should believe and consider the Catholic tradition fixed once and for all. Similarly, "philosophers" charge "scientists" with having to stick to paradigms that men of science have long ago discarded. Or, for that matter, "scientists" tend to imagine that philosophers just do not have the tools to understand them. For the relations between science and philosophy, see my *Ontonomía de la Ciencia* (Madrid: Gredos, 1961).

[41] See also my study "The Myth of Pluralism—The Tower of Babel," *Cross Currents* 29, no. 2 (Summer 1979): 197–230. In Volume VI, Part 2 of this *Opera Omnia*.

[42] It would be interesting to relate together H. Nakamura's *Ways of Thinking of Eastern Peoples* (Honolulu: East-West Center, 1964), and M. Heidegger, *Was heisst Denken?* (Tübingen: Niemeyer, 1954).

[43] I have inserted this paragraph after the discussion of this paper at the Georgetown University celebration of the Centennial Symposium in honor of Teilhard de Chardin, in order to circumvent some possible misunderstandings.

Nonhistorical Consciousness

Nonhistorical consciousness informs the prevalent worldview and self-understanding of so-called prehistoric Man, from time immemorial up until the commonly accepted beginning of the historical period of humankind. This does not mean, however, that prehistoric Man belongs only to the chronological prehistoric past. Nonhistorical consciousness is a contemporary kairological reality, not only for the so-called primitive, but also for the modern cosmopolitan dweller. One of the reasons I propose to call the religiousness of these cultures *primordial* is that they represent something primordial in every human being. This nonhistorical time-awareness, which fosters a vision of life and thus of reality different from the historical vision, is one example.

The decisive break is the invention and spread of writing. That old Egyptian legend related by Plato of the king berating his fellow-God for having invented Script represents this mutation.[44] With the invention of Script, past events acquire a consistency of their

---

[44] Plato, *Phaedrus* 274–75. It may be worthwhile to reproduce the entire passage:

> SOCRATES: But there remains the question of propriety and impropriety in writing, that is to say the conditions which make it proper or improper. Isn't that so?
>
> PHAEDRUS: Yes.
>
> SOCRATES: Now do you know how we may best please God, in practice and theory, in this matter of words?
>
> PHAEDRUS: No indeed. Do you?
>
> SOCRATES: I can tell you the tradition that has come down from our forefathers, but they alone know the truth of it. However, if we could discover that for ourselves, should we still be concerned with the fancies of mankind?
>
> PHAEDRUS: What a ridiculous question! But tell me the tradition you speak of.
>
> SOCRATES: Very well. The story is that in the region of Naucratis in Egypt there dwelt one of the old gods of the country, the god to whom the bird called Ibis is sacred, his own name being Theuth. He it was that invented number and calculation, geometry and astronomy, not to speak of draughts and dice, and above all writing. Now the king of the whole country at that time was Thamus, who dwelt in the great city of Upper Egypt which the Greeks call Egyptian Thebes, while Thamus they call Ammon. To him came Theuth, and revealed his arts, saying that they ought to be passed on to the Egyptians in general. Thamus asked what was the use of them all, and when Theuth explained, he condemned what he thought the bad points and praised what he thought the good. On each art, we are told, Thamus had plenty of views both for and against; it would take too long to give them in detail. But when it came to writing Theuth said, "Here, o king, is a branch of learning that will make the people of Egypt wiser and improve their memories; my discovery provides a recipe for memory and wisdom." But the king answered and said, "O man full of arts, to one it is given to create the things of art, and to another to judge what measure of harm and of profit they have for those that shall employ them. And so it is that you, by reason of your tender regard for the writing that is your offspring, have declared the very opposite of its true effect. If men learn this, it will implant forgetfulness in their souls; they will cease to exercise memory because they rely on that which is written, calling things to remembrance no longer from within themselves, but by means of external marks. What you have discovered is a recipe not for memory, but for reminder. And it is no true wisdom that you offer your disciples, but only its semblance, for by telling them of many things without teaching them you will make them seem to know much, while for the most part they know nothing, and as men filled, not with wisdom, but with the conceit of wisdom, they will be a burden to their fellows.

Trans. R. Hackforth, *Plato: The Collected Dialogues*, ed. Edith Hamilton and Huntington Cairns (Princeton, NJ: Bollingen/Pantheon, 1961), 520.

own without the need of personal involvement; they may become (external) reminders without being (internal) memories. They are simply written down in some archives. From this moment forward, your life can be encoded not only in your memory and your flesh but in external devices (the writings), which can bear witness for or against you and vouch for events that are—because you have perhaps forgotten them—not entirely real to you. Past events acquire independent reality. They can be stored, frozen, so to speak, fossilized in special devices of clay, stone, leaves, or artificial materials. They do not need to be accumulated in Man's memory and to permeate the present. But they can be brought back to mind by the political leader or resurrected by the prophet, for they are still encoded in Man's brain and language. Above all, they can be projected into the future as the accumulated experience of past generations. We may recall that a Mediterranean city, Byblos, became famous for its parchment, and some Mediterranean religions have become even more famous for calling the "Bible" their cornerstone. Historical consciousness emerges, as it were, from a more generalized nonhistorical consciousness and gathers its power with the invention of human Script. With this, time acquires a certain independence in regard to Man. The human being will have to reconquer time and henceforward sets out in search of time lost or time to come.

Prehistorical Man, on the contrary, lives mainly in *space*, and is oriented especially to his particular "place" in the universe. Time is subsidiary to space. An autonomous (human) time is not of much import for his consciousness. Time is cosmic, or rather anthropocosmic, for the separation of the cosmic and the human is not (yet) made. In other words, time is natural, not cultural. The seasons of the Earth measure time, not the exploits of Man, as in historical eras.[45] The human beings are agriculturalists and/or hunters, settlers and/or nomads. Biological or vital functions, in the noblest but also most elementary sense of the word, occupy their minds and hearts: human attention is concentrated on birth, puberty, marriage, death, eating, playing, dreaming, and also, I would assume very importantly, on speaking. Work is done in order to eat, drink, and be protected by clothing and a house. But we must not forget that to eat, drink, sleep, mate, and so on are all *theocosmic* and not just "biological" acts. Work is done primarily for the living, for life to go on from the ancestors to the descendants, for the world to continue. But living means "to walk in Beauty," as the Navajo would say, to enjoy life, to be open to the beauty of nature, the joy of human intercourse on all levels, the ecstasy of self-discovery and the complex numinous relationships with supernatural and superhuman powers. Men go to war to rescue a woman, to wreak vengeance, to obtain better hunting or plowing grounds, and perhaps also to humiliate their neighbors, or eventually even to conquer an empty space . . . but they do not march into the *future*. What would it mean to them? That is left to the Alexanders, Akbars, and Napoleons of the historical period.

The world of prehistorical Man, his environment (*circunstantia, Umwelt*) is the *theocosmos*: the divinized universe. It is not a "world of Men," but neither is it the "world of Gods" as a separate and superior realm hovering over the human. Man shares the world with the Gods. He still drinks *Soma* with the Gods.[46] The Gods do not yet form a clan of their own, as they will

---

[45] See the classic study by M. P. Nilsson, *Primitive Time-Reckoning: A Study in the Origins and First Development of the Art of Counting Time among the Primitive and Early Culture Peoples* (Lund: C. W. K. Gleerup, 1920), for examples, data, and arguments.

[46] See *RV* X.135.1; although, significantly, it is a hymn describing the ancestors in the realm of Yama.

do when history is about to begin. It is the world of history that views the prehistorical world as "full of Gods."[47] This is a vision from the outside. In the nonhistorical consciousness, it is the world itself that is divinized, or rather divine. The divine permeates the cosmos. The forces of Nature are all divine. Nature is "supernatural," so to speak. Or rather, Nature is that which is being "natured," born—from or of the divine. Prehistorical Man's home, his background, is a cosmotheological one. *Harmony* is the supreme principle—which does not mean that it has been achieved. The meaning of life consists both in entering into harmony with nature and in enhancing it.[48]

Prehistorical Man certainly has clear ideas of past, present, and future. The mother may worry about her children or the grandfather about his crops, as do historical human beings. But their time is not, I submit, historical; that is, it is not centered on Man as an accumulation of the past with which to build "historical reality." What is not assimilated or not desired is discarded.[49] Time is not there to build a society or to create a better future. You are not the owner but the "enjoyer" of your time. Time is the day or the night. Time is an old Man or a God, a gift of the past. It is the rhythm of Nature, not the construct of culture. One tribe may want to overpower another, to have better or larger pastures, but the idea of an Empire, a Kingdom, a Church, a collective enterprise different from what Nature does or separated from the rhythms of the cosmos, makes no sense to prehistorical Man.[50] The meaning of life does not consist in building a Great Society on Earth, a powerful organization, but rather in enjoying life in the best possible way.[51] Prehistorical

---

[47] See the famous pre-Socratic sentence attributed by Aristotle to Thales (*De Anima* I.5 [411a7–8], and already reported by Plato (*Laws* X [899b]): "Of all the planets, of the moon, of years and months and all seasons, what other story shall we have to tell than just this same, that since soul, or souls, and those souls good with perfect goodness, have proved to be the causes of all, these souls we hold to be gods, whether they direct the universe by inhabiting bodies, like animated beings, or whatever the manner of their action? Will any man who shares this belief bear to hear it said that all things are not 'full of gods'?" Trans. A. E. Taylor, *Plato, The Collected Dialogues,* op. cit., 1455. See also Aristotle's *Metaphysics* I.3 (938b20–27) and Augustine's *De Civitate Dei* VII.6 (MPL 41:199) on Varro's dictum of the world's elements "full of souls."

[48] An important aspect that would throw light on a characterization of this first mode of consciousness would be a study on human attitudes toward sex. See E. Aguilar, *Vers una sexologia de la religió* (Barcelona: Edicions 62, 1982), where the scattered data on Paleolithic Man are gathered with a view to determining both our present deepest instincts and the basic experience of prehistoric Man.

[49] *Non numero horas nisi serenas* [I do not reckon but the sunny hours], says an ancient sundial.

[50] See the significant passage of Hegel: "Was wir eigentlich unter Afrika verstehen, das is das Geschichtlose und Unaufgeschlossene, das noch ganz im natürlichen Geiste befangen ist, und das hier bloss an der Schwelle der Weltgeschichte vorgeführt werden musste" [What we properly understand by Africa, is the unhistorical, undeveloped spirit, still involved in the conditions of mere nature, and which had to be presented here only as on the threshold of world history]. *Die Vernunft in der Geschichte* (*Reason in History*), J. Hoffmeister, ed. *Philosophische Bibliothek*, 171, 5th ed., 1955, p. 234. In Ritter, ed., *Historisches Worterbuch der Philosophie* (*Historical Dictionary of Philosophy*), op. cit., vol. 3, 1974, s.v. "Geschichtslosigkeit," where J. Burckhardt's opinion is also given: The barbarism of the "barbarian" is precisely this "Geschichtlosigkeit" (lack of any sense of history).

[51] The bibliography is already becoming immense. See the recent studies: F. Gillies, "The Bantu Concept of Time," *Religion* 10 (Spring 1980): 16–30; J. Murungi, "Toward an African Conception of Time," *IPU* 20, no. 4 (December 1980): 407–16 (on Ameru time-reckoning); A. Kagame, "The Empirical Apperception of Time and the Conception of History in Bantu Thought," in UNESCO, *Cultures and Time* (Paris: UNESCO, 1976), 89–116.

Man cannot believe, for instance, that a powerful State could enhance the value of the lives of its individuals.[52]

Eschatology coincides with the end of one's own life.[53] You begin every day anew. Each day has enough of its own weight.[54]

This nonhistorical consciousness could also be called the *prescriptural mentality*. It is difficult for a historical mentality to imagine life without Scripture. Nonhistorical consciousness entrusts everything to memory—not to reminders. The past is present only insofar as memory and the patterns of daily life preserve it. The presence of the past is in the living of it, in every detail of life. The legends are in the telling, just as there is no song until it is sung. Accumulation of knowledge is possible only to the extent to which one can digest it. Food can be gathered in silos, but knowledge has to be actualized, and memory is the only treasure house. Tradition is the very life of the present. The sense of life does not lie in what I still have to live, but in what I have already lived, and especially in what I am living. Death is not frightening. In a sense, death does not lie in front of me but just behind me.[55] When I was born, I overcame death, and the more I live the more I am distancing myself from my (deadly) non-being before the time I was.[56] I can put my life at stake at any moment. It is not that I am playing with death. I am playing with life.[57] I do not need to capitalize on life. Life is not just the continuation of a passive state of being, not just the inertia of a static situation, but a constant struggle, the active participation in the cycles of Nature in which life does not die.[58] The bearer of life passes it on and thus he does not pass away, because the bearer is just what he carries. A quenched torch is not a torch; the torch is the living flame.

---

[52] Hegel had already seen that "das Historische" begins where "die Zeit des Heroentums," that is, the age of the culture hero, ends. *Werke*, ed. H. Glockner, 14:256ff. (in Ritter, op. cit.).

[53] It is significant that the most obvious meaning of the Second Coming, as described in the New Testament, and the resurrection of the flesh, as maintained by the dogma of the church, namely that it all happens in a nonhistorical context, has been almost overlooked in Christian exegesis. To put it quickly: individual Final Judgment and humanity's Last Judgment, for the individual, coalesce. The Second Coming arrives at the death of each human being. The resurrection is with our identical body of flesh and bones, that is, now. See R. Panikkar, "La Eucaristía y la Resurrección de la Carne" (1952), reprinted in *Humanismo y Cruz* (Madrid: Rialp, 1963), 335–52. In Volume III, Part 1 of this *Opera Omnia*.

[54] Mt 6:34.

[55] See R. Panikkar, "The Time of Death, the Death of Time. An Indian Reflection," in *Meletē Thanatou / La réflexion sur la mort*, Ecole Libre de Philosophie "Plethon," Second Symposium International de Philosophie (Athens, 1977), 102–21.

[56] Cf., for instance, the typical Buddhist mentality, where Long-ch'en Rab-jampa said in the fourteenth century, "The suffering of birth is more fearsome than that of death." *Dharmacatur-ratnamāla* 1, trans. A. Berzin, *The Four-Themed Precious Garland* (Dharamsala: Library of Tibetan Works and Archives, 1979), 19.

[57] Many of the hunters' customs that have prevailed until our times among the military and which books of history record as gladiators, soldiers' bravery, duels, etc., could be adduced as examples. The most recent one could be gathered from the—on the other hand frightening remarks—of the president of the United States of America, senators, and congressional representatives, when two Libyan planes were shot down over the coast of Libya on August 19, 1981. Just an exercise to prove that "America has the muscle to back up its words" (Ronald Reagan, *Santa Barbara News-Press*, August 21, 1981, 1). You look at the present and the past, but not at the future. The difference, however, with modern weapons in a volatile world cannot be overestimated.

[58] See *CU* VI.11.3.

It is significant to reflect on the fact that in monetary terms, while prehistorical Man uses roughly 90 percent of his income for food, the citizen of the so-called (historically) developed countries spends only 10 percent. But food for "natural" Man is not just swallowing proteins or preserving health. Food is dynamic communion with the entire universe, food is sharing in the cosmic metabolism, it is the symbol of life, the intercourse with all that there is, the greatest bond among humans and equally the greatest sign of fellowship.[59] The vital needs of historical Man lie elsewhere.[60]

If Joy is the main value for nonhistorical consciousness and Joy is real in the present, Hope is the basic value of historical Man, and Hope is tested in controlling and dominating the future. You cannot enjoy three square meals a day, but you can very well produce and accumulate unlimited foodstuffs for use as future political and military weapons.

But prehistorical Man is haunted by the past. If he forgets it, then only those who can remember have the knowledge and the power. Tradition is powerful because it transmits the past. The forgotten past becomes what later is called the mythical past. Cult makes it present. Liturgical time is not historical: the past irrupts into the present; the present transforms the future. Since at least the Upper Paleolithic period (around 35,000 BCE) we find the same custom of burial, which is Man's first known way of reacting to time.[61]

We have been saying "prehistorical Man" as a concession to historical consciousness and in order to stress the kairological dynamism as seen from a historical perspective. For this reason, I have called this first moment "nonhistorical consciousness." If, in fact, a certain type of this consciousness is represented by the so-called prehistoric peoples, another type of the same consciousness has existed in far more recent cultures, like most of the major traditions of Asia. The time-awareness there is certainly nonhistorical, and it would be improper to suggest that these cultures must now catch the last wagon of historical consciousness, as we shall have opportunity to explain. One of the most powerful factors in the world today is the myth of history, which renders plausible the effort to spread the Western-originated technological worldview around the world under the pretext of its universality.[62]

But before we proceed further, we still have to characterize the other two moments.

---

[59] Cf., for example, the Vedic texts on food, which although already of a late period still reflect this mentality, in R. Panikkar, *The Vedic Experience* (Los Angeles/Berkeley: University of California Press, 1977), 224–37. Volume IV, Part 1 of this *Opera Omnia*.

[60] "You North Americans—some business executive was complaining—eat in between the working hours; we South Americans just work between the hours of eating!"

[61] Cf., for data and elaboration, S. G. F. Brandon, *History, Time and Deity* (Manchester: Manchester University Press, 1965). Brandon's overall thesis "is that religion has stemmed from man's consciousness of Time, and that his reaction to Time has found a variety of expressions including the deification of Time." See "The Deification of Time," *Studium Generale* 23 (1970): 485–97.

[62] From this viewpoint, both the so-called First and Second Worlds, the liberal capitalist and the socialist capitalist ideologies, are just two variations on the same historical myth. For an understanding of the Second World as "those (few) countries which, at somewhat different times but far ahead of the rest, were able to take advantage of the techniques while escaping the mental, political or economic control of the First World," see D. V. Coutinho, *Cross Currents* 18 (Fall 1968). Yet our present-day situation shows that what might have been a difference at the beginning has been eroded if not destroyed by the very power of technology (from the First World).

Historical Consciousness

In the second moment, the previous kairological phase is not discarded but it is progressively superseded, or at least counterbalanced.[63] This new period, the period of Script, also marks the passage from *agri*culture to *civil*ization, that is, from the village to the city. The village, like the fields and Nature, does not have that specific time that we today call human. City time is not so much cosmic as it is historical. It does not move so much with the sun as with the clock.[64]

Historical time is not just human time, although historical Man tends to identify them. This identification gives birth to the myth of history. Historical time is that particular (human) time-consciousness that believes in the autonomy of the "human" race vis-à-vis the time of terrestrial and supraterrestrial entities. And this historical time, called "human" time, is mainly understood as the thrust toward the *future*—in which the fullness of existence or definitive welfare, be this of the individual, the tribe, the nation, or all humankind, will be achieved. This human time implies the conviction that we are in bondage, not yet completed, and for that reason we must struggle against Nature, against fate, against the Earth or matter. It is a struggle for freedom against anything supposedly antagonistic to Man. Our destiny is (in) the Future.

While nonhistorical time-consciousness may find Man's fullness in each temporal moment, historical time is indefinite and needs to be "rescued" (redeemed[65]) in eternity or in a qualitatively different future, if Man is to be saved from the Sisyphean despair of never achieving anything or reaching any goal. Historical Man, unlike prehistorical Man, who stands in greater or lesser harmony with Nature, believes himself to be in dialectical opposition to Nature. The civilized Man is the nonnatural (cultural) human being.[66] Both the belief in a future eternity and the belief in an eternal future belong to the same need that historical consciousness feels, namely, to transcend temporality.

Here transcendence is the main category. You have to transcend time.[67] You have always to go beyond and ahead.[68] You have to travel and conquer space. You have to set sail for the Indies, even if you get no farther than the Americas. You have to fly to the moon and explore beyond the limits of your power, even if it explodes in your hands (or over the heads of the yellow Japanese), even if genetic manipulation will make you a puppet in your brave new world. You cannot stop.

---

[63] It should be clear that I do not subscribe to the simplistic evolutionary theory still prevalent today in many history and history of religions books, which regards "prehistoric Man" as an undifferentiated and unevolved primitive whom "we" have now left completely behind us. . . . The process is much more complex, and we find today not only in the so infuriatingly called underdeveloped countries, but also (fortunately) in each of us, strong traces of primordial Man.

[64] "Abstract time became the new medium of existence," says L. Mumford in his chapter "The Monastery and the Clock," where he defends the thesis that "the application of quantitative methods of thought to the study of nature had its first manifestation in the regular measurement of time." With the clock, "Eternity ceased gradually to serve as the measure and focus of human actions" (*Technics and Civilization* (1934; New York: Harcourt, Brace and World, 1963), 12–18.

[65] See Eph 5:16.

[66] See the popular distinctions between Nature/Culture, World/Person, Nature/Grace (Supernature), Man/Animals, Spirit (Mind)/Matter, etc.

[67] Ut ergo tu sis, transcende tempus [In order to be, transcend time], says the first European, the African Augustine, *Tractates on the Gospel of John* 38, n. 10.

[68] *Plus ultra* [further beyond] was the motto of Charles V of Europe.

Immanence, on the other hand, is the main category of nonhistorical consciousness. We should draw attention here to the double meaning of the word *immanence*.[69] It is significant that from the perspective of historical consciousness the concept of immanence has been interpreted as a sort of negative transcendence; otherwise immanence, for a historical mentality, would be synonymous with identity.[70] But immanence can also be understood in a nonhistorical way, and in this case it means neither negative transcendence nor identity. That the divine Spirit, to give an example, is immanent in us does not mean that God dwells in us in such an interior way that we are transcendent, so to speak, with respect to the Spirit—who would then be demoted to the status of an inner guest. Nor does it mean that there is a sort of monistic identity between the "two" (God and the soul). It means (although the word *meaning* may not be appropriate here) that we may be able to distinguish—but not separate—them, that they are neither one nor two, without for that matter saying that the distinction is only an epistemological one. The mystics, in the historical world, indeed have such an experience. But one does not need to be a mystic at all in order to have such a "vision" of things.

Nonhistorical consciousness is geared to immanence, we said, as historical Man is to transcendence. For this nonhistorical consciousness to be happy, to realize its own full humanity, there is no need to go out and conquer the moon or another space or (in a male-dominated society) another woman, just for the sake of having another experience. Instead one tries to discover what one is and what one has, one prefers to be spectator rather than actor, one will perhaps kill one's woman before just trying another one—or if she has gone off with another male.[71]

Village life has, in this sense, no "historical" future.[72] Even today, if you want to have a career, you go to the city.[73] Village time has its seasons, its past and future; the year is its unit; but the presiding value is the present as conditioned by the past. And for the present, for the encounter with a friend, the celebration of a feast, a marriage, or for going to war, village Man may easily endanger and even sell his entire future.[74] The fight against the dowry system in India, for instance, is bound to fail (like Western-style family planning) if the problem is not

---

[69] See R. Panikkar, *The Trinity and the Religious Experience of Man* (Maryknoll, NY: Orbis Books, 1973), 29ff.; 33ff.; 59ff.. In Volume VIII of this *Opera Omnia*.

[70] See R. Panikkar, *Le mystère du culte dans l'hindouisme et le Christianisme* (Paris: Cerf, 1970), 29–41. This is the reason why the historical West has so often considered as pantheism and monism the trend toward immanence of many Eastern worldviews. In Volume VII of this *Opera Omnia*.

[71] The example of the male-female relationship should be taken *cum grano salis* and understood in this context without extrapolation. What is suggested here is that sexuality can also be envisaged under the attitude of transcendence and that of immanence. Androgyny and the interiorization of the *śakti* could be examples of the latter.

[72] Cf., for instance, J. S. Mbiti, "The African Conception of Time," *Africa* 8 (1967), and other writings of the same author, who maintains that African traditions have "virtually no concept of the future," although his view is contested by F. Gillies, art. cit.

[73] As the saying goes, "In the village, young man, you have no future. You'd better take a job in the city."

[74] "Are you going to live in debt for the rest of your life? Don't you realize that this momentary celebration of just a few days will represent a mortgage on your future?" says the Westernized "well-to-do" Man to whom the villager has gone to ask for a loan for the marriage of his daughter. The villager understands so little of this discourse that he is hardly capable of replying, "But don't you understand that life is made of such moments? Don't you realize that life is only worth living if we celebrate it by giving it away? Are you not capable of eating time, assimilating it and making it your own, so that you don't have to slip on it as if it were something external to you?"

tackled at this deep anthropological level.[75] It may be worth noting that the alleged incapacity, in the eyes of so many "social workers," of so-called undeveloped peoples to accept and adopt the "benefits" of modernity may simply be (human) nature's reaction to external onslaughts. The modernized technocrats call it the passive resistance of the primitive mentality, impervious to change and suspicious of technical improvements—all "for their own benefit," of course. This instinctive resistance of the "natives" is very often their defense mechanism for self-identity and survival. At any rate, the greatest rupture introduced by modern technology in nontechnological cultures is precisely the breakdown of their autochthonous rhythms by the introduction of a foreign time-consciousness.[76]

It may spare us long pages of description to recall a familiar story from the biblical tradition and to become aware of the biased sympathy of that tradition for its hero, considering his dubious, lying character.[77] Esau was a prehistorical Man; Jacob had historical consciousness. The former was unconcerned about the future and found in the exquisite taste of a potful of lentils the fulfillment of the present, and thus of life.[78] Esau cared nothing for his historical destiny. Instead, he believed in the symbolism of eating.[79] Jacob was concerned with what has been the dominant feature of Semitic civilization: the coming of the Kingdom—variously called promised land, nation, church, heaven, paradise, justice, liberation, or whatever. Jacob understood the meaning of his grandfather's move out of the city of Ur and into the future. . . . He was eager to be the heir. Esau did not care about history, about historical vocation, historical destiny, about a task to be performed by the power of his or God's will outside and beyond the actual reach of his person. His sense of transcendence was not temporal. The Indian peasant who sells off his entire future for the dowry of his daughter, or the African family that consumes all its reserves for the great annual celebration, are on the side of Esau. Christ irritated the children of Jacob when he told them to let the day take care of itself and not to worry about the morrow.[80] Historical Man has to think about the future and has to live toward it. Prehistorical Man has no historical role to play or function to perform. His life is lived in the present, although often haunted by the past. He sings and lives like *la cigale*, while

---

[75] And at this level, of course, the problem presents itself in a different light.

[76] This begins to be felt even by modern Westerners in their own lives. The proliferation of technological means for overcoming the limitations of space and time is now reverting and producing precisely the contrary effect. Cf., as an example, J. P. Dupuy, "L'encombrement de l'espace et celui du temps" [The congestion of space and time), *Esprit* 10 (October 1980): 68–80. Also especially noteworthy is Ivan Illich's essay "Energy and Equity" (London: Calder & Boyars, 1974), reprinted in Illich, *Toward a History of Needs* (New York: Bantam, 1980), 131–72.

[77] See Gen 27:1ff. Would it be fair to say that historical cities, kingdoms, and countries have mostly been founded on violence, blood, and deceit? History only leaves a place for the victors. *Vae victis!*

[78] It is remarkable how Esau has been downgraded as a glutton eager only to fill a biological need—as if Brahman were not food and the Eucharist an eating, as if communion with Nature were to the shame of "civilized" Man, as if, again, it is only the future that counts. The basic distinction emphasized by J. Maritain and which—through O. Lacombe, L. Gaudet, R.C. Zaehner, and others—has often been blurred in the history of religions, between immanent nature-mysticism (natural) and transcendent encounter with the living God (supernatural), may also have the same origin in this historical interpretation of reality, which is then superimposed on nonhistorical worldviews.

[79] Gen 25:29–32. Cf., by way of example, the Vedic texts on food in R. Panikkar, *The Vedic Experience*, op. cit., 224–37: Food is Brahman! See also G. Deleury, *Le modèle indou* (Paris: Hachette, 1978), the chapter on "Les manières de table," 21–40.

[80] See Mt 6:34, etc.

historical Man works and hoards treasures like *la fourmi* of La Fontaine's fable. Again, any bank official in the villages of India or elsewhere will tell you how these "primitive" people have no idea of savings and wring his hands over how difficult it is to "educate" them into the pan-economic ideology. Now they are told that to look after their old age they will need not grandchildren but money—inflation notwithstanding. Historical time is under the spell of the future and the guidance of reason. What Esau did was not reasonable, nor was it what Christ preached.

People and peoples are set whirling into motion; their movement accelerates not because they want to overcome space or be victorious over it, as nomadic tribes or prehistorical Man might do, but because they want to conquer *time*, as well as to demonstrate their excellence and superiority over others (a superhuman role). Wars are waged to make the victors great and their children powerful. Man works under the mirage of a historical future to be achieved: a great empire to be built, a better future to be conquered, an education for the children, to make ends meet, and so on.[81] The entire modern economic system is based on *credit*, that is, the mortgage of the future.[82]

This sense of purposefulness and ambition are the essence of modern education. Modern science means the ability to foresee the future, so that you may control where the ball is going to fall, or predict when the eclipse is going to occur, or ensure your longevity. We need only substitute atoms, bombs, chromosomes, and epidemics for balls and upheavals, inflations, crystallizations, amalgams, and synthetic products for eclipses, and we have spanned six thousand years of human "science"—the knowledge and control of those parameters expressible in terms of space and time.[83] Bear in mind that what we call science, understood as the attempt to control empirical causality, began as magic.[84] The paramount question here is to know *how* things will happen in space and time—because then you can *control* them.[85] Space and time become the paradigms of reality. Something is real for us when we can locate it on the grid of spatiotemporal Cartesian coordinates. From here we immediately deduce that something is real when it is a fact, and when the "fact" belongs to the past, it has to be a historical fact. Jesus is considered to be real if he is a historical figure—whereas Kṛṣṇa, for the nonhistorical Hindū mentality, would lose his reality if he were to be described as only a historical personality.

Historical consciousness did not reach its maturity until the birth of modern Western science, although its origins are much more ancient, as any history of civilization or science will tell us.[86] Both forms of consciousness are intermingled. One does not have to accept Kant's conception of time and space as forms a priori to our sensibility to realize that cultures

---

[81] See R. Panikkar, "The Mirage of the Future," *Teilhard Review* (London) 8, no. 2 (June 1973): 42–45.

[82] If time—this linear time—were to stop, the whole system would collapse. The "most powerful nation in the world" has, of course, the highest budget deficit.

[83] See I. Barbour, *Issues in Science and Religion* (New York: Harper & Row, 1966).

[84] See the keen observation by Freud in his essay "Der Mann Moses und die monotheistiche Religion"[Moses and monotheism]: "In Grunde ruth ja alle Magie, die Vorläuterin unserer technik, auf dieser Voraussetzuung (dem Glauben an die 'Allsnacht der Gedanken')" [All magic, the predecessor of science, is basically founded on these premises (faith in the "omnipotence of thought")]. In *Gesammelte werke*, vol. 16 (Stuttgart: Fischer, 1959 [3rd ed. 1968]), 221.

[85] See Nietzsche's saying in *Thus Spake Zarathustra*: "Wherever I found the living, there I found the will to power," as quoted by R. May, *Power and Violence* (New York: W. W. Norton, 1972), 19, trying to show that "power is essential for all living things."

[86] See the monumental work of P. Duhem, *Le système du monde* (Paris: A. Hermann, 1913–1917).

and civilizations have not always experienced the two of them as intrinsically connected, first of all, and then not always in the same manner.

The world of historical Man, his environment (*circunstancia, Umwelt*) is the *anthropocosmos*, the human world, the universe of Man. Historical Man is not inserted in the evolution of the cosmos; his destiny has little to do with the fate of the stars, the phases of the moon, the seasons, or the rivers.[87] He lives in what he believes to be a superior world, the human one; cold and heat, day and night, rain and drought have been overcome. He is not dependent on the seasons, and as little as possible on the climate. The seasonal feasts of the Catholic Church, to take an example from a relatively traditional institution, have practically disappeared.[88] Nature has been tamed and subjugated. It has been demythicized; there is nothing mysterious about it. Its secrets have been unraveled and its power channeled into megawattage and megatonnage of all sorts. Historical consciousness has overcome the fear of Nature. The meaning of life is not to be found in the cosmic cycle but in the human one, in society, which is a human creation. *Justice* is the supreme principle—which does not mean that it has been achieved. Nor has historical consciousness gained all the hearts and minds of our contemporaries. Prehistorical attitudes and reactions are still powerful.

By the same token, the world of historical Man is not the world of the spirits. Angels, *apsaras*, devils, dwarves, elves, *devatās*, sirens, goblins, seraphim, *bhūtas*, and the like have all been, if not completely done away with, rendered impotent and subservient to human reason. In any event, these ghosts have no history, and historical Man's life no longer unfolds on such a stage—despite occasional outbursts of the ghostly, irrational unconscious.[89] The only scene is the historical arena. With the DDT of his reason, Man has allegedly rendered all these "forces" innocuous. If at all, they are energies to be studied by psychoanalysts, psychiatrists, parapsychologists (if need be), physicists, and so forth. Historical life is a display of Man's possibilities before his fellow humans. Historical Man stands alone in the world theater—without Gods or other beings, living or inanimate. If some still accept God, he is transcendent, impassive, perhaps good for another life, but certainly not about to meddle in human affairs. God has left the world to the strivings of Men.[90]

If the discovery of Script could be said to have been the decisive break between prehistorical and historical consciousness, the corresponding event here—which opens up the posthistorical period—is the discovery or invention of the internal self-destructive power of the atom. So powerful is its nature that it has ceased to be what it was purported

---

[87] "Neque enim propter stellas homo, sed stellae propter hominem factae sunt" [Man was not made for the sake of the stars; rather, the stars were made for the sake of man], says Gregory the Great, reflecting the "superiority complex" of the emerging Western Christian consciousness. This attitude is comprehensible as a reaction against the tyranny of the *stoikeia tou kosmou*, the elements of the world, which characterizes the first Christian centuries of European civilization. See Panikkar, *Humanismo y Cruz,* 123ff.

[88] Quatember days are forgotten; the night of St. John the Baptist remains popular only in some corners of southern Europe and Quebec; the cosmological meaning of Christmas and the Epiphany have almost faded away; the rogation triduum before Ascension has been practically abolished; the feasts of the Guardian Angels and of the three great Archangels have been artificially heaped together. Processions for rain, blessings for a good harvest and for domestic animals have remained as folklore remnants in but a few "undeveloped" countrysides.

[89] More than 25 percent of all hospital beds in the United States are in psychiatric wards, and many mental patients roam the streets.

[90] See Eccl 3:11.

to be: *akṣaram*, indestructible. It has ceased to be *atomos*, indivisible, ultimately simple, and in a certain sense, everlasting. The splitting of the *atomos* has also exploded historical consciousness.[91]

We are not yet fully aware of the anthropological (and not only political and sociological) consequences of this fact. The change is qualitative, not only in weaponry and technology, not only in the nature of war and the mechanism of the economy, but also in the newly emerging self-understanding of Man. When Becquerel less than a century ago (1896) proved that the atom was destructible and thus not immutable, he shook the belief of millennia of civilization: that the world is made of some permanent elements, whether they are called elements, ideas, or principles. At any rate, the atom stood for the consistency of things held to be permanent and thus reliable. The atom corresponded to the old idea of substance. If nothing "sub-stands" anything, historical consciousness is at a loss. There is no platform, no beginning from which anything can unfold and upon which can be accumulated being, experiences, energies, or whatever. Modern physical science knows better, but old beliefs die hard. At least elementary particles and their interaction with energy seemed immutable. Now this also is put in question.[92] Nothing seems to escape the corrosive passing of time. Or perhaps time itself is a constituent of a more embracing reality.[93]

This change may well represent the end of the Western period of humankind. There is no doubt that the acme of historical consciousness is tied not only to the Judeo-Christian-Islamic tradition but also to Western dominance of the entire planet, even if the name for such dominance is science and technology. The grandeur of the idealistic view of history, of a Schelling calling history "the eternal poem of the divine Reason,"[94] or Hegel's identification of history with reason,[95] or Marx's equation of history and

---

[91] This idea of the importance of the splitting of the atom has often been expressed, but most of the time in connection with the first explosion of an atomic weapon on human "targets": "This atomic bomb is the Second Coming in wrath," said Winston Churchill the day after the explosion. "If I were asked to name the most important date in the history of the human race, I would answer without hesitation, August 6, 1945" (Arthur Koestler). "The explosion of the first atomic bomb has become a para-historical phenomenon. It is not a memory, it is a perpetual experience, outside history. . . . It has no relation to time. It belongs to motionless eternity" (Pedro Arrupe). (Emphasis mine and quotations from J. Garrison, *The Plutonium Culture* [New York: Continuum, 1981]).

[92] See S. Wienberg, "The Decay of the Proton," *Scientific American,* June 1981, 64–75. The popularized subtitle says, "The proton is known to have a lifetime at least 10,100 times the age of the universe, but theory indicates that it may not live forever. If it is not immortal, all ordinary matter will ultimately disintegrate."

[93] This is, in fact, the hypothesis of this essay.

[94] "Nichts, das heiliger ware als die Geschichte, dieser grosse Spiegel des Weltgeistes, dieses ewige Gedicht des göttlichen Verstandes" [Nothing is more sacred than history, this great mirror of the spirit of the world, this eternal poem of divine understanding], *Werke,* op. cit., 5:289, 306, 309 (in G. Scholtz's entry "Geschichte" in Ritter's *Wörterbuch* 3:364).

[95] "Ich will über den vorläufigen Begriff der Philosophie der Weltgeschichte" [I would like to talk about the preliminary concept of philosophy in world history]. So begins Hegel's lecture on *Die Vernunft in der Geschichte.* "Zunächst dies bemerken, dass, wie ich gesagt habe, man in erster Linie der Philosophie den Vorwurf macht, das sie mit Gendanken an die Geschichte gehe und diese nach Gedanken betrachte. Der einzige Gedanke, den sie mitbringt, ist aber der einfache Gedanke der Vernunft, dass die Vernunft die Welt beherrscht, dass es also auch in der Weltgeschichte vernünftig zugegangen ist" [I would like first of all to observe that, as I have said, philosophy is primarily reproached for treating history with thought and considering it on the basis of thought. The sole thought which philosophy brings to the treatment of history is the simple concept of *Reason*; that Reason is the law of the world and that, there-

science,[96] or even more recent characterizations of Man as history:[97] all this comes to an end.[98]

The Crisis of History

As long as several historical realms and empires of all sorts were on the planet, Men could go on believing that the cruelties and inconsistencies of one system could be corrected by another, and that, at least theoretically, historical existence was the destiny of the human being. To be sure, many empires supposed they had conquered, dominated, or at least influenced the entire human race, but we know that until now not a single historical regime has pervaded the four corners of the world. Nor have we yet come to such a pass, and this gives us some small respite.[99] But science and technology are on the brink of penetrating everywhere, and the pan-economic ideology is more and more becoming the only system of "communication." Moreover, the world situation is dominated by the politics and policies of the two so-called superpowers and their respective (more or less reluctant or "nonaligned") satellites. We are fast heading toward one single System, despite the dialectical divergences of the protagonists on the world scene. It is this situation that leads ever more people to wonder whether such an impasse can really be resolved simply by emigrating from a socialist country to a capitalist one, by improving the System, or by transcending history altogether. This is what I must perforce call not *a* historical crisis à la Toynbee, but *the* crisis of history, that is, the crisis of historical consciousness as the underlying common and prevalent self-understanding of Modern Western Man and his cultural satellites.

Of course it is quite obvious that a numerical majority of the peoples of the Earth do not (yet?) live within these parameters. Nonetheless, their lives are increasingly affected by the historical power. Let us try to catch a glimpse of the situation.

First of all, we have to distinguish three final stages: the end of history, the end of time, and the end of Man. Before the secular spirit made its inroads into the Western mind, the majority of the world believed in the end of Man. Even if there may be a second cosmic cycle, this Man, as we know him, comes to an end—and generally by catastrophe. If in the Hindū and other Oriental traditions there are indefinite *kalpas* or cosmic periods, in the Abrahamic traditions there is only one. But the final act is a catastrophe. I am not speaking *directly* about this.[100]

---

fore, in world history, things have come about rationally]. Some pages later, he says "ihr Individuum [of history] ist der Weltgeist" [the subject (of history) is the World Spirit], and further on: "Das eine ist das Geschichtliche, dass der Grieche Anaxagoras zuerst gesagt habe, dass der Nus, der Verstand überhaubt oder die Vernunft, die Welt regiere" [The first is the historical fact of the Greek, Anaxagorus, who was the first to point out that Nous, understanding in general or Reason, rules the world].

[96] "Wir kennen nur eine einzige Wissenschaft, die Wissenschaft der Geschichte" [We know only one science, the science of history], K. Marx and F. Engels, *Werke* (Ostberlin, 1956–1968), 3:18 (in Ritter, *Wörterbuch,* op. cit., 3:374). Marx says something more than that all science is historical: "Die Geschichte ist unser Eins und Alles" [History is our One and All] (ibid.).

[97] See Heidegger's *Sein und Zeit,* op. cit., passim.

[98] See G. Scholtz's excellent article, "Geschichte," in Ritter's *Wörterbuch,* op. cit., for useful information and references.

[99] I am saying that not only are the Brazilian and African jungles the "lungs" of the Earth, but that the so-called underdeveloped peoples are all that prevents the System from exploding. Once these peoples are "developed," there will indeed be no exit.

[100] This is the strictly theological problem that in the Christian tradition is called the *parousia* or *Second Coming*. Historians of religion call it the Millennium, and modern theological thinking

I am also not speaking about the end of time, but about the end of history. I am precisely disentangling these two issues by questioning the assumption that Man is exclusively a historical being.[101] So I am not addressing myself to the traditional theological question, but presenting an anthropological problem. The myth of progress has practically collapsed.[102] The *historical* situation of the world today is nothing less than desperate.[103] There is really no issue of "development" for the famished masses who make up over half the world's population.[104] There is no consolation for the millions who have been mentally and physically handicapped by malnutrition.[105] It is no answer to proclaim that modern technology *can* overcome all these shortcomings when in fact it *cannot* alleviate the present predicament of those who are in the meantime victims of this situation, and it *does not* solve all the problems it could (utopically) resolve. What is worse, people have lost all hope that the lot of their children is somehow going to be better. And their common sense prevails. They are already in the third generation of those "evangelized" by the hope of a technical paradise, and they have reached the end of their tether.[106] This is the situation today: the heavenly Paradise has lost its grip on most people. A life of privation here, a vale of tears now, a bad karma in this life so that I may be rewarded later on with a heavenly Garden, a city of Brahman, a vision of God, or a more comfortable rebirth—all these are rapidly receding myths.[107] Election discourses and traditional religious preachings may still stir

---

distinguishes between the History of Salvation and human history.

[101] It is significant that J. Pieper's *Über das Ende der Zeit* speaks about the end of history. See the English translation, *The End of Time* (New York: Pantheon, 1954).

[102] Vladimir Solovyev wrote in his last book, *Three Conversations*, in 1900: "I am of the opinion that progress, that is noticeably accelerated progress, is always a symptom of the end." And thus Alfred Weber, after the Second World War: "The outcome of history up to now is that mankind is returning to the dread of the world and existence that is felt by primitive peoples." "Der vierte Mensch oder der Zusammenbruch der geschichtlichen Kultur" [The fourth man or the collapse of historical culture]) (*Die Wandlung* [1948]: 283). In J. Pieper, op. cit., 73, 75.

[103] Typical in this respect is the conclusion of William I. Thompson in his widely read book of some years ago, *At the Edge of History* (New York: Harper & Row, 1971): "Western Civilization is drawing to a close in an age of apocalyptic turmoil. . . . Birth and death are ultimately confusing; to make sense of them we will have to make our peace with myth. . . . At the edge of history, history itself can no longer help us, and only myth remains equal to reality. . . . And now we sleep in the brief interval between the lightning and the thunder" (163).

[104] Cf., by way of example, Susan George, *How the Other Half Dies: The Reasons for World Hunger* (London: Penguin, 1976).

[105] The figures are staggering and irreversible. All we can do is try to prevent the situation from worsening. And this is only a theoretical hope, as the experience of the last thirty years sufficiently demonstrates.

[106] Food, that gift of the Gods that, according to the *Bhagavad Gītā*, makes a thief of anyone who enjoys it alone without giving anything in return (III.12), has become a weapon, a military weapon in the hands of the so-called world powers (see George, *How the Other Half Dies*, op. cit.). The United States alone, that is, 6 percent of the world's population, consumes 34 percent and controls over 60 percent of the world's energy (some years ago the figure was 40 percent). See S. Turquie, "Efficacité et limites de l'arme céréaliere" [Efficacy and limitations of grain as a weapon], *Le Monde Diplomatique*, no. 312 (March 1980), as a concrete example of speculation regarding US policy against the USSR after the invasion of Afghanistan.

[107] "Sic transeamus per bona temporalia, ut non amittamus aeterna" [May we pass through the good things of the temporal world so as not to lose those of the eternal one], Collect of the Latin Liturgy, Third Sunday after Pentecost, is an excellent prayer, provided it is not interpreted as an evasion of earthly

the masses for an emotional moment, but the human race is becoming more and more immune to such societal viruses. The goods have to be delivered now, and not when God and the (that is, my) party is going to win.

But there is not only despair among the poor. There is equally disenchantment among the rich. The poor of the world still retain a certain prehistorical religiosity that gives them something to hold on to. . . . Those who live in scientific and technological comfort have discarded the Gods and now find that their practical Supreme Value shows signs of radical impotence.[108] The rich could justify their comforts by persuading themselves that "in due time" the masses would also enjoy them. Now we can no longer believe it. It is ingrained in the System that the rich get richer and the poor poorer.[109] But no solution is at hand, and we have lost innocence.[110] Postindustrial society is becoming increasingly conscious that the trend of the present world cannot be stopped. Standstill would amount to chaos.[111] Armaments proliferate to maddening proportions—and have to, or else the present economic system would collapse tomorrow.[112] The pan-economic society is bound to explode sooner or later.[113] If you quantify everything and put a price tag on every human value, the *humanum* vanishes and gives way to the *monetale*. Every "human" good becomes subservient to its monetary value. Some privileged people may prosper, but happiness will elude them. Yet there is still more to it: today we realize that *the people* will not prosper, only some individuals, groups, classes, corporations, or nations.[114] An economy based on mere profit is bound to burst the day you have no more markets to make the operation profitable, because all the "others" are

responsibilities, postponing the heavenly reward to some later "time" or "other" world. Many examples from other traditions could also be given.

[108] The literature is already bewildering. Cf., for instance, the study by D. Yankelovich, "New Rules in American Life," *Psychology Today,* April 1981, 35ff., which, although limited to the United States, serves as an indicator of the trend of technological societies.

[109] See the many penetrating analyses of Denis Goulet on so-called Development, e.g., *The Cruel Choice*, op. cit.; *A New Moral Order* (Maryknoll, NY: Orbis Books, 1974).

[110] If the world were to use the amount of paper that the United States consumes in two years, no tree would be left on the planet. If the peoples of the Earth were to consume units of nonrenewable energy at the rate the United States is consuming them, energy exhaustion of the world would come during our generation.

[111] Cf., nevertheless, the efforts at changing economies by gearing them into other fields, as reported in *The UNESCO Courier—The Arms Race* (April 1979).

[112] Approximately 60 percent of the worldwide economy of the historically and economically "developed" countries is geared directly or indirectly to armaments and so-called defense. If such markets were to disappear, their economies would collapse, and—since theirs is a way of life based on economic values—their entire civilization would also collapse. See the recent UNESCO Bulletins dedicated to armaments: *The UNESCO Courier—The Arms Race* (April 1979), and *A Farewell to Arms* (September 1980).

[113] Modern science fiction literature is proliferating. Novels about the end of the world abound. See Gore Vidal's *Kalki* and Morris West's *The Clowns of God*, just as examples.

[114] The studies on neocolonialism, as the examples of Brazil and India show, are most revealing. Because of the size of these two countries, the experiment can still go on, but the price paid in lack of freedom and surfeit of suffering is also well known. The "prosperity" of such a country is due to the 5 percent of the population who are in contact with foreign markets and can take advantage—that is, exploit the fact—of cheap domestic labor. This 5 percent benefits by a factor of thousands of percent. Fifteen percent of the people share, in varying proportions, the fringe benefits from the "welfare" of the first minority, and 80 percent of the people live in worse conditions than before the "economic boom" and "industrial progress."

living at a much lower standard than you are. Commerce means exchange, not profit. But who in the modern world would be satisfied with just exchanging goods? The moment that human values become monetizable, you need an incentive to run commerce.[115] Profit, not the joy of discovery or the curiosity of novelty or pride in your courage, becomes strictly necessary.[116]

---

[115] The shift in meaning of the word *economy* is significant. From *oikos*, house, and *nomos*, law, order; that is, the order of the house, the household, the administration of Man's housing (*vivienda* in classical Spanish is still both house and lifestyle, way of living), it has come to mean the monetary aspect of all human transactions.

[116] The art of bargaining and the human aspect of "shopping" in the so-called underdeveloped countries, in contrast to the stiff, joyless, and callous reaction of "developed" individuals buying in these "primitive" shops that do not have "fixed" prices, is a quite ordinary example. The objectification—and thus dehumanization—of human relations begins. Commerce has lost any relation to human intercourse. Still, human nature seems reluctant to admit such a prostitution. Employees in the supermarkets are quite familiar with the gossip and intimate chatter of their clientele, despite "self-service" and credit cards. See the fine irony of the contemporary Spanish poet J. M. Pernan in his poem "Feria de abril en Jerez":

> Y es que Andalucía
> es una señora de tanta hidalguía
> que apenas le importa "lo materiá."
>
> Ella es la inventora de esta fantasía
> de comprar, y vender y mercar
> entre risas, fiestas, coplas y alegría
> juntando a la par
> negocio y poesía …
> La Feria es un modo de disimular.
>
> Un modo elegante
> de comprar y vender,
> Se lo oía decir a un tratante:
> —Hay que ser inglés,
> pa hacer un negocio
> poniendole a un socio
> un parte con veinte palabras medías
> que cada palabra cuesta un dinerá:
> "Compro vagón muelle cinco tonelás
> Stop. Urge envío …" ¡Que cursilería!
> En Andalucía
> con veinte palabras no hay ni pa empezá …
> ¡Que al trato hay que darle su poco de sá! …
>
> Lo de menos, quizás, es la venta.
> Lo de más es la gracia, el aqué,
> y el hacer que no vuelvo y volvé,
> y darle al negocio su sal y pimienta,
> como debe sé.
>
> Negocio y Poesía: ¡Feria de Jerez!
> ¡Rumbo y elegancia de esta raza vieja
> que gasta diez duros en vino y almejas
> vendiendo una cosa que no vale tres!

("April Fair in Jerez": The thing is, Andalusia / is a lady of such nobility/ that she cares little for the "material." / She is the inventor of this fantasy / of buying and selling and 'bargaining' /

To this day, among the tribes of Nagaland in northeastern India, rice is not *sold,* that is, one does not speculate with the elementary needs of life; they do not have a market value but a human value.[117] Fundamental human needs should be out of the economic bounds. We do not eat human flesh, not because it is not good or nutritious, but because it is human. Yet today, even if we do not kill our fellows to eat their flesh, we let them sell their rice and starve in consequence.[118]

We had best consider for a moment some examples. The entire world economy today, and with it the world of politics as well, is geared to the historical future under the name of growth and the power of credit.[119] And here the trouble begins. The modern world is beginning to surmise that there may well be limits to growth.[120] In the world of the Spirit, growth has no limits, because the Spirit as such has no limits: growth does not mean *more* but *better.* So here we have another theological idea gone berserk: a theological thought (the infinity of God) becomes a cosmological belief (the infinity of matter). But in terms of quantifiable matter, better has to mean more: more accumulation of more finite entities into a finite receptacle. Growth of this sort can quickly become cancerous. No wonder that cancer is the modern epidemic! Nowadays, faced incontrovertibly with the finite material resources of the planet, the urge to grow has been vitiated. But the momentum of growth seems inexorable. . . . It cannot stop itself unless a qualitative change takes place, and the hope for such a change has been the congruous Marxian worldview. Otherwise a catastrophe or a dictatorship is welcomed, if only to contain the runaway growth—because those who can have more at the price of others having less will not divest themselves of their advantages out of sheer moral principles. Of course a mere cataclysm would only lead people to repeat

---

amidst laughter, festivity, rhyme and merriment / bringing together / trade and poetry . . . / The Fair is a way of disguise, / an elegant way / to buy and sell. / I once heard it said to a merchant: / —You have to be English, / to make a deal / by wiring a partner / twenty half words, well chosen, / as every word costs money, / "buying 5 ton freight wagon / Stop. Urgent shipment . . ." How coarse! / In Andalusia / you cannot even begin with twenty words . . . / you must add a little salt to your dealings . . . / Less, perhaps, is the value of the sale / but more grace there is here, / and the way I do not turn back and then I do / adding salt and pepper to the bargaining, / as it should be. / Commerce and poetry: the Fair of Jerez! / the regality and elegance of this old race / that spends ten coins on wine and clams / while selling something that is not worth three!].

From Jose María Pernan, *Obras Completas: Poesía,* Torno I (Madrid: Escelicer, 1947), 429–30.

[117] At harvest time every family receives all the rice necessary for the season and keeps it in great baskets in the first portico of the house. There are private and communal paddy fields. Only now has the "real estate" business begun to get a foothold. And, incidentally, as of 1980 there have hardly ever been any cases of psychotic illnesses.

[118] See the evidence produced by S. George, op. cit., and the documentation cited below from *Le Monde Diplomatique.*

[119] "Le monnaie de crédit sert ainsi dans le systéme capitaliste à projeter dans Ie futur une production accrue grâce a l'utilisation immédiate d'un volume augmente de force de travail" [Credit money is thus used in the capitalist system to project . . . into the future an increased production through the immediate use of an expanded manpower] (G. Kleinschmidt, "Revenir à l'etalon-or?," *Le Monde Diplomatique,* May 1980). Or again: "Des lors, en érigeant la recherche de la richesse pour elle-même en finalité du systéme, le capitalisme devra substituer une normalisation monetaire nouvelle à celle héritée des economies pre-capitalistes" [Therefore, in setting the pursuit of wealth for its own sake as the goal of the system, capitalism will be obliged to substitute a new normalization for that inherited from pre-capitalist economies] (ibid.).

[120] See, as a single example, the well-known study by the Club of Rome, Donella H. Meadows et al. *The Limits to Growth,* (New York: Universe Books, 1972).

the vicious circle all over again. Most of the words of warning we hear today were already articulated after World War I, but no heed was paid to them. He who rides the tiger cannot dismount. And this seems to be the predicament of our modern world.[121]

Let us keep to the example of the modern economy. Capitalism is geared to profit and, by an internal logic, to the maximum of profit. The passage from the *optimum* to the *maximum* is linked with the passage from the present to the future.[122] Credit means mortgaging the future in the hope that work will redeem it in due time. Here again the model is one of infinite time.[123] We are impelled to live toward the future. Disenchantment sets in when we can no longer work for the problematic welfare of our great-grandchildren, because even for those we can still see around us, the System is ineffective. Historical consciousness finds itself in an impasse. Historical consciousness seeks its fulfillment in the future, but the internal logic of an economy of profit and growth, unlike a lifestyle of contentment and self-sufficiency, inherently obliges one to mortgage the future. You do not grow from the inside, like a living organism, but by enrichment and accumulation from the outside. Such a situation is literally a *mort-gage*: a pledge to die once the markets become saturated and the victims, called clients, reach the limits of their endurance.[124] Historical Man claims to control and forge his destiny. Yet the present human predicament seems utterly to have escaped his control.[125] And this problem of control produces the current crisis of historical consciousness.[126]

---

[121] Cryptically, in a slightly different sense, but also prophetically, M. Heidegger writes: "Die Geschichte geht, wo sie echt ist, nicht zugrunde, indem sie nur aufhört und ver-endet wie das Tier, Geschichte geht nur geschichtlich zugrunde" [Where history is genuine, it does not perish merely by ending and expiring like an animal; it perishes only *historically*], *Einführung in die Metaphysik* (*Introduction to Metaphysics*) (Tübingen: Niemeyer, 1966), 144.

[122] As an example of the intrinsic dynamism of the pan-economic ideology, both capitalist and socialist, See the by now well-studied problem of contemporary hunger. See the series of articles in *Le Monde Diplomatique*, May 1980, showing how "Par une perversion de la science et de la technologie, les méthodes de production sont portées à un degree de sophistication que seules justifient les lois de la plus-value et du profit. L'énorme concentration des capitaux et autre moyens élimine le paysan, et sa sagesse millénaire, au profit d'exploitations plus 'rentable' economiquement" [By perverting science and technology, methods of production are brought to a degree of sophistication that only the laws of surplus value and profit justify. The enormous concentration of capital and other means does away with the peasant and his ancient wisdom in favor of more economically "profitable" operations] (13).

[123] An analysis of the budgets of individuals, societies, and especially of states, indicates that living with increasing deficits can lead either to a *sanatio in radice* (bankruptcy) or to a takeover by the creditors, once they are powerful enough. One cannot go on indefinitely with a negative budget.

[124] The bibliography today is immense. Cf., as a single example, the multivoiced dialogue in A. Birou and P. M. Henry, *Toward a Redefinition of Development* (English edition, ed. J. P. Schlegel) (Oxford: Pergamon Press, 1977).

[125] "Geschichtsbewusstsein ist Sympton der Endzeit" [Historical awareness is a symptom of the endtime], says Erwin Reisner, quoted by E. M. Cioran, *Écartèlement* (Paris: Gallimard, 1979), 17, who adds, "C'est toujours par détraquement que l'on épie l'avenir" [It is always by failure that we study the future] (18); and again: "Rien de plus aisé que de dénoncer l'histoire; rien en revanche de plus ardu que de s'en arracher quand c'est d'elle qu'on emerge et qu'elle ne se laisse pas oublier" [Nothing is easier than to denounce history; on the other hand, nothing is more arduous than to win free of it, for it is from history that we emerge and it will not let us forget it] (18–19). "La fin de l'histoire est inscrite dans ces commencements,—l'histoire, l'homme en proie au temps, portant les stigmates qui définissent à la fois le temps et l'homme" [the end of history is inscribed in its beginnings—history, man at grips with time, bearing the stigmata that define both time and man] (39).

[126] "De meme que les theologiens parlent a juste titre de notre epoque comme d'une epoque

Totally different is the economic vision of most traditional cultures, which are so often labeled "primitive." They function under three assumptions that are at loggerheads with the modern pan-economic ideology:

1. Regional welfare versus a global economy
2. Regional self-sufficiency versus global profit
3. Limits to the value and restrictions of the field of the economy versus extrapolating it as a universal value in a universal field

It is clear that by embracing the entire planet, modern communications have undermined assumptions 1 and 2. But it is also clear that the change (often called progress) is proving to be worse than the previous stage.[127] Self-sufficiency is destroyed in favor of profit the moment you accept the principle of interest.[128] And profit is only for the successful ones. Success here means to be *better off* than your neighbor. The medieval Western theologians who argued against usury as an antinatural device, that is, against the idea that money generates money[129]—were not so wrong, after all, when they pointed out not only the anti-evangelical spirit of the practice but also the principle of exploitation of Man by Man inherent in the modern economy.[130] The very System calls for human exploitation.[131] It is abuse as a System.[132] But we have reached the limit: global profit is self-contradictory. The British, the Banias, the Medicos can only expand as long as there are underprivileged masses.[133] Now we reach three limits: of humanity, of its patience, and of the Earth itself. There are not many new markets left; there is not much endurance left in the people, now conscious of being exploited by the System; and energy consumption can no longer be expanded without devastating ecological convulsions. The internal economic dialectic is deceptively simple. In a closed system, the

---

postchretienne de meme on parlera un jour de l'heure et du malheur de vivre en pleine posthistoire. . . . Le temps historiques est un temps si tendu qu'on voit mal comment il pourra ne pas eclater" [Just as theologians rightly speak of ours as a post-Christian age, some day we shall hear of the splendors and miseries of living in a posthistorical epoch. . . . Historical time is so tense, so strained, that it is hard to see how it can keep from exploding] (ibid.). Or again, "L'homme fait l'histoire; a son tour l'histoire le defait" [Man makes history; in turn, history unmakes man] (42).

[127] See Ivan D. Illich, *Tools for Conviviality* (New York: Harper & Row, 1973), as well as Illich's many other incisive critiques of "development."

[128] See the four articles of Thomas Aquinas, *Sum. Theol.*, II-II, q.78: *De peccato usurae*, where he keeps to the doctrine of the Church, traditional since the first Councils, and yet already makes the obligatory distinctions for a new financial order.

[129] The dictum comes from Aristotle's *Politics* I.3.23.

[130] Cf., e.g., the article "Usury" in the *Encyclopedia of Religion and Ethics*, ed. J. Hastings (1921; Edinburgh, T and T Clark, 1971).

[131] Islamic theology said much the same. In some Islamic countries today, the banks do not lend money at interest, but share as partners in the investments and gains of their clients.

[132] For the situation of foreign workers in 1979 in a democratic and "civilized" country like France, see J. Benoit, *Comme esclaves* (Paris: Alain Moreau, 1980). The so-called immigrants in France represent 11 percent of the wage-earning population; yet their proportion of wounded or dead is between 22 percent and 50 percent, etc.

[133] For how a highly "advanced" country with no problems of overpopulation, scarcity of land or economic resources treats its original inhabitants, see S. Hargous, *Les indiens de Canada* (Paris: Ramsay, 1980), and also *Journal Monchanin* (Quebec) 12, no. 1 (January–March 1979): "Political Self-Determination of Native Peoples" (issue no. 62).

profit of one party entails the loss of another party. The only way to widen the system is to multiply money. This is inflation. It gives momentary relief to those who do not need it for subsistence, but thrusts deeper into the pit those who are at the bottom.

Modern economy goes hand in hand with an egalitarian society. Once all hierarchical distinctions are leveled down—no castes, no guilds, no aristocracies—the only differentiating factor becomes money, which is one's way of distinguishing oneself from others.

The contemporary political panorama is no longer that of a children's quarrel, and the social disintegration cannot be brought under control. Competitive society is bound to self-destruct. If success means reaching the top, the moment others are alerted that they too can reach it, they will try to destroy you, and one another after that. Past and present examples are only too blatant. The situation is not that of a battle between the good guys and the bad guys, the white and the black, Americans and Russians, women and men, believers and unbelievers, and so on. The struggle is with the System to which the human world seems to be inextricably bound: the technological and pan-economic ideology.[134]

Again, it is not convincing to say that technology *in itself* is not bad or that money *as such* is a handy invention; because there is no *in itself* and *as such*. Abstractions will not do, just as reason alone will not solve any human problems, because the human situation is not an exclusively rational one. Abstraction is a good scientific method but inapplicable to human questions, because nothing human can be subtracted from Man without changing the very variables of the problem.

My contention is that the contemporary technologic–pan-economic ideology is intrinsically connected both with historical consciousness and with the specific character that consciousness has taken in the Judeo-Christian-Islamic-Marxist-Western world. The Western roots of modern science have been sufficiently studied, and this is equally the case with technology, which could only be what it has turned out to be with the collaboration of the present economic System of the West.[135] The entire predominant System today presupposes not only a certain epistemology and anthropology linked with the cosmology of modern science, but ultimately an entire ontology.[136]

Paolo Freire's "conscientization" and most of the movements for achieving political consciousness in Latin America, Africa, and Asia represent the painful passage of the prehistorical consciousness of so-called illiterate masses into historical consciousness.[137] In fact they are passing from the prescriptural mentality to a historical mentality.[138] The

---

[134] The world today includes roughly 200 million people living in concentration camps called slums, favelas, ghettos, bidonvilles, and the like. By the year 2000 most probably some billion or more people will be living in the subhuman conditions of the "inner cities" or outer slums of the "great cities" of the world. See B. Granotier, *La planète des Bidonvilles* (Paris: Seuil, 1980).

[135] As one fully elaborated example, see the extensive analysis, references, and bibliography of Lewis Mumford's two-volume magnum opus, *Technics and Civilization: The Myth of the Machine* (New York: Harcourt, Brace & World, 1967), and *The Pentagon of Power* (New York: Harcourt, Brace & World, 1970), a thoroughgoing critique of the megamachine of Western technological culture.

[136] See R. Panikkar, "Mythos und *Logos*. Mythologische und rationale Weltrichten" in H. P. Dürr and W. Ch. Zimmerli, eds., *Geist und Natur* (Bern: Scherz, 1989), 206–20.

[137] We should carefully distinguish between the theology of liberation in Latin America and other movements for liberation on other continents. Yet all seem to have in common "awareness building" and the assimilation of historical categories.

[138] See the political posters contesting US involvement in Latin America, which say, *Tomar la Historia en Nuestras Propias Manos* [Taking history into our own hands] (from a mural of the Casa de los Chicanos at the University of California, Santa Barbara, May 1, 1981).

villagers, and even more the recent immigrants into urban slums, are being exploited due to their lack of historical consciousness. Modern political and social reforms tend to "conscientize" these people by giving them a sense of history, by inciting them to be actors in history and authors of their own destiny, instead of mere objects of exploitation.[139] They are taught to organize themselves and struggle for their rights. It is when they enter history, however, that they discover the great deception: they have come too late, and can never be the masters of history.[140]

Let us put it in very crude terms. Many people are afraid of a World War III and a major atomic catastrophe. (Another example of projecting our fears as well as our joys into the future.) Those who feel such panic are generally the well-to-do denizens of the first and second worlds. But for two-thirds of the people of the world, that cataclysm has *already* come.[141] Please ask not only those living in sub-animal conditions (again, much over one-third of humankind); please ask the millions of displaced persons, and take a look at the geopolitical chart of the world (since one can scarcely call it a human map): gulags, concentration camps, persecution, and real wars on every continent. *World War III has already come*, and the atomic phase of it will be only the predictable outcome and final act of a drama that is now not only Myrdal's "Asian Drama" but a world tragedy of massive proportions and devastating implications.[142]

I have elaborated these more sociological aspects of the contemporary world so as to emphasize the urgency of the question, its importance, and the existential background for a transhistorical consciousness. This latter is no longer the privilege of an aristocracy but begins to be the common lot of the people and peoples of the Earth in their search for survival amid the internal and external strains of modern life.[143]

---

[139] "La conscientisation n'est pas la simple prise de conscience. La libération permanente des hommes ou leur humanisation ne s'opère pas à l'intérieur de leur conscience mais dans l'*histoire* qu'ile doivent constamment faire et refaire" [Consciousness is not just becoming aware. The permanent liberation of men or their humanisation does not take place in their consciousness but in the *history* that they must constantly make and remake], say D. Von der Weid and G. Poitevin with reference to Paolo Freire, *Inde. Les parias de l'espoir* (Paris: Ed. d'Harmattan, 1978), 112 (emphasis added).

[140] This would be my warning to all movements of "conscientization" in countries on the way to (Western) development. Each culture is a whole. Adoption of short-term advantages is a Trojan horse that brings with it the inevitable destruction of traditional structures. On the other hand, isolation is no answer, either, nor are most traditions capable of responding on their own to the needs of contemporary Man.

[141] During the Year of the Child (1979), a study by the pediatricians of Kerala reported that 60 percent of the children of that state are likely to grow dull-brained due to protein deficiency. But India in 1978 earned 230 crores of rupees ($2.3 billion) in foreign exchange by exporting fish and fish products (and Kerala is a fish-consuming population!). The Indian Army in 1979 rejected more than 50 percent of the candidates between the ages of 17 and 21 on medical grounds, and only 15 to 20 percent were found fit. While the diet of those in the United States and Europe includes 35 percent of protein-rich foodstuffs, the African diet includes only 23 percent, Latin America 20 percent, and India 10 percent (and in India, 60 percent of the diet is cereals, compared to 9 percent in the United States). Report by C. J. Samuel in *The Indian Express*.

[142] From the Second World War to 1980, there have been over 130 wars fought on this "peaceful" Earth. From 1500 BCE until 1860 there had been at least (for these have been registered) eight thousand peace treaties, of which the majority contain a clause alluding to permanent, not to say eternal, peace. See Bouthoul, *Huit mille traites de Paix* (Paris, 1948), 11. In A. Corradini, "The Development of Disarmament Education as a Distinct Field of Study," *Bulletin of Peace Proposals* (International Peace Research Institute, Oslo) (March 1980): 220.

[143] Here I would also situate the renaissance of interest in monasticism and the contemplative life

In sum, the historical imperative has failed.[144] All messianisms lose their raison d'être.[145] And yet the two great political superpowers of the day both have in common the messianic idea that they represent and embody the salvation of the world.[146] At this eleventh hour, however, the impasse begins to appear with greater and greater lucidity to more and more people. The symptoms are legion: the possibility of global human self-destruction, the depletion of the Earth and the conquest of space, the planetary interdependence of humankind and the universal vulnerability to any clever individual or self-seeking group, the increasing fears and indeed the new defense mechanisms for survival—no longer geared to a more powerful technology but to a new thrust toward life, independent of the powers that be. The conviction is equally gaining ground that the present-day economic System can no longer be controlled by external factors, that it is, on the contrary, this very System that conditions the options and imposes its dominance. Reform is no longer a solution, and revolution only amounts to turning the same mechanism upside down.

History has become not a dream but a nightmare. Man, said to be a historical being, discovers that he cannot make history. Dictatorships render the people powerless, and democracies have failed not only in the praxis but in the theory. The individual—when there are millions of them—does not really count, any more than a single dollar counts when the transaction is on the order of billions. The individual is only a powerless fraction in a mass. In order to have power, one would need to cease being an average person—since to join with others to form a pressure group requires above-average means, especially when the group has to be of a size that only technology can manage. The majority has become a mass, which is ill-equipped to discover any truth.[147] Moreover, when the issues at stake are global questions, issues of survival and not just technicalities, what justification has a country (or its ruling elite) or a group of countries for imposing the burden of its policies on the rest of humankind? The minority can bow to the majority when it comes to driving on the right

---

among people in the postindustrial regions of the world. Cf., for example, Norman O. Brown citing Jakob Boehme:

> To rise from history to mystery is to experience the resurrection of the body here now, as an eternal reality; to experience the *parousia*, the presence in the present, which is the spirit; to experience the reincarnation of the incarnation, the second coming; which is his coming in us.
>
> Our life is as a fire dampened, or as a fire shut up in stone. Dear children, it must blaze, and not remain smoldering, smothered. Historical faith is moldy matter—*der historische Glaube ist ein Moder*—it must be set on fire: the soul must break out of the reasoning of this world into the life of Christ, into Christ's flesh and blood; then it receives the fuel which makes it blaze. There must be seriousness; history reaches not Christ's flesh and blood. (Boehme, *De Incarnatione Verbi* II.vii.1.)

From Brown, *Love's Body* (New York: Vintage, 1966), 214.

[144] We need only to consider the historical folly of the world situation in terms of the dialectic between the superpowers and the lethal armaments proliferating on the planet.

[145] This is the great challenge to the Abrahamic religions—traditional or secular—in the form of Empire, Church, Democracy, Science, or Technology.

[146] See E. Jahn, "The Tactical and Peace-Political Concept of Détente," *Bulletin of Peace Proposals* 12, no. 1 (1981): 33–43, where it is shown that none of the "superpowers" have abandoned their belief that peace and justice on Earth can only be brought about if their respective ideologies triumph—by war, or by détente.

[147] See J. Ortega y Gasset, *La rebelión de las masas, Obras Completas*, vol. 4 (Madrid: Revista de Occidente, 1966), 113–312, or the English translation, *The Revolt of the Masses* (New York: Mentor Books, 1950).

or the left side of the road or changing the decimal system, but when you are threatened in your very being, the limits of tolerance have been reached.[148]

And yet the individual is left with the conviction that he or she can do little to alter the force of circumstances, the inertia of the System, or the dynamics of power. More and more the conviction dawns upon the human spirit that the meaning of life does not lie in the future or in shaping society or transforming Nature, but in life itself, lived in its present and actual depth. To this recently more visible—although not altogether novel—moment in human consciousness we now turn our attention.

Transhistorical Consciousness

This third form of consciousness is coming more and more to the fore.[149]

The two others are far from having disappeared, and to be sure, this third form has always been in the air in the shape of metaphysical insights and mystical experiences. But today it is gathering momentum, and by virtue of principles elaborated by the sociology of knowledge, it is also changing in character.[150]

As symptoms of the crisis of historical civilization and attempts to find a way out, there are today all over the world movements for peace, nonviolence, return to the Earth, disarmament, ecology, world federation, and what have you, right down to macrobiotics. Most of these point to a transhistorical mood, but they should take heed lest they contribute to prolonging the agony of life in an unjust System by not being radical enough. Without something of a transhistorical dimension, even these movements run the risk of being coopted into the System. An example would be the "social services" that allow "business as usual" to march on unabated without the bad conscience occasioned by coming face-to-face with its victims, merely because some good souls are taking care of them.[151] We may, and even must, join in the efforts for a better world and a more equitable social order, but we should not deceive ourselves. It is here that the function of the true intellectual and/or contemplative becomes paramount. What we need is a radically different alternative, not just patchwork reform of the abuses of the existing System—in spite of the fact that any practical steps toward this alternative will have to begin with the status quo and try to convert it into a *fluxus quo* conducive to a New Heaven and a New Earth, if this much-used and -abused image is still permissible. In any event, such an alternative demands nothing short of a radical change in consciousness.

Let me suggest at least one of the roots of this radical change. In Western parlance, I would put it that we are witnessing the passage from monotheism to trinity, that is, from a monotheistic worldview to a trinitarian vision. In Eastern words, it is the overcoming of dualism

---

[148] See R. Panikkar, *Myth, Faith and Hermeneutics*, chapter 2, "Tolerance, Ideology and Myth."

[149] Transhistorical consciousness pierces *through* history to its transtemporal core. The exceptional use of "posthistorical" in this paper should be emphatically distinguished from the "posthistoric man" of Roderick Seidenberg's classic study of the same name, which dissects the new barbarism of contemporary institutions and processes that have (pre)fabricated a lethal collective automaton out of the image of God (Seidenberg, *Posthistoric Man: An Inquiry* [Chapel Hill, NC, 1950]). See also L. Mumford's powerful essay "PostHistoric Man," responding to Seidenberg's analysis, which appears in Mumford, *Interpretations and Forecasts, 1922–1972* (New York: Harcourt, Brace, Jovanovich, 1973), chapter 34, 376–87.

[150] Here is where I see the existential and practical import of this study.

[151] The proof of the present untenable situation is that such "works of mercy" have become tragic: you are a scoundrel if you don't perform them, and a traitor if you do. Again, another pointer toward the transhistorical.

by *advaita*, that is, the transition from a two-story model of the universe to a nondualistic conception of reality. In philosophical language, it boils down to finding the middle path between the Scylla of dualism and the Charybdis of monism.[152] In a more contemporary way of speaking, we could say that it amounts to experiencing the sacredness of the secular.[153] I mean by secularity the conviction of the irreducible character of time, that is, the sense that Being and time are inextricably connected. Time is experienced as a constitutive dimension of Being; there is no atemporal Being. *Sacred secularity* is an expression meaning that this very secularity is inserted in a reality that is not exhausted by its temporality. Being is temporal, but is also "more" and "other" than this. Now this "more" is no mere juxtaposition—as if eternity, for instance, would arrive "after" time, or as if a supratemporal Being were temporal "plus" something else, or merely atemporal. Similarly, this "other" is not another Being that does not share temporality. I would use the word *tempiternity* to express this unity. Employing another neologism,[154] I have called *cosmotheandrism* the experience of the equally irreducible character of the divine, the human, and the cosmic (freedom, consciousness and matter), so that reality—being one—cannot be reduced to a single principle. This is, in my opinion, the basis for a change that is truly pluralistic.

If we take pluralism not as a political strategy but as a word representing the ultimate structure of reality, we shall have to overcome the assumption of a single human pattern of intelligibility.[155] At this level, all words break down.[156] It may be that there is only one scheme of intelligibility, but we cannot postulate it a priori. It may also be that there is a peculiar awareness of dimensions of reality that simply does not fit into the category of intelligibility.[157] We may be aware of Matter or of the Spirit and yet be unable to call them intelligible—not only de facto, because *we* cannot (*quoad nos*) know it, but de jure (*quoad se*), because they do not belong to the order of intelligibility.

The underlying hypothesis of monotheism is that there is a Supreme Mind to which all things are intelligible, so that if *quoad nos* beings are not transparent, *quoad se*—that is, for God—all reality is intelligible.[158] It would not be fair to criticize this metaphysical hypothesis by underscoring the dangers of manipulation and the abuses

---

[152] See my many studies elaborating and applying this assumption, e.g., "Ṛta-tattva: Preface to a Hindu-Christian Theology," *Jeevadhara* 49 (January–February 1979): 6–63; and *The Trinity and the Religious Experience of Man* (Maryknoll, NY: Orbis Books, 1973).

[153] See my book *Culto y secularizacion* (Madrid: Marova, 1979), especially 58–61 and 90–100. See also H. Fingarette, *Confucius: The Secular as Sacred* (New York: Harper & Row, 1972). In Volume XI of this *Opera Omnia*.

[154] "Il n'y a que les termes nouveaux qui fassent peine et qui réveillent l'attention" [It is only new terms that tire and reawaken attention], says Malebranche, *Traité de morale*, part 1, chapter 6, para. 8.

[155] See R. Panikkar, "The Myth of Pluralism—The Tower of Babel," *Cross Currents* 29, no. 2 (Summer 1979). In Volume VI, Part 1 of this *Opera Omnia*.

[156] See the Upaniṣadic dictum: "Whence the words recoil, together with the mind, unable to reach it—who knows that bliss of Brahman has no fear" (*TU* II.4.1; see also II.9.1).

[157] In the wake of the Greek philosophers, the Latin Scholastics distinguished between the knowledge of an existence and that of an essence. On this basis, moreover, Descartes and Leibniz elaborated the entire problematic surrounding the Ontological Argument.

[158] See the Thomistic principles: "Deus enim cognoscendo se, cognoscit omnem creaturam" [God, knowing himself, knows every creature] (*Sum. Theol.* I, q.34, a.3), and J. Pieper's answer to J.-P. Sartre that existence is not prior to essence because there is an Existence identical to its Essence (God). We could equally adduce Spinoza or Hegel regarding the ultimate intelligibility of Being.

it has led to in all sorts of caesaro-papisms, totalitarianisms, and colonialisms, East and West.[159] The problem is of a deeper nature.[160]

To say that we are beginning to witness the end of history does not have to mean the end of Man. Yet the ordeal is going to have historical proportions, precisely if we are to bring history to a close. In this crucible of the modern world, only the mystic will survive.[161] All the others are going to disintegrate: they will be unable to resist either the physical strictures or the psychic strains.[162] And this disintegration will include the so-called middle classes, which, for the moment, can eat adequately and do not try to take a stand on any slippery decision-making platforms. The bourgeois, that is, the inhabitants of the burghs, are today the denizens of the megalopolis: bombarded by noise, haunted by fear, drowned in "information," propagandized into stupefaction; people anonymous to one another, without clean air to breathe or open space for human—and not just animal—intimacy, with no free time at all because time itself is now in bondage.[163] There is no real *scholé*, leisure, and time is no longer free.[164]

The mystic, or at least a certain kind of mystic, has a transhistorical experience. He or she does not situate things along the course of linear time. Theirs is a vision that includes the three times: past, present, and future.[165] An example is the difference between the popular belief in the Semitic religions of a "creation" at the beginning of the world, understanding this creation as an event situated in the past, and the interpretation often given by metaphysicians and mystics: that the "creation" and "conservation" of the universe by God are not two separate acts, and that creation is a continuous process.[166] Scholastic theology affirms that the simplicity of God obliges us to say that the very act by which God begets the Son creates the world.[167] The eternal intratrinitarian process and the temporal extratrinitarian

---

[159] Cf., e.g., F. Heer, *Europäische Geistesgeschichte* (Stuttgart: Kohlhamrner, 1953).

[160] See S. Breton, *Unicité et Monothéisme* (Paris: Cerf, 1981). On totally different lines, see David C. Miller, *The New Polytheism. Rebirth of the Gods and Goddesses* (New York: Harper & Row, 1974).

[161] This was the cryptic leitmotif of my collection of essays of over thirty years ago, published as *Humanismo y Cruz* (Madrid: Rialp, 1963).

[162] The statistics on mental illness are revealing, even without speculating about increases in violence, suicides, assassinations, crime rates, etc.

[163] See E. Castelli, *Il tempo esaurito* (Padua: CEDAM, 1968), and also *Il simbolismo del tempo*, ed. E. Castelli (Rome: Istituto di Studi Filosofici, 1973).

[164] The very shift in the meaning of the words tells some of the story. To *negotiate*, in English, means to manage, to convert into money. The Latin *negotium* is rightly translated as "business": to be busy, that is, to have *nec-otium* (no leisure). And here *otium* certainly means peace, calmness, tranquility. See "affair," from the Latin *ad facere*, to do, to be done: ado (trouble, fuss). See equally the etymologies of the German *Geschäft* ("was man zu schaffen hat," what one has to do, produce, create) and *Handeln*, commerce (to handle, that is, to make with the hands: arts and crafts). Even more revealing is the etymology of work in the Latin languages (*trabajo, travail*, etc.) from *tri-palium*, an instrument of torture (as still in the English travail—and also travel!). If *scholé* means leisure, rest, ease, *scholía* means to be busy (nervous due to lack of time), occupation, business.

[165] "Tolle tempus, occidens est oriens" [Eliminate time, and evening is morning—or West is East], as Meister Eckhart so pregnantly puts it. *Expositio Sancti Evangelii sec. Iohannem* 8 (*LW* iii.9).

[166] See my Hindu-Christian essay in this regard, "The Myth of Prajāpati: The Originating Fault or Creative Immolation," in *Myth, Faith and Henmeneutics*, op. cit.

[167] "Pater enim, intelligendo se et Filium et Spiritum Sanctum et omnia alia quae eius scientia continentur, concipit Verbum: ut sic tota Trinitas Verbo dicatur, et etiam omnis creatura" [For the Father, by understanding Himself, the Son and the Holy Ghost, and all other things comprised in this

act ultimately coalesce in their source. In this vision, the fulfillment of my life does not need to depend on the fulfillment of the historical future of my nation, people, race, or even of humankind. I am somewhat independent of the strictures of historical events. If the end of my life is the destruction of all *karmas* still binding me to the temporal flux, then the meaning of human life no longer lies in the historical fulfillment of a mission but in the realization of the human being.[168]

Prehistorical Man was fearful of Nature, but he managed in his own way to come to terms with Mother Earth or the Earth Goddess. Now Big Brother and his twin, technology, are frightening historical Man, who tries desperately to cope with them. Prehistorical Man had to take his distance from Nature, so to speak, in order to survive as Man. This alienation from Nature made him Man and differentiated him from the animals—for better or worse. Modern, that is, historical, Man has now to separate himself from *the System* in order to live as Man. This salutary severance, this weaning from the System, will differentiate those who succeed in preserving their humanness from the robots, victims of the System: ants, work addicts, cogs in the megamachine, "bits" identified by number in the ubiquitous computers' memory banks. Withdrawal from the System does not necessarily mean flight into the mountains or mere escapism from history. It certainly does mean a pilgrimage to the "high places" of the human spirit and the human Earth, as well as an overcoming of the historical obsession. But it also means keeping one's hands and heart free to help fellow beings on their way to this new conscientization. Perhaps we could call it *Realization*.

Here are some of the traits of this Realization: Nonhistorical consciousness sees life mainly in the interplay between the past and the present; the future has hardly any weight. Historical consciousness is busy discharging the past into the future; the present is just the intersection of the two. Transhistorical consciousness attempts to integrate past and future into the present; past and future are seen as mere abstractions. Not only has the two-story building of prehistorical Man collapsed, but the one-story building of historical Man is also a shambles. The two-story building was the cosmological image of traditional religions: now and here are only the time and place for the struggle to attain the happiness of salvation elsewhere and after.

Here is where we should situate Buddhism, as that wisdom that is based on the experience of the momentariness of our existence, without accumulations from the past or expectations for the future. We have here an example of a nonhistorical but certainly not prehistorical mentality: the Buddhist *kṣaṇavāda* or doctrine of the momentariness of all things (of all *dharmas*). Reality is basically discontinuous.[169] We create time. Time does not sustain us like a mother. It is our child. The only reality is the creative instant. History is woven from the detritus, as it were, of authentic human activity, and of any activity. History may have to do with *karma*.[170] Both are factors impinging on our lives, and we must rid ourselves of them.

---

knowledge, conceives the Word; so that thus the whole Trinity is "spoken" in the Word; and likewise also all creatures] (Thomas Aquinas, *Sum. Theol.* I, q.34, a.1).

[168] See the *hodie*, the *today* of the Easter liturgy in the Christian rite. Today the world is redeemed, because today it is created and today risen again.

[169] See L. Silburn, *Instant et cause. Le discontinu dans la pensée philosophique de l'Inde* (Paris: Vrin, 1955). Silburn remarks that there has been a general incomprehension regarding this fundamental Buddhist tenet.

[170] See R. Panikkar, "Time and History in the Tradition of India: KĀLA and karma," in UNESCO, *Cultures and Time* (Paris: UNESCO Press, 1976), 63–88.

Human life is more than just an accretion from the past and a projection into the future. It is both (and together) the *ex* and the *sistence* that constitute our being. This is why only by in-sisting on the ex-sistence are we saved. And this is the experience of contemplatives. They live the present in all its in-tensity and in this tension discover the in-tentionality and in-tegrity of life, the tempiternal, ineffable core that is full in every authentic moment. It is the *Nunc dimittis* of old Simeon realizing that his life had been fulfilled in the vision of the Messiah,[171] or the *hodie* of Christ to the good thief:[172] Paradise is the today, in the *hic et nunc*, but not in their everyday banality or in the externals of death and suffering. That is why, I submit, Christ said to the good thief: "You shall be. . . ." The future of the today is not tomorrow; it is in trespassing the in-authenticity of the day in order to reach the *today* in which paradise abides. The meaning of life is not tomorrow, but today.[173] To be sure, between the two moments there is a chasm, there is an abyss. This abyss is death. One has to have overcome death in one way or another. Only then have we the carefree living of the mystics, the nonaccumulation of riches of the gospel, the transcending of space and time of the hindū, the momentariness *kṣaṇikatva*) of the Buddhist, the *wu* of the Chinese, and so forth.[174]

The novelty of the phenomenon is the increasingly societal aspect of this transhistorical consciousness on the contemporary scene.[175] It is no longer some few individuals who attempt to overcome historical consciousness by crossing to the other shore and experiencing the transtemporal, the tempiternal. There are increasing numbers of people in the historical world impelled to this breakthrough in their consciousness out of sheer survival necessity, due to the stifling closeness of the System and the universal strictures of the modern predicament. It is precisely the instinct for survival that throws many toward the other shore of time and space, because the spatiotemporal framework of this Earth is being polluted and prostituted beyond measure by the mechanized robots of the megamachine, all victims of the technological cancer.

We are assisting at a change in the relationship between the sociological strongholds of these forms of consciousness. Preindustrial societies tended to be inclined to nonhistorical consciousness—not only in the East, but also in the West.[176] Now postindustrial societies are becoming more and more open to transhistorical consciousness while the "elites" of the preindustrial societies are trying to change the mode of consciousness of their people in

---

[171] See Lk 2:25–32. He saw in Jesus Christ the fullness of time.

[172] See Lk 23:43.

[173] See the astonishing injunction of the Gospel not to worry about the morrow, or be concerned, or remember, *me merimnāte* [v. 25], Mt. 6:19–34. See the same *amerímnos* (free from care—without memory, and without divided being) of 1 Cor 7:32. See Phil 4:6.

[174] The great temptation of all religions is to cut the constitutive tension between the *ex* and the *sistence*, the temporal and the eternal, the *vyāvahārika* and the *pāramārthika*, the *saṃsāra* and the *nirvāṇa*, the earthly and the heavenly, appearance and reality, the phenomenon and the *noumenon*, the bad and the good, the tares and the wheat, the secular and the sacred, etc.

[175] Although the phenomenon is not reducible to the so-called New Religions, they offer a good example. See J. Needleman and G. Baker, eds., *Understanding the New Religions* (New York: Seabury, 1978), for an exclusively North American approach. See also G. Lanczkowski, *Die neuen Religionen* (Frankfurt a.M.: Fischer, 1974), for a world panorama, and the previous studies by G. Guariglia, V. Lanternari, and E. Benz.

[176] See the words of Milan Kundera, the exiled Czech writer living in Paris, as reported by the *Christian Science Monitor* (July 29, 1981, B2): "The small nations of central Europe have never pretended to make history. They have always been its victims. Hegel and his cult of history could never have been a Czech or a Hungarian. Kafka could never have been a Russian."

order to introduce the historical consciousness that is a prerequisite for industrialization or revolution.[177]

The generalized belief of the nonhistorical mentality, which still penetrates deeply into historical times (we spoke of kairological moments) is this: only a very few reach salvation.[178] Salvation is a privilege.[179] Reality is hierarchical. Just as only one is the king or only a few seeds among millions bear fruit, so the elect are the exceptions among Men. The others are either aborted from this new life or will be given other chances in successive births. Heaven is for the few; the gate is narrow; few are chosen. All this is in the realm of transcendence or the "next" life, even if understood mythically.

Historical consciousness transforms this belief in another world into a historical vocation to a historical future.[180] The historical belief in Israel of a certain type of Judaism, and in the perfect society of a certain type of Marxism, could offer us two typical examples, although we could also adduce many a Christian and Muslim belief. Fulfillment is in the future.[181]

The religious crisis of historical humanity sets in when the conviction dawns that this future does not look very bright in either the vertical or the horizontal direction. Another world as a sublimated replica of this one loses credibility, and another world in the near or distant future has, practically speaking, missed its chance to carry any power of conviction. Confronted with this situation, transhistorical consciousness gains ground among the peoples.

But the democratization of modern consciousness, the leveling down of the hierarchical structure of the universe, destroys the belief that salvation or realization is a privilege. Man wants the fulfillment of life not only here and now for the select few, but for everybody. This means that there is now emerging a new myth that the fullness of life—or more simply, its meaning—has to be attained not only in this world, as the mystics have always stressed, but for everyone. This salvation, understood as human fulfillment, cannot be tied to, or belong to, one race, one culture, or one religion. Modern conscience feels that it has to be universal, within reach of everybody. Yet it is obvious that this is not the case; a substantial propor-tion of the five billion humans have not even reached the minimum level of the *humanum*. This impasse fosters the emergence of transhistorical consciousness on a societal level, once the great temptation is resisted: the fall into hedonistic indulgence in the merely temporal moment by those who can selfishly afford it. This may be said to be the traditional touch-stone of authentic spirituality. Escapism from the people, instant self-gratification, selfish elitism, and blindness to the historical predicament of Man would be just the opposite of the transhistorical consciousness I am describing.[182]

---

[177] "The scheme through which industrial society churns out its past has been called history," says Ivan Illich in his polemical style: "Vernacular Gender," *Tecno-politica* (Cuernavaca), Doc. 07.81, p. 58.

[178] See *BG* III.32; IV.40; VII.3.19; IX.3; XII.5; etc.

[179] This has been the persistent belief of humankind throughout the ages, following the cosmological paradigm that only a tiny little portion of any given plane reaches the higher one: more water than earth and more earth than plants: these are more numerous than animals and animals outnumber Men. So the elect are also fewer in number. To reach a higher birth or total release is a privilege, perhaps a calling, and thus a duty—but not a right, certainly not a birthright; it would have to be a re-birth-right.

[180] See K. Rahner, *Zur Theologie der Zukunft* (Munich: DTV, 1971).

[181] "Comment lui assigner un but? (à l'histoire) Si elle en avait un, elle ne l'atteindrait qu'une fois parvenue à son terme" [How to assign it a goal? If it had one, history would reach it only once it had reached its term], writes E. M. Cioran in *Écartèlement*, op. cit., 42. He also refers to "ce défi à la contemplation qu'est l'histoire" [that defiance to contemplation which is history] (60).

[182] Here are the causes for the flourishing of so many "New Religions" and sects promising to deliver the goods for their members here and now. And here also are the dangers of confusing transh-

*   *   *

Summing up, the background of prehistorical Man is the *theocosmos*: he finds himself in friendship and confrontation with the *numina*, the natural and divine forces. His scenario is the divinized cosmos.[183] He lives mainly turned toward the past. He worships his ancestors.

The horizon of historical Man is *history*: he finds himself in collaboration and struggle with human *society* of the past, present, and future. His world is the human world. He lives mainly turned toward the future. He worships the God that shall be.

The emerging myth of transhistorical Man assumes a more or less conscious *theanthropocosmic* vision of the universe: he finds himself, in varying degrees of harmony and tension, within a cosmotheandric *reality* in which all the forces of the universe—from electromagnetic to divine, from angelic to human—are intertwined. He lives mainly in the present. He is very cautious in worshiping. If at all, he would reverence the intersection of past and future, of the divine and the human. Prehistorical Man has *fate*.[184] He is part and parcel of the universe. Historical Man steers *destiny*.[185] He predestines where he stands. He arranges his own life. Transhistorical Man lives his *lot*.[186] He is involved in the total adventure of reality by participating in the portion "allotted" to him or by willingly shaping the part that he is.

The prehistorical mentality does not have to justify Man's existence to itself or to others. The human being simply lives, like any other living being. Historical consciousness has to justify, that is, to prove, the value of Man's existence by his *doing*, that is, by creating or producing his own world with its values. Modern Man is a worker.[187] Transhistorical Man has lost both the prehistorical naiveté and the historical optimism/pessimism. He feels the urge to be what he is supposed to be by occupying his proper place in the universe.

The world of transhistorical Man, his environment, is the cosmotheandric universe. The renewed interest in astrology, for instance, is due not merely to the desire to know

---

istorical consciousness with the desire for instantaneous gratification, pleasure, well-being—and thus the role of drugs.

[183] See the traditional Hindu homologation (since the *Śatapatha Brāhmaṇa*, vg. VI.1.1.1–15; VI.1.1.2.1–13; XI.1.6.1–11) between the four types of beings created by Brahmā and the four times of the world (and thus of the day): Dawn is the time of Men; Daylight is the time of the Gods; Evening twilight the time of the Fathers (ancestors, *pitṛs*); and Night the time of the Demons. Man's life is inter-twined with these four dimensions of time, the highest God, according to the *AV* XIX.53–54.

[184] *Fate* is from the Latin *fatum*, past participle of *fari*, to speak; thus the past participle means the spoken, that is, the definitive sentence spoken by the Gods; but also with the connotations of fame and fable, which open up room for freedom.

[185] From the Latin *destinare*, to determine, arrange, make firm, establish; from *de-stanare*, to settle, fix; from *stare*, to stand. (Compare Sanskrit *sthānam*, place, stand.) See also Novalis's phrase describing the true historian as the "Liebhaber des Schicksals." *Schriften*, ed. J. Minor (1932), 2:315. In Scholts, art. cit.

[186] From the Old English *hlot*: portion, choice, and also decision (German *Los*); an object used to assign more or less by chance, casting lots for a reward, a duty, etc. (see lottery, to allot, etc.). In ancient German, it conserved the meaning of "Opferanteil der Götter, Opferblut" and, of course, "Erbschaft," inheritance. See Latin *clavis*, key; *claudere*, to close; etc. Not etymologically but semantically connected with *moira* (the greek Destiny), with the original meaning of "lot, portion." The verb *meíromai* means to participate. See *meros*, part, portion; *merizo*, to divide. See the Latin *mereo*, I merit, in the sense that I gain, that is, gain a portion, merit a part (of the profit of the work or action).

[187] See the spanish Constitution of the Second Republic (of 1931): "España es una república de trabajadores de todas clases" [*Spain* is a democratic *republic* of *workers* of all *classes*]. See the Marxist ideology: In the USSR, it is illegal not to work.

what will happen, how a marriage or a business will develop, but to the increasing awareness that personal destiny is linked both with the fate of society and with the adventure of
the entire cosmos. As another example, we may cite the renewal of popular religiosity and
the proliferation of so many new religious movements expressing people's thirst to connect
again not only with the human world but with the universe at large, where humans are not
the only conditioning forces. The destiny of Man is not just a historical existence. It is linked
with the life of the Earth (ecological interlude and with the entire fate of reality, the divine
not excluded. God or the Gods are again incarnated and share in the destiny of the whole
universe. We are all in the same boat, which is not just this planet Earth but the entire mystery
of life, consciousness, existence. *Love* is the supreme principle, the linking force that brings
everything together. But we have already hinted at the main reason for the awakening of such
consciousness: life has to make sense even when all the idols—progress, civilization, peace,
prosperity, paradise—fail. To make virtue of such a necessity does not make the virtue any
less real, once it is truly achieved.[188]

We could formulate the same fundamental intuition from a personalistic perspective.
All Men want to reach salvation. I take this statement to be a qualified tautology. All Men
want to acquire the fullness of what they believe they are called to be. All Men want to be
happy—another translation of the same tautology. But it is a qualified tautology, because it
implies that all Men want to reach the meaning of their lives, and it opens the door to different
understandings of that meaning by calling it salvation and allowing a variety of notions as to
what this salvation may be. Now we could describe three fundamentally different interpretations or experiences of this salvation, according to the predominant degree of consciousness.
In most religions we find the three types, although with differing emphases. For purposes of
our discourse, we may call one *nirvāṇa*, the other *sôteria*, and *mokṣa* the third.[189]

Nirvāṇa, as the name indicates, would suggest here a "blowing out," an exhaustion of
the burning material, an escape from the strictures of the prison of space and time and thus
of matter. I save myself by allowing *saṃsāra*, this world, to fall quietly away, even if to do so
I must put up with it for the time being and do my duty. My salvation consists in the realization that I was already immortal, except that I was enmeshed in this trap of matter. The
examples here would run from Plato and the Gnostics to Mahavira and the Vedantins. They
cross religious boundaries, because the source could be said to be the personal experience
that my being is ultimately pure consciousness (or simply a soul) and that this consciousness
or soul has nothing to do with my body or, ultimately, with matter.

Soteria, as the name indicates, implies a being whole and healthy, protected and well. It
entails a belief in the possibility of transforming the structures of space and time into something that will provide Man with the very fullness of his being. One is saved when one reaches
that condition of a New Heaven and a New Earth where the deep and authentic nature of
everything will shine forth in its true state and make manifest the universal harmony that is
now veiled, distorted, or rotten—owing to whatever disorder: personal, cosmic, or divine.
Immortality is not something that belongs to one's nature but something that belongs to
the redeemed structures of the transformed universe. It has to be not only conquered but
re-created, as it were. It is a new creation. The examples here would run from Paul and the

---

[188] The name of Nietzsche, with his ambivalent attack on history, should be mentioned here.

[189] I have to insist that these three words are used here as codes for the trends described, and are
in no way directly linked with Buddhism or Christianity or Hinduism. My reflection here is a cross-
cultural one, not a comparative enterprise.

Christian Fathers to Abhinavagupta and the Tantrikas. They cross religious boundaries because the source could be said to be the personal experience that my being is a mixture of spirit and matter that has not yet arrived at its complete fusion, and that this integration is ultimately the very meaning of reality.

Now it is clear that if the ideal of salvation is *nirvāṇa*, the historical development of the world is a very secondary process, relevant only insofar as it touches one's self directly, making one suffer or giving one enough to eat and live on, so that one may pursue the real goal of one's life.[190] Contrariwise, if the ideal of salvation is *sôteria*, the historical development of the world impinges directly on my own realization and that of all my fellow beings. To be engaged in the historical process of transforming humankind is the means for salvation.[191]

Traditional religions have been inclined to interpret salvation as *nirvāṇa* in a more or less radical or qualified manner. So traditional Christians would consider this world not as an obstacle, perhaps, but as a means to attain the other, the real one. Modern movements such as Marxism and humanism have been inclined to interpret salvation as *sôteria* in a more or less radical or qualified manner. The great crisis of our times is that *nirvāṇa* has ceased to be credible to a great part of the world, mainly to that part of humankind that has been touched by the ideology of modern science. And, at the same time, *sôteria* has equally lost its credibility for a great part of humankind presently facing the no-exit of the present pan-economic ideology. Is there any way out of the dilemma? Is there a transhistorical human experience above and beyond the nonhistorical *nirvāṇa* and the historical *sôteria*? If *nirvāṇa* is fundamentally transcendent, and *sôteria* immanent, *mokṣa* could be the code for this rather nondualistic interpretation of the problem. The peoples of the world thirst for this integral liberation, not only from the chains of an unjust social order, but equally from the limitations of a confining, selfish ego.

In sum, transhistorical consciousness is not worried about the future because time is not experienced as linear or as an accumulation and enrichment of moments past, but as the symbol of something that does not exist without Man but cannot be identified with him either. It is neither the City of God nor the City of Man that transhistorical Man is about to build. He or she would rather concentrate on building or bringing to completion the microcosm that is Man, both individually and collectively: mirroring and transforming the macrocosm altogether.

Separated, any one of these three modes of consciousness is insufficient to bear the burden of being human. Not unlike the androgynous character of Man (in spite of the differentiation between male and female), these three modes are all intertwined in human life, although kairologically distributed.

My essay here has been to render plausible the thesis that the exclusive dominance of the myth of history, on the one hand, and historical consciousness, on the other, are both coming to an end. Man is embarking upon a new venture, about which we know only that

---

[190] The common observation of Westerners coming to India—that the population is selfish and insensitive to the issues of common comfort, work, and civilization—stems from the fact that all these concerns are not ultimately taken seriously. It is all played by ear, according to circumstances, without any of the convictions of the Western type of work ethic.

[191] The seriousness of the Latin American "theology of liberation" has often been misunderstood in traditional Christian circles as mere social work or a dilution of the transcendent nature of the Christian kingdom of God. It all depends on whether this kingdom is already there, or is to be expected, or built in collaboration between Man and God—that is, whether salvation is interpreted as *nirvāṇa* or *sôteria*. Gandhi's *satyagraha* for a Rāmraj (a divine kingdom) also goes in the same direction.

we shall act the more freely the more we allow the internal dynamism of our deepest being to express itself, without projecting beforehand what we are to do and to be. We are creatively participating in the very existence of the cosmotheandric reality.

Postscript

We may glean some idea of what it means to live in a nonhistorical world by considering the cosmic consciousness of many Indic sages still living today: here history is not the backdrop to a life of struggle for a better future, worry over what will come tomorrow, or anxiety about whatever we shall be doing with our fellow human beings in the daily activities of the marketplace.

Historical existence, by contrast, is probably best reflected in the media environment purveyed by modern newspapers, radio, and television. Today's "hero," that is, the Man of the media culture, is the concerned citizen, ever anxious to know what was afoot yesterday among the "giants" . . . those larger-than-life figures striding across the front page or the television news, making their marks in the fields of politics, sports, finance, and probably also in the so-called arts and culture, nowadays mainly the stage or screen.

The Man of today's media culture, this "information consumer," is the common citizen of the megalopolis—linked up by satellites and computer networks, of course, with all the other citizens in all the other megalopolises of the world. He or she strives mightily to know "what's going on outside," and yet is totally unconcerned with "what's going in inside," that is, with what happens in the internal universe, those profound recesses of reality to which a psyche has access, or at least an inkling, when it digs down deeply enough into that cosmic dimension of reality I have tried to describe in this essay. Human gatherings, even religious gatherings—the "ecclesia"—tend by and large to coagulate on the surface of history, attempting to better the human social condition or that future condition called Heaven, utopia, or whatever.

The human being is the subject, active and passive, of history. That is all. I am not criticizing. I am describing.

The cosmic consciousness one can still discover—indeed, live—today is of another kind altogether. You simply live there with the stars, the mountains, and the animals, with the spirits of past and future. You witness all the faces and facets of the cosmic struggle. Are you ill? Your own ailments are not just dysfunctions of your organism, but somatic reflections of cosmic disturbances with multiple causes, one of which can obviously also be a viral infection. Are you well? A walk in the mountains with this state of consciousness is no less than a stroll among the galaxies, a sharing in the dynamism of the universe, and a wholly new measure of time. Looking at the lilies of the field is not then a romantic gesture (as one might admire the beauty of a painting), but a touching-with one's own hand and eye and intellect—of that layer of reality that remains hidden to those who can see everything but don't look at anything.

In such a life there is nowhere to go, because the movement of the universe is not lineal. There is nothing to reach for, because what one has to do is to bear witness, and thus to share, even also to cause, the very movement of the spheres. There is nevertheless a great task to achieve: perfecting that micro-universe we call ourselves, "realizing" ourselves in the sense of the classical Indic spirituality. Concern for eternity is not synonymous with anxiety about the future.

The "end of Man," then, is not individual happiness but full participation in the realization of the universe—in which one finds as well one's "own" joy (obviously not "owned" in the sense of private property). You need not worry about your own salvation or even perfection. You let live, you let be. You don't feel so much the need to interfere with Nature as to enhance, collaborate, and "allow" her to be. In this vision, plainly, a God is needed. Nature is not a blind force, but has a divine channel, or Lord, or even creator (if you think so). What is important is the realization that to follow Nature does not mean to follow blind mechanical forces, but to obey a divine plan, or rather a divine reality, which reveals itself to us in the shape(s) of all that we call Nature.

Perhaps it is the hermit who seeks to get out of the world of history, who does not play the game of social success and historical future. Yet he is still linked with reality, and with the human reality. The pitfall of religious orders lies in not keeping the balance between time and eternity exemplified in the very lives of their members: the pure and cosmic ideal of the individual monk transcending space and time is often countered (not to say perverted) by the superior's worry about the future and the continuation of the order (parallel to the "national security" obsession of modern states).

The cosmotheandric vocation is also a calling to the inner discovery of a lifestyle that is not exclusively historical. You do not postpone everything for the future, you do not become entangled in the world of means (always the irresistible temptation of technology). May I call this transhistorical consciousness the mystical awareness? It is a consciousness that supersedes time—or rather that reaches the fullness of time, since the three times are simultaneously experienced. Then the whole universe holds together, then I am the contemporary of Christ as well as of Plato, the end of the world has already come, or rather is constantly coming . . . along with its beginning. Then my individuality touches everything and everybody and yet I *am* all the more: *aham brahman*. The end of the world will come before some of you die, said Christ. "Today you shall be with me in Paradise." Then (that is, now) resurrection and also reincarnation make sense. The meaning of life is not something you can make a career out of, nor yet something you can postpone discovering until after death. And this is the paradox: I am all the more myself, my self, the more my ego has disappeared. I am then everybody and everything—but from a unique angle, so to speak.

Sharing in the unfolding of Life; assisting at the cosmic display of all the forces of the universe; witnessing the deployment of time; playing with the dynamic factors of life; enjoying the mysteries of knowing and no less the mystery of living; waking not haunted by the doings of the day ahead, but gifted with the being bestowed in the present; not wanting oneself to succeed at the price of others' defeat, or wanting to "distinguish" oneself by doing something "extra"-ordinary, as if the ordinary were not enough; just walking in the divine Presence, as the ancients used to say, being conscious of the systole and diastole of the world; feeling the very assimilation and disassimilation of the cosmos on both the macro- and the micro-cosmic scales, lending sensitivity to the stars and atoms, being the mirror of the universe and reflecting it without distorting it; suffering as well in one's own flesh the disorders of the world, being oneself the laboratory where the antibodies or medicines are created, not being unaware of the forces of evil or the trends of history, but not allowing oneself to be suffocated by them either; each of us overpowering these demons in our own personal lives, understanding the songs of the birds, the sounds of the woods, and even all the human noises as part of the vitality of reality expanding, living, breathing in and out, not just to go somewhere else (and never arrive), but just to be, to live, to exist on all the planes of existence at the same time: the tempiternal explosion of the adventure of Be-ing . . . *this is transhistorical existence.*

4

THE MIRAGE OF THE FUTURE

Man cannot live without myths. Man cannot live either without changing his myths. The myth of changing myths is so purely a myth that like most myths it is not seen as being such. A myth is something in which you believe without believing that you believe in it.

One of the most powerful myths today is the myth of the future. It also provides a nonintellectual pattern where participation is possible. This is another important function of myths. It offers a model where people of different ideas can agree. Marxists and Christians, traditionalists and progressives, as well as people from the East and the West seem to agree that we are facing the future and that the future constitutes one of the most basic problems today. From Christian hope to scientific futurology, from absolute future to objective and subjective future we find today a vast gamut of opinions and discourse. The future is a real myth: an all-encompassing container of more than one act of intellectual content.

This does not deny the importance of the future. On the contrary it underscores it. You may no longer believe in the promised land or in the celestial paradise, but you would not do without the incorporation of the future in your life, and most probably the entire Western interpretation of the Jewish or Christian myth is shifted toward this new myth of the future. The forms can take all the possible nuances of the complex Western mind.

I would not like to undermine such a healthy myth. I would like only to prevent its idolatry, and to curb an unbounded enthusiasm. I would like only to prevent this myth of the future from fading away too early before having yielded all its potentiality.

I submit that this myth of the future should be analogous to the one that gave it birth. It is all based on a peculiar experience of time. By and large, time is seen in the contemporary world as something positive and real. But we shall not enter now into the mire of time—rather, we shall remain with the mirage of the future.

Hardly anyone will deny, I presume, that the new shaman in the West since the Renaissance, and even more especially in our contemporary culture, is the "science-man." He is powerful, he knows the future, he can manipulate so many things—perhaps in the near future we will be able to manipulate even birth, sex, and specific human characteristics, to destroy life, to create it, to conquer space, and so on. He has an ambivalent power, like all shamans, for good and for bad, a power that is in him, a power that is not only higher than but independent of himself. The most marvelous power that the modern shaman, that "science-man" has, is power over time. If the future does not obey him, at least it is open to him. He can foretell the course of the stars, and even more, he can foresee the behavior of matter and the course of events. The last offspring of this science-man, the sociologist, heir of the psychologist of a few decades ago, can even foresee human events, not only of individuals but also of societies.

Theologians and philosophers want also to have their share in the conquest of the future. They had the intemporal and the eternal domain of their own, but now only a few people seem interested in such values, and the men of letters are worried as to how they too can say something important regarding the future. In point of fact, were they not pioneers in this field by reason of their interest in time, history, and the like? And now everyone is interested in futurology.

The future came thus to acquire the character of a myth as it was the unsought and yet almost self-introducing answer to so many human problems. What a certain type of world-view would call heaven; and another, paradise; and a third, the end of society; and a fourth, the goal of human life; and a fifth, the aim of human development and so on, now found a common word: the future. All agreed on this formal aspect: that the answer was somehow involved with a future stage in which salvation, peace, relaxation, happiness, integration, and the like would be acquired. How this stage would be acquired, how this stage would look was open to discussion, but all agreed that it was a future stage. The future, a future that has no content of itself, and no need of further conceptual precision in order to be accepted as future, was emerging more and more as a real myth: the "thing" is that there is a future as end, goal, aim, and the like. What or how this future "is" becomes a second question. This is again the question of the form in which a myth is clothed, so a phenomenology of myth tells us. A myth is a cloak that can cover innumerable conceptual forms.

"The Future Is Ours"

The discussions on the subject are enlightening. "We have the real conception of the future," say those on the one hand, and the others reply, "We are the genuine representatives of the future and not you who project in it all your unfulfilled desires." A third party criticizes the first two for some other reason, but, and this is the important factor for us, everyone claims that the "future" is theirs. This belongs to the very structure of a myth. When theologians discussed the attributes of God and people fought regarding different notions of this central theological problem, then God was a myth. All wanted "God." The only quarrel was that the "others" did not apparently have the right concept. Something of the kind happens now with the myth of the future. "God is the real future," some will go so far to say, combining in a very significant way these two notions and proving by this very fact what I am trying to point out: that the future is a myth wherein the opposites seem to coalesce—as is the case in almost all myths.

I have called this myth a healthy myth, and I repeat that in no way do I wish to undermine its power, despite my intention of eventually transforming it a little by this process of intellectual clarification.

"There will always be wars," some say. "No, there will be a time, (a future) in which there will be no wars," says the opposite view. The former statement was held traditionally by those who used to believe that there was a nontemporal realm in which there will be no wars. The latter statement was traditionally linked with the earnest struggle for a better future world that was prompted by the belief that there is no other world, or it is very problematic, not human, and the like. Belief in the future played the same role as belief in heaven. Very different ideologically, they were very equivalent functionally. Again, this is another characteristic of the myth. The bitter dispute between these two conceptions is understandable. To affirm that there will always be wars amounts, in the eyes of the others, to passive resignation if not criminal connivance with the forces of evil. To put all human effort into eliminating war on earth, and thus to neglect the more vital and existentially undelayable issue of human personal existence would seem equally unjust to those who do not live in the future, or only for the future, but who live in and for the present, and who are not satisfied with being utilized simply as tools for future generations. The tension should not be minimized. If the future of man is man, why should I not sacrifice in holocaust the relatively small number of those who are an obstacle to this development, be their names Ukrainians, blacks, infidels, believers, Jews, communists, Christians, Nazis, imperialists, leftists, or old or incurable sick people? But if, on the contrary, the future of man is not man, why bother about anything more than the service that I can do for the other without too great an inconvenience on my part? "Sine magno incommode,"[1] a certain theology would say. What has not been done for the sake of heaven that has also not been performed for the sake of the future?

The "Incarnation" of Heaven?

On the horizontal and secular level, the future has been the heir of the vertical and sacred heaven. This passage has brought about a certain purification of the idea of man's ultimate destiny, but it carries with it the danger of obliterating other dimensions of the human being that are not sufficiently considered in the "model" of the future.

Going back to the old model would probably not do, and certainly not do for those who have gone through the process of expecting from the future the salvation of man, or at least those who see in the future the only possible meaning of human life. The "incarnation" of heaven in the image of the future, that is, bringing down to the temporal level the image of an a-temporal reality, is not altogether a negative process, even under the assumption that there is a timeless "heaven." This kind of heaven had for a long time assumed a role that the present degree of consciousness no longer requires it to assume. The timeless heaven can no longer be a kind of refuge for the shortcomings of man or a justification for his laziness or lack of involvement.

Yet to admit that the future, even if called absolute, or written with a capital letter, can supplant all the functions of the a-temporal heaven is another extreme that may be equally one-sided and insufficient.

My point is this: an analysis of the experience of the present shows that it contains a temporally irreducible element. Likewise, an analysis of the experience of the future shows that there is also a temporally irreducible element, which not only prevents the manipulation of the future (even assuming that one could univocally determine or know it) but also prevents treating the future as an exclusively temporal parameter.

It seems to me that this is more than just a question of words. It would be only a verbal matter if one were saying: you understand by future only the temporal factor, and you, for your part, understand by future something else that you call nontemporal. But this is not the case. The so-called nontemporal factor is, in my opinion, inbuilt into the very temporal structure of the future, so that there would be no future without this timeless factor, nor would there be any timeless factor without the temporal structure of the future are only two perspectives conveying something that is Advaitic, that is, nondualistic in character.

Though the underlying assumption of this hypothesis may be that there is no time without the timeless, and that there is nothing timeless without being "at the same time" temporal, we would prefer not to discuss now this far-reaching thesis, but rather to concentrate on the concrete problem of the tempiternal nature of the human future. I may also be dispensed with justifying the introduction of this neologism. It stands for the nondualistic constitution of human "time" as something neither merely temporal (as other beings may be) but as tempiternal, that is, endowed with a sui generis temporality that we call tempiternity, at least for reasons of expediency.

---

[1] "Without great difficulty."

At this point the title of this paper enters the picture. It points out that the future may only be experienced as future insofar as it is a mirage. What is a mirage? It is (the experience of) something real in an unreal space. The image is real though formed in an unusual way. The location of the image is wrong; it is misleading. It is the experience of a wonder, a miracle, one might say playing upon the same etymology of the words "miracle" and "mirage." The image is an advance of the space, so to speak. The image occurs at a place where the "imaged" thing does not exist. The mirage is a peculiar blend of reality and unreality. Similarly with the experience of the future. It exists and yet it does not exist. It is a mental construction, on the one hand, and it is an experiential reality on the other. The future about which we are talking is not, of course, the mere projection of one's wishes, of the simple prolongation of the present. It is a real future, a future that is supposed to happen, to come and to become real—just as the past is not my conception of it, but that which actually happened. The real future is that future that can assert the claim it is going to become present, that it is going to happen, to cease to be future in order to become present. To say, "1985!" has no meaning whatsoever unless it is accompanied by a certain representation of the shape of the world in that particular year.

Futurology Shapes the Future

This future presents some important features. It has a claim to reality both as future and as potentially (or rather, I would prefer to say, "futurally") present. It is neither merely present, nor simply an elucubration of our mind, nor a projection of our will. Future, real future, is only that reality that will really happen. The future is the still-to-happen reality, and not the mere possibility of an event. To belong to the realm of the merely possible or to belong to the domain of the future are two fundamentally different things. The future is, now, precisely that which will happen, though we do not know, what it "is," that is, what it "shall be." This future has a very specific degree of freedom that the present does not have. The speculation and interpretation of the future contribute to its configuration, that is, to making it really future. The image of the future has a futurology power, one might say. In other words, there is in the present already something of the future as future, for the future depends, even if only in part, on my believing in it, on my interpreting it, or on my elaborating on it. Futurology is important in a peculiar sense in which other sciences are not: it shapes and forms to a certain extent its very subject matter: the future itself. The future not only "is" as it "shall-be": it also "shall-be" as it actually "is."

But this also means that the future does not exist, or simply "is" not, to those for whom it shall be not. My future is only that which will cease some time to be future in order to become present. Short of this it is no real future but only a would-be future, a pseudo-future, the appearance but not the reality of future. I am what shall be. My future is not an abstract and merely possible "future," but only that particular future that is going to be my future; in other words, future is not merely "future-parameter-time," the prolongation of a homogeneous and merely formal dimension called properly or improperly "time," but future is that portion of reality that is not yet, though it shall-be (or, playing with a grammatical subtlety, it will-be). All this means that future without a subject is not real future.

A Future without Me?

The problem now emerges clearly enough to enable us to face the concrete and often anguished question: what am I going to be in the future? Supposing that "I" shall no longer live in 1985. Can I, in that case, still speak of a future? Is there no meaning at all if I speak or think or even worry about 1985? Am I so selfish, or self-centered, that I propose to take interest in 1985 only insofar as the possibility of my survival until then? In other words, has the future a meaning only if there is a subject? And if that is true, what about serious thinking about the years of the coming century when certainly I shall not be there?

Now, who is the subject of the future? It cannot be my ego, except in a very limited, selfish, and also uninteresting way. Futurology, like astrology, begins to deteriorate the moment in which it becomes subject to individualistic interpretations and individualistic uses. Can the subject of the future be humanity at large? If "humanity" has nothing to do with me, it also has nothing to do with you, my contemporary, and in that case all our speculation about the future is only glib and barren talk; humanity would in that case refer only to those living at that time in which the future will be present.

If we are not present, somehow, in humanity, and if there is a total disconnection between us and that future that we are not going to see, then several assumptions would follow, such as: speaking about the future makes no sense, or Man can be dealt with like so many atoms, or the study of the future is the simple analysis of the governing laws of a given present moment and its extrapolation in time. But if futurology, human futurology, is more than applied physics, or sociological guesswork under the name of probability and statistics, we have to find its subject matter in the real human nature.

The real subject of the future can only be that real part of me, of you, of all of us, which is going to be real at the time when that particular future will be present. Certainly humanity may be said to be the subject of the future, but not an abstract humanity. On the contrary, it is that humanity that is real in every one of us, that human-ness that, in addition to my ego, will perdure and endure the bite of time and go on with other names and shapes and yet carry the same living flame of which my ego was only a bearer for the "time-being."

This means that the future is real future insofar as there is a real subject for which that future becomes present. This means, further, that we can only speak of a real future insofar as we are involved in that subject of the future. This amounts to saying that our involvement in the world goes much beyond the limited involvement of our psychological ego, that we are really concerned with the future because our persons transcend by far the boundaries of the ego, that is, there is another element in us that is not exhausted in our ego.

I shall not elaborate here on the law of *karman* or on the distinction between man as an individual and as a person. (To speak of man as an individual is, in my opinion, totally insufficient and eventually wrong.) One of the many openings of the person is also toward the future. It is an opening that proceeds in a nontemporal way. The manner in which the future is in the present cannot be a temporal manner. If it were such, it could only be as present, but then it would no longer be the future, but a future already domesticated, converted into present.

Even if we add that it is potentially there, this potentiality cannot be a temporal one. The future cannot be present in the present as past or as future or as present without ceasing to be future or ceasing to be present. It can only be in the present if it is there in a nontemporal way, if there is in the human person another element that cannot be reduced to the temporal. This is surely not the rational consciousness; otherwise by this means we could reach and foresee the future, which is not at all the normal case. Here we enter again into the non-*logos* structure of man, into that other dimension alluded to at the beginning of this paper.

In order to start a real confrontation with the future, we have to face the future as future, and not as present, and not as a wishful projection extricated from an extrapolation of the past. This is only possible if we detect the non-temporal element of the future and see also that this element is efficient in the present. Beyond all doubt, this non-temporal element transcends our ego. Not only mystics and parapsychological experts know something about this; also any human lover, and the ordinary man, has the experience that his existence is not merely a temporal accumulation of qualities at a given point. To show this is not our purpose here and now. It suffices to say that any confrontation with the future has to confront the real future, and not a ghost—and to do this, the confrontation in one way or another has to transcend time without trying to escape it, or to postulate and project outside time another second reality. To go more deeply into this experience may be perhaps one of the most exhilarating and fruitful concerns of our times. The future is only the mirage of the future, but a mirage is a wonderful thing.

5

The Future Does Not Come Later

Reflecting on tradition is traditional, on the one hand, because this has always been done, but it is, on the other hand, an undertaking against tradition.[1] Genuine tradition is distinguished from education, and even from cultivation, for tradition is further transmitted and simultaneously deepened in a lively or spontaneous way, that is, it is not programmable. Such a manner of handing down can be handled neither on order nor according to individual preference. One cannot manipulate tradition. It is a process that belongs to the life of a culture as such. No individual can dominate tradition. When one starts asking about a tradition, that tradition is literally put in question because one is no longer posing a question about the true tradition but is asking about its history, about a truly valid concept, which cannot, however, replace tradition as such.

Yet this questioning essentially belongs to our era. We cannot avoid it. But we need to be aware of the fact that the meaning of tradition cannot be investigated because what we ask about is no longer tradition but spiritual heritage, historical customs, or whatever else. We can only ask about the past, and even when we ask about the present, it is, so to speak, treated as an object of the past. By contrast, tradition is the load of a past that is ever present. The meaning of a tradition lies precisely in the obviousness with which that tradition makes every other question possible without itself being placed in question. Otherwise, it is not tradition but historical consciousness, historical reflection, or whatever.

The fact that a people with no historical consciousness possesses an even greater sense of tradition could indicate the mythical character of genuine tradition. There are values that dissolve as one interprets them. Any need to interpret them already shows that one no longer believes in them. Tradition is by nature esoteric. Reflection on tradition no longer belongs to actual tradition. Tradition indeed provides the weapons for revolution, even generates them, so to speak, but it operates rather in uncritical and unconscious elements of a revolution than in the supposed values for which a revolution fights. One must hand down the packet of tradition as a "deposit"; if subjected to analysis by reason, intentionally opened, the tradition evaporates like the aroma from an opened bottle of perfume.

But general reflections on the meaning of tradition are not what concern me here; I instead try to use a concrete example to illuminate one aspect of the contemporary situation of world culture. Formulated on the level of personal experience, it could be titled "The future does not come later," which is meant to imply that the well-known linear experience of time seems to have broken down today. Expressed in more academic language, it would be titled "The re-mythologization of time." And the same idea would appear in a philosophical costume as "The declining myth of temporal causality." All this, however, requires explanation.

---

[1] First published as "Die Zukunft kommt nicht später," in *Vom Sinn der Tradition*, Hrsg. L Reinisch (Munich: Beck, 1970), 53–64.

I should first reveal my connection to the material on whose basis I venture my hypothesis. It is material from *three worlds*, and indeed in almost all possible meanings of the sentence. I can scarcely say that I have one foot in Europe and another in Asia, for I stand with a third in the New World, which should not be too quickly identified with the old Occident. In addition, the three traditional worlds, if I am allowed to say so, are also not totally unknown to me: I mean the heavens, or the world of theology; the earth, or the world of philosophy; and the underworld, or the world of science, not without reason called natural science. Furthermore, I would like to claim that I feel as much at home among the three generations of our time; I mean the young, the middle, and the older generations. This is no autobiographical confession but a simple presentation of the sources of my experience.

The concrete example with which I wish to illustrate my more general hypothesis is the problem of the protesting youth, which is much discussed and, in my opinion, often misunderstood, or even more concrete, the situation of student agitation in the whole world.

The first thought that speaks for my hypothesis is the universality of the phenomenon. It is too absurd or too improbable that such a worldwide occurrence should have no common root. I can appeal to the situation in Berlin to explain what is taking place at the University; I can also point to the economic reasons that correspond to the unsatisfying situation of India's Universities; I can take into account the political situation of Spain, the spiritual state of France, or the social factors of North American students, along with all the internal and external problems; I can suggest the mentality of Africa, the history of Latin America, the idiosyncrasy of Great Britain, the trauma of Japan, and so forth as factors in the widespread unrest and various occurrences. But nobody can deny one thing: namely, that the current phenomenon is universal, which makes probable at least that the particular and situational causes do not suffice for explanation and that a universal reason could also exist.

This common reason must be more deeply anchored in the issue, that is, it must arise from this universal situation. The explanation that it has something to do with a worldwide communist conspiracy, or the like, seems too childish and superficial to me. Childish because it "slyly" wants to be superior to the ivory-tower pondering of philosophers. Superficial because even in the case of such a conspiracy really existing—which, by the way, one must not consider excluded—first, this conspiracy does nothing other than misuse the given situation (and precisely this requires explanation), and second, such a conspiracy is itself a phenomenon that requires explanation. So, I try here to trace this deeper reason rooted in the very nature of the situation.

I suggest the following hypothesis for that purpose. Taking place before our eyes today is a change in a fundamental human myth at least three thousand or four thousand years old, a mutation in human consciousness that could perhaps be expressed as the dying of the temporal-causality myth. Here lies the actual reason for the so-called problem of the young generation. I first explain the issue and then try to corroborate the hypothesis with the example mentioned.

The principle of noncontradiction is undoubtedly a cornerstone not only of Western but actually of world civilization for perhaps three or four thousand years. But Parmenides and Aristotle introduced the temporal condition in their formulation of this principle: a thing cannot at the same time be and not be, that is, "A" cannot at the same time be "A" and "Non-A." Of course, "A" can certainly be first "A" and later "Non-A," but when the "later" is omitted, there seems to be an incompatibility between "A" and "Non-A." The question is: What happens if the time factor is taken away? What would such a world look like?

Mystics have reflected on this since time immemorial. Or perhaps better, they have always yearned for that. In timeless eternity prevails the *coincidentia oppositorum*, the *Aufhebung*[2] of contradictions. The implicit presupposition of all such schools of thoughts, however, was that in such a realm—whether called heaven, the true reality, the Being, or God—time is no real measurement, that the temporal reality there is only temporary or even simply an illusion. The temporal world is *saeculum*, "secular," because that is the original meaning of this probably Etruscan word: lifetime, line of succession, then extended to the world ages, whereby the world sets the floating, flowing, changeable reality against the lasting, true, firm, static, unchangeable reality.

What is new in our *saeculum*, in our era, in this eon, however, lies precisely in the fact that our time is not being robbed of its character of reality but that it is losing its privilege of causality. In other words: we are today experiencing the end—or more accurately the onset of the dissolution—of thinking and experiencing in a temporal-teleological manner. Machines and computers will be presenting causal connections from now on, while humankind and its time are entering a new knowledge of freedom—and thus also a new risk.

Overcoming contradictions by eliminating time as an unreal or at least unimportant factor is no longer the point, rather that we no longer grant time any causal power. Time is not understood as illusion, for it is real and perhaps even experienced as the whole of reality; it is no cause, however, for it causes nothing. It is the reality that is here present, all together, whereas temporal progression is no longer a causal chain. There is no temporal hierarchy, no privileging of beginnings. The myth of beginnings—"In the beginning, God created the heavens and the earth," "In the beginning was the Word"—is destroyed. Rather, one would understand that God creates—or rather *will* create—the heavens and the earth at the end, or that the Word is at the end, or rather *will* be. But that is said only as an aside.

What I want to express here is that time is no longer used or seen as a causal instrument. I need not use or waste time to employ it for other purposes—not even future time—no, not at all. Time itself possesses no power of causality, and there is consequently a democratization of time, such that past or preceding time is no longer the best, nor is it more powerful or even necessary for reaching a later time. Sequentiality is no longer considered an ontological process, but even more, it is no longer considered a causal chain.

In other words, this new consciousness destroys the previous, so far self-evident chain of means and purposes, at least in their temporal dimension.

After this abstract phrasing, I would like to repeat the same thoughts by means of the current consciousness and world feeling of the student generation. I think that, in this way, much of what otherwise remains incomprehensible can be taken into account and explained, for the same youthful generation perhaps does not know how to express it and, as long as this generation remains so young and sincere, cannot formulate it at all. Perhaps through that, a dialogue and a certain mitigation of the tension can also become possible. If this hypothesis should prove true, then the consequences would be of great practical significance.

What above all agitates and angers students today? These students, moreover, undoubtedly represent the remainder of the youth, who are perhaps so busy with other life-sustaining activities that they have no time to occupy themselves with these problems. Little surprise, then, that time again takes revenge here.

---

[2] *Editorial note*: Panikkar here employs the famous Hegelian term meaning the process of both taking something away and preserving it on a higher level (*auf-heben*). A literal translation of the Latin expression would simply be "coincidence of the opposites."

The students are above all agitated when they feel that they are being treated as instruments, as means to goals, even when these goals are themselves, that is, their own *later* coming future. "You should study now, my son, so that you become a man *later*, you should prepare now for your life so that you can really live *later* and participate in political, academic, and social life *later*." All this sounds like the general formula promoted in various places: "You should behave well on earth to reach heaven *later*; you should save now so that you can enjoy your well-earned credit *later*; you should respect girls so that you can be happy with your own wife *later*; you should not curse the Americans or other powerful groups too loudly and crudely so that we can obtain our complete independence *later*; you should obey now so that you yourself can command *later*, . . ." and so on.

To interpret young people's reactions to such maxims as simply negative and nihilistic would be wrong, in my opinion. What the younger generation finds most unacceptable is the temporal hierarchy, the temporal privilege, the temporal components. Merely because state B temporally follows A does not necessarily mean that B is or should be lesser or inferior to A. Are not the power and authority of nearly all parents, teachers, priests, and superiors based on temporal priority? They are there earlier: they have more "time" and thus more power. Has it not even been considered a sign of genuine humility to ascribe one's privileges not to one's own achievements or value but to one's age? Is not the right of the first owner yet a source of power and even of acknowledged privileges? I am thinking not only of the rights of the firstborn or the first owner and occupier but also of all privileges based only on temporal priority, in the misjudging of various other values. Does this not mean the suppression of quality and truth in favor of a general quantification through time?

In a technological era, one has perhaps no means to judge that a vehicle approaching an intersection from the left is possibly in a greater hurry than one with priority merely because it approaches from the right. Similarly, society may thus consider necessary the creation of a general quantification based on the temporal dimension of events, but such means neither that this should be an exclusively universal law nor that there can be no other worldview.

"From *mythos* to *logos*" expresses a beautiful and generally acknowledged sentence that also reflects the process of humankind's development. But *logos* itself has a certain characteristic of myth, and that, incidentally, is the reason why the process can occur without the complete self-alienation of Man. One such mythical feature of *logos* over the last three or four millennia has actually been that of temporal sequence, understood as ontological causality. One could ascribe all of natural science to solving the uncritical equation: *post hoc, propter hoc.* What is already obvious in the realm of natural science—just because one phenomenon comes after another doesn't make the first the cause of the second—is not yet obvious in the anthropological and sociological spheres, and even less so in the ontological one. Parents are still seen as the cause of their children, above all because they come earlier, educators as the cause of education because they possess knowledge earlier, and the older supposedly have the right to shape the society according to their standards because they came earlier.

The reaction of today's youth is indicative. They no longer wish to *prepare* for life but to *live*, they no longer endure being regarded as provisional or on the way but want to experience the *eschatological*, that is, the time to come, in the present. Expecting has completely separated itself from hoping. One expects nothing because one does not want to wait. One feels disappointed and frustrated when hope is prolonged and delayed till the future. One wants a social order that is not based on the causality of time.

The whole discussion about means and purpose, or rather, means and goals, becomes incomprehensible and sounds confusing. When the ends do not justify the means, how are the means then justified? When they justify themselves, they then cease being means; they are then goals in themselves, so one should not regard them as means and therefore not manipulate them or view them only as a function of putative goals.

The worldview of such a consciousness is eschatological. The world is a game: the temporal factors all possess the same value, and space is no longer a dimension necessary to go through, nor is time a span worth utilizing. One desires liberation from the tyranny of time and space. Everything is connected: mystical tendencies, interplanetary travel, eschatological consciousness, anticausal thinking, and so on.

A question now arises: can one construct a world with such a world experience? Probably not, and that is the weakness of the young generation. But without such a world experience, one can also surely not construct a world today; that is in turn the weakness of the older generation. Dialogue is necessary here, working together required.

Let us briefly return to our students. Students demand to be respected as full human beings, not merely as students, and to be allowed to participate in the human life of individuals as well as of society. They in fact demand it not as a gracious and benevolent concession on the part of the older generation but as a generally acknowledged right. To regard university as a novitiate for life is taken by them as degrading, politics as a taboo for those not yet initiated as a residue of primitive customs, and society as structured like a hierarchical pyramid as unacceptable. University should not be a place in which various techniques are transmitted, but a place where various generations consciously pursue a life in common. An educator is not someone who knows more but a person of the older generation, whose vocation consists in living together with younger people because that person considers life not as a contest over productivity but as something that needs to be lived and experienced. Universities therefore can and must be places of peace and tolerance; still more, places where seeking occurs that cannot occur elsewhere. That is probably the deepest concern. This naturally has various affects in various areas: in politics, education, religion, social consciousness, and so on.

Here I summarize: The future is no genuine reality, no more than the past. The present, however, is laden with both. They are called tradition and hope. Tradition, real and living tradition, belongs not to the past; and hope is likewise related not just to the future. The true future does not come later, it is already there in the hope.

Birth, or rather, mere existence, confers the right for a fully human life, not work or individual capabilities or achievements; being-human, not age, is crucial. What is real (*wirklich*) is not my efficiency (*Wirkungskraft*, a confusion that is simply immoral); what is real is my existence. A society whose legitimacy depends upon productivity or utilitarianism offends against human dignity, and a competitive system amounts to the bestial law of the jungle and nothing else.

Time is not decisive, or better said, the past and the future, as such, are the main enemies of authentic existence; time is no source of privileges, neither has it some magical power of causality. And yet—and this is the essential difference in comparison with other times—time is no illusion, but a real factor. But time is measured not through its sequence, rather through its degree of presence. The last can easily be the first. Whether one has worked the whole day or just one hour makes no difference.[3] The criteria of life are other than that. Time resists its own quantification and rationalization.

How should one achieve a goal, however, if the means are not there to be used as means? I could work out an answer as follows. First of all, much of what has until now been considered only as means should be taken as an end in itself. Second—and this is the new thing—the

---

[3] See Mt 19:30–20:16.

time factor should no longer be considered a means. Time has been democratized, not only with regard to eternity, but also with regard to itself. Any time is equally sacred or secular; time cannot be divided such that some times become enslaved in the service of other times. Being a child or being old, practicing music at home or performing in a concert hall, studying for its own sake or using what is studied, time for learning or time for teaching, they all are equivalent times because real time is life and life has value in itself, not in its achievements.

There is no boredom (*Langeweile*, "long-while"), for all "whiles" are all equally short. One lives not *for* something, say, for a questionable future. Rather, one lives simply because all points of life are equally distant from an invisible central point.

The future comes, surely it comes—but not later.

6

Sacred Space Is the Real Space

Jesus said to them:
"When you make the two one,
and make the inside like the outside,
and the outside like the inside,
and the upper side like the under side . . .
then you shall enter [the Kingdom]."

—Gospel according to Thomas (Coptic) 22

Space is the ultimate fabric of reality.[1] We are also space. This space expands in nine directions, which I attempt to describe with the divine symbol of the door (*janua*, from the God Janus, and *porta*, from the God *Portunus*).

An Open Gate: Symbol of Potentiality, Universal Receptacle

Our experience of space begins probably with the awareness of external distances. We see through an open gate. The child's awareness of distance goes together with the distinction between himself and the others. For the undivided consciousness of a child, (spatial) separation also means (intellectual) distinction: distances constitute the outer space, and distinctions make the inner space. Two spatially inseparable entities would be indistinguishable.[2]

Inner space and outer space are the two faces of one and the same Reality. Inner space is not a metaphor taken from the outer space. This primacy given to exteriority by some cultures represents a split in human consciousness, if not balanced with interiority. The primordial and universal experience of space, far from being circumscribed to the outer space, is a holistic one: the inner and the outer aspects are complementary.

This fact of one single word symbolizing a reality both spiritual and material is not an exception. In Chinese Buddhism, for example, the word *agha*—coming from the Sanskrit *ākāśa* (ethereal space)—indicates both the visible matter and the invisible void. In Western

---

[1] In *Concepts of Space, Ancient and Modern*, ed. Kapila Vatsyayan (New Delhi: Abhinav Publications, 1991).

[2] This is the mathematical and philosophical problem of the *identitas indiscernibilium*. See my "Singularity and Individuality: The Double Principle of Individuation," *Revue internationale de philosophie* 111–112 (1975): 141–65. In Volume X, Part 2 of this *Opera Omnia*.

languages, however, the word "ether," of Greek origin, has become obsolete after having been dismissed by modern science as a superfluous hypothesis.

The most traditional conception of the universe is a sacramental one, seeing each material reality as imbued with a spiritual component, as a carrier of physical and psychic forces. *Kabod* in Hebrew means both weight, preciousness, and (God's) glory. *Pneuma* in Greek means wind, breath, and spirit, and even in many texts of St. Paul we cannot make out whether he refers to the human or divine spirit. *Ātman* in Sanskrit means body, soul, and self. *Salus* in Latin means both health and salvation.

When most of the old traditions refer to the primordial elements, they mean a reality that is at the same time material, spiritual, and even divine. The same could be said of the elements of the pre-Socratics. The water of Thales, for instance, is certainly not H_2O.

In brief, the separation between inner and outer space, identified respectively with spiritual and material, is a rather modern conception. Space may be conceived as the container that makes any content possible because it is as much container as content. Space is that within which things happen and are, because space is equally *within* things.[3] Space is a primordial reality that does not belong to our categorization of things into "inner" and "outer," subjective and objective, material and spiritual, created and divine.

"All that is, the inner and the outer, is within space," says an *Upaniṣad*. "As far as there is *ākāśa*, so far also there is *ākāśa* within the heart. . . . Within it, indeed, are contained both heaven and earth, both fire and wind, both sun and moon, lightning and the stars, both what one possesses here and what one does not possess; everything is contained within it."[4] The Upaniṣadic tradition equates *ākāśa* to *ātman*. Plato says that space (*chôra*) "provides a habitat for all created things"[5].

We may begin with a truism: space is everywhere, it is both the "where" (*ubi*) and the place (*situs*) of things. Everything is somewhere because it is situated, and in relationship with the whole. Being is being-with (*co-esse*) but also being-in (*in-esse*). This amounts to recognizing that space is everything, but not "all" of everything. Space coexists with everything. Nothing can surround space since *that* would again be space—we could say, paraphrasing Aristotle.[6] But how could it be otherwise without destroying all intelligibility to space?

Our first approach is that of an open gate. Properly speaking, an open gate is no gate at all. We are already *in*—and equally *out*. Janus, the God of the Gate, had a double face, the symbol of ambivalence. This means that, in spite of all our holistic and intuitive methods, we need the rigor and effort of partial approaches, that is, we have to open the doors through specialization: one gate or another. The problems arise when we forget that our entrance was only a hole we made in the complete building—or when we lose sight of the fact that our hole does not introduce us into the building but leads us outside it, since the temple we are considering does not stand "over there" but encompasses us. We are part of it.

A Closed Gate:
The Modern Fragmentation of Knowledge

The growth of a person, as well as cultural maturity, is accomplished by means of distinctions. The child grows by "discriminating" more and more. Culture distinguishes and deepens knowledge by means of specialization. So we begin to distinguish between spaces: right and

---

[3] See *CU* VIII.1.3.

[4] *BU* II.10. See 1 Pet 3:4 for the Christian tradition, especially as interpreted by mystics.

[5] *Timaeus* 52A.

[6] See *Phys*. III.6 (206a8ff.).

left, up and down, east and west, physical and psychic, terrestrial and astronomical, inner and outer. But distinctions should not lead to separation.[7]

In some cultures, space has become mainly a physical notion, and only by extension a spiritual one. Yet space is an all-encompassing category, as African cultures still remind us. But modern Man has succeeded in fragmenting knowledge up to the extent of disintegration, ignoring that the fragmentation of knowledge entails the fragmentation of the knowing subject. There is nothing wrong with specialized skills; the problem is that authentic knowledge cannot be fragmented without affecting the knower.

Space—converted into an objectifiable or specialized notion—has been reduced to a sort of Newtonian extension, a kind of empty box where the movement of bodies takes place. When space is conceived just as exteriority, we can speak of inner space only metaphorically. No "place" here for the inner space, not even for distinctions between space and space in different places. All physical space is homogeneous, and generally isomorphous. The same yardstick is used to measure the distances between the stars and those within a molecule.

We have here an unavoidably political problem. Should we pay tribute to a certain scientific Modernity and call "space" only the external space of physical bodies? Or should we keep to a more traditional and holistic use of the word? It is certainly semantics—but our languages are languages spoken by Man, a political animal, and they shape the world we live in. I suggest that it is an unnecessary tribute to Modernity to restrict the use of the word "space" to the physical sense, as it would amount to another defeat of traditional cultures in front of the all-invading technological complex.

One example may suffice. Most traditional religions live in contemporaneity and coexistence with the ancestors, who are present around us. They obviously cannot coexist in a Newtonian space: there is no place for the dead there. The *svargaloka* (heaven) of Hindū tradition is strictly linked with a Hindū cosmology. The same for the corresponding Christian notions. Heaven and hell have to be spatial if they have to be real, but it would be absurd to ascribe them to some physical localization in the sense of modern science. We cannot conceive them as being located in an astronomical outer space, nor in a merely subjective—or metaphorical—inner space. Either heaven and hell do not exist, or we need another notion of space altogether, another *where*, another conception of existence. There is no theology without cosmology, and vice versa.

In a word, the notion of space has also been fragmented. Modern space is closed: to enter it, we have to use the philosophical gate on the right, that is, the direction that usually indicates the place of tradition.

The Gate on the Right:
Three Different Philosophical Insights

If inner space is only "space" by analogy with the outer space, what is the *primum analogatum*?

Reality reveals itself to us through our organs of perception. These organs are intertwined, although we may give predominance to one or another, or even deny the existence of one of them. Our notion of Reality will accordingly vary. We distinguish three spheres of the Real because our means of knowledge are ultimately three. The Greek philosopher Plato, representing the West, would call them the sensible, the intelligible, and the mystical. The Indian philosopher Madhva, summing up a great part of the Indic philosophical specula-

---

[7] See my "*Colligite Fragmenta*: For an Integration of Reality," in F. A. Eigo, ed., *From Alienation to At-one-ness* (Philadelphia: Villanova University Press, 1977).

tion, calls them the five senses that perceive (*indriyas*), the mind that infers (*manas*), and the spirit that intuits (*sākṣin*).

a. If our viewpoint begins and ends with the sensory data, space will be considered fundamentally as physical distance between bodies. By extrapolation and metaphorically, space will also refer to spiritual space as the "place" that allows the human unfolding of life.

b. If our emphasis lies on the intelligible reality, space will refer primarily to that which makes distinctions possible. Space will here be the symbol for the underlying basis of all multiplicity.

c. If our view is directed toward the experience of the ineffable, that which "lies" above and beyond (again a spatial metaphor) the sensible and the intelligible, space will then be the invisible "container," potentiality, emptiness in which *diversity* of beings is possible, the bosom enclosing everything. Space will then be directly related to *kenon, śunyatā, asat,* emptiness, non-being.

A philosophy of space would have to consider these three different insights, thus making us aware that the temple of Reality has many dimensions. We can therefore enter it from the left, the side being considered—in our times—the symbol for newness and a certain nonconformism.

The Gate on the Left:
An Effort at Integration

Our thesis defends the *Advaitic* or a-dualist relationship between inner and outer space. This means that we neither identify inner and outer space, nor differentiate the two in such a way so as to make only one of them the real space, and the other a subordinate notion. This implies that we can perceive a space that grounds both the inner and the outer dimension.

The dichotomy between inner and outer space corresponds to the opposition between subject and object. The outer space is considered to be "objective," even if all objectivity were to be a projection of the mind (materialist monism). The inner space, on the contrary, is supposed to be within us; it is "subjective," even if the whole subjectivity may amount to the whole of Reality (idealist monism).

Outer space means especially the "physical" *distances*. Inner space seems to refer fundamentally to the awareness of *distinctions*. Psychology, epistemology, and philosophy deal with inner spaces; the natural sciences with outer spaces—but it looks like the "twins" have been for a long time on no speaking terms.

The commonality of the notion of time creates a bridge between the Sciences and the Humanities. Both spaces, in fact, cannot dispense with time. Physical space is not conceivable without time. Nor has inner space any meaning if the temporal experience is excluded. Thus, the space-time scheme seems to be common to all human disciplines. But this time-space is still far from the holistic experience of space we are looking for.

We shall have to leave our temple again and enter through the rear—a more humble way to go into any building.

The Rear Entrance:
The Architectonic Science

We now focus on one old and central discipline that is both a science and an art, and which in Western languages carries the ambitious name of architecture. *Archi-tektonia*: the art of the principles, the chief of the crafts, the most important *technê*, the work of the Primordial Builder.

Scientia architectonica amounts, still in eighteenth-century Europe, to *philosophia prima* or ontology. Leibniz sees God as the architect of the universe. Even for Kant architecture has the connotation of wholeness. Up until Schleiermacher, architecture suggests the systematic gathering of a multiplicity under a whole. The architect is not the "engineer," the man with a great *ingenium* (technological mind), but the head of the artists, the imitator of the Creator. Gaudí was an architect, and he—most significantly—built both temples and houses and gardens.

The traditional architect became the "builder of houses" (*oiko-domos*) for God and the people. A house is not a box, and much less a garage. A house was, to Man, the main symbol for being in the world, the proper space in which to live and handle things. Agriculture was the cultivation of the fields, while architecture was there to make possible the cultivation of the soul within the human space: Man's habitat. The house represents the cultural world, and architecture the art and science of building a cultural system, that is, human life.

The old Jewish wisdom knew it well: a house is not a haphazard construction according to the whims of Man. "A house is built by wisdom" (Prov 24:3), and Wisdom is the firstborn of God, the model of the works of YHWH.[8] The house is the continuation of the creative power of God with the collaboration of Man. In the Christian tradition, St. Paul uses this double metaphor: "You are God's *agriculture*, you are God's *building*" (1 Cor 3:9).

Three currents of thought run through the wisdom of etymology:

1. The house (*domus, oikos*) is the home, the family, the basic human group (the husband is bound to the house, the spouse is *casado, casada*—from *casa*, house—in Spanish, etc.), that is, the *human* element.

2. The house is the building, the construction, the shaped space, the timber used for it, that is, the *natural* element.

3. The house is the enclosed circle within which one is centered and also protected (cf. the Sanskrit *damayati*, Greek *damazô*, and Latin *domare*: to tame and also to bind), that is, the *cultural* element.

Architecture is the link between the human and cosmic order, *ṛta* and *dharma* combined. Any true architect, even nowadays, would affirm that true architecture is something more than simply manipulating the outer space with technological means; it is intimately connected to anthropology, nor is it independent of cosmology. An architect does not build a den for the individual, he rather shapes space as a manifestation of human life within the cosmos.

The function of the architect is not that of exclusively creating an outer space, nor is the task of the artist that of merely describing an inner space. Both belong together. This is why the good architect is an artist, just as the authentic poet is much more than a versifier. Their actions are not individualistic performances. To build houses for the exclusive sake of monetary profit, or to do verses, paintings or pots *only* for sale is a human and cosmic aberration.[9] The architect is the shaper of a space in which people can breathe, live, enjoy. This space is an expression of the genius of a person, a generation, or a culture. It does not imply conformism or mere repetition, it requires creativity. True tradition never repeats the old.

The architect "senses" the space of his time, while the poet rhymes the times of his space. The architect "expresses" what "impresses" the people of a particular cultural period. The

---

[8] See Prov 8:1 and 22, etc.

[9] My criticism of modern society is not against qualitative emulation, but against quantitative competition. See my three studies on "Alternatives to Modern Culture" *Inter-Culture* 77 (1982): 2–68. In Volume XI of this *Opera Omnia*.

creative architect lets space emerge from a non-place, from a *u-topia*. The creative genius lets the thing that has not (yet) found its *topos* be incarnated in space, become space.

When classical traditions tell us that the artist has to undergo purification, contemplate, and/or follow some rituals, they are telling us that there is no real outer space without an inner space, and that the arrow will not hit the target if the target is not in our heart. But, equally, the outer shells somebody else creates will also condition our interior.

I am speaking of something much more primordial than the psychological influence of a building on the tenant. I have in mind something much deeper than the aesthetic taste of the architect to choose places and shapes pleasing to the eyes or comfortable to the senses of the beholder or user. The true architect creates not only shapes but also, in a sense, space itself. I am referring to the intrinsic link between the inner and the outer, the spiritual and the material, the cosmic and the human—and also the divine.

It is my "inner space," my sense of distinction, of discernment (*viveka*), which will open up for me the sense of place, distance, and orientation, that is, the "outer space." We live in a space that we ourselves help to create. But, at the same time, it is the space in which we find ourselves living that will shape our lives, taste, feelings. The artist is the person who breaks this vicious circle. The traditional *ars architectonica* lets us immediately breathe in a space that cannot be exclusively "located" within or without. Body and soul are not separable.

"Artistic" here means the poetic activity of shaping a new world out of the very world in which we are already living. We create our own space as much as space creates us. Spatiality is a "human existential."[10] But this spatiality is not an exclusively inner world in which we live with our own thoughts, dreams, and actions, and much less can it be identified with the external places, buildings, cities in which we exist. They pervade each other, so that the one is impossible without the other.

The architect is not a tailor. Spatiality is much more than clothes to wear, and more than an amorphous or empty "place" within which we move. It is part of ourselves. The architect is the first technician, the co-shaper of that space that we are or will become. Living enough time in any environment shapes both the environment and ourselves. The shoes take the shape of our feet, and, in the old couples, the spouses resemble each other; thus Space is both an active and a passive anthropological configuration.

All this has very practical effects. To live in a rented house is like wearing somebody else's clothes, or even like borrowing a foreign body; it is like having an artificial limb. To have lost this sensitivity is one of the results of the technocratic civilization.

A prefabricated house is like a prefabricated (transplanted) kidney: an emergency solution. Most modern apartments in a big city are no longer natural habitats or cultural places, but prefabricated prostheses. Time and space are not neutral, objective values, and for sale.

It is against human dignity to sell one's own time and one's own space—like to sell one's own body. The outer cannot exist without the inner, and vice versa. The indwelling in a place is not the occupying of a certain number of square meters on neutral grounds. The tragic expropriations of Papua and New Guinea, the no less tragic Israeli-Palestinian war, the gypsies and poor people evicted from suburbs where they have lived for generations . . . furnish us with dramatic examples of this conflict of cosmologies. Space is part of those who live in it, of their own being.

---

[10] The expression is redundant if by "existential" we understand something constitutively belonging to the ontological structure of Man, the existing being. Heidegger calls *Existenzialen* the "Seinscharaktere des Daseins" (the Being-features of *Dasein*, the Being-There).

Having approached our building by an indirect way, we should face it now straight from the front gate, that is, from an anthropological viewpoint.

The Front Gate:
Space as Human Landscape

The English word *country* (from the French *contrée*), the Italian and Spanish *contrada*, the Portuguese and Catalan *encontrada* vaguely remind us of the Latin *contra*, "against." The German *Gegend* also has the same meaning and the same origin. The accepted etymology may not be correct; yet, historically, it has conveyed the suggestion of a land, a place "in front of" (against) us.

Objects are objects because they are situated in front of us, in a territory. We are in dialectical relation with the objects that have been "thrown in front of us" (*ob-iecta*) to form our territory. A territory is something objective spreading in front of us. Peoples wage war to conquer a new territory. The *Conquistadores* went, like the astronauts go, to the discovery of new frontiers, to the conquest of the other, the *aliud*, with the consequent danger of alienation, as history shows.

Something very different is the landscape. It is not sheer objectivity, it is part of us. We are not without landscape; landscape is not without us. Landscape is not in front of us as an objective datum. Landscape is not just "inscape," a merely subjective mood. The landscape is our native or natural *regio* (region, homeland), that is, that which *regit* (supports) us, and not simply something around us, external to ourselves. It is neither exclusively interior to not merely around us. It is our spatiality.

We live *in* a country, but we are not *in* a landscape. We *are* landscape, although not only landscape. This landscape is part of our spatiality, which can neither be equated with the *topos* or *locus* of the Aristotelian tradition nor with the *chôra* or general habitat of all things in the Platonic sense. This spatiality is indivisible from the concrete landscape which *we are* and which allows us to *move*.

We are landscape and we move within it, not as tourists going to foreign places, but as pilgrims reaching our real centers. We are not limited to our physiological bodies, and the landscape is neither like a bigger or subtler body nor like a clothing we wear. Space would then be the general abstract noun for spatiality, an "existential" proper to Man.

Animals are in deep symbiosis with the place in which they live. They live in a territory, and their territory is vital to them. Man is spatiality not so much because he needs a territory, but because, while knowing himself to be spatial and corporeal, he knows at the same time that space belongs to him. This space is his own landscape. Spatiality is not primarily what makes distance possible, but what makes *nearness* possible. Spatiality makes it possible to people to establish a mutual polarity, that is, it turns them into neighbors. We are sharers in space as we are sharers of the word. *Homo loquens* is *homo spatialis*: there is a deep relationship between these two aspects.

The experience of language may help us realize that we *are* space. We have two forms of speaking. The one is to chatter, to go on repeating learned things and preconceived opinions. The other is when we "inhabit" the words we say, when language is the very "house" of our being, when we live in the very words we utter, when each sentence comes out of a concrete experience in time and space—an experience we allow to crystallize, as it were, in the words that flow spontaneously out of our whole being.

We do not think such words beforehand, we do not calculate them, nor do we arrange them trying to make an impression on our hearers, nor even *reflecting* on the meaning of what we say. We simply say it, we inhabit those very words, they are a revelation of what we truly are and not the result of what we "want" to say.

Those words are truly sacraments. They create the proper space into which they draw the listeners as a whirlwind engulfs those near it. These authentic words themselves create a space that encompasses both us and the listeners. It has been written that we will have to give account of every idle word (Mt 12:36), that is, of every word that does not effect what it says, because it is deprived of inner energy.

Landscape is the space that we are, not just outer space, not just "surroundings." As our home is not just a comfortable place or a useful shelter, landscape is not only an inner space either or a product of our imagination. Landscape transcends our individuality, but is part and parcel of our personhood.

Modern individualism is the great obstacle to our becoming aware of our own spatiality, which cannot be so easily individualized and privatized, as it belongs to the person, not to the ego.

The implications are far reaching. We humans are not foreigners of this planet: we belong together. The so-called time-lag, that is, the uneasiness after a long jet journey, because it has disturbed within us the temporal rhythms of nature, is well known. Less studied is the "space-lag" due to the same phenomenon, generally less felt because modern habitats (from airports to hotels) are artificially homogeneous.

In a word, Man is not only soul, nor only soul and body: Man is also society and cosmos.[11] The animals, plants, and the Earth are not just useful or dangerous creatures. They are deeply linked with us, like space itself. Each person is a microcosm. The correspondences between the inner and the outer, the *here* and *there*, are the warp and woof of Reality, say the *Upaniṣads*.

Our spatiality is a human feature. "Outside" landscape, we could not *be*. The flight into astronomical space may betray modern Man's will to "fly away" from himself. And yet we cannot escape "naked" to our outer planetary flights. When we decide to, we have anyway to take our earthly space, our atmosphere, and our space shuttle with us.

The ecological consequences lie at hand. We *are* space, we do not simply *dwell* in it, therefore we cannot decide to give up landscape: we would stifle.

Man is not only a corporeal being, he is also "inscape" and landscape. Landscape not only forms, but also "in-forms" the human being. A person without a proper landscape becomes dehumanized, as can be seen in the overcongested urban conglomerations and in the slums of many big cities. Dehumanization occurs when we lack the vital space that constitutes part of Man's life.

Many of the problems of immigrants have to do with environment. The reason is deeper than a simple lack of familiarity; it has to do with the "inscape" of each individual who, in his or her turn, is linked to the landscape. This is also the case with modern urbanism. Modern technological megalopolises force people into straitjackets that change their very constitution.

Man, however, is not the whole of reality, nor is space the whole of Man. Man is more than spatiality, and space is also more than just a human feature. This is why our front-door analysis is not enough. We shall have to climb to the heights of the temple and try to have a look from the top. We shall have to break the roof[12] of the house in order to discover the divine dimension.

---

[11] See my "Der Mensch, ein trinitarisches Mysterium," in R. Panikkar and W. Strolz, eds., *Die Verantwortung des Menschen für eine bewohnbare Welt im Christentum, Hinduismus und Buddhismus* (Freiburg: Herder, 1985), 147–90. In Volume VIII of this *Opera Omnia*.

[12] See Mk 2:4.

The Upper Gate:
Sacred Space, the Real Space

Sacred space is simply real space, and not a geometrical abstraction. The sacred space is the real space encompassing distances, distinctions, and diversity. Profane space is partial space, that is, specialized space. Physical space is profane space, as also an exclusively inner space would be. There is space when our existence is open (spacious). We suffocate when we narcissistically close ourselves within our monads. The landscape that permits us to fully *be* is created by a sacred action.

Many liturgies, from the Amerindian to the Christian, begin by creating a proper space where fellowship with one another and with the Divine may be manifested. In India, music does the same: it begins by creating a space where the singing, playing, and worshiping can take place. This space is neither exclusively exterior nor exclusively interior; it is both, like us, who have an "interior" and an "exterior" at the same time.

Let us remember that the word "space," from Latin *spatium* (from the verb *patere*), means to lie open, patent (cf. the Spanish *patio*, an open courtyard). This sense of openness and freedom seems to be common to the Indo-European words. *Chôra* is the word Plato uses:[13] it means emptiness, free space, open land, and also a finite region, an inhabited land, but not fenced.

In Sanskrit, *ākāśa* means a free or open or empty space. It suggests "that which lets things be seen" and thus allows us to see, to know: that which allows things to manifest themselves. It is the place of revelation, as it were. Things *are* insofar as they are spatial.

Sacred space as real space is neither subjective nor objective; it is prior to those categories. The *vāstupuruṣamaṇḍala* of Indic architecture offers us a perfect example: the ritual diagram (*maṇḍala*) describes the concrete descent of *Puruṣa*, the primal Reality, into a localized entity, *vāstu*. Space is that which makes the manifestation of Reality possible. Reality, inasmuch as it is manifested, is spatial, although space is not the whole of Reality.

In Hebrew, space as *maqom* and *merchab* is one of the names of God. More properly, *maqom* is the habitat of wild animals, then habitat in the sense of house, and more specifically God's house, that is, the temple, the shelter of YHWH himself. As in most old traditions, here it is also difficult to separate the temple on earth from the temple in heaven. In sacred space, both meet.

This is so much so that St. Paul will say that heaven is the proper space of Man, the genuine and everlasting house, not as an external dwelling place, as if space were an empty box within which we move (see 2 Cor 5:1–2). Once we lose our space, we lose our heaven. We are space, which is the divine "place" where we truly are. It is obvious that all this has no meaning in a Galilean-Newtonian-Einsteinian cosmology. It is also obvious that the idea of heaven as a lofty parking place for deceased souls has dwindled away.

Astrology also studies the spatial connections between astral bodies and human beings, looking for the "hearth" of Man. This inner space is also the astrological space. The astrological connections are not causal connections (as if being born under one constellation were the cause of our character) but spatial relationships—of a space that is both inner and outer. The stars feed on the Earth's breath, said Heraclitus.[14] The stars of the firmament—says Origen—are the bodies of those angels that have condescended to remain in the physical universe in order to serve the cosmos and collaborate to the universal restoration of all beings.

---

[13] *Timaeus* 52Aff.
[14] Quoted by Aetius II.17.4.

The inner/outer space is the space that constitutes us. It requires a sense of orientation, which is inbuilt in our own existence. We are not solipsistic entities, but humans-in-the-world. We are our world and not just along *with* our world or *in* it.[15] All prepositions are here superfluous; we may just say that we are our world, although this being-world does not exhaust us.

Perhaps music is the best introduction to the experience of space. Music is rhythm, number, movement, sound. The word "music" comes from the Greek *mousikê*, something which—through rhythm—unites language, verse, music, and dance. Not without reason two of the classical philosophical systems of India, *nyāya* and *vaiśeṣika*, consider sound (*śabda*) the specific quality (*guṇa*) of space (*ākāśa*). The experience of music is a main door to the experience of space, which is at the same time inner and outer.

Without outer space, there is no music. Without inner space, music is only psychological noise. Rhythm is the movement of inner and outer space at the same time. Would music be the true measurement of time in space?[16] We would then unify two classical definitions of music: the science of numbers, and the art of melody. "Heaven and Earth do not exist without music," Pythagoras is supposed to have said.[17]

Having soared up to the "music of the spheres," we should now come down to the depths of the human being and enter that gate underneath, which leads us to an analysis of human existence.

The Inferior Gate:
Space as the Extension of Existence

Augustine described time as a certain *distension* of our *existence*.[18] We could recover the word and call space the corresponding *extension* (*dilatatio, Ausdehnung*) of our being. We are, we exist distended in time and extended in space. Existence is both (temporal) distension and (spatial) extension. There is a specifically human time that we may call temporality. There is, similarly, a specifically human space that we may call spatiality. Space, I have suggested elsewhere, presents a cosmotheandric, that is material, divine, and human.[19]

The spatial character extension of human existence, as understood here, has little to do with the Cartesian dualism of matter as *res extensa* and spirit as *res cogitans*. It is our entire existence that is extended—and intellectual as well. Indeed, our spatial *extension* is correlated to the temporal *distension* of our being, although not reducible to it.

The fact that our beings are distended in time and extended in space means that they exist not all at once or as a whole, but extended and distended along space and time. Putting it the other way around, time and space are both constitutive of existence and not extrinsic to it. Now, this extension is both inner and outer and makes for distances, distinctions, and diversities.

There is a tension in each being that unfolds in temporal distension and spatial extension. The human beings show a tension spreading in space (similar to their tension unfolding in time); they show an inner face and an outer face, and as it were, they have not filled the whole space.

---

[15] The well-known formula of J. Ortega y Gasset, "Yo soy yo y mi circumstancia," could be complemented by saying that the "circumstance" is part of our "in-stance" and "ek-sistence."

[16] See Augustine, "Quid autem metimur nisi tempus in aliquo spatio?" (*Confessions* XI.21.27): "What is then what we measure if not time in some space?"

[17] Quoted by Cassiodorus, *Institutiones* II.5.2.

[18] *Confessions* XI.23.30.

[19] R. Panikkar, *The Cosmotheandric Experience* (Maryknoll, NY: Orbis Books, 1993). In Volume VIII of this *Opera Omnia*.

This extension allows growth, movement, and change—in space. Space is that feature of existence, ultimately of Being, that makes "room" for movement. Movement is inherent to Being because it is movement in space and it belongs to Being. Things do not move in an empty space: things themselves are spatial, space being of the same essence of Reality.

The ultimate tension is not between spirit and matter, but between freedom and bondage. Space is neither material nor immaterial, but it can be the *locus* of freedom or the "place" of constraint.

The *Advaitic* Experience of Space

It would amount to misunderstanding the *Advaitic* experience of space, to imagine this experience as a synthesis between inner and outer space. It is rather the opposite—although, for cultural reasons, it was more expedient to proceed analytically so as to reintegrate the "two" spaces into Space.

The *Advaitic* experience grasps immediately the "two" as "non-two," and is aware of "their" mutual and constitutive dynamism: the one space is not without the other, because the very nature of space is constituted by the primordial relationship between the "two." We say "primordial relationship" because we could not say that the "two" spaces make the "one" space, nor the opposite, that is, that the "one" space manifests itself in the "two." We should rather speak of the radical a-duality of the "two" without either of them losing their relative reality. The relation is not one, the poles are needed; it is not two either, the relation is not the poles. There is neither one nor two.

Advaita is neither monism nor dualism. There is a dynamic and constitutive relationship, so that each of the poles of the relationship is the whole, because we can in no way isolate the poles without destroying them, as they would thus cease to be poles. If we were to suppress the one pole, the other would automatically disappear. Polarity itself is the primordial reality. Where is the wind when it does not blow? Where is Man when he does not live? There is no wind without blowing, there is no Man without living, there is no *outer* without *inner*, nor *inner* without *outer*.

The *Advaitic* experience has a formidable difficulty, especially for our times. It elicits the fear, even the terror of losing control, that upsets our obsession for security. The *Advaitic* experience implies the abandonment of the sovereign leadership of the *logos*, without—for that matter—falling into irrationality.

The rational/irrational dilemma is an ultimate dilemma from a rationalistic point of view. "A-rational," however, does not need to be irrational. It is not about transgressing the strictness of thought. Reality is not reducible to intelligibility. We stutter, we suggest, we symbolize, speak by approximations, innuendos, *dhvanis*, use parables and metaphors as feeble devices. The *ṛṣi*—the sage of the *Vedas*—sings, but the song is only in the singing, not in its notation or in our thinking or speaking about it.

The *Advaitic* experience of space is thus neither that of inner nor that of outer space but, as it were, that of the one in the other. In the inner we discover the outer, and in the outer the inner.

Should we say, then, that the true architect is the shaper of silence? "And the brethren remained silent" after the Lord had spoken, says a Buddhist sacred text.[20] "*Brahman* is Silence,"

---

[20] *Mahāparanibbāna-sutta* VI.7.

says a lost *Upaniṣad*.[21] Out of Silence the Word came, repeats the Christian tradition.[22] "*Wu wei*," murmurs the Chinese sage.[23]

The wise Jājñavalkya told his wife Gārgi,

> *That which is above the sky*
> *and below the earth,*
> *that which is called past, present and future:*
> *all this is warped and woven on ākāśa, the ethereal space.*[24]

—the sacred space.

---

[21] Quoted by Śāṅkara in his *BSB* III.2.17.

[22] Ignatius of Antioch., *Epistle to the Magnesians* VIII.1 (PG 5:669).

[23] Laotzu, *passim.* E.g., "The way of heaven [*T'ien Tao*] is one of non-activity [*wu wei*]."

[24] *BU* III.8.3.

SECTION II

SCIENCE AND TECHNOLOGY

1

MAX PLANCK (1858–1947)

Gewissenhaftigkeit und Treue, das sind die Führer.[1]

The Man

As of the past school year, the University of Göttingen's renowned *Physics Colloquiums* are once again being punctually held.[2] From 1945 on, the mature Planck was able to have the satisfaction of seeing how these were not only restored to their old splendor, but also how they actually surpassed it. The minds who, by virtue of the political circumstances, converged in Göttingen could yield nothing less. But Heisenberg will no longer be able to visit the school during this new term because since the spring of 1946 he has been trying, with much success, to once again resuscitate the Kaiser-Wilhelm-Institute of Physics, nor will the mature Planck receive an invitation from Max von Laue, the current president of the Max-Planck-Institute, or from Arnold Eucken, the dean of the Faculty. Max Planck in fact passed away at the beginning of the school year.

By now, a general knowledge of the works of Max Planck is part of the common cultural heritage of our times. Everybody knows that quantum theory, which introduces a new conception in Physics, is one of the pillars on which modern science rests. Energy, that physical enigma that causes the transformation of bodies, is not a continuous magnitude, as was believed until Planck; rather it varies in "jolts" and therefore appears to be composed of indivisible units.

But things may be a bit more complex and cannot, perhaps, be rigorously expressed with so much simplicity. To draw a sketch of Planck's personality and of his work is the intent of the present paper.

* * *

His brief, yet dense, scientific biography has just seen the light; it constitutes a true monument in the history of Physics during this century, and above all, it contains an extraordinary treasure of psychological material for the interesting problems of investigation and discovery.[3]

---

[1] "Care and devotion, here is the [only] *Guides*," which term, in German, clearly contrasts the *Führer*: Max Planck, *Wege zur physikalischen Erkenntnis* (Leipzig, 1934), 66.

[2] First published in *Arbor* (Madrid) 24 (1947): 387–406. Translated from Spanish by Carla Ros.

[3] M. Planck, *Wissenschaftliche Selbstbiographie* [Scientific autobiography], published by E. Abderhalden in *Neue Züricher Zeitung*, nos. 1986ff. (October 11–24, 1947).

Max Planck was born in Kiel in 1858. When he was nine years old, he and his family moved to Munich, where he attended the gymnasium. His passion for science was awakened early, at school. In the classrooms of the Maximilian-Gymnasium, the young Planck listened, entranced, to his professor of Mathematics, Hermann Müller, who explained physical laws with diagrams and clear examples. It was an influence that Planck picked up at the time and that would last throughout his life. Clarity and precision would later be characteristics of all his work.

"I will never forget," he writes in his autobiography, "the description that Müller gave us [about the principle of conservation of energy] of a bricklayer who painstakingly drags a heavy stone up to the roof of a house. The effort exerted is not lost, rather it remains stored there, intact, perhaps for years, until one day the stone gets detached and falls on the head of someone." This classic example would later become famous in Physics.

Planck would struggle for years against the best physicists of his time in order to free them from the pernicious influence of this simile. It is one of the scientists' great temptations—incidentally—to believe they have explained something when they have found a mechanical paradigm to visualize it. This is the mechanistic prejudice. If—Planck used to repeat, insistently and all alone—the natural interchange of heat between two bodies, one with a high temperature and another with a low one, can be explained through the simile of how a certain weight falls from a certain height, then the demonstration of the famous irreversibility in the second principle of thermodynamics (the law of entropy) is superfluous, as well as the existence of an absolute zero in temperature, since—if we let ourselves be influenced by the mechanical example—it would only be possible to measure differences in "level" between two temperatures.

The Milieu

It is highly significant to hear from Planck's own mouth, in his autobiography, that what led him to science at a young age and made him later become passionate about it was "the absolutely non-obvious fact that our laws of thinking concord with the regularities that we perceive from the external world in the course of our impressions; that is, that it be possible for Man to reach conclusions about those regularities solely through thinking." We cannot forget that we are in the Germany of the 1870s, where Kant and Idealism were ubiquitous and had penetrated in all of European culture.

Planck thus approaches science with highly philosophical concerns, like Newton, the father of classical physics.[4] But the German physicist's implicit conceptual premises are those elaborated by Kant. This is the drama involving science during the nineteenth century and even currently, and Planck himself is its most genuine personification of it.

The president of the Kaiser-Wilhelm-Gesellschaft is dramatically, though half-consciously, torn between two poles: the Kantian idealism he has received and the scientific realism he has practiced. We must bear this tension in mind in order to understand many of his affirmations. Ultimately he is a complete realist, even a naïve one, who expresses himself in Kantian terms.

His sharp intelligence, and even more so his profound common sense, lead him to affirm, in the aforementioned autobiography, that "it is of fundamental importance that the external world represent something independent of us and that [it be] something absolute, in front of which we find ourselves." Furthermore, he adds in all honesty that already in his youth,

---

[4] A comparison of these two geniuses of Physics would be very interesting. A parallelism can even be established in their longevity, as Newton lived to be eighty-five, and Planck, eighty-nine.

"the search for laws that are valid for this absolute [the external world] seemed to me to be the most beautiful scientific mission of all my life." Planck resists being an idealist, despite the fact that he poses science's criteriological problems in Kantian terms—and his resistance will contribute considerably to the future blossoming of realism.

A scientist *cannot* be an idealist; he lives with too much proximity the fact that the outside world is independent of the laws of his own thinking and that of every created spirit, and that such laws only come close to the reality of things asymptotically and with much insecurity—in both the common and the scientific senses of the word. The incompatible tension between the Kantian-Cartesian philosophical concepts that the scientists resorted to and the results and demands of the experimental sciences constitutes the main problem of current cosmology.[5] It is altogether another thing when traditional Aristotelian-Thomist concepts of reality are used.

*   *   *

With captivating simplicity Planck himself describes his first steps in the world of science. Not everything were successes. During his university studies (three years in Munich and a fourth year in Berlin) he continues to be enthusiastic about Physics, but admits to being disenchanted with his teachers. While one can hold that his professors in Munich "were only locally relevant," in Berlin he studied under Hermann Helmholtz and Gustav Kirchhoff. In his autobiography he provides a masterful description of these great physicists of the nineteenth century. One can imagine the boring, and boredom-inducing, Helmholtz and the elegant and cold Kirchhoff unable to quench the young and audacious Planck's zeal for knowledge. Nevertheless, in honor to truth, Planck confesses to having learned much from his professors. While, as we will see, in philosophy we must assume that he was an autodidact, in science he was connected to the most authentic scientific tradition.

He then submerges himself in books and delves into the investigations of Rudolf Clausius on the second principle of thermodynamics. Clausius is his true teacher; Planck reads his texts avidly and is under the impression that he is finally centered. In 1879 he completes his doctoral dissertation on problems related to Clausian entropy.

In his old age, Planck remembers the scientific loneliness of his youth. Similar to what happened to Newton, his first publications had no resonance.[6] "The impression this text had on the physicists of the time was equal to zero,"[7] he writes in reference to his thesis. He barely passed the examination, and only because he was known to be a good student. Hemholtz did not even read his thesis, and Kirchhoff flat out rejected it; Clausius was in Bonn, unreachable to Planck's attempts to visit, and he never answered Planck's letters, just like Carl Neumann from Leipzig. Every vocation has its trials and every man who fulfills his mission must overcome the despondency that is brought upon him by the "great men," those who are satisfied by their own routines. The encounter with "Philistinism" belongs to the destiny of all sincere and great men. The Dutch Academy of Sciences did not admit for publication the then celebrated work of Van't Hoff on gases, and London's reply to the first attempts of formulating the great periodic law of the elements was that perhaps it would be better to catalogue them in alphabetical order. *Eppur si muove....*[8]

---

[5] See my "La entropía y el fin del mundo," *Revista de Filosofía* 13 (1945): 311ff.

[6] See Leonardo Villena, "Sir Isaac Newton," *Arbor* 17: 319ff.

[7] *Autobiography.*

[8] "And yet, it *does* move," as Galileo was reported to say.

Planck stakes all his noble ambition on becoming famous when, sometime in those years while he was *Privatdozent* in Munich, he decides to sign up for the contest announced by Göttingen's Faculty of Philosophy in 1884 that would award the best study on the essence of energy in 1887. Planck was given the second prize. In the existing discussion between Helmholtz and Weber (let us recall Weber's law), Planck leaned toward the former; but it was Weber who was a professor in Göttingen. Notwithstanding, this was the time when public recognition of his merits began.

In 1885 he is called to Kiel as *Extraordinarius* in Theoretical Physics. Planck confesses that the day of his nomination was one of the happiest in his life. He was twenty-seven years old, and he was then able to become emancipated from his family. But happiness is never complete: the nomination had not been a consequence of his scientific prestige, but rather of the existing and long-lasting friendship between his father and the Physics professor at Kiel.

In 1889, after Kirchhoff's death, Planck went on to substitute him in his chair in Berlin, first as *Extraordinarius* and then finally as *Ordinarius* as of 1892. This is the time of his scientific maturity, as he himself acknowledges. We are now on the eve of 1900 when, along with the new century, Planck inaugurates a new era for Physics with his brilliant hypothesis on quanta. He is already over forty years old.

The Gestation of the Discovery

"Things happen *as if* bodies attracted each other . . . *et hypotheses non fingo*" (I do not venture hypotheses), wrote the discreet Newton when he formulated his law of universal gravitation. And this was exactly the position the prudent Planck took when he introduced the discontinuous *variation* of energy in the well-known problem of black-body radiation.

There are two types of hypotheses that have been repeated throughout the history of human thought. Some are stridently revolutionary, due not only to the scientific work of their discoverers, but also to their fantasy. Generally, after a short period of absolute supremacy, they fall from grace and are then reduced to their just limits. The Theory of Relativity is a good example. Others, on the other hand, start out as humble partial hypotheses and then progress uninterruptedly until they end up at the head of a certain discipline.[9] *Amice, ascende superius!* Planck's hypothesis has been of the latter type. What began as a simple particular constant, a straightforward working hypothesis to explain a specific problem, gradually became one of the fundamental postulates of all of physico-mathematical science.

The specific problem may have been a small one, but it had to tackle the concept of energy that "along with the notions of space and time is the only thing common to all the diverse fields of physics."[10] Planck, as an authentic man of science, is interested in specific and particular problems but never loses sight of the general vision or forgets the more universal philosophical reflection that provide meaning to scientific issues and put them in their place.[11] The problem of energy inspired him; it was his "favourite subject."[12]

But there is more. By virtue of his philosophical interests, Planck places himself within the line of tradition, and through this he touches upon a profound and real problem that has troubled Man throughout time. This is a very important datum for any study of the

---

[9] Planck himself recognizes this evolution in his theory. See *Physikalische Gesetzlichkeit,* 1926. In *Wege zur physikalischen Erkenntnis,* 170.

[10] See *Wege zur physikalischen Erkenntnis,* 7.

[11] See *Wege zur physikalischen Erkenntnis,* 282ff.

[12] *Autobiography.*

psychological process of discovery and invention. How can our minds conceive and later fulfill brilliant intuitions that begin as shy hypotheses and end up as audacious and undisputed theories? The apple falling is banal—to cite Newton's classical example—but the decisive fact is the repercussion of this fact in a mind that is concerned with the issue.[13]

A little before Planck was born, in 1850, Robert Mayer wrote his classical study "on the mechanical equivalent of heat";[14] five years before, he had already published some "considerations on the forces of inanimate nature."[15] These texts posed in the field of science the profound metaphysical concern which in Kant is formulated as the problem of the conservation of *substance*; in Leibniz, as the law of the conservation of *force*; in Descartes, as the principle of conservation of *movement*; and in Scholastic philosophy, as the matter of *impulse*, intimately related to the great problem of the dynamism of being.[16] Planck properly belongs to this line of thought. His concerns are profoundly philosophical, which is why the transcendence of his discovery is so great. The investigation also leads to some dead trails. But the fruitful paths can only be traveled by those who place themselves in the authentic perspective discovered by philosophy.[17]

With the theory of relativity, Einstein forces us to revise the concepts of space and time. With quantum theory, Planck profoundly modifies the physico-mathematical concept of energy.

What space, time, and energy, these fundamental dimensions of physical events, are in their essence in the physical world is not something that physico-mathematics can tell us.[18] Their intimate reality escapes the methods of the latter, in the same way that the soul fled in face of the surgeon's scalpel, which was never able to *come across* it—as the already decadent nineteenth-century materialism vociferously proclaimed in a challenge of sorts. Fortunately, there were never any blithe apologists who affirmed to have come across the soul because, if they had been able to, they would have ipso facto turned it into a material thing, therefore destroying its very essence.

The physico-mathematician merely has to confront the mathematical, quantitative, if you wish, design of physical reality. The underlying substance, matter (which is the foundation), escapes his methods of quantitative, phenomenal experimentation[19]—although, vice versa, quantity and therefore the entire physico-mathematic construction only makes sense if it is supported by a precise physical reality (substance). Thus, ultimately, physico-mathematics has many things to say about the intimate texture of bodies.[20]

Planck always intuited this distinction more or less rigorously. This is why he was very careful not to say that "the essence of quantum theory is the extension of the atomic principle to the explanation of nature,"[21] and not to connect his conception to the cosmological

---

[13] See my "Investigación," *Revista de Filosofía* 2/3: 389ff.

[14] *Über das mechanische Äquivalent der Wärme.*

[15] *Bemerkungen über die Kräfte der unbelebten Natur.*

[16] As far as I know, a profound study on the conservation of energy from this global point of view is still to be written.

[17] In 1933, Planck gave a conference on this problem of invention, which on its own constitutes a true monument to psychological observation: *Ursprung und Auswirkung wissenschaftlicher Ideen* (in *Wege zur physikalischen Erkenntnis*, 260ff.).

[18] Even if energy is not a simple dimension for physico-mathematics, it still is so physically.

[19] See my "La ciencia biomatemática," in *Arbor* 3 (1944).

[20] This does not mean that there are no mathematical formulas for physical processes that have no direct physical representation.

[21] This is, for example, what it says in the October 6, 1947, article in the *Manchester Guardian*

doctrines of Democritus from twenty-five centuries earlier, as is usually disclosed in superficial popularizations. Only someone like W. Ostwald, "strongly inclined by nature to systematisation"—as Planck himself accurately characterizes him[22]—could create a philosophical *energetism* by defending the identity of energy with Being itself.

We must ponder the prudence and sobriety with which Planck explained the appearance and development of his theory in his speech upon receiving the Nobel Prize in 1920.[23] There was a strictly scientific problem that had interested him for a long time: "The distribution of energy in the normal spectrum of radiant heat."[24] Later he realizes, however, the reason he was troubled by this problem: "This so-called normal distribution of energy represents something absolute and, because the search in pursuit of the absolute always seemed to me to be the most beautiful task of investigation, I dedicated myself to its study with great intensity."[25]

The "Quantum" of Action, a Universal Constant

Even though the scientific genesis of quantum theory is well known and has already been sufficiently popularized, it is interesting to point out some general considerations about its evolution here.

It is truly instructive to collate the twofold explanation that Planck himself makes of his discovery. He explains his personal work in the aforementioned speech (1920) and again summarizes it toward the end of his life in his autobiography. For the latter he uses the speech from the Nobel Prize, as can be seen by the fact that there are six entire paragraphs copied from it almost literally. Since the biography is of a more anecdotal and confidential nature and the speech of a more scientific one, with quotes from original papers, in the former he eliminates some of the more general sentences he had pronounced in Stockholm;[26] but, on the other hand, he adds others that reveal a greater consciousness of the meaning of his theory.

In neither case, however, does Planck venture to say anything about the intimate essence of the function that had so inspired him and whose hidden behavior he had just discovered: energy. Planck's prudence in this regard is extreme. On June 25, 1935, he gives a speech about Leibniz in the session of the Prussian Academy of Sciences in Berlin,[27] where he continuously speaks about the "principle of continuity" as capital in the Leibnizian system, without even minimally alluding to whether his quantum theory, according to him, contradicts or reinforces such a principle. Planck sees the ultimate cosmological problem, but he eludes it systematically. Recognizing himself to be ignorant of more profound problems is not the lesser merit of an investigator. A naïve mind would be liable to think that energy should pose no problem whatsoever for the discoverer of quanta, but Planck repeatedly alludes—perhaps to calm himself—to the fact that "the investigator's appeasement and happiness does not lie in stillness of possession, but rather in the continuous growth of knowledge."[28]

The bare scientific process is, all in all, sufficiently exhilarating. Planck discovers his formula and calculates its constant, which, because it represents the product of energy over

---

dedicated to Planck's death; and analogously in the one of October 5, 1947, in the *New York Times*.

[22] *Autobiography.*

[23] See *Wege zur physikalischen Erkenntnis*, 68ff.

[24] Ibid., 69.

[25] *Autobiography.*

[26] See for example, *Wege zur physikalischen Erkenntnis*, 72.

[27] In *Zeitschrift für Naturforschung* (Wiesbaden, 1935), 298ff.

[28] In *Die Physik im Kampf um die Weltanschauung* (Leipzig, 1937), 25.

a certain period of time, he calls *elementary quantum of action* according to classic physics terminology.[29] For the time being it is only one more physico-mathematic constant, and Planck himself has doubts about its meaning within physics. He then diligently tries to frame his formula and his constant within the terminology of classic physics, against his colleagues' judgment, who consider "the series of years" and "the much work" he devoted to it time lost.

Planck merely proposed the alternative:

> Either the quantum of action was a fictitious magnitude . . . , or there lay a real physical
> notion beneath the deduction of the law of radiation, [and] then the quantum of
> action should play a fundamental role; at that point something completely new was
> being announced, something unprecedented to date, which seemed to be called to
> radically transform the way we think about physics—which, since the discovery
> of infinitesimal calculus by Leibniz and Newton, rested on the assumption of the
> monotony [continuity] of all causal connections.[30]

These are perhaps the most audacious words he ever pronounced.[31]

"Experience made the decision fall in favor of the second alternative."[32] Planck describes with contained, though contagious, scientific enthusiasm how his constant was adopted by the most diverse researchers in their respective areas of expertise, thus becoming a universal constant in physics. Einstein, Nernst, Debye, Bjerrum, von Bahr, Rubens, Hettner, Sackur, Stern, Tetrode, Millikan, Bohr, Sommerfeld, Schrödinger, and so on, use it and introduce it in all of physics.

It is certainly exhilarating to follow the steps of the triumphal progress of the humble numerical value of a small constant, and to witness how it gradually falls perfectly into place in the calculation of the most varied physical phenomena. The constant h must represent something real. It is understandable that one be surprised to see the coincidence of the laws of his *thinking* and the independent *being* he has before him.

And yet Planck proceeds step by step, slowly. He does not regret having spent long years trying to find a solution to the problem inside of classic physics, as the failure of his efforts has allowed him to better realize the importance and significance of his theory.[33] Furthermore, the prudent physicist clarifies in 1920 that "a real quantum theory has not yet been created with the introduction of the quantum of action,"[34] not only because of the problems which at the time he foresaw as very serious,[35] but also because of the difference that he had always suspected existed (although he did not have the adequate conceptual system to express it rigorously) between the physico-mathematical behavior of a function and its physical reality.[36]

---

[29] The first value of h, Planck's constant, which he himself calculated was 6.55×10^{-27}, practically the same as the value adopted in 1937 (Milikan–von Friesen, etc.), $6.610 + 0.012 \times 10^{-27}$ and as the one calculated in 1911 by Birge, $6,6242 \times 10^{-27}$ *erg sec.*

[30] *Wege zur physikalischen Erkenntnis*, 76–77. This text is also repeated in his autobiography.

[31] *Wege zur physikalischen Erkenntnis*, 171ff., where he seems to admit that energy is discrete, though without categorically affirming it.

[32] Again in *Wege zur physikalischen Erkenntnis*, 76–77.

[33] *Autobiography*.

[34] *Wege zur physikalischen Erkenntnis*, 81.

[35] As to the problem of the energy of a quantum of light after emission. This is the classical divergence between Huygens and Newton.

[36] See my "El indeterminismo científico," *Anales de Física y Química* (Madrid) 396 (1945): 584ff.

Planck does not skip the philosophical problem, though he does not face it head on. Many physicists of a lesser magnitude have often lacked the authentic humility of the true researcher.[37]

Despite his temperance, the excitement on the afternoon of October 19, 1900, in the session of the Berlin Physics Society must have been considerable.[38] Through one of those intuitions that only geniuses know how to transmit, the physicists in attendance suspected that the motto *Natura non facit saltus*[39] of antiquity, which the liberal century of the *laissez faire, laissez passer* had been so attached to, had finally reached its end; and that the material world as an object of the creation of a Spirit also participated in the palpitating dynamism of the entire Being. The kingdom of earth also[40] suffers violence.

Planck, who used to limit himself to personal intimacies, tells us nothing of these sessions. In the account of his life, he merely relates that the following morning his colleague Rubens met him and told him that he had spent the night calculating Planck's formula with his own data, and that the calculations coincided fully. That constant must have possessed some kind of value for such a methodical Teuton to lose his hours of sleep in recalculating the numerical value of a simple formula!

For the time being, it is a simple theoretical interest, which only attracts the authentic men of science, who consider utilitarianism treason and actively flee from it. Our Berlinese professor of Theoretical Physics abhors utilitarianism.[41] Another generation will speak of the atomic bomb, radar, and so on. One of the hard trials facing any investigator is having to struggle against a practical-minded environment that brands him a parasite. And one does not always have the serenity of a Faraday, who, when asked by Gladstone, the great politician, about the practical utility of his discovery (which, as we now know, has made the industrial use of electricity possible), frankly responded, "Sir, you will soon be able to collect new taxes!"

Quantum Physics

What, then, is the real meaning of the quantum theory with reference to the "discrete" nature of energy?

It contains an obvious discontinuity; but the problem lies in knowing if such a discretion lies in energy *itself* or in its *variation*; and in the second place, if the discontinuous *manifestation* of energy allows us to deduce something about the very *nature* of physical energy.

The cornerstone, the ultimate reality that physics must confront, is matter, as that from which all bodies are constituted. Matter is physically determined by a series of qualities whose quantification (quantitative aspect) gives place to the different physico-mathematical units. Matter is inserted in a spatiotemporal net, but at the same time it acts upon and influences

---

[37] When leaving the complex and learned conference of a notable physicist who tried to amaze the auditorium by considering the problem of the intimate nature of light solved—not from the physico-mathematical point of view (Bohr's principle of complementarity), but rather from the physical one—somebody made the following comment: "My most sincere conclusion is this: on Mondays, Wednesdays and Fridays I believe in the undulatory theory; on Tuesdays, Thursdays and Saturdays I defend the corpuscular hypothesis."

[38] That day Planck explained his new formula of radiation. Weeks later, on December 14, 1900, he read his famous communication "Zur Theorie des Gesetzes der Energie im Normalspektrum" [For a theory of the law of energy in the normal spectrum].

[39] "Nature does not proceed by leaps."

[40] As well as the Kingdom of Heaven (Mt 11:12).

[41] Planck in his article on Leibniz (*Wege zur physikalischen Erkenntnis*, 298).

other bodies, it moves. At bottom, this is the great metaphysical problem of movement. There is something in bodies, some coefficient of activity, of dynamism, that they must possess (force, work, energy, action) that explains change in matter. We are here transcending physico-mathematics in order to penetrate into physics in the Aristotelian sense of the word. There is something in matter that is the cause of its activity. Is this "something," which is postulated by philosophy, and whose effects physics captures, and whose manifestations physico-mathematics measures and represents by a function, discrete or continuous?

If we pose the problem like this, its solution is already discernible. It makes no sense to speak of the discontinuity of that which is not quantitative. It makes no sense to say that a sound, a color, a smell as such—not as longitudes of waves, molecules, and so on—are discrete. Perhaps the ancient theory of impulses can still teach us something.[42]

But pinpointing a problem is one thing and solving it is another altogether. What is here under discussion is the physico-mathematical function which represents physical energy.

Energy, that internal force that is able to carry out work, only *manifested* itself in a discrete mode; better yet, it was only *observable* in discontinuous variations. That is to say, in order for mathematical calculations to adapt to *experimental* reality, the physico-mathematical magnitude known as energy could not adopt any value whatsoever, but rather only a few multiples of the universal constant calculated by Planck. In *mathematical* (not physical) terms, energy appeared as discontinuous; it was not represented by any continuous function that always allowed the interpolation of any intermediate value.

Yet, once primitive quantum physics was surpassed by current quantum mechanics, *continuous changes* of energy (pure translations and perturbed systems) were reintroduced, relegating discontinuous variation to periodic movements. Thus, not even physico-mathematical energy is rigorously discontinuous, as experimentally it behaves both ways.

And yet, what happens to *physical* energy properly said? What can we deduce about its nature as of its behavior? An investigation on the intimate essence of energy is still to be undertaken, and almost even to be rigorously and philosophically posed.[43]

It is emblematic that the University of Göttingen did not award Planck the first prize sixty years ago: in fact, his brilliant reply did not exactly answer the question of *essence*, but rather only of the *behavior* of energy. The investigation aimed at the first prize is still pending.

* * *

Quantum theory properly said has had a long and slow evolution. We can distinguish three definitely concluded stages and a contemporary era.

In the first phase, the constant h is introduced; it is the quantum of action as a universal physical constant. The main steps toward this were taken by Planck in 1900 with his famous formula; by Einstein in 1905 when he applied the theory to luminous radiation (photons);[44] and by Bohr in 1913 when he introduced the idea of quantum in the study of the atom's structure.

The second stage ends in 1927 with Heisenberg's principle of indetermination. In the history of science there have been very few years of such high scientific density as those

---

[42] The arduous philosophical problem of the essence of energy is not our concern here.

[43] For a more detailed description of the metaphysical, physical, and physico-mathematical levels in our penetration into reality, see my *El indeterminismo científico*, op. cit.

[44] Einstein defends the corpuscular model of radiation as a heuristic hypothesis without daring, quite prudently, to affirm its specific significance for Physics. See "Über einen die Erzeugung und Verwandlung des Lichtes betreffenden heuristischen Gesichtspunkt," *Annals of Physics* 17, no. 132 (1905).

between 1925 and 1927. During these years we see the emergence of the transcendental investigations of Luis de Broglie (waves-corpuscles), Erwin Schrödinger (fundamental equations of quantum mechanics), Werner Heisenberg (uncertainty principle), Paul A. M. Dirac (matrix mechanics), Born, Jordan, and others.[45]

The final stage begins after 1927; it is one in which scientists seriously concern themselves with the physical interpretation of their mathematical theories. It is the age of extra-scientific studies, in which Planck does not participate in the least, since he had in fact anticipated them by some years.

From 1936, or more precisely from 1939, a new era can be foreseen. From a "sensational" point of view, it is the Atomic era. From the more serene point of view of a history of science, it could be characterized as the beginning of the reconciliation between classic and modern physics, between Newton and Planck. Quantum mechanics harmonizes continuous and discontinuous variations of energy. It is now said that classical quantum physics has been surpassed. This is the point of departure for the fusion of these two perspectives into a more profound vision of reality.[46]

*   *   *

In this brief text we are only concerned with reporting Planck's personal work in the third stage we mentioned.

While scientific evolution followed its course, Planck turned to studying Philosophy (an excellent example for our scientists![47]), although, unfortunately, he had nobody to help him surmount the atmosphere that dominated almost all German philosophy faculties, which at the very least must be characterized as being excessively historical, if not downright historicist. In his writings he demonstrates not only a genuinely philosophical preoccupation, but also ample erudition.[48] But if we interpret the silence present in his autobiography (so explicit, on the other hand, in reference to personal friendships) as actual data, we must deduce that Planck did not have close contacts with any one philosophical personality who may exercise a determined influence over him. This explains many things. Philosophical autodidacticism is rarely free of serious gaps.

Causality

Among the philosophical problems that troubled Planck throughout his life, the principle of causality occupies a central place. Most of his monographs are directly or indirectly about this topic.

---

[45] In 1926 Planck describes the situation of Physics at the time as a *Sturm und Drangperiode*, "a very stormy period / a true epoch of *Sturm und Drang*" (*Wege zur physikalischen Erkenntnis*, 177).

[46] See the countless general works that have appeared in the last few years, trying to give a unitary vision of the physical world in connection with philosophy, both on the part of scientists as well as of philosophers. Let us recall, for example, Herman Bavinck, Weyl, Eddington, Oliver Lodge, Whitehead, Zimmer, Dingler, von Weizsäcker, Haering, M. de Broglie, Meyerson, Becher, Wenzl, Driesch, Maritain, Pesch, Hoenen, etc.

[47] In fact, he recommends it emphatically. Cf., for example, *Wege zur physikalischen Erkenntnis*, 177, and indirectly, 282ff.

[48] See, for example, the vast philosophical documentation in his article on *Kausalgesetz und Willensfreiheit*, "causal law and free will" (*Wege zur physikalischen Erkenntnis*, 87ff., specifically 93ff.).

The problem of the principle of conservation of energy, which constituted the starting point of his scientific speculation, soon led him to consider causality as the key to such a principle. It is obvious that this first principle of Thermodynamics and of all of Physics rests on the validity of causality. Energy—we may say—is preserved precisely in order to be later detected as the *cause* of subsequent transformations.[49]

Planck begins by using this principle scientifically, without any reflexive considerations about it.[50] But he will soon realize the importance that such a principle of causality entails, since all of science rests on it.[51] He will defend this affirmation, one way[52] or another,[53] throughout his entire life.[54]

Here Planck demonstrates great philosophical sense. The entire problem of physical laws rests on causality, even if it is posed through probabilistic laws that presuppose it.[55] Moreover, Planck recognizes, with profound insight, that science and philosophy must collaborate tightly if we are to achieve a complete conception of the physical world.[56] While some of his current disciples declare that they are going to attempt "a philosophical interpretation of quantum physics free of all metaphysics,"[57] the actual founder of the discipline repeatedly and sincerely recognized that "physical science cannot advance without a certain dose of metaphysics."[58]

But Planck's philosophical concerns, imbued with Kantianism, are even more profound.[59] After studying the "unity of the physical conception of the world"[60] and describing "the worldview provided by the new physics,"[61] he goes on to tackle the place that physics has in any conception of the world.[62] And with this he fully penetrates not only into the philosophical problems of science but also into philosophy itself.

This leads him to the final stage of spiritual reflection: religion. Although the reigning environment in his time period tended to completely disassociate the religious field from the scientific one, the actual facts and the evolution of his very own spirit fully lead him to this ultimate sphere of Reality. It is curious to observe, for example, how he systematically eludes the name of God in his long article on "causal law and free will,"[63] despite constantly alluding to Him. Nevertheless, he confesses himself to be fully religious, just as true scientists have always been—he writes.[64] Later on, he tackles the religious problem directly, be it occasionally

---

[49] See my *El indeterminismo científico*, 599.

[50] See his *Die Einheit des physikalischen Weltbildes*, 1908 (included in *Wege zur physikalischen Erkenntnis*).

[51] *Wege zur physikalischen Erkenntnis*, 49ff., specifically 53.

[52] Ibd., 65.

[53] See *Der Kausalbegriff in der Physik* (Leipzig, 1932), 26.

[54] See *Determinismus oder Indeterminismus* (Leipzig, 1938).

[55] *Wege zur physikalischen Erkenntnis*, 147ff.

[56] Ibid., 104ff.

[57] Hans Reichenbach, *Philosophic Foundations of Quantum Mechanics* (Los Angeles: Berkeley & Co., 1946), vii.

[58] *Wege zur physikalischen Erkenntnis*, 177.

[59] As proof of the Kantian influence on him, see *Wege zur physikalischen Erkenntnis*, 32 and 100, etc.

[60] *Die Einheit des physikalischen Weltbildes* (Leiden, 1908).

[61] *Das Weltbild der neuen Physik* (1929).

[62] *Die Physik im Kampf um die Weltanschauung* (1935).

[63] Op. cit. Only once does the name of God appear, at the end of a quote from St. Paul.

[64] *Wege zur physikalischen Erkenntnis*, 126–27.

in diverse papers;[65] be it, without fear of the word, in a simple Christmas article;[66] be it more seriously, years later, in a direct manner.[67]

But it is also through the problem of causality that Planck reverts from physics to philosophy and ultimately to religion.

Planck carefully analyzes the validity of the principle of causality. After affirming its absolute value within the field of the physical sciences, he goes on to examine its role in the world of the spirit. This leads him to the problem of freedom, which constitutes the other pole of his philosophical concerns.[68] If causality ruled the entire world—he says—there would be no room for freedom. And in the wake of Kant, Planck cannot renounce to moral law[69] or to the primacy of ethics above the rest of disciplines, nor can he in any way reduce the absolute value of the righteous will.[70]

Planck's sharp intelligence, which makes him be realistic despite his Kantian formation,[71] also helps him overcome the cold and unilateral rationalism of so many scientists. In the same historic year 1900, along with Planck's communication, the first volume of the monumental work by Edmund Husserl, *Logical Investigations*, appears. It must be pointed out that, while the philosopher still[72] adheres to the possibility of "philosophy as a rigorous science"[73] by eliminating from it any premises that may "contaminate" it, the scientist's common sense affirms that "there is perhaps no other statement that has caused as much damage because of its false conception as the one about the lack of presuppositions in science."[74] This is the other problem that will concern him throughout his life.[75]

*   *   *

It is perhaps inopportune to criticize Planck's theory of causality in a rigorously philosophical plane. We would then need to discuss his clever, though not original, distinction between the physical validity of the principle of causality and its logical necessity. For Planck, the principle of causality flows from the actual logical structure of our thinking. It is not, thus, either a Kantian category or a supreme logical principle. This point could be debated; but if it is admitted, we cannot anyway identify the principle of causality with that of sufficient reason, as Planck implicitly does, when he sees the *reasons* for human actions as their efficient *causes*.[76]

---

[65]   See, for example, his aforementioned article on Leibniz.

[66]   *Wege zur physikalischen Erkenntnis*, 281ff. This article refers almost exclusively to natural scientific "faith," or, to put it another way, to the human hope for truth as an indispensable assumption of science.

[67]   *Religion und Naturwissenschaft* (1937).

[68]   See also *Vom Wesen der Willensfreiheit* (1936).

[69]   *Wege zur physikalischen Erkenntnis*, 127.

[70]   See *Die Physik im Kampf um die Weltanschauung*, 32.

[71]   See again as proof, his 1930 conference on *Positivismus und reale Außenwelt* [Positivism and the reality of the external world] (*Wege zur physikalischen Erkenntnis*, 208ff.).

[72]   I say "still" because neo-Kantianism had especially stressed the *Voraussetzungslosigkeit* [lack of conditions] of philosophy.

[73]   E. Husserl, *Philosophie als strenge Wissenschaft* (Tübingen, 1911), 1:289ff.

[74]   *Wege zur physikalischen Erkenntnis*, 282.

[75]   See one of his last papers: "Der Sinn der exakten Wissenschaften," *Geist der Zeit* (1942): 566ff.

[76]   See *Kausalgesetz und Willensfreiheit*, 115ff.

For Planck, causality is a "heuristic principle, an indicator, the most valuable navigator we possess to lead us through the thick chaos of events."[77] But in Planck we must understand his intentions more than his formulations. And his intentions—better yet, his most profound convictions—are quite patent.

The physical world is dominated by the most absolute causality, and this in a way that is "totally independent of the peculiarity of the investigator's spirit";[78] that is to say, "it would maintain its meaning even if there was absolutely no knowing subject."[79] Therefore, causality regulates both the macroscopic as well as the microscopic world; it governs classical physics as well as quantum physics.[80] Another thing is the impossibility of reaching an exact determination of a process because of Heisenberg's Uncertainty Principle.[81]

On the other hand, there is "only one point, one sole point in the wide and incommensurable world of nature and of the spirit, which is inaccessible and will forever remain unreachable to any causal consideration, not only in the practical order, but also even in the logical one: this point is one's own I."[82] This is how Planck saves the world of the spirit. Even if, for Planck, the reasons for which the spirit operates are also causes subject to the principle of causality,[83] there exists a human person's depth that is free of this causal chain. Next to "causality's *have-to*, there is the moral *must*."[84] And this is when we see the appearance of "character, instead of intelligence; religious faith, instead of scientific knowledge."[85]

Planck makes an effort to recognize the spiritual sphere above the material one, but his scientific temperament requires proof of the liberation of the law of causality in the world of spirit. This is characteristic of his reasoning:[86] the reasons because of which Man decides are the cause of his actions; but the knowledge of such a motive of the will can originate a new motivation, and so successively. The personal "I" breaks this chain wherever it wishes. This is where freedom begins. This is why future human events are unforeseeable; but, on the other hand, these events are calculable, that is, they already belong to the causal chain, once they have been carried out.[87]

* * *

In sum, whoever is able to get to the bottom of things, disregarding their more or less close-fitting dress, will always find in Planck's philosophical works a rich volume of observations and arguments that allow one to go deeper into the vision of the physical world that surrounds us and of the psychic one that impregnates us.

If Planck, this restless scientist always in search of suprascientific truth, had lived during the Middle Ages, in which religious faith strove to become increasingly more comprehensible,

---

[77] *Wege zur physikalischen Erkenntnis*, 26.
[78] *Kausalgesetz und Willensfreiheit*, 117.
[79] Ibid., 118.
[80] *Wege zur physikalischen Erkenntnis*, 65.
[81] See M. Planck, *Sinn und Grenzen der exakten Wissenschaft* (Leipzig, 1942).
[82] *Kausalgesetz und Willensfreiheit*, 115.
[83] Ibid.
[84] Ibid., 123.
[85] Ibid.
[86] See *Wege zur physikalischen Erkenntnis*, 165.
[87] See also *Wege zur physikalischen Erkenntnis*, 65ff.

the *Summa* of his works would doubtlessly have been bestowed the following subtitle: *Scientia quaerens philosophiam!*[88]

His Life's Work

This is the setting of extrascientific ideas in which this extraordinary man of science set his physical investigations, and that gave him the unitary conception of human life that makes all his work so appealing. He does not want to think without life, or religion without thinking;[89] precisely because he is open to all spheres of Being, he realizes both Man's small-ness and the greatness of his mission.[90]

Some people tried to show Planck as the prototype of the *Faustic nature* of the "German Race."[91] Rereading his texts, one can find no traits that may justify such an epithet. His rather passive political actions—letting himself be honored by the German authorities, doing good to whoever he could, but without making too great an effort to protect those who were perse-cuted—manifest a harmonic, rather placid nature. His field was not that of practical action.[92]

Toward the end of his life, the mature Planck maintains an intense scientific epistolary activity. But he is not a mummified scientist, and one is pleasingly surprised to see the polite words he interchanges with Sommerfeld, in which both sides use poetry to communicate more beautifully to each other.[93]

Neither does one see the characteristic hubris of Goethe's Faust in him. Despite being the founder of the deepest ground of current Physics (much more important than relativity[94]), he is never swelled with pride because of his exclusive paternity. If he laid down the first stone in the building of the new Physics, it is a building that all modern physicists have collaborated to erect. This is ultimately a greater merit than the one of creating a hypothesis that is so personal that it cannot be put in the hands of strangers without degenerating, as has happened so many times in the history of human thought.

What are possibly the last lines he wrote for the public can be found in a letter addressed to the Swiss periodical *Atlantis*, from a few months ago, for an issue dedicated to the University of Göttingen, where so many leading German scientists met after the war.[95] It consists of only one short paragraph, which portrays his temperament and manifests his ideals:

> After the loss of my home in Berlin and the political catastrophe which caught me in Elba, my wife and I have moved to Göttingen, city of my Planck ancestors, in order to avoid becoming Russians. At eighty-nine years old I can no longer produce

---

[88] Please forgive the anachronism of the use of the modern concept of science in a medieval context.

[89] See *Kausalgesetz und Willensfreiheit*, 124.

[90] See M. Planck, "El sentido íntimo de las ciencias exactas," *Revista Nacional de Educación* (Madrid) 32–33 (1943): 77–78, where he is pleased to once again use, in his own way, Newton's happy comparison of himself to a simple child playing next to the sea.

[91] See, for example, most German high school physics books written as of 1933.

[92] One of his sons, who was active in the German Ministry of Foreign Affairs, was executed at the time of the conspiracy against Hitler planned by Gördeler and von Stauffenberg.

[93] According to what he himself reveals in his autobiography.

[94] See the same emphatic affirmation in Maurice de Broglie, *Átomos, radioactividad, transmutaciones* (Buenos Aires, 1940), 71.

[95] It is interesting to learn that, along with the scientists mentioned at the beginning, one finds there: A. Windhaus, Th. Valentiner, H. J. Iward, H. F. Rein, O. Hahn, Nicolai Hartmann, G. Misch, H. Nohl, etc.

scientifically. What remains for me is the possibility of following the progress that my work has channelized, and every once in a while, of repeating my conferences and giving satisfaction to the desires of the people and especially of the young ones, avid for truth and knowledge.[96]

Planck was a tireless investigator and a passionate truth seeker; while we wait for History's definitive judgment, we could apply to him Goethe's happy expression, the same expression with which Planck ended one of his best conferences in Berlin:[97]

> *Wer immer strebend sich bemüht,*
> *Den können wir erlösen.*[98]

---

[96] *Atlantis* 19, no. 6 (1947): 223.

[97] *Die Physik im Kampf um die Weltanschauung* (Leipzig, 1937), 32.

[98] "He who always strived, following his aspirations—here is whom we will save!"

2

ONTONOMY OF SCIENCE

Introduction: The Atom of Time[1]

Sed omnia in mensura, et numero, et pondere disposuisti.

—*Wis 11:21*

Despite the numerous issues it tackles, this book does not aspire to be a collection of thoughts; it wishes, instead, to be the demonstration of *one* adequately developed and exemplified thought. This germinal—and from my point of view, fertile—thought is the following: Reality is simultaneously one and multiple—though not in the same sense. It is one in the absolute sense, as God is the only *Being* and outside of Him there is nothing, and *beings* neither increase nor modify the Supreme Being. And it is multiple in that all of the absolute nature of Being is not, in fact, enough to eliminate the enigmatic and difficult, though undeniable, presence of beings. Furthermore, at the very core of the one and only Being there is a Trinity, not exactly numerical, to which we must ultimately refer every divine and nondivine ontological problem. But even within the realm of beings, reality is one and multiple at once: creation is ontologically one and it is simultaneously varied. Therefore we cannot underscore one aspect in detriment of the other. For example, we must not accentuate the difference between matter and spirit so much, lest we fall into a radical dualism, nor must we only consider their unity, in such a way that cosmological monism is not overcome. Moreover—and with this we arrive at the third plane of unity and multiplicity, which is our own—the material universe itself is one and multiple at once. The material being is one, and any partial consideration of a "physical" problem is, at the very least, truncated; any closed vision of *one* being in itself is, at the very least, an abuse. But the material being is also multiple and, consequently, any exclusively deductive reflection will be, at the very least, imperfect; any general formulation will be blind or insensitive to the particularisms that constitute the multiplicity of beings. If God is one and not multiple since His Trinity is something like the full expression of His unity, matter as the last link in the scale of beings is practically more multiple than single or, at the very least, its multiplicity holds almost more consistency than its unity.

Since Science and Philosophy speak to us about physical reality, they represent this tension, this danger, as well as this adventure. By means of the transcendental realism that this book attempts to defend, we mean to guarantee unity without losing the analogy and to maintain diversity without falling into dualism. Science and Philosophy complement—and need—each other mutually; only their harmonic symbiosis can offer a vision of physical reality that is not disfigured.

---

[1] The author decided to only include the Introduction and the Contents of *Ontonomía de la ciencia* (Madrid: Gredos, 1961), in the *Opera Omnia* as he considered that the book was outdated from a scientific point of view. Translated from the Spanish by Carla Ros.

Yet, like any other harmonic solution, this synthesis requires a renunciation. Without such renunciation, the alluded complementariness turns into mere opposition and rude antagonism. Science, in one word, must renounce to reifying or substantializing its concepts, to assuming a subject (which would be more than physical) that is the foundation of physical operations; ultimately, it must renounce to a conception of the world (because the *world* is not physical). Philosophy, in turn, must renounce to its inveterate prejudice of believing itself to be self-sufficient, both from above as well as from below. From above because it is not the ultimate wisdom, and from below because it can no longer overlook Science and base itself in mere a prioristic constructions or in prescientific conceptions of the physical world.

But this mutual renunciation—if it is authentic—also entails an advantage: the salvation of the soul, of Physics and of Philosophy.

Physics is saved because it reaches its complete *ontonomy*, which allows it to develop freely within its own field without foreign interferences and to enjoy a collaboration of greater service. And Philosophy is also purified, as renouncing to an anachronistic and ineffective tutelage allows for the possibility of an efficient development as "server" of the suggestions and recommendations that Science affords it—as in Christianity, the roles are inverted—without because of this losing its proper ground, a ground that we could call specific rather than "its own."

However, this investigation does not intend to make us reach this synthesis. It is a very imperfect investigation, not only due to the double imperfection that affects, in the first place, any human creation and in the second place, the specific issue of the Philosophy of Science in which a synthesis has not been yet attained in our present day, but also because it must recognize a third and very important imperfection from the start. This essay is imperfect insofar as it is radically unfinished; I would almost even dare to say that it is truncated, as in fact it is something along the lines of the cosmological testimony of an intellectual life which, after having been intensely dedicated to the problems of Science—even of experimental Science—as a catharsis of the spirit, has abandoned these grounds to live in other dimensions. I do not, thus, give excessive value to this work. I know that the possibility of a much deeper penetration exists, a more profound dimension that is barely indicated here, an enigma that is very superior to that which these pages may make one imagine. I can now discern and "suffer" these problems, but I leave it in the hands of others—those who may have the time, the temperament, the ability (and obligation)—to do the real work and reap the possible positive suggestions from these chapters on the path to a real synthesis.

I do not, however, believe that the ideas that are gathered here, fruit of a decade of cosmological activity that ended in 1950, are altogether insignificant or that making them known is not worthwhile. They are not the last word in scientific Philosophy, as in these past years much has been written that is more valuable and more up to date—to the point that these reflections may already appear practically archaic. Nor are they the most powerful exclamation on this particular subject, that is, a new theory or the outline of a synthesis or a previously unpublished solution. Their interest lies perhaps in their propaedeutic nature—not precisely didactic—and in their intrinsic potentiality. Furthermore, despite the delay with which these studies are now published, which not only takes away from their currentness but also from their value; despite the fact that, consequently, they cannot be "updated" and I have had to revise them without notes, or books, or any sort of auxiliary matter, we hope that they still hold a peculiar philosophical value and even a theological one, as they have gone through a metaphysical filter of more than ten years. We suppose that what remains possesses, at the very least, a certain amount of purity. In other words: everything that is spoken, written, and thought is always, consciously or unconsciously, a function of the whole. Only if the whole has been more or less perceived will the part not be out of focus. More than a decade ago I wrote about spiral formation and about Science as theological propaedeutic, and in a note I added that I should not write anything about cosmology before having reached a certain theological synthesis. This awareness of being in the second turn of the spiral is the justification for publishing these pages now.

*   *   *

If it is at all possible to summarize, in an introduction, what is to be stated later, I here attempt to do so by simply commenting on the title: *The Ontonomy of Science*.

The experimental sciences of our day and age, that is to say, the physico-mathematical sciences, are presently going through the second stage of their development and thus they find themselves in the position of being able to overcome it, thus reaching the third stage of maturity and a coming of age. Contributing to such an overcoming forms part of the immediate end of the present study.

After an initial stage in which Science lived protected and sheltered, but also suffocated and tied down, by Philosophy, which heteronomically dictated its laws to all the other types of knowledge, it became emancipated, claiming complete *autonomy* for itself; this led to scientism, to believing in Progress, and so on. It is now, once the euphoria of independence has diminished and Science's sense of responsibility has grown as a consequence of seeing its results applied both to itself and to man and society at large, that the conditions for the third, *ontonomical,* stage are prepared.

In the same way that the modern machine—which is also an offspring of Science through Technique—has enslaved and still enslaves man and yet, in our time period, we are already able to perceive the overcoming of machinism since the man who is used to machines simply uses them as *quasi*-natural instruments without letting himself be dominated by them; in the same way—I was saying—that we no longer need a specialized—and enslaved—chauffeur to drive a car, analogously, the *autonomy* that Science demanded for itself in face of the paternalistic *heteronomy* in which it lived subjected to Philosophy is giving way to a harmonious *ontonomy* that allows us to interrogate Science within human culture without unilateral totalitarianisms.

In face of the other two extreme postures, I call *ontonomy* the recognition or development of the laws that are proper to each sphere of being or of human activity, with a distinction between the superior and inferior spheres, but without separation or unjustified interferences.

Ontonomy is sensible to the peculiarities of each being or type of being—without absolutizing those regularities as if other beings did not exist (autonomy), or enslaving them in the service of higher entities, as if the inferior being did not also have its own laws (heteronomy).[2]

Neither is all of reality revealed by Science—or by Philosophy—(heteronomy), nor is scientific knowledge completely foreign to or does it supplant philosophical knowledge (autonomy). Science has its own nature and its peculiar sphere which, on the other hand, have internal and constitutive connections with Philosophy.

To clear the way and find the place of Science among man's different types of knowledge is the intention of the present study. But we will limit ourselves to the study of only one of these connections and in a very partial and introductory way. We thus disregard the study of the relationship between Science and other forms of knowledge, be these pre- or a-scientific, and we only tackle a few aspects of the problem of the relationship between Science and Philosophy.

---

[2] See R. Panikkar, "Le concept d'ontonomie," in *Actes du XIè Congrès International de Philosophie* (Amsterdam: Louvain, 1953), 3:182ff.

Within this limited framework, our efforts can be summarized by saying that we are trying to develop some of the ontonomic principles of Science:

Methodological, on the one hand, by showing how Science possesses its own peculiar mensurative method that conditions both the quantitative dimension of the reality it apprehends as well as the nature of Science itself.

Criteriological, on the other, in a twofold sense: objective and subjective. *Objective* insofar as we will try to show that the object of Science is given in a formal sui generis predicamental abstraction. *Subjective* insofar as the scientist, in order to do Science, uses a characteristic functional thinking in face of the traditional predicative thinking of Philosophy.

Metaphysical, finally, by pointing out that Science only apprehends one sphere of being, which, even though it is different from the rest, it is not exiled from the totality of being; that is to say, that there is a distinction between Physics and Metaphysics, but no absolute independence.

All of these considerations would have a very relative value or, at the very least, a predominantly philosophical one, if we did not try to exemplify and to show the validity of such principles in current problems of the Science of our times.

After an introduction, of a more anthropomorphic nature than an aseptically scientific or rigorously philosophical one, we go on to study the evolution of the concept of Science from a point of view that merely aspires to complement what has been written on this particular subject in the past few years.

Then there are two chapters dedicated to the development of some of the points mentioned that I believe to be interesting for a theory of the ontonomy of Science. In these I elaborate a series of principles whose visibility intends to be exemplified by the study of the specific problems that constitute the content of the remaining four chapters.

Needless to say, the bibliography indicated in each chapter does not aspire to be either selective or exhaustive, or even to be up to date. It represents part of the books that I was able to consult throughout my scientific voyage and that I consider it my duty to record here, even if there are many other works to which I am in debt that are not mentioned here due to the special—somewhat nomadic—circumstances in which I am finishing this modest investigation.

* * *

It is my pleasure to manifest my gratitude here to O. Foz, L. M. Garrido, E. Gutiérrez, J. M. López Roca, O. Market, L. Polo, and R. Roquer, who have had the courtesy of reading this manuscript and assisting me with their valuable observations. In previous years I also maintained fruitful conversations with J. Arellano, R. Saumells, M. Siguán, X. Zubiri, and many others to whom I would also like to express my gratitude. This investigation was accepted as a doctoral dissertation in the Faculty of Sciences of the University of Madrid with a tribunal formed by the chairs A. Ipiens, A. Ríus, E. Gutiérrez Ríos, J. Baltá, and A. González Álvarez. Not only because of the maximum qualification they gave this thesis, but also because of their constant support and collaboration, I would like to convey my most expressive appreciation here to them.

Barcelona
August 6, 1958
Feast of the Transfiguration of Our Lord

* * *

Contents of *Ontonomy of Science*

A. PRINCIPLES

  I.   SCIENTIFIC AND PHILOSOPHICAL
1. Mutual Incomprehension
2. Objections from the Philosophers
   a. Negative
   b. Positive
3. Critiques from the Scientists
4. Mutual Collaboration

Bibliography

  II. THE EVOLUTION OF THE CONCEPT OF SCIENCE
1. The Genesis of Scientific Knowledge
2. Certain Aspects of "Modern" Problems
   a. The Problem of Confidence
   b. The Matter of Interest
   c. The Methodological Question
   d. Philosophical Science
3. The Birth of Science
4. Physico-Mathematical Sciences
   a. Their Origin
   b. Their Nature

Bibliography

  III. SCIENTIFIC KNOWLEDGE AND PHILOSOPHICAL KNOWLEDGE
1. Scientific Criteriology
2. Substantive Thinking and Functional Thinking
3. The Despoilment of Substance in the Nature of Bodies
4. The Movement of Bodies

Bibliography

  IV. THE COSMIC SENSE OF SCIENCE
1. Physics and Metaphysics
   a. The Dangers of Pure Formalist Thinking
   b. Meta-Physics
      i. There Is No Metaphysics without Physics
      ii. There Is No Physics without Metaphysics
2. Cosmic Vision

Bibliography

B. EXAMPLES

  V. BIOMATHEMATICS AND BIOPOIESIS
1. Biomathematical Science
   a. The "Unitary Theory" of Physical and Biological Phenomena
   b. Biomathematical Sciences
2. Vita in vitro

3

THE NARROW DOOR OF KNOWLEDGE

Sense, Reason, and Faith

Preface

For almost half a millennium the subject of this book has affected the fulcrum upon which Western culture rests, the culture which has been steadily, and not always peaceably, invading the planet.* This study, however, does not seek to address this problem in all its complexity, or even provide solutions; it simply sets out to touch on certain issues relating to the phenomenon of modern science in relation to other forms and manners of knowledge.

Every specific problem, however, is not independent from the whole and, accordingly, cannot be properly treated without a more or less explicit vision of this totality. Just as there is no elementary particle without its field. Everything is connected with everything, and the individual or particular can only be so insofar as it is a part of the whole. This "whole" cannot be arrived at as the sum of particular knowledges. It can only be reached through the gateway of wisdom. This is the gate that opens us up to plenitude (to *pan, sarvam, pūrṇam*), to the ideal of humanity since the beginning of *homo sapiens*. This gateway is narrow because it requires a pure heart, an emptiness that is not easy to attain: this is the path of wisdom, the experience full of Life, the mystic experience.

With this we have already made reference to the content of this book: wisdom, science, and knowledge. We shall be looking more particularly at the last two of these very specifically. Science and knowledge are not the same thing, despite their common etymology, but they are closely related. There is no true science without knowledge. Furthermore there is no knowledge worthy of the name that does not in some way include or incorporate the subject that knows. Knowledge (*gnôsis*) without love is "puffed up," making us arrogant, say the Scriptures.[1] This is the great temptation of all science, and of modern science especially. Yet we cannot separate science from those who cultivate it. The so-called objective is so, precisely to the extent that there is a subject that defines its criteria. What is more, there is no knowledge if the latter does not in some way take into account the whole of the object being known. But this totality is not the sum of its parts, as was clear to the pre-Socratic philosophers several centuries before Plato. Another sort of human activity would be called for, apart from the scientific method. Modern science, based on analysis and measurement,

---

* Original text: *La porta stretta della conoscenza. Sensi ragione e fede* (Milan: Rizzoli, 2005). Reviewed by the author in *La puerta estrecha del conocimiento* (Barcelona: Herder, 2009). Translated by David John Sutcliffe.

[1] 1 Cor 8:1.

does not claim to "save" mankind; knowledge can and does do so—although in this case together with love.

Three words of the Hellenic tradition could have constituted the title of this work: *epistêmê, gnôsis, melôs,* terms that we might translate somewhat freely as science, knowledge, and melody, taking this last to be the *harmony* between the other two. Melody as the background music to this essay; the harmony of reality does not exclude provisional discord, which can however be overcome, or which according to some can only find solution in God, or at the end of time. Harmony, on the other hand, cannot be discovered by dialectic reason, which has to "see" one thing after another. Awareness of harmony is possible only when we integrate the third dimension of reality, visible to intuition, the third eye, love, the mystic, or whatever we call it. That is, harmony between the three human forms of contact with reality: sensitivity, reason, and faith—to use the three symbols.[2] Mastery of one of these, or even of two, is not enough, but rather their interpenetration in a relationship of interdependence, that is to say, *advaita.* This intuition as represented by wisdom underlies this study, but is not explicitly discussed.

Knowledge, while it is different from love, cannot be separated from it, nor can science from knowledge, nor physics from theology. *Colligite fragmenta*[3] (gather up the fragments so that nothing may be lost) has been the motto of my life. Harmony, on the other hand, cannot be captured separately by any of the three forms. Knowledge of harmony is only made possible by integrating the three dimensions of reality spontaneously, that is to say, in freedom. It is for this reason that being pure in heart is not merely a moral precept, but above all something demanded by knowledge. The pure in heart shall see God[4]—that is, reality.

The subtitle, too, should be clearly understood. Modern-day science is *opus rationis,* a brilliant monument to human reason based on measurability, and thus it is the quantification of the real. *Omnia in mesura et numero et pondere disposuisti (Thou hast ordered all things in measure, number, and weight)*[5] could be its central maxim. This motto, however, is incomplete. At the beginning of his *Confessions,* St. Augustine quotes a psalm and then goes on to quote another: *Et sapientiae tuae non est numerus,*[6] which is usually translated as if the wisdom of God were infinite, incommensurable, in accord with other passages in the Bible. The seventy say: *Kai tês suneseos autou ouk estin arithmos,* which may be translated as having the opposite meaning, saying, "For his intelligence numbers do not exist." The infinite is not a limitless quantity, nor is it an infinite number, which, as a matter of fact does not exist except as a—doubtless most useful—mental concept. In other words mathematical infinity is not the same as the reality of an intelligence that is wisdom, knowledge, intuition, vision, and so on. The abstract force of mathematics, however, offers a finite mind a way of approaching the infinite, if only mathematically.

In other words, science about the infinite is not knowledge of the infinite. The science of the infinite, or rather *about* the infinite, constitutes an extraordinary effort of the mind and its ability to extrapolate conceptual thought. Modern mathematics is a brilliant indication of this. Infinite knowledge is another "thing," and is not the same as knowledge about the infinite, but rather a metaphor for hypothetically infinite knowledge, that is to say, limitless knowledge. The limits of knowledge have to do with the limits of the object that is known.

---

[2] 1 Jn 1:1.
[3] Jn 6:12.
[4] Mt 5:8.
[5] Wis 11:20.
[6] Ps 146:5.

If there is infinite knowledge, this cannot be exhausted by an object that will limit it. Every object, when it is known, has its limits, and if we "imagine" it to be infinite, this is because we do not know its limits and we "think" we have not been able to reach them because "behind" them we will not find a reason for there being something else. In a word, the infinite cannot be *thought*—and here is where it differs from calculus. Put another way, infinite knowledge is the equivalent of infinite ignorance, the awareness that we do not expend or exhaust the knowledge of a thing or of knowledge itself. Knowledge of the limits is equivalent to recognition of our ignorance (of beyond what we know).

It could be said that wisdom is not measurable, quantity has its limits in the quantifiable, and in any case reality is not necessarily that. Reality has no reason whatsoever that compels it to be intelligible. We have thus arrived at the postulate of Parmenides, the father of Western culture in general and of modern science in particular: thought (*noein*) reveals to us what being is (*einai*). Indeed, from a more extreme point of view they are one and the same thing. An intercultural approach is needed to realize just how serious the effect of this postulate is.

So what is left, then? Are we barred from knowledge of reality? We still have the third eye, the mystical consciousness, the intuition of the supramental—the Spirit, in a word. Is this the traditional threefold anthropology or cosmotheandric vision[7]—which has nothing to do with the sometime very popular question of the supernatural? Neither science nor knowledge can tell us more than a part of what is reality or man.

There is no infinite knowledge, but there is the possibility of knowledge of the whole, a limited holistic knowledge. This is the field of faith. Faith is also knowledge, but of a different type from scientific knowledge.[8] For a long time there was no conflict between the two because scientific *epistémê* was subjected to theological *gnosis*. However, the former ceased to be *ancilla theologiae* centuries ago, and that is where the conflict came in. This conflict has many root causes, and the principal one of these goes back, arguably, to the emancipation of science from a theology that, abusing its power, had failed to notice that the new situation needed a new growth and a change.

The current situation is almost the opposite: it is theology that follows along in the wake of science. The *ontonomy* of these two forms of thinking has almost been forgotten.[9] The *nomos* of theology is not the *nomos* of science, and it is not a question of theology submitting to science nor of science submitting to theology. By *nomos* we mean not so much law as the order (*dharma, tao, taxis, ordo*) within each individual with respect to the whole. Such a relationship depends on an *on*, a reality, on a being that is polyvalent and multiform. In the same way, certain philosophers from Aristotle onward tell us that being can be said in many ways (*pollachôs legetai*).

However, we do not have to do with an *anomia* or anarchy, but rather an *ontonomy*, of a relationship between two modes of knowledge that are in any case human.[10]

---

[7] Cosmotheandric: a word that expresses the integrated relationship of the World, God, and Man: the *kosmos*, *theos*, and *anthropos* are the three poles of the trinitarian reality in constant communion one with another. There is no moment when these three dimensions are not present, in one form or another, in reality. This vision surpasses both the theocentric and anthropocentric views.

[8] Heb 11:1–3.

[9] Ontonomy is the recognition and the respect for the natural (hierarchic) order of each sphere of being within a harmonic whole; autonomy defends the independence of each sphere of being; heteronomy is the dominion of one sphere over another.

[10] This was the theme of my doctoral thesis in Sciences in 1958, published in 1961 with the title of *Ontonomía de la ciencia*. See the previous chapter.

The pages that follow do not elaborate on these considerations, but nonetheless they are predicated on them. For that reason, referring to them was necessary.

The underlying idea in this essay is the solution and healing of the anthropological schizophrenia of our time and the conviction that the solution here does not lie in dialectic synthesis, but in a deepening of man's life itself, to overcome the dichotomy between theory and praxis, between the (philosophical and scientific) intellectual life on the one hand and the spiritual life on the other—vividly exemplified by the dislocation between science and knowledge.[11]

The merit of this book, hopefully, is that it offers an alternative to the *mythos* of history, reinforced in hindsight by modern science, which forms the backdrop against which modern man tends to think of reality. Our criticism of science is neither sociological nor epistemological; it relates to the vision of the world implicit in contemporary scientific culture. If the gateway to knowledge is in itself narrow, but not actually barred, modern science represents rather a window that allows us to see a dimension of the real, but which does not offer us a way in, except as mind, and thus only in an abstract rather than ontological manner. The *logos* is not separate from spirit (*pneuma*).

But what is more, the *logos*, as word, cannot be separated from sound. Hence our subtitle, which includes our *senses*, although we will not do justice to this first key to knowledge, without which the other two (*reason* and *faith*) will not open the Gateway for us. The fact that to be able to talk about sensitivity (or feeling) one would have to have experienced it is what has led us to concentrate on knowledge while often forgetting the role of the senses—as has, in any case, happened with faith. Completely human knowledge requires the use of the three keys in their correct hierarchy.

The ancients talked of a *mundus sensibilis* and of a *mundus inteligibilis*, running the risk of slipping into the dualism of the modern world. The very word "senses" has a double connotation: on the one hand "the senses" (meaning *Sinnlichkeit*, sensuality, carnality) in terms of knowledge of the senses, of feeling, and on the other "the senses" (meaning *Empfindlichkeit*, feeling, *voluptas*, sensitivity, sensitiveness). We use the word in the first of the two meanings: the bodily senses, sensations, as the first key to knowledge. The question of *aesthesis* (sensation) is so broad that, without forgetting it, we have concentrated on the problems of intellectual knowledge.[12]

There is a further peculiarity to note about this study: its underlying interculturality, which relativizes some of the *mythoi* of modernity, accepted uncritically as they normally are. Such myths include the myth of the supremacy of reason, philosophy as *opus rationis*, the universality of science, and the linear nature of time. The author is critical of the dogmas of modernity, and while not undervaluing them, he does not take them to be fixed anchor points in his reflections. These pages are a synthetic reworking of an issue I have been thinking about for many years. I have striven to be as clear and as brief as possible, without falling into the currently rife trap of superficiality. Technical terms, both those of philosophy and of science, have been avoided as much as possible. This is not a difficult book, but it needs to be read unhurriedly, slowly even, in the same way as it was written.

The world situation in this century calls for a radical overhaul (the paradox is apt) of the parameters of modern consciousness in force over recent millennia. Life is constant renewal.

---

[11] See for example Cantore (1977), Zohar (1990), Peacocke (2001), Nicolescu (2002) . . . , all of which represent an effort to overcome this separation.

[12] The contemporary bibliography on senses/sensitivity is immense. There is a useful summary in Naumann-Beyer (2003).

The corollary of such audacity requires that we have the humility to know that we are fallible.

I wish to express my gratitude to friends and critics who have accompanied me during the long gestation of this work and its thinking. I am especially grateful to Milena Carrara and to Germán Ancochea, who have been concerned with this book, working on the basis of various previous articles written in different languages, encouraging me, what is more, to go more deeply into certain topics to achieve the most harmonious presentation possible.

Milarupa
Easter 2005

Scientific Thought and Christian Thought:
Phenomenological Reflection

An observation needs to be made at the outset of this first section of the book, to avoid a possible misunderstanding that can easily arise, especially where interpreting things in the light of Western society—characterized as it is by specialization and interest in the specialization of things to the point of identifying things in terms of their specific differences. To equate these two forms of thought (Christian and scientific) would be just as mistaken as treating them as opposites, forgetting that both are "thoughts."[13]

Without now addressing the big question, "What is thought?" we can't forget the famous phrase of Heidegger's: "Science does not think."[14] He considered thought as going well beyond simple logical manipulation of facts. We are referring here to "thought" in its more general sense of mental activity, the activity of the mind. Science, in effect, can be considered as a particular activity of the mind. In line with the classifying genius of the West, taking classification to its limits, we could say that science calculates, theology believes, and philosophy thinks. But this issue does not form a part of our "phenomenological reflection" here. We cannot reduce thought, as an activity characteristic of mankind, to fit into any of these compartments. Christianity and science are both human activities, and this affirmation provides the point of departure for our reflections.

The intellectual world of the West, more particularly after Plato and Aristotle (leaving aside poetic language and language that we condescendingly call "vulgar") has virtually come to identify the word with the concept. This identification is actually necessary for the language of modern science, but not for philosophy, despite a tendency to the contrary in analytical philosophy. Thus we have come to view a word as the expression of a concept and not of a reality. This is the origin of much misunderstanding. One thing is the anarchy of language where a word can mean just about anything, and quite another thing to fall into the trap of univocal paradigms, forgetting the difference between concept and word. The art of translation is so tricky precisely because it has to translate words and not just concepts. It would be an impoverishment of knowledge if this were to be reduced to simply concepts. Concepts also allow analogies, but then analogies require a *primum analogatum* and to be intelligible. Metaphor, allegory, and symbolic interpretation are a fundamental part of human language and cannot be reduced to concepts. "Clear and distinct ideas" (Descartes) are a postulate of reasoning. Put another way, the language of science is basically and fundamentally conceptual,

---

[13] In the autumn of 1992, the Fundació Joan Maragall of Barcelona organized an international symposium on "Scientific Thought and Christian Thought." The author took part in the roundtable, discussing the ideas that are here compiled and reworked.

[14] See Heidegger, *Was heisst Denken?* (Tübingen: Niemeyer, 1954), 4.

directed at the observable world. The language of faith is fundamentally symbolic, orientated intentionally toward reality. It should be remembered that, in Hebrew, *dabar* (word) means both word and deed, thing or event. And that in the primordial traditions (the Mesopotamian tradition, for example) Man is considered the word of God in the form of divine event.[15]

The much-debated question of the conflict between "science and faith," so typical of the previous century, is still, despite being wrongly conceived, interesting to many intellectuals. I suspect the reader will capture the deliberate use of theological words used to refer to science, and vice versa, scientific language referring to religion. No one has a monopoly over words—and in any case, irony has heuristic value. I underline this point to avoid misunderstandings.

We have said that the conflict between "science and faith" is a problem bedeviled by its underlying premises: the problem is not really between science (reason) and faith, but rather arises in the conflict between possible conclusions drawn from certain scientific knowledge on the one hand, and a body of belief on the other. But not, in any case, with *faith*.[16] Faith, as I have reiterated on so many occasions, is a constitutive dimension of Man, an existential opening up *to*. . . . Faith is the *faculty* eminently a part of Man, of opening up consciously (and not necessarily by dint of reflection) on the Infinite, God, Nothing, the Unknown, the Void, and so on, where any naming seems superfluous, out of place, since strictly speaking faith has no object. To be able to refer to the object of faith we have to interpret it according to the categories of the culture in question. These interpretations constitute the beliefs that characterize the different visions of reality related to different religions and worldviews. In any case, the expression "Christian faith" is misleading, in that it refers to the Christian interpretation of faith, and thus to Christian *belief*. If we speak of the Christian faith, then we should also speak of the Hindū, Islamic, atheist, and scientific faiths. . . . I mean that the noun (faith) should have a meaning in itself in transcendental relationship with the qualifiers. Faith always manifests in a belief. The immensity of the problem will allow us to make only a few simple points, which I shall present in thesis form.

The first part of this volume is not in fact a philosophical reflection on the nature of science and religion, but rather a phenomenological description of these two great events of our age. By phenomenology I mean a simple description of both Christian and scientific phenomena—as they would appear to the eyes of a "neutral" observer. We know that such an observer does not exist and so such a thing is not possible, but caricatures are frequently useful in bringing to our notice less evident aspects of reality.

Modern Science

1. *Modern science is a novum of scarcely half a millennium's standing.*

The roots of modern science go back into the mists of time. Its predecessors were the civilizations of Egypt and India, the Platonists and nominalists of ancient Greece, to name just a few. Around 1600, to put a date to it, and with Galileo (1564–1642) to put a name, we come up against a *novum*. There is, at all events, a difference between traditional science and modern science. The first mentioned, traditional science, consists of *scientia, gnôsis, jñana,* which is to say learning that will bring plenitude, joy, salvation . . . insofar as knowledge leads to an ever greater assimilation of reality on the part of the knower. Indeed, it is thought that Man is *homo sapiens*—and that wisdom will lead mankind to its plenitude (realization,

---

[15] See Trebolle Barrera (2004) and Garcia Recio (2004: 54). In the two Sumerian languages (Inim) and Acaddian (Awatum) no distinction is made between word and deed; see Mander (2004).

[16] By belief, we mean the interpretation of faith according to a specific religion or culture.

salvation, etc.). Modern science, on the other hand, is at bottom a form of calculation that does not presume to take in Man as a whole, nor provide us with redemptive knowledge, because it is assumed that we are rational animals, and that rationality will lead us to understand one particular aspect of reality—one that many in this day and age believe to be the most important, and without which, admittedly, we could not exist. In this limited sense too, modern science "saves" us.

Modern science exhibits at least three general characteristics:

a.   It is *an intellectual construction*

i.   based on a very particular form of observation: that of the quantifiable aspect of reality;

ii.   generally justified by experimentation, that is to say, by means of more or less induced variation in the observable data, which allows projection of this behavior onto space-time coordinates, in this way constituting a body of doctrine;

iii.   that arises out of confidence in mathematical rationality: a coherent system of deductions based on axioms previously postulated on pragmatic or a priori grounds. It should not be forgotten that modern science developed mathematics, making mathematics its "bible" and providing its "exegesis."

b.   It is a *social edifice* to all intents and purposes the most important of the modern world. Its church is formed of three pillars that mutually reinforce each other: the "teaching body," the "priests," and the "organization"—that is to say, the scientists, the technocrats, and the economy. States, nations, universities, multinationals, and other present-day institutions all respect, accept, and support this impressive edifice, one considered so solid that it is difficult to imagine that it will not last "forever." "It will endure until the end of time." Modern science is an indisputable component of this present civilization, a powerful institution that has spread all over the world. It is flexible and believes itself capable of modification (*scientia semper est reformanda*), but not that it is mortal. The "gates of hell shall not prevail."[17]

c.   It is a *cultural world* that dominates our way of thinking and of seeing reality, still intimately and often secretly allied with its "secular arm," technology—which is something very different from *technē*. Modern science is not just an assembly of knowledge, it is a politico-social institution; it is also *forma mentis*, a way of seeing reality and interpreting facts and events that present themselves to human consciousness. This is a scientific ideology, just as there is a scientific myth[18] that dominates modern culture: according to this myth, what is scientific is guaranteed to be sound, to be superior, and indeed to be the truth.

Science has influenced, almost in totalitarian fashion, the thinking habits of modern man (although has generally not done so consciously). As equitable a thinker as David Jou,[19] when formulating the three fundamental cosmological questions, does not question the essence of

---

[17]   Mt 16:18.

[18]   Myth is the horizon of human comprehension that provides a backdrop for intelligibility. Myth is accepted a-critically. Mythical consciousness is the organ with which we participate in myth— which we refer to as *mythos* to distinguish it from the vulgar conception of myth. It is in a unique relationship with *logos*. Reality, before reaching us as an object of cognitive reflection, reaches us in the form of *mythos*. Once cognition has taken place, this knowledge becomes *logos*. This process is known as de-mythologization, a process that eliminates *mythos* as such. But a new *mythos* will emerge to give intelligibility to the new knowledge.

[19]   Who took part in the symposium mentioned in footnote 13.

the universe, nor does he ask what the universe, life, and intelligence are. Instead, he asks a question that he considers "neutral" on what are the "origins of life and intelligence." This is a scientific evolutionary mode of thinking, as we shall have occasion to see. It has us believe that explaining the genesis of a phenomenon is the equivalent of *knowing* it.

We should not forget that the culture provides the backdrop against which these questions are formulated. The question on the origin of things, which replaces questions on being or essence, conditions all scientifically based culture. The question on origins presupposes a dynamic conception within a linear view of time. The question itself presupposes evolution, which leads us to classify historical periods as either developed or undeveloped—or developing, as we euphemistically say.

2. *Scientific thought is a particular, limited way of thinking.*

By "thinking" I mean that human activity by whose means Man arrives at the intelligibility of a thing. And by "intelligibility" I refer not simply to the rational evidence, but also the acceptance of the truth of an object as illuminated by the human faculty that the medieval philosophers called "intellect," to distinguish it from "reason"—although in this field there is a bewildering diversity of terms. In any case, the scientific mode of thinking is conditioned by its method. This method is characterized by

   a.   *Active abstraction.* Scientific thought, in effect, abstracts a part of reality, the part that can be measured. None of the aspects of reality that present themselves as good or bad, threatening or seductive, beautiful or ugly, undetectable to the five senses or bearers of nonrational messages, enter directly into scientific thought. The latter is content to extract the quantifiable parameters of (observable) phenomena, basing itself more or less explicitly on the assumption that this algebra (with its deductive operations in rational logic) will reveal to us the (pragmatic) behavior of the phenomena that we set out to describe. In this way it can predict, monitor, control, calculate, and formulate laws on the behavior (though not the nature) of observable phenomena.

   b.   *Passive abstraction*, that is to say, disregarding all that does not enter into the parameters of the method. In other words, it excludes any element that cannot be intrinsically objectified, such as the intentions of the thinker, the ethics of the thought, or any other extrapolation foreign to the scientific enterprise. This does not mean that scientists (who tend to be among the most sociologically intelligent men and women) do not have many other valid intentions and concerns, such as doing good and extending the benefits of science to all. In the same way that the missionaries of past centuries wanted to save souls and ensure they went to heaven, these latter-day "missionaries" want to save bodies and extend peace and well-being to all.

   c.   *Abstention from pronouncing on other aspects of reality*, limiting itself to the possibility of establishing scientific laws underwritten by the mathematics that sustain them and having passed the test of falsability. For that reason, unique or singular phenomena are excluded from the field of scientific thought. Thus, just as there was formerly a clear distinction made between the natural and the supernatural, the religious and the political, a quite analogous distinction is currently made between the scientific and the nonscientific. It is the same myth in a different guise. Myths are reluctant to die, and they survive the very conceptual systems that were founded on them.

3. *The scientific worldview is monocultural, monorational, and pragmatically self-sufficient.*

By "worldview" is meant the vision of reality characteristic of a given culture and something that underlies every religion. Such a worldview would be the background against which human perceptions are situated, more or less instinctively, in such a way that they make some sense or are in some way intelligible. The worldview is the way that we, in our human consciousness, perceive the world. Here we deliberately distinguish worldview from cosmology, which is the vision that modern science has of the cosmos, where the word *cosmos* already has its particular meaning as a scientific object as understood by modern science. The world of astrology and the world of alchemy, for example, do not form part of scientific cosmology, but they do in either case presuppose a particular worldview or cosmovision.[20]

The scientific worldview is:

a. *Monocultural*. It is no coincidence that modern science originated in Christian Europe around half a millennium ago, and that it followed in the footsteps of the Platonic tradition that introduced such concepts as objective reality, although in point of fact Platonic objective reality was a much broader concept than its modern scientific equivalent. Platonic concepts represent the ideas of the Platonic world. Philosophy debates whether mathematics can be seen as a world that acts as an intermediary between Platonic ideas and material reality. In any case scientific concepts are algorithms. Modern science feels at home in this culture of Western origin. To capture the difference, think, for instance, of the Veda-Upaniṣadic culture in which the concepts are not in fact concepts but states of consciousness that are objectified to indicate their solidity and the validity of the categories in question. Analyzing the nature of concepts, within Hellenic culture, is the equivalent (homeomorphically speaking)[21] in the Vedic-Upaniṣadic culture of asking oneself what these objects *feel*, and *how* they feel. It would be a methodological error to write this off as anthropomorphism. Recall that other cultures have forms of thinking in which what counts is uniqueness rather than repeatability, the resistance to comprehension rather than rational transparency (noetics). Eastern philosophies are based on the repeatability of things (*saṃsara*) and they do so precisely to affirm that this world of phenomena is an illusion.

Here I am not criticizing monoculturalism; I am saying rather that we should be conscious of it. If we do not want to defend a totalitarian conception of cultural evolution, in which each new "advance" contains all previous stages and where that which is scientific represents the highest rung of human evolution, we need to recognize that the other worldviews can have their own validity, although relative, in the same way as the scientific worldview does and, therefore, the latter needs to be relativized—put into relative perspective—while underlining the fact that relativity does not mean relativism.

b. *Monorational*. The modern scientific view of the world claims to be rational, in the sense of mathematical rationality (which category would surely include Heisenberg, Gödel, non-Euclidean geometry, and so forth). All that cannot be brought into line with this type of rationality, which is seen as universal in this cosmology, is regarded as inoperative or directly false. Modern science studies only that which is reasonably possible: hence the tendency of present-day culture to prove rationally that God exists, since otherwise (it is thought) such an entity would not be real. The angels as symbols of spiritual reality, for example, cannot form part of scientific cosmology, since they are neither scientifically verifiable nor experimentally controllable. Love is explained as a movement of attraction motivated by sentiments that stem from psycho-physical affinity. It is only when the object to be studied is quantifiable and, therefore, controllable (if

---

[20] By cosmovision I do not mean what Heidegger calls *Weltbild* (image of the world) in his lecture in 1938, in which he describes it as a characteristic of "modernity" (*Neuzeit*).

[21] Homomorphism: a third-degree analogy that points up the equivalent function of two or more symbols—God and Brahman, for example.

only statistically) that scientific interpretation becomes possible. Science knows how to wait and knows that it has not yet deciphered all the enigmas of the universe. The world, said Galileo, is written in mathematical characters. Modern science also consists of the work of deciphering, but it knows that reading nature's writing is a considerably more complex operation. Science has to know how to carry out the exegesis of the book of nature, just as Christianity has to know how to read the book of Revelation—so it was said even in Galileo's time.

This monorationality should not be absolute in its resolve, but open enough to be able to admit without difficulty that phenomena that have not entered (yet) into the field or scope of science may do so in the future—as has happened more than once. It can be accepted quite easily that people believe in angels and in "mad love" (as Ramon Llull would say), but these have no place in the world of science; they may gain their place later if they have the patience to wait. Scientific hope looks to the future, while religious hope looks to the invisible.

c. *Self-sufficient.* This could also be termed "self-regulating" (self-moderating). Scientific cosmology is sufficient unto itself, like a society that is self-perpetuating setting up new leaders from its ranks. Science does not fix its own contents; it is prepared even to change paradigms, but demands that this need has to be demonstrated—within the paradigms that it itself recognizes. It has no dogmas of content, only of method and working hypothesis; it is open to dialogue, but a dialogue that it finds comprehensible, which it terms "rational language"—and believes it to be universal.

The great lesson of modern science inheres in its methodological rigor and precision of observation, together with its freedom from preconceived ideas, which will only be accepted if they pass a rigorous "scientific" examination—something that philosophers will subsequently call a vicious circle because it is a priori limited to what is rationally possible. In the last instance, the great virtue of science as a heuristic method resides in its flexibility: it knows itself to be limited, fallible, and provisional. Science as a scientific activity (not as a technical-scientific institution) does not have preestablished interests. It does not hesitate to scandalize or throw off-balance those who put their hopes in already-overcome hypotheses.

In less scientific terms it can be stated that modern science has no need whatsoever for God: it does not need this hypothesis, which could be accepted without difficulty by the scientist, but is superfluous for science. Modern science does not hunger and thirst after firm bases: it can live with the provisional. It is not absolute, it is proteiform. Thus, paradoxically it is able to believe that *extra scientiam, nulla salus* (outside of science there is no salvation). It is sufficiently open and tolerant, but within its own limits.

Christian Theology

1. *Christianity is a novum of scarcely two millennia standing.*
    The roots of Christianity go back into the mists of time. Its predecessors were the Egyptian religion, Zoroastrianism, and the prophets of Israel, to mention just a few. But something new happened around the year 753 CE after the founding of Rome, to give a date, and with Jesus of Nazareth, to cite a name.
    There has always been a difference between traditional religions and Christianity. The former are, generically speaking, religions of redemption and paths of cosmic consciousness, insofar as Man is considered part of the cosmos. The latter, on the other hand, is predicated on the condition that the incarnation of the Divine has taken place in a historical man and, indirectly, in history itself, because Man is considered the king of creation.

This traditional Christianity (currently facing a crisis) is characterized by at least three aspects:

    a.   It is *an intellectual construction*:

        i.   Based on spiritual experience having its origins in the impact caused by Jesus of Nazareth and continued by the Christ—the name generally given to the risen Jesus. I refer to the personal experience of the Christian, without which one cannot talk about the *faith* of Christians.

        ii.   Justified by a conscious interpretation not just of the historical facts but of the experiences that have been accumulating over the centuries. I refer to interpretation not simply by an individual but by a tradition that has led the Christian faith to crystallize in a series of more or less integrated beliefs.

        iii.   The result of self-comprehension within the Judeo-Hellenistic cultural matrix to which have been added Gothic and other later elements. It should not be forgotten that Christianity is a profoundly Mediterranean intellectual and spiritual construction. The entire Bible is steeped in the Semitic mentality. Bread and wine, to take just one example, are typical Mediterranean symbols.

    b.   It is *a social edifice,* and was for many centuries the most important social edifice of the European world and of many of its colonies, merged with the political and economic powers for more than a thousand years. The states, the nations, the universities, the social classes, and the public laws all accepted the primacy of the church in the life of the peoples. This institution is sustained by three pillars that mutually support each other: the masters, the experts, and the church—that is to say, a body of doctrine, practical application, and a complex organization. The churches are powerful institutions that have spread all over the world and that seek to become "inculturate" (uncultured) in any existing culture—such that they *semper sunt reformandae,* but imperishable.

    c.   It is *a cultural world.* Although the church has lost power almost everywhere in the world, the patterns of thinking in modern societies are Christian, or at least eminently shaped by what could be called Christian culture, whether orthodox or secularized. And not just the ideas. The *forma mentis* of the contemporary world is fundamentally Christian in character, having received the full impact of the Western world. This mental set includes the sense of history, the conviction that there is a duality between spirit and matter, the notion of linear time, and consciousness of individuality. Christians of the Latin rite remember perhaps that at Advent tide the Bible readings in the liturgy speak of the peace that will reign when all peoples in the world have submitted to Jehovah (Yahweh) and walk in the light of the Lord. The cut-and-dried secularized version of all that is the conviction that peace will reign when all on Earth have a world government, a global democracy, a single global market, a world bank. . . . Many of the so-called alternative movements share this ideal, although with reservations.

Let us not forget that modern secularized culture acts in the same framework as the Christian *mythos,* although often in dialectic opposition to the Christian *logos.* To give an example: the majority of those who consider themselves "atheists" are not strictly that, but rather "antimonotheists."

2.   Christian thought is a particular, limited way of thinking.

By "Christian thought" I mean a way of thinking that seeks to see reality thematically in the light of personal Christian experience and the accumulated interpretation of the Christian tradition. Christian thinking could be characterized as evincing the following aspects, among others:

a. *Exegetic thinking.* While many of us might want to consider Christianity (or at least Christendom) as a religion of the Word, it can be seen that for some centuries now it has been a religion of the Book rather than of the Word—as are all Abrahamic religions in practice, with the exception of the "mystic" movements. It is also true that an important role has been attributed to tradition, especially in the Orthodox and Catholic interpretations, always however subordinated to that of Scripture, which evidently needs interpretation, that is to say exegesis, of narratives and historic traditions.

Although the concept of Scripture is currently facing a crisis, because of hermeneutic modern-day thought, Christian self-comprehension interprets itself as an intellectual elaboration that arises from what are known as "revealed facts." Interpreting them correctly, then, is all. Many of the old controversies between "science and faith" have been read as either conflict or harmony between the facts of so-called revelation and the data provided by science, arguing that there cannot be contradictions between these two since both come from God. The fact that in our times a minority oppose this view and wish to reinstate experience as pertaining to the most authentic origins of Christian thought does not alter the fact that the predominant aspect of Christian identity is based on interpretation of the Scriptures. There is a surprising parallel between the application of logical methodology in the elaboration of scientific data and a similar application in the elaboration of biblical "fact," as we have said.

b. *Exclusive thinking*—considered universal. For the very fact that Christianity believes it is on the road, albeit an *asintotic* one, to truth, Christian thought considers that in being faithful to this truth it cannot contradict its own basic intuitions, since these are all considered the revelations of an omniscient God. Tolerance is possible, and indeed necessary, but thought cannot betray its own self and accept error. The formula *ex ecclesiam nulla salus* (outside the church, there is no salvation) may express this attitude, leaving aside many possible interpretations. Precisely this has made Christian thought very mindful and sensitive about unity. He or she who is saved is not just any being in an undifferentiated series of individuals, but rather a unique being, and thus incomparable. For centuries Christian thought has not found it unacceptable that only the few will obtain salvation, which indicates an anthropology very different from the currently dominant one. In contrast to scientific objectivism, here we have extreme subjectivism. What counts is the subject. Nonetheless, the parallels with science are surprising, although in scientific circles, they do not talk of *exclusivism* (the need for exclusion) but rather of "rigor" and "accuracy." For example: 2 + 2 is exactly 4 and we can't accept it being 4.001. Even the laws of subatomic physics and Heisenberg's uncertainty principle presuppose rigorous if problematic causality—problematic because not individually measurable.

c. *Existential thought.* Christian thought has always claimed to be a redemptive science. Without faith there is no redemption, but the act of faith is a free act. The method, that is to say the path, is an existential path—it seeks to lead one to liberation, to the plenitude of man, or if you like, to heaven, to the vision of beatitude, to divinization, to happiness, and so on. It has to be recognized, however, that in spite of the baroque nature of a good deal of Christian thought, the latter has avoided providing a total explanation of reality and has concentrated instead on trying to articulate the meaning of our pilgrimage as *homo viator* toward our goal. The Bible—and theologians stress this—is not a science book or a history book, but a simple description of what will help Man to attain salvation. Christian thought refers to the plenitude of man—understood in the modern sense as an individual. Here we see a sharp difference with scientific thought, which is essentialist in tendency and ideally is objective—as we have indicated.

3. *The Christian cosmovision or worldview is (mono)theistic, anthropocentric, and a-critical.*

      a. *Monotheistic.* I dispense with the parentheses here to maintain the parallel with scientific cosmology and because, in essence, the greater part of the Christian tradition over these two millennia has (still) not overcome the monotheist schema inherited from its most important matrix, the Hebrew religion. The Christian worldview defends the idea of God as the creator of heaven and earth, either because this is the interpretation expounded by the Bible, or because it is the confirmation of a more long-standing intuition that the world did not get created on its own, nor contains within itself the reason for its existence—which is then projected on a God the creator. In the course of the Christian dialogue with the surrounding world, God has been considered the soul of the universe giving life to the world, a world that thus comes to be his organism (pantheism); or as the architect of the universe, and thus the result of a divine plan (Platonism, etc.); or as a divine watchmaker who guarantees the order of the world (Newton, Leibniz); or as the almighty engineer who makes everything work (many modern scientists); or as a creator God who gives being to all things (according to many philosophers). In one way or another, however, the Christian God is cause (creator), and the world is his effect (creature). This could be the moment to recall that the great challenge for Christian thought on the threshold of the third millennium consists in overcoming monotheism, entering deeply into the experience of the radical Trinity, as I have called it elsewhere, and developing its meaning.[22]

      b. *Anthropocentric.* Man is the center of the universe, of course not in a spatial sense, but the Christian vision of reality is basically interested in mankind and its salvation. The incarnation is for the benefit of Man, although Paul tells us that all creation benefits from it. God, to paraphrase St. Gregory the Great, becomes not a star but a man. Christianity is not interested in how things are going in heaven, we could add citing Galileo, but how to go to heaven. Christian cosmology is seen as based on Man. What medieval commentators called *curiositas* and considered a sin was the desire to delve into matters having no bearing on the plenitude of human life. God became Man, so that Man could become God. The cosmos was conceded only relative and secondary importance.

That the Earth might be the center of the universe does not mean that our planet is situated at the center of the scientific coordinates of space; the meaning is not cosmological but rather one of cosmovision or worldview. That modern Man, while accepting scientific cosmology, still believes himself to be the center of reality in the midst of a marginal galaxy of the astronomic world remains incongruous. This is an instance of the imbalance of the present-day Christian worldview. This brings us to the third point.

      c. *A-critical.* Unlike scientific cosmology, the Christian worldview is not the result of thematic reflection. Christian thought has slowly but steadily incarnated or become fleshed out with the world, accepting (albeit reluctantly and belatedly) the vision of the world that it was slowly encountering. In a certain sense, a specific Christian cosmovision does not exist. Christian thought has limited itself to declaring non-Christian those visions of the world that it considered incompatible with its own. Despite that, it has progressively adopted the *cosmovision* that has come to prevail under the influence of science. Think not just of Ptolemy and Copernicus, but equally of Michel Servet, Pasteur, and the present-day problems to do with evolution, the Eucharist, and the resurrection. I have written elsewhere that the *Divine Comedy* represents the ultimate expression of the Western worldview, and in effect Dante's writings constitute a Christian vision of the

---

[22] See Panikkar (1998).

world where everything that happens is situated in its place and acquires meaning. From Pythagoras to Dante, the West has had a largely homogeneous worldview; subsequently, Western civilization has produced no other global view of reality, despite the (brilliant but unsuccessful) effort by Goethe in *Faust*. The most recent worldview has confined itself to dismantling, piece by piece, that which preceded it, because it did not consider it convincing (insofar as it did not explain phenomena) without however replacing it with anything else. We still find ourselves, in spite of the well-meaning efforts of a Teilhard de Chardin, apologetically subordinating Christian thought to the scientific.

Christian thought has progressively adapted itself in greater or lesser measure to the cosmological reforms as they have been proposed, but without advancing a cosmology of its own. Most if not all the so-called Christian theologies have yielded to the prevailing dualism and have taken on the visions of the world (and of Man) compatible with what they thought was God.

This phenomenological description, as simplified and ironic as it is, can help us to clarify the terms of the apparent conflict between "science and religion," which still raises so many hackles.

Encounter or Disencounter?

It is not possible for us living in the modern world to turn our backs on science. Christians are no exception, but the price they have to pay, especially if they have been trained up in the world of science, involves what amounts to a sort of cultural schizophrenia. Having described the scientific and Christian circles, let us now look at points where they converge and points of divergence.

We have emphasized that the origins of Christianity and of science stem from the same cultural origins and that they have developed their intuitions and discoveries within the same tradition. Now the West is beginning to become aware of the role of other cultures. To put it briefly, all human questions that do not bear interculturality in mind will continue to be affected by the colonial syndrome—that is to say, they will be monocultural and will not be able to provide satisfactory answers since they are wrongly framed.

Monoculturality leads to the identification of a human problem with the cultural framework needed for its formulation. Knowing only one language will make it very difficult to separate a word from its meaning. The name is not the thing, but if the latter has only one name, denying the name will deny the thing. We shall be giving examples of this in due course.

1. The conflict between modern science and Christianity is more a conflict between worldviews than between reason and faith.

We began by saying, in a very general way, that any human statement needs the framework of a worldview, latent or manifest, to mean something. To put it another way: no text is meaningful out of a context. What is more, one and the same text can have different meanings depending on the context in which it is inserted.

In short, the conflict is not so much between faith and reason as between the beliefs of the religions and the affirmations of science—that is to say, between the different interpretations of reality according to the means that we *believe* we have at our disposition.

Applying this need of a framework to our specific case, we could say that all statements made by science need a context of a worldview to take them out of the realm of pure mathematics or abstraction and acquire a physical meaning, to be able to express something about reality. What Galileo and Bellarmine argued about, for instance, was not just how the heavens operated, but how to go to heaven. The cosmovision or worldview of the day could not separate these two questions, and Galileo could not unite them. That is how the conflict arose—a conflict that had nothing to do with the Christian faith: both interlocutors desired to be good Christians. The conflict had to do with the vision of the world necessary for the Christian faith to be credible, or at least reasonable. It was a clash of worldviews.

$1 + 2 = 3$ does not mean anything (other than being a mathematical formula) until this equation is interpreted in a specific everyday setting, in other words within a (setting with a) worldview. The celebrated incompatibility between the particle and wave theories of matter arises only when we imagine that particles and waves are real representations of what is arrived at by two systems of differential equations.

In the same way, all theological statements need the context of a worldview to acquire a meaning that will be able to confront the assertions of science. If the heaven of the theologians had nothing to do with spatial or psychological space, it would just be a lifeless abstraction. Regarding a purely abstract conception of God, in the sense of an a-cosmic experience, sciences in the modern sense will have nothing say. But then we should need to add that theology is not applicable to man. It will be necessary to descend into the arena of a God creator of the world, that is, a God with a cosmic function, to be able to set up a dialogue with science: then we could argue about the world, not before—we should have descended to the level of the worldview.

Here we should complete our first *excursus filosoficus* on the father of Western thought who lived twenty centuries ago: Parmenides. With admittedly many ifs and buts, Parmenides has made practically the whole of the Western world believe (I say believe) that being (*to on*) on the one hand, and what our thoughts (*nous*) construct, produce, discover, say about it on the other, are intrinsically related (not to say identical). In short, our ideas on reality are at the least an image of it, so that what science and theology tell us is not a mere abstraction, but one that reflects reality—even if this is the reality of the ideal world of idealism. To express it in another way, both Christian thought and scientific thought set out to say something about reality—so we cannot evade the problem.

I limit myself to two brief examples.

a.   *Evolutionism.* Perhaps no other subject has caused such rivers of ink to flow, until the present, as this one. We shall be able, therefore, to give no more than a broad outline.

What does the theory of evolution state? The term is so generic that it will be necessary at the outset to establish a distinction between micro- and macro-evolution, between restricted and total transformation, between the evolution of the species and that of all reality, between historical and eschatological evolution, and so on. We will not be going into specific problems therefore, but look at evolutionism as an ideology.

The problem of evolution is not so much the cluster of scientific theories (or hypotheses) as the mentality that makes them plausible. This is an aspect common to all forms of evolutionism. What we have to do with here is the *forma mentis* we apply to reach a certain level of intelligibility of phenomena. Evolutionism spread so rapidly because this way of thinking is co-natural—shares the same nature—as modern scientific thinking. Modern-day science does not set out to tell us what things are, but simply to describe the behavior of things (the regular behavior within the realm of the possible). Describing their behavior is equivalent to revealing the gestation, that is to say the origin and subsequent development, of the phenomena—in a word, their evolution. "Knowledge" of the past will enable us to foresee the future, and this is what interests science. To put it briefly, here "worldview" or "cosmovision" equals "cosmogeny," while "intelligibility" equals "temporal explanation." We mean "explanation" here in its most literal sense: that which unfolds a phenomenon in its temporality, extending the event (that is, the evolution of a phenomenon) in space and distending it in time, as it appears extended and distended before our eyes. The implicit hypothesis would be that in this unfolding there is real continuity, and the continuity is genetic, intrinsic. Thus this is real evolution and not (as a certain Buddhist conception might have it) a succession of instantaneous moments that we connect up mentally, like a film, so that we have the impression that what precedes is the cause or origin of what comes after, deducing a *propter hoc* from a *post hoc*. Indeed, evolutionism thinks to have understood a phenomenon when this is seen unfolded, distended in time, or unwound in space.

Having reached this point, we have to single out three problems: an *anthropomorphic* one, an *epistemological* one, and a *metaphysical* one.

The anthropomorphic problem consists in extending awareness of personal evolution to all observable phenomena. We remember our childhood, our growing up, and having a certain awareness of our continuity, we attribute the change to the development of a certain substance (our self), which remains there developing (that is, evolving) from an origin that gives us the key understanding what we are. This is the implicit assumption in the question on origins. When we then ask about the origin of things or about the meaning of evolution, we project our personal self-awareness on all reality and adopt a human model of thought. This, obviously, is an anthropomorphism.

It will be advisable, however, to check whether and to what extent this anthropomorphism could be avoided. What did Pythagoras mean when he said that "man is the measure of all things"? What does the *Ṛg-Veda* mean when it sings that "man is all"? What did Aristotle mean when he said that "the soul, in some way, is everything"? Or a variety of Christianity when it affirms that man is the end (the aim) of creation? At times man becomes the condiment for all dishes, but we would do well to be aware of that, and to distinguish the condiment from the food. All that man touches has the imprint of man. All objectivity is objective for a subject. Is this the anthropomorphism of evolutionism?

An example from the field of theology will prove useful to throw into relief the parallels we have noted between evolutionism, scientific thought, and the Western mentality, especially in its Judeo-Christian aspect. I refer to the ontologization of the law, a result of symbiosis between the spirit of the Torah (Divine law) and Roman legal genius. The consequences here are many, and have shaped Western society. Let us look at an example that many may find forced, simply because the *mythos* that it seeks to describe has penetrated into the fabric of Christian civilization, which represents a qualified paradigm of the above-mentioned symbiosis—to the point that, all too often, one speaks of Judeo-Christianity as if it were a single religion. The example is that of apostolic succession, which is an instance of practical evolutionism. What makes the bishop of Rome a bishop, or a bishop of any other see, is episcopal ordination, the sacrament, the initiation, a fresh and discontinuous act, and not the judicial succession of the episcopal charisma passed on from one to another. Today, however, while granting the distinction between legitimacy and validity, more weight is given to succession than to the sacramental ordination—the initiation will be accorded to the successor, rather than naming as successor the one who has been "ordained." The judicial order is thus ontologized; the historical genealogy is interpreted in an evolutionary sense: charisma itself is passed from one to another. I have no intentions here of casting doubt on apostolic succession; my intention is to underscore the communion in the *mythos*. However that may be, everything is interrelated.

The deeper problem of evolution does not concern the temporal origin of man or the cosmos. The question is more fundamental, one where our identity and our dignity are at stake. What is man? An epiphenomenon of the cosmos, a hastening traveler, or a microcosm that reflects all reality. From the *material* point of view, it is ridiculous to take the human body seriously as the central reference of reality, despite its complexity. There are myriads of bodies in the universe and each one is different. From the point of view of the *soul*, we do not know if there are other conscious beings in the universe, but there is a cultural communion that allows us a certain *unanimity* (a common soul). From the point of view of the spirit, we experience the infinitude and the oneness of each human being, but clearly this cannot be demonstrated: if this were so, the basis of the proof would be more fundamental than the *probando*, that is, the experience in itself. The spirit is not "private property." Properly speaking there is no Zeitgeist (spirit of the times), there are just certain latent characteristics common to a particular age.

When trinitarian theology affirms that man is the son of God, repeating in a new form an intuition that is also found in Egypt and in other cultures, it means that man is not an instrument, a means for something else, not an intermediate being in an undefined chain of beings. Instead man possesses a personal dignity that is an end in itself; this is divine, or rather, the corporeality, the humanity, and the divinity are three inseparable dimensions of his being—as I have explained elsewhere.[23]

We repeat: the problem with evolutionism is not knowing *how* a being evolves, but to know whether evolution allows us to know what this being *is:* Who am I? and Who are you? We cannot reduce man to a chain of individuals.

If it is maintained that science does not concern itself with this problem, then reason cannot be more than an unstable dualism, since after all science is a human construction. "What is man?" the *Vedas* wonder, and a Hebrew psalm asks the same question. And we often forget that the question itself is the answer. Man is a being who asks, "Who am I?"—and not just, "Where did I come from, and where am I going?" All men and women will at some moment in their lives ask who they are, often without being conscious of the fact that the question involves their dignity, what they truly are: *homo quaerens*, a being conscious of the fact that they do not know, because we cannot know the infinite, but simply become it, *be it*.

But when the West adds a predicate to the question (unlike the *Vedas*), its mind already betrays its tendency to objectify all knowledge (*quaerens fidem, beatitudinem, regnum Dei, iustiam, pacem, infinitudinem*), which immediately leads it to classify, compare, and in the last instance ignore the advice of the Gospels: judge not—in spite of all the deliberations about the phrase that affirm that the sun shines upon the good and evil, and the rain falls on the just and the unjust alike.[24]

It can be seen, then, that the question of evolutionism touches the very point of balance upon which human dignity rests. The contemporary debate over the human genome is an instance of this.[25]

The second problem, related to the first, is *epistemological*. We have insinuated that modern science is *epistémê* and not *gnôsis*: knowledge of a particular aspect of reality and not awareness, consciousness of reality. While the term *epistémê* has multiple meanings, we should perhaps clear up many questions if we reserve it precisely for scientific knowledge.

---

[23] See Panikkar (2004).

[24] Mt 5:45.

[25] See Scott Eastham, "Worldviews in Collision: The Challenge of Genetic Engineering," *Journal Interculture* (Montreal), no. 145 (October 2003).

Trusting the etymology rather than the history of the word, we could say that *epistêmê* is a true *epi-stamai* (*istêmi*, from the root *stà*), that is, a "putting before us" of things like a parade of models so that they appear before our eyes to be evaluated and classified. And if we wished to be even more subtle, we could recall that the matrix of *epi* does not just connote "before," but also "upon." *Epistêmê* would then be that form of knowledge that situates before, but also *upon* things, not just to know them but to control them, dominate them, and be able to predict what they will do, how they will behave—not an advantage to be sniffed at.

Scientific thought is certainly *epistêmê*. Christian thought would be more exactly *gnôsis*, in accordance with all the tradition—distinguishing it from so-called gnosticism. In recent centuries, Christianity, suffering from an understandable inferiority complex and an equally understandable tendency to apology, has sought to accede to the prestigious status of "scientific thought." To do so, it has resorted on occasions to veritable acrobatics for wanting to be *epistêmê* like the rest, always in the end having to beat a retreat. Christian thought is not "information," it is awareness—it does not depend on observation but on experience.

What is the theory of evolution good for, in that case? It offers us a model for how things have evolved with the passing of time, reducing the macroscopic leaps to little theoretical microscopic variations. Here too, the influence of the scientific method's format is evident: we do not know how one species becomes another, from an invertebrate to a vertebrate, for example, but we can experience evolution within our species. It will then be easy to extrapolate. Having reduced reality to quantifiable parameters, excluding qualitative change (passing from one wavelength to another, we observe a change in color) and following the model of differential calculus (on an infinitesimal scale) we have no difficulty in accepting a change from C to T (from a cat to a tiger). What does not appear in our experiments we project on temporal magnitudes, and in this way, the change is minimal. I don't think Christian thought can contribute much in this area, unless, as we thought, in this hypothetical fashion parade of models, of species (of animals or beings) the dignity of man is seen to be compromised, his destiny, and compatibility with the Divine nature—not wishing, however, to go into the question of the nature of the divine mystery at this point.

To sum up: the problem of evolution is a question of worldview or "cosmovision."

So, what does Christian thought think about evolution? Let us go back to the fundamental point: What does Christian thought mean? Furthermore, what right does "Christian thought" have to judge other ways of thinking? Some Scholastics, such as some Hindū philosophers, solved the problem with the theory of the double truth, which in the long run, however, does not stand up. Christian thinking over the centuries of history has believed in a hierarchical world, in which each successive higher level contained, and in some degree governed, the lower spheres of beings, and wherein every being arose, emanated, was caused or produced by the higher spheres, until the highest sphere was reached—the ultimate cause and origin. It was thought that this hierarchy was inscribed in nature herself or derived from the Ultimate Cause, such that it was no problem to find that living creatures sprang out of mud and dung. This evolution was not understood as a metaphor, but as a physical fact. The problem comes when this evolutionary view is transferred from physics to metaphysics, from behavioral hypothesis to cosmological hypothesis—which brings us back to the question of worldview.

The third problem is *metaphysical*. We have already referred to the fact that the answer to how a thing has evolved is very useful, but it does not reveal to us the mystery of the thing. We cannot separate the two matters because the genesis of any being throws light for us on its being, but we need to distinguish them since we cannot confuse what something *is* with *how* it came to be. To see them as the same would in itself presuppose evolutionism. And here the theophysical problem arises:[26] what is Being?

Scientific thought does not tackle the metaphysical question, unless indirectly, yet it cannot set it to one side. Nor can theology be confused with metaphysics or the so-called onto-theology. But man is not able to renounce the quest for intelligibility within the limits of the possible.

In the last instance the problem of evolutionism enters in contact with Christian thinking when it wishes to say what *we are*.

It is significant that the so-called conflict between Christian thought and the theory of evolution does not arise until the point at which both science and theology disregard their own limits and engage with the question of worldview (cosmovision) within their respective fields. If science is limited to the quantifiable and the demonstrable, then the theory of evolution is not scientific. If religion limited itself to the end and purpose of man, evolution could be an acceptable hypothesis to the extent that it explains, offers, or guarantees a space for the destiny of the person.

The metaphysical problem of evolution is as ancient as the problem of change, that is to say, how a being can retain its own identity even while changing. The classical distinction between permanent substance and accidental change only shifts the problem along. But then, what changes? This is the well-known question of becoming, that is, the relationship between identity and difference—a classical problem in philosophy that goes back to Parmenides and Heraclitus.[27] Posed thus, the problem has no solution other than going back to premises: who gave human reason authority over reality? Again we touch on the theophysical issue of physics' ultimate foundation: metaphysics.

b. *The resurrection of Jesus Christ.* According to Christian tradition, the physical fact of the resurrection is central to Christian faith.

It should be obvious that faith in the resurrection cannot be reduced to accepting the belief of the first disciples, which has to be interpreted as a subjective experience that freed such psychic energy that it made them the founders of what came to be the Christian religion. The whole Christian edifice cannot rest on the subjectivity of a few disciples, as intense and sincere as their experience might have been. What is more, (Christian) faith should be personal, and thus immediate, like all existential experience. It cannot be content with being "faith" in the faith of others, the trusting acceptance of the testimony of a handful of privileged people. If "scientific faith" has to pass through the sieve of rational verification, Christian faith ought to pass through the sieve of Christic experience. Believing does not mean a-critical submission to the one authority or the one reason; rather it means obedience, as intelligent *listening*, to mankind's sources of truth: the triple *empireia* of the senses, reason, and faith, all involved in the same experience. By existential experience we mean the awareness that such an experience changes our lives. The rest is mere intellectual reductionism. So as not to break the tie with rationalism, I have written that the "Christ experience" is also critical in that one cannot ignore the rights of the intellect—that is to say, the intelligibility of such experience. It is not a question of subordinating either experience to reason or reason to experience (spiritual experience in this case). The first attitude is rationalist, the second "faithism" or mechanical faith. It is a question, however, of a benign circle, as I have said on many occasions. This is not a dialectical issue; it is a dialogal one. Without this

---

[26] Theophysics is a science in which physics and theology are not separate; they are in an onto-nomical relationship.

[27] *Dicitur autem creatur fluvius* [The creature is like a river], says an oft-used text in the Middle Ages.

experience, there can be no faith worth the name. Faith without works is dead (is not faith), say the Christian Scriptures. Faith without the contribution of the sensitivity, intelligence, and the "third eye," say the Scholastics, is superstition and is not able to sustain a life. The Samaritans did not have faith in Jesus because of what the Samaritan woman told them of her conversation with him at the well (*propter tuam loquelam* [for your word]), but because of their own experience of him.

What comes to us as reality is always a datum, a gift, grace—but not necessarily a truth. The truth is filtered by the interpretation it receives, which in turn depends on many factors.[28] Hence the necessary collaboration between the three sources of human knowledge: the senses, reason, and faith, in the words of the subtitle of this volume.

Faith in Jesus's resurrection believes in the physical, that is to say real, resurrection of Jesus of Nazareth; but if it is not accompanied by a personal experience, it is not faith, but simple acceptance of an incomprehensible fact, an absurd one in the light of rational thought.

However, what does "physical body" mean? What is corporeality? And once again, this is not a problem of simple physics but of cosmovision. It is not a question of superficial acceptance of the resurrection and defending a "scientific" cosmology, imagining a sort of immortality of the proteins and nervous system of Jesus's body, present in the Eucharist or in any hidden place in space, which materializes before believers in a way we cannot now verify. That would be incredible from all points of view, not to say absurd. In any case, we should not confuse the immortality of the soul (Plato) with the resurrection of the body.

It is an instructive historic—and indeed ironic—fact that Christian theology, which prided itself on being the queen of the sciences, *regina scientiarum*, has ended up being their slave. The classic apologies have become the adaptation of Christian intuitions to the scientific paradigms.

The Scholastics of the Middle Ages understood this well and did not hesitate to follow the opposite method, adapting their concepts to the matter, space, and time of their Christian experience, to thus be able to explain what they believed in. In this, they were precursors of the scientific spirit; they interpreted empirical data, but from an insensible *empireia*, and sought to explain reality based on this experience. This was not a case of an *intellectus quae-rens fidem* (an intellect seeking to believe) but of a *fides quaerens intellectum* (faith seeking comprehension) and above all a *quaerens* (constant seeking). Faith is not a superstructure or an appendage to reason, it is a form of knowledge, like sensitivity (use of the senses). But faith is not apodictic knowledge, rational evidence. It could be called an inferior kind of knowledge, if the criterion were certainty, but on the other hand it would be called superior if adhesion to experience took root in life itself. There are martyrs of the faith and not so many martyrs of reason—although fanaticism is a danger. A hymn in the *Ṛg-Veda* describes the origin of the world and ends by saying that those who contemplate creation in the highest surely know from whence creation issued, or perhaps they do not.[29] The supreme knowledge is *agnosia*, ignorance, where the mystic locates the experience of faith. In a word, faith is consciousness of another order.

Basing themselves on Plato and Aristotle, and carrying out operations of authentic spiritual alchemy, the medieval philosophers were able to present a worldview (cosmovision) that rendered their beliefs *credible*. Today, however, this worldview no longer convinces us. Their vision atrophied and the medieval formulae have lost life and consistency.

---

[28] Elsewhere, in English, I have allowed myself a play on words: "truth lies in the interpretation" (in both senses!).

[29] *RV* X.129.7.

Here we have a real problem. It is clear that we are faced with two visions of reality: one that believes that physical laws really reflect the behavior of bodies, and another that believes that bodies can come to life again, so that eternal life is possible even in the body. Eternity has no duration, it is not time. It is wrong to translate "eternal life" to mean "life that lasts forever," just as it is disorientating to confuse *bios* (physiological life) with *zoé* (human-divine life). The Gospels called *zoe*, eternal life, literally "vital force," which I have translated as tempiternity[30] (*āyus* in Sanskrit) because it is not temporal, but transcends time. "Ut ergo et tu sis transcende tempus" (So that you also are, transcend time), says St. Augustine with lapidary force.

Christian thought is obliged, it seems, to change the vision of the world of science and state that the body is something more than the material system described by a physiologist scientifically.

The scientific data are not disputed, simply they are only partial. Christian thought, as so many other anthropologies say, does not reduce man to being a rational animal. Our example ought, however, to offer a credible alternative without having recourse to the easy solution of saying it was a miracle. The most traditional theology states that the Eucharist is not a miracle, because no so-called physical laws are altered. We cannot criticize the physical conception of the body if we do not work on a more convincing "Christian" conception of the body and its reality. To say that this is a fact of faith to which only the members of an esoteric club have access is to sidestep the issue and is equivalent to defending a magic theory of faith, which is not to deny that this experience will not be possible without overcoming a certain superficiality of human life. Thus, just as the intellectual life goes beyond the life of the senses, the life of faith cannot be limited to the rational life. Symbiosis is imperative.

Throughout the history of human thought, two theories have been formulated in response to the problem here discussed, a problem not just for Christianity. As we shall reiterate one more time, the issue can be reduced to asking which we trust more: the experience of reason or that of faith—though in any case the problem of reconciling the two remains.

A first hypothesis is that of the so-called theory of the double truth, one truth that is valid for the material, the sublunar world, the *vyāvahārika*, the physical world, and the other for the supernatural world, the *empireo*, the *pāramarthika*, the metaphysical realm. There is always, however, the question of how to harmonize both sets of truths without sliding into personal, cultural, and cosmic schizophrenia.

The second hypothesis is mysticism as a whole experience, which includes the third dimension of reality—what we see with our "third eye," which is how faith is referred to in some traditions, the Christian tradition included. If we accept that the body is no more than what modern science has told us, at least until recently, we should abandon our faith in the resurrection and in the real presence of Jesus in the Eucharist, and indeed in the world, if we want to retain a degree of rationality. Reason has to be surmounted but not eliminated. Here, Christian thinking cannot just be pulled along behind science, it should formulate its own worldview. What it cannot do is add to the confusion. The conflict is real and is a conflict between worldviews.

In these cases, Christian thinking should take the initiative and be creative. It is not enough to say that modern science is shortsighted and deprives us methodologically and a priori of the inclusion of the third dimension in the body of knowledge on man. What is needed is

---

[30] Tempiternity expresses an experience that is not dialectically opposed to either the eternal or the temporal. Instead there is an interaction between the two within a broader swathe of human experience and divine transcendence. The eternal is experienced in the temporal and the temporal in the eternal, in a seamless unity.

to elaborate this notion and recognize that, for the last few centuries, Christian thinking is in crisis, is in tow, is defensive in its attitude, with its strategic withdrawals, a situation that might lead one to conclude that there is no authentic scientific thought. To confront this problem, half a century ago I started a project to which I gave the name *theophysics*.[31] Not having been able to continue with this systematically, I shall provide a summary now. It is about taking the Christian worldview seriously, not so much adapting physics to theology as developing a vision of reality in which Christian intuitions are neither an appendix nor a supplement, but a raising of awareness of the "nature" of things: the *Christian existentiality*. It should be remembered that faith is not against reason but is a different sort of knowledge. The challenge in any case continues.

I cannot avoid voicing a suspicion: that Christian thought, having sought to monopolize the ambit of religious thought, is paying dearly for it now—having been practically displaced by scientific thought. The contribution of other cultures would constitute substantial capital. It would then be seen that many of Christianity's intuitions that seem incompatible with science would be acceptable in other cultures, in the eyes of other visions of the world. It could be that life, space, time, matter, and so forth are not what science describes or defines but in fact much more, while science just describes certain aspects of the realities that we designate with these names. It could be that we have to emancipate ourselves from the dominion of science over human thought. And let it not be said that these other views were (or are) "precritical" conceptions of reality, because it is not a question here of turning back the clock, but of allowing cross-fertilization from these other visions of the world without renouncing the discoveries of "modernity." It is significant that so many supposedly "liberal" and "progressive" attempts to explain the resurrection of the body take refuge in psychological, spiritual, or esoteric refinement, and precisely abandon the body. On the other hand, many "conservative" interpretations verge on magic or superstition. Perhaps a symbiosis between science and the visions of other cultures would be much more fertile. How then can we believe in the resurrection? Above all, let us not suffer what Aristotle in his *Metaphysics* calls "the constriction of the truth" ("ab ipsa veritate coacta," *anagkazomenoi*). Faith is a free act and cannot be constrained. The truth shall set us free, say the Christian Scriptures. It is faith in the resurrection that affords us our joie de vivre. It is not for nothing that the resurrection constitutes the center of "Christian" thought. I would venture the following considerations.

Jesus dies and is buried. Soon after, the tomb is found to be empty and not even his enemies dispute the fact. Jesus appears several times, eats with his own people, and lets himself be touched. The resurrection is the transformation of Jesus into the Christ. Christ is Jesus resurrected. Jesus is now only a memory. Christ on the other hand is alive and real. This realness is not just anamnesic or psychic, it is also physical and corporeal: it is a presence that is real, quite as real as a morsel of bread or a poor man who hungers. In the Eucharist it is not the bread that changes into Christ, but rather Christ who transforms himself or manifests himself in the bread, and is recognized as such in the liturgy that celebrates it. This Christ-anointed, firstborn, mystic body, life, alpha and omega, light, beginning, body, matter, is the central symbol of reality for Christians. Perhaps the body is much more than what science tells us it is. Other dimensions of physical reality go beyond the scope and reach of science. To paraphrase the evangelical message in the Prologue to the Gospel of St. John—"In Principio est Verbum [...] et Verbum caro factum est":[32] "In the Beginning there was the Word made flesh"—I would observe that this does not mean a Beginning (void)

---

[31] See Panikkar (1961).

[32] Jn 1:1–4.

that afterward became flesh, but that in the Beginning there was the flesh—without going into the problematic question of the "Beginning."

We are so accustomed to scientific distinctions that we hasten to explain, solely in scientific terms, the individual problem of the physiology of Jesus's body as if the resurrection were a chemical transmutation. "You did it to me," said Jesus, referring to any act, whether good or bad, done to one's neighbor; the same Jesus who was bold enough to say, "Before Abraham was, I am." In this sense, the Christian congregation called believers "the body of Christ," of that Christ who had existed before the beginning of the world, as the book of the Wisdom of Solomon suggests and as many religious traditions also affirm. A "fulfilled" man according to many religions is the homeomorphic equivalent of a resuscitated (resurrected) one, and the vision of reality thereby takes on new depths: "Who hath seen me, hath seen the Father." Belief in the resurrection is the equivalent of recognizing in Christ a symbol (*the* symbol, for Christians) of universal solidarity and the divine nature of all reality. The vision is complete: who has not seen the father has not seen me.

Surrexit, non est hic. He hath risen, he is not here (nor in any "here") they said, announcing this for the first time, these messengers or angels (bringers of good tidings). Jesus went his way when they would make him king. Jesus vanished, as he did in Emmaus and as always, from any limiting "here." But *resurrexi et adhuc tecum*, "I rose from the dead and am still among you," so we sing in the Latin liturgy echoing a psalm: He is nowhere, yet is with us and within us; in each of *us* that is authentically so. Man is more than just a body animated by a (rational) soul—more, not less.

I mean by this that if we are not able, *minutis minuendis,* to realize the experience of our own resurrection (something implicit in the liturgy, and not pertaining to linear time), we shall never grasp the meaning of the resurrection of Christ and with Christ. Neither the resurrection nor eternal life, together with hope, can be expectations of the future in linear time. They are founded upon a different worldview. "If Christ had been born a thousand times in Bethlehem and not been born in you, you would be lost forever." So says Christian mysticism in the words of Angelus Silesius. We are accustomed to interpreting the *kerygma* of the resurrection in the Semitic context of a "story of salvation." The salvation of someone certainly takes place in the story, but this is not a historical fact. Time does not have to be interpreted as linear time.[33] Christian resurrection appears after the death of the ego, as the Gospel writer John teaches us and as the mystics also tell us.

The challenge is not a small one. The resurrection is the central point of the revelation; almost all religions in the world speak of a celestial or heavenly state, celestial not temporal, but illuminated, realized, fulfilled, and so many other homeomorphic equivalents. We have already said that eternity is not a long time that never comes to an end, and similarly space is not a container within which bodies move. We have stated, too, that man is not just a developed or advanced ape or a mere energized body and that religions are not simple systems of ethics of conduct. The change is much more fundamental; it touches the very foundations of reality. There is a lack, especially in modern man, of a cosmic sense of human existence, the cosmotheandric vision of reality. In other words, matter is an abstraction in the same

---

[33] It is significant that the many explanations provided by modern theology of the resurrection that I have been able to consult (K. Barth, R. Bultmann, M. Scheler, A. Gehlen, M. Buber, D. Sölle, J. M. Pohier, J. Moltmann, E. Schillebeeckx, W. Pannenberg, M. Faraijó, N. Lohfink, W. Marsen, A. Torres Queiruga, . . .) do not dispute the myth of history— semiotic and linear. Christians call Jesus Lord of history, but they have made him a slave of it.

way as God is, or Man. We need to distinguish, but not separate. The resurrection of Jesus is the confirmation of what has been said.

An observation is necessary here. To explain the resurrection, we have used the facts of the Scriptures, but faith in the resurrection is not based on any exegesis, but on an experience inspired by Scripture, and that uses the words of the sacred books to make it comprehensible.

The challenge for modern-day science in this respect is positive: it obliges us to think about the nature of reality, including physical reality. I repeat that faith is a form of knowledge, and for that reason cannot avoid scientific knowledge.

In synthesis, if the resurrection is the central fact of the Christian message, and cannot be considered as a mere appendage, it should therefore radically transform our existence and vision of reality. The contribution of interculturality can be very valuable here. I don't say that "awakening," "realization," "fulfillment," and "born again" are the same concept, but they are certainly homeomorphic equivalents. The task of theophysics is to help us to undergo an experience of the world that is congruent with the great intuitions of mankind. As I have already stated, this I believe is the task of the third millennium.

2. *The cosmological difference is the difference between fundamental myths.*

In addition to the list of multiple differences—ontological, theological, transcendental—that modern thought has studied and still studies, we ought to add the difference of worldview or cosmovision: that is, the cosmological difference that cannot be confused with the others. Each culture has, in effect, its vision of the *cosmos*—that is to say, of reality. This difference has been practically forgotten thanks to the reigning monoculturalism and the almost absolute hegemony of rationality in the predominant culture in recent centuries. The cosmological difference (distinguishing aspect) is based on the diversity of myths, and comparative mythology cannot follow the rules of a single -logy, as still happens most often. But we cannot and should not look at this complex issue at this point. It is enough, however, to have raised the point.

What we have here is the question, on the one hand, of recognizing different visions of the world, different cosmologies, and on the other, of acknowledging an important point: that there is a difference between our experience of the world (which becomes, when it is conscious, our *logos* of the world) and the world as such. This last is not a Kantian world "in itself," which can *appear* different for everyone, or at least for every culture. There is not one single world (*noumenon*) for each of us, nor many visions, many *Weltanschauungen*, of this single unique world. It is not a case of there being one "objective" world that we all then subjectivize in our own way. The world is neither objective nor subjective, but rather is at a point where the objective and subjective worlds meet.

The cosmological difference is that which exists between the *mythos* of the cosmos, in what we believe we experience, and the *logos* of the cosmos, about which we philosophize. This will lead to the relativization of all cosmovisions, which, as I have mentioned before, does not mean descending into relativism.

We have already seen that conflicts that can be defined as between "science" and "faith" are conflicts that take place in the arena of the world, in the area of cosmovisions or worldviews. If scientific thought is not content with just being a strictly formal (mathematical) formulation, Christian thought is not content with simply being considerations concerning the ideal (eschatological) world—rather, both have a bearing on what one side and another call "reality," or "the world," in this context—a world that as we have said is not necessarily the same.

The hermeneutic difference is what exists between any text and its interpretation, which includes, involves, the context together with the pretext that is concealed within every text.

The cosmological difference, in contrast, is what there is between the text, together with its interpretation, and what I call the warp and weft, the place of the text in the totality of existing cosmologies. Pretext, text, context, and warp and weft form the tissue of reality as the human spirit is able to know it. Let us look at two examples of each of the four cases.

"God created the Heaven and the Earth."

"Any transformation of energy in any isolated system will produce an increase in entropy."

To interpret these two statements correctly, we need to integrate them into the above-mentioned *quaternitas*. As the four factors are interdependent, it is immaterial which one we start with.

a.   *Texts*. Each text constitutes the raw material of the interpretation. The text has a body, content, objectivity, and says much more than the author actually intended. What the text says depends not just on what is written, but also on what is read into it—that is to say, the readerly perspective. The correct reading of a text also involves the reader. Already in the sixth century before Christ, Pythagoras said that purity of living (*katharsis*) opens the door to knowledge. And the last father of the Western church, Pope Gregory the Great, affirmed that the words of Scripture grew at the same time as the sense of the reader ("[...] verbi sacri eloqui [...] iuxta sensum legentibus per intellectum crescunt")—this being a principle that certain literal exegesis has forgotten. All text that is read—that is, spoken—is a new event. The text is not just objective. Its object also includes or implies the reader. Out of context, the two statements cited above on creation and on entropy may "say" something completely different. If a being, beyond the physical world, has caused galaxies, and our Earth in particular, to emerge out of the void, we could also imagine this God as perhaps something like a source of heat or a concentration of primordial energy that—located beyond the system of the astronomical universe—acted with neither need nor reason to cause the Earth to appear out of the no-universe and then give it a kind of secret code that would manifest with the passing of time. Read in this way, the text could serve to confirm the scientific interpretation, going considerably beyond the bounds of the interpretation of the Pentateuch. Conversely, our scientific text could be used in the Christian ambit as a metaphor to explain that every-thing has a price and that if we do not open ourselves to the infinite—that is to say, if we do not break the closed circle of contingency—salvation is not possible. We can do nothing: we need a source of divine energy that will allow us to overcome death. If we do not charge ourselves with divine energy that will maintain "the difference of potential" and that comes out of transcendence, we are all condemned to death and hell.

We could continue exploring this text as we have been doing here. Basing ourselves on the law of entropy, we could set out to demonstrate the end of the world, Christian escha-tology, and the contingency of the created. This would take us away from the text, however, with the danger of pseudo-science and pseudo-theology and the risk of undue extrapolation.

If we were now to give the biblical a Buddhist context, the result would be different again. It might be interpreted as saying that when all was in peace because nothing existed, not even time, *something* (without time, space, or anything at all) suddenly appeared and set about making this world of heaven and earth—which perhaps exists only in (our) mind.

If we were to transfer the scientific text to a Hindū context, to take one example, we would read it as if it said that energy, which is a spiritual quality and irreducible to any means, is in this text considered to be a material and measurable thing that will condemn us to lose our freedom and make us believe that we can exist in a closed system. The second law of thermodynamics would be equated with the law of karma—and so on.

b. *Contexts.* Within these respective contexts, the religious text concerning the creation tells us that the Supreme Being, Life eternal and primordial, the Absolute, has extended his adventure by setting about producing all things, such that the whole universe is nothing more than a game or adventure of a con-tingent, tangential reality, one that coincides tangentially with the divine immensity, such that this universe is nothing in and of itself and yet is all (that is to say, divine) in its point of contact with the tangential. It tells us that all things are creatures, that is to say, divine in one way and nothing in another—ex-tensions in space, dis-tensions in time, in-tensions in the mind, ex-istences in Being—which exist insofar as they preserve this dynamic tension between an immanent divine presence and a transcendent absence. Creation is *ex nihilo* because it is solely *a Deo*. Creation is *creatio continua* as scholars used to say: if God creates, it is here and now that he (still) creates.

The second text, the scientific one, read in its context has it that energy, meaning the ability to do work or apply a force (such as necessary to move a mass or oppose gravity) remains constant if no external obstacles are put in its way, and that when this happens heat is produced, heat that is furthermore endowed with a sort of inertia that, in the absence of external influences, will cause it to be aligned in one particular direction. It follows that continuous movement is not possible, that nothing can pass through two equal states, and that this universe has a history, a beginning and an end.

We should be making undue extrapolations if we were to deduce from the first text that the world is an isolated system, or from the second that the world is contingent. In summary, every text encloses a meaning, in its own context, which holds out the possibility of under-standing it, of criticizing it, and also of making it say what it does not "say."

c. *Pretexts.* One can carry out an examination of the pretexts of a text by examining its contexts, as we have said, determining the way the author of the text uses it with an intentionality—an intentionality that will be all the more effective to the extent that it is concealed and is identified with the text, so that it seems that what is speaking is the text itself.

The ancients knew this very well when they maintained that behind all sacred Scriptures there was the hidden force of revelation that wished to tell us something. The message of a sacred text is not what it "says," but rather what the inspiration behind it meant it to say. For that reason, the interpretation of a text needs faith, as tradition has always insisted. If the author is unknown, and we do not know the context, then it will be all the more difficult to understand the text. It is necessary to know who is talking in order to know what is being talked about, unless this no longer forms part of the original context, as happens in meetings between scientists or meetings between theologians. The right that the church assumes to interpret Scripture for us is that (only) it (the church) knows the pretexts. No text is purely objective, that is to say, without pretext. There is no doubt that the first of the two texts, on the creation, is to establish monotheism in all its aspects. Subsequent Christian reading of the text has interpreted it as creation out of nothing, given that its pretext was to seek to contradict the Platonic tradition when it spoke of a demiurge giving form to raw material that was not only eternal but divine. This was something that Christians could not accept in that they thought that it contradicted not only what the text says (creation out of nothing is not very explicit in Genesis) but also what was actually meant by the authors and the inspiration behind the text. We shall spare the reader the vast bibliography on this subject.

The Old Testament Scriptures, beginning with the sacred books of Moses, are, in their turn, the pretext to preserve, stimulate, and indeed create the identity and cohesion of the children of Israel. As is well known, they are writings revised *postfactum*. The New Testament is not immune, either, to the apologetic intentions of the Gospel writers and the other writers of holy Scripture. It would be ingenuous to forget this, and it would lead to fundamentalist readings dehumanizing the writers themselves. All writers aspire to something, perhaps just to telling the truth—"their" truth.

In the same way, the debate over perpetual motion and over the constant quantity of energy (to an extent a vicious circle, since it introduces the idea of potential energy to maintain the quantity constant) constitutes the pretext for the study of heat and arriving at Clausius's famous formulation that ushered in the second law of thermodynamics. The Industrial Revolution is in full swing. Energy is indispensable, and the most obvious source is heat. There is a need to find the relationship between the two. The formula emerges as vital for the dawning industrial age. There is no debate here about the sex of the angels (why bother?) but about the forms energy takes, a subject that has implications for everyone. The history of science is full of such pretexts, and one of the most famous is that of Galileo. Indeed, the promoter of scientific objectivity is laden with extraordinary subjective pathos. His texts are a pretext to show the errors of the Aristotelians and the priority to be given to the natural (divine and eternal) revelation of the "great Book of Nature" over the positive revelation of Scripture, which latter should be read with the key provided by the former. Or, to use his own words, "It is theology which should be interpreted in the light of scientific fact and not the other way round"—because science, as he saw it, simply interprets the facts of nature (which he considered divine).

There is no text, then, that does not conceal many pretexts, knowledge of which will provide the hermeneutic keys to understand any text. Hermeneutics cannot be a completely objectifiable science, precisely because a part of its "object" is the subject itself, which both reveals and conceals itself in the text. It is not possible to reduce a text to objective dimensions; the intent involves the author, and to know the author it is not sufficient to know how to read the text. As the medieval knights knew well, behind every blade there was the hand of a knight . . . and a lady who caused him to wield it. Behind the current debate in schools across the United States on the theories of creation and evolution there are interests that are not just ideological, but generated at times by millions of dollars. The Hammurabi text, the Aśoka inscriptions, and the Egyptian obelisks all have very many intentions, sometimes secret, sometimes manifest, and mostly unconscious. In short, scientific thought and "Christian thought" are not two formal structures of pure thought. Behind every thought is the thinker and his "lady" (not necessarily a woman). It could just as easily be a goddess, a sage, an idea, or an ambition—but in any case, a lover. Paraphrasing Dante we could say, "love that moves the heart and the other texts."

     d. *Warp and weft.* Man cannot desist from seeking to understand, nor be able to understand things if these have not been reduced to a degree of harmony against a holistic background. We should perhaps add that this human longing is a constituent part of man's makeup, a project that is continually frustrated, but that is the human condition. It is necessary here to make a distinction between to com-prehend and to under-stand. Comprehension is rational and requires "reduction" to an intelligible unit. Reason fixes and imprisons its own "object." To understand something, on the other hand, involves an understanding that goes beyond comprehension. In this case the intellect does not capture and imprison the thing, but approaches it.

The warp and weft is the cosmovision in which the contexts are situated and tends toward understanding rather than comprehension. The book of Genesis can speak to us of God, and Clausius can describe entropy for us. Both of them, however, are speaking to us, and speaking of the world we live in. It is precisely here in the warp and weft that it becomes essential to be familiar with the *mythos*, the ambit that includes different contexts and where a warp and weft is constructed that is not based on the same laws as the texts. To put it another way: the meeting between scientific and religious thought should not take place either in the field of theology or of science. The game should be played on neutral ground. Both kinds of thought, therefore, are to be situated in the field of the *logos*, of the (not necessarily rational) word, and both aspire for this to be favorable to them. Thus if we want the relationship we are looking for to be truly impartial, neither dialectal reason nor theological intellect are enough. This is the trap into which many good intentions have fallen. For that reason, the dialogue between religion and science is something considerably more serious than ecumenism "just in case." At stake here is human nature itself, if we do not wish to descend into irrationalism, and a-critical, sterile scientific and religious commonplaces.

The method to be adopted for this dialogue is not dialectal (the dialectic is not universal) but rather *dialogal*: the very platform for consensus or dissent is constructed through dialogue. From the point of view of interpretation, I have introduced the notion of *diatopic hermeneutics,* in that the points of departure (the *topoi*) will not necessarily be common to both sides. A comparative history of ideas would be useful here, but the warp and weft I am talking about is something more than the idea.[34] Indeed, capturing the human warp and weft is anything but an easy task. However, being aware of the problem is a big step forward in itself.

All of us live in a particular context. Scientific thought and Christian thought form a part of a basic Western cultural context, even if its contents may vary from individual to individual. All culture is a kind of macro-context that, in a sense, it is possible to come to know, but the warp and weft does not allow there to be a supersystem that includes it. For that to be, there would need to be a superstructure for that, and so on ad infinitum. No human being can embrace the total spectrum of human existence; no one can allow themselves the luxury of saying what mankind is—not until the last woman on the last island at the end of the ages has said the last word. Humanity is not a thing, nor can human consciousness ever be absolutely objectified. *Homo loquens.*

For this alone, the warp and weft opens us up to the *mythos* and not to mythology, which in itself means a submission of *mythos* to *logos*. And if the error of other times was a-critical submission to the *mythos*, now it is the belief, contrariwise, that we have demystified reality thanks to science.

Text, context, and warp and weft form the human *fabric*. Every one of us participates more or less actively in the construction of the warp and weft of our own existence, but this is inserted into the *fabric* that has been woven before us, in the world in which we live and in the culture that surrounds us. Neither scientific thought nor Christian thought forms the whole of this *fabric* of human life. Perhaps another word here for *fabric* would be *worldview*. But metaphors are dangerous. Fabric suggests unity, oneness, whereas worldviews are distinctive. We ought, therefore, to emphasize that the fabric can be of many different hues and be formed of different weaves. In any case, the human fabric cannot be seen; in the first place because it is simply too vast, second because we are immersed within it, and third because it is not (yet) finished.

The fabric is not ours. The world in which we live, the universe of which we are conscious, is not the result of our thoughts, but neither is it a "reality" in itself, unique for us, a datum, absolute. Reality is not the fruit of our interpretation, since we ourselves, with our interpretation, belong to the same reality and we modify it. The world is given to us not like an object

---

[34] See, among others, Nakamura (1992).

to investigate or like an object of thought, but like a gift, like something that embraces us, where we can live and discover our objects. In a word, reality is not given to us like the *logos*, but offered as a *mythos*, like the horizon in which we in our turn situate our idea of the world.

The differences of worldviews (cosmovisions) derive from the hiatus between this world of ours given by the *mythos*, and the world that is also ours, revealed in the *logos*. This makes any absolutization impossible, because any interpretation is visibly inserted in a *mythos* that enables it and, consequently, limits it. I have spoken elsewhere of the *pars pro toto* effect: we see *totum in parte*; the *part* represents the *totum*, but is not it.

3. *The task of our time is the provisional symbiosis of human knowledge.*

I take *sym-biosis* to mean not so much co-existence as conviviality in the sense of sharing life.

Some fifty years ago I established a difference between synthesis and system, and defended synthesis as the overcoming of the cultural schizophrenia of our times, without this becoming a system that has to be coherent—closed, in the last analysis. The fragmentation of knowledge has resulted in the fragmentation of the knower. Today, however, the connotations of the word "synthesis" are closer to that of "synthetic," almost making advisable a change of metaphor, and a switch from chemistry to biology (from synthesis to symbiosis). But in no way does this have to do with system. To achieve unity of information, integrating criteria are needed. System is an edifice that is constructed, a *summa* that is worked on to be totally coherent. If the connecting thread is the Christian creed, we will make theology the *regina scientiarum*; if it is calculation-based science, all other types of knowledge will be *ancillae scientiae*.

Symbiosis, on the other hand, does not have preconceived plans or integrative criteria. Systems are constructed, symbiosis is lived; system is artificial, symbiosis is natural. Life is precisely this coordination and this living-togetherness. Any outside interference wounds it and can be justified only as therapeutic surgery to return things to a natural state of affairs, as far as this is possible. In any case, we could think of alchemy as Paracelsus understood it, that is to say as creative participation of human genius in the task of getting the universe to reach its plenitude, given that, according to the alchemists, God left the work uncompleted so that Man might bring it to its fullness. So, as we have said, we have not made the texture of our lives ourselves, we received it. In this respect there is a difference between scientific thought and Christian thought: the first interprets the fabric as data to comprehend and to use, and the second sees the fabric as a gift to enjoy and be thankful for. These attitudes are not incompatible, in fact, but it is not easy to conjugate them. This way of understanding primordial data, this receptivity to gifts poured out, is more a function of the *mythos* than the *logos*. Hence the function of the *mythos* can be seen as essential.[35]

The problems run deep and the one we are focusing on here particularly so. A more superficial approach would not solve it.

After so many centuries of more or less considerable tensions, with casualties on both sides (casualties precisely among the more intelligent and sensitive), not only has Christianity lost ground, but science too has sacrificed a good part of its harmony and complementarity. It would seem then that the time has come to reach something more than a political peace, as they now seem to want to achieve with Galileo. The way to achieve this task would not seem to be by decree, although an intelligent policy, lacking in other times, could prove extremely helpful. If we have become aware of the world situation, we cannot content ourselves with defensive or apologetic attitudes—for example, when we speak of the great worth of Christianity and the unworthiness of Christians, the nobility of science and the misuse of technology. These are

---

[35] "The true philosopher is a lover of myths," said Aristotle.

instances of the fragmentation that needs to be overcome. How do we get to know Christianity if not through the praxis of Christians? How to know science if not by seeing the use to which it is put? "By their fruits ye shall know them." Neither Christianity nor science are discarnate ideas or theories that exist only in the realm of the ideal. We are not discussing mathematical hypotheses here, but human realities; not two abstractions, but rather the life itself of mankind.

Symbiosis is not attained with the victory of one or the other side, nor through well-intentioned compromises or demonstrations of civil tolerance. Symbiosis is lived, like the healthy functioning of any living organism, be it biological, sociological, or cultural. It is not a question of favoring one set of knowledge by denigrating the other, nor of establishing a more or less a priori hierarchy. It is a question of opening to the light, wherever it might come from, which to use the words of the Gospels is the life of man—of *homo sapiens*.

I repeat that the current situation leads us to radically reconsider the direction of our human adventure over the last few millennia. For this an intercultural approach is necessary.

We ought, however, to be keeping to our subject. I shall confine myself here to suggesting three points where the symbiosis between science and Christianity would be possible—or, changing metaphors, suggesting three bridges we can use to set up communication. The first of the three is essential and implies consequences for the general problematic. The other two are simply examples of possible mutual fecundation.

    a. *The* agnôsia *of all* gnôsis *(the ignorance of all knowledge)*. After the lessons of history and the observations of the "sociology of knowledge," it should be evident that all knowledge is not only integrated into time and space, but is the function of these two factors, and thus intrinsically transitory. What one age defends is modified or even rejected by another. And this happens as much in the world of scientific thought as in Christian thought. Tolerance was heresy in the seventeenth century and a virtue in the nineteenth and twentieth.

This *agnôsia* refers not only to what lies well beyond the limits, but rather to what penetrates the very heart of what is known, to the extent that it is known. Something is known consciously when it is known that it is known. This is the weakness of reflection, of pondering, which weakens knowledge but makes it more human. Otherwise this would be fanaticism. Brahman, pure consciousness (*cit*), does not even know that it is Brahman—so says the Vedanta. Apart from being a father, which is purely relation, God the father in no wise *is*—so confirms Christian theology. Knowing that something is known itself introduces a knower of this knowing (that it is known) distinguishable from what is known, and this in a sense leaves it in the penumbra—given that this awareness is turned on the knowing that this is known and not on the thing (being known). When the knower knows itself, it ceases to be the knower and becomes the known—I do not wish to go into this problem at this point. There are, however, more things to say. In knowing something, despite our identification with it, we are aware that we do not exhaust it; we do not eliminate its mystery, nor do we phagocyte it totally. This does not happen in the case of scientific knowledge, which is abstract. The resistance of the thing that is known reveals to us that it is real. Light only illuminates an opaque mass, which is what allows us to see what we see. If it were completely transparent it would be invisible (unknowable). The very thought of divine omniscience is impaired by the assumption, presupposition, that Being is totally knowable—that is, part of the Parmenidian doctrine according to which Thinking is coextensive with Being.

A *first corollary* leads us to the double reality of all knowledge.

The first relativity, as we have said, is that which sees a relationship between knowledge and being. All true knowledge reveals being, but does not necessarily exhaust it. The second relativity affects us more directly: it is that which sets up a relationship between pretext,

text, context, and warp and weft, and thus leaves space for scientific thought and Christian thought, each in its own field.

Nature's apparent obedience to the conceptual schemes of human intelligence provides one of thought's most passionately debated themes. "See how the sky and sea obey me!" a scientist might well exclaim enthusiastically. In the same way contemplation (including Christian contemplation) can wax enthusiastic over the luminosity all things take on, with the mysterious beauty of reality and its infinite light.

In summary, all knowledge is knowledge of the knowable—of reality. All being is a mystery. Mysticism is aware of this. Night, the void, darkness, these make possible the light, *gnôsis*. "Blessed are those who have attained absolute *agnôsia* [ignorance]," said Evagrius Ponticus in the fourth century. For that reason, we have written that symbiosis, the task of our time, is constantly provisional and not for that reason less viable. Contingency is graven on the very heart of reality. Idolatry (taking any being, idea, or belief as absolute, our notion of the Absolute not excepted) is the greatest of sins.

This attitude cannot be called agnosticism, which is the renunciation of the search, of the *quaerens*, as we have said. The Gods love the shadows, says the *Veda*, and Yahweh dwells in darkness, echoes the Bible. Put very simply, agnostics know that they do not know, mystics do not know that they know; the former are aware of their ignorance (and suffer for it), while the latter are not aware that they know (and enjoy this). Science "is puffed up," says St. Paul, in a phrase that however we need to interpret correctly. "Unknown to him who knows, known to him who does not know," says the *Keno-Upaniṣad*. Those are saved who do works of mercy without knowing they do them to me, repeats St. Matthew. "Cloud of unknowing," says the medieval mystic. To put it philosophically, epistemology has no power of redemption. Straight is the gate to knowledge but is closed to no one.

A *second corollary* is the intellectual possibility of overcoming rationalism without denying reason, which however has the right of veto. "Knowledge" is not the equivalent of "rational knowledge." There are many forms of rationality, but there are also many forms of intelligibility, and overarching the two, there are many forms of consciousness.

A *third corollary* has not just to do with the possibility but also the advisability of mutual fertilization between cultures. Not one of them, singly, can manage the situation in which mankind currently finds itself. Today, interculturality is much more than an academic luxury, it is a vital necessity for human survival. *Conviviality*,[36] which we mentioned earlier, does not just concern thought or theory, but needs to manifest in human praxis. It may be that no culture can teach anything to any other, but every culture can and should learn from the others. I dare say that only those cultures that know how to learn from the others will survive, which does not mean letting the others take control, much less colonize one. To learn, here, means to assimilate without losing identity.

A *fourth corollary* may be even more important, given that mankind's ability to live together depends on it: the justification of pluralism. The fact that man finds visions of the world that are incompatible and philosophies that are incommensurate only means that man "experiences" his constituent limits: in other words, his contingency. Modern individualism has made plausible individual humility (I'm so small that I cannot open the door to knowledge) but collective pride (we, all of us—Christians, atheists, laypeople, Hindūs—have the keys of the door to knowledge).

    b. *The limits of scientific thought.* What we have said makes it plain that scientific thought is a specific, limited way not only of approaching reality but of thinking.

---

[36] Full communion of life.

Thinking traditionally, scientific thought can be classed with calculation or with the ability to predict the course of phenomena. This is in effect a kind of knowledge that is possible without love, which has given up pretensions of knowing, as opposed to knowing about, something and confines itself to determining laws on the behavior of phenomena. The triumph of our present-day scientific age has made scientific thinking the paradigm for all thought; its influence in all branches of knowledge, philosophy included, is undeniable.

We might almost say it has taken over the monopoly of the very words that have been the mainstay and vehicle of the great intuitions of humanity. Thus, for example, "time," "mass," "weight," "space," "energy," "body," and to a certain extent "mankind," "animal," and so on, seem sometimes to have only the meaning that science gives to those terms, which is something measurable or at least able to be experimented about.

The other side of the coin is, however, just as undeniable. In the first place, the triumph of science would not have been possible had there not been other deep causes for this, not reducible to the human thirst for power. If science has dominated the world scene to the point of seeming universal, and has permeated the entire world, to all practical purposes replacing other forms of knowledge, then there must be something in its nature or that of mankind that has made its predominance possible.

In other words, scientific knowledge has had the most spectacular results concerning reality. Mathematical calculation, as axiomatic and formal as it may seem, has secured real power over things. The physical world seems to obey what scientific reason calculates. Scientific knowledge is a cognitive factor of the first order. But as we have said repeatedly, there are many other forms of knowledge apart from scientific knowledge.

The limits of scientific thought, however, cannot be reduced only to the limited number of its objects, but also to the limited form of its methods, as we have already seen. The limitations on thought are twofold:

    i.   Not all reality is scientifically thinkable. There are other forms of thought that reveal other aspects of reality.

    ii.   Not all reality is thinkable; and while there might be non-scientific thinking that can open reality up to us, thought does not exhaust either Being or reality.

Formulated theoretically, these statements seem rather obvious. However, in the practice of a large part of humanity, life presents itself as so complicated that there is precious little time left to cultivate what in Latin was called *otium*, which these days is considered a vice, construed as idleness. It is not surprising then that cultivating the Spirit in oneself has been put on the back burner and has almost become the specialty of a caste.

    c.   *The relativization of Christian thought.* Christian thought, either for complex historical reasons or because of features of the human mind reinforced by the Western European character (not Jewish precisely), has come to think of itself as universal, and this happened when it came to be thought that "truth" is a synonym for "universal," and this latter a synonym for "absolute universality."

Having summarized the limits of scientific thought in two points, we can do the same with Christian thought:

    i.   Not all reality can be reduced to a Christian interpretation of such—that is, we cannot rule out a priori other potentially valid interpretations of reality.

    ii.   Not all reality is Christic, not even eschatologically speaking. This is the mystery of evil—or, if preferred, the symbol of hell.

We are not concerned now with Christian dogma, but rather with the realization that these dogmas are only valid if one is aware of their limits, that is to say, the specific, limited context that confers on them their meaning. Thus, for example, all that might be said about an "absolute" God will always be subject to the limitation and contingency of human interpretation and reception.

The word that represents this necessary recognition of these cultural and religious limits is *pluralism.*

Not a few are wary of this term and are right, to a certain extent, to criticize it if one takes it to involve repudiation of the truth and a dallying with self-destructive relativism. What has not been done in the name of God, religion, or democracy? We can always abuse any word. Pluralism does not mean either "plurality" or "relativism," nor "chaos." On the one hand it means "relativity" and thus excludes any absolutism, while on the other it means the experience of human contingency. If we pointed to, and criticized, the undue extrapolations of science, now we have to recognize that this has also been the case with some "Christian thought," and continues to be so.

Let us recall what we said above about pretexts, texts, contexts, and warp and weft.

Christian thought harbors a certain fearfulness of losing its primacy among the worldviews—perhaps more because of Hegel than the Gospels. At all events, recognition of the relativity of Christianity does not take away any of its truth—although this may have been understood until now as an attack on the Christian vision of truth or reality. Being conscious of one's own limits is the first step to overcoming them. Christians should not be afraid. Christ himself recognized that there was a Mystery, the Father, who was above him. But that is not our problem now.

Physics and Theophysics:
Philosophical Reflection

The period in which theological science represented the totality of knowledge was followed by other periods in which the different branches of human knowledge gradually became independent from theology and, as a reaction, have wanted to sever all connection with it. The context of this reaction is where we have to situate the beginnings of modern science. This is the "official version," which does not mean it is not the truth, nor that theology does not have its share of the responsibility. But what is often forgotten, nevertheless, is the price that has been paid for this independence: the fragmentation of knowledge into more or less specialized fields, and the atrophy of holistic knowledge—which cannot be the sum of the gamut of specialized "sciences."

It is in any case a matter of concern that, for several centuries now, theology has been largely absent from the tremendous effort man is making to get to know the physical world from both the practical and speculative standpoints. Theology was considered fundamentally as a "contemplative" science (in the strict sense) and thus was little concerned with transforming the world or investigating it and, more passive than modern science, never set out to conquer it. I refer to theology as knowledge, because many religions, understood as praxis, have in effect wished to "convert" the world, to save it. Yet frequently they have invited us to flee from it. Christian spirituality has evolved to a certain extent: from a monastic attitude, which practically ignored the world, it has slowly moved toward a secular position. In a similar way, theology as a whole, after its initial focus on the problem of a transcendental Divinity, has come down to *ad extra* realities, to the extent of interesting itself in the structures of actual being. The theology of liberation could well be an instance of this—as experienced in the reaction of the more classical reaches of theology, accusing the former of having "lowered itself" to analyze merely human (political) issues.

These days we are witnessing an increasing interest in what I have called "sacred secularity."[37] Thus, just as it would be erroneous for secular spirituality to want to undermine what the monastic tradition, for example, has elaborated and developed, in the same way it would be equally erroneous to claim that a theology "of earthly realities" or of science could dispense with traditional theology.[38] Not only does one complete the other, but each interpenetrates and fertilizes the other, while being, often, mutually critical. In reality, everything is connected with everything else: *sarvam sarvātmakam*, said the ancients. The smallest energetic change in the ultimate elemental particles is something that happens in the heart of the Trinity. We are in the Trinity—but we do not yet have the intellectual wherewithal to manage the new intuitions.

There is still, however, the fact that, until now, relatively little has been written about the integral nature of reality. Science perhaps needed to get things out of its system, on its own, and it was not a good moment to bother her too much on her honeymoon with knowledge and wisdom. However, times are changing.

It was needful, too, for theology to get down from its throne as sovereign queen and emancipate itself from the fear of pantheism, which has made it prone to a very understandable degree of dualism in the ambit of monotheism. So as not to confuse God with the World, it was thought necessary to accentuate the difference between the two. So as not to reduce the world to mere appearances it has been necessary to attribute substantiality to it. This dualism is responsible for the dichotomy we have alluded to—not resolved either by the opposite reaction of monotheism.

This relationship of theology with the scientific world has gone through various stages that are beginning to be studied. Not only Galileo, but also Copernicus, Tycho Brahe, and indeed Descartes too, drastically so (while carefully prepared by postmedieval nominalism), all represented the exile of theology from the world of science. In the face of excessive intrusion, the territories were politely divided up. A worthy retirement was secured for the *regina scientiarum* so that it could cultivate its own garden, that of a God seemingly interested only in souls and their salvation, or what it saw fit to reveal to us. "Without questioning in the slightest the truth of the faith, and wishing like any faithful Christian to go to Heaven." Descartes thought to put aside all discordant opinions and trust only in reason (*his* reason) to discover the truth of things.

For a certain time philosophy acted as a bridge between science and theology, but slowly and surely its hybrid nature led it toward rationality and so it separated from theology, causing it to lose its autonomy, inducing it to become one of the positive sciences. It thus ceased to exist as philosophy and became just another variant of scientific activity. To illustrate what I mean, you only have to open at random any book of theology written in the Middle Ages, and then one written in the modern or contemporary era. The first will be full of references to the physical sciences of its day: spontaneous generation, the theory of heat, of the humors, of fire, are used as examples or often supply the actual foundation of philosophical theories on knowledge, on the creation, on the analogy of being. To understand the extent to which not just philosophy but theology and the very formulation of dogma are indebted to the cosmological theories of their time, you need simply to turn to the admirable (but unknown) works of Albert Mitterer.[39] We immediately become aware that the content of

---

[37] See Panikkar (2004). In Volume XI of this *Opera Omnia*.

[38] In 1952, at the insistence of Hedwig von Skoda (founder of Equipes internacionales de renaissance chretienne), I taught a course on "Theologie der irdischen Gegebenheiten" [Theology of earthly realities].

[39] See, for instance, Mitterer (1948).

Christian doctrine, dogma included, has this debt to the cosmological theories of earlier times, without which the doctrine would be misinterpreted. Modern theology, on the other hand, seems to move in a disincarnate world, of pure spirits, and even the latter are lacking in psychological laws. They are far away from present-day science—and so the dogma seems to have dropped out of the clouds.

Nonetheless the reciprocal distancing between science and theology has never been total. Theology, despite everything, has maintained a certain presence within science itself as a result of the moral imperative that science has always felt. The example of many nuclear scientists of today is not one of people bristling with scruples nor of pure moralists, but of scientists who are aware of the complexity of the issues. The debate on atomic questions, genetic engineering, and so on is not exempt of moral concern, regardless of how this is resolved. When science of Hitler's Germany carried out experiments on human beings to advance medical knowledge, the universal conscience of science itself rebelled—and even today when this is done, it is kept secret.[40] Furthermore, we can see that one of science's incentives is its concern to solve the more human problems of existence, like food and housing, not to mention health—although here we see the intrinsic link between technological science and the economy. Science has never lost interest in humanity, and has never freed itself from moral concern; even when the separation had become evident, science stated that it was benevolent, improving the quality of life or at least serving the cause of "Progress"—all of these being moral categories.[41] The formula of science for science's sake, paralleling that of art for art's sake, is anything but scientific. That science latterly became allied with the economy, as theology had earlier done with politics, is another problem that we cannot ignore, but cannot go into at this moment. Modern science is not pure, in either sense of the word, nor is theology.

Theology is still present, above all with a negative moral tone, with vetoes that transcend the order of science, which nevertheless science bends before or rebels. Science, for example, has not yet found physiological differences between human beings and animals, yet it has refused to put them on the same level. It accepts that a chimpanzee may be killed for "scientific" experiments, but not a man—until now!

Theology is also present in terms of positive moral dicta that invite science to pursue one path instead of another, and to help mankind with its most urgent problems. When science, for example, has put itself at the service of the state, it has done so, despite multiple abuses, following a moral imperative that it felt within it. Similarly, the step from science to technology was not taken, in the first place, for economic motives of exploitation or power-seeking, but out of a moral impulse that pushes science to be useful and of service to humanity. This is so even if this impulse might afterward be corrupted or distorted into serving just one class, one collective, one nation, one race, or one economy—with the concomitant theoretical "justifications" for which philosophy and theology are also responsible.

I am mounting this defense of pure science so as not to err on the side of pessimistic criticism that sees evil everywhere. My criticism is not moral and extrinsic to science, but is directed at the fragmentation of knowledge or, better, the abandoning of a different (not to say superior) level of knowing of the particular "brands of knowledge." We have already noted that science is not pure, among other things because there is no pure science, that is, detached from Man. One thing is abstraction, and another the dislocating of a particular field of knowledge from knowledge of the whole.

---

[40] See, for instance, Eastham, op. cit.

[41] See, for example, Heisig (2003) and criticism of the invasion of the human body by modern medicine, and the by-now classic work by Illich (1976).

There was a time when scientific research was considered dangerous for the faith, and thus not advisable from the Christian point of view. We are still paying today for the harm done by that attitude. But the reasons for it are comprehensible on both sides. Classical (that is, rational) science has no need for a "prime mover," which may not even be necessary for its calculations. Classical (that is, monotheistic) theology cannot accept the *ontonomy* of science.

At the present time scientists who are immersed in the scientific world, and at the same time are firm believers, cannot fail to feel a profound tension and at times even opposition, not so much in the doctrinal order as in the more subtle order of the very approach to the problems and areas of interests. It cannot be denied that the religious and the Christian modalities are frequently antagonistic. This has led to the creation of watertight compartments, often not the result of cowardice but a healthy defensive reaction. While there is not a *theophysics* worthy of that name (call it what you will), the scientist who is also a believer will continue to feel a certain chronic malaise because of the exclusively positivist dimension of science. In the first part of this book, on the subject of Jesus's resurrection, we limited ourselves to referring to what might be a conception of the corporeal (or of matter) more in line with a theophysical vision of reality—but here we can only touch on the problem.

In Western culture a philosophy is slowly taking hold that does not seek to ignore science and that is able to be more than just "scientific" (providing epistemological analysis of scientific knowledge). This philosophy is, at least de facto, allied to theology. Philosophy reminds science that there are other things besides scientific objects. But there is more: oftentimes philosophy emerges in the very innermost of science, without it needing to be imported from outside. Think for example of the emergence of psychiatry and psychology from out of science's depths: they emerged within its heart, but soon transcended its bounds—because they engaged with man. At the same time it is significant to note how so many physicists cannot resist the temptation of writing their book on philosophy, which once again is symptomatic of the fact that the separation between science and theology is neither natural nor permanent.

Finally, theology itself is steadily appearing on the scientific scene, so much so that today it is normal to speak of a "theology of earthly realities," a "theology of work," and of the *consecratio mundi*. Despite the fact that the ideas circulating on this are still rudimentary, there is discussion not only of the theology of human love and of free time, but of technology itself and of the machine. The problems will out, anyway, and cannot be reduced to generic alarm bells of a moral order, such as for example the case of biogenetics or nanotechnology, without wishing to enter into any specific field at this moment.

In summary, the relationship between physics and theology is intrinsic and not only because they coincide in certain areas such as the moral. Both disciplines refer to reality and converge on man. We can now proceed to offer a few notes on this problem.

Theophysics

The word could sound extravagant for those accustomed to the "*politique de domaines séparées*" and perhaps still fearful of theologians intruding into worldly matters because of the papal caesaropapism—which was intellectual too—of a few centuries ago. It has to be said immediately that the *theos* of theophysics is not necessarily the God of rigid monotheism—and certainly not a God of substance, even if personal. Let us not forget that the person, here, is purely relational. Theophysics seeks simply to emphasize that the science of material reality (physics) also belongs *ontonomically* to theology, because the *logos* modified by *theos* seeks to embrace the whole of reality—"embrace" here being a metaphor of lovingness rather than possession.

We repeat that the *theos* of theophysics is that divine mystery that permeates all reality and does not dwell alone in a *topos ouranios*, in a transcendent heaven; this is an incarnate, Trinitarian God—to stick to Christian language.

It is significant that modern authors, despite the opening there has been to Buddhism and Hinduism, can and do still move within a monotheist mode of thinking. Monotheism is not solely the belief in one God, in a Supreme Being, it is also a form of thought that makes this possible: the supremacy of rationality—that is to say, the belief that reality can be reduced to one sole principle. Monotheism is the *mythos* that makes belief in a supreme God plausible. By way of introduction we shall outline certain characteristics of this presumed theophysics.[42]

1. The Cosmotheandric Problematic

The vision that derives from a conception of reality that does not exclude God leads us in the first place to not making Man a stranger to the world.[43] An extreme position here would be the ingenuous and possibly archaic conception of man as one thing among many, without discrimination or distinction; but the other extreme is to take reason and indeed the spirit so seriously, and being so proud of this "privilege," that we forget Man is dust of the earth and the *humus* of this planet, contingent along with the other beings, while yet self-aware. However, if things are looked at theophysically, there is not Man on one side and the world on the other, but rather an *anthropocosmos*, the first element of a still more total reality that in turn culminates in a *theocosmos* in which God is still the God *of* the world, and the world is still the world *of* God—without for now specifying the (*advaita*) sense here of the genitives. Theophysics needs a new language. But, to return to the *cosmotheandric* vision, we see that in it, not only is the soul not separate from the body, but that the Earth and Man are similarly not antagonistic and divided, in the same way that Man and God, while different, are not separable except mentally. But the mind, as we have said, is not the judge of reality. There is a positive symbiosis that extends to allowing a *certain* reconciliation between man and the machine—without condemning all machines as dehumanizing, although the danger is real enough. The ultimate reason for this is at the deepest level based on the fact that men and machines (however material and technical) are not two things that are completely heterogeneous from each other. In this sense it would be necessary to distinguish between machines of the first and second degree. The former are an extension of the body and use natural energy. The latter are independent, and their laws are independent from ours.

This unity between man and the cosmos, which is gradually being revealed to us, is redolent with consequences in all fields. The connection that is these days accepted between the soul and the body, for example, overcomes the dualism that has corroded much of Western culture. Overcoming post-Cartesian (and ultimately Platonic) dualism, which has swung between defending Man as a pure spirit and defending Man as consisting of a soul and a body, considered to be two separate substances, the unity of Man is now considered at a more profound level. This has led to the contemporary vision of a positive asceticism that does not despise or undervalue the body and also the fully human concept of mysticism itself, which cannot be completely a-cosmic and incorporeal. Things themselves take on a new dimension as we rediscover the ancient relationship between them and man.

When Christ walked on the water this was something more than thaumaturgics, and when the saint preached to the fishes he was something more than a poet. The living stones

---

[42] The term *theophysics* was introduced in Panikkar (1961).

[43] See Wilber (1998), where he speaks of three eyes— of the senses, of reason, and spiritual (which we have called of faith to keep to the tradition). Faith is also knowledge.

of the Buddhist and Christian Scriptures, the living water, the supertemporal fire, the burning bush that burned yet was not consumed, the rubies and emeralds of the heavenly Jerusalem, the many wings and eyes of the celestial beasts, the sacrificial lamb that yet lives . . . all represent something more than primitivism or Hebrew folklore, something more than simple metaphors needing to be "demystified" or read as "metaphysical." In summary, *theophysics* is the basis and foundation of what we have termed *ecophysics*[44]—to be distinguished from ecology, which is a movement that is almost exclusively pragmatic.

Nonetheless, theophysics is not limited to a classically "theological" vision of a created world, but seeks to go much further. It seeks above all to see the God of things, or God in things, and to see things in God. It doesn't claim to see God Transcendent, the Other (*alius*) by means of a telescope that sees beyond things. Instead it aspires to see as through a microscope the most recondite aspect of what things themselves are, their most intimate nucleus, their meta-physical constitution—in other words, expecting to see God inseparable from things (*alter*). To do this it does not have recourse to contemplation of the *great beyond*, but to rigorous observation of the *great right here*.

It should be made clear that theophysics, as understood here, is not compatible with a an exclusively transcendent and absolutely monotheist *theos*. The Trinity should reclaim its rightful place. God is essentially relationship, and in this relationship there is Man and also the Cosmos.[45]

There is a need to return to a tripartite anthropology that considers Man to be formed of body, soul, and spirit. As a body we are living matter, as a soul we are consciousness, as spirit we are divine. Man is material, conscious, and divine in his very nature, where nature is not just *physis*.

A linguistic observation is pertinent here. Language, above all alphabetical language, is individuating. If we say water, we do not say air; if we say Man, we do not say God; if we talk of Justice, we do not talk of Love. Yet there is not, nor can there be, water without air, Man without God, Love without Justice—and vice versa. Concepts individuate, while symbols connect—they are always meta-physical. However, when capturing polarity or being conscious of harmony (or disharmony), scientific knowledge proves to be of no use. The latter only sees compatibility or incompatibility—it is only as men and women, as people, that scientists are able to perceive harmony. Older Chinese and Japanese thought went in this direction: a haiku says what it does *not* say. The Sybil suggests, the parable is not univocal. . . . But, on the other hand, we cannot make a blend of everything and we should distinguish, although not separate. To think is to do more than calculate or achieve clear and distinct ideas. Thus, if we say Man, we are not saying either God or Matter, but rather this *microcosmos* and *microtheos* that do not exist either without Matter or God. In a word, Man and God are simple abstractions.

2. Tempiternal Temporality
Because of its particularity of wishing to offer us a nondivided (*advaita*) vision of reality without separating it from its fundament, theophysics positively values linear time but is not imprisoned by it—imprisoned in two directions: vertical (tempiternal) and also horizontal (temporal). The cross is a symbol of this because it cannot have one arm without the other. No being is complete until he or she is a pilgrim, no structure is finished (and thus no affirmation is definitive) until it has used up its *ontic* itinerary, at least in a non-Buddhist conception of reality (Buddhism would express this using different terminology). On the other hand,

---

[44] See Panikkar (2004).
[45] See Panikkar (1994b).

theophysics will be wary of transcending time by dispensing with it and directly assuming an a-temporal vision of things, as if the temporality of things were a mere accident. The theophysical vision is not a-temporal, much less eternal; it is tempiternal. It does not "see" things *sub specie aeternitatis*, it sees them temporally, but from a tempiternal perspective: *sub specie tempernitatis*. That is, it provides us with a vision of a being or process that transcends their temporal venture in their immanence, offering us the constitutive opening of a being that insofar as it *is*, presents a temporality that is still developing. Hence the humility and the provisionality characteristic of theophysics. Seeking to reveal things to the maximum, since it sees them as being divine, it feels obliged to say the minimum, given that this divine adventure *ad extra* is still developing in time and space. Theophysics does not deny the possibility of stepping outside of time, but it recognizes that in this case it will not be physical, and so cannot be theophysical.

Theophysics needs a new language, but has none other than that formed by the old words. The Being that is God is rather (or *also*?) Non-Being since the category (of being) is not to be applied to the godhead. Yet we have no alternative (Non-Being implies Being). In the same way, reality seen from the standpoint of theophysics is transcendent in its immanence and immanent in its transcendence. It is like the real shadow of Being—to continue using the same language. Certain Indian philosophers speak of the World (and of Matter) as the Body of God, while stating that God in no wise *is* body, but *has* a body. Theophysics recognizes the distinction between the Divine (*Theos*) and the Material (*Physis*) but does not separate them—just as it does not separate time from eternity (eternity does not come after time).

Theophysics offers, therefore, something more than a univocal vision of reality. Paradoxically, the most-used metaphor for knowing, especially in the West, is vision, sight. However, human sight always sees an ensemble, a combination of things at the same time—a polarity, and never (or almost never) a single object. When theophysics focuses on time, for instance, it captures above all the temporal aspect, and thus eschatological nature, of concrete things. The eschatological vision here represents an end of time that, like the mathematical limit of a converging series, continues to belong to that same series and has not yet overcome the barrier of time and space. But on the other hand, it captures the three times together in the single real present. The past is a memory and the future a projection. The new Heaven and the new Earth of the book of Revelation, and re-absorption in Brahman as in certain *Upanisads*, to give just a couple of examples, take on primordial importance for theophysics.

This line of thinking is not just an awkward appendage to theophysics, unlike the state of affairs in classical theology, and even more so in physico-mathematical science. Eschatology is precisely the vision of the finality and end of matter, and also of the body and other physical entities. The theophysical standpoint keeps us constantly open and prepared for any eventuality while things are (in being) and time continues on its way. To what extent we can permit themselves extrapolations and be able to say something about that which now "is," based on what "will be," is actually the delicate and important task of theophysics. To put it another way, what we call space, time, matter, light, and other physical *phenomena* have a theophysical dimension that completes the quantitative one and that is not merely aesthetic. For too long, holistic knowledge has been separated from purely physical and material science.

Death and resurrection, for instance, are two categories fundamental to this theophysical concept of the universe. While a being, a process, or any kind of factor or datum has not "died," it has not completed its time or its mission. Nothing valid could be affirmed if the dimension of the resurrection were not directly connected with death. The law of the transformation of energy is not linear temporality, and in general the principles of thermodynamics, and the law of karma, to give two examples, gain considerable light from this perspective. Theophysics is to be found always *in fieri*, in becoming.

To sum up: the time of theophysics is not linear time, which starts at the beginning and goes on to the end; its category is not so much speed or distance (which latter is always between two bodies) so much as density, so to speak: time more or less laden with intensity—as in any case common sense would tell us. An hour of anguish or sleep or joy or pain will not all have the same sixty minutes. Real time is not homogeneous. We can refer to a time as more or less full, but not a time that is longer or shorter. The phrase in the Gospels about the fullness of time (*plêroma tôn kairôn*) takes on a completely new sense here, which theophysics should clarify.

Let us take the adjective "eschatological" in the most literal sense: at the end of *logos*, at the far limit of *logos*, there where the spirit could be located. Theophysics seeks to present us with physical reality without separating the latter from the totality of the real: not separating physics from its constitutive connection with the divine mystery (which is not something foreign to matter) it finds the eschatological dimension, situated at the very limit of logic. This is not, therefore, a defining concept, but rather the limit of a concept, of which however we are conscious. This experience of time is profoundly different from the great *mythos* of the West, above the monotheist West, not to mention the great dogma of history as the place where both the human and cosmic events of life take place. I am not saying that the *mythos* of history is false, but that history is the *mythos* that offers us the horizon from which emerges what we apprehend as reality—which brings us to another characteristic.

Theophysics presents, lastly, a vision of the material world that is authentically theological, in the sense we discussed earlier—that is to say, it is a vision of God that reveals itself to be immanent in the universe, not just in the universe as a whole, but in the concrete yet mysterious detail that physics reveals and theophysics reworks and takes to a deeper level. There is an a-dual, *advaita* relationship between physics and theophysics. This is not, then, a resorting to pantheism, but a freeing oneself of one's fears. Things are not God, but without God they simply *are not*. God is not a part of things, above all because God does not have parts. The Creator (should we want to use such language) does not withdraw after the act of creation. Creation and conservation are the same act. Creation is a continuous act—or to put it in a more traditional fashion, an eternal act, or a tempiternal act, as I should prefer to call it. As we have already noted, theophysics does not simply give us a new vision of physics, but a new vision of God.

Theophysics, however, is above all physics, a physics that has not however been segregated from reality by means of abstractions that end up becoming rigid and mere conceptual structures (generally mathematical ones). Matter is not an accident of the real; theophysics is an essential part of theology—if we wish to continue using this term. Where there is no physics, there can be no theophysics; but the concept of physics here is considered in all senses of the word, not excluding the most up-to-date phenomenological and mathematical ones. A certain brand of cosmology, in its classical form, maintained that Aristotelian physics allowed contact with reality and thus offered a platform to hark back to ultimate reality. But modern science, thanks to the very fact of renouncing affirmations concerning the true nature of things, has thought to enjoy total independence from theology, claiming not to make metaphysical statements. This was the historical misunderstanding between Roberto Bellarmine and Galileo Galilei. In a classical context of confrontation, the latter had his reasons, but seen from a wider point of view it was insufficient. One cannot "alienate" a science from the domain of the being of things (and thus from that of Being) just because it does not

refer to the nature of reality. Unquestionably, such a science will not offer a base to be able
to work back causally to substance-God, but this does not mean that there is not a link with
the divinity, one that is even greater than that of epistemological causality. What interests
us here is simply to underline the way in which the scientific-mathematical vision of reality
reveals an aspect of this reality, and of ultimate reality, which is certainly not transcendent,
but is immanent; a link with that reality that so many traditions know as God.

The theological dimension of theophysics becomes clearer when we consider that
it represents a way of approaching physical reality with all the means available to us for
achieving knowledge of such reality, without ruling out faith. Here, too, when we talk of
faith we do not see it divorced from other forms of knowledge. Indeed, faith always bears on
intellectual knowledge, and frequently does so on rationality. There is no sense, for example,
in postulating that animals have faith. The vision of faith neither excludes nor sweeps aside
scientific considerations—furthermore, in our case it needs them and presupposes them.
Second, when we speak of faith we do not mean a sort of simple acceptance of the "articles
of faith" or "revealed fact," as intellectually elaborated propositions to be manipulated and
recombined with "scientific truths," to harmonize them and conjugate them, preparing the
ground for subsequent interesting deductions. Above all, true theology is not a mere science
of conclusions drawn from the so-called revealed facts. For a fact to be revealed it should be
recognized as such, and accordingly the conclusions will be those drawn from facts recognized by faith as facts of faith—which is a vicious circle. When we say that theophysics, apart
from being physics, is true theology we mean that it represents a positive and vital symbiosis
between an *intellectus quaerens fidem,* and a *fides quaerens intellectum* (between an intellect
in search of faith, and a faith in search of intelligibility), which as an opening and a path
renders us sufficiently sensitive to be able to discover the real and recondite dimension of
things. This is a far cry from the intention of getting faith to concord with reason, or theology
with science. Theophysics has a different task, a task that stems from within faith and sees
the material world in a light that does not exclude reason, but completes and enriches it.

We are not talking here about unquestioning faith. We have labeled this aspect of theophysics "contemplative" in the original sense of the word, which does not mean no interest in
the material world, but seeing the world as a temple, a symbol of the human-divine dwelling
as something holy—the "sacred secularity."

To be able now to show the fecundity of theophysics we need to look at some examples
and illustrate how a theophysical vision of the world sheds new light on both physics and
theology.

On physics, on the one hand, because it restores to it that dignity of science over the
real, that is to say theological, where the *theos* is not a purely transcendental being estranged
from material reality. Theophysics is not mere abstract (or metaphysical) cerebration, a
discipline that confines its activity and its interests to simple processes, formulae, and
patterns able to generate the satisfaction of reason or power over men and nature. The
dignity of physics is much more than all that, and theophysics makes it conscious of this
fact. What we are saying here obviously does not detract from the extraordinary value
of mental abstraction—although we have to remember that Pythagorean numbers were
something more than algorithms in the modern sense. In any case, theophysics redirects
physics to the very heart of reality. There physics too deciphers the revelation of God
immanent in material reality, to use traditional language.

On theology, on the other hand, it sheds new light above all because it reconciles it with
the scientific world, which had practically separated itself from theology. At the same time

this contact vivifies it and enriches it. Fundamentally, however, it does so because it revalues the material world and gives a "theophysical" value to the corporeal and thus to sensitivity—the world of the senses. From the Christian standpoint it takes seriously the centrality of the incarnation and in general the dignity of material reality, overcoming and healing the cultural schizophrenia of our times without incurring traditional monism. The theological dimension of material creation can only come from the contribution of theophysics. Let us look at an example.

3. Simultaneity

Among the many *aporias* that contemporary physics is heir to, both in post-Newtonian physics and post-Cartesian philosophy, with repercussions upon even Planck and Einstein, there is the problem of the so-called synchronicity or apparent a-causality of many subatomic phenomena.[46] The instances of synchronicity were first observed in psychology and studied principally by Carl Jung, but today analogous phenomena are observed in contemporary physics. The best-known paradoxes are the wave/particle behavior of elementary particles and Neil Bohr's theory of complementarity: the relevant instances are too numerous not to require a revision of the very foundations of physics.[47] How, for example, can two events at the subatomic level be simultaneous without there being mutual information (Bell's theorem, etc.)? It is here that the contribution of theophysics becomes indispensable, because the physics, after introducing the human factor (the observer who modifies the observed), has left out an essential variable: the *theos* understood not as a separate entity, but seen to be related to the phenomenon itself (*ontonomy*).

The hypotheses put forward range from simple physics to metaphysics, but there has not yet been the daring to take the final step, thanks to a noncritical and unsatisfactory conception of the divinity. Hence the importance of the cosmotheandric viewpoint, which does not split up reality into watertight compartments, without (to reiterate) erring into monism.

We can assemble some of these theories, without going into them in their complex detail. In this field, physics, anthropology, and theology converge. Our lesson here has purely heuristic value.

Resuming, and simplifying, we could divide into three groups the hypotheses that have emerged to deal with the new information.

In Bohr's *complementarity*, waves and particles are considered complementary hypotheses—although the complementarity supposes a common background that remains inexplicable—otherwise neither of the two hypotheses could completely explain the phenomenon. For Bohr it was simpler because he recognized that the observer modified the observed, and thus it is the experiment that introduces complementarity.

All particles have their momentum (mass times velocity) and their position (within the whole), but we cannot measure one without modifying the other. This has led to use of the term "instrumentalism," according to which all our elucubrations on physical reality depend on the instruments of observation. No one these days disputes this fact. The problem inheres, however, in the question of the degree of dependence between the observed and

---

[46] The great names of Heisenberg, Bohr, Schrödinger, Dirac, Bell, Pauli, Prigogine, Bohm . . . , to stay within physics, and without leaving out Jung, who can serve as an example. See for physics the extensive bibliography in Panikkar (1961), Cantore (1977), and Barbour (1990). And in relation to Jung, Mansfield (1999).

[47] See Mansfield (1999) for the many examples it contains and its connection (which few books on science have) with Jung's work.

the observer. Observation unquestionably modifies the phenomenon being observed, but it is not clear whether this is the only cause of the new behavior of the particle, since the new behavior is unpredictable.

Complementarity is, in any case, the first wound in dialectical thought based on the principle of noncontradiction. The phenomena appear to be contradictory because they are seen from a different perspective, but the fact remains that the two hypotheses (wave and particle) offer a satisfactory explanation for the complete phenomenon. It is not so much a question here of complementarity as the possibility of a double explanation. This in fact brings us to the second hypothesis.

The paradox is due, then, to *limitations in our knowledge* of the laws of nature, as Planck, Einstein, and more recently David Bohm have maintained. Bohm hypothesized the existence of hidden variables, which led him to formulate the notion of an *implicate order*, which becomes explicit only with our observations. What seems to us a-causal is due to our ignorance of the more hidden laws of nature. To summarize: a certain *critical realism* causes us to note that our knowledge of the world is only partial and that, therefore, we cannot draw apodictic conclusions. This too can hardly be denied.

The *idealist hypotheses* seem to be the most plausible in that to deny them one needs to use the same ideas—with the danger of creating a vicious circle. We are prisoners of our ideas, or rather our (ideal) world is the prison from which we cannot escape. The *noumenon* is unknowable or nonexistent. This hypothesis comes in an enormous variety of forms. There is no doubt that our mind participates in and influences, but it cannot be proved that physical reality, knowledge of which assuredly depends on our ideas of it, is a purely ideal entity without its own consistency. That an ontonomically independent reality exists is plausible enough. If the opposite were true, the behavior of particles would be theoretically determined, and there are strong suspicions that this is not so.

We could cite the great names of idealist philosophy, from Berkeley and Kant down to the recent mentalist hypotheses of Victor Mansfield—who simply affirms that all objects of experience are a factor of our mind—although it cannot be shown (without creating a vicious circle) that they are *only* that. Parmenides's dogma shows up yet again.

These three hypotheses do not in any sense claim to be exhaustive, but they give us an idea of the issues. Theophysics does not give us one single, univocal answer. In terms of the different problems, it accepts most of the hypotheses and situates them against a more harmonious background without unifying the different solutions, but also without letting them disperse in the dualism of mathematical laws on one hand and the patterns described by physics on the other—and, more importantly, without the (schizophrenic) divorce between the sciences of matter and those of the psyche, with God poised like a separate entity. The dualisms can be overcome without descending into monism. This is the wisdom of the *advaita* (a-duality) as we have repeatedly maintained.

The connection that exists between man (the observer) and the world (the observed) is at this stage indisputable. Cartesian dualism can no longer be sustained. Body and soul are not two independent entities. Mind and matter are not separable, although different. The relationship between the cosmos and the divine continues to be problematic, and the study of this is the specific task of theophysics. We have already said that God is relationship (in a very real sense) with man—the radical trinity—but we have left in the penumbra the relationship between God and the cosmos. It is true that some theologians speak of the continuing creation, and of the immanence of God, but fear of descending into pantheism lingers in many minds in that the rigid monotheism of a supreme being in substance and transcendence still has not been overcome. If God is absolute, such a Being cannot have more than a *relatio rationis* with the world (an unreal, purely mental relationship) as certain Scholastics maintained—against the Christian dogma of the Incarnation. The alternative is neither atheism nor polytheism, it is the trinitarian vision, as I have sought to explain elsewhere.[48] The task before theophysics is not to argue about God, but to reflect upon the world in the light of the divine mystery, which in any case implies a certain conception of divinity. The so-called natural laws, for instance, are not considered to be immutable fact, but simply empirical ones, as could be said also of human reason. We cannot therefore talk of universal constants in a universe we know only incompletely without making unwarranted extrapolations, and recognizing that we make our reason the universal judge of reality. This does not mean that, accepting the immutability of the created (and thus also of "reason" in its relationship with reality) we cannot postulate firm principles—*rebus sic stantibus*, the Latins used to say. But perhaps neither God nor the World (nor Man) are static entities.

Many of the *aporias* we have cited in this overview do not seem to be insuperable, because they have to be in a broader (or deeper) context. We can take as an example the subatomic phenomenon of simultaneity.

We would prefer to speak of simultaneity rather than synchronicity, which is the term used both in psychology and in science. The *chronos* of the word seems to once again suggest linear time, which is the origin of many difficulties. Simultaneity, on the other hand, refers to both time and space.[49] *Simultas* in fact means to be together, although the word also has temporal connotations. We have lost the sense of the *contiguity* of reality and we continually interpret it in a dualistic manner. Things touch. Contiguity does not just mean proximity, but also that the beings touch (from the Indo-European root *tag-, tango*, I touch, from which are derived *tangent* and *contingent*). Bodies touch, are contiguous, simultaneous. Reality is a whole, integral (*integer*): all its constituents touch. In this touching there are not two bodies, but neither is there just one: the touching is the tangent (at one point) of the contingency; it is simultaneous, but awareness of it is not necessarily simultaneous. Once again, the *advaita*.

This touching has been expressed in different contexts in many cultural traditions that speak of the world as the body of God, and this includes the Christian tradition, which speaks of the Mystic Body of Christ.[50]

The body is a theophysical symbol and not just a material one: furthermore, matter is a simple mental abstraction. And in any case reality is neither one nor multiple. Neither numbers nor quantities are adequate metaphors for reality, which is prior and cannot be reduced to numbers and quantities alone. "Everything is connected with everything else." This is an intercultural and all but universal intuition (*pratīyasamutpāda, quodlibet in quodlibet*, etc.) There is a relationship of inter-in-dependence in all reality. All beings have their degree of freedom, which confers dignity on them and which deserves our respect. We have called this intrinsic relationship *ontonomy*.

---

[48] See Panikkar (1998).

[49] The Indo-European root of the word simultaneity, from *simul*, is *sem* (in Sanskrit *samah* and in English, *same*). The Greek word *hama*, too, refers to contiguity both in space and time.

[50] I am advised at times not to use terms like Mystic Body, Body of God, or Divine Force, because such expressions have been abused and so they may disorientate or irritate lay mentalities and scientific minds, just as in the past one was advised not to use expressions which, while not formally heretical, were *piarum auribus offensivae* (offensive to pious ears). However, it is important to explain the meaning of the words we use.

"Le prévisible n'est pas libre," said Simone Weil. The world of physico-mathematics is not free, although to us it may not seem predetermined. Neither the World, nor Man, nor God are slaves of Parmenides's dogma, which gives no room for freedom and makes reality the slave of logic. Life is constant novelty, creation is continuing, the law of inertia is valid for reason and for physics, but reality has no need to submit to the laws of ontology. We only need to look at the cultures that are not monotheistic to realize that "Divine Right" is a "blasphemy," as is the image of a legislator God who has to submit to His own laws—although free to indulge in whims (miracles) with the pretext that they are His laws (forgive the caricature). Recall what we said in the first part: modern science is a monocultural construct—brilliant but not universal, as we shall see below. Contemporary physics is currently moving toward a theophysical vision of reality. The body is not just an inert mass, nor is matter independent of the soul and the spirit. Its relationship is *ontonomic*, that is, nondual. The chasm of dualism is being gradually overcome. God and the World are not two separate entities, although they are different, as logic attests.

This is not a question of turning back the clock—to continue to use a metaphor from linear time. Modern physics should make another leap forward. We repeat that theophysics constitutes a new vision both of matter and of God, and also of Man.

The correlations of the cosmotheandric view are true correlations, that is, they are two-directional. The hierarchy of reality is a constitutive correlation, then—not from higher to lower, but in the true sense of the word, thus they are of a "sacred order." So, just as "A is twice B," so "B is half of A," in theophysics it is said that if God is God of the World, the World is the World of God (in a hierarchic relationship).

To maintain the unity of physical laws and adapt them to the harmony and the beauty of reality, medieval cosmology had adopted the Aristotelian idea of potentiality, which afterward was surreptitiously taken up by modern physics speaking of *potential energy*, a pure construct of the mind intended to safeguard the rationality of physics. This allows precognition of "the law of conservation of energy," as a postulate of the mind afterward transferred to physics. We can find a parallel with this intrusion of the mind into the field of physics with the introduction, at one time, of ether (*aether*) as a pure physical relation to explain rationally the propagation of electromagnetic waves—a theory that was afterward abandoned as superfluous and replaced with that of the general theory of relativity. The *actio in distans* was and indeed still is a problem that physics alone cannot resolve. I suspect that the "fifth element" was actually introduced by Empedocles to maintain the theophysical unity of the universe. Ether allowed one to believe in the contiguity of things, that is to say, in the unity and harmony of the universe.

The potentiality of nondeterministic contemporary physics presents a modality that is essentially different from that of classical physics, which continues with the deterministic template of Laplace and the individualistic interpretation of reality. However, the behavior of potential energy in classical physics is not known, cannot be determined; we cannot know what it will be; it presents radical indetermination. The behavior of the particles is not determined a priori—and the law of probability does not apply.

The laws of probability do not necessarily recognize the degrees of liberty of matter. They still accept the universality of the efficient cause; our interference modifies the behavior of what is observed, and we do not know the trajectory of the particle (in the example that is already a classic)—a trajectory, which, however, is theoretically already fixed. The classic probabilities accept causality. Contemporary physics accepts correlations. These are not causal, they are correlative—although to varying degrees. God and the World for instance are in a correlation, a hierarchic correlation and not an egalitarian one. We can think of a God without a world, although in fact there is no God without a World; we cannot think however of a World without an ultimate referent (God)—which in an extreme case would be the World itself.

Theophysics is not in a position to resolve all the problems of quantum physics that we have referred to, but with it many of them cease to be. A modern postulate continues to be the necessity of information that can be transmitted at a (maximum?) speed of light based on the relative position of the transmitter. The senses, as the first key to knowledge, can help us to accept and understand that simultaneity is possible because it needs no transmitter (intermediary). The palpable touch of one body with another needs no transmission; it is immediate, and accordingly its effect is similarly immediate—although my awareness of the touch needs a nervous system able to transmit the information to the brain so that I become aware of it. This connection of everything with everything is explained in terms of the universe as one single body, a mystical, spiritual, subtle body, and so on. But here the term "body" does not just mean inert matter. The root *krp* (from which *corpus* is derived) means "form," "beauty." Beauty is an attribute of reality, of reality as yet undivided, that is to say, *cosmotheandric*. There is no body without God, but also there is no God without body (not in the abstract, but in fact). The body of God is not separated from him (although different) and can only be so in the abstract mind.

The simultaneity of contemporary physics is then plausible and not irrational. We have constructed our world according to the parameters of classical science, and the latter are showing themselves to be incompatible with the phenomena of simultaneity. The problem would not occur if, having used the three eyes of knowledge, we had arrived at another vision of the World. There is no vicious circle here, instead it is a vital circle, which, as I have explained elsewhere, has its origins in human contingency—and, thus, also in our thoughts, but not necessarily in reality. *Anagkê stênai* (we need to stop somewhere), the Greeks used to say.

Many *aporias* of (essentially contingent) human thought would be cleared up if we abstained from projecting our thoughts on reality. Zeno of Elea's paradox in the fifth century BCE is due to this extrapolation of thought outside its field (although Zeno merely intended to criticize the Pythagoreans). For swift-footed Achilles to catch up with the slow tortoise, he had to run half the distance, then the other half, and so on, ad infinitum. Zeno's argument was that when Achilles reached the spot where the tortoise had been it would have already advanced a little, and this would be repeated again, and again. Thus Achilles could never succeed in catching up with the tortoise, because he had to pass through an infinite number of intermediate stages. Not for nothing, some have considered Zeno to be Parmenides's disciple. The space, a product of thought (infinitely divisible), is not a real space, but modern science has not yet completely outgrown Parmenides.

We have spoken of the narrow gate of knowledge, and not of three gates that open onto three worlds: the divine, the human, and the material. This thought lies at the basis of Jung's thinking too, when he speaks of *Unus Mundus*. But not even through the door of knowledge can we enter into contact fully with all reality. We are contingent, we touch reality at one certain point, which however allows those who have their three eyes wide open to "see" reality.

That does not mean that reality does not have three dimensions that we need to distinguish but not separate. The door of knowledge is open, though narrow, but that is only the door. We shall need to cross the threshold and walk out into open country. The human being is *homo viator*, a pilgrim in a virgin land.

The Origin of the Cosmos

In cosmotheandric intuition, the problem of the cosmos's temporal origin is not presented as a dualism between an eternal God and a temporal world, because the basis of reality is the trinitarian *perichôrêsis* and not a substance. Accordingly, we are not to be speculating here over a God creator and putting upon Him the enigmas of the human mind, but rather developing a distinctive vision that, without eliminating the mystery of reality, does not just project it exclusively upon a transcendent Supreme Being. In the cosmotheandric vision, or that of the *radical trinity*, God, World, and Man *are not* one without the other, and asking which came first is like a childish game to find out who is the winner in this temporal race. The word "origin" could mean hierarchy—that is, "sacred order" (*holoarchy*, says Ken Wilber) as for instance in the case of Father regarding Son, yet without the Son there can be no Father (and vice versa); or it could mean temporal order. Theophysics is aware of the fact that talking about the world's temporal origin, that is, of its *beginning*, is equivalent to inquiring into the source of God—forgetting that God *is* the Beginning. In other words, the issue of the Beginning is a pseudo-issue—also philosophically so, because "before" time is already a temporal notion, inasmuch as it is the same as asking oneself what time is there (was there) before time.

This problem, however, has a long history owing to the fact that the abstract concept has become independent from concrete thought.

So as to not complicate things and stray from our topic, I shall refrain from enlarging upon another (similarly theological and Christian) hypothesis, which from a cosmotheandric point of view has no need of the physical dogma of creation. In brief, the first phrase in Genesis ("God created Heaven and Earth") should be surpassed or overridden by John 1:3 ("All things came into being [*egeneto*] through Him"—the *Logos*).

When we get to the crux of the matter, theophysics is not only the hidden driving force behind scientific research, it has also been the conscious aspiration for most of the founders of modern science. Newton said that his theological works were just as important as his scientific contribution. The works of a Kepler or a Copernicus run along the same lines as the effusions of an Augustine or an Anselm. The theological conflicts with Galileo, and with nearly all other scientists, arose precisely because the separation of dominions seemed a far more serious blasphemy than the other conflicts that inevitably arose at that time.

Nor are more modern investigators excluded from the yearning for a global not to say mystical conception of the universe. Planck, along with Einstein and Heisenberg, to name just a few, all exhibit this yearning.

"O qui lumine Naturae, desiderium in nobis promoves luminis Gratiae, ut per id transferas nos in lumen Gloriae; gratia ago Tibi Creator, Domine, quia delectasti me in factura Tua, et in operibus manuum tuarum exultavi," wrote Kepler in his book on science. (Oh, thou through the splendor of Nature, which stirs up within us the desire of the light of Glory, as to transport us to the light of Glory, I give thee thanks, Creator and Lord, because you have made me revel in what you have done and hence I have exulted in the work of your hands.)

Let us take a look at some of the details of this question.

1. The Question of the "Beginning of the Cosmos"

One of the common concepts of the theology of creation influenced (albeit indirectly, but much more than we commonly suppose) that concept of science that places the "creative act of God" at the beginning of time (Descartes's *chiquenaude*). As such, once God had created the world, He, as Creator, could rest on the seventh day and limit himself to maintaining the universe and exercising a kind of supervision as chief engineer. Plainly, science cannot show excessive estimation for a God whose task has consisted in starting up the universe and is now limited to "patching up the holes" for which science is yet to find an explanation, and to beating a strategic retreat once the scientific explanation appears. This is obviously a caricature, but physics too, on its own, cannot say much on the subject of creation. Scientists who are also believers find themselves, much to their concern, caught within a dichotomy that favors neither their faith nor their reasoning. They then stumble into the doctrinal dualism and personal schizophrenia we have already mentioned, which makes nonbelievers laugh. As St. Thomas Aquinas says, that "mundum non semper fuisse" (the world has not always existed) cannot be demonstrated, and "sole fide tenetur," that is, only through faith do we know that the world had a beginning.[51] Theophysics would have us see, among other things, that the issue of the beginning of the cosmos is not a problem about which physics can say very much—and neither can the Bible, since what Aquinas calls by this name is no more than the literal, and hence rational, interpretation of the first words of Genesis: "In the beginning God created heaven and earth."

The word "beginning" is generally attributed a strictly temporal meaning, although it is often used in translations of words from other languages where it has nothing to do with the modern concept of temporality. When the hymn *Hiranyagarbha* from the *Ṛg-Veda*, the Prologue of the Gospel according to John, and other cosmogonies say *agre, en archê*, or similar expressions, they do not fundamentally indicate a temporal beginning and even less one in linear time. Within this context, the *beginning of the Cosmos* is, strictly speaking, a metacosmic notion and has nothing to do with a zero time.

This would be a clear example of the danger of a complete *algorithmization* of physical reality, believing that the mathematical world of physics is a truthful mirror of physical reality. Zero time allows for—1 (minus one) time, as if time were represented by a mathematical series.[52] As we have already mentioned, real time is immeasurable.

Already in their time, the Christian Scholastics debated whether the cosmos could exist *ab aeterno*, and many of them did not find this to be contradictory. The philosophical idea of creation could perfectly be seen as a *creatio ab aeterno*, given that there is not a time when God is not Creator—even though the expression is disorientating, because eternity does not allow for an *ab*. The very expression *ab aeterno* is contradictory.

Another idea common to the Scholastics was that God constantly creates the world because in God there is no time: and hence, *creatio* (creation) is continuous. The image of an architect and, even worse, one of the engineers who works for a given time and then is conceded a long *sabbath*, an indefinite vacation, was considered a purely childish and unconvincing interpretation of the Bible. That which gives life, the Father of many traditions, is not a divine watchmaker, the author of a mechanical world. More than one human tradition, as we have said, affirms that the world is the Body of God—and thus concomitant with Him and not necessarily identical to Him. All the perplexities of theodicy that arose to justify the Lisbon earthquake centuries ago or the more recent tsunami in Southeast Asia are not problems for theophysics, as that *theos* does not exist.

The *beginning* of the Cosmos refers to the Foundation, the ultimate Matter, the Sustenance (*skambha*), the Self of the universe as the *Atharva-veda* sings. According to a predominant intuition, this universe needs a Foundation (*Grund*)—even though it has at times been defined as *Ungrund* (foundationless). This is the idea of the contingency that thinks of the cosmos as tangential to this Base (*Grund*). This then at a certain point *touches* (*cum-tangere*) something

[51] *Sum. Theol.* I, q.46, a.2.
[52] See Balmés's two volumes (2003–2004).

that is "more": more stable, more real ... than the actual cosmos. These are complex issues, and after all, our ancestors were not so stupid.

We should add that, as victims of monoculturalism, we tend to evaluate older cosmologies using the parameters of our modern scientific cosmology. From the moment that we have no other but our own, we forget that our own parameters are just as relative as the cosmologies of former days. We tend to forget (to give an example closer to us than the more ancient cosmology of Jainism) that the categories of the Ptolemaic universe were not those of Copernicus and, as such, cannot be compared without further ado. The Gods, spirits, a material heaven, a qualitative space, a human nature linked to the living earth, these were the essential ingredients of the Ptolemaic universe, which practically vanished from the Copernican system. We tend to read these systems as if they were two different texts, forgetting that the comparison of contexts requires an interpretation different from that of texts.

To summarize, the relativization of the whole ancient vision of the world, which is easy for us to recognize, should also go in tandem with the relativization of our own vision of the world—a much more difficult thing to do, as it constitutes our *mythos*, something that can only be discerned from an intercultural perspective.

To put it another way, creation is not a thing of the past, but rather of the present; the creating "*fiat*" is not an act at the world's (temporal) beginning, but rather, it is the tempiternal act of God with which He creates all things throughout time, which is an act in the present. Any contemplative seer "sees" that "God" gives life *today* and *now* to the world. God is not alone at the beginning and at the end of the world, but rather is creating the universe while it is, subsists, and develops. All theories of evolution are no more than a reaction against a static concept of the universe, which a post-Cartesian conception of reality had instilled in us. In these issues theology is not an added supplement to physics, but rather its most profound dimension, its invisible soul, which saves us from concern about the past and obsession with the future. All the works these days on the expansion of the universe, on the origin of life, on evolution, on the essence of cybernetics, or on automation are ultimately theological issues that neither physics-mathematics alone, nor theology *ad usum* can resolve in an adequate manner. The real problems of the world also implicate man and that other aspect of reality that is divine mystery. God is not foreign to the world.

The question of the "beginning" of this world is posed at bottom because it puts *what* this world is and "*how* in fact *this* world started" on the same plane. The *this* is substituted by the "*how* of its development." The *this* remains as mysterious today as it was millennia ago, although shifting our gaze to the *how* seems to me to stray from our metaphysical concerns. Contemporaries of the "New World Order" console themselves with the conviction that metaphysical and cosmological issues cannot be resolved and as such concentrate on scientific issues. Some of them, however, seem to have the intuition that there is something else. We have reached the core of the problem.

2. *The Philosophical Problem*

The *beginning* is plainly a temporal concept. It refers to time. So then, time is related to change. We could refer to Newton's first law (without asking ourselves if it had not already been formulated by Galileo, or at least applied from the moment that its roots were discovered originally in Greece) and state that if there were no change whatsoever, time would completely lack any meaning.

We could say that time is the "measurement of change," employing the word measurement (*metron*) with a different meaning from the original, attributed to the first of the Seven Sages of Greece, Kleoboulos of Lindus, when he said *metro ariston*, that is, measurement, moderation, caution, the sense of limits, weighing up . . . is the best thing. Nevertheless, with the discovery of machines to calculate change, the internal *metron* of all things, time has become an external measurement of this movement. The original vision was different. All things happen "in" time, because time is that quality of "things" that "allows" them to happen. The universe has always been thought of as being alive, and time is its breathing (*prāṇa, brahman, Atem*). We have already cited the ancient Greeks, who described life, *zôê*, as "the time of being," *chronos tou einai* (Hesychius), while the *Atharva-veda* speaks of time as the supreme deity upon which the whole world rests. Time, like space, is intrinsic to beings; things *are* time and do not just transit through it.

The investigating spirit of man wishes to travel in "time" and wants to know the beginning of the cosmos, "the origins of the universe." We see things and events that happen again and again. We desire to return, ascend, or descend to the origins of each and every thing. It is easier to search for origins along a temporal path than to dive deep into the abyss of the Self. Moreover, the human mind seems to ask itself whether the origins are at the beginning or at the end, if things are pushed from the source or pulled toward the end. Some cultures are predominantly *archaeological*—they look toward the past. Other cultures, not excluding those in phase with Aristotle, are more *eschatological*—that is, they look toward the end and think that the generating energy is at the end and not at the beginning. It was said that God acted as the final cause, or, according to Aristotle's beautiful expression, *ôs erômenon*, as the beloved, the desired, as an erotic magnetic force. And it is true that sometimes we know some things better by knowing what they are going to be than ascertaining what they have been.

We are, then, making a distinction between "origin" and "beginning." Perhaps to be able to know the origin, that is, the source that has been the generator of an event, we should wait a little, learn to be patient, and direct our attention toward the *telos*, toward the eschatology. In contrast, modern culture believes it can know the present better by knowing the past—hence the importance given to history derives. There is also much interest in the future, but from a linear and historic perspective. It is known that many human civilizations do not have a linear idea of the temporal process and even less one that runs straight. We have absolutely no proof that time runs in a straight line, a curve, a sinusoid, a spiral, a discontinuous surface, or anything else for that matter. It is difficult to overcome the spatial image of temporality.

To speak of the beginning of the cosmos in this sense is equivalent to asking oneself where this present world came from, where the dynamism that governs changes we see in our cosmos came from, while the very question about what this cosmos is remains open. The traditional cosmos was centered on the solar system surrounded by incredible lights (stars) that indicated, without a doubt, that we are not alone in the universe. Medieval Europeans made a strict difference between events in the normal *sublunar* world (below the moon, or rather, on the earth), *sub sole* events (events under the sun, that is, in the cosmos), and the meaning of all these *sub specie aeternitatis* (from the aspect of eternity)—where everything takes on its true value: the famous celestial spheres.

How did this cosmos begin? The issue that underlies the question and that endows it with importance is the following: to what extent does the answer help us understand the present-day cosmos and our presence within it?

At this point we should now return to the topic of the first part of this book: evolutionist thought.

As we have pointed out, Darwin's evolution of the species (and subsequent elaborations) is one thing and social Darwinism is another, and yet another is the theory of evolution as a *forma mentis*, which we have called evolutionist *thought*. All three theories, while interconnected, should be distinguished, although it might be that the last-mentioned gives credibility to the other two. To reiterate what we have just said more succinctly: evolutionist thought springs from the conviction that genesis is equivalent to evolution and understanding the evolution of a process leads to understanding the process itself. In other words, this is the conviction that to discover the *how* of a process (how it is presented, developed, manifested . . .) leads to knowledge of the *what* (what that process is). In brief, becoming is being: the answer to Parmenides is provided by Heraclitus. From this standpoint, the *nature* or *physis* of a phenomenon is inseparably linked to its birth, to its genesis, to its becoming.

The human mind, while recognizing that there is an intrinsic relationship, resists identifying Being with Becoming. We should not remain tied to immutable essences (constitutive elements), yet neither should we drown in the treacherous slough of pure evolution. To know the beginning of a phenomenon is of inestimable value, but this knowledge alone is insufficient. A thing is not known without also knowing its end.

Evolutionist thought leads us to be contented with a simple explanation of *how* something has evolved. We definitely know we are descendants of our parents, and the same goes for other animals. We know how crystals are formed and perhaps we also know how the surface of the earth has developed through the ages. It is this precious knowledge that opens up the possibility for us to foresee some models of behavior and also formulate certain rules: all this gathering of knowledge, however, does not reveal to us our own nature, nor that of an animal, a crystal, or the Earth. If we concentrate exclusively on trying to know how the past has become the present, we can easily let what I have called the *tempiternal present* escape us. In brief, the beginning of the cosmos does not yield the key to understanding the cosmos; the universe's temporal unfolding keeps secret what the universe itself is. Nature has a history and its unveiling shows models, proportions suggestions, and allows us to establish certain laws, yet the formulation of *how* does not substitute *what*. Reality is a constant novelty. To deduce from the present situation in the world how it was millennia ago is not exactly the same as deducing how people, say, in Italy lived in the Middle Ages by observing the contemporary political situation. Nature is less voluble than man, yet to suppose that it is just inert "matter" that obeys deterministic laws is an unfounded hypothesis. Matter also has its level of freedom.

We might not even need to know about the beginning of the cosmos to gain enough knowledge about what that very cosmos is. Perhaps knowledge of a sufficiently long enough segment of its existence will enable us to consciously live within it. The televised image of an unknown landscape will speak to us just to the extent that we are capable of appreciating the landscapes around us. If we do not appreciate a flower, we shall not be able to discover the beauty of a garden. I would go further and question whether traveling along the highway of linear time might be the only or even the best way to embrace the knowledge of the universe.

I can simplify all this with a reference to the origin of *homo sapiens*.

If we wish to know what *homo sapiens* is, first of all we have to try to find one or, rather, various examples. There are many all around us. We shall soon discover things in common as well as individual differences. We then elaborate a complex scientific anthropology. At a given moment, nevertheless, we shall stumble upon the fact that each and every one of us is a special example of *homo sapiens*: ourselves. We research and seek to apply all known anthropology to ourselves. We then become aware of something: all our anthropological knowledge ignores what we really wish to know, the oneness (singularity) of each of us. Hence, we discover that each one of us is unique and, as such, not an object of scientific knowledge or susceptible to classification. Everything can be classified, with the exception of the classifier and the classificatory criteria—which would have the need of other criteria, and on and on ad infinitum. The knowledge of a certain beginning of myself and of others will certainly help me to understand *homo sapiens* better. I know *homo sapiens* has evolved and that thousands of years ago it was in part different and partly the same. The differences will help me to enlarge upon what is more and what is less important (essential) in *homo sapiens*. Nonetheless, this knowledge of *homo sapiens* is not the same as comprehension of myself (or my Self). To be able to understand the mystery of mankind, our suffering, our happiness, our worries, our certainties, our dreams, our desires, our knowledge of ourselves and our *ātman*, our previsions, our myths, our loves and our hates, our oceanic feeling and our freedom, our thought and what that is based upon—in short, to be able to understand the reality that I *am* and my neighbor *is*—we may need many kinds of means, parameters, introspections, and considerations other than those required to reflect on the evolution of *homo sapiens*, on its ancestors or what influence a DNA molecule can have on a protein chain—however interesting the latter may seem to molecular biology.

3. *The Scientific Issue (the "Big Bang")*

The question mark hovering over the *beginning of the cosmos* has a different connotation in "modern science." We have already mentioned that modern science is not here understood as being a modernization of the *scientia, gnôsis, jñāna* of ancient cultures, but rather the scientific paradigm of "new science" up to contemporary scientists, including the recent shift in paradigm.

Let us take the Big Bang theory as a symbol, because the physical-mathematical weakness of this hypothesis is known (that apart from its ontologization of time), yet its fascination is unquestionable as it seems to proportion the missing link sought by modern physical science and the cosmological thirst of mankind (who wish to have a model of the universe).[53]

We could have employed more "scientific" language, which in this case would be more mathematical language, and comment upon Dirac's 1928 equations, the problem of antimatter, the theories of the formation of galaxies, of black holes, of nature's four fundamental forces, of nucleo-synthesis, of cosmic rays, and so on, but theophysics, while still recognizing the value of mathematics, does not lose sight of the whole and hence does not stray from physical reality and man who lives within it.

One certain brand of science extrapolates to conceptual forms and speaks to us of the "expansion of the universe," rather than sticking to describing observations of this evidence which is indirect in that it does not go beyond deductions based on variation of the spectrum of galaxies and extrapolation from observations made of our Milky Way (in spite of Hubble's hypothesis in 1929) that the farther away a galaxy the more "rapidly" the distance between the two parts increases. These variations would therefore imply increasingly less density in the constitutive elements of galaxies. This is interpreted as showing the "age of galaxies," as if we were dealing with the age of a human being or real expansion in space, such as seen in clouds growing in the sky. But when science thinks about the beginning of such expansion, of time related to the starting point, a temporal beginning (as if the theory of relativity applied only to space and not to time), we find ourselves fairly and squarely immersed in a cosmovision.[54]

---

[53] See the beautiful book by Nicolescu (2002), who takes the Big Bang hypothesis very seriously, basing himself on calculations on particle physics. Cf., however, his liberating statement, "L'acte créateur scientifique ne peut pas *être* réduit à la simple *évidence* empirique" [The scientific creative act cannot be reduced to simple empirical evidence], 161.

[54] To obtain a materialistic vision of science, which distances itself from "metaphysical materialism" to defend scientific materialism, see the interesting work by Bellone (1973).

Analogously, a certain brand of Christianity claims that "at the beginning of time" a God creator brought this material world into existence and that He continues to support it, if not exactly like an Atlas God, then in a more metaphysical manner certainly, while still physical. When He is presented as "spirit," "father," "architect, "engineer," or the like, we find ourselves totally in the terrain of cosmovision. We have now left aside the formal theological thought of the mystery of God and we apply it to what is known as the "universe," forgetting that "one must not make an image of God," since "no one has seen God," as Moses and St. John the Evangelist, among others, have said.

Which are then the poles of the discussion? They are simply two conceptions of the world: one that postulates the creation of a real world wrought by the hands of a God (in one specific view of the world) and another in which divine intervention does not appear (excepting perhaps at the beginning of time, so as to be able to find a place still for God).

They are two opposed worldviews, but while the former seems intrinsic to the Christian vision of life, the latter is a compromise. The former is a strictly monotheistic conception of the universe; the latter tends to separate God from the World and leaves a place for a primordial energy or mysterious Force. The more conciliatory among theologians recognize God as having at least one role: of having given a "initial fillip," as Blaise Pascal said about Descartes's metaphysical system, or provided the honorary kickoff that started the game; the more conciliatory scientists, on their side, consider themselves satisfied if they are guaranteed a policy of separated competences: each one in their own terrain. God remains a stranger to the scientific terrain, except for the fact of having started up a "Creation," which follows his rules—*deduced* from the world's behavior.

The most severe scientists would tell us that all this is superfluous and without any scientific meaning whatsoever: that God is not only a superfluous hypothesis, but also a harmful one. The most rigorous theologians, in turn, would add that a *deus ex machina* at the beginning or at the end of this cosmic comedy is a caricature of that which is divine: the beginning of the universe would not be a problem for physics—in any case, it would be for metaphysics.

The problem can then be formulated from a double viewpoint. On one hand, a philosophical one, "*What is the relationship between God and the world*?" and on the other, scientific, "*What is the relationship between the world and the* Big Bang *theory (or analogous theories)*?" Yet, which world are we speaking about? If after reaching this point we believe we can abandon metaphysics and lean only upon physics, we shall immediately find ourselves embroiled in a battlefield of cosmovisions (worldviews). As ancient myths said, the world is a battle being fought between Gods (angels and demons included) and men. In short, this is the conflict between theology and science. Nevertheless, it is not a question here of Christian or scientific faith, but rather of our acceptance of the vision of the world we have, taking into account what specifically Christian thought and specific scientific thought say about the world. We concentrate here on Christian thought, as in other religions the issue is not regarded or it is treated in a much different manner. To begin with, we should investigate whether Christianity and science are talking about the same "world" and analyze the "instruments of observation" both use as, depending on which are adopted, the world thus "revealed" will change. And if we are told it concerns the world in the ordinary sense, we will then enter completely into the myth of the cosmovision that underlies the two forms of knowledge and take for granted that it is the same.

What then does scientific thought tell us? Much about abstract mathematics, something about the Big Bang, and precious little about the real world.[55]

---

[55] See the ambitious study by Barrow-Tipler (1998), which seeks to show the limits and indispens-

What does Christian thought tell us? Much about the Incarnation and about the resurrection of man, something about creation, and very little about the physical world.

This dialogue cannot be dialectic because we do not know whether the same *legein* are involved—from the same narration—but it should be *dialogical*, scrutinizing the *logoi*—the different registers of language.

What does "Christian thought" tell us about the Big Bang?

Christian thought could say, on one hand, that it has not taken the physical time of the universe into consideration. Neither the "Beginning" in the Bible nor St. John's account refer to the "beginning of physical time." On the other hand, the Big Bang theory seems to take it that the beginning of this world was due to an energetic force within matter itself, which has continued to be in the state of expansion. To ask oneself if the Big Bang is compatible or not with Christian thought is a methodologically inappropriate and philosophically captious question. *Methodologically inappropriate* because it presupposes uncritical recognition of the tribunal of discursive reasoning, as if this could decide upon the truth of two different epistemological propositions by applying the criterion of compatibility and of rational noncontradiction to them, without having previously established whether the two propositions have the same reference. *Philosophically captious* because it seems to boil Christian thought down to a crystallized body of doctrines (and, as such, we should speak of "Christian doctrine" or better still, of "doctrines accepted by Christians") or those reduced to a very particular exegesis of the Bible).

This exegesis would consist in both the rational interpretation of a text as information (as in scientific thought) and in the interpretation of the Bible in the light of a form of knowledge that differs from scientific knowledge. So, without going into the nature of this kind of knowledge, we are seeking to understand if it is possible to start out from something comparable to the hypothesis of the Big Bang.

Leaving aside the formidable philosophical and theological difficulties inherent in Christian interpretation, and the necessity (once denied by St. Thomas) of a "beginning of creation," let us limit ourselves to considering whether the Bible can actually tell us something about the Big Bang.

The first answer is that the Bible tells us nothing. The second should explain whether "Christian thought" can be content with being a mere exegesis of the Bible (something that many Christian thinkers would not accept). The third would, on one hand, have to explain how historical Christian tradition has interpreted those phrases in the Bible that speak of the creation of the world and, on the other, whether these relate to the same world. The fourth answer would be the properly hermeneutic one and would be of interest to scientists: to determine, if possible, an interpretation of biblical narration in harmony or discord with the Big Bang hypothesis.

Not much philosophical or historic speculation is needed to realize that one only has to change a text's context and approach it with a different pretext, for the text to say exactly what we wish it to say.

This is the methodologically weak point of all *componenda*. "God created heaven and earth in six days." Leaving aside the mystery of the sentence's subject ("God") and the ambiguity of the verb ("create"), we can begin to interpret the meaning of "six days" and "heaven and earth" in the light of whatever we wish them to mean. Consequently, it seems obvious, reducing "Christian thought" to the search for affinity with scientific hypothesis not only denies it all autonomy and, as such, all credibility, but reduces it to a subordinate version of scientific thought. This would then be recognized as the paradigm of rationality.

ability of the human factor in any calculation— with extensive bibliography.

In brief, there is a literal Christian interpretation (six days of twenty-four hours each), and a literal scientific interpretation (15 billion years). It is, then, a double issue. First, there is the metaphysical issue: what is the world's (nontemporal) Origin? Second, there is the anthropological one: what does man's dignity become if he is only an individual afoot in a practically infinite universe?

To shed some light on the first issue it is necessary to distinguish between the problematic *beginning* of linear time and the metaphysical *origin* of Existence and Man—problems that go beyond the fields both of modern science and traditional theology. As for the second issue, it is necessary to overcome the contemporary *mythos* of privileging *quantity*, which to a great extent comes from the influence of science on modern man.

We have already made reference to the abandoning of the Big Bang hypothesis by many researchers as well as modern science's incapacity, currently, to provide a model of the universe. Scientific cosmology restricts itself to a search for mathematical parameters that agree with the observations of some experiments and can, therefore, be applied predictively to be able to monitor specific phenomenon and, in this case, suggest that the known universe's "age" is estimated at 15 billion years. What is attractive about the Big Bang hypothesis is that, despite all due reservations, it presents us with a fundamentally energy-based account of the putative evolution of our material universe. But the issue regarding the origin of the cosmos is not only a mathematical or scientific question or a confrontation of these ambits, but in any case, a legitimate cosmological question in a wider sense: what is the temporal origin of our universe?

There could be many other *kalpas*, many other universes, and our cosmic beginning could well not be an absolute beginning. Then the question arises, thanks to modern science, whether or not we can have some say on the human question of the temporal origin of our cosmos. Human destiny seems to be tied to that of the universe, and this universe would seem to have revealed how old it is to modern physics.

We do not relate to time with the same sense that other cultures attribute this term. We speak of *chronon*, the natural physical-mathematical time unit, considered to be constant. This unit can also be the minute-second as a practical partition of solar or subatomic movement, resorting to an anthropomorphic or, better still, materio-morphic model. We could simply say that, having to cover the shortest possible distance (otherwise, the force of attraction would prevail) at the maximum speed, we could extrapolate a time unit that we could call a *chronon*. What is important to us at this moment is the cosmological model, whether the expression "beginning of the cosmos" should be taken as referring to our universe.

I shall restrict myself to taking into consideration just three points:

    a.   The universe in question is the astronomical universe accepted by modern science based on the fragile theory of the constant speed of light, of the variation of colors in the spectrum, and the (paradoxical) behavior of elemental particles. While we only have some modest information about the world beyond the Solar System and even scantier information about that beyond the Milky Way, science maintains that these physical-mathematical rules are valid throughout the universe and states the constancy of these rules in an extrapolation that goes far beyond the limits of possible verification, as all instruments of verification are linked to the "verifier" (man). Contemporary astrophysics has carried out important experiments that qualify what we have said; yet we have not yet left the solar system nor have we been able to overcome the subjectivity of the experimenter. Man is the measure of all things, as Pythagoras said and we continue to repeat.

Modern findings are fascinating and important. But the enormous progress in the field of physical-mathematics, and this partly in experiments on the solar system, does not mean we can extrapolate without any foundation. Rather, it indicates that we should be cautious, avoiding hasty conclusions and sweeping cosmological applications.

Even supposing we could find the point of union (unification) of the four physical forces (electromagnetic, gravitational, and weak and strong nuclear forces) in the so-called unified theory (something we are still waiting for), we shall still find ourselves considering exclusively physical "energies." And also the singularity of moment zero in time, which in itself lies beyond all scientific approaches, and does not permit any kind of conclusion. Aside from reducing the cosmos to a mere hotchpotch of forces, we have to face the fact that other dimensions of reality have been ignored.

b.   Our second observation is more important; it depends totally on words, but we do not have anything else. Physical-mathematical time is not cosmological time; it is not real time, according to the value that in practice all world cultures have given to this word. The time of modern science is a physical-mathematical parameter, a quantifiable magnitude, the measure of an objective relationship between static space and velocity. Without doubt a very important factor, yet not the same as that "reality" or entity that other cultures have labeled *time*. Thus, we find ourselves faced with a vicious circle, as velocity is already intrinsically correlated with time; inasmuch, to measure time itself we need time—something that undoubtedly serves to measure time but does not tell us what time is. And any and every clock will always have to move at the same (constant) speed to be able to measure time.

Having relativized (not to say ridiculed) all other cosmologies, we should not now place modern scientific cosmology in an absolutely position as the only one that is fit to replace the others and supply us with a true model of the universe. A clear-cut distinction should be made between modern cosmology (the global scientific theory of the cosmos) and other traditional cosmologies or "cosmovisions" (visions of the universe that other cultures have)—yet the last word has still not been said.

We can all agree with the fact that my age is the expression of my time, yet the age of a stone—and, analogically speaking, the age of the universe—needs a different measure to the *metron* of my personal time. After all, time is one of those words that defies both objectivization (time with no subject that perceives or suffers change is not time), and subjectivization (for time to exist, things must really change, which requires an immutable or independent background). Time is neither a subjective nor objective entity. Time is real, but it is neither "there" (objective), inasmuch as there is a same time for everyone, nor is it "here" (subjective), in such a way as it would make it a private affair for each and every one of us. Time is relation and relation is relative.

The idea of the beginning of the cosmos is probably an anthropomorphism. We have had a beginning because we define our ego as something that began with our birth. The Earth has had a beginning because we restrict the Earth to that ensemble of matter with a specific form which we call our planet: which, nonetheless, does not mean at the same time the absolute beginning of this "matter" that "later on" becomes a planet. Yet the beginning of the cosmos seems to point toward an absolute beginning, and this concept is rather ambiguous. There is a beginning if it is seen in relation to something for which it is a beginning. This "something" "before" the beginning cannot exist temporally, in time—otherwise it could not be an absolute beginning. In other words, we can conceive "something" lacking a beginning, but not an absolute beginning, because something is a beginning only when it is related to something else, and, as such, it is not absolute. The very notion of a beginning is a relative notion. To play around with Not-being as if it *were* a being is not correct. If the world is temporal, there is no beginning to the cosmos, as being temporal there will always be a beginning *before* our beginning. If the world is eternal, it cannot have a beginning because eternity (no time) cannot be *before* the world, and therefore it cannot be its beginning. Are we not, therefore, dealing with a pseudo-problem as we have been suggesting since the very *beginning*?

     c.   Does this perhaps mean that God or religion do not belong to scientific thought or that scientific thought, as such, should be intrinsically a-theist and a-religious? It all depends on our concept of science and our idea of God; yet however we wish to see it, our reflections on the beginning of the cosmos cannot be based upon a preformulated concept of God or religion that would align in favor or against the existence of this beginning.

In other words, if the cosmological conception of earlier times conditions the idea of God, the present-day scientific vision of the universe conditions our vision of God in the same way. Both theology and science speak to us of a real world. We cannot subordinate science to theology, nor theology to science. The great challenge of our time precisely consists in the fact that these two great human activities cannot find a degree of harmony without there being a radical mutation of both. The term *theophysics* seeks to symbolize the *ontonomy* between both of them. What follows are certain reflections on the matter.

Substantial Thought and Functional Thought

The Self is not primordially substance: the West has heard this from Heraclitus onward, but never really believed it until the great revolution unleashed by modern science. This is not a new issue. Some pre-Socratic philosophers—the Scholastics, for instance—had already seen this, but modern science has embodied this new vision in the common world, so to speak. Indeed, modern science would seem to avoid the Aristotelian problem of substance, denying in its scientific speculations any importance to predicative thought, for which qualities are nothing more than quantifiable attributes of substance. Nevertheless, it should be said that this "great revolution" was preceded by Christian trinitarian intuition according to which God is not substance (in which case it would be tri-theism) but rather more like a relation, even if, since Constantine, monotheism has been prevalent.

In any case, a strong intellectual ascesis is needed to go beyond predicative thought. Asking oneself what an electron is has no meaning if we do not first overcome the primacy of substance, and give consistency to the world of simple functions. Just as the question regarding the *being* of a geometric shape has a different meaning from the question of the *being* of a billiard ball or a Dutch cheese, the question of the *being* of an electron, of a wave, of a proton, or of a photon has a different meaning from the analogical question about the being of an atom of lead, of a water molecule, or a piece of wood. Philosophy that has gone beyond Platonism knows very well that when we speculate about love, the will, or freedom we are not talking about substances, but rather relationships. A certain medieval cosmology perhaps forgot this, reifying the forces of nature. In short, the self is not only substance.

We have criticized evolutionism by saying that with it science does not answer the question of what man *is*; yet one must add that science responds to this criticism by explaining how man *functions*, thus inverting the dogma of a certain line of philosophy that affirmed that the functioning of a thing is determined by what that thing *is* (*operari sequitur esse*), and instead saying the opposite, that something is in terms of its function (*esse sequitur operari*) and that only the functioning of a being can reveal to us what it is—as we have already said. At bottom, the categories of substances and accidents are anthromorphisms from which science frees us.

The being of subatomic phenomenon, for instance, is not substantial, but rather it is simply accidental, to continue using Aristotelian categories. What are these "beings" then? Here is where the theory of abstraction presents us with an answer to the obscure enigma veiling the ultimate questions of the universe. These "beings" are physical-mathematical properties of matter—that is, they are quantitative behavior patterns, pure processes, or quantifiable qualities—if you prefer. Modern physics denies that its affirmations might have substantial validity. Modern science measures, calculates, tests, experiments yet it does not give answers to what there is "behind" phenomena, because it does not believe that being coincides with substance and has it that physical-mathematical realities are not substantial.

The historical process is known. Man, early on, just by thinking, came to recognize the existence of *atómoi*, the ultimate individual particles and foundation of all existing bodies. Whether we are speaking of traditional cosmology's four classical elements or of a higher number of atoms, the approach would be the same. Technical processes have enabled us to reach these cornerstones of matter, but these same processes (which have obtained results owing to the application of quantitative methods, that is, functional thought) have proceeded to isolate (and here we have the problem) not precisely particles, but rather energies, processes, effects, and so on, which have no substantial consistency whatsoever, yet do possess a sui generis reality, which in traditional language we could call "accidents" and which would be better described as *functions*.

Qualifying what we previously mentioned, to ask oneself what a "fractal" is, for instance, makes no sense if the being of the fractal is interpreted as a substance. Fractals are a function—but a function also *is*.

If we wish to call a function an accident, we should not interpret these accidents in an overly anthropomorphic way (like the accidents that occur to human beings), nor in Aristotelian terms as being dependent on substances. While the main accidents of psychosomatic substance are qualities and habits that have their roots embedded in human substance itself, and that modify it intrinsically, the accidents in question are of a different kind and represent a prevailing quantitative aspect—they are functions with their own *ontonomy*. Their connection with material substance is of a different kind from human accidents, because their relation, their *esse in* and *esse ad* (staying with the medieval Scholastics), is of another kind: that of a mutual inter-in-dependence. This is functional thought. Although modern science cannot be reduced to physics alone, we can take it as being paradigmatic and make it the focal point of our examples.

One of the great contributions of modern science to human thought, bringing man closer to the truth, is functional thought. Functions too (which are not substances) similarly reveal to us what being is like. *How* a "thing" functions, how a phenomenon behaves, does not directly reveal the substance, the being of this thing or the essence of that phenomenon, but perhaps we do not have any other access to what this thing or phenomenon is other than observing *how* it functions. We cannot confuse the being with the functioning of this being but, very frequently, being is only revealed in its functioning and, thus, knowing the *how* of a thing is not a secondary matter.

What's more, the functioning of being seems to follow paths, models, behavior patterns that appear to obey the rules of logical thought. The fact that bodies fall belongs to simple experience; moreover, the fact that bodies seem to follow—indeed obey—regularities that our logical thought discovers is a true revelation concerning the nature of bodies. It is not enough to say that we have "deduced" the regularities from the repetition of simple observations, since we discover the same laws (in this case that of falling objects) when we extrapolate to very different conditions. We cannot state that nature obeys the mind, yet we should recognize the fact that there is a marvelous and mysterious harmony between nature and our logical minds. To make the issue still more complex and surprising, we discover that this relationship is not automatic, because we also realize the experience of freedom, that is to say, that nature, especially human nature, can "decide," although within certain limits, *not* to obey such laws.

In summary, theophysics aids us not only in understanding the harmony of the universe, but also to see that our access to reality cannot disregard intellectual experience. It is necessary to experience the exciting realization that nature seems to follow these patterns that our mind has discovered. Physical science from past centuries was born of this enthusiasm: nature obeys the logic of the human mind. This scientific ecstasy with which true scientists experiment is, nevertheless, just a first leap on the springboard of the mind toward reaching spiritual or mystical experience. What is discovered then is not just logical determinism, but also the freedom of nature, which is the solution to Parmenides's dogma on the "slavery" of reality vis-à-vis thought. We ought immediately to add that this harmony of the universe is not necessarily moral harmony.

Science's functional thought does not eliminate predicative thought, but it puts it in its place. Phenomenology occupies the place of substantialist metaphysics.

1.   Substance and Accidents

Science has its own specific field and explores the aspect of reality proper to it, whether in terms of quantitative "accidents" of matter or quantifiable entities or qualities of intra-matter that are much less accessible to our immediate understanding.

We are not developing here a metaphysics of the functions of physics. Science provides us with the data but is not concerned with elaborating a theory of the meaning of the reality it deals with. Science limits itself to describing phenomena without setting out to solve the problem of the level of reality they are concerned with.

The categories of substance and accident are too closely linked to predicative thought, preventing us from looking more deeply into the specific class of peculiar being discovered by physical-mathematics. An accident, according to predicative thought, is a way of being dependent on substance, *upon* which it is supported, while in functional thought a function is independent of substance and is considered in a relational "self," that is, in a field.

This kind of philosophical conceptualization can also proceed through abstractions and consider the function as being separated and isolated, yet with one basic difference. While certain traditional philosophical thought considers the essence of an accident to be its pure accidental being—that is, in its own peculiarity but referred to a substance (for instance, a color in itself is a quality of bodies)—scientific thought considers functions in *themselves*, yet without substantializing them: they are conceived as functions or functional aspects of something that on its own is nothing else but this function. However much our thought wishes to be independent, we cannot contemplate these functions within a substantial scheme, but rather do so in a temporal-spatial framework. Functional thought inquires into the happening of things insofar as it identifies such with a temporal *flow* or refers it to a spatial *being*.

If traditional cosmological thought is, therefore, a substantial-based thinking even when it is concerned with the accidental, scientific thought, in contrast, is a spatial-temporal mode of thinking. The former's connecting thread is the *ousia* of things, their substance; their essence if you will; the latter's connecting thread is the spatial-temporal structure of beings. Time and space are the "forms" or "categories" of functional thought. It is not a coincidence that Kant wished to establish a conceptual scheme for science.

It would be worthwhile to underline this fact, as in certain brands of philosophy there is a tendency to minimize science's *philosophical* importance, reducing it to simple technique—of thought, but of a very restricted kind. I mean that the so-called scientific revolution is not simply the introduction of machines or the change in lifestyle after the Renaissance, but rather a true revolution of thought, and as such, philosophy—and thus of man's life upon the Earth. The great breakthroughs of modern science are not only due to its power, through its alliance with technology, but also for having "touched" upon an aspect of philosophical knowledge, that is, understanding, that had been forgotten by certain (theoretical) philosophy. The problems here are in any case not so simple. Buddhist cosmovision, for instance, is much more co-natural with the scientific mentality, and nonetheless, modern science did not develop in the East where important technical discoveries were made, but in the West. Thought is certainly important, yet man is more than just a *res cogitans*. In other words, *praxis* is not possible without there being a *theory* that sustains it, but the latter (*theory*) alone is not the cause of *praxis*.

2. Material Being

Things *are* not only in a metaphysical dimension; they *are* also while they are in a spatial-temporal dimension. Science, with its functional thought, would reveal the spatial-temporal structure of the cosmos to us.

As modern science has stemmed from (dialectical and not always cordial) dialogue with the philosophy of its time with its Greek (and Scholastic) roots, a few brief paragraphs in this philosophical language could be of some help to us for clearing up the terms of this issue.

It is of no use, then, to substantialize space and time, to think of them as substances, as supports, the hypostases of the events of scientific phenomena. This mistake, understandable in a phase of transition between two ways of thought and during a period when science was gestating, proves fatal for both the development of the latter and its relationship with philosophy. Space and time are not in competition with substance, they are something else, of which analysis is not called for at this moment. We are also saying that it is no use epistemologically "substantializing" time and space as a priori forms of knowledge (Kant)—making epistemology the "substitute" for metaphysics and thus clearing the way for idealism.

Nevertheless, it is perhaps an opportune moment to add that the true being of things is not only their mere *existing* (*extra nihilum*), but also their complex *in-sisting* (*in tempore et spatio*). The "created" *being* is not just once, nor in fact *is*, properly speaking. Rather it finds itself *being* and in due course will *be*. In this "being that is being," being is more important than becoming. To be is a verb and in this verb there is a spatial-temporal path. This aspect of bodies that is noncomplementary but rather constitutive is revealed to us by physics and is further elaborated by theophysics where it has not lost ground. It is here that the dogma of incarnation should have its impact! Or, perhaps also, the other way round, incarnation is the specific creed of this human intuition. This commentary, which would appear strange to modern science, belongs fairly and squarely in theophysics—although we shall not linger over this idea here. Science puts us in contact with the cosmic vision of the universe as if it were a spatial-temporal whole in development. It can be considered an individual being or an isolated property, yet this consideration will always be partial, not only because there are *other* beings and other properties alongside the "case" in hand but rather because this "case" contains within it a constitutive reference, an open valency, an essential relationship with the *whole*. This "link" is not fortuitous, yet neither is it a logical or causal connection: it is a constitutive part of the warp and weft of reality. To take words seriously, this "link" (bond or binding) is the religious dimension that "re-binds" us to reality as a whole, yet without harming the ontonomy of all beings, such that their inter-in-dependence is not lost. Any kind of dichotomy of reality is an open wound that cannot heal unless through integrating a part with the whole. The entire universe is a dynamic universe in movement and organization, on its way toward a plenitude about which science, or philosophy as *opus rationis,* can do no more than stammer with half-formed meanings that which any nonreductionist philosophy can and should encompass. Not to dogmatize upon the whole, but rather to compose a fuller vision, however unattainable, fragile, enigmatic, and mysterious it might be, with a respectful and hopeful approach. This may seem like a paradox, but it could be a gloss of the *Âvetāśvatara-Upaniṣad,* which sees the divine potential of reality obscured by its own qualities (its own attributes).[56]

To return to the modern science, only if we recognize this double dimension of our thought can science's statements be explained and numerous *aporias* in physics be clarified. Among the best known are the impossibility of simultaneously measuring a subatomic particle's velocity and its position, and the antinomy between the particle and wave models, according to which apparently irreconcilable aspects of these particles' behavior are observed. Equally as well known, for instance, are the difficulties that arise from taking it that light and other micro-physical wave movements have a trajectory (given that they do not seem to manifest at intermediate points), Gödel's theorem, Dirac's equation, and so on. One passionate issue, which is now beginning to be studied, is the well-known phenomenon of *synchronicity.*[57]

What happens is that these paradoxes manifest when we interpret scientific results with substantial thought, instead of applying the more adequate functional thought to help us comprehend what science is telling us.

For instance, we have hypothesized (and hypostatized) in the electron a series of properties of atoms and of matter in general, or better said, we have considered the electron as a substantial particle, instead of a function, as a group of properties that express the specific behavior of . . . nothing else, unless it be the electron itself! This, instead of considering it in itself precisely as such behavior, defined by its properties—although in the end, at bottom, these are phenomena of the material being, and indeed of reality. Thus it becomes explicable that the electron, for instance, is not in any particular place, that it may be represented *as* a wave, like a cloud that surrounds the nucleus. If the electron *were* a particle, this would be inexplicable, along with its physical-mathematical indeterminacy. The electron has no substantiality that distinguishes it from other electrons; what is more, we cannot guarantee that at the end of a process the electron will be the same. Furthermore, physics considers this hypothesis to be senseless, and then we understand why it is right: the electron is not a particle, it is not a substance. And this lack of its own individual features goes, from the physical-mathematical point of view, for any kind of subatomic formation. "Particles" are not substances, they are functions.

3. *Physics and Metaphysics*

Physics is not metaphysics, yet neither can metaphysics be identified with philosophy. A linguistic and conceptually disorientating anarchy reigns in this field. This anarchy can effectively disorientate thinking in physics, and scientific thought in general, which seeks to speak with a single voice and ideally prefers "clear and distinct ideas." In contrast, the plurality of the same notions in metaphysics, ontology, wisdom, philosophy (without mentioning notions from other cultures) is inherent to the subject we are dealing with, since the human

---

[56] This phrase is practically untranslatable without adding a long commentary: *apaśyam devātma-śva-guṇair nigū ḍhām.*

[57] See Mansfield (1999).

condition obstinately resists uniformity and rejects all kinds of unison. The fact that there is not just one conception of what philosophy is must therefore be seen as positive and a sign of the richness of man. It is as disorientating to interpret some physical phenomena with substantialist thought as it is illegitimate to project the axioms of mathematical thought upon reality as a whole.

Without getting into the discussion over what metaphysics is and whether it is mono-theistic, substantialist, epistemologistical, ontological, or positivist with respect to our problem, here we understand this term to designate the attempts of the human mind to find a foundation to physics as a science of empirical reality, even if this *empireia* is considered realist, critical, or idealist.

Something very different, on the other hand, occurs with modern science. Science, in the sense of the natural sciences, presents a double uniformity of the object and method in intrinsic relationship. The object of science is nature observed with the scientific method, that is, with direct or indirect sensory observation and the possible integration of this into a conceptual system. This explains why science is right (without this necessarily overturning philosophy) when it defends the statistical character of its laws and the (conceptual) hypothesis of the probabilistic behavior of elemental entities.

In the same way, owing to the discovery of relationships of uncertainty, a series of more or less important considerations are often expressed concerning the nature of physical science and human knowledge itself. They are mostly extrapolations lacking in scientific rigor and philosophical value. The degree of freedom of elemental particles, for instance, could provide us with a metaphor, yet it has little to do with human freedom. The idea that matter is full of holes is a vulgarization of the particle nature of matter and not a means to make the resurrection more comprehensible; the theory of relativity is not an argument to defend pluralism, and so forth. There is, however, an example of scientific pluralism. It is a known fact that quantum physics is not compatible with the general theory of relativity, and that the more recent string theory does not solve the problem, as it similarly does not explain the phenomenon of black holes in the universe. Despite that, calculations based on these theories offer results that are verifiable within certain limits. Neither human reason nor the purest logic can offer us an indisputably definitive vision of reality. Perhaps we need a third eye, that of the spirit (of the above-mentioned tripartite anthropology) not indeed to obtain for us "certainty and security" but to bring us peace and joy—not as factors foreign to the human adventure on our way toward our plenitude, but as qualities intrinsic to our very nature.

We ought, however, to get back to our thoughts on the topic in hand.

The relationship between physics and metaphysics is based precisely on their difference. At most, modern science, as the dominant form of thinking of the elites of the world (not all elites however), can provide us with the point of departure for certain metaphors.

Metaphysics, like theology, seeks to find the meaningfulness of reality, insofar as this is possible. Science has no such pretensions, but its descriptions too have their repercussions on the real, although in their own particular way. Metaphysics cannot afford to ignore them. Let us look at a few examples. Science goes beyond its own limits if it seeks to give us a vision of the world, but the cosmic vision of man cannot dispense with the contributions of science. The relationship between physics and metaphysics is an asymmetrical one. Physics does not offer a vision of the world, but it provides material for metaphysics, so that any metaphysics that ignores physics ceases to be valid. Metaphysics needs to listen to physics, but the latter should decide if it has been properly interpreted by the former.

Man is more than a physical entity and maybe for that reason has always sought to formulate the laws of the physical world as particular instances of more general metaphysical laws that are valid for all being. With the same purpose but in an opposite sense, formulations have at times been extrapolated that remain excessively physico-mathematical in orientation, as springboards to arriving at the laws of the mind. All spheres of reality have their *ontonomy*, and we need to be cautious with our extrapolations.

It is instructive to observe this need for unification of our reason, and the pressing need that man has to use speculation to arrive at a complete synthesis, of which man is himself an example. In view of this tendency, the Scholastics extrapolated top downward, so to speak, while many modern scientists extrapolate bottom upward. The former, interested primarily in the world of the spirit, confined themselves to applying to the material world the laws they discovered in the world of the spirit. We should not be content with dismissing this as anthropomorphism, to label it thus and think to have done with it. Pythagoras's maxim, mentioned earlier, is ambiguous: man is not the measure of all things, but rather its measurer. We are not the *metron* of them, but rather their *metriotês*—their measure, moderation, and limit, we might say, playing with words. All that man does, thinks, or wants bears the imprint of humanity.

In classical antiquity and in medieval times, for example, they talked of love and of hate in the natural world, and attributed to bodies the affinities, family relationships, and inclinations like those they believed to exist in the world of the psyche. Medieval physics, accustomed to qualitative differences in that way solved the problem of what caused changes to bodies. It is precisely this point that modern observers think laughable, finding terms like *vis dormitiva*, *curativa*, and so on to be infantile. The world of qualities has been supplanted by the world of quantities.

Modern science, for its part, following the epidemic of quantitative exclusivism and of an irreducible and irreconcilable dualism between nature and spirit, has started to react in the opposite direction.[58] We do not speak of the love of one body for another, or the amorous attraction of the Earth as its natural home, or the tendency of one substance to seek union with another. Instead we speak of the force of gravity, of the indeterminacy of psychic acts— yet we still use expressions like the attraction between bodies and so on.

Mankind has now arrived at the point where it seeks to understand the spiritual world by means of the physical world, whereas formerly it was the contrary. Materialist and spiritual monism are simply two examples of this unifying tendency of man, yearning to attain plenitude. Indeed, as early as the thirteenth century, Ramon Llull, in his *Arbor Scientiae* V.5, gives an all-encompassing definition of philosophy: "Lo filòsof ama saber la veritat de les coses" (The philosopher loves to know the truth of things), and goes on to speak of the double movement "en pujant e en davallant" (ascending and descending) to arrive at the truth.

There is no question that knowledge of the world of the spirit helps us to know about the reactions of matter. Without certain analogous processes operating in our inner world we should be profoundly incapable of understanding what happens in the outer universe. Furthermore, an in-depth study of the behavior patterns of matter provides us with a clear paradigm of analogous regularities that can be observed similarly in the spiritual realm. This is the harmony we referred to in the Preface.

The world is a whole, and our age in particular is probably becoming mature enough to be able to contemplate the synthesis that our culture thirsts for and needs.

But there is more: this interpretation of matter and the spirit not only allows us to formulate laws that can be applied analogically to other worlds, it makes it possible to observe the

---

[58] See as a specific example the study *Intercultural Theology III* (Hollenweger 1988).

mutual interference that obtain between the two. They are steps that lead to the overcoming of spirit-matter duality, without thereby entering into extreme monism.

This question has been studied above all in human beings, who, as such, possess a spiritual and a material side, intimately interlinked and united; there is no reason, however, to restrict this to humans.

Pantheism has it that the world has a divine nature. This is an error, but not one of excess but rather defect—because sufficient audacity (faith) is lacking to discover in all things that divine spirit that really *is* in them, which feeds them and brings them into being without, for all that, either things or God losing their distinctive nature. "The divine embraces all nature," said Aristotle in his *Metaphysics*. "Knowing God is the plenitude of science [*plenitudo scientiae*]," said St. Bernard, but this *scientiae* is *gnôsis* and this *gnôsis* implies becoming God, not an exclusively transcendental God, but immanent too—that is to say, God as Trinity. Using traditional language, we could repeat very schematically: God *is*, but not only is (and not exhaustively) in the divine *nature*: Being is, but beings are—if we choose to employ this ontological terminology, which is not the only one, nor perhaps the best. We need to avoid rendering uniform the complex variety of the universe, but there is nothing wrong in seeking the relatedness of all things and finding in them traces of the Trinity itself. At bottom, it is not just the Trinity that is reflected in the beings of the world, but also it is the beings of the world that reflect the Trinity. This is what many traditions mean when they assert the mirror nature of the universe; everything reflects everything else. One can, therefore, turn the phrase around: in the Trinity we find traces of Reality itself. There is a need to be bold in our conceptions but aware of the unilateral and imperfect nature of our intuitions, even the most brilliant of them. Error is a truth that we abuse. The so-called laws of nature are not laws of a (nonexistent) abstract nature, nor laws of the human spirit. They are regularities of the cosmotheandric "complex."

To sum up, there can be no metaphysics without physics. The beginning of knowledge starts with sensitivity, that is, with knowledge of the physical world. Having changed our knowledge of physics, metaphysics cannot continue to be the same. But on the other hand, there can be no physics without metaphysics. All physics imply metaphysics. Our interpretation of physics depends on the underlying metaphysics, and the concepts of physics itself—such as time, matter, space, energy, and so on—predate all measurement and physical experiment.

Once again, the a-dual wisdom of the *advaita* makes its appearance.

The Limits of Science and of Knowledge: A Critical Reflection

We have already said that science does not constitute the full extent of knowledge, and that, above all, if it is not separated from love, represents the most noble aspect of the human being, that is to say, one's communion with reality. We realize ourselves, become real, by knowing, and we know when we identify ourselves with reality. We iterate that authentic knowledge is inseparable from love: both are forces that are both centripetal and centrifugal, which move the universe—"the sky and the other stars," to quote the last line of the *Divine Comedy*. We become real by knowing, being born along with what we know in accordance with the most widely accepted etymology (although contested today). "Connaître, naître ensemble," says Paul Valéry.

The gateway to knowledge is not closed. It is open to all human beings, but not wide open; on the contrary it is a narrow entrance. Man does not receive the gift of the true life immediately, at birth. One needs still to be reborn (to reality). This is the privilege of man.

This rebirth is not automatic. Human life is not only physiological, *bios*, it is also *zôê*, the divine grace that we need to know how to receive. The so-called beatific vision is full knowledge, as Christian theology says.

I shall not give way to the temptation of describing other possible keys to the doorway of knowledge. The old doorway lacked even the doors, but merely indicated the threshold. Entering through a *gopuram*, one of the great gateways to the temple, was the equivalent of an initiation—for that reason, not all could enter.

The threshold has no barriers, but it marks, in any case, a limit: All who have cultivated themselves, to echo Cicero, who defined philosophy as *cultura animi* (culture of the soul). The sciences are specialized bodies of learning, but knowledge is not a specialization; it cannot be split, it is holistic consciousness. Were we not conscious of what we know, this would not be knowledge, says the *Upaniṣad*.

The problems are exorbitant. We limit ourselves just to certain specific cases.

Science Is Neither Neutral nor Universal

Knowledge, we have said, is the noblest quality that human beings possess. Mankind, precisely for this knowledge, feels itself to be the lord of creation. When this knowledge reaches its limits, man still wants to know more, "to be as God,"[59] knowing the tree of good and evil, without waiting for *kairos*, the incarnation of the divine in Man. This is what Original sin is, according to the Bible. This knowledge claims to be universal: truth is made absolute and objective, and seeks to be so for all comers. The more perfect knowledge is, the more universal it believes itself to be. Yet, not putting limits on knowledge means seeking to ignore the "limited" condition of Man. This is the first problem that we shall be dealing with, above all in the specific case of scientific knowledge: modern science's surprising discoveries have made us believe that scientific knowledge is universal.

1. *The tendency toward Universalization*
   I shall begin with a little story.
   A young man with tears in his eyes and a letter in his hand laments, "Every single day, for the past two years, I've written a letter to my fiancée, and now she writes and tells me she's going to marry the postman."
   For more than two hundred years we have related to science as if it were the go-between that has kept us informed about the nature of reality, so it's no wonder that we have fallen in love with her. Admittedly, criticizing a loved one is not easy. Some, however, perhaps being more sensitive to the state of the world, are beginning to wake up from the Galilean dream of nature being writ in mathematical language, and from the millennial dream of a lost paradise. Modern science is just a go-between. We might cite ancient wisdom, which probably originated in Central Asia around the fourth millennium before Christ, of which Pythagoras is the best-known exponent in Europe. We know that the wise man from Samos not only spent some time in Egypt but also received his initiation in Babylonia. This wisdom states that nature's language is music, which does in fact have a mathematical structure, yet cannot be reduced to such. "Âabdabrahman" (Brahman [is] Word), states an Indian tradition; "*In the beginning was the Word*," echoes Christian tradition. Elsewhere I have written about the Holy Quaternity of the Word: speaker, sound, sense, and interlocutor. But let us get back to the adventure of modern science over the last centuries.

---

[59] Gen 3:5.

These days we hear of such things as "radical innovations," "Asian values," and "respect for other cultures." Nevertheless, in practice we in the West continually fall back on the habitual Western mentality. This is natural: no one can jump on their own shadow, and language betrays us. We can, however, be aware of the fact that *homo technologicus* is not the only variety of human species or culture, and still carry on living (and so, likely enough, also thinking) in accordance with the technological model. In effect, it seems that the paradigm of Western or Westernized modern man's thinking is the scientific one. Nonetheless, the current crises oblige us to reflect upon the present scientific order. On this, I shall limit myself to just a few personal reflections.

There is a very subtle tendency toward universality in both the (modern) concept of science and the (rational) conceptions of philosophy: a tendency toward thinking that science and philosophy are neutral concepts and, therefore, apt for any culture as such. Just think about Kant's criterion on moral action: our behavior is moral when it can rise to a universal level. A human invariant (knowledge in this case) is not necessarily a cultural universal (object of knowledge), as we shall now go on to see. Each culture has its own categories.

As we have pointed out, precisely the stupendous and certainly spectacular discoveries of the originally European technological civilization have led many to believe that the historical period we are living in represents a decisive turning point in world history. Be that as it may, this belief leads us to a reflection upon our human condition running deeper than the habitual self-criticism of every age. We should avoid a-critically devolving into a forced attempt at solving problems without before having carefully reflected upon the meaning of our own existence and that of the world. We need new categories and a truly contemplative spirit.

Naturally, the universalizing syndrome that we witness every day is not new in human history. While different in nature, we can think of at least some powerful attempts at universalization. I refer to three religions and four ideologies, which are closely interconnected among themselves.

Buddhism, Christianity, and Islam all have believed that they had a message to transmit to the whole world and, in a certain sense, the right to go forth and proselytize throughout that world. At the same time, European *rationalism* believed that *its* comprehension of rationality was a universal phenomenon. *Marxism* (which is an offshoot of the former) also believed itself to be a universal instrument for social justice. And, while being less theoretical and more practical, we ought really to mention *capitalism*, the pan-economic ideology. Our last example on this list is *science*.

As a consequence of the ideologies mentioned, plus not a little input from monotheistic thought, the conviction has arisen that modern science and technology should take on a redemptive role similar to the other above-mentioned tendencies. As a corollary, we could equally consider similar universalizing tendencies expressed in more political terms: world democracy and world government, among other similar items. An equivalent word to universalization is globalization—a term that these days provokes heated ideological arguments. In our case, the globalization of science is tantamount to the empire of scientific rationality.[60]

We should learn from history and pay attention to the voices of other cultures—and at least stop assuming that we are the only representatives of civilization who can carry the content of all human wisdom.

The study of cultures shows us that each civilization has chosen some mundane values to make sacred. The modern "civil religion" has enshrined science and technology in the same

---

[60] We have sufficient example of this in the definitions given in the 1974 edition of the *Encyclopedia Britannica*.

way as in other periods they placed the mantle of the divine, mysterious and sacred, upon other beings or notions. The history of religions is a truly fascinating discipline from which we should learn—overcoming as necessary the syndrome of viewing religion as some kind of sect.

Globalization is not only the result of techno-science's penetration of a large part of the world. This has been made possible owing to the present-day reigning *mythos* of rationality, as we have already pointed out. Making reason the sole method to reach intelligibility allows us to encounter a common "denominator" in the most diverse cultural variations—along with the consequent danger of forgetting the many "numerators." Globalization represents this rational abstraction—quite apart from its political and economic aspects.

2. *The Power of Mental Abstraction*

Probably owing to the fascination exercised by the extraordinary power of abstraction of the human intellect, other equally indispensable aspects of reality are undervalued if not actually discarded, and these aspects are essential to obtaining a more complete vision of the world.

Mathematical terminology tells us something of importance about the structure of reality, yet it is not the only language of that which is real. Moreover, reality cannot be brought down to a mere linguistic expression, although language is a constitutive dimension of man.

By synthesizing humanity's extensive history, we can draw a distinction between *human invariants* and *cultural universals*.

All people, as human beings, eat, sleep, speak, grow, think, and so forth. These are human invariants.

But our understanding, interpretation, and thus the efficacy of these very acts differ depending on varying human cultures. In some traditions, eating is symbiosis with nature or the Gods, or is a eucharistic act; for others, it is a biological process or simply a gesture of living together or what you will. To sum up, the power of the mind's abstraction allows one to attribute more than one meaning to the same act. But a simple, necessarily abstract common denominator cannot do justice to the complex experience of a given culture. On this basis then, there are no *cultural universals*, whereas we can find analogies and partial identities across many cultures. Also reflections on human nature, on natural law, along with other similar notions may evince a very different idea of this presumed human nature, not exempt from specific cultural connotations. One important case in point is the debate over the universality of human rights.

In a comparable fashion, education could be seen as a human invariant, if one thinks of it *formally* as a collaboration between various generations to help the younger ones acquire the plenitude of their humanity, aside from the fact that plenitude and humanity can be interpreted in very different ways as also the necessary means of attaining such perfection.

Going back to our point, *techné* ("art" in Greek) can be considered a human invariant. All human beings use and manipulate the external world to their own advantages, benefit, and improvement. *Technology*, however, is a special case, a transformation of this *techné*. This is generated by a particular culture, more precisely by a particular development of *techné* in this culture that has continued to use machines of the second order (which use nonnatural sources of energy). If we translate "technology" to other non-European languages, we shall immediately see the difference. *Techné* makes a reference to the spirit (in-spiration); technology is linked to a kind of cognitive *know-how* (*techno-logos*). Technology is not a cultural universal, much less a human invariant.

The reason that modern science was believed to be a cultural universal derives from the above-mentioned power of abstraction. Of course, formal concepts are indeed universal, yet only within systems with shared conventions. The sum of $2 + 2 = 4$, for instance, is universally valid, yet only to the extent that 2 and 2 remain formal signs, which in turn have meaning only within a generally shared axiomatic theory of numbers (most of the time unconsciously present). But if we add two cows and two angels there may be a problem. And the abstraction "two cows" already abstracts from each of the cows what it really is. Each cow can formally be a cow, yet materially each cow is unique. It cannot be substituted by another. If instead of cow we substitute man here, we should be appalled, surely, if we condemned an innocent person in the place of someone who is guilty, because after all 1 = 1. Man as a universal concept is only a formal notion, deprived of what we consider our own most precious personal value. People as such are uncountable. We are all sons and daughters, but children are not interchangeable for their respective mothers.

But let us seek to deepen our reflection upon modern science and technology.

3. *Specificity of Modern Science*

In practically all traditions of humanity, science has meant the fruit gathered and more or less systematized from the tree of knowledge: in practice, the most effective human means for coming into intimate contact with reality. Knowing means assimilating, becoming one with the thing known. "To know Brahman is to become Brahman," it says in the *Upaniṣad*; "The human soul [*psyché*] is in a way all things," stated Aristotle (and the Scholastics repeated); "Each one of us is a microcosm," stated the pre-Socratics; "To know *pratītya-samutpāda* [the universal concatenation of all things] means attaining illumination," says Buddhism, and so on. In this sense science does nothing but repeat a human archetype: knowledge has an intrinsic redemptive power when the object of knowledge is God, Man, or simply Reality. This "science" is knowledge, and this knowledge is not exclusively theoretical. With the fragmentation of knowing (that is, with specialization), however, knowledge loses its holistic nature—thus salvation is reduced to mere material well-being. Whole knowledge is inseparable from love; it is the human way of attaining perfection, liberation, plenitude.

Modern science has renounced these "lofty goals" and has been content to be able to calculate, foresee, control, and succeed in somehow capturing the behavior of a given problem. In other words, the "problem" does not refer to human comprehension (the essence of something), but rather to a phenomenon that is the object of an empirical observation or logical operation. And all this along with an important restriction: this phenomenon must be repeatable, to such an extent that it becomes a controllable model. A one-off event is not conducive to scientific knowledge. This leads us to the ironic etymological resonance of *cogitare* with *co-agitare*—as they remarked in the Middle Ages. Today, too, thinking is not synonymous with knowing.

At all events, modern science has taken on a word with a thousand years standing, *scientiae*, and has changed, not to say distorted, its meaning. Now then, because of its overwhelming success in the modern world, this means, rather than integrating what is traditional, it replaces it. In any case, not an unusual happening.

Time, for example, is now not seen as "the life of beings," as the Greeks perceived temporal reality; *space* has little to do with the classical Indian *ākāśa*, the fifth element, the bosom of all things (to fall back on an imperfect analogy); the *body*, as *śarīra*, is not, for instance a more or less sophisticated machine brought to life by a soul; what we translate as *life* is not considered to be the individual's private property, as the Greeks knew well, distinguishing *zôê* from *bios*, and we could go on.

In brief, modern science is neither *neutral* nor *universal*.

Modern science is not *neutral*, that is, it is not without a very particular value, to the extent that it cannot become part of any culture without modifying it.

I do not wish now to comment in detail on the ambiguous notion of science as *value-free*, in the sense of disinterested. Modern science could be interpreted as a positive, negative, or ambivalent value, but definitely not as lacking in value. And, to this effect, those who maintain that it is value-free interpret this freedom from whatever "value" as the most positive value of all—as laden with human value.

On the contrary, we could say that modern science possesses enormous value—and also a great power. Nevertheless, this value is not universal, but rather specifically linked to the culture it has been generated by, that which is known as modern culture, which these days involves not only the West and the white race. Modern science embodies the power and creativity of one single and particular culture. It is a powerful cultural phenomenon: the proof inhering (for better or worse) in the fact that it is widespread throughout the world. It is not neutral: it is actually the bearer of a particular cosmology.

Nor is it *universal*. It is not extensive in time (obviously) nor in space, nor history, nor geography.

In reality, one only has to live in any other culture in the modern world to become aware of the fact that there are radically different approaches not only to life and death, but also to matter, time, space, the body, and other fundamental notions, not to mention social and political matters. This is arguably an important factor in explaining the current state of chaotic affairs in many countries: Western civilization, which is imposed upon them through the dominant class, is scarcely natural, not to say unnatural, for them. This leads us to affirm that the introduction of modern science into other cultures can represent a foreign body in their tissue. If these other cultures are not up to absorbing and transforming it, perhaps because it has come upon them so quickly and on such a massive scale, science becomes a Trojan horse that destabilizes the very intimate fiber of the culture into which it has penetrated. This produces a symbolic destruction comparable to cultural genocide. If science is not universal, its universalization not only destroys other cultures' outward way of life, but also their way of thinking and indeed living. At the base of colonialism is faith in the values of one particular culture as apt for the whole of humanity—hence its pretension to universality.

The "justification" that has it that modern (that is, Western) culture is superior, so that its introduction means "progress," is debatable and leads to one of its fundamental characteristics becoming apparent: the specialization and, accordingly, fragmentation of knowing which goes together with the individualistic vision of humanity. The automatic washing machine obviously represents progress compared to washing by hand in cold water, yet it cannot be completely separated from the industrial and economic complex that makes the use of washing machines possible.

The dream that it could be possible to serve two masters and guarantee a pacific cohabitation between a modern scientific ideology and traditional cultures betrays a superficial conception of both traditional cultures and modern science. Cultures are not simply folklore, nor is modern science just pure experimentation or mental lucubration.

It is true that the life of cultures is more resistant and more adaptable than the life of particular individuals. An apparent and briefly lasting success does not prove very much. We have relativized other cosmologies and visions of the world. It is important that we should also relativize—put into perspective—our own predominant cosmology. The emergence of esotericism and fundamentalism in all fields of life should be a warning to us. Nature resists uniformity.

And here is the dilemma: either we believe that the whole history of humanity has a single line of development, such that the scientific breakthroughs of our times resume and replace the wisdom coming from all previous civilizations, or, *on the contrary,* we recognize the fact that the unfolding of human creativity is able to go along lines and take on form that cannot be confined within one single system. Logically, we should mention the third possibility of unequal coexistence, in which "superior" or stronger values supplant the weaker ones—in a more or less violent manner.

In the first case, taking the first view, we should be ready to maintain the opinion that other cultures are fated to disappear and yield their place to "our" scientific culture. We can proceed according to this point of view by avoiding forcing the pace, but also without euphemism or the cultivation of false hopes that a peaceful coexistence or at least marginal existence for the others might be possible.

In taking the second view, we would work toward a healthy pluralism that allows cohabitation and coexistence of civilizations, by accepting that no single culture, religion, or tradition is able to claim the right to represent the range of human experience or the power to reduce the diversity of humanity to just one form, widespread as the latter might be. For this cohabitation to be operative, it is necessary to overcome dialectical thought along with mere rational thinking. In a word, it is necessary to put *metanoia*, the overcoming of *noûs*, into practice, as I have repeatedly said.

In the third instance, we should be conscious of the fact that culture is more than nature. In nature, the law of the jungle prevails, where the stronger devour the weaker. Overcoming this is the challenge of our times—as well as being particularly urgent, as without this *metanoia* humanity will destroy itself. With the dominant anthropology we are returning to the law of the jungle—although the euphemism employed for this is competition.

This task could be fascinating, and this is what I would define as creativity: overcoming the mind's inertia—and that of history. Human freedom is not just the ability every one of us has to take particular decisions chosen from a range of possible ones. It also entails the cosmic power of collaborating in humanity's destiny. This is our responsibility, and perhaps the most formidable human value, both in the East and West. To say it in ancient words, "synergoi tou theou"—(to be) God's coworkers.[61] Unfortunately, when we say "God" we often make him an idol.

We have already made reference to the specificity of modern science. First, the experimental and quantitative *method* entails a very particular vision of (inductive and deductive) *reason*. Its *field* is quite specific too, although these days it tends to extend to other fields of reality. One example is medicine in general and psychoanalysis in particular. The field of science is yet to cover the whole of reality. But we cannot raise barriers between peoples and cultures. The issue is not resolved in an office or in any way artificially. A human problem cannot ignore man.

Science and Parascience

I shall begin with a quote from Rabindranath Tagore: "The greatest error in modern life is to have given so much importance to things that, in reality, do not have it." And this could be completed by adding: "and to have forgotten about the things that really are important."

Once Confucius was asked what he advised should be done in the Southern kingdom, where the situation was going so badly. Confucius replied by saying that the first thing to be done was to return to words their original meaning.

What do we mean when we use the word *science*, and what do we wish to say when we say *parascience*? If we search for a univocal answer, we will arrive at the issue of power: *science*

---

[61] 1 Thess 3:2.

is what scientists know as science and *parascience* is what scientists say is "pseudo-science." Hence, we would have clear concepts as long as we accept that the dominant power defines what should be understood by science and parascience. Accordingly, I propose beginning with an interdisciplinary consideration, followed by intercultural one.

1. Interdisciplinarity and Interculturality

From the *interdisciplinary* point of view, the standard opinion not only represents the interpretation of the present-day dominant culture, but is in any case totally legitimate.

We are in need of criteria to be able to distinguish and keep free from all imitation, approximation, and deformation this not only noble but very complex activity that is science. Hence, it is right and proper that the scientific community should declare itself against any endorsing of non- or antiscientific mystifications.

From the interdisciplinary viewpoint, I would like to underline the fact that very hetero-genic meanings have been grouped together under the umbrella of *parascience,* and point out a symptom that we need to be particularly critical about: the concepts of orthodox and heterodox. These sometimes flourish at a subliminal level, while at other times these are expressed all too explicitly in "scientific" circles. It seems that scientists are the orthodox practitioners and parascientists the heterodox ones. And while we may not want to conduct a witch hunt, we feel responsible for scientific orthodoxy and combat heterodoxy as in olden times, with obviously different procedures, yet with the same *forma mentis.* This then is a historic and slightly ironic observation. To put it in another less historic but still ironic way, what is frequently surprising is scientists' "belief." And when we say "belief," we do not mean fanaticism, just that scientists *believe* in what they are doing. Let us not forget that true faith is always accompanied by skepticism and doubt. Modern science tolerates various opinions, yet it insists upon the approval of dogma, known as fundamental postulates (otherwise, it says, there would be confusion and anarchy) and taking no notice of Confucius's advice.

From the intercultural point of view, we should recognize the fact that Roger Garaudy bluntly affirmed (exaggerating maybe, yet once in a while it is good to hear it said): "The West is an accident." An accidental event. I would say rather that it is an accident in the other sense, a most important, meaningful historical collision that now dominates the world. In any case, each culture is a galaxy, and we cannot transfer criteria from one culture to another: not even the criterion of truth, not even that of goodness. And this implies a *radical relativity* (which, I reiterate, is not relativism) that should be respected.

We should bear in mind that in the intercultural sense, science is not the monopoly of the West, nor can it be equated with a Galilean, Cartesian, or Einsteinian variety of modern science from previous centuries, along with all their well-known predecessors, but can be traced back to antiquity, to Aristotle, Plato, and beyond.

There are other historic and cultural *veins* that we cannot ignore. That would mean subsiding back into the sort of colonialism that believes that the parameters of one single culture can be the judge of the enormous range of human experience. Because of this I have cited Tagore, who, a product of his time and wishing to be condescending, "anglicized" his name Thakur, changing it to Tagore.

Our formulation begins with what is a philological irony from the intercultural point of view. The prefix *para,* in Latin, is related to *pare* and with *ap-par-ent* (the same root as *peer*—an interlocutor of the same class). Hence, *parascience* has taken on the meaning of something similar to science, with the ambivalence of something that resembles science or has the appearance of being scientific without properly being so, and thus having a pejorative sense. *Para,* in Latin, can also mean neighbor to or opposite. *Para* is an originally Indo-European word commonly used in Sanskrit with a precisely opposite meaning. Rather than denoting something that isn't up to the mark, or is a deformation or imitation of something, in Sanskrit it is the surpassing, the perfection of something. Just take a look at common words such as *parabrahman* (supreme spirit), *paramārtha* (ultimate truth), *Parameśthin* (main chief), and so forth. There are around fifty words in which the Sanskrit *para* is (like *meta* sometimes) that which qualitatively surpasses the qualified substantive's parameters. This results in the irony that the word *parascience* could legitimately express not the idea of pre-science or *pseudo*-science, but rather the opposite, something that science has yet to achieve. It would then be this more profound and general, superior knowledge that modern science has not attained, accomplished, or realized.

Science is, as we have said, knowledge. Nevertheless, there are many kinds of knowledge, and modern science (determined as it is by its three characteristics of objectivity, rationality, and dialectics) is one of them. However, such science does not understand all kinds of knowledge: it does not understand artistic or religious knowledge, for instance, or critical knowledge of oneself (not its object). As we have already said, modern science is a quite restricted form of knowledge.

Now it would be necessary to establish the difference between knowledge and rationality. We could consider rationality to be a method that leads us to some kind of rational evidence and knowledge, on the contrary, as awareness or perception of things that are not necessarily rationally intelligible. I employ the expression "awareness" in the same way as the German *Gewahrsein* to distinguish it from *Bewusstsein* or being conscious. There is one kind of awareness of things that responds to the whole criteria of criticism, skepticism, and self-valuation (I'm not talking about verification or falsification, which pertain to other paradigms), yet which cannot be identified with rational intelligibility. That there are parasciences in the sense of pseudo-science is something on which we could all agree. I am talking about something else.

2. Reductionisms

A simple reading of ślokas 5 to 11 of the *yogasūtra* by Patañjali would provide us with a radically different vision of the meaning of knowledge relative to the form we call "scientific," telling us that the word "science," in the sense of *gnôsis*, and even more so, in the sense of *jñāna* (knowledge), cannot be boiled down to just the modern concept of science.

Here is a summary of these ślokas without commenting upon them. There are five mental processes:

- *pramāṇa*: means to acquire rational knowledge; perception, observation, induction and deduction, testimony.
- *viparyaya:* knowledge of error, form, confusion.
- *vikalpa:* creative imagination, knowledge of words, knowledge of nonmaterial things.
- *nidrā:* dreams, experience, inexistence.
- *smṛti:* memory, knowledge of what is absent, remembered tradition.

It would be worth reminding ourselves of the notion of *vijñāna-māyā-kośa* (the veil of knowledge) from the *Vedānta*, which frees us from the risk of confusing reality with any of its veils (*velam entis*, the veil of being, according to Meister Eckhart), including the veiling (*kośa*) of knowledge (*vijñāna*). Parascience would hence be (ironically speaking) the surpassing of all knowledge.

Within the West's intercultural, scientific, and philosophic situation, one should be able to encounter some kind of reference point that would allow us to overcome both seclusion within the fortress of strict science, and the a-critical opening up to "anything goes"; and at the same time provide us with more complete knowledge, free from caricature, of our very own Western tradition. Interculturality is important for this reason. Let me give an example.

If, observing from another continent, we said that Western medicine is a system for making money, we should not be totally in the wrong, yet for an exponent of modern science this would be a caricature. The observation might be true as far as it goes, yet it would certainly not represent what a genuine doctor would say that medicine was about. If we said that alchemy was a system that was limited to changing lead and other minerals into gold, this would be the same kind of caricature as saying that medicine is a certain class's system to line its pockets and retain its power. We should be being ironic about alchemy, too, if we say it is a more or less primitive procedure to produce the philosopher's stone. This would be a distortion, a caricature of what alchemy has been about for centuries.

Alchemy is based on the conviction there is a harmony between matter and man, just as astrology is based on the harmony between microcosm and macrocosm. The false impression given of astrology (and both sides are responsible for this) derives from the identification of astrological connections with causal relationships, as, for instance, the theory that if born under a certain constellation, one's character would inevitably have specific characteristics. This is a distortion and spurious application of causality to a way of thinking that sets out to study the co-relationships between microcosms and macrocosms, yet does not accept efficient causality.

Returning to the example of Western alchemy and astrology, we observe that there are the three characteristics of parascience that are equally to be found in China, India, and other places; I would sum them up by saying that they have to do with the overcoming of a threefold reductionism: anthropocentric, epistemological, and intellectual.

a. *Anthropocentric.* The first characteristic of much parascience is the wish to overcome *anthropocentric reductionism.* Man is *not* alone, nor is man alone in the universe. This fact is somewhat constitutive, so that here solipsistic self-sufficiency is impossible at all levels. God is not alone either. Nor is human thought or human nature the private property of the individual. There is a universal concatenation. Everything is related to everything else, both in heaven and in all concerning matter and man, yet this is not a causal relationship, a deterministic relationship, and nor is it so constant that it could be set down once and for all, as a physical law understood in the modern sense. Physical laws are the laws of *physis*, that is, laws of nature, and nature is alive, as its name indicates, and not just inert matter. Yet there are still other kinds of relationships. To forget about these would lead to isolation and solipsism, not only sociologically, but above all in the intellectual, philosophical, and scientific sense. We are not beings sundered from the planet upon which we move or from the sun from which we receive blessings or hurt, or from the universe from which we proceed. In the first place, it is necessary to overcome anthropocentric reductionism, which leads us to think that, being human, we are sufficient unto ourselves. In fact, self-sufficiency does not work enough even for us to be aware of the reality we live in. Everything has its repercussion on man. This is the basis of the Vedantic *karman*, the *śivaita sarvamsarvātmakam*, the Buddhist *pratītyasamutpāda*, and also the Chinese and Pythagorean cosmovisions—a basis which lasted up until the Renaissance in the West. Nicholas of Cusa in his time was still able to state, concisely, "Quodlibet in quodlibet" (Each thing is in each thing). There is a universal *perichôrêsis*, a co-relationship in one of whose centers Man is to be found, the *maius miraculum*, the greatest of all miracles according to St. Augustine, to Islam, and to the cabalistic and

Christian medieval Renaissances, to name just four sources. Man is certainly a center, that is, one pole of the radical Trinity. There are three poles, where three is not a number (by making it a number, we revert to mere rational interpretation). Overcoming anthropocentrism is not achieved by relying on theocentrism and even less on materialism. It again concerns *perichôrêsis*—which one becomes aware of through the three organs of knowledge: the senses, mind, and spirit (sensibility, reason, and faith). It is difficult to live a fully human life with only that which is on sale in the supermarket—including the cultural one.

    b. *Epistemological.* The *second reductionism* that parascience seeks to overcome is *epistemological reduction*—that is, the reduction of knowledge to rational intelligibility. First, parascience does not limit itself to a more or less verifiable rational science, but seeks to introduce other phenomena, those that slip through the net of rational intelligence, into the field of human knowledge.

The field of knowledge is far more extensive than the field of science. This is a challenge for parascience (in the noble sense of the word), which leads to overcoming the epistemological dichotomy, that is, to the indissoluble nature of the object/subject binomial. Every object and all objectivity are object and objectivity for a subject. The very concepts of objectivity and subjectivity are intrinsically connected. There would be no objectivity if it were not for subjectivity. Whether subjectivity arises from the individual or from the group or the Zeitgeist (spirit of the time), we leave for philosophers to debate. I shall just say that there is no epistemology that is not based upon ontology, and that scientific epistemology stems from a very specific cosmology, however widespread and however convincing it might seem to us. This is the power of *mythos*—the *mythos* of a scientific worldview, in this case.

I am resuming what I was saying earlier. Faith is a conscious experience, hence it is also knowledge, yet it is knowledge that has no object, it is not objective, without this meaning that it is merely subjective. The object of faith is not naked faith, but belief: the intellectual interpretation of the act of faith. The confusion between faith and belief has been the basis of many historic misunderstandings of primary importance. Faith is not apodictic knowledge.[62] Faith is not knowledge of an objective truth; it is more like awareness of nonsubjective vacuity. It is the opening onto that which is invisible.[63]

    c. *Rational.* The *third reductionism* is what I call *rational reductionism*, for the lack of a better expression. Knowledge is not only epistemological; neither is it solely rational. But man is not knowledge alone. Mystics talk about a touch that is neither perceptible nor intellectual, yet about which there is a certain mode of knowledge, something we can talk or babble about: "Un no sé qué que quedan balbuciendo" (something or other, which they babble on about) (St. John of the Cross), "the cloud of unknowing" of the Anglo-Saxon mystic, the "*docta ignorantia*" of Nicholas of Cusa or of the Areopagite, the "blessed ones who have attained infinite ignorance [*agnôsia*]" of Evagrius Ponticus and Maximus the Confessor—not to mention countless Oriental sources. Is it possible to talk about this? If by talking we mean comprehending (*intellegere*) what is said, it certainly is not, yet if the word goes beyond its rationality, it certainly is: it is talked about and it is understood as not being nonsense.[64] I cannot understand a statement I do not comprehend, yet I can be aware of the fact that I do not understand it. Words (*śabda, vāc, dabar, logos*)

---

[62] Mic 9:24.
[63] Heb 11:1.
[64] The actual evolution of the verb *intellegere* (from *-lego, legere*, collect) is significant, from discernment, care, preoccupation, interest, and also love, it has come to mean rational intelligibility.

go beyond their intelligibility, and we are conscious of this fact. It is this consciousness (the lack of rationality) that distinguishes this conscious ignorance from madness. We have already mentioned that knowing is an ontical act and not only an epistemological one, that knowing something means becoming the object that is known and that the consciousness of this union is important yet secondary. "Lord, when have we seen thee hungry, thirsty, naked?"[65] Or as an *Upaniṣad* states, "Unknown [*avijñātam*] for those who know, known [*vijñātam*] for those who do not know."[66] Parascience is conscious of the fact that it would be reductionism to exclude this kind of consciousness—which at this moment we cannot digress further upon.

3. *Parascience*

Parascience, taken in its better sense, does not seek to be solely objective, much less subjective, which is not easy to accept in "our" technocratic civilization that has set up a dichotomy between what is objective and what is subjective. Paracelsus, the humanist and physician, speaks to us, just as do all genuine representatives of parascience, of the purification of the heart as an indispensable condition to obtain true knowledge. We have believed to such an extent in the object/subject dichotomy that we consider the purity of intentions of one's life to be one thing and objective knowledge (investigation) another. Parascience seeks to bridge this gap. In alchemy, for instance, it is said that if we do not overcome the dualism between object and subject, what is proposed with alchemical activity (which consists of man's collaboration in enabling the universe to fulfill its aim) will never be achieved. According to Paracelsus and many others, God left the universe incomplete so that man could complete it. Therefore, the universe's perfection is entrusted to man's historico-cosmic function, so that history, knowledge, and activity become three factors of the same reality.

In the earliest text on alchemy translated into Latin from Arabic, there is a dialogue between the Moorish king Khalid and a certain wise man by the name of Morieno (which could be Mariano and, as such, Christian): "Is there a material that is germane to alchemical activity? What material ought we to use?" asked the king of the wise man. "That which is within you and always in yourselves," was his answer.

We cannot be separated from ourselves during scientific or parascientific activity. There is an existential lie in which our existence is not authentic, true, and transparent. Pureness of heart is not just a moral commandment, but also a requirement of knowledge and of Being. Without a pure heart, authentic science cannot be realized, if the word is to mean more than simple logical calculation. It is not enough to say that science is just a specialization and that not everything is reducible to science, nor that modern science can be identified with science in general. Yet we can say that science is a specifically human activity (and not just something man shares with other species), and we cannot alienate it from the "humanity" of man.

For some time now, we have been saying that we are in the dawning of a new age, and that, as such, we cannot continue to use patches and poultices to resolve the problems of humankind and the Earth.[67] Parascience may well be of aid to us, if not as a model, then at least as a stimulus.

From the philosophical viewpoint, this represents the weak spot of Parmenides's scheme, which identifies thinking with being and that for more than two-and-a-half millennia has been the compulsory reference point of the Indo-European world. Thus reality is destined

---

[65] Matt 25:35–36.
[66] *KenU* II.3.
[67] See Rosenberg (1971; 1984).

to be the slave of thought. We have even constrained God to obey logical laws, and we have made him stick to them. The most that so-called believers have conceded to this watchmaker engineer God is that, from time to time he "suspends" his physical laws, for instance, in the case of miracles.

It is somewhat childish to want to save faith in God by turning him into a great mathematical Spirit. The totem pole would then be mathematics, with the difference that totems are symbols, whereas mathematics is science. The parallelism, however, points to the same mentality.

St. Peter Damian (an unpopular philosopher for political as well as other reasons) clearly expresses this concept when saying, *de potentia Dei absoluta*, God could have not only avoided the destruction of Jerusalem at the hands of the Romans or captivity in Babylon, but rather the *already* accomplished historical act would never have happened.

To put it another way, for the universe to function it should not have to comply with any of the laws that some claim to know. Perhaps the very nature of the universe does not allow itself to be imprisoned by any kind of law. We should indeed apply ourselves to the principle of noncontradiction to be able to *think* properly, yet reality is not obliged to obey thought. This attitude might turn out to be very dangerous if we apply it to ourselves and to our *thinking,* but reality retains a degree of freedom of which we can only be aware. Reality is free and, therefore, inscrutable to the mind. Because of this, true knowledge is not only adaptation (of the mind to reality), but rather identification (of both). That is why, as we have said, pureness of the heart is not an epistemological requisite, but rather an ontic and ontological demand. Knowledge is something more than the activity of an abstract mind or of an epistemological act. Only the pure in heart will see . . . God, reality, the truth that alone can "set us free"[68] if this very truth is free of the constriction of logical thought, without this signifying anarchy.

This is the great challenge of our times.[69] It is not by chance that man refuses to be labeled by any kind of law. The so-called freedom of the children of God is not a moral freedom, but pertains to very being itself when it is pure. The principle of noncontradiction is a principle that refers to speech and, as such, also logical thinking, but not (necessarily) to reality. I put "necessarily" in parentheses as there is an ontological necessity that governs human logic, but that cannot be extrapolated from reality.

Perhaps we have not truly realized that living humanly upon the Earth does not mean conforming to moral, physical, or religious laws of any kind. "Those who are born of the Spirit [which is the Spirit of Truth and Freedom] do not know from whence they come nor whither they go."[70] Man is not a machine. If the principle of replicability is not a criterion of the reality of a phenomenon, perhaps it will not be a criterion of its intelligibility either. In human life an unrepeatable event, a look, a smile, an intuition, a suspicion, all have a value that does not become imprisoned in repeatability. This means, if we reduce knowledge to what can be repeated, and to that which can be formulated with laws, the result is impoverishment. All this constitutes a revolution we are still not ready to live: Nevertheless, I do believe that we should begin to consciously experience freedom—which of course is not anarchy. And this is our great hope: that as with all scientific discoveries, it is when faced with the impossible that light breaks through and changes happen.

---

[68] Jn 8:32.

[69] See Schestow (1944) for the description of a similar problematic to the one cited here, although in a different context.

[70] John 3:8.

All that we have said in this chapter does not contradict previous comments on science's wonderment on discovering that, to an extent, the harmony of reality is not anarchy nor is it irrational *anomie*. The Spirit of God, to metaphorically cite Genesis, moved upon the face of the waters.[71] Freedom belongs to the Spirit and is above creatureliness.

Science and Knowledge

Science is not man in full, yet neither is knowledge. Moreover, man himself is not the whole of reality. What is more, science and knowledge both have a natural tendency to embrace the whole of reality: man is a *mikrokosmos* and a *mikrotheos*. Stated in more academic fashion, this is the *pars pro toto* syndrome or the intrinsic correlation between the microcosm and macrocosm. Stated politically, the temptation toward totalitarianism forms part of human nature. The word presently in vogue is no longer imperialism, colonialism, or something similar, it is now globalization. Human wisdom, nevertheless, also consists in resisting this temptation without destroying its natural roots. Science and knowledge have an aspiration toward wholeness, to all, to God, theophysicists would say—yet not to an exclusively transcendent, nor rigidly monotheist God, as we have already pointed out.

The individual is not all, obviously, nor does consciousness reach to the limits of the universe, nor does science have the pretension of being able to examine all that is knowable. However, there is a *plus ultra* instinct in the human being that cannot be stifled. This is what was meant by the affirmation that man is the image of Divinity. "Not man for the stars [*propter stellas*], but rather the stars have been made for man," as St. Gregory the Great said in a polemic manner; St. Thomas echoed him when stating that "the wise man [*sapiens homo*] dominates even the stars."

To the modern ear, used to the analytical language of contemporary science, these phrases seem grandiloquent and verging on the magical. We have cited them as they give the opportunity to underline the difference between (modern) science and (traditional) knowledge. Knowledge is participative. Man knows when he *participates* humanly, that is, consciously, in the dynamism of reality, when he takes part in the Intelligence or in the Word, as stated in the *Vedas* and repeated in the Gospels, not far from the Aristotelian intuition regarding the *psyché* that, in a certain manner, is everything. Man, on the other hand, knows *scientifically* when he explains the behavior of phenomena. Knowledge is metaphysical, science is epistemological. Science provides us with information on phenomena; knowledge, although at very diverse levels, makes us participate in the essence of things.

A priori limits cannot be set on science or knowledge, yet one should and can say that they still have not reached their limits, even if there is an essential difference between the two. Knowledge is a human invariant. All human beings know themselves, although to different degrees; they know others, the cosmos they form part of and also their limits, as well as their ignorance. They are aware that "Rationalibiter comprehendit incomprehensibile esse" (It is reasonably understood that there is something incomprehensible), to use a phrase of St. Anselm; that is, it is known that all is not known, that the incomprehensible also exists, and this consciousness brings about the awareness of the existence of Mystery. Or, to put it in another way, the World, Man, and God are known, if imperfectly: the cosmotheandrical reality. Modern science is also knowledge that, because of its power, sometimes becomes a synonym for absolute knowledge. All knowledge worthy of the name, scientists say, should aspire to become "scientific" knowledge. We do not wish at this moment to offer a critique

---

[71] Gen 1:2.

of this opinion, which at a given time became popular and which is still dangerous for its reductionism, although now on the wane.

We should like, on the other hand, to underline three aspects of human knowledge that to us seem to be vitally important to humanity.

1. The Contemplative Attitude

Contemplation is not (inductive or deductive) reasoning, but rather the more feminine attitude of total openness to reality, without any preconceptions and interferences. *Meleta to pân* (Cultivate the whole): this was the maxim of Periandros of Corinth, one of the Seven Sages of Greece, who lived at least six centuries before Christ. This advice takes for granted, however, that one of the first steps toward cultivating the whole consists in overcoming one's own individuality and reacquiring the sense of the person. Man is not an individual, but a person; that is, one knot in the infinite web of relationships. The isolated individual, therefore, is no more than an exclusively formal abstraction, inexistent in reality. The individual only exists in the abstract mind. I certainly exist, yet only in relationships with everyone else, with the World and the Infinite. Only by surpassing the individual can one establish empathy, a relation, a love, and also acquire consciousness, not of all things but rather of a whole—in a way that is not closed in on itself. One then becomes conscious of the solidarity, of the web that unites us to the whole of reality, to the divine, to the material, and to the spiritual. If my thought alienates me, separates me, it is not authentic thought, but rather calculus, abstraction.

Forgetfulness of the contemplative dimension has led the West into the temptation of wishing to "prove" God's existence and objectivize and thus rationalize him—with the fine pretext of believing in him. I am aware of the fact that the words I am using (God, dimension, contemplative, mystic, holistic . . .) have connotations that may not do justice to what I am seeking to get across. One cannot think God, since God is not an object, but rather a pole of a relationship of which we form a part. This is the Trinity. I can be conscious of this mystery, which I can call God or use some other word. Buddhists do not have need of this word, nor of the hypothesis. Nevertheless, they are conscious of the mystery, of the unknowable, and perhaps they broaden the meaning of thinking. Let me not be misunderstood. I am not saying that all cultures believe in God, yet I am stating that there are homeomorphic equivalents: third-degree analogies that perform equivalent functions in each culture to provide a specific image of reality.

The strength of symbolic thinking needs to be brought back instead of limiting ourselves to thinking concepts and, because of this, being obliged to "thinking" only *with* concepts, combining their compatibility in accordance with logical laws—and even worse if concepts are translated into algebraic signs, however useful they might be in certain rational operations. To discover the reality that symbolic thinking reveals to us is a route that scientific culture still has to travel. Distinction without separation in this double form of thinking is important if we would redress the contemporary situation. We are coming to one of the most important moments in modern science's trajectory, as it is beginning to discover its own limits. We are far from the naïve optimism of Marcelin Berthelot, the famous chemist who in 1884 could proclaim that, thanks to scientific progress, there were no longer any mysteries in the world.

The word "contemplation" is not adequate if it is taken exclusively to mean immersion in a state of introversion. It was Cicero who translated the Greek word *theoreia* as contemplation, uniting the cognitive aspect with the capacity of man to act upon reality.

There are three ways to become open to reality, as we have already said: the empirical knowledge of the senses, intellectual knowledge, and mystic intuition, the latter being a word that has become so contaminated that it can no longer convey what in fact it means.

It refers to a third kind of more holistic, more loving, and more immediate consciousness, that is, experiential, yet not permitting conceptualization. Given that the whole is not the sum of the parts, one does not reach it by analyzing its parts and then adding them together, but rather through a complete experience that includes all three eyes, that is, the senses, the intellect and that other sense, to which we have given the name mysticism—and that in phenomenological terms could be termed faith. But in all real knowledge the three eyes (the three organs of knowledge) act together. The fragmentation of knowing has led to the fragmentation of human life. It is important to regain the sense of wholeness, yet not a closed wholeness, but rather a complete one—where there is no need to understand it in its pejorative sense. Language betrays us, but we can be conscious of this betrayal.

Let us say it again: man is not exiled on this earth and condemned to not knowing the whole, that is, reality. We are not talking, however, about scientific knowledge. The *tò pân* of pre-Socratic philosophy is neither analytic nor rational knowledge. It is the knowledge of the third eye, which Christian tradition (the Vittorinos, for instance) has called *oculus fidei*, the eye of faith, obviously not of the "truth of faith," but rather of a third dimension of reality that could be named in many different ways: Self, Mystery, the meaning of life, God, and so on. For this knowledge to be real and, as such, true knowledge, it cannot be separated from the other two eyes (the senses and reason). This is the contemplative attitude. One then understands why it is the path toward freedom and happiness.[72]

2. The Experience of Time

Kairon gnôthi (Know the moment). This was said by Pittacus of Mytilene, another of the Seven Sages. The *kairos* is not linear, homogeneous time that cannot be stopped. "Be conscious of the moment," it could be translated perhaps, without forgetting that each moment is unique.

Man does not live *in* time as if following a path. Man *is* time. Everyone is *his own* time, time that is qualitatively different from that of anyone else. Here we come to one of the myths of modern science, which would have us think that time is an exclusively quantifiable variant like space—which it is not. There is much more to it. Conceptual knowledge of time is not real time. I can certainly experience the passage of my life, yet this is neither knowing the *kairos* nor myself. Every life is unique, nontransferable, not reducible to conceptual and thus abstract knowledge; science, on the other hand, is abstract knowledge. Nonverifiable, unrepeatable, immediate knowledge that cannot have a demonstrable claim to truth does not pertain to the field of science. And yet the most important treasure of our lives, as we have said, is to be found in unrepeatable, nonreplicable moments. We only really live in the present. Also, when we speak of the past or future we speak of them in the present. We should remember that the present is not solely a moment of time; it is the moment lived in its totality, which I have named *tempiternal*, since while being temporal it is charged with eternity.

Time is the life of each and every thing, not the unfolding of events against a uniform and common background. This backdrop is an abstraction, a mental hypothesis. As we are time, our time is not a commodity, although these days it is frequently reduced to this.

One of the most difficult and profound challenges of interculturality is recovering the experience of time—not as something that is up for sale, a highway, or something that oscillates back and forth, but rather as *tempiternity*. Eternity and time in themselves do not exist; what does exist is tempiternity, which opens up to our consciousness the experience

---

[72] See Schestow (1994) for the description of a similar problematic to what we have shown, although in a different context.

of each moment's unique value. This is what the Buddhist theory of the atomicity of time teaches us, but also a beautiful psalm does so: "Miserere mei, Domine, quia sum pauper et unicus"[73] (Have mercy, Lord, for I am poor and unique). Each one of us is irreplaceable. This sense of uniqueness is a call to dignity, to responsibility, to the knowledge of one's own value. Every human being is unique and, therefore, incomparable, unclassifiable. My *karman* cannot be repeated as long as it is mine. Science's time is measurable—and, as such, it has to be homogeneous.

The Big Bang theory, for instance, as I have previously said, presupposes a quantifiable and constant time, which in turn requires the (gratuitous) hypothesis of universal constants—otherwise the physico-mathematics cannot not work. We cannot confuse the measurement of time with the experience of time. This latter is personal and not objective, nor can it be made objective.

The knowledge of time (*kairos*) is equivalent to self-knowledge, as tradition also says, and this knowledge opens us up to the knowledge of God (Plato) and of all things (Muhammad). Obviously, it is not an individualized knowledge, but rather that participation that we mentioned earlier and, as a consequence, knowledge of all, as in reality everything is connected; this leads us to our next point.

3. *The Thirst for Authenticity*

Esthe su (Be yourself). The Platonic invitation to *be ourselves* speaks to us of man's yearning to realize the Self. The last line in Plato's last letter (addressed to Dionysius II of Syracuse) says, "Ho auto isthi" (Be yourself). The "fall" begins when this *autos*, this Self, is identified with an ego separated from all (egocentrism). One almost universal principle of the traditions of humanity tells us that within man there is a natural aspiration toward wholeness, in which happiness is found. However, Man is a complex being and searches for this plenitude in sundry places: in science, in knowledge, in others, in love, in the *ātman* as an individual or as Brahman (God), and more.

Science arises in the final analysis from this desire that tempted Eve in Paradise, that of wanting to be *as* God, perhaps to accelerate the process or to be content with being *as* God and not fully divine—as we are told by the nondual wisdom of the *advaita* or the Trinity. In this sense, even if modern science has renounced such ideals, the impulse that moves the best of scientists to continual research is the desire for Truth and Beauty.

In summary: Man thirsts for Science and Knowledge. Neither of them are solipsistic values. Reality is relationality—*advaita*, trinity. Let us return to another Greek sage's wisdom (while qualifying it)—Heraclitus of Ephesus: The whole is dynamic. Infinity is infinite because it can never be reached. Science and knowledge are truly themselves when they communicate this sense of the provisional, of infinity, of divinity: "The sun is new each day." Reality is rhythm, and we are in it.

This infinity, for the very reason that it has no limits, can have no criteria outside itself. Physicists, from the Greeks until the dawn of modern science, following Plato, believed that the orbits of planets were circular precisely because, in the absence of any proof to the contrary, the circle was thought the most perfect geometrical figure, hence, the most beautiful and, consequently, the most convincing.

To be authentic, as the word suggests, means being fully *autos*, that is, the Self. The description Yahweh gives of himself in the Bible is no different: "I am that I am." All of us are called to this authenticity, as we have pointed out. When both science and knowledge

---

[73] Ps 24:16.

are authentic, they are moved by this aspiration—and not by the desire for power or fame. There is no ulterior motive in authentic scientific or philosophic research nor, at bottom, the human impulse toward plenitude. All beings have this natural inclination toward God, as nearly all traditions of humanity say in one way or another. For too long we have accepted the primacy of teleology—whose justification comes in its penultimate field. Man thirsts for infinity, or rather, man's thirst is unquenchable, yet this thirst is not the fruit of the will; it is very different from desire, which has to be overcome, as Buddhism and also the Gospels state.[74]

Ultimate actions, such as real love, are produced without asking *why*, without a final cause, as it says in the *Bhagavad-gītā*. Love has no "perchene," stated the Italian mystics. All traditions accentuate purity of heart as a condition to attaining happiness and inner peace.

Epilogue

The common thread throughout these pages has not been an analytical review. Despite any impression of dispersion, of following many sidetracks and detours in the process of our exposition, there is an inner coherence here that is not syncretism. The *advaita* intuition is not the synthesis between dialectic systems, nor between monism and dualism; it is the holistic vision that goes beyond logical thought. Upon the basis of some specific issues we have sought to recover the *harmony* between human beings' many different activities, but without thereby destroying *ontonomy*. Pluralism is one thing, belonging to human nature, and another is the *anomie* of an anarchic world, as we have already said.

In spite of its aspect of conciliation between different branches of knowledge, the subliminal message of this book goes further. Starting with the latent conflict between modern science and a "religious" vision of the world, it is not insensible to the current human condition of our times. We find ourselves at a crucial moment in history. We cannot go back in time, and if we continue in the same direction as we are going, it will lead us to a catastrophe of planetary proportions. Man is truly a mortal being, and there is no need to fear death. Cultures are also perishable, yet their death is neither sudden nor total. Life does not die, the *Vedas* state, but rather it is transformed; and the transformation of a culture is in the hands of those who are not content with negative criticism alone, however important it may be, but who are searching for a true metamorphosis, even though the price they have to pay could be their lives. Human life is not automatic; it is free. Our responsibility derives from this. Perhaps technology has made us believe that without any effort we can live a fully human life. These issues are not unrelated to our problem.

From this study's metahistorical perspective we can state that both modern Science and traditional Philosophy are mortal values, but death is not absolute. Man, whose nature is not exclusively cultural, outlives culture, although he himself is transformed. This transformation supposes the beginning of a new culture. Cultural rhythms are not, however, biological.

The dominant culture of our times is telling us in the language of ecology that we cannot go on like that, yet the ecological problem cannot be solved while leaving technoscience intact. And this is not possible without calling modern science, which supports it, into question. The correlations are intimate, but this science is possible only within a cosmology that makes it plausible—monotheism and all. Theology is also in crisis. This crisis affects the West, but also all the other cultures and religions in the world. The door of knowledge is becoming increasingly narrow, despite the splendid windows of scientific "knowledge."

---

[74] Matt 16:25ff.

In other words, the problem of modern science cannot be dealt with by extricating ourselves from its underlying cosmology. The true problem is modernity's worldview. On the other hand, modernity cannot be "demonized" because it has produced negative results. This is a much more complex issue. As we have shown in this book and in other places, it means entering another *mythos*—a *mythos* that is slowly yet spontaneously coming into being everywhere. These pages seek to serve as a catalyst.

Thus, it is not a case of breaking down the doors of knowledge that man has been accumulating over the centuries, nor of resorting to purely ethical reforms, such as seeking the right use of technology, for example. What we need is a new cosmology that involves the very conception of what is Divine: a cosmotheandrical *metanoia* is needed.

Contemporary science is beginning to feel this necessity because man is the subject of scientific activity. An example would be useful here. The so-called string theory from the eighties, which was intended to resolve the wave-particle dilemma and the issue of nature's four elemental forces, did not come up with the hoped-for results; yet the "superstring theory" of more recent years has shown (but not proved) that when it is believed one has resolved one question, other new unresolved problems spring up. For instance, when science accepted the theory of "black holes" (into which energy, and, hence, all types of information seem to disappear), Hawking found exceptions. The determinism and coherence, without which rationality enters into crisis, do not appear as criteria for absolute truth. Physicists trust that, *in the future*, an answer will be found to the exceptions, but meanwhile we have to be contented with provisionality. In other words, contemporary physics is again seen to be unable to avoid mystery. This is also of use as a remedy for another kind of dogmatism, the religious kind, which has frequently given the impression that theology could offer all the answers. Symbiosis is necessary and healthy.

In other words, despite the conventional heading of this "epilogue," there is no *epi-logos*, no "last word." Contingency is constitutive, but mankind is becoming aware, and this is precisely where its dignity resides. Mystery is not life, but rather inheres in the consciousness man has of it.

As such, it would have been presumptuous, not to say premature, as we observed in the preface, to confront the problem in all its complexity. *Faith* is the basis of that which does not appear,[75] yet reason saves us from fanaticism and our senses reveal our contingence to us. We have simply skipped our way through some specific issues that illustrate a more general problem. Provisionality forms part of the human condition. All fanaticism is suspect.

What we have said does not seek to be a solely negative criticism of the current situation, but rather to underline the importance of anthropological change for contemporary humanity. Not everyone shares our way of thinking, and one vision or policy should not be imposed, but rather be open to dialogue. The door of knowledge is narrow, not closed, and we should open it up together.

---

[75] Heb 11:1.

4

THE AMBIGUITY OF SCIENCE

In one of the "novenaries" in which I usually gather my reflections on various subjects, I speak of the need to discover the limits of science, which has been extrapolated from the scientific field and has spread like a cancer in the mentality of modern Man, both Eastern and Western.[1] Science is no longer the monopoly of Europe and the West. In India there are more than two million scientists, one million of whom are dedicated to the army (for the national defense), like 55 percent of all the world's scientists anyway.

Relativizing Science

What can we do with science? First of all, not worship it as if it were the golden calf. Second, avoid its allure.

Third, get over what science has wanted us to believe, that is, that it offers the explanation of reality—something that true scientists have never wanted to do. As there is a cosmological vacuum in the civilization where science has prospered, scientific explanations have been converted into cosmological explanations. Seen from a certain perspective, the theory of the "Big Bang," for example, is of such an extraordinary naivety that, if one did not think that the world currently has almost three million soldiers and the madness of arms race exists, one would be inclined to believe that this thing is not possible among "wise men" (*Homo sapiens*).

Fourth, go beyond the justification of the "favorite child" of science, technology, which makes us believe, thanks to propaganda, that it is indispensable for our lives, so that without allotropic medicine, without antibiotics (which ironically means "anti-life"), without everything that the scientific mentality has introduced, Man would die of hunger and disease. This is simply false.

Fifth, and most important as it is also the most obvious, discover the internal limits of science. Contemporary science, for example, that of Sheldrake, Capra, Prigogine, or David Bohm—which I would like to distinguish from modern science—is no longer, and significantly so, the science of causality, nor the science that seeks to explain everything with mathematical paradigms; it is a wholly diverse conception, arising from an internal crisis of science, where probability itself is in the dock. Science perhaps, from this point of view, is itself reaching its own limits, and this is a very important moment. In a few days I will attend a conference on "Science and Spirituality," where, together with the names I have already mentioned and other people, we will discuss this theme. It cannot be denied that in the last three hundred years the most important part of the globe has lived with this belief, and if we seek respect for Pygmies, we can also respect countries that believe they are overdeveloped because they

---

[1] A talk published as "Ambiguità della scienza," *L'Altrapagina* (Città di Castello) (1992).

have a scientific mentality, but they should be treated with the same methods, that is to say, they should be relativized. Science itself is beginning to discover its own limits.

The most immediate consequence would be a complete review of the form of primary and secondary school education in all those countries in which Science has a pride of place that truly kills creativity and spontaneity, and prevents the joy and real education of young people. This brings to mind Gandhi's affirmation, which maintains that the only way to develop intelligence is the exercise of craftsmanship and the use of one's own hands. We could thus overcome that sort of Western fatalism that believes we cannot do without the technical-scientific corporation. The longer-term consequence is what I have called "emancipation from technology."

Technique and Technology

I distinguish between *technê* and technology, between the first-degree machine and the second-degree machine. *Technê*, which we can translate with "technique" but which could be translated with "art," is the heritage of all cultures. All cultures have *technê*, that is, a certain manipulation of matter and the material world, and also of the nonmaterial word, for human well-being—a certain practice of art, articulating things and using all possibilities inherent in nature for the people's well-being. *Technê* is not only the hammer or sails but it is all that which uses primary forms of energy. With this *technê* the first-degree machine, the tool, can be made. This tool is good or bad depending on the use I make of it; the pen or the hammer is good or bad according to its use, so it is ambivalent.

This does not occur with the second-degree machine, with what I would call "technology." It is only our mind's inertia that prevents us from seeing this phenomenon clearly.

And it is no coincidence that development has occurred principally within European civilization. Within the Chinese civilization, for example, there was a moment, in the fourteenth century, of extraordinary momentum, when people became acutely aware of the need for a breakthrough, in order not to arrive at the atomic bomb and therefore the destruction of the world. In the West, on the other hand, we got there without interruption, so that we do not even have a word to explain what is not a cultural universal, not *technê*, not patrimony of all peoples, but technology. Technology leads to technocracy: the *kratos*, power, resides in this way of using the second-degree machine. The second-degree machine is made not naturally, but using first-degree machines that permit the transformation of forms of energy and the realization of acceleration. I am thinking of the atomic accelerators at CERN, for example. The second-degree machine not only conditions our habits, but even compels us, otherwise we will go bankrupt. Thus, our lifestyle changes, our lives change, our way of thinking changes.

This is a rapid analysis of the first-degree machine and of this second-degree tool, which have different laws and different accelerations: let us not forget this law (which we all now know), that a quantitative change also generates a qualitative change. This is why I repudiate that modern technology is neutral and universal. *Technê* is governed by the spirit; you must be "inspired" and then you will find everything, even joy, and then you do not have any need or wish to be paid, because what fulfills you is not even monetizable. Thus begins a process of demonetization of culture that I would like to examine more deeply. Instead, in technology, ratio has substituted *technê* and so . . . Châteauneuf-du-Pape![2] There are five thousand reasons to abandon the production of wine from the "Castelli" near Rome, the "Frascati." Nowadays

---

[2] A vintage French wine. [*Editorial note*]

you either produce five million bottles or it is not possible, it is not profitable: this is the quantitative change one is compelled to make, otherwise one can do nothing. And we begin to have another conception of life . . . and, evidently, also another wine.

Going beyond Scientific Knowledge

I do not mean to demonize science nor even technology. I have specified enough what we must not do with science, but perhaps I have not sufficiently developed what we can do. I have spoken of emancipation from technology, of reducing science to its limits, and third, which I did not elaborate enough, of going beyond modern science, since in contemporary science there are enormously positive starting points for this surmounting. However—and this is what my debate focuses on with, for example, Prigogine, the Nobel Prize winner for Physics with whom I have debated several times—I do not agree with him about reducing everything to science, although he enormously opens the limits, the boundaries, and the conception of this science. Modern science, including contemporary science so far, is linked to measurements and excludes unique events: a unique event is not a subject for science. But for me, and perhaps for human life, unique and unrepeatable events are the most important and decisive ones—and yet they are not a subject for science.

Science consists in understanding, in knowing. I have analyzed this attitude at length and shown that the word "understand" or the word "know" can have two meanings: the meaning that modern science uses and the sense in which other traditions, including Western tradition, has used it. If "science" after Bacon (it is he who states that "knowledge is power") means being able not only to control but to know the behavior of phenomena, for me this understanding or knowing is not how the majority of humanity, including the West, interpreted these words. There is a very specialized, very abridged form of "understanding and knowing," which is calculating, forecasting, having a certain knowledge of regular behaviors and also of chaotic situations (of "chaos" in the physical sense of the word), which leads us to great trust and a great result: the science of the "positive."

I spent seven years doing nothing but science. Science is a fascinating human activity, not only for the rigor and the method that are required in scientific research, but also for all the effort of finding and extricating the behaviors and the mysteries of Nature, albeit doing violence to "her." Science uses the greatest things human beings have done: it would be absolutely contrary to my opinion to want to say anything negative about science in this sense. But science has extrapolated in an unscientific manner, wanting to become cosmology and wanting to supplant all other forms of knowledge. It may be that this has occurred not as a consequence of science but through the fault of theologians, who practiced a completely absurd, narrow-minded theology, but this is not the point at issue. The responsibility is that of Bellarmine, if you like, and all the theology of his time, but this is another matter. It is precisely the wish to have a scientific discussion carried out scientifically that leads me to say what I am trying to say. But I absolutely do not want to give the impression of demonizing science, or not recognizing that science has done anything positive.

I would like to be wary of the desire to turn back to the prescientific and a-critical age, to the romanticism of villages and the simple life—not only because we cannot turn back, which is in itself a tautology, but because I think that the scientific phenomenon in this sense is an . . . I was going to say essential, but I would say existential contribution that cannot be removed from the blossoming of human life. But, as often happens in people's spiritual life, what was a great means for many positive realizations can at a certain moment become an obstacle.

This, in my opinion, is the situation in which modern science finds itself today, not to mention now the relationship of science with technology, which appears to have a different attitude, although technology is a hybrid, and nowadays modern science cannot be practiced without profit, and so on, but this is a wholly different topic.

The Ambiguous Relationship
between Science and Cosmology

The relationship between science and cosmology should also be studied much more in depth. My thesis, synthetically expressed, is that science offers us an element, a parameter for cosmology that we need, but the two things cannot be identified with each other, and we cannot have a cosmology that is exclusively the fruit of scientific research. For this reason, I have a bone to pick with scientists who want to make a cosmology of science. Stephen Hawking's best-seller, *A Brief History of Time*, is the clearest example of this.

At this point we need to exercise a double criticism. One refers to the a-scientific extrapolation to pass from scientific knowledge to cosmological intuitions. I think that modern science does not give us a vision of the world and does not want to give us one, but it is we who, unable to live without cosmology, take the only thing we have at hand, that is, all the imposing scientific construct, and make a cosmology of it. It seems that this is what is happening.

My second criticism regards the epistemological foundations of science. Before embarking on the topic, I would like to make an observation of a sociological nature. As I have also lived in purely scientific environments, where I worked passionately on mesons with Yukawa, and on photosynthesis, I realized that in certain circles taboos always exist. A taboo for seminaries in the past was sex; in seminaries sex was not spoken about. Among psychoanalysts another taboo, which we tried to break down with some friends, is talking about God: one does not speak of God. In many circles it is not possible to criticize science because "science is universal and neutral; 2 and 2 makes 4 everywhere." I even contest the fact that 2 and 2 makes 4 everywhere: it only happens where the 2 and the 4 do not mean anything. But this is not the point.

I think, however, that taboos are still operating, although I believe that scientists, from the sociological point of view, are among the most intelligent people in society.

I do not, however, want to criticize either scientism or techno-science. My criticism—in the technical sense of the word—is epistemological, focusing on the epistemological foundations of science as knowledge. I am speaking of post-Galilean modern science, of science that mathematicizes, which in order to express anything needs recurring parameters, which are quantitative and, in a certain way, comprehensible, although not immediately intelligible, as happens in the calculus of probability, non-Euclidean geometry, or matrices, which have opened up to science extraordinarily profound and fecund fields. So, my speech is strictly philosophical and limits itself to identifying the limits of modern science as knowledge of reality.

The Internal Limits of Scientific Knowledge

Science must proceed by abstractions, which is obvious. And my criticism is that science uses not only a first abstraction, but a second, a third, a fourth: that is, in any problem we must extract sub-problems and find sub-systems. Physical chemistry is a classic example, but nowadays macrobiology and microbiology are also beginning to do it. We can in a certain way find out the behavior of these sub-systems and deduce the rules that permit it.

I maintain two things: first, that even if we could find all the internal regularities and the behaviors of all the sub-systems or sub-sub-systems, these or their integration still would not give us the behavior of the system. And today both in meteorology and in Prigogine's "field problem," in the systems of disorder, even in science itself, the point has been reached of accepting that the recognition of sub-systems and the integral of sub-systems does not lead to knowledge of the system. This means that we are going outside reality to find its integration.

My second criticism is that all science, understood as this physical-mathematical knowledge of reality, is an abstraction both of objective reality and (an even more serious fact) of the knowing subject. The knowing subject must use, so to speak, the scientific telescope of mathematical abstraction, but reality, both in the subject and in the object, is much more multicolored—as reality, not as a "thing."

So, to find the inner limits of scientific activity: this is my criticism. Within scientific activity there is much to learn for me, and I think it is one of the fields of knowledge that, sociologically speaking, has made the most progress in the history of mankind. No resentment for the scientific world or for science, but maybe criticism for its predominance in society (but this is another level), and above all, rebellion against this reduction of thinking and knowing to calculating, in the most radical form of the term.

I have explained many times that the philological origin of the two great Indo-European cultural roots is this activity for which Man is Man: thinking. *Pensare* (thinking) is like *pesare* (weighing). The two roots are *men* and *med*. From *men* comes *mens—mentis*, *mein*, *mensura*, and also, in Anglo-Saxon and Germanic languages, *mount*, which derives from *moon*, because the moon is used to measure, mind, and so measure, the quantity, the quantification, the study of behaviors of a certain reality that can be translated in mathematically measurable terms.

Colors, before the discovery of the significance of waves and frequencies, could not be measured; therefore, colors (see Goethe) did not belong to science. Today we have discovered the parameters of correlation, and we can say yellow, green, and so on, because we have found a certain length, a certain number of angstroms, a certain frequency that allows us to establish a correlation; but no one, not even today, would identify the number of angstroms that defines green with the color green. There are many other things in the color green. There are also many other things in the moon. Ask dogs what happens when there is an eclipse, ask poets or lovers . . . but we now think that the moon is a physical body and that is all, and that the rest are pretty metaphors for those who are not yet scientists. My criticism is against this reductionism, not against what science can tell us about the weight, density, atmosphere, craters, and all the other aspects of the moon. The *mens* makes a Man a Man, and so anything that goes against rationality, rigor, and measure is obscurantism.

The other root is *med*, from which, very significantly, come the words "medicine," "meditation," and "moderate" (in both senses of the word: as being modest and therefore having the sense of the situation, and in the sense of leading a group). A "moderator" is he who leads, but who leads adapting himself to reality, having a sixth sense to see how things should be conducted, because he has seen and felt something more. "Medicine" is the form of *mederi*, to make you reach salvation, *salus*; health and salvation, *soter* and *soteria*, which in Sanskrit is *sarvam*, which means "everything." And "meditation" is this entering into harmony with reality without forcing it. The instrument of science, on the other hand, is the experiment, which does a certain violence to what I have before me. I try to keep a certain number of fixed points, I establish some variables, I incise with anything, I see how the objects react to my intervention, and I take note of their reactions.

Observation, Experiment, Experience

The other form of knowledge, which has been somewhat neglected and which is perhaps the most important for creative incentive, is observation. Observation is different from experiment. When Faraday, six years before making the discovery that has permitted all our technological civilization, writes in his diary, "to convert magnetism into electricity," this intuition was not the result of any experiment, but of an observation. When Kekulé, traveling on a hot summer's afternoon on a London bus, passes London Zoo and sees that the monkeys are climbing on top of each other waving their arms, this sparks in his mind the structure of carbon, the carbon hexagon. It was not an experiment; it was an observation. Then he spent all night, he says, reflecting on this vision: he conjectures that this is valid for carbon and hydrogen, and he begins to find the structure of all organic chemistry. "Je commençais à supposer" (I started to suppose), says Lavoisier. Everything is connected, but experiment is not observation. Perhaps observation is typical of the genius, or the patient man, but it is without doubt available to all: we all can observe.

We have lost this capacity for observation because observation requires patience, the respect of rhythms (I could cite Newton's apple). Observation does not do violence to reality; it lets reality speak to you, approach you, and you open yourself by observing. We have almost forgotten observation because we deal with experiment, in which we proceed much faster. We carry out experiments on everything, even sexology (or at least a certain type of sexology; another type is much wiser) and psychology conduct experiments. There is also observation, but often the balance is not very stable. Observation is another window on reality, less violent than the experiment because it accepts determined rhythms in entering into contact with the Real, with the awareness that the observer enters into a relationship with the observed that is such that the former can modify the latter. The great self-incrimination of the West is that we had to wait until 1927 or 1928, when his book was published, before Heisenberg spoke to us of the Uncertainty Principle. If we needed to wait for Heisenberg to understand that the observer modifies the observation, it means that we had lost the sense of observation.

There is another great capacity that has remained rather underdeveloped, and it is experience. If observation has something of a centrifugal direction, experience has a centripetal direction. That is to say, I am the one who is modified, the thing is a part of me, I have opened myself up and reality has entered me from outside and has become a part of me.

Correctly combining experience, observation, and experiment, and not only focusing on experiment: this is my central suggestion when I speak of science. And I would not like to be interpreted hastily as someone who wants to curb science, an attitude that I consider wrong.

The Classifier Is Not in the Classification

With regard to evolution, I would like to observe that it is part of observation, and for this reason many say that evolution is not a science, but a very useful work hypothesis that helps to give a certain framework to numerous facts. I have some reservations about evolution, both from the logical and scientific point of view, at least in the sense the word is used today. I do not have the authority to say whether evolution or non-evolution is a hypothesis that is plausible or probable or proven in the field of the evolution of the species. As regards a global sense of the evolution of the cosmos, I think it is a very useful and very plausible hypothesis, but I cannot accept evolution as a philosophy for the following reason: evolution is the result of the West's inclination to classify; from Aristotle, through Porphyry, up to modern science there has been constant classifying. Things are classified: sulfuric acid is not sulfurous or sulfide, species A is not species B, sub-species C is different from sub-species D, and so on.

It is this classification that permits us to see a relationship, and even an evolution, if we project a static situation into a dynamic paradigm, in a time that is conferred a certain movement, as occurs in the stills used to make up a film. But two things, as a matter of principle, cannot enter into any classification (and modern science is fundamentally based on classifying): the criterion of classification, which cannot enter into classification without giving rise to a vicious circle, and the classifier.

And when I ask what Man is, and I am told an animal, a biped, speaking, wise, *habilis*, originating from ants,[3] sooner or later than the Pithecanthropus or the Homo erectus or the Neanderthal Man . . . I realize that all classifications omit one thing, which is the thing that interests me and which perhaps interests each of us: what I am, not what is "Man" in the third person. Man, who is the classifier, cannot find the answer by putting himself in the classification. So, no evolutionary answer based on any classification can tell me who the classifier is. This question is the true tragedy of the young people today, who want to know what the classifier is, while we respond with classifications. The classifier is another thing: it is the human, or cosmotheandric, Mystery (divine, human, material).

And we find ourselves once again before the limits of the theory of evolution.

---

[3] In the "post-Flood" tale in Greek mythology. [n.d.t.]

5

Technocentrism

Some Theses on Technology

Discussions on technology are usually set within the context of Western culture, for technology is originally a phenomenon of the West.[1] But it has now overflowed its initial cultural boundaries into many other places. The importance of technology throughout the world has given rise to intercultural problems of such magnitude that it cannot be ignored. The problems of technology can no longer be approached exclusively from a monocultural point of view. The following theses aim at making us aware of the technocentrism of a great part of our contemporary culture: a phenomenon that is threatening to turn into ideology.

Rather than pronouncing value judgments, I try to limit myself to a description of the topic. I use the word "technology" not as the "science of techniques" (as geology means "science of the Earth"), but as a short form for "technological system," that is, to express the technocratic complex that embraces the whole of contemporary human life. However, Western mentality should not be identified with technology. On the contrary, among young generations, there exists in the West today a strong reaction against technology's ascendency, even stronger than that still spreading among the elites of Africa and Asia, who remain fascinated by it. The problem is so big that we can here just sketch some traits of it in the form of a thesis, without being able to develop them as they would deserve. First of all, I present some reflections about technology in itself, and then submit it to critique from an intercultural viewpoint.

Intracultural Reflections

Mutation—There Is an Essential Difference between Traditional Technique and Contemporary Technology

Although the word "technique" seems to belong to the order of *technê*, technology introduces an essential mutation into *technê*. Technique is art, *poiêtikê technê*, wherein the human mind integrates itself into matter to produce an artifact (pottery, music, poetry, a building, and so on) that may enhance the beauty and well-being of human life. One must be inspired not only to create poetry but also to produce any sort of technical activity (*technê*). In one sense, technical activity is a human activity that modifies the material world and establishes

---

[1] *Editorial note*: First published in André Merrier, ed., *Philosophie et Technique* (Institut International de Philosophie, 1984), 61–72; original English translation (*Philosophic Issues in Christian Perspective* 7, 1986) by Maurice M. Belval, here revised on the basis of a longer and modified version worked out by Panikkar in later years.

in it a new symbiosis with Man. When this activity is institutionalized, it starts to be a part of human affairs, of culture in general, which consists in cultivating not only the earth but also all that contributes to the enrichment of human life.

Technology, however, arises when the mind, the *pneuma*, is replaced by the *ratio*, the *logos* (in the narrowest sense). Into *techné* there is introduced an *arithmetic*, that is, a *rhythm* (the fruit of a *mens*, *mensura*), and then the product of the technique can be reproduced numerically, as soon as one knows its numeric code. Although each artifact has its proper style and, in a way, is unique, technology demands at least the possibility of multiplicity. To produce a few hundred bottles of wine from a few acres of vineyard with the natural bouquet of that soil may still be an art. But there is a moment in which quantitative changes bring about qualitative changes. To fill some million bottles and export them to all continents so as to render the operation profitable is feasible—just, it is no longer the function of *techné* but of technology. A mutation has occurred that we nearly ignored. To produce a single car in the world would, in theory, be an artistic creation, but it is not feasible. It is not possible to produce just the few gallons of gasoline and the few hundred pounds of steel and rubber needed for a single car. Technique makes use of the tool produced through human ingenuity: this is the first-order tool. Technology needs special machines, the second-order tools, that impose their own—special and independent—rules upon Man. The second-degree machine becomes indispensable, and Man must yield to the exigencies of its operation. The first-degree tool, on the other hand, is subordinate to Man. I have examined these differences elsewhere.

Techné is achieved by means of first-order instruments. Technology is itself an instrument, which soon, however, turns into an end. Activity, work, or fabrication, referring to *Homo faber*, are the words I wish to reserve for technique, whereas toil, labor is the keyword of technological system. Man is no longer an artist; he has become a laborer. He no longer works to a work of his own, for his own well-being: he is not a "work(mak)er," but he works for someone whom he does not know, and with whom he would probably not get along well, for a *salary* that will not only let him eat salt (*salarium*) but do everything he wants—apparently. He no longer stands proudly on his feet, resting on Mother Earth, nor walks with his head held up to heaven. He sits on wheels, on a concrete road, and must look only in front of himself. The route has been already chosen by others.

Technological Civilization—
Technology Is More Than Applied Science

The fragmentation of modern Western thought, euphemistically called "specialization" but in fact consisting in the hypostatization of conceptual abstractions as if they were separate entities, often considers technology as the simple application of scientific discoveries. This is indeed inaccurate. Modern science is, of course, an element of technology; but the latter does not exist outside the economic, social, ideological ensemble that furnishes the variety of constitutive elements needed. Technology is a complex fact whose scientific element is not the only aspect to be taken into consideration. A computer does not represent solely the channeling of an electronic movement; its operation implies a thorough ordering of matter and human life. The construction of an ordinary airplane, for instance, requires the combined activity of thousands of people and operations: the electrolysis of aluminum, the monitoring of electrical energy, the manufacture of composite machines, motors, and so on, and instruments (altimeters, antennas, radio direction finders, and such), and so forth. This airplane requires millions of years for its fuel, and it is designed for millions of human beings who will use it as a means of transportation. A plane does not only help you fly: it *makes* you fly.

In all technological undertaking, a distinction must be drawn between the purely speculative (scientific) procedure and its realization. What is labor for the technologist may be creative work (*techné*) for the scientist responsible for the project. The scientist is often an artist, a creator. The engineer planning some new undertaking may also experience the feeling of creating. Infra-atomic research, however anti-natural, is a fascinating activity (death, as well as atomic decomposition in the sun, is not against nature, but a murder is—even when Man splits the atom).

But we lost this sensitiveness. Even the transition from science to technology can offer a creative element for the businessman who launches into a practical financial and commercial operation by following as carefully prepared a strategy as that of a commanding general on the battlefield, and, like him, can enjoy the beauty of an artistic creation. It is this satisfaction that accompanies all human activity, even pretechnological activity, making it so fascinating. But the technological system does not stop with the design; it seeks to put into practice what has been designed.

And *praxis* is more than theory. Designing a new type of plane, like designing a new weapon, can be a great intellectual success, a true creation of the human mind. But a thrilling war strategy is not war; the design of a new machine is not the same as the millions of real machines produced for the purpose of computing, killing, or producing. Technology also includes its practical realization; technology is a *praxis* as well as a *theôria*. And saying that theory is good even if the resulting praxis can be evil is like saying that hate is good as long as you do not put it into practice.

Technocracy as the Specific (Dominant?) Character of Contemporary Western Civilization

Each culture has and has had its proper techniques, and several cultures have common techniques; but only contemporary Western civilization offers this unique fact of technology.

No matter what the objections of *Veda* enthusiasts may be, it is unquestionable that planes, televisions, computers, and so on have never before existed on earth. But this state of affairs is not accidental, de facto: it is essential, de jure. Technology is essentially linked to the culture that has brought it about. In a word, technology is the child of a given culture, and it is intrinsically bound to it.

Now, can it be maintained that the dominant character of contemporary Western civilization is technology? In order to come to a decision on that point, it would be necessary to come to an agreement on the axiology to be applied. It is from the point of view of the vision underlying the technological system that technology seems to dominate the world. Those who attach but slight importance to historical reality and to the power of matter will not admit that technology might be a dominant force. They will consider it as a negligible fact. And it is this negligence, or even contempt for technology on the part of certain traditional cultures, that has allowed Western civilization to invade the world almost without resistance from most other cultures—what I have elsewhere called the "Trojan Horse Syndrome."

Cross-Cultural Questions

Technocentrism—Technology Is Not Universalizable as If It Were a Cultural Invariant

Technology Is Not Neutral. The universalization of technology implies the Westernizing of the world and the destruction of the other cultures that rest on visions of reality that are incompatible with the modern Western presuppositions of technology. Technology is therefore not neutral. It can germinate only in a modern soil and develop only in a Westernized climate.

The extent to which other cultures can survive, can preserve their identity, and avoid reduction to marginal folklore remains a huge problem that cannot be solved a priori, or in general, for all traditional cultural forms. And, if certain human cultures are sooner or later condemned to disappear because of the invasion of technology, those who live in those cultures, instead of being deceived with the mirage of progress and the promise of a "happy future," should be told openly that the price of this future happiness will be the extinction of their culture. The victors alone will survive.

Let us see how technology, far from being neutral, is in fact intrinsically linked to Western culture, and feeds on it.

The Specific Features of Technology. The myth of technological civilization contains a set of "mythems"[2] that cannot be found in most cultures. The fact that the incompatibility of technology with traditional cultures has not been noticed, and that it has been thought that technology could be subjected to the lifestyles of different cultures, proves that there has been no dialogue among cultures during this technological avalanche. Fundamental belief in a linear evolution of the human species has prevailed, according to the parameters of eighteenth- and nineteenth-century European culture. And I would not necessarily wish to accuse the technocrats of bad faith. It is a question of the sociology of knowledge. With the scientist intoxication of the past centuries, Western culture could not do otherwise.

Ontonomy Is Impossible—
Technology Is Autonomous,
It Is Independent Both of Man and Nature

The West today, after awful experiences such as the massacre, during the twentieth century, of 100 million people precisely by means of technology, is awakening from a dream in which Man was able to master the technological system. The more Man penetrates the world of technology, the less he succeeds in finding a way out, so he becomes more and more fatalistic. Man now thinks that it is impossible to get rid of the technological system. And this is what dictates the lifestyle, the dominant values, and the rhythms of the collectivity, and even a large part of the forms of thought, not to mention the arms race, the growth of the multinational companies, and the proliferation of machines, that nobody seems to be able to stop.

The second-order machine has its own regularities, which depend neither on natural laws nor on anthropological laws. It is no accident that we speak of the end of metaphysics and that sociology has become the queen of humanistic disciplines.

One no longer considers what being *is* or *ought to be* or *why* things are, but only notices *how* they behave or react. Statistics, computer science, and experimentation have methodological primacy. The megalopolis, a typical example of the second-order machine, furnishes proof in support of this thesis. Human life has lost all ontonomy: the person does not count. To survive, one must conform not only to regulations on traffic, taxes, unions, banks, inflation, insurance, and so on, but especially to regulations concerning salaried labor—all external constraints on human nature. And more specifically, we have lost our relationship with space and time meant as anthropological categories, and we became prisoners of a time and a space that are scientific abstractions.

---

[2] I call "mythems" the intellectual contents that are present in any given myth—and are often mythic, and not necessarily conceptual. I understand myth as that which provides the horizon of intelligibility, or the sense of reality disclosed by a certain *mythologoumenon* (cosmogonic narrative).

We are subjected to the great Man-built machine. One may say that the nontechnological Man was subject to cold, epidemics, floods, seasons, and such. I would answer that
the *techné* can solve the majority of these problems, and that there is no need of going
back to some primitivism. It is not about idealizing past times. The point is to discover
the meaning of life and the nature of human joy, and seek to determine whether, in this
respect, technology has brought us forward or backward. I have elsewhere dealt with the
regression from *Homo sapiens*—who included *Homo faber* (wisdom means "making")—to
Homo habilis.

There is good reason to speak of modern Man as a hybrid between animal and machine.
Human and cosmic interdependences have always existed. And in a well-ordered cosmos the
possibility has also always existed for a harmonious balance that might be called "ontonomous"
(the *nomos* of *on*, the intrinsic order of being) midway between a heteronomous dependence
of domination and an autonomous independence of dispersion and isolation.

Primacy of the Machine—
Technology Depends on a Mechanical
and Gravitational World

The words "mechanical" and "machine" could serve as symbols for expressing the essence
of technology. "Mechanical" was used in modern languages before "machine," to which it
is related. Apart from the original pejorative meaning (still used nowadays) of ruse and
artificial ingenuity still preserved in the word "machination," and the sad memory linked
to the Latin *machina* (the platform upon which slaves were exposed for public sale), the
original Greek *méchané* (cf. *méchos*) means instrument, the means of reaching something
(and, therefore, ruse). It is also close to the Gothic *magan* (*mazan*) meaning power (cf. the
German verb *vermögen*, from the root *magh*: to be capable of, to be able). Technology refers
to the realm of machines, whereas technique belongs to the world of instruments (tools).
The power of the tool comes from Man; that of the machine, from the outside. The source
of the energy of a tool is *ingenium*, that of the first-order machine is directed nature (wind,
water, and so on), and that of the second-order machine is transformed nature (chemistry,
atomic power, and so on). We must therefore make a distinction between first-order tool
and second-order machine.

Independently of these etymological hints, the vision that sustains technology is that of
a post-Galilean and post-Newtonian world in which the concepts of mass, force, speed, and
especially acceleration (hence also gravitation) determine the human and cosmic structures
and behavior. There is no room for angels moving the planets (as Newton still believed),
or for domains in which the law of entropy does not count. All of that is relegated to the
world of magic. *Siddhi, tapas, mantras*, like everything that is called miraculous, is set
aside, outside the real world, not to mention, of course, *apsaras, asuras*, spirits, demons,
and other beings that are autonomous centers of operation. Even prayer has degenerated
into a lever to move or urge God's will, instead of being one of the powers that move the
universe ("il sole e l'altre stelle"[3]). Poets are allowed to speak to us of the Gods who can
perhaps still exercise control over Man, but machines are off-limits to divine powers.
Technology is impermeable to all the incantations of the other cultures; but, vice versa, a
technological civilization cannot prosper wherever the Gods do not obey the second law
of thermodynamics.

---

[3] "The sun and the other stars"—the last words of the *Divine Comedy*.

Anthropocentrism—
Technology Presupposes That Man Is Essentially Different
from, and Superior to, Nature

It was not an accident that technology emerged and developed in a world ruled by the Semite conception of the universe, where Man is the master of Nature, and not one more thing in her bosom. No one in the West seems to object to the current language that speaks of exploitation: agricultural, mining, and so on. The Earth and animals are exploited to draw from them a profit for Man, king of the universe. Many authors speak—and rightly so—of the instrumentality of technology (Huber) and of the extension of the human will in nature (Hersch), or more explicitly, of "bending physical determinism to human ends" (Hersch). Human dignity does not rest on the fact of *being* (and thus being human), but on the capacity for dominating Nature.

Once again, a large number of human cultures do not share this opinion: they would condemn as truly unjust this exploitation and domination of Nature, which they consider as unnecessary, self-defeating indeed, for the full development of humankind. According to this view, Man is not an exception in creation, but, on the one hand, is part of the universe and, on the other, is the meeting point of the cosmos, and all the more human in that the destiny of the universe is being worked out in him. Human freedom is a cosmic power, not merely a psychological capacity to choose.

Interventionism—
The Method Proper to Technology Is Experimentation

For technology, the method of knowing does not consist in the contemplation of things or in a participation (even to identification) with reality, but in an intervention called experimentation. Modern science is born out of experimentation, which is now applied everywhere. Anyone familiar with hospital practice realizes the extent to which the sick are subjected to experimentation. But let us think about psychology, anthropology, and sociology, not to mention physics. Experimentation is now the acceptable procedure with animals, with things, and even with humans. A situation is modified at will for testing the results of an intervention. Human activity is not considered as a collaboration with the rhythms of nature, for personal development and the harmony of the universe, but as labor—labor regarded as production, modification, domination, and, for most, as a punishment to be endured, a means of living and of earning not indeed one's own life,[4] but the conditions that make it possible. It is altogether evident that this conception is foreign to many cultures, even in the West. The passive resistance of the peoples of Asia and Africa to labor, for example, is neither a sign of laziness nor lack of interest on their part: they simply do not think of the universe as a big machine, or Man as a part of that machine.

And what is meditation if not a radical confidence in the fundamental harmony of reality? In meditation, we are only asked to settle down so that things may sediment and find their proper place. In a *cosmos*, each entity has a natural place. In a technological civilization, there is no room for contemplation. On the contrary, one must immediately intervene: action no longer flows out of a contemplative plenitude, but itself takes the initiative—and, alas, very often only by virtue of the previous inertia of thought.

---

[4] See Mt 16:26.

Objectivism—Technology Presupposes That Reality Is
Objectifiable and Thus Subject to Thought

If Hegel defined philosophy as the *Anstrengung des Begriffes* (the effort of concept), technology can be described as the crystallization or objectification of concepts. Concepts, once formed, can be fixed inside machines that guarantee constant and precise functioning, like in the machine of our brain. Reality can become the object of thought because it is objectifiable. This objectification makes reality immutable and constant, in such a way as to make sure scientific knowledge attainable, since it does not change. You can rely on the constructions of the scientific-technological enterprise. Thought is the warden of Being: Being cannot escape. Thus, machines can be built that work, and Man can rely on them. The fact that a part of contemporary Physics has stepped beyond rough paradigms of objectivity gives some reason of hope toward science, but it does not deny what we just said about the objectivistic ground of technology.

Would technology be possible if real processes did not follow the laws of logic, or even those of probability? It is well known that a large number of traditional cultures do not believe in the sequence of logical causality as the law governing the universe. Logic is good enough for the *logos*, but Reality is not exhausted by it. Many cultures do not mean to rent an apartment in the big house built by technology: they think that the price is too high.

Interchangeability—
Space and Time in Technology Are Independent
of Human Space and Time

The criterion of truth, or rather of exactness for all experimentation, is its inherent capacity for repetition. Technology is based on that certitude. Without a constant and homogeneous time, no machine could function, no modern city (a typical example of the mega-machine) could get along.

When an experiment yields the same results over and over again, it probably is disclosing a scientific law. But what would become of human relations if we could always foresee the behavior of another? Human space and time are intrinsic to each human being, whereas the space and time in which machines move are supposedly neutral and universal.

A machine can be adapted to one place or another, just provided that the different values of its parameters—such as the force of gravity, temperature, and so on—are calculated in the different places. But technology lays claim to a geographical universality that is foreign to many cultures.

The predominantly qualitative universality of Christianity became more and more geographical universality once Christians began to travel, five centuries ago. Marxism and, almost at the same time, technological universalism first emerged out of this environment. Technological universalism is in direct conflict with cultures and religions that do not want to sacrifice their identity and lose themselves in a world without castes, skin colors, and dialects. This universalism is another example of the clash between technology and culture. According to various cultures, many human goods, such as the religious ones, for instance— like a good wine—cannot be exported because they are not neutral with respect to space and time, whereas technology believes itself to be universally exportable.

Some may object that the human experience of the West testifies to the same distance between the technological world and other dimensions of life, and that these other dimensions coexist peacefully with the technological world, thanks to a distinction of levels. We may counter that, apart from the sickness of the West, here the process that led to the invasion of life by technology was due to an endogenous and evolutionary movement, whereas in other parts of the world the movement is exogenous and "revolutionary"—not to mention its destructive impact on traditional structures everywhere, even in the West.

Anti-Animism—The Inertia of Matter

For our technological civilization, matter is dead; it has its own laws that are independent of the laws of life and those of Man. Technology makes progress at the expense of the animist beliefs of humanity, which are considered irrational.

Technological progress entails quantification of biological, sociological, historical, and anthropological phenomena. The Western world smiles when it hears about Iroquois asking pardon and even permission from a tree before cutting it, or when workmen in India are seen covering their machines with flowers and honoring them with acts of *pūjā* during certain festivities. Yet the animism of many cultures, though often despised by the modern world, partly because it is frequently expressed rather grossly, is far from having disappeared, and represents nowadays an undeniable cultural force, incompatible with technological mechanism. Technology is violence against Nature; Nature can be now described as "vanquished in its mystery and conquered in its forces" (Bachelard).

It is, equally, a sign of hope the fact that the West is now remembering about the *anima mundi*, which was a common belief still after the Renaissance, and that it now tries to reformulate the "Gaia hypothesis" with "scientific" arguments. But all this will not bring about much technology.

Nominalism—Science Presupposes an Epistemological Nominalism, and Technology an Ontological Nominalism

It is true that part of postrelativist and postquantum science has become problematic unto itself and is seeking other presuppositions, but it is also true that the technological civilization is based on a conception of reality that many cultures lack. Nominalism assumes that all that we can know of reality is expressed in common terms, which are only labels or signs superimposed on things. Ideas are merely mathematical abstractions that make science possible. With this epistemological paradigm, technology creates a world for Man to live in—a world of quantifiable entities with labels attached to them for their proper manipulation. But this is not the belief of many past and present cultures. The scientific and technological method of dividing a problem into its parts, for example, as was recommended by Descartes and looks obvious when repairing a machine, presupposes a nominalistic attitude according to which the whole is the same as the sum of its parts. That sounds incomprehensible to more than one culture.

Quantifiability—Technology Makes Sense Only in a Quantifiable Universe

The realm of science is the measurable. Science proceeds by measuring. We can only measure something if we succeed in reducing the phenomenon in question to discrete units. Science calculates, or as Heidegger put it, "Science does not think."

Science assumes that there is a quantifiable element in reality, but it does not necessarily reduce reality to *quanta*. Properly speaking, modern science does not even claim to give an explanation of the world. It measures behaviors and, by discovering some constant patterns, is able to predict events of many kinds. A true scientist is humble; he or she does not want to change science into philosophy. It may happen, however, that Science *does* turn into Philosophy because of the current cosmological vacuum.

Technology does something more: it multiplies. As we have said, *one* car is an impossibility. Technology requires not only thousands of cars, but also thousands of users and thousands of miles of roads. We enter into the world of quantity and acceleration. Without acceleration, technology is impossible. Technology is the world of the quantitative "more" ("faster!"). Time is just a quantitative factor that is pliable to acceleration. What cannot be measured does not "count"—the pun is revealing. But we insist in saying that all this is no cultural invariant.

Control—The Epistemological Mood of Technology Is One of Knowledge as Power

The Baconian dictum "Knowledge is power" corresponds to the use of knowledge in the technological enterprise. We are in the Cartesian world: without epistemological certainty there is only ontological insecurity. If there are many diverging opinions, I cannot trust them. I have to find it by and for myself. I need to know with certainty in order to be secure. I cannot trust the beliefs of the community: I need criteria, which, obviously, can only rest with *me*. I am the final judge. Descartes did not say, "*Cogitamus, ergo sumus*" (We think, therefore we are). The decisive point is not that "we" think, but that "[*ego*] *cogito*." The only sure *cogitatum* is "I myself," ego. Only I can be the ultimate criterion. I need to have my and others' opinions under control, as they could be wrong, and that is dangerous. Control is indispensable.

Technology promises this control. It offers power. It is objective power, what technology has, not subjective authority. Power owns us: muscles, money, armies, and now knowledge. Authority is conferred on someone, it is recognized by someone else: *other* people give it. Technology, on the contrary, profited from the authority of science and converted it into power. Technology offers the means to transform the natural organism of a human society into a well-run organization—provided, of course, it does not break down or is not threatened by another, more powerful organization with greater technological expertise. The arms race, for instance, is inbuilt in the technocratic complex: it is a condition needed to survive.

Instrumentation—Technology Is the World of Means

The field of technology is the instrument. It deals with making instruments, and making them useful. But they are complicated and require training. The instruments are *for* something, but that end is not discussed. We presuppose that these instruments will facilitate (speed up) matters and do it quicker and better. What the "it" is or what the "matters" are is not questioned. First, we have to learn, at least, to use the instruments. Afterward, we are promised, we will discover how useful they are.

Technology allows us the better use of ever better instruments for something outside its realm. Man eats, walks, loves, speaks, studies, plays, understands, sees, and so on, for the sake of those activities themselves. Technology does not stop at itself. If it did, it would revert into *technê*—and disappear. Technology needs acceleration, that is, the creation of ever better instruments. And we ourselves become "in-strumented."

*   *   *

My "refrain" is very simple: the great temptation of the West is Messianism. The West demolished some Messianisms, but it now seems that it has collectively fallen prey to another—and all the more dangerous as, in this case, the West is no longer in front of a human face, of someone who can be nailed to a cross or fought in a war.

On the other end, disenchantments can be as dangerous as enthusiasms, or even more than that, and pendular reactions are equally unsatisfying. Nor would it prove a solution to come out of one technological intoxication and fall into another. The emancipation from technology that I indirectly present as an alternative is, above all, a spiritual movement of the whole person, that is, of Man prior to the great dichotomy between individual and society.

We have overcome many racial, religious, and other self-centrisms. Now we must face the great challenge of technocentrism. And for that, we need a new innocence.

6

EMANCIPATION FROM TECHNOLOGY

The Thesis

"Is the notion of development an indispensable requirement in order to face today's world situation?"

Before coming to grips directly with the question, let me reformulate it so that I may offer a better answer. You know how questions condition answers. I see in the request itself an example of one of the most insidious characteristics of technology: it presents itself as an accomplished fact and then declares itself indispensable (to solve the problems it itself has created).

My intention here is not to analyze the assumptions behind the question, that is, there must be something that is indispensable, one must face the situation and consequently confront it, the world situation is catastrophic if one diagnoses it on the basis of economic criteria, and so on. It is precisely because of the gravity of the situation that I avoid such an analysis, my intention being to avoid all unnecessary considerations that could distract us from the issue.

Within such a context, I would reformulate the question as follows: is there something indispensable for contemporary Man? And my answer would be quite traditional: yes, only one thing is indispensable, the One of so many cultural traditions, the *unum necessarium* of the Gospel,[1] for example. I thereby wish to emphasize that the indispensable is a whole, a "One" (although it is constituted of many parts, as the Gospel asserts), so that one cannot give a "specialized" answer that would rest on its own autonomy, and localize it in the political, or economic, or religious order, or in any realm. To say that the ills of Man are economic, moral, or social, that they are external or only internal to him, would mean to approach them only partially and not to take reality into account. Everything is interconnected (*pratītyasamutpāda*). We are here touching upon the cosmotheandric problem.

Having said this, I limit myself to the question raised by the so-called development.

Development

Development may be understood in the following ways.

The Symbol of People's Well-Being
and the Perfection of the Human Person

However, I would not give this symbol the name of "development." The word "development" has too specific a connotation to be used as synonymous with perfection, salvation, liberation; it suggests a whole set of values that are not transcultural universals. For example:

---

[1] Lk 10:41.

the conception of progress under a particular form, of linear time, of a dependency between material goods and human well-being, and so on. Even if the word "development" does express the search for human perfection in a given culture, one should look for the homeomorphic equivalents of its notion within other cultures.[2]

We are again in the presence of a colonialist syndrome: its monoculturalistic nature confuses the part with the whole (*pars pro toto*). Development can mean perfection, human fulfillment, happiness, in a given culture, but it cannot be simply identified with human perfection. Of course, no word has a universal meaning, but some words do reach a degree of abstraction that enables them to encompass more than one universe of discourse, while others are too narrowly linked with a single cultural universe.

I do not undertake here a research into the homeomorphic equivalents, that is to say, the set of word-symbols that fulfill an equivalent function in the respective cultural systems. Nor do I undertake a linguistic analysis. Consider, for example, the connotations that the word *realization* would have: movement toward human realization, aid to realization, realized life, realized village, and so on.

My answer, although arising from semantics, is clear: such a development is not indispensable, because it is not the same as the *humanum*. The latter would be a modern word (and again undoubtedly limited) to express "the necessary thing."

Not to accept the word "development" as the unique model, and to refuse the Westernization of the world, does not at all mean a criticism against the enormous "developments" of Western culture, and even less a sort of narcissistic stagnation, smugly satisfied with the actual state of other cultures. Let me stress, once and for all, that cultures must strive to free themselves from everything that impedes the realization of human happiness. When I reject a certain type of development, it is not a matter of wishing to remain in abject poverty and repugnant filthiness, while doing nothing against inhuman exploitation and social injustice, remaining insensitive to the respect and dignity of the human person. Nor is it a call to embrace romantic simplicity or negative asceticism. On the contrary, it is an invitation to a radical transformation and to a full human realization; one that does not exclude the other part of the cosmos, and that takes the very destiny of the Divine into consideration. It is an appeal to self-realization, perfection, change, struggle against evil, improvement of life, and of the conditions for a humane existence: sanitary, economic, intellectual, and so on. I am simply reacting against the monopoly of *one* symbol.

The Modern Western Model of Human Fulfillment

The Western Man has his own ideal of development and/or perfection in all realms. It is a grandiose conception, but this human paradigm is not the only one among the world's traditions. To consider it as the ultimate ideal for all cultures smacks of the same colonialist attitude mentioned above, which does not take the other cultures of humankind into consideration. There are often attempts, of course, to soften the rigidity of this conception through practical adaptations to other local cultures. They are allowed to subsist at the folkloric level, they are tolerated within marginal reservations, but "the world" must develop along the paradigm of a single culture, which is said to be "global."

---

[2] The Hindi words used to name development are: *vikāsa*, expansion, flowering, evolution; *vṛddhi*, progress, growth, advancement, increase; *parivardhana*, increase; *baratī*, with the same meaning as the preceding words, and also abundance, progression, prosperity; *unnati*, elevation, height, swelling, growth, etc.; each of these words expressing the notion of growth, in whatever context.

My answer to the question is again very clear: no! This form of development is neither indispensable nor desirable for humankind. If one accepts cultural pluralism, one must also accept and maintain a different conception of human nature and of human joy. This type of development is not universal. It is linked to one single culture.

The Utilization of Modern Technology

This third interpretation is the most widespread, the most subtle, and, perhaps also for these reasons, the most dangerous. Development is here presented to us as being at the service not only of Man in general but also of particular cultures. Most of the time, it does not come out as an ideology, but as a simple instrument—therefore supposedly neutral—for people and governments to use as they see fit. Those who advocate this want to "depoliticize" development—and hence accept that most of the capital be indigenous, that technological transfers be controlled by the native experts, and even that benefits remain in the country. "Developed" countries open their doors to the young people of "nondeveloped" countries, thus giving them the opportunity to study and become specialists. Even the Christian churches, often at the root of a certain Westernization, collaborate in "development" as a manifestation of love.

My third answer is equally: no! Technology, in this case synonymous with development—and contrary to *techné*, art—is not neutral.

It cannot be an instrument at the service of a culture and of a way of life that are foreign to it. It is utilized by an elite trained along the model of Western culture, but it represents a Trojan horse—introduced by this elite—that unleashes confusion, corruption, and chaos in a great part of the world called "developing," a euphemism meaning "on the way to degradation and destruction."

Elsewhere I tried to show the Western roots of modern technology and its monocultural character. So I can now take it for granted, and move on to more existential questions. I will henceforth be speaking about technological development.

Some Options

The present state of the world is that of nation-States, or simply States that pretend to be the mouthpieces of nations. It is also that of transnational corporations well committed to so-called development. We must start from the historical situation that is our own.

In connection with this factual situation, there are a number of possible options, all leading to practical attitudes that cannot be described here because they depend on each country's concrete conditions. The situations in Paraguay, Ghana, and India are not identical, despite the insulting common denominator of "Third World." I will mention three options.

Development to the Utmost

This is the radical option. Since we must develop, we might as well do it to the utmost, and rapidly. We shall thus spare ourselves slow agonies and avoid creating victims in the coming centuries. If the West has succeeded, why should other countries fail? Their peoples are not less gifted, intelligent, and capable than the West—beware of racism!

Although this option—in theory—is no longer prevalent, in practice it is still very powerful in the political realm of many States and major groupings. Even if this conviction has not been the sole motivating force behind the multinational corporations and certain dictatorships, the latter's ways of acting can serve as exemplifications. Most peoples, it is said, are not ready to live under a democratic regime, because they do not possess sufficient

SPACE, TIME, AND SCIENCE

maturity. They still need an authoritarian regime to maintain order (no one says, "Their first need is to be civilized," but that is exactly what they think), indeed to promote modernization and industrialization. There is a will to convert most countries into efficient technocracies where telephones work, trains leave and arrive on schedule, corruption is unmasked, and the individual can become aware of being a cog in the gear of the mega-machine. The price to pay for such a "development" will be high, depending on the country and its circumstances: militarism, dictatorship, repressive measures against possible terrorists—but it is all worth it. Look at TV advertisements: don't they offer a technological paradise if we buy the products presented to us under a seductive light?

The main reasons why this option appears unacceptable to me are the following:

Sacrifice of the person. The dignity of the human person can no longer be safeguarded when one is ready to sacrifice contemporary generations to a better future.

Crushing of other cultures. The result of putting this option into practice would be to crush all those cultures and lifestyles that are incompatible with development. Techno-logical civilization would become the sole dominating force of the universe. This form of development, which is a Western phenomenon, is not co-natural to many peoples. And except for a few elitist minorities that succeed in conforming to it, the majority of their people will find no affinity between that civilization and their own. They do not see in that mechanized world a ground or an atmosphere that can be favorable to the realization of the human person and to creativity. Their natural talents are unable to come out and to bloom in a climate so totally foreign to their being. Many of these humble peoples experience a sort of latent frustration because of their incapacity to adapt to machines, speed, and so on. They feel uprooted and marginalized in a society that does not offer them the possibility to contribute to its "development."

The Impossibility of Its Realization on a Human Scale. This development cannot be realized on a world scale. The world's resources are insufficient to allow all human beings to adopt a life standard equal to that of the "developed" countries. An example: the United States, which represents 6 percent of the world's population, consumes almost 40 percent of the nonrenewable energy resources of this planet. If everyone were to adopt this "standard" of living, in two years there would be no trees left on this planet, to cite only one of the catastrophic results of such a global consumption of energy.

Issues of Implementation. The only way this type of development could be implemented is if we were to profit from it, with the collaboration of the other 15 percent who could profit from it in a collateral way. As to the remaining 80 percent of humankind, they would be condemned to misery. We already see signs of this process in Brazil, in India, and in the world in general.

One must not jump too quickly to the conclusion that such an option is unacceptable and impossible to realize, and hence that one must reject it. If one reflects on genetics, biology, the subatomic world—in short, on our high-powered technology and on the hybrid man-machine that it creates—one may well think that human culture is simply following, at an accelerated pace, the dynamics of Nature. More than 90 percent of inorganic matter was necessary to produce a minimum of organic matter, and a considerably greater waste was necessary for the succeeding passages to vegetable, animal, and human life. Why should Man be the last link in this evolution? The "incest" between Man and artificial nature could give rise to a socio-bio-genetical mutation of the world and produce new beings as distinct from us as we are from (other) animals. Does Man hold the fate of evolution in his hands? Is Man more than pure evolutionary nature? Or are we doomed to be carried away by the maelstrom of a cosmic evolution, in spite of Heisenberg's principle of uncertainty and of the principles of free choice of anthropoids? The *Homo technologicus* would then be a sequel to the *Homo sapiens*.

So, although we here seriously deal with peace and pacifism, we are not considering what the US president or a USSR leader has said or done last week; we are looking at the problem of humankind's future. Do we wish to follow the direction of cosmic evolution at the price of sacrificing Man for the sake of a few elites who would then become "supermen"? Or do we hold to the inviolability of the dignity of the human being?

Mitigated Development

This option asserts itself out of an attitude of concern. It wants to "humanize development," to "reintegrate it within its own realm and limits," to introduce an "organic development," and to place it at the service of Man—in short, to control it.

All these slogans, however well-intentioned, do not point to a way that is feasible in itself, nor that is respectful of the differences among the human traditions. The Western type of development is, one could say, almost synonymous with industrialization and with the introduction of technology throughout the planet. I limit myself here to technology, which is different from *technê*, and which represents the mechanization of nature and of human life.

The Autonomy of Technology and Its Uncontrollability. The humanization of technology is an impossibility. It is technology that changes the very meaning of the *humanum*. One must live in other cultures to realize the inhuman face that technology presents to "under-developed" peoples when they have not yet become intoxicated by propaganda. One cannot control technology. Heidegger foresaw this very well—without entering into sociological details. When one considers a megalopolis of 5 million inhabitants and an airline fleet of 150 jet aircraft (not to speak of the military machinery), when the ownership of a car has become indispensable for running daily errands, one can no longer state that technology is at the service of Man. It is at the service of the "services" that it can deliver, but these services are already set and imposed by the mega-machine. Technology only makes sense to those who have been brainwashed by its "basic gospel." It has aroused in them the desire to commit their lives in that direction, firmly convinced that this type of revolution will transform their mortal lives and change the face of the Earth. But, in the process, they have snuffed out the ideals of people belonging to other cultural universes.

Its Elitism. The advantages of technology are reserved to an elite. If 0.00001 percent of the world population own a television set, 10 percent a car, 0.001 percent a private airplane, 20 percent can travel by airplane, if a few nations have developed the atomic bomb, and if the number of satellites is less than one per million persons, that is, if only a few can benefit from the advantages offered by technology, use it to their advantage, and direct it—without, nevertheless, being able to escape the slavery in which it keeps them—this small number, seen from the outside, can give the impression of enjoying its benefits.[3] But these soon disappear in the inextricable bottlenecks, not only on the highways, in the skies, and on the airwaves, but also in the confusion of satellite messages and information with which we are daily bombarded to such a saturation point as to be non-assimilable. As soon as they are no longer reserved to an elite, they can no longer subsist.

---

[3] Figures refer to the year of publication of the article—1988.

SPACE, TIME, AND SCIENCE

It belongs to the very nature of technology to have an autonomy of its own, to which Man must submit. If human culture has transformed our nature, *techniculture* is now in the process of bringing about a new anthropological transformation. Is this change going in the right direction? Could it be led to promote a greater hominization rather than an ever greater technologization?

Coexistence and Apartheid. The relationship between technology and cultures is neither one of neutrality nor one of subordination. It is one of supplantation. Technology is the offspring of a specific culture. It secretes its own civilization, which will swallow up the other cultures of humankind if it succeeds in taking root across the planet. It may perhaps tolerate some cultural reservations like those of North American natives, and these reservations of a new type will include three-quarters of the world population. Perhaps all other cultures are condemned to extinction, but one should be aware of it.

Let us not fool ourselves.[4] The pan-economic ideology of a technologized world is dominated by inexorable laws.

First: Money calls for money. Money flows from where there is little to where there is more of it. This is "profit," without which the mega-machine cannot work.

Second: In a closed system—and the world today is a closed system—the growth (progress, wealth . . .) of one section of the system implies, and often causes, the poverty of the other section. Technology is based on acceleration, even acceleration of natural rhythms. But these rhythms are the very ones that bring about a harmonious recycling with Nature, for Nature acts as a living organism.

So, coexistence between cultures and technology is not possible. Nor is slavery, for the slaves, at least, were useful. All that remains is apartheid or extermination.

Emancipation from Technology

This is another possible option. It is not an attitude of violent or dialectical confrontation—the latter would be doomed to failure anyway, since the technocrats are more powerful—but one of real emancipation from the grip of technological civilization upon human life.

Such an emancipation cannot ignore the status quo of a world that is highly technologized in its body and soul. It can only be brought about by a *dismantling* of the technocratic system and not by its destruction.

This dismantling cannot be achieved through artificial constraints that would run counter to the technological impetus. In fact, no form of dictatorship can succeed in breaking this impetus; it would require a power superior to technological power. The remedy would be worse than the disease.

Nor can the dismantling be brought about through forms of negative asceticism. The motivation would be weak. It is not a matter, here, of going back to the past, or despising the positive achievements of humankind.

Furthermore, it is not a question of putting obstacles in the way of human creativity, of repressing the joy of living or lessening the quality of life. On the contrary, it is a question of the real growth of Man and of his unique contribution to the authentic cosmotheandric adventure of the universe.

---

[4] Only one example, among thousands. Back in the 1960s, Nigeria was the greatest *exporter* of food. In 1983 it was the greatest *importer* of food. But this datum does not tell us about the hundreds of thousands of human beings who suffer atrociously from this condition, often at the price of their lives.

This emancipation can only take place through a serious conversion—*metanoia*—of the technologized world, on the basis of a profound meditation on the actual malaise of humankind. Today's inevitable encounters between the technological world and the wisdom of the various religious and cultural traditions could be at the origin of a dialogue between cultures and technology. The dialogue will be *dialogical* only if there is a mutual trust among the various movements that are already advancing toward a liberation of Man. These dialogues should not aim at solving technological problems, but at studying the fundamental questions of human life.

Today's climate is favorable for such an endeavor. The inferiority complex of many cultures is beginning to disappear, in part at least. And so is the superiority complex of the Western civilization (although it is not limited to the West). War—which is a direct product of technology—has caused, during this century, more than 100 million victims. We know that this same technology has in fact, indirectly, made countless other victims by creating demographic and food imbalances, and so on. We live under the constant threat of nuclear war and of the destruction of the planet even in the absence of any war. These major facts, these justified fears have sensitized a portion of humanity to today's situation. The question being asked is the very one that Man has been asking since the *Upaniṣads*: that of Being and Non-Being—a question that today is inevitable, not only from the individual but also from the collective point of view.

To better elucidate what I mean by emancipation from technology, I will describe, by contrast, what the technological civilization represents.

The Technological Universe

When speaking of technology, we cannot stop at an accelerator (of elementary particles) nor at complicated electronic machines. We cannot isolate this machine from what has made it possible and from its use by human beings, which is its sole justification: the machine implies a whole world from which we cannot abstract. In short, the technological world is an autonomous world. The world of the mega-machine has substituted itself to that of nature. Man no longer lives in a natural universe, but he moves in an artificial one. The advent of technology has raised his hopes of being fully protected, the master of elements, and even of being happy. But his experience is not one of full security. He undertakes excursions, picnics in the natural world, but these are just temporary escapes to breathe and to renew the strength necessary in order to be better able to work in what is called the real world, that is, the world of the machine.

In the technological world, it is reason that dominates. The angels and the Gods have no place. It *does* allow room for meditation: no one will prevent you from practicing it; you can even devote to it whatever time you wish, provided you do so in your "free" time (hence the other hours are not). But such a universe, where there is no room for meditation, is one that has lost its reality and its justification. A cross at the crossroads, statues of the Virgin, of St. Michael, altars to the spirits, temples to Śiva or the local Gods, chapels on hilltops, shrines at the base of trees, burning incense sticks—all this no longer has a meaning in a technological world. It is seen as superstition. It is tolerated with a certain condescension toward those who have not "evolved" yet. In fact, such "superstitions" are to be found in developing countries. The physical presence of the *numinous* is precisely one of the signs that these peoples are not developed.

What draws a smile, sometimes, is to see Muslims interrupt their factory work, spread their carpets, and prostrate themselves to pray in the direction of Mecca. But the smile is quickly wiped off one's face when this institutionalized religiousness, in a totalitarian setting, becomes an instrument of power and a means for development. Then traditional sacredness starts to be seen as degraded. All of a sudden, one realizes that the two things don't go together. If one wishes to identify God with machines, he is considered as a person falling prey to unwholesome theocracy.

The technological world, of its very nature, is a world without God. Personal beliefs in a God are respected, but in the realm of one's private life; technology leaves no room for metaphysics. Theologians and philosophers are free to think and say what they like best about a God which hovers over the world. However, God is also and essentially a cosmological concept; He is related to the world inasmuch as He is its creator, its "inspirer," its soul, its providence, its domain, its being, etc. But the technological world is atheistic. It has no room for God. He is totally unnecessary. His presence would destroy the entire structure. He can certainly exist outside or even above the technological world, but He has nothing to do *inside* it.

In that universe, the superior force is Man, or rather impersonal Man, a certain type of humanity—or perhaps the Laws of Science, but mostly the technocrats. In a mechanized world, there is, at most, the need for a supreme engineer, but this "clockmaker" of a cheap apologetics that comes from the era of the naïve optimism of technological adolescence is precisely Man, or the spirit of Laplace if we wish—ultimately a "superman," "beyond freedom and dignity." Modern astronomy astounds us with its physical majesty, with its complexity as a perfect machine. There is, therein, no God or Gods that can be measured. They have no work to accomplish in that astral world. It is the *deus otiosus*: He set the machine in motion, now He is at rest.

Let us just consider the difference between a "metaphysics of light" that takes "God is light"[5] seriously, and a physics of light that believes seriously that "light is energy" (physical obviously, that is to say, the capacity to produce work, $E = \frac{1}{2} mv^2$, or simply $E = mc^2$).

What I have just said, in other words, is that the technological world is one of the objective productions of Man; indeed it is the historical world par excellence. History is here understood simply as the human phenomenon, and Man as a historical animal. Of course, there is history and history. But here it is about a human-based history, the history of external and temporal facts. It is a history without angels, without Gods, without devils and *asuras*—a history of *Homo faber* only, although rich with instruments of all sorts, standing on an inert platform called the terrestrial globe. Even animals play no role in it. Elephants and camels are no longer needed to wage war, nor horses to plow the earth. What matters are atoms and computers, in any case electronics. Man no longer moves around in the cosmos but in history, in the cage of history that he built for himself.

Man's life on earth mostly unfolds alongside the machine. This companionship is not without conflict. Sometimes it does bring a certain amount of pleasure—which usually comes from an excessive zeal toward this machine, to which Man is devoted and to which he devotes extra time. Man no longer lives in communion—nor in struggle—with the angels, the planets, the spirits. His life unfolds in human history. His fate is tied down to this planet, that he considers a dead thing, a material base upon which to set his feet, subject (as he himself still is) to the "law of gravitation," a scientific dogma unknown up until a few centuries ago.

Man no longer lives in a world where miracles are natural, where he is aware of being someone in a universe that is alive, and that is not limited to the solar system as modern science quite often believes. In the technological world, the spirit is not incarnated, but Man is mechanized (*enmachiné*). He is a prisoner of the machine. One only needs to live

⁵ See *RV* I.1.1; *RV* I.115.1; 1 Jn 1:5, etc.

in another culture to realize it. For example, the spontaneous reaction of the Asian peoples toward the threat of the atomic bomb is revealing. They feel no anguish at the thought that the planet may be reduced to ashes. They live in a non-Newtonian and a-historical world. They do not feel that their life is threatened by the total disappearance of this "world," because their world is different.

I am not saying that it would be better not to worry, I am not defending outdated cosmologies: I am criticizing the technological world, and trying to show that Man is suffocating in it. So, when I speak of an emancipation from technology, I suggest an exit from the technological cosmos, the liberation of cosmology from a purely historical world governed by the laws of mechanics. What I propose is that we should widen our human horizon. I am not advocating a return to an ancient world as ferocious and rigid as the present one, nor alienation, escape, the search for a refuge in an imaginary world of fairy tales. The new universe has yet to emerge. That is why I focus my criticism on the technological world. I would like to be a philosopher rather than a poet, although both can well go together. It is the contemporary poet's role to describe the *cosmotheandrica commedia*.

The technological world has yet another aspect. It presents itself as tributary of the scientific worldview. All of science can be reduced to the formula "S is P." It tells us something (P) about S. It is the world of predicates. Even when it speaks of subjects, it tells us *what* S is. It transforms the subject into a predicate of its scientific knowledge. It is the world of objectivity.

Technology seems to bring a solution to practical problems, apparently in an objective way and outside all subjective participation. The subjective factor is, at most, a temporary imperfection that needs to be gradually objectified. For example, if I own a dishwasher or a water pump or any other such gadget, I manage things on my own, no longer needing to enter into relationship with people who formerly carried out the functions of my machines. That is what we say when we affirm that machines make us self-sufficient.[6]

A textile factory, newly built in a village, provides a job to many people, but it will also take away the livelihood of a great number of families of weavers. It will also affect the human relations between the villagers and cause their breakdown, if not through modernization of human life, at least by introducing acceleration: one may become rich ten or a hundred times more quickly than by following the rhythms of nature. One begins by the artificial race against time—and one ends in the arms race. It is the same syndrome. If mail is electronically processed, the subjective element is not necessary and personal factors are seen as obstacles. Communication today has become a science (even at the level of psychology). It is no longer an art.

In a word, technology breaks down the anthropocosmic correlations of which the *Upaniṣads* are a model. Things work automatically; processes become objective. Today, one no longer prays for rain, which is fine, but what is not so fine is that rain has been removed from the seasonal rhythms, from the lunar cycle, from the village customs, and it has broken all relationship with the universe of Man and of things (one just needs to have money and technological know-how to build a dam and to open it up when required).

Another example. In nonindustrialized countries, shopping in bazaars is an art and a school, and all purchases include an indispensable personal factor. Fixed prices are a new invention introduced by mass production. But in a bazaar each piece of merchandise is unique, and its

---

[6] Two professors—whom I know well—had met many times at international conferences where the technological devices were flawless. They had been just colleagues for many years. Once, in a place in the Middle East, technology failed (meals, rooms, airplanes, reservations . . .). They needed this technological crash to discover each other, and become true friends!

price is a function of the total network of relationships that makes it what it is. There is a big difference, also, between choosing the cloth and giving it to a tailor who will make a shirt for me, and buying one of those mass-produced anonymous shirts that may not always fit my size. The technological world, which claims to provide more free time, does not allow one to "waste one's time" in bargaining for merchandise. Love, human warmth, personal relations, dialogue, the heart-to-heart, the play of minds, are automatically eliminated.

In a word, relationships created by *techné* are human relations, whereas those imposed by technology are objective. One is not grateful to a tractor in the same way as one thanks an ox cart or an animal-drawn plow. The master craftsman has a personal relationship with his apprentices; he transmits his very self, whereas the administrative manager has formal relationships with his subordinates. The latter have received their training in some college, and if they do not prove good cogs in the wheel, they will simply be replaced. It cannot be otherwise. Anyone who has taken part in meeting of the board of directors of a large company knows that, when they speak of production, budget, and profit, they must abstract from the human beings that their employees are. In such a case, they can build a hospital or a temple, but cannot be concerned with persons.

One should not interpret these sentences as a sort of nostalgia for the medieval guilds, for also at that time there was a form of despotism. What we are faced with here is the very structure of the technological system and of the world that it is creating in order to subsist.

To find new structures that are human and not dehumanizing for our times is one of the most pressing tasks to be accomplished. Hence the importance of our groping and experiments in the practical realm.

Milestones for Emancipation

Here are some points of reference that may be of some help in our efforts to emancipate from technology.

Conscientization. One should begin with a critique of those false notions that are quite widespread and of the opinions held by the technocratic complex in its own interest. I can only list a few of them:

- "Technology is absolutely indispensable to feed and support the current world population and to solve the problems of contemporary Man." But, as a matter of fact, technology (not *techné*) solves only, and imperfectly, problems that it itself has created.
- "Allotropic medicine, with all its technological baggage, is an indispensable requisite for the health of humankind." We ignore the existence and value of other forms of medicine. We often confuse medicine with hygiene, and we tend to forget that, according to the World Health Organization (1983), among the 20,000 drugs produced in the world, 90 percent were superfluous or dangerous. Furthermore, we have to mention the institutionalization of modern medicine, which enslaves it to the technological system.
- "The pan-economic ideology is indispensable to a civilization on a world scale, with a common market, and for an equitable distribution of wealth." We have not yet emerged from the colonial mentality, which recognizes *one* model of civilization.
- "Only technological comfort can supply the means for a truly human life, free from all fear and constraint." We forget that technology brings its own anxieties and insecurities with it, and we confuse a rational attitude with a technological one.

- "Only a megalopolis can provide an advanced cultural or really refined life (theatre, opera, music, poetry, science . . .)." Aside from the elitism of such an assertion (only 10 percent of the population is capable of real culture, because we need at least one million citizens to enable us to have a refined cultural life), we confuse culture with passive and bourgeois enjoyment, which stifles "geniuses," and we mistake the real human creativity, which is not in the genius but in all Men.
- "There is no other alternative for an economically just life: either liberal or State capitalism." We want to drive everyone into the Western dead end (either the Atlantic or the Soviet one).
- "The Earth and its resources are at the service of Man, who is the king of creation." And we are unaware of the *terricide* we are committing against Mother Earth, nor of the profanation of matter, since we have lost a sensitivity that is still alive in other cultures.
- "We must, in practice, simplify things, reduce them to the language of computers: black or white." On the other hand, we must demystify the idols created by the mass media, which are forced to simplify human situations and theoretical problems, but feed false facts. Reality is then reduced to simplistic formulas: the theology of liberation is pure Marxism; the Hindu caste system is intrinsically incompatible with the growth of the human being; North America is nothing but imperialism; communists are the devil on earth; members of African tribes are "savages and primitives"; Christianity is essentially violent and proselytizing; Hinduism is idolatrous, and so on.

All those assertions must be qualified in relation to precise contexts. We could extend the list, but these examples will suffice.

Deconditioning of Man. "Emancipation from technology" is a short form for *emancipation of Man from the grip of technology*. But this is only a means or an intermediate stage, since it is a matter, finally, of the liberation of Man as a whole—period. It is a question of his salvation, his perfection, his joy, whatever word is used to express the end or destiny of the universe, because here Man is not the "individual," but a microcosm, the crossroad of all reality.

One must underscore this with force, because, in talks on the subject, one easily ends up accepting the rules of the game of the technological world: *the problem posed by technology is not technological but human*. It is the destiny of Man that is at stake. We are dealing here with human nature.

It is not a question of finding new antipollution agents or inventing a defensive weapon more sophisticated than missiles. It is a question of raising radical questions on the nature of Man and the structure of reality, in short, human joy, and to examine the role of technology at the service of the human ideal.[7] I insist: the change in mentality must be radical. That is why we need intercultural exchanges. The weight of vested material interests is too great to let us think we can change things without some great upheaval. Can we avoid a major

---

[7] International meetings, in this light, often look pathetic, be it about the United Nations, UNESCO, the nonaligned countries, the World Health Organization, etc. The meeting of the Commonwealth in New Delhi, November 1983, could provide an example of the lack of realism in the face of the world situation: enormous goodwill, sincere exchanges between people of different ideologies, in-depth specialized studies, but all is bogged down and sinking more and more fatally, because no one even envisions the possibility of reexamining the fundamental assumptions upon which the present system is based. "He who rides a tiger," says an Indian proverb, "cannot dismount it."

catastrophe? Furthermore, these vested interests are not exclusively material; there is also an inertia of thought, besides the inertia of action.

This being said, we must wonder: to what degree does technology liberate, or, on the contrary, enslave Man more and more?[8]

Culture consists in cultivating some interior and exterior spaces of the human being for a fullness of life. In the past, I introduced the word *techniculture* to stress that agriculture was no longer the model of culture. Today I ask: after more than one century of experiencing technological civilization, is humanity heading in the right direction? There are so many signs and cries that force us to raise the fundamental question of the meaning of life, not only from an individualistic viewpoint, but also from a historical, sociological, and even cosmological perspective—for example, the drive that propels Westerners, particularly the youth, toward a simple and natural way of life; Man's aspiration to autarchy toward the machine; the desire to safeguard the artistic ("technical," in the Greek sense of the word) *consciousness*; the thirst for a religiosity that liberates from the stifling nature of a mechanized universe (and of a scientific vision of the universe), and for an authentic joy.

Isn't it significant that poets and artists, ever since the beginning of the century, and more than thinkers and philosophers, have often been warning us against the decline of human life, in striking contrast with the shallow optimism of technology enthusiasts? Even scientists like Einstein, Heisenberg, and Oppenheimer had a foreboding of the *Mene, Tekel, Peres*[9] of technological civilization. Man seems to wither within the cosmology of a universe that has come out of some initial "Big Bang." He feels imprisoned in a world that is only 14 billion years old, and, since he cannot see what another world could consist of, he poses himself the fundamental question of the meaning of life, and he contests the context in which he lives. Mysticism—to use a word that is dangerous because of its polysemous character—is not an appendix to cosmology or a luxury for anthropology. It is the whole vision of the universe that is called into question. It is not a matter, here, of knowing if the introduction of a tractor in an Indian village is going to be profitable to some, while other families will starve. What we are asking is whether three-quarters of humankind will or will not be reduced to slavery, and if Man himself, and as a whole, is not in the process of losing his humanity.[10]

---

[8] See, for example, the contradictory language of modern India in *The Hindu*, one of the major newspapers in the country. Every day, it publishes on its last page a brief commentary on a Hindu religious topic; most of the time it is an abstract of a conference held by a *swami* or spiritual master. On November 14, 1983, the title of the article was "Unshared Wealth Is Useless" (p. 16). But page 7, devoted to "Management," contained two articles, two paragraphs, four lesser advertisements, and half a page of advertising with a picture of a *gopuram* (entrance tower of a Hindu temple) inside which one could see pictures showing the inside and outside of a vast industrial complex, with the following words attributed to Pandit J. Nehru: "I look upon these works as temples of Modern India . . . ," and followed by a long advertising notice from an industrial company. One of the articles, "Impact of Technology on Organization Structure," by an Indian author, uses the following jargon: "Rapid change poses problems of obsolescence. It also creates problems of assimilation and adjustment in other systems. Since in the framework of the socio-technical system, technology is related both as an input and as an output to the strategic system, the social system and the managerial system, it is important to understand the impact of technology on corporate strategy, management systems and social behavior." And in the same newspaper there was a conclusion from a meeting of the FAO in Rome: "The Sahara desert has crept south up to 200 km in a single year." The development of technology?

[9] See Dan 5:25.

[10] Gone are the days when one could write, "By intercalating a more and more perfected mechanism between man and raw nature, technology causes the progressive disappearance of menial labour

Distinction between "Labor" and "Work." In the technological world, work (human activity) is confused with labor. For more than a century, but more so since the Russian Revolution, the West has been riding a wave of optimism and infatuation with labor—an infatuation that is quite understandable after centuries of feudalism. The West would talk about the "nobility" of labor and even about a theology of labor. But, in the course of time, the fire of enthusiasm was extinguished by both praxis and theory: praxis has shown that labor degrades Man, and theory has demonstrated that labor is not a creative activity. I say "labor" and not human work / creative activity. The confusion between the two is at the source of the current uneasiness in the world of labor.

Marx's vision was right: the worker should be given back not only his/her dignity but also that which, with it, belongs to him/her, that is, the fruits of his/her labor. But the fruit of "work" is not the product of "labor." It is not production-line activity that brings about the kind of well-being necessary for a human life to be lived in dignity—but the activity of the carpenter, the craftsman, the artist, and even the philosopher and scientist. In short, the activity of the *poietic* Man (ποιητικος ανθρωπος, the maker). Not only is it unjust that the "sur-plus" and the "plus-value" be accumulated by the few, but labor itself represents an objectification of reality that kills life. Marx spoke that language because in his time Man was already beginning to be alienated from his creative activity—precisely through salaried labor. Salary is like a bread crumb that is thrown to the laborer so that he may survive and continue to labor in the interest of the Capital. The fruit of the worker's work is his happiness, the satisfaction that comes from being a builder of reality, a co-creator of life, the awareness that one is realizing one's true self.

The fundamental difference between technological labor and the activity of *Homo faber* is the following: *poietic* activity consists in a human contribution to the unfolding of the entire universe. It is the *techné*, the applying of human intelligence to the discovery of things and of their behavior in view of a more perfect cosmic and human life. It is a discovery, a revelation, and not an interference of Man as master and lord of nature. There is such a thing as a human creation, but it belongs to the order of self, of life, of *ātman*. We could quote Paracelsus's definition of alchemy: God has left the things of the universe to be fulfilled. It is Man's duty to bring them to their fulfillment. The art by which this is done is alchemy. It cultivates both the earth and Man. It improves Nature.

Technological labor, on the contrary, displaces creativity and turns everything into an object that is cut off from Man and Nature. Its aim, through the process of acceleration (origin of the *New Science*) and through an active intervention into the natural process, is to produce objects that may be useful to Man. Hence the means of production must be under control, and in this system, competition and profit become inevitable. The earth is no longer cultivated in order to live. It is interfered with in order to extract a profit from it. It is exploited. Man is also exploited, interfered with: he is, so to speak, the raw material employed in and transformed by technological activity. One conquers Nature. One domesticates Man.

I have tried to show elsewhere how acceleration represents the violation of the rhythms of Nature, for Man's sake, and how technology is a violence done to Reality, again for the sake of Man.

---

which formerly made of man a slave of nature; it also allows one to gradually liberate more and more of the spiritual potential dormant in each one of us." A. O. Dondeune, "Technique et religion," at the 13th Meeting of Pax Romana, Louvain, July 1959; then published in *Foi et Technique* (Paris: Plon, 1960), 17.

There exist, in certain traditions, an extreme sensitivity to life and an infinite respect for reality. Thus, according to the Jaina vision of the universe, the whole cosmos is alive; the earth, the waters, the wind, vegetation, the animals are, like Man, *jīvas*, living substances, conscious, capable—in varying degrees, depending on the category they belong to—of full awakening and spiritual realization. Technology, under whatever form, is a source of *hiṃsā* (violence) and therefore must be rejected. Obviously, such a trust in the ultimate harmony of the cosmos requires a deep-seated optimism. The biblical conception, on the other hand, sees nothing anti-natural in Man's intervention in Nature and, consequently, is not foreign to the birth of technology. Let us add, however, that the only intervention that would be justifiable would be the one that serves Man's Humanness and contributes to the advent of a new earth and a new heaven.

In 1776 Adam Smith said, after Locke (1690), that labor is the measure of the value of things. Such a statement has a meaning only in an industrialized world that is oriented toward the maximum of productivity; such a view is unconcerned with a natural relationship with Nature, with "synergetic" relationship with reality. The tree "rejoices" when we cut away some of its branches; the forest breathes better when we clear the undergrowth; the cow is grateful when we milk her too-full udders after the suckling of the calf. The iron mineral is *more* iron after being purified. But labor, in modern society, has no connection with human life and with Nature. It is only the source of the value of things (A. Smith). Marx clearly saw that we were not giving this value all the importance it had. But the problem that preoccupies us concerns primarily the critique of industrialized society as a type of human society. "To do an inventory or the critique of our civilization," wrote Simone Weil, consists "in bringing to light, in a precise manner, the trap which has made Man a slave of his own creations." This trap, in my opinion, is that of domination (the human *hubris* that wants to extend his power over the rest of creation: the Bible is again implicated), which supplants the fundamental attitude of harmony and συνεργεια with the world.

The efforts of industrialized society to convince the workers of not yet "developed" countries to join the labor force, thus falling into servitude, are well known, from Spain and southern Italy to Africa and India. This effort at "modernization" is called discipline, saving, progress, civilization, modernity, even education. It consists in integrating the workers into the mega-machine in such a way that they can no longer escape.

Reaffirming the Value of Craftsmanship. I would have preferred to speak of reaffirming the value of the arts, since we still speak of "master of arts," liberal arts, fine arts, mechanical arts, and so on; but because the word is presently reserved to aesthetics, we can keep the word *craftsmanship*, a word that is closer to *craftsman*, *Homo faber*.

In any case, the idea is to recognize and give all due importance to the *art of living*, along with its subsidiary arts: the *Trivium* (Grammar, Rhetoric, Logic), the *Quadrivium* (Arithmetic, Geometry, Astrology, Music), as well as medicine, fine arts, and so on.

To draw a line of demarcation between *technê* and technology is no easy matter, and the boundaries are perhaps fluid. Electricity, for example, as a channeling of electrons, would belong to the mechanical arts, and its direct utilization by Man would belong to *technê*. But the utilization of electricity in the construction of second-order machines would represent a form of violence. Such is the case of the atomic accelerator (bombardment of electrons, or other elementary particles, in order to experiment *in vivo* with living matter). In the same order of experimentation, some have not hesitated to torture human beings for the advancement of science.

The intrinsic criterion that allows to set limits, although in a flexible and sometimes uncertain manner, is *violence*. But it is not always easy to detect it in its true nature, all the more so in the political and social realms.

The extrinsic criterion is *human freedom*, understood in the broader scale of humankind, not in the restricted scale of the individual. Slavery can liberate the master but chain up the slave. Technology does bring certain benefits to the boss, but it turns the worker into a cog of the mega-machine, and so forth. When Man is obliged to utilize the machine because, otherwise, his job would not be profitable, when he is forced to submit to its exigencies, we have both feet in the domain of technological civilization.

Here also the margin is broad, and the problem complex. But to persist in disparaging technology does not lead to anything positive, especially if we know that its impetus is an irreversible one. Let us rather try, first and foremost, to study the possibility—and its concrete application—of an alternative beginning from a culture of craftsmanship. The Marxist-inspired statement "Man is a worker" carries a very positive meaning. It says that every human being is an artist, and that his own creation belongs to him. Otherwise, there is a dehumanizing alienation. Contemplation is also a creative act.

The jump from *techné* to technology takes place when an impersonal *ratio* of the order of quantity replaces the inspired human spirit who creates something of a craftsmanlike nature. Technology is of the quantitative order, while *techné* is of the qualitative order. We can imagine anything, even a robot painting pictures to decorate a prefabricated house, but we would then find ourselves in full cultural degeneracy.

Techné is not at all limited to making clay pots and clocks. It could, in an alliance with science, be at the heart of a new civilization—perhaps the one after the technological exaltation of our times.

Provisional Alternatives. Three major movements are currently coexisting throughout the world:

a. A movement oriented toward technological growth. It still believes in development, and most of the elites in non-Western countries want it.

b. A movement that rejects technology. It can be mainly found among the young generation in the Western countries. These young people are turning toward a postindustrialized and postmodern life. They are irritated, exasperated, revolting, sometimes desperate opponents of a cold, artificial, mechanized world, which they feel powerless to change, and whose suicidal march they are unable to stop. Hence their deep commitment to opposing movements: pacifism, ecology, spiritual communities of all sorts.

c. A group-based movement that seeks to introduce positive alternatives in a limited milieu, either in the economic, social, religious, or other fields. Young protesters and those who look for an ideal that may give a meaning to their lives often take up this direction.

This movement and the previous one often overlap, but we must distinguish between the tendency to a wholesale rejection of the present world and the one that seeks to build a new world within the existing one, without trying to directly destroy it. A certain hope seems to dawn upon these groups: the human organism, like a snake, will shed its old skin for a new and more beautiful one; a new humanity is emerging.

Some groups belonging to the second movement do use technology in order to correct its alleged abuses. Nonviolence here is essential, but to make it effective, they feel the urge to transform it into a power capable of changing society, and they often call on technology to do so.

The groups of the third movement put an emphasis on praxis, on the viable implementation of alternatives.

All of this gives us points of reference, which are milestones for a liberation of Man from the grip of technology. Perhaps a merging between the groups of the second and third movements could be important and positive, for technology is sufficiently powerful to isolate the groups of the third kind and reduce them to a tolerated "apartheid," all the while pursuing, without interference, its course of technologizing the whole world.

New Wisdom

If the preceding section underlined the importance of praxis, we should now stress the not less important role of theory—in symbiosis, of course, with praxis.

The problems are far from being solved. We are still groping. We lack solid anthropological foundations for a cultural pluralism. Monism, which leads to cultural monophormism, is not a solution. Nor is a scattered plurality of little "kingdoms" closed in upon themselves. The cultures of the Earth have hardly begun to dialogue. When they did meet, it was almost always on the battlefields of wars or commerce. The present situation puts us in a position where we must be attentive to each other, and act together at the various levels of reality.

The dialogical dialogue has become today indispensable. That is the direction in which I am directing my effort.

7

Cosmic Evolution

Human History and Trinitarian Life

Permit me a preliminary and personal remark.* The first time I heard Teilhard's name was in Salamanca, in the late forties, when people asked me about the influence a certain French Jesuit had upon me. I was intrigued, but could not lay hands on any of his writings. People still insisted on the similarity and thought he had an influence on me. Perhaps there are many other ways of passing a message! Only much later I had the occasion of coming to know his thought. I have even directed a PhD dissertation on him. Yet I am not an expert on him—and what is worse, probably I cannot be called a Teilhardian. You will hear today a different voice.

At the beginning of this century, Bertrand Russell published a book with the title *Why I Am Not a Christian*. Reading it almost a century later, one gets the impression that many Christians would agree with almost everything that Russell says, and yet, or precisely for those reasons, draw the opposite conclusion. To be sure, truth does not shackle one, one does not possess truth, but rather, if at all, one is possessed by it—as Thomas Aquinas says. Certainly, the dogmas are not fixed and rigid statements to imprison the flight of Man[1]—toward the divine mystery, but *media qua,* channels or rather telescopes that direct us much beyond themselves—as the Scholastics clearly affirmed. Truly, Christian freedom is not just to bow down in front of the last Führer of that particular community, or blind obedience to laws, but the power that flows from the conviction that the Sabbath is made for Man and not vice versa. In fact to be a Christian does not mean to believe that God created the world in six days, short or long, in twenty-four hours, or during some millennia or whatever, but to have discovered in Christ the symbol of the entire reality. In short, one tends to draw the conclusion that for those very reasons that Bertrand Russell says that he is not a Christian I am a Christian. Or, at least, to be theologically precise (for *why* one is a Christian has no "reason" beyond the why—it is grace), those reasons would legitimate the acceptance of that religion. I am not doubting Russell's encounter with many Christians representing the attitude

---

* Text of the lecture the author held at the Teilhard Centre for the Future of Man, London, 1990, then published in *Teilhard Review* 25, no. 3: 61–71.

[1] Once and for all I explain that we need a single word for *anthropos* and not split names, thus favoring modern fragmentation. And this name is Man (whether it comes from the root *man,* to think, or not). It is still unconscious patriarchalism to concede males the privilege on Man (and also swallow the almost insulting etymology of *wo-man*). In order to avoid misunderstanding I write the word with capital M, and use the pronoun *it (neutrum)* waiting for an *utrum.* I also capitalize Man for analogous reasons as tradition capitalizes God, and Teilhard capitalized Earth. This is the triad of the cosmotheandric intuition.

he castigates, I am only saying that they do not represent Christianness as I understand it, and I suppose that is true for the majority of us.

It would be revealing indeed to compare that book with a still shorter paper that Teilhard wrote in Peking in 1934 and published first in 1969: *Comment je Crois*. But I have referred to Russell's book because my lecture could probably bear the title "Why I Am Not a Teilhardian," and perhaps years later, readers may interpret my position as truly Teilhardian. Teilhard would be the last indeed in rejecting evolution, even of his thought and our interpretations. What encourages me, besides what I have said of Russell, is a remarkable passage of Teilhard's *Le Milieu Divin*:

> Créer, ou organiser, de l'énergie matérielle, de la vérité ou de la beauté, c'est un tourment intérieur qui enlève celui qui s'y hasarde à la vie paisible et reployée où gît proprement le vice de l'égoisme et de l'attachement.

> To create, or to organize material energy, or truth, or beauty is an internal suffering which robs the person who dares [to enter into that kind of creative activity] the comfortable and self-centered life which in fact constitutes the vice of selfishness and attachment.

He goes on to say,

> Non seulement pour être un bon ouvrier de la Terre, l'homme doit quitter une première fois sa tranquillité et son repos, mais il lui faut savoir abandonner sans cesse, pour de formes meilleures, les formes premières (de son industrie, de son art, de sa pensée). S'arrêter à jouir, à posséder, serait une faute contre l'action. Encore et encore, il faut se surpasser, s'arracher à soi-même, laisser à chaque instant derrière soi les ébauches les plus aimées.

> In order to be a good worker of the Earth Man must abandon not only one first time its tranquility and its restfulness, but Man does need to know how continually to abandon in favor of better forms, the first forms of its industry, its art, its thoughts. To stop at just enjoying, or [even worse], possessing, this would be a sin against action. Again and again one needs to overcome oneself, to tear oneself away from oneself, and leave behind every instant the projects one is most attached to.

This is the sign of a great Man: not to be attached to what one has probably created with effort, or as he said, with interior torture. I detect here the *tapas* of the Vedic tradition. If we have to follow his footsteps, he would not be satisfied by our repeating his ideas, following in his track, and not trying to do exactly what he demands from himself, "s'arracher à soi-même"—abandon everything, and jump again and again into the newness of life, of creativity, into the beauty of everything that is new every day, every moment.

No doubt, Teilhard was a pioneer. But no doubt also, due to many causes and reasons, not the least the acceleration of our times, the mutation that he surmised is now much clearer in front of us.

I would like, in dialectical communion with Teilhard, to underline three main topics that will explain why I made this kind of ambivalent introduction, of not being Teilhardian and of being with Teilhard. As the Mahābhārata says, everything triadic is perfect. So Evolution, History, and Trinity are the three "small" problems of my meditation. But before that, I should preface my brief comments by again another threefold consideration in order to delimit the perspective of my talk.

Evolution refers to modern *science*. This science is fruit of the Western culture. And this fact is not accidental. My first point will then have to be a cross-cultural reflection. *History* refers to *humanities* at large. My second point will try to situate our question historically. *Trinity* is a theological notion. My third remark will then be to emphasize a central and often neglected human attitude.

Another preliminary remark, I could put it very quickly in academic parlance by saying that the nature of cross-cultural studies does not formally consist in research about other cultures. It does not consist in knowing what others have known or have discovered. Indology, Orientalism, or however we name it, previously with great exotic admiration or condescension and now with great sympathy and desire to learn, is not directly a cross-cultural activity. We all have to know a little more about the world. This is a must. But this is not cross-cultural studies. To study the cultures of others has been done more or less ever since the beginning of time. A real cross-cultural attitude demands that the very *paradigms,* the very *categories,* the very "forms of thinking," and the *presuppositions* of that other culture become integrated in the very vision I have of my own culture and the other culture. It is not a new object; it is that the scenario changes. It is not that there are new things in the panorama; it is that the panorama is a different one. It is not something by which I enrich myself with more knowledge and more information, so that eventually I may have better business; but it is an activity by which I attain a kind of introspection that changes my "forms," in the word of Teilhard, my very patterns of understanding. Cross-cultural studies challenge my own securities and starting points. It is a dangerous thing indeed.

My second preliminary point regards "Teilhard's Cosmology in the Light of Other Cultures," as the subtitle indicates. As I well know, Pierre Teilhard de Chardin had to fight basically on two fronts: in the arena of a rather religiously agnostic or indifferent science, and in the theatre of a rather world-denying and *microdoxic* Christianity. He rescues for science the spiritual and the transcendent. He saves for Christianity the material and the scientific. There is no need for me to specify further.

We cannot ask him to struggle with the same intensity on a third front: the cross-cultural scene. We all know the linearity of his evolutionary schemes and the meaning of his convergence of religions, about which Ursula King[2] so tellingly writes. For him there is basically one single *phylum* in history. I would call it the Abrahamic *phylum* and within it the scientific ideology. We need to situate Teilhard—thus History.

My third *prenotandum* could be said to be methodological. It has to do with the way to approach such questions. There are two words in the dictionary that today should be shunned, and yet they are absolutely unavoidable. We have been using them in a thousand different manners, and yet we do not have substitutes. The one I am not going to speak about is love; the other one I am going to comment on for a moment is contemplation. Contemplation is required. If we live in this hectic inner, and not only outer, trepidation; if we live under this constant bombardment of *news*—and I have just heard that in Ethiopia something terrible has happened, but two minutes later they tell me that in Bangladesh something else happens, and while I am thinking what I am going to do in Bangladesh something else happens, and while I am thinking what I am going to do in Bangladesh, I hear that somewhere in Ireland,

---

[2] Referring to the book *The Spirit of One Earth* by Ursula King, who chaired the meeting where the author delivered this lecture.

or somewhere else . . . , and then these other poor people dying of hunger and the disaster in the Philippines. . . . I can understand a second glass of beer and going to sleep. We are paralyzed. What can we do? Nothing? Become slowly callous? Mere thinking does not help much. Things are so complicated, the information is so variegated and often contradictory, and there are so many areas in which we should be experts, that we renounce thought and action. Praxis is often of little avail. Do we pour money into a charitable enterprise that perpetuates colonialism and dependence? Do we jump into one front at the expense of being utilized by the powers that be, perhaps against our own good intentions?

Contemplation pierces through this double barrier. Thought leads to private ideas; contemplation leads to action. But there is a difference when compared with activism. It is an action suffused with thought—and love. It is false contemplation if I do not engage myself into that which I am supposedly contemplating. I am part of the solution but also part of the problem. Contemplation is prior to the split between theory and praxis—in spite of the fact that Cicero translated *theoria* with *contemplatio*. Contemplation itself is enlightened action. I may be allowed to play freely on a Sufi story. "What is contemplation?" the disciple asked the master, and the reply was, "Contemplation is wisdom"; "And what is wisdom?"; "Wisdom is to see." And the disciple asks: "To see *what?*" "To see the eagle in the egg, the butterfly in the caterpillar, the saint in the sinner," was the answer. But seeing is not just looking at the appearances. It is this seeing that brings forth the eagle, the butterfly, the saint. If we do not see the eagle in the egg, the butterfly in the caterpillar, and the saint in the sinner, we don't see. We are blind and barren. This means that what is required is not just moral holiness but *intellectual* sanctity. I insist in this threefold comment that provides the concrete background of my talk: The radical mutation in our times could probably be well expressed in the three names of the title: Evolution, History, Trinity.

Evolution

I am not going to repeat here what most of you know of Teilhard's thought perhaps better than I. I am going to jump a step ahead and dare to challenge the common vision of evolution.

A few years ago, Seyyed Hussein Nasr in his Gifford Lectures, *Knowledge and Sacred*, wrote a most blatant attack against Darwinism and evolution in general. He complains that "this type of thought" has entered even "into the realm of Catholic theology itself" and has produced "that Darwinization of theology, and the surrender of this queen of the sciences to the microscope, which is represented by Teilhard de Chardin." He goes on to say, "From the traditional point of view Teilhard represents an idolatry which makes the final phase of the desacralization of knowledge and being, the devouring of the Eternal by the temporal process, if such were to be possible."

He calls Teilhard's effort "to synthesize science and religion" a "fantastic mental sublimation of a crass materialism," and accuses him of "reduction of vital energy to physical energy." Nasr adds, "Teilhard saw the world of nature as, in a sense, 'Marxist,' that is solely determined by temporal and historical processes."

I am not going to enter into the controversy. I have already said that Teilhard's cultural parameters are the natural sciences and the Catholic theology of his time. Seen from another perspective there is much to learn from the criticisms we just heard. Here lies the enormous difficulty of cross-cultural studies. We tend to extrapolate our own views, forgetting the context that gives meaning to any text. What I have called *diatopical hermeneutics* should be here at work.

I feel that in many aspects Teilhard would have said to Nasr that it was not his intention to desacralize anything.

Repetons-le: en vertu de la Crèation, et plus encore, de l'Incarnation, *rien n'est profane*, ici bas a qui sait voir. Tout est sacré, au contraire, pour qui distingue, en chaque créature, la parcelle d'être élu soumise à l'attraction du Christ en voie de consommation.

We repeat: by virtue of Creation, and even more of the Incarnation, nothing is profane, down here to those who know how to see. Everything is sacred, on the contrary, for those who distinguish, in every creature, the particle of being elected subjected to the attraction of Christ in the process of being consumed.

On the other hand, I can also understand that Nasr would have retorted that in a wider context Teilhard's thoughts were a betrayal of Christian tradition. But I shall abstain from analyzing whether Nasr's interpretation of Teilhard is correct. I shall limit myself to the more general problem of *cosmic evolution,* as the title of the lecture indicates.

We all know how many of the so-called believers have responded to the overwhelming evidence of the evolution of the species and the less overwhelming extrapolation of the evolution of the universe: "All this may be good and well, but, above, beyond, and 'engineering' all this, there is an infinite God who, we believed before, 'did create' all those creatures; but we now 'know' that he masterminded the evolutionary meta-genetic code, and on the seventh day he took rest." This certainly changes theology, that is, it gives another idea of God, and on the whole for conventional believers it has worked satisfactorily. It is the typical and modern dualistic answer: on earth it may be evolution, but in heaven it is not so. This answer, however, satisfies neither scientists nor theologians. Not the scientists, for this purely transcendent God is a scientific superfluous hypothesis. It is not needed. They can explain everything without assuming such a transcendent agency. It may very well be that this God does exist, they will condescendingly concede, and "He" may satisfy the extrascientific needs of people, but science remains atheist. It does not satisfy theologians either, for such a *Deus otiosus* or merely *ingeniosus* would be a mere caricature of what practically all traditions have understood by the word "God."

Teilhard was too much of a scientist and of a theologian to be satisfied with a merely "material" evolution. His cosmic evolution cannot leave God untouched. God is not "*en dehors de la melée,*" an outsider. He knew that the "law" of evolution is somewhat "anterior" metaphysically, or at least logically anterior, to the actual evolution, even if the "law" is not a causal one. Agreeing or not with Teilhard, his merit lies in the fact of having put, and suffered, the problem in its intellectual and human dimensions.

Tempted as I am to intervene in the polemics I restrain myself from doing so. There are scores of studies on the subject, and you do not need now another one. I shall fulfill my duty, however, by mentioning, instead, my main difficulty with evolutionary thinking. And I stress *thinking,* and not just the theory of evolution. I am not approaching the scientific view on evolution, nor the cosmo-theological vision of it. I am limiting myself to the evolutionary mental makeup, prior to both science and theology.

I could formulate my objection epistemologically (ontologically rather) and anthropologically.

From the point of view of a theory of knowledge, the evolutionary thinking presupposes that objectification is a proper method to arrive at real things, at reality, at stating what is the case. It will maintain that the evolutionary description of the world, in spite of being provisional, open, and tentative, is an objective one, that is, a real one. We can put it on the blackboard, as it were. We say something about the world.

My concern is this. Where is the subject, the knowing subject? If it evolves along with the objective explanation, we should not be able to detect any evolutionary change. Only a diachronical vision can detect the alleged evolution, that is, only in relation with the accelerated or retarded phases of the knowing subject. It is then a subjective judgment. If the subject, or our intellect, does not evolve, this means that it is somewhat outside the evolutionary process. We need then somehow to absolutize our viewpoint, which does not run with all the other beings toward a future. It is a point outside evolution that makes possible the very idea of evolution.

I am jumping like a monkey, but this should be allowed, speaking of evolution. Once we have the species all neatly classified we detect a hierarchy among them. And once we project our thinking on an objectifiable temporal line, once we project it on Cartesian coordinates, we have, first, the evolution of the species, and extrapolating, the evolution of the entire universe.

It is sensible enough. It suffices to put it all on a blackboard or make a slide of it and everybody is convinced.

Now, besides the fact that not all thinking needs to be classificatory, one thing at least we cannot classify. I said, at least, because many a system of thought would defend that, by definition, God is so infinite and unique that it is not a classifiable entity either. Whatever the case about God may be, still another thing absolutely cannot be classified: we cannot classify the classifier! I mean, of course, in the same classification in which we classify all the rest.

If we ask with the *Upaniṣad, ko' ham?* (who am I?), the answer cannot be "a rational animal." That is, the answer cannot be a classification that includes the classifier.

The answer cannot be a genus and a specific difference. I can classify all human beings according to some agreed-upon criterion, but I cannot classify the classifier. And the question about "who am I" is asking about the classifier. It is the I who I am who puts the question. I am not asking what *is* Man. I am asking who I *am*, and even who we *are*. To say *animal rationale* or *animal loquens* does not answer the question, which is not about the *is*, but about the *am*.

Incidentally, Aristotle's famous definition just referred to does not say this. He did not write that Man is a speaking animal and much less a rational animal. He wrote that "among the living only in Man the *logos* transists." The *logos* is not the private property of Man. The *logos* graces Man, as it were, descends upon Man, as I have commented elsewhere.

Incidentally also, the word Aristotle uses for living (beings) is not *bios,* the individual life of our bio-graphy, but *zoe,* the living power of our *zo-ology.* How many Christian scruples would have been spared if the usual Greek distinction between *bios* and *zoe* had been interiorized! Christ does not speak of eternal *bios,* of an "eternal" biography, as if he were flattering our ego. Apart from the meaning of *aiínios,* which is not exactly what many mean by "eternal," the "eternal life" Christ promises is eternal *zôê,* a life that does not admit its own destruction, infinite life, a life about which the *Chāndogya-Upaniṣad (CU* VI.10.3) says that it does not die: *na jīvo mryata.* Otherwise it would not be life. This is the human experience of life. This is what is asked when we proffer, "Who am I?" and "Who are we?"

We want to know who we really are and not to which class we belong. The question cannot be answered by any classification. It cannot be objectified. It concerns the same classifier. It is demeaning to assume that when we ask about our identity, that when we try to search into the depths of our human experience, that when we ask about the knower, that being which questions everything, we could be satisfied with an answer that at best would swallow the subject into an objectifiable entity.

The question about ourselves cannot be answered by any objectifiable response, because, in the last instance, we do not ask about any-thing, but become aware of ourselves as question, as a questioning being. We may recall that untranslatable sentence by the African Augustine in his *Confessions*, which has all the ambivalence of the Dative: *quaestio mihi factus sum*. We may literally translate, "I made a question of myself," but it gives a wrong flavor, because of the genitive. I am myself a question for me, I have become a question to myself, I discover myself as a questioning being, i.e. as the classifier, and not the classified. In his moving prayer, Augustine does not ask God to give him all the answers. This would destroy his questioning spirit. Man is capable of questioning, even the cosmic evolution, because in a way there is something more to reality than an evolving universe.

We could formulate it philosophically, saying that Man is that existence whose self-understanding belongs essentially to what Man is. Therefore, to know what Man is, one has to know what Man thinks of itself, so that until the last woman on the last island in the last continent has her voice heard and has spoken, nobody on earth has the right to exhaustively say what Man is. The human being is such a unique being, precisely because its self-understanding belongs to the very essence of what one is. All the rest is natural history or whatever it is, but not my I, that's not what we are. The objective method makes us blind to what we are.

To make a very long story short, let me read a poem that combines Latin, German, and English—because the motto is Latin, the inspiration is German, and the poem is Geoffrey Hill's "Chorale-Prelude: *Ave Regina Caelorum*." I think the Sisters here would like to know that a poet like him is directly inspired by "Es ist ein Land verloren" from Paul Celan's *Die Niemandsrose* (1963):

> *There is a land called Lost*
> *   at peace inside our heads.*
> *The moon full on the frost*
> *   vivifies these stone heads.*
> *Moods of the verb 'to stare'*
> *   split selfhoods, conjugate*
> *ice-facets from the air,*
> *   the light glazing the light.*
> *Look at us, Queen of Heaven.*
> *   Our solitude drift by*
> *your solitudes, the seven*
> *   dead stars in your sky.*

That kind of reality is a human phenomenon. It is not classifiable. Each time it is unique, and in each of us it touches an intransferable chord and irrepeatible reality. Any common denominator is an abstraction and any description an approximation. It is a type of reality to which we resonate and the cats don't. It is of a radically different order.

This does not allow us to decree Man as the absolute king of creation. We know what disasters this produces. But human hubris is the opposite to the human consciousness of its own abyssal depths. My point is simply the irreducibility of the human factor, the truly human element, to any merely cosmic evolution.

This leads us immediately to our second part, about which I have to be deceptively brief.

Human History

On purpose my long title speaks about history and not just Man. I am not defending immobilism. I am all for Cosmic Evolution, only that I would not include the entire reality within it—not because the Cosmos may not evolve, but because the Cosmos "is" not the entire Reality. Man is a historical being. Man changes, evolves, and in this dynamism it shares the destiny of the Cosmos. Man is not separable from the Cosmos. But it is not identical with it; not exhaustively reducible to it. They belong together but each has its proper *ontonomy*.

Some years ago (1981) I wrote in the *Teilhard Review* an article titled "Is History the Measure of Man?" The plain answer was, No. As I have so often said, History is the Western myth, the horizon of reality, the background over against which we situate human events and in which we insert human meaning. If Christ did not have historical existence, Christianity, for most Christians, would collapse. Kṛṣṇa does not need historical existence in order to be real. The two myths are different.

An example will introduce us briefly into what I want to say. The Abrahamic religions have stressed so much God acting in history, God leading his people in history from exoduses, crusades, and caliphates, that many a contemporary theologian finds it difficult to do theology any longer, to speak about God, after Auschwitz. We should not minimize Auschwitz but we should not single out this case only. What about the probably 45 million Africans deported to the Americas to be sold as slaves, and with hardly any official Christian voice protesting? What about Kurds, Gypsies, and so many others? What about slavery as an institution? And what about our modern predicament? My point is about all the Auschwitzes together. It is a drama that we have had to wait until Auschwitz in order to be convinced that the myth of the God of History collapses. A God of History, engaged in history as the Lord of history, has lost credibility.

In short, neither is history the measure of Man nor Man (and much less history) the measure of God. Historical destiny is real, humanity as a whole may go somewhere, but any one of us is not just a number, a piece of a chain, indistinguishable as a grain of sand of Abraham's descendance. Man is more than just a historical being. History may go its way. But Man is not drowned in history. The historical destiny of humanity is not identical with the personal drama of every single Man. The Christian tradition has daring formulations: "Le Chrétien se reconnait comme fonction de diviniser le Monde en Jesus Christ," wrote Teilhard.

Man is image of God, a temple of the Trinity, Man's personal destiny is to become God. Man becomes God. God does not become God. The scar of temporality forever remains in human nature. The divinization of Man has not to wait until the end of times. It is the calling of each Man. Human dignity is not a farce, an abstraction, or something belonging to the human collectivity alone. In every one of us there is the destiny of reality. Man is a nonquantifiable being. Each Man is unique. Ultimately each being is also unique. But my point here is to affirm that, whatever the cosmic evolution may be, each of us has something "else," a mysterious "factor" irreducible to any cosmic evolution.

Having said this I have to emphasize with no less force that the alternative is not sheer individualism, "salvation of the individual soul," spiritual liberal capitalism. The belief in such aberration has triggered the opposite reaction.

My uniqueness is not my singularity. The uniqueness and thus the dignity of Man is not an individualistic conception, a quantifiable category. History is not extrinsic to Man, not just a place where we, unhistorical beings, dwell for a while. Our situation in time as well as in space belongs essentially to our existence. Man is a person, not an individual. And a person is a knot in a net of relationships. In every one of us there is the entire reality. And yet this indwelling is the mystery of the person. The ancient Indians had it clearly formulated, the *pratītyasamutpāda* of Buddhism tells us that all is related to all; the *sarvam-sarvātmakam* of Kashmiri Shivaism tells us also that everything is an epitome of everything.

It should be clear that I am not limiting the cosmic evolution to matter and reserving something else for Man. Teilhard is right in insisting that our destiny is common, that we are part of the entire process, that we have to overcome any type of such lethal dualisms. This will be, I hope, clearer in the third part of our lecture.

Trinitarian Life

The higher we climb the pyramid not only the more important the topic, also shorter is the time at my disposal. I shall sum it all up in three statements.

a. *The Trinity is not a Christian exclusivity.* It is not something exclusively Christian. We find the idea of the Trinity practically in all traditions of the world. Of course there are different names and diverging interpretations of this belief, but almost everywhere we find expressed the experience that the Divine presents a threefold manifestation, a triadic basis (*hypostasis*). According to the idea of the Divine, of course, this *saccidānanda* will be differently interpreted.

Put it differently, the idea of a divine Trinity is neither a human conundrum that only God could reveal, nor an idea to be found in Christianity only. This is simply a matter of History of Religions.

The Christian idea of an exclusively revealed dogma to Christians comes not only from a certain ignorance of other traditions, but also, and perhaps mainly, from the conviction that truth has a certain exclusivistic character. If Christianity is true or revealed, it was believed other religions could not be also true and revealed in the same sense. If Israel is chosen, other people are not chosen, and the like. This comes, as I have explained elsewhere, from the application of the principle of noncontradiction as an exclusive criterion for truth.

b. *The Trinity is not a divine monopoly.* It does not belong in an exclusive way to what some call God. Besides what Christian tradition has called the immanent Trinity (*ab intra*) and the economic one (*ad extra*), I submit, there is the radical Trinity (*in omnibus*). This is what I have called the cosmotheandric or theanthropocosmic intuition, the vision that the entire reality is a Trinity of God (infinity and freedom), Man (consciousness and love), and Matter (time and space).

I agree that I would need more time to make it plausible. It may not do, for instance, to state that the I, Thou, and It is also a symbol of this radical Trinity. The one is not the other, and yet none of them is without the other. We can speak of a totally mutual correspondence, or equality.

In fact, History of Religions shows us that this intuition is almost universal. There is God, a Source, an Origin, an Abyss, Silence, Nothingness, Non-Being. There is also an Image, a Result, a Book, a World, an Offspring, a People, Being. There is, further, a Return, a Love, an all-permeating Energy, a Spirit. There is Heaven, Earth, and Man, etc. This fact is so general that we should be ready to entertain the idea that it belongs to the very structure of our mind. But this does not weaken what we said before. It could well be that our mind is so structured, precisely because reality itself is trinitarian.

c. *The real Trinity is not triadic.* Seen from the interior, as it were, the Trinity is not Three anything. There are not three "things." We would then need the famous and justly condemned *quaternitas,* an extra fourth platform from which the three would appear as such. All the conundrums of the Trinity stem from envisaging it from the outside. We meet then three entities that claim to be different and identical, which is absurd.

Seen from the inside, the Trinity would appear concentrical, as it were. The Father, to choose Christian terminology for brevity and clarity's sake, is only such because it has a Son. Father implies Son and vice versa. The Father and Son can only be such because there is a Spirit that unites and distinguishes both. But this again is speculation.

To see the Trinity from within, in fact, is as impossible as to see it from without. We can only "see" it, that is, experience it from our own human vantage point which cannot claim to be the "objective" inside, the center, as it were, nor outside it. We experience something above and something below, and both intrinsically related to us. We experience, at the same time, that although we are in the middle, as it were, the center is not in us. Many a religious tradition has deduced that the center is above, in God. I for one, would not subscribe to any (man-made) theocentrism. I would rather defend that there is no center at all, because the relationship is constitutive. The *perichoresis* or *circumincessio* of classical Christian theology, the *pratityasamutpada* or radical relativity of Buddhism, and so on.

I have tried to present the same idea more philosophically, saying that the underlying intuition is the non-duality of Reality, the *advaita* of so many traditions including Christianity. Reality is not three, or not two for that matter. What would then be the link? It is not one either. We cannot deny the differences and shrink all into an undifferentiated monism, material or spiritual. Reality is irreducible to one or to many; it is neither one nor two. The Trinity is the most universal vision of this Advaitic intuition.

It would be not too difficult for me to co-opt Teilhard into this vision. Ultimately any authentic thinker is struck by reality and reflects and refracts it according to its own genius. Each true thinker in a way is a revelation of this reality. When we plunge into the profound vision of our ancestors, we sense that we are in deep communion in spite of shades, lights, perspectives, and one-sidedness we would like to overcome. In spite of the fact that Teilhard is of yesterday, the science and theology of his time have done a big jump. I may have substantial qualifications to make to his science and his theology. But this is not the most important. Says Teilhard in *Le Milieu Divin,*

> Qu'est-ce qu'en effet être *sainte,* pour une creature, sinon adhérer à Dieu au maximum de ses puissances? et qu'est-ce qu'adhérer à Dieu au maximum, sinon remplir dans le Monde organizé autour du Christ, la fonction exacte, humble ou éminente à laquelle, par nature et par surnature, elle est destinée?

> What does it actually mean to be holy, for a creature, if not to adhere to God to the fullest of one's strength? and what does it mean to adhere to God as much as possible, if not to carry out the exact, humble, or eminent function to which, by nature or by supernature, she is destined?

> When I read him I discover something more than mere ideas. I discover the poet, the saint, the Man. And then I understand: I stand-under the spell of his life and vision.

BIBLIOGRAPHY

Abram, D. 1996. *The Spell of the Sensuous*. New York: Pantheon Books.

Agazzi, E. 1992. *Il bene, il male e la scienza*. Milan: Rusconi.

Aguilar, E. 1981. *Vers una sexologia de la religion*. Barcelona: Ediciones 62.

Aristotle. *Metaphysics* I.3 (938b20–27); IV.2 (297; 1003a33); IV.11 (219b1).

Bachelard, G. 1991. *Le nouvel esprit scientifique*, 4th ed. Paris: Quadrige-PUF.

Balmès, M. 2003. *L'énigme des mathématiques. La mathématisation du réel et la Métaphysique.* Tome 1. Bern: Peter Lang.

Barbour, I. 1971. *Issues in Science and Religion*. New York: Harper Torchbooks.

———. 1980. *Technology, Environment, and Human Values*. New York: Praeger.

———. 1990. *Religion in an Age of Science*. The Gifford Lectures, 1989–1991, vol. 1. New York: HarperCollins.

———. 1996. *Issues in Science and Religion*. New York: Harper & Row.

———. 2004. *El encuentro entre ciencia y religión*. Santander: Sal Terrae.

Barfield, O. 1957. *Saving the Appearances: A Study in Idolatry*. London: Faber & Faber.

Barrow, J., and F. J. Tipler. 1998. *The Anthropic Cosmological Principle*. Oxford: Oxford University Press.

Bellone, E. 1973. *I modelli e la concezione del mondo nella fisica moderna da Laplace a Bohr*. Col. Filosofia della scienza 14. Milan: Feltrinelli.

Berry, T. 1988. *The Dream of the Earth*. San Francisco: Sierra Club Books.

Berry, T., and T. Clarke. 1997. *Reconciliación con la Tierra*. Santiago: Cuatro Vientos.

Birch, C., J. Francis, P. Gregorios, et al., eds. 1978. *Faith, Science, and the Future: Preparatory Readings for the 1979 Conference of the World Council of Churches*. Geneva: World Council of Churches.

Biron, A., and P. M. Henry. 1977. *Toward a Redefinition of Development*. New York: Pergamon Press.

Bohm, D. 1981. *Wholeness and the Implicate Order*. London: Routledge & Kegan Paul.

Böttger, B. 1974. "Indische Perspektiven." *Neues Hochland* 66, no. 3 (May–June): 235–45.

Bouthoul, G. 1948. *Huit mille traites de Paix*. Paris: Julliard.

Brague, R. 1999. *La sagesse du monde*. Col. L'Esprit de la Cité. Paris: Fayard.

Brandon, S. G. F. 1965. *History, Time and Deity*. Manchester: Manchester University Press.

Breton S. 1981. *Unicité et Monothéisme*. Paris: Cerf.

Brunner, F. 1954. *Science et réalité*. Paris: Aubier-Montaigne.

Bruno, G. *Cena de le Ceneri*. Dialogo IV.

Burtt, E. A. 1954. *The Metaphysical Foundations of Modern Science*. New York: Doubleday Anchor.

Butterfield, H. 1951. *The Origins of Modern Science, 1300–1800*. New York: MacMillan.

Cantore, E. 1988. *L'uomo scientifico. Il significato umanistico della scienza*. Bologna: Ed. Dehoniane.

Caporale, R., ed. 1976. *Vecchi e nuovi Dei*. Turin: Valentino, 521–44.

Capra, F. 1975. *The Tao of Physics: An Exploration of the Parallels between Modern Physics and Eastern Mysticism*. Boulder, CO: Shambhala.

——. 1987. *Das neue Denken. Die Entstehung eines ganzheitlichen Weltbildes im Spannungsfeld zwischen Naturwissenschaft und Mystik*. Bern: Scherz.

Casel, O. 1968. *Das Christliche Opfermysterium*. Graz: Styria.

Cassé, M. 2001. *Du vide et de la creation*. Paris: Éditions Odile Jacob.

Castelli, E. 1954. *Les présupposés d'une théologie de l'histoire*. Paris: Vrin.

——. 1959. *L'enquête quotidienne*. Paris: PUF.

——. 1970. *Le temps invertébré*. Paris: Aubier.

Cazenave, M., ed. 1998. *Dictionnaire de l'ignorance. Aux frontières de la science*. Col. Sciences d'aujourd'hui. Paris: Albin Michel.

Chenu, M. D. 1952. *Pour une théologie du travail*, in *Esprit*.

Cioran, E. M. 1976. *The Trouble with Being Born*. New York: Viking.

Corradini, A. 1980. "The Development on Disarmament Education as a Distinct Field of Study, *Bulletin of Peace Proposals*, International Peace Research Institute (March): 230.

de Broglie, M. 1940. Átomos, radiactividad, trasmutaciones. Buenos Aires: Libreria, p. 71.

de Santillana, G., 1955. *The Crime of Galileo*. Chicago: University of Chicago Press.

——. 1966. *Le origini del pensiero scientifico. Da Anassimandro a Proclo, 600 a.C.–500 d.C.* Florence: Sansoni.

Deleury, G. 1978. *Le modèle indou*. Paris: Hacette.

Diels, H., and W. Kranz. 1934. *Die Fragmente der Vorsokratiker*. Berlin: Fragm. 52.

Dolch, H. 1954. *Kausalität im Verständnis des Theologen und der Begründer neuzeitlicher Physik*. Fribourg: Herder.

Dondeune, A. 1960. "Technique et religion." At the Thirteenth Assembly of Pax Romana, Louvain. *Foi et Technique*. Paris: Plon, p. 17.

Dou, A. 1993. *Els científics i la fe Cristiana*. Barcelona: Claret.

Dubarle, D. 1967. *Approche d'une théologie de la science*. Paris: Cerf.

Duhem, P. 1913. *Le système du Monde*. 5 vols. Paris: A. Hermann et fils.

Dumont, L. 1982. "A Modified View of Our Origins: The Christian Beginnings of Modern Individualism." In *Religion* : Vol. 12, No. 1, pp. 1–27.

Dupuy, J. P. 1980. "L'encombrement de l'espace et celui du temps." *Esprit*, no. 10: 68–80.

Dürr, H.-P., and F.-T. Gottwald, eds. 1997. *Rupert Sheldrake in der Diskussion. Das Wagnis einer neuen Wissenschaft des Lebens*. Bern: Scherz.

Eastham, S. 2005. "World Visions in Collision. The Challenge of Genetic Engineering." *InterCulture* (Montreal), no. 145.

Ebner, F. 1952. *Das Wort und die geistigen Realitäten*. Freiburg: Herder.

Einstein, A. 1905. "*Über einen die Erzeugung und Verwandlung des Lichtes betreffenden heuristischen Gesichtspunkt*." *Annalen der Physik* 17: 132–48.

Eliade, M. 1952. *Images et Symboles*. Paris: Gallimard, p. 113.

——. 1957 and 1959. in *The Sacred and the Profane*. New York: Harcourt, Brace & World.

——. 1959. *Cosmos and History*. New York: Harper.

——. 1967. *From Primitive to Zen*. New York: Harper.

Ferguson, M. 1980. *The Aquarian Conspiracy*. Los Angeles: J. P. Tarcher.

Ferrer Iñareta, A. 2005. *La biblia de oro. La Biblia de la era cuántica*. Barcelona: Evana.

Fingarette, H. 1972. *Confucius: The Secular as Sacred*. New York: Harper & Row.

Fraser, J. T. 1975. *Of Time, Passion and Knowledge*, Braziller, New York.

———, ed. 1966. *The Voice of Time*. New York: Braziller.

Fraser, J. T., et al., eds. 1978. *The Study of Time. III*, Works of Internarional Society for the Study of Time. New York: Springer.

Frauwallner, E. 1956. *Geschichte der Indischen Philosophie*. II. Salzburg: Otto Müller, p. 111.

Gal-Or, B. 1987. *Cosmology, Physics and Philosophy*. 2nd ed. New York: Springer-Verlag.

García Recio, J. 2004. "Ojos contemplativos y apuntes de mística en Mesopotamia." In J. Martin Velasco, ed., *La experiencia mística* (Madrid: Trotta).

Garrison, J. 1981. *The Plutonium Culture*. New York: Continuum.

George, S. 1976. *How the Other Half Dies: The Real Reasons for World Hunger*. London: Penguin.

Gilles, F. 1980. "The Bantu Concept of Time." *Religion* 10 (Spring): 16–30.

Goulet, D. 1971. *The Cruel Choice*. New York: Atheneum.

———. 1974. *A New Moral Order*. Maryknoll, NY: Orbis.

Granotier, B. 1980. *La planète des Bidonvilles*. Paris: Seuil.

Greene, B. 2005. *L'Univers elegant*. Col. Folio Crítica Essais. Paris: Gallimard.

Groupe 21. 2001. *Mémoire du XXI siècle. Cahier 3–4: Création et transcréation*. Paris: Éditions du Rocher.

Guardini, R. 1940. *Die letzten Dinge*. Würzburg: Werkbind-Velag.

Gupta, S. 1974. "The Concept of Time: East and West." *Teilhard Review* 9, no. 2 (June): 40.

Hargous, S. 1980. *Les Indiens de Canada*. Paris: Ramsey.

Haught, J. F. 1984. *The Cosmic Adventure: Science, Religion and the Quest for Purpose*. New York: Paulist.

Hegel, G. W. F. 1807/1955. "Die Vernunft in der Geschichte." In *Philosophische Bibliothek*, ed. J. Hoffmeister 171a, 5th ed., p. 234.

Heidegger, M. 1954. *Was heisst Denken?* Tübingen: Niemeyer.

———. 1972. *Sein und Zeit*. 12th ed. Tübingen: Niemeyer, §73, p. 379.

Heisig, J. W. 2001. *Dialogues at One Inch above the Ground*. New York: Crossroad.

Hofstetter, A. 2004. *Earth-Friendly: Revisioning Science and Spirituality through Aristotle, Thomas Aquinas, and Rudolf Steiner*. Great Barrington, VT: Lindisfarne.

Hollenweger, W. 1988. *Geist und Materie*. Munich: Kaiser.

Hottois, G. 1984. *Le signe et la technique, La philosophie à l'épreuve de la technique*. Paris: Aubier, L'invention Philosophique.

Husserl, E. 1911. *Philosophie als strenge Wissenschaft*. Vol. 1. Tübingen, pp. 289ff.

Ignatius of Antioch. *Epistle to the Magnesians*. VIII.1 (PG 5.669).

Illich. I. 1973. *Tools for Conviviality*. New York: Harper & Row.

———. 1974. *Energy and Equity*. London: Calder & Boyars; reprinted in *Toward a History of Needs* (New York: Bantam, 1980), 131–72.

———. 1976. *Limits to Medicine*. London: M Boyars.

Jabès, E. 1976. *The Book of Questions*. Middletown, CT: Wesleyan University Press.

Jain, E. 1981. "The Tactical and Peace-Political Concept of Détente." *Bulletin of Peace Proposals* 12, no. 1: 33–43.

Jaki, S. L. 1978. *The Road of Science and the Ways to God*. The Gifford Lectures, 1974–1975 and 1975–1976. Chicago: University of Chicago Press.

James, E. 1969. *Creation and Cosmology*. Leiden: Brill.

Jou, D. 1992. *Algunes qüestions sobre ciència i fe*. Col. Quaderns de la Fundació Joan Maragall 10. Barcelona: Claret.

Kakuska, R., cur. 1984. *Andere Wirklichkeiten: die neue Konvergenz von Naturwissenschaften und spirituellen Traditionen*. Munich: Dianus-Trikont.

Karuvelil, G. 2004. "The Science-Religion Dialogue: The Cognitive Issues." *Vidyajyoti: Journal of Theological Reflection* (Delhi) 11, no. 68: 799–812.

King, U. 1986. *The Spirit of One Earth.* St. Paul, MN: Paragon House.

Koyré, A. 1968. *Études newtoniennes.* Col. Bibliothèque des Idées. Paris: Gallimard.

———. 1971. *Études d'histoire de la pensée scientifique.* Col. Bibliothèque des Idées. Paris: Gallimard.

Kuhn, T. S. 1970. "The Structure of Scientific Revolutions." In *International Encyclopedia of Unified Science.* Vol. 2, no. 2. Chicago: University of Chicago Press.

Küppers, B.-O., cur. 2000. *Die Einheit der Wirklichkeit. Zum Wissenschaftsverständnis der Gegenwart.* Munich: Wilhelm Fink Verlag.

Laín-Entralgo, P. 1957. "La espera y la esperanza." In *Revista de Occidente.* Madrid.

Lanczakovski, G. 1974. *Die Neuen Religionen.* Frankfurt am Main: Fischer.

Laotzu. *T'ien Tao* [The way to heaven].

Leibniz, 1935. *Zeitschrift für Naturforschung* (Wiesbaden): 298ff.

———. 1937. *Die Physik im Kampf um die Weltanschauung.* Leipzig: p. 25.

Lonergan, A., and C. Richards, eds. 1998. *Thomas Berry and the New Cosmology.* New London, CT: Twenty-Third Publications.

Lubac, H de. 1944. *Corpus Mysticum.* Paris: Aubier.

Lutz-Bachmann, M., A. Fidora, and A. Niederberger, eds. 2005. *Metaphysics in the Twelfth Century: On the Relationships among Philosophy, Science and Theology.* Turnhout, Belgium: Brepols

Mahadevan, T. M. P. 1954. *Time and the Timeless.* Madras: Upanishad Vihar.

Mander, P. 2004. "Una civiltà tradizionale: la Mesopotamia sumerica e il Sacro." In *Corpo Spirituale e Terra Celeste.* Melide, Switzerland: Holos International.

Mansfield, V. 1999. *Synchronicity: Science and Soul-Making.* Chicago: Open Court.

Margenau, H., and R. A. Varghese, eds. 1993. *Cosmos, Bios, Theos: Scientists Reflect on Science, God, and the Origins of the Universe, Life, and Homo Sapiens.* 2nd ed. LaSalle, IL: Open Court.

Maritain, J. 1946. *Distinguer pour unir, ou Les degrés du savoir.* 5th ed. Paris: Desclée de Brouwer.

Martín Velasco, J., ed. 2004. *La experiencia mística.* Madrid: Trotta.

May, R. 1972. *Power and Violence.* New York: W. W. Norton, p. 19.

Mbiti, J. S. 1967. *The African Conception of Time.* Africa VIII.

Meadows, D. H., et al. 1972. *The Limits to Growth.* The Club of Rome. New York: Universe Books.

Mercier, A. 1969. "Science and Responsibility." *Studi Internazionali di Filosofia* (Turin) 197: 1–126.

Miller, D. C. 1974. *The New Polytheism: Rebirth of the Gods and Goddess.* New York: Harper & Row.

Mitterer, A. 1935. *Das Ringen der alten Stoff-Form, Metaphysik mit der heutigen.* Stoff-Physik: Innsbruck.

———. 1936. *Wesensart Wandel und Aartensystem der physikalischen Körperwelt,* s/I (A. Weger).

———. 1948. *Philosophie und Theologie.* Wien: Herder.

Moltmann, J. 2003. *Science and Wisdom.* Minneapolis: Fortress.

Mumford, L. 1951. *The Conduct of Life.* New York: Harcourt, Brace.

———. 1967. *Technics and Civilization.* New York: Harcourt, Brace & World.

———. 1970. *The Pentagon of Power.* New York: Harcourt, Brace & World.

———. 1973. *Interpretations and Forecasts, 1922–1972.* New York: Harcourt, Brace, Jovanovich, 376–87.

Murungi, J. 1980. "Toward an African Conception of Time." *IPU* 20, no. 4 (December): 407–16.

Nagel, E., and J. R. Newman. 1958. *Gödel's Proof.* New York: New York University Press.

Nakamura, H. 1964. *Ways of Thinking of Eastern Peoples.* Honolulu: East-West Center.

———. 1992. *A Comparative History of Ideas.* Delhi: Motilal Banarsidass.

Nandy, A. 1990. *Science, Hegemony, and Violence: A Requiem for Modernity.* New Delhi: Oxford University Press.

Narlikar, J. V. 1987. *La estructura del universe.* Madrid: Alianza Universidad.

———. 1988. *The Primeval Universe.* Opus Books. Oxford: Oxford University Press.

Naumann-Beyer, W. 2003. "Sinnlichkeit." In K.-H. Barck, *Ästhetische Grundbegriffe* (Stuttgart-Weiman: J. B. Metzler), 5: 534–77.

Nedelman, J., ed. 1955. *Science, Religion, and Reality.* New York: Braziller.

Nedelman, J., and G. Baker. 1978. *Understanding the New Religions.* New York: Seabury.

Nicolescu, B. 2002. *Nous, la particule et le monde.* Paris: Éditions du Rocher.

———, ed. 2003. *Le sacré aujourd'hui.* Paris: Éditions du Rocher.

Nilsson, M. P. 1920. *Primitive Time-Reckoning: A Study in the Origins and First Development of the Art of Counting Time among the Primitive and Early Culture Peoples.* Lund: C. W. K. Gleerup.

Ortega y Gasset, J. 1930. "La rebelión de las masas." In *Obras Completas*, vol. 4 (Madrid: Revista de Occidente, 1966, vol. 2).

Panikkar, R. 1942. "Investigación." *Revista de Filosofía* (Madrid) 2/3: 389.

———. 1945. "El indeterminismo científico." *Anales de Física y Química* (Madrid) 396: 584ff.

———. 1945. "La entropía y el fin del mundo." *Revista de Filosofía* 13: 311ff.

———. 1947. "Max Planck (1858–1947)." *Arbor* (Madrid) 24: 387–406.

———. 1953. "Le concept d'ontonomie." In *Actes du XI Congrès Internationale de Philosophie*, vol. 3 (Amsterdam: Louvain), 182ff.

———. 1961. *Ontonomía de la ciencia. Sobre el sentido de la ciencia y sus relaciones con la filosofía.* Madrid: Gredos.

———. 1962. "Tecnica e spiritualità nel terzo mondo." *Tecnica e Uomo* (Rome) 7/8: 50–52.

———. 1963. *Humanismo y Cruz.* Madrid: Rialp.

———. 1964. "Technique et temps: La technochronie." In E. Castelli, cur., *Tecnica e casistica* (Padova: CEDAM), 195–229; in *Pax Romana Journal* (Fribourg) 2 (1968): 3–6, 26–27.

———. 1966. "Filosofia e scienza. Problemi e rapporti di due significative espressioni della cultura contemporanea." *Civiltà delle Macchine* (Rome) 1: 19–30.

———. 1967. "La Faute Originante ou l'Immolation Créatrice. Le Mythe de Prajapati." In E. Castelli, ed., *Le Mythe de la Peine* (Paris: Aubier, 1967), 65–100, esp. 70–79.

———. 1967. "Progresso scientifico e contesto cultural." *Civiltà delle Macchine* (Rome) 3: 3–13.

———. 1968. "El Cero." *Indice* (Madrid) 23, no. 227: 13–14.

———. 1970. "Le mystère du culte dans l'Hindouisme et le Christianisme," in particolare il cap. "Le culte et le Temps" (Paris: Cerf), 43–52. In Volume VII of this *Opera Omnia*.

———. 1971. "La loi du karma et la dimension historique de l'homme." In E. Castelli, cur., *Herméneutique et Eschatologie* (Paris: Aubier), 205–30.

———. 1971. *Zur theologie der Zukunft.* Munich: DTV.

———. 1972. *El concepto de naturaleza. Análisis histórico y metafísico de un concepto.* 2nd rev. ed. Madrid: CSIC (1st ed. 1951).

———. 1972. "The Law of Karman and the Historical Dimension of Man." *Philosophy East and West* 22, no. 1: 25–43. In Volume IX/1 of this *Opera Omnia*.

——. 1973. *The Trinity and the Religions: Experience of Man*. Maryknoll, NY: Orbis Books.

——. 1975. "Singularity and Individuality: The Double Principle of Individuation." *Revue Internationale de Philosophie* (Bruxelles) 19, no. 111–112: 141–66.

——. 1977. "Creation and Nothingness. Creation: ex nihilo sed non in nihilum. Nothingness: ad quem sed non a quo." *Theologische Zeitschrift* 33 (*Festgabe für Fritz Buri zum 70 Geburtstag*) (Basel): 344–52.

——. 1979. *Culto y secularización. Apuntes para una antropología litúrgica*. Madrid: Marova, 58ff. In Volume IX/1 of this *Opera Omnia*.

——. 1979. "Machines and Men." *Frontier* (London) 13, no. 2: 91–95.

——. 1982. "Alternative(s) à la culture modern." *Interculture* (Montreal) 77: 26–68.

——. 1983. *Proceedings of the XVI World Congress of Philosophy, 1978*, Düsseldorf.

——. 1984. "L'émancipation de la technologie." *Interculture* (Montreal) 85: 22–37.

——. 1984. "The Destiny of Technological Civilisation: An Ancient Buddhist Legend: Romavisaya." *Alternatives* (New York / Delhi) 10, no. 2: 237–53.

——. 1986. "Some Theses on Technology." In *Logos Philosophic Issues in Christian Perspective* vol. 7. University of Santa Clara: 115–24.

——. 1988. *La Trinidad*. Madrid: Siruela.

——. 1988. "L'émancipation de la technologie." In R. Vachon, ed., *Alternatives au développement* (Montreal: Centre Interculturel Monchanin), 293–313.

——. 1990. "Antinomias entre la cosmología moderna y las cosmologías tradicionales." In H. Beck and I. Quiles (curr.), *Entwicklung zur Menschlichkeit durch Begegnung westlicher und östlicher Kultur* (Frankfurt am Main: Lang, 1988), 213–19.

——. 1990. "Cosmic Evolution, Human History and Trinitarian Life." *Teilhard Review* (London) 25, no.3: 62–71.

——. 1993/XXXIII. *The Cosmotheandric Experience*. Maryknoll, NY: Orbis Books. In Volume VIII of this *Opera Omnia*.

——. 1993/XXXIV. *Ecosofia: la nuova saggezza—Per una spiritualità della terra*. Assisi: Cittadella; new ed.: *Ecosofia. La saggezza della Terra* (Milan: Jaca Book, 2015/LXXIV).

——. 1994. "Pensamiento científico y pensamiento cristiano." *Cuadernos Fe y Secularidad* 25, Maliaño: Sal Terrae.

——. 1996. "Modern Science and Technology Are Neither Neutral nor Universal." In *Forum Engelberg, VII Conference, Europe-Asia: Science and Technology for Their Future* (Zurich: Hochschul Verlag an der ETH), 205–9.

——. 1996. Preface to A. Mercier, *God, World and Time* (Bern: Peter Lang), 11–13.

——. 1997. "Ciencia y paraciencia." *Moralia, Revista de ciencias morales* (Madrid) 20, no. 1: 89–96.

——. 2000. *Mito, fede ed ermeneutica. Il triplice velo della realtà*. Milan: Jaca Books.

——. 2003/XXXII. *La nuova innocenza*. Sotto il Monte: Servitium, 155–68.

Pannenberg, W. 2001. "La questione di Dio creatore." *Communio, Rivista Internazionale di Teologia e Cultura* (Milan) 180 (November–December): 29–40.

Paty, M. 2004. "Genèse de la causalité physique." *Revue Philosophique de Louvain* 3: 417–45.

Peacocke, A. 2001. *Paths from Science toward God. The End of All Our Exploring*. Oxford: One World Publications.

Pemàn, J. M. 1947. *Obras Completas: Poesía*. Buenos Aires: Escelicer, 429–30.

Planck, M. 1908. *Die Einheit des physikalischen Weltbildes*. Leipzig: S. Hirzel.

——. 1926. *Physikalische Gesetzlichkeit*. Leipzig: Ambrosius Barth.

——. 1929. *Das Weltbild der neuen Physik*. Leipzig: Zweite, unveränderte Auflage.

———. 1932. *Der Kausalbegriff in der Physik.* Leipzig, p. 26.

———. 1934. *Wege zur physikalischen Erkenntnis.* Leipzig, p. 66.

———. 1935. *Die Physik im Kampf um die Weltanschauung.* Leipzig: Harnack-Haus in Berlin-Dahlem.

———. 1936. *Vom Wesen der Willensfreiheit.* Leipzig: Vortrag.

———. 1938. *Determinismus oder Indeterminismus.* Leipzig.

———. 1942. *Der Sinn der exakten Wissenschaften.* In *Geist der Zeit,* pp. 566ff.

———. 1944. *Sinn und Grenzen der exakten Wissenschaft.* Leipzig: Verl. Hirzel.

———. 1947. "Wissenschaftliche Selbstbiographie." *Neue Züricher Zeitung* (October 11–24), E. Abderhalden, 1986.

Pokorny, J. 1959. *Indogermanisches etymologisches Wörterbuch.* Bern-Munich: Francke.

Polkinghorne, J. 1987. *Scienza e fede.* Milan: Mondadori.

Price, L. 1956. *Dialogues of Alfred North Whitehead.* New York: Mentor Books.

Prigogine, I., and I. Stengers. 2004. *La nueva alianza. Metamorfosis de la ciencia.* 6th imp. Madrid: Alianza Editorial.

Prodi, G. 1974. *La scienza, il potere, la critica.* Bologna: Il Mulino.

Rahner, K. 1965. *Marxistische Utopie und christliche Zukunft des Menschen.* In Rahner, *Schriften zur Theologie,* vol. 6, *Neuere Schriften* (Einsiedeln: Benzinger), 77–88.

Ravindra, R., ed. 1991. *Science and Spirit.* New York: Paragon House.

Reichenbach, H. 1946. *Philosophic Foundations of Quantum Mechanics.* Los Angeles: Berkeley & Co., p. vii.

Rose, H., and S. Rose. 1980. *La radicalización de la ciencia.* Sacramento: Nueva Imagen.

Rosen, E., cur. 1967. *Kepler's Somnium: Dream, or Posthumous Work on Lunar Astrology.* Madison: University of Wisconsin Press.

Rosenberg, A. 1971. *Durchbruch zur Zukunft. Der Mensch im Wassermann-Zeitalter.* Bietigheim: Turm Verlag.

———. 1984. *Zeichen am Himmel, Das Weltbild der Astrologie.* Munich: Kösel.

Rossi, A. 2002. *Il mito del mercato.* Troina: Città Aperta.

Satyavrat, Â. 1963. *Essays on Indology.* Delhi, pp. 174ff.

Schell, J. 1982. *The Fate of the Earth.* New York: Alfred Knopf.

Schestow, L. 1994. *Athen und Jerusalem.* Trans. from Russian. Munich: Matches & Seitz.

Schleftelowitz, J. 1929. *Die Zeit als Schicksalsgöttin in der Indischen und Iranischen Religion.* Stuttgart: Kohlhammer.

Schumacher, B., and E. Castro, eds. 1996. *Penser l'homme et la science / Betrachtungen zum Thema Mensch und Wissenschaft. Mélanges offerts à Evandro Agazzi à l'occasion de ses soixante ans.* Fribourg: Éditions Universitaires Friburg.

Sheldrake, R. 1983. *A New Science of Life.* London: Paladin Book–Granada Publishing.

Silburn, L. 1955. *Instant and Cause.* Paris: Vrin, p. 43.

———. 1961. *Le Vijnana Bhairava.* Paris: De Boccard, p. 69.

Sini, C. 2000. *Idoli della conoscenza.* Milan: R. Cortina.

Soler Gil, F. J., ed. 2005. *Dios y las cosmologías modernas.* Madrid: BAC.

Soler, L. 2004, "Établir des correspondances entre théories physiques incommensurables." *Review Philosophique de Louvain* 3: 446–76.

Sontag, F., and M. D. Bryant, eds. 1982. *God, The Contemporary Discussion.* New York: Rose of Sharon Press.

Strolz, W., ed. 1985. *Die Verantwortung des Menschen für eine bewohnbare Welt im Christentum, Hinduismus und Buddhismus.* Freiburg: Herder, 147–90.

Sullivan, J. W. 1949. *The Limitations of Science: A Creative Scientist's Approach to the Unknown*. New York: Mentor Books.

Swimme, B., and T. Berry. 1992. *The Universe Story*. New York: HarperCollins.

Tada, T. 2000. *Fe y ciencia. Ciencia y religion*. Vitoria-Gasteiz: Luz Pradera.

Tarnas, R. 1993. *The Passion of the Western Mind*. New York: Ballantine Books.

Teilhard de Chardin, Pierre. 1957. *La vision du passé*. Paris: Editions du Seuil, p. 184.

Thompson, L. 1961. *Toward a Science of Mankind*. New York: McGraw-Hill.

Thompson, W. I. 1971. *At the Edge of History*. New York: Harper & Row.

Torres Queiruga, A. 2003. *Repensar la Resurrección*. Madrid: Trotta.

Toynbee, A. 1976. *Mankind and Mother Earth*. New York: Oxford University Press.

Trebolle Barrera, J. 2004. "La mística en los textos veterotestamentarios." In J. Martín Velasco, ed., *La experiencia mística* (Madrid: Trotta).

Turquie, S. 1980. "Efficacité et limites de l'arme céréalière." *Le Monde Diplomatique* 312.

Van Melsen, A. G. 1970. *Science and Responsibility*. Pittsburgh, PA: Duquesne University Press.

Villena, L. 1946. "Sir Isaac Newton." *Arbor* 17: 319ff.

von Wesendonck, O. 1931. "Kālavāda and the Zervanite System." *Journal of the Royal Asiatic Society* (January): 108–09.

Warnach, V. 1960. "Vom Wesen des kultischen Opfers." In B. Neunheuser, ed., *Opfer Christi und Opfer der Kirche* (Dusseldorf: Patmos), 29–74.

Wasmuth, E. 1945. *Der Mensch and die Denkmaschine*: Köln: Jacob Hegner.

Weinberg, S. 1981. "The Decay of the Proton." *Scientific American* (June): 64–75.

Whitehead, A. N. 1948. *Essays in Science and Philosophy*. New York: Philosophical Library, p. 73.

———. 1948. *Science and the Modern World*. New York: Mentor Books.

———. 1955. *Adventures of Ideas: A Brilliant History of Mankind's Great Thoughts*. New York: Mentor Books.

———. 1957. *The Concept of Nature*. Ann Arbor: University of Michigan Press.

Wilber, K. 1998. *The Marriage of Sense and Soul*. New York: Random House.

Yankelovich, D. 1981. "New Rules in American Life: Searching for Self-Fulfillment in a World Turned Upside Down." *Psychology Today* 15: 35–91.

Yukawa, H. 1973. *Creativity and Intuition: A Physicist Looks at East and West*. Tokyo: Kodansha International.

Zohar, D. 1990. *The Quantum Self*. London: Bloomsbury.

GLOSSARY

All terms are Sanskrit or English unless otherwise specified

adhyātma: the highest self (*paramatman*); the main or primordial self; the intimate Self of every being; individual appearance.

advaita: nondualism (*a-dvaita*). Spiritual intuition that sees ultimate reality as neither monistic nor dualistic. The recognition that the merely quantitative problem of the one and the many in dialectical reasoning does not apply to the realm of ultimate reality. The latter, in fact, possesses polarities that cannot be divided into multiple separate units; not to be confused with monism.

agnihotra: the daily fire sacrifice performed morning and evening in all homes of the high castes, which consists of an oblation of milk sprinkled on the fire.

aiôn (Gr.): cosmic time, eternity; also, a period of life.

ākāśa: air, sky, space, ether, emptiness (void), atmosphere, the fifth of the primordial elements (*mahābhūtāni*), which is the element of sound. It is all-pervading and infinite and, therefore, often identified with Brahman.

aporia (Gr.): difficulty that prevents one from going beyond reason, dead end.

arhat: ascetic, saint, the highest and most noble figure of Theravada Buddhism.

āyus: vital force, vitality, life, temporal existence, the length of life granted to man. See Greek *aiôn*, aeons.

bhakti-mārga: the path of love and devotion, one of the three classical spiritual paths (*karma-mārga, jñāna-mārga*).

bhuman: infinity, fullness.

bodhisattva: the enlightened one. In particular, in Mahāyāna Buddhism, he who, having attained liberation on earth, makes a vow to help all other beings attain liberation before they enter *nirvāṇa*.

Brahmā: the creator God (cf. the "Trinity," later Brahmā, Viṣṇu, Śiva). It is not important in the *Veda* but in later periods it inherits many of the characteristics of Prajāpati.

chôra (Gr.): space, region, place.

circumincessio (Lat.): compenetration of the three Persons of the Trinity. Corresponds to the Greek *perichoresis*.

Dasein (Ger.): being here; real, existing man; a term used mainly by M. Heidegger; human existence.

empeiria (Gr.): experience, practice, dexterity (experience—practical as opposed to theoretical activity—as the only valid source of knowledge).

himsā: violence (*ahimsā*: nonviolence) The root *hims-* from *han-* means to hurt, to kill.

homeomorphic: that which performs a similar function.

hypostasis (Gr.): "that which stands beneath": substance, person. A key and controversial word in the first disputes regarding the Trinity, especially due to the ambiguity of its Latin traduction.

313

jīva: living being (from *jīv-*, to live); the soul in its individuality, as opposed to *ātman*, the universal soul. There are as many *jīva* as individual living beings.

jīvanmukta: "liberated while alive and embodied," the highest category of the holy or fulfilled person who has reached the destination in this life and, therefore, in the human body; he who has fulfilled his *ātman-brahman* ontological identity; he who has reached his own being, becoming totally integrated.

jñāna-mārga: the path of knowledge, contemplation, and intuitive vision; one of the three classic paths of spiritual experience, generally considered superior to those of *karman* and *bhakti*, although many *bhakta* regard *jñāna* as merely as form of *bhakti*.

kairos (Gr.): time, opportune moment, crucial point at which the destiny changes phase, epoch.

kāla: time, appropriate time, destiny, death. In the *Atharva-veda* and the *Mahābhārata* it is celebrated as a great power that determines all things, hence its meaning of destiny and even death (*māhakāla*).

kṣaṇa: the instant, temporal moment.

kālaśakti: the power of time.

kalpa: a period of the world, a cosmic time of variable length.

Kṛṣṇa: *avatāra* of Viṣṇu (lit. "the black one") and one of the most popular Gods. He does not appear in the *Veda*, but he is the revealer of the *Bhagavad-gītā*. He is the divine child and the shepherd God of Vṛndāvana, the incarnation of love and the playful God par excellence.

lokasaṃgraha: the "keeping together, maintaining of the world" by the wise man and the saint through the sacred or liturgical action (concept of *Bhagavad-gītā*).

madhya: the middle; what is in the middle.

maṇḍala: lit. "circle." Mystic representation of all reality; a pictorial illustration of the homology between the microcosm (man) and the macrocosm (the universe).

mantra: prayer, sacred formula (from the root *man-*, to think), sacred word, a Vedic text or verse.

mārga: road, path, way.

metanoia (Gr.): transformation, change of mentality or heart, conversion; going beyond (*meta*) the mental or rational (*nous*).

mokṣa: ultimate liberation from *saṃsāra*, the cycle of births and deaths, and from *karman*, ignorance and limitation: salvation. Homeomorphic equivalent of *sōtēria*.

nirvāṇa: lit. "the going out [of the flame]," extinction. The word does not refer to a condition, but indicates liberation from all dichotomy and conditioning, whether it be birth and death, time and space, being and non-being, ignorance and knowledge, or final extinction including time, space, and being; the ultimate destination for Buddhism and Jainism.

nous (Gr.): mind, thought, intellect, reason.

nyāya: one of the six brahmanic darsanas, copied by Gautama in his *Nyāyasutra*. The real meaning of *nyāya* is logic or method, analytical investigation.

ontonomy: intrinsic connection of an entity in relation to the totality of Being, the constitutive order (*nomos*) of every being as Being (*on*), harmony that allows the interdependence of all things.

pāramārthika: ultimate level, ultimate reality, true reality.

parousia (Gr.): the return, the presence, the second coming of Christ.

pars in toto (Lat.): the part in the whole.

pars pro toto (Lat.): the part that represents the whole.

perichôrêsis (Gr.): notion of the early church Trinitarian doctrine describing the interpenetration of divine persons. Corresponds to the Latin *circumincessio*.

physis (Gr.): nature.

plêrôma (Gr.): fullness, the full, complete.

Prajāpati: "Lord of creatures," the primordial God, Father of the Gods and all beings. His position is central in the *Brāhmaṇa*.

prāṇa: vital breath, life, the breath of life, the vital force that holds the body together.

pratītyasamutpāda: Buddhist doctrine of the "conditioned genesis" or "dependent origination," which claims that nothing exists for itself but carries within itself the conditions for its own existence, and that everything is mutually conditioned in the cycle of existence.

pratibandha: preventing or braking force.

pratiṣṭhā: foundation, support, base.

Puruṣa: the Person, the spirit, man. Both the primordial man of the cosmic dimension (*Rigveda*) and the "inner man," the spiritual person existing within man (*Upaniṣad*).

sādhu: straight, leading straight to the goal, good, just. A good person, renunciant, monk, or ascetic.

śakti: energy, potency, divine power, the creative energy of God. The active, dynamic—feminine—aspect of reality or of a God (generally of Śiva). Personified as the goddess Śakti, consort of Śiva with a creative function.

saṃsāra: the impermanent phenomenic world and the condition of identification with it, the temporal existence, the cycle of births and deaths, of conditioned existences; state of dependence and slavery.

sarvam anityam: everything is transient.

satcitānanda: represents three possible attempts to define *brahman* or absolute reality.

siddhi: perfection, perfect capacity or faculty. Psychic faculties that may appear as a by-product of spiritual development.

śloka: stanza, verse, usually *anuṣṭubh* (four times eight syllables), epic meter.

sôteria (Gr.): salvation, liberation, redemption.

tapas: lit. heat; hence inner energy, spiritual fervor or ardor, austerity, asceticism, penitence. One of the forms of primordial energy, along with *kāma*.

tempiternity: nonseparation between time and eternity.

vāyu: air, wind, personified as a God in the *Veda*.

vrata: vow, religious observance.

vyāvahārika: "relating to earthly matters, to mundane life," i.e., the earthly way of seeing, the practical perspective; the relative level.

INDEX OF ORIGINAL TEXTS IN THIS VOLUME

The Ambiguity of Science. Original text in *L'Altrapagina* (Città di Castello) (1992). Translated by Daniella Engel.

"Technocentrism: Some Theses on Technology." Original article: "El tecnocentrisme: algunes tesis sobre tecnologia." In A. Merrier, cur., *Philosophie et Technique* (Institut International de Philosophie, 1984), 61–72; enlarged in *La nueva Innocència* (Barcelona: Proa, 1998).

"Emancipation from Technology." Original text: "L'émancipation de la technologie." *Interculture* (Montreal) 85: 22–37.

"The Cosmic Evolution." Text of the conference at the Teilhard Centre for the Future of Man, London, 1990; then published in *Teilhard Review* 25, no. 3: 61–71.

INDEX OF NAMES

About the Author

An international authority on spirituality, the study of religions, and intercultural dialogue, Raimon Panikkar made intercultural and dialogical pluralism one of the hallmarks of his research, becoming a master "bridge builder," tireless in the promotion of dialogue between Western culture and the great Oriental Hindū and Buddhist traditions.

Born in 1918 in Barcelona of a Spanish Catholic mother and an Indian Hindū father, he was part of a plurality of traditions: Indian and European, Hindū and Christian, scientific and humanistic.

Panikkar held degrees in chemistry, philosophy, and theology, and was ordained a Catholic priest in 1946. He delivered courses and lectures in major European, Indian, and American universities.

A member of the International Institute of Philosophy (Paris), of the permanent Tribunal of the Peoples (Rome), and of the UNESCO Commission for intercultural dialogue, he also founded various philosophical journals and intercultural study centers. He held conferences in each of the five continents (including the renowned Gifford Lectures in 1988–1989 on "Trinity and Atheism").

Panikkar received international recognitions, including honorary doctorates from the University of the Balearic Islands in 1997, the University of Tübingen in 2004, Urbino in 2005, and Girona in 2008, as well as prizes ranging from the "Premio Menéndez Pelayo de Humanidades" for his book *El concepto de naturaleza* in Madrid in 1946 to the "Premio Nonino 2001 a un maestro del nostro tempo" in Italy.

Panikkar lived in Tavertet in the Catalonian Mountains, where he continued his contemplative experience and cultural activities from 1982 until his death on August 26, 2010. There he founded and presided over the intercultural study center Vivarium. Panikkar published more than fifty books in various languages and hundreds of articles on the philosophy of religion, theology, the philosophy of science, metaphysics, and Indology.

From the dialogue between religions to the peaceful cohabitation of peoples; from reflections on the future of the technological society to major work on political and social intelligence; from the recognition that all interreligious dialogue is based on an intrareligious dialogue to the promotion of open knowledge of other religions, of which he is a mediator; from his penetrating analysis of the crisis in spirituality to the practice of meditation and the rediscovery of his monastic identity; from the invitation of *colligite fragmenta* as a path toward the integration of reality to the proposal of a new innocence, Panikkar embodies a personal journey of fulfillment.

Among his most important publications with Orbis are *The Trinity and the Religious Experience of Man* (1973); *Worship and Secular Man* (1973); *The Unknown Christ of Hinduism* (1981); *The Silence of God* (1989); *Cosmotheandric Experience* (1993); and *Christophany* (2004).